WOTAKOI:
LOVE IS HARD FOR OTAKU

FUJITA

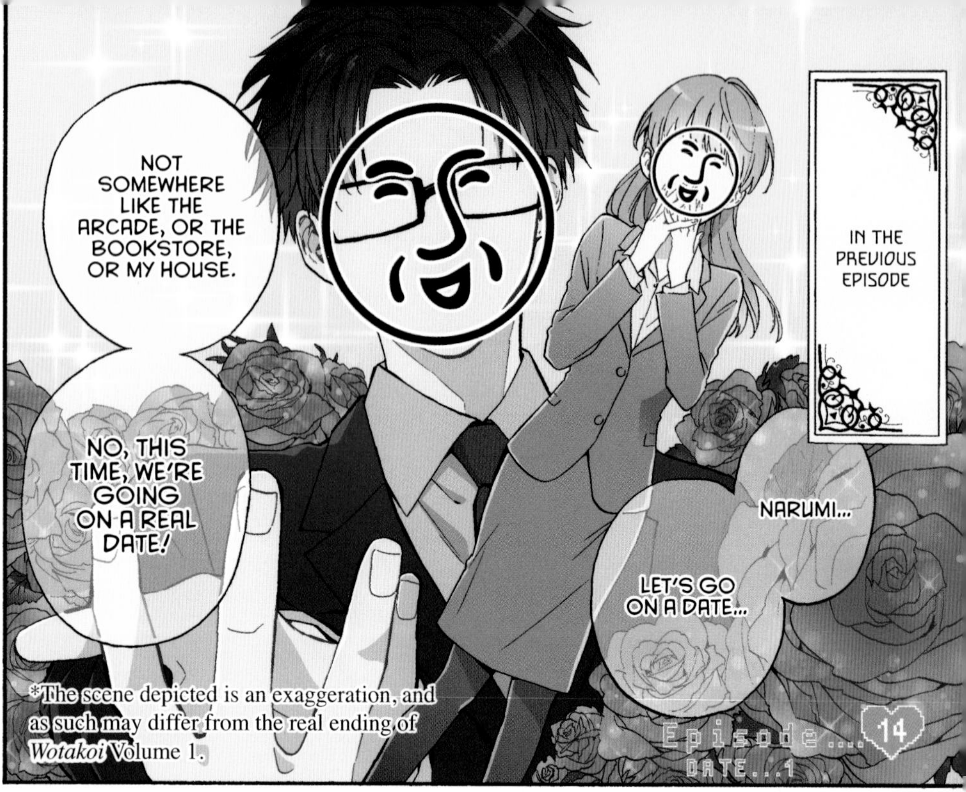
IN THE PREVIOUS EPISODE
NARUMI...
LET'S GO ON A DATE...
NOT SOMEWHERE LIKE THE ARCADE, OR THE BOOKSTORE, OR MY HOUSE.
NO, THIS TIME, WE'RE GOING ON A REAL DATE!
*The scene depicted is an exaggeration, and as such may differ from the real ending of *Wotakoi* Volume 1.
Episode....14
DATE...1

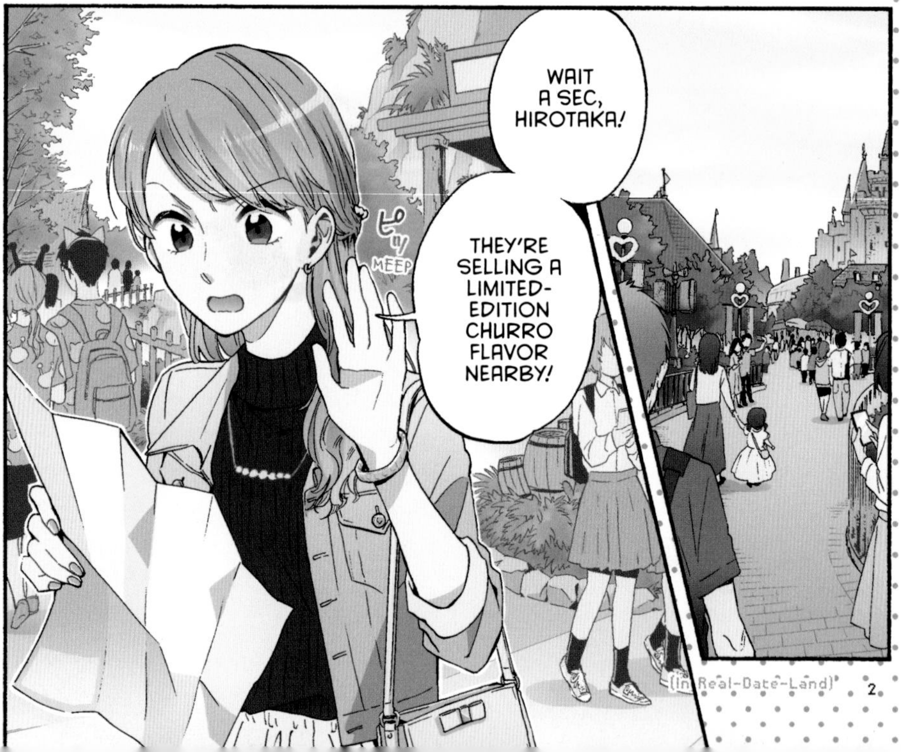
WAIT A SEC, HIROTAKA!
THEY'RE SELLING A LIMITED-EDITION CHURRO FLAVOR NEARBY!
ピッ
MEEP
(In Real-Date-Land)

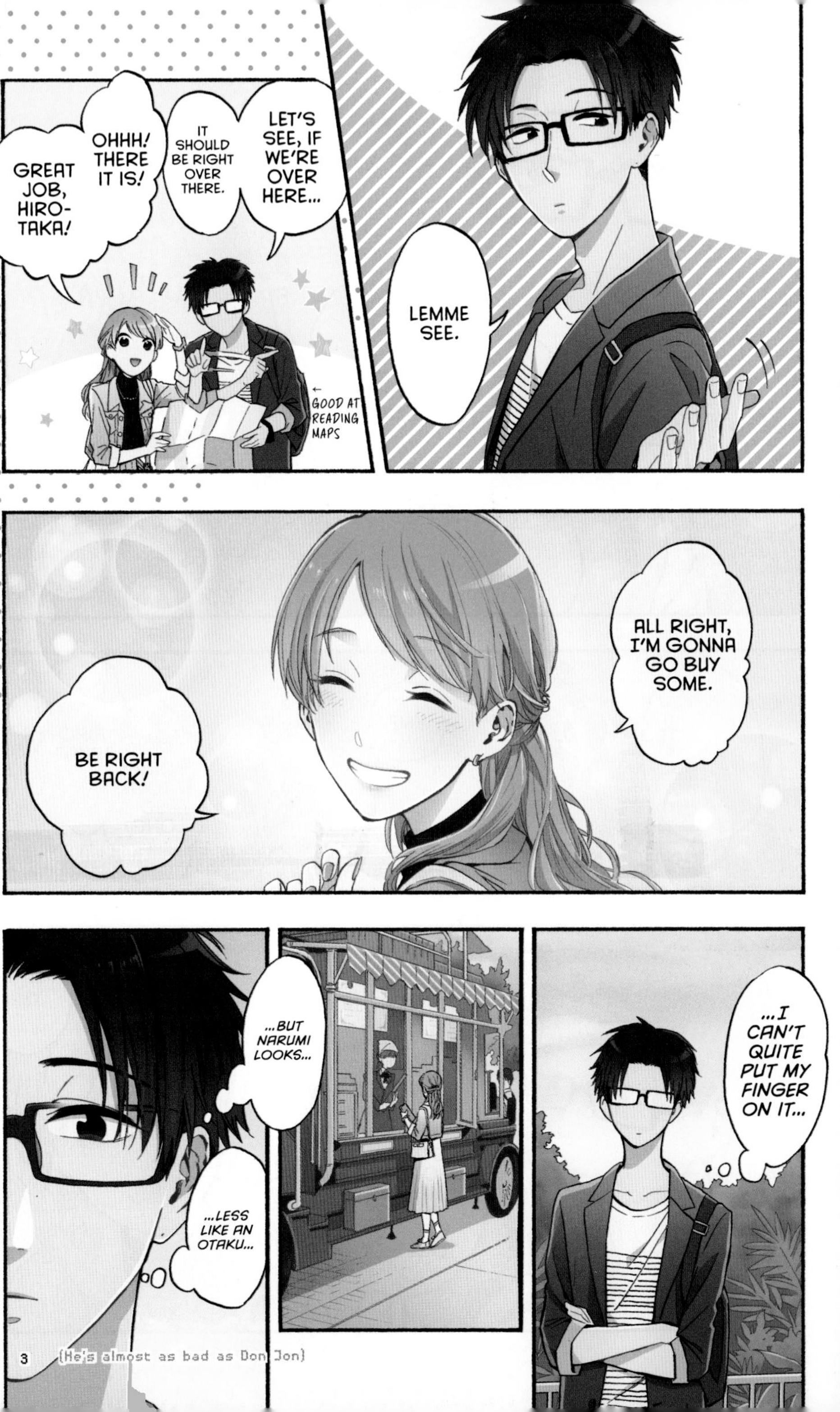
LEMME SEE.
LET'S SEE, IF WE'RE OVER HERE...
IT SHOULD BE RIGHT OVER THERE.
OHHH! THERE IT IS!
GREAT JOB, HIRO-TAKA!
← GOOD AT READING MAPS
ALL RIGHT, I'M GONNA GO BUY SOME.
BE RIGHT BACK!
...I CAN'T QUITE PUT MY FINGER ON IT...
...BUT NARUMI LOOKS...
...LESS LIKE AN OTAKU...

 [He's almost as bad as Don Jon]

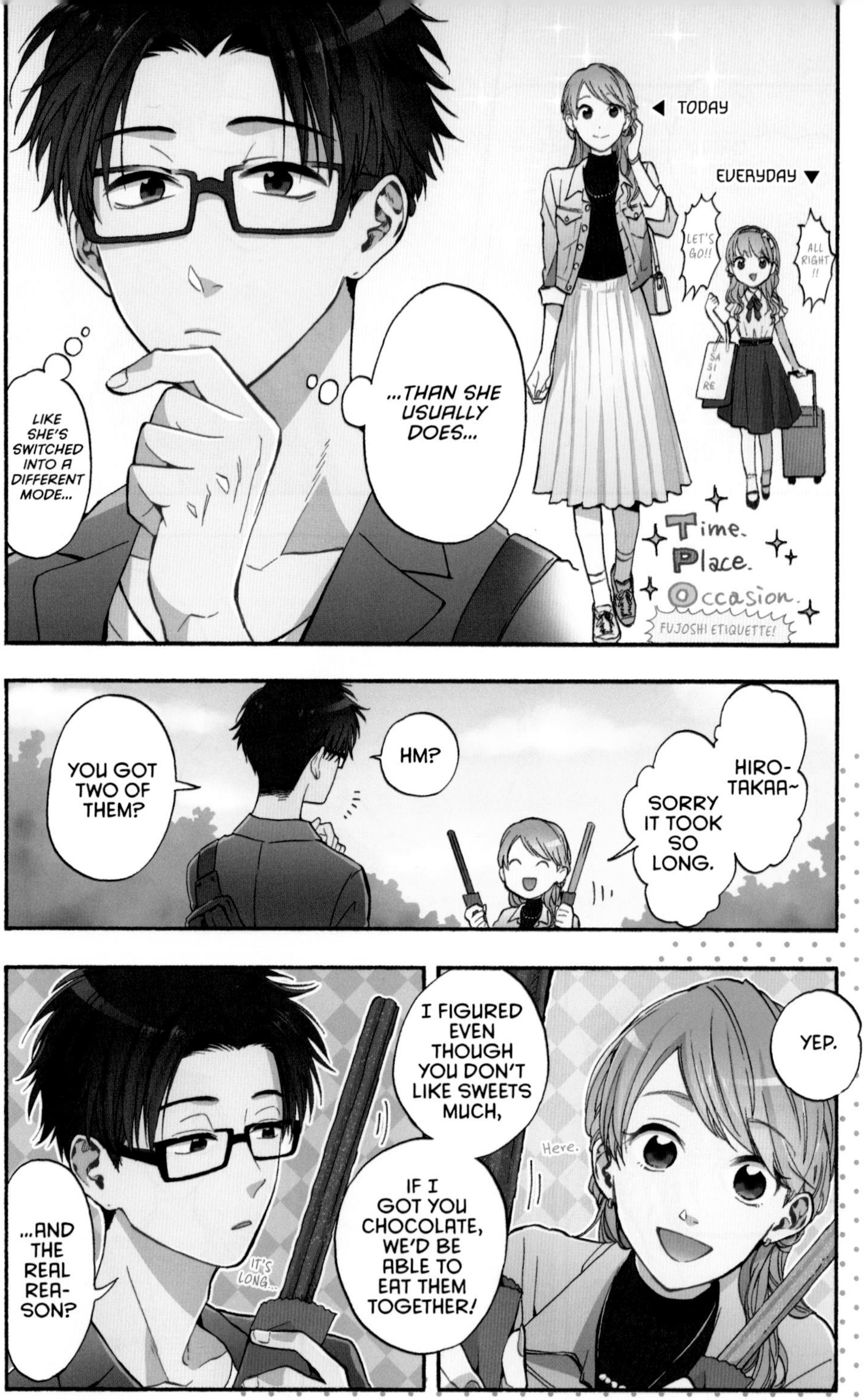
◀ TODAY
EVERYDAY ▼
LET'S GO!!
ALL RIGHT!!
SASIIRE
Time. Place. Occasion.
FUJOSHI ETIQUETTE!
...THAN SHE USUALLY DOES...
LIKE SHE'S SWITCHED INTO A DIFFERENT MODE...
HIRO-TAKAA~
SORRY IT TOOK SO LONG.
HM?
YOU GOT TWO OF THEM?
YEP.
I FIGURED EVEN THOUGH YOU DON'T LIKE SWEETS MUCH,
Here.
IF I GOT YOU CHOCOLATE, WE'D BE ABLE TO EAT THEM TOGETHER!
IT'S LONG...
...AND THE REAL REASON?

(Eating them is a daunting task)

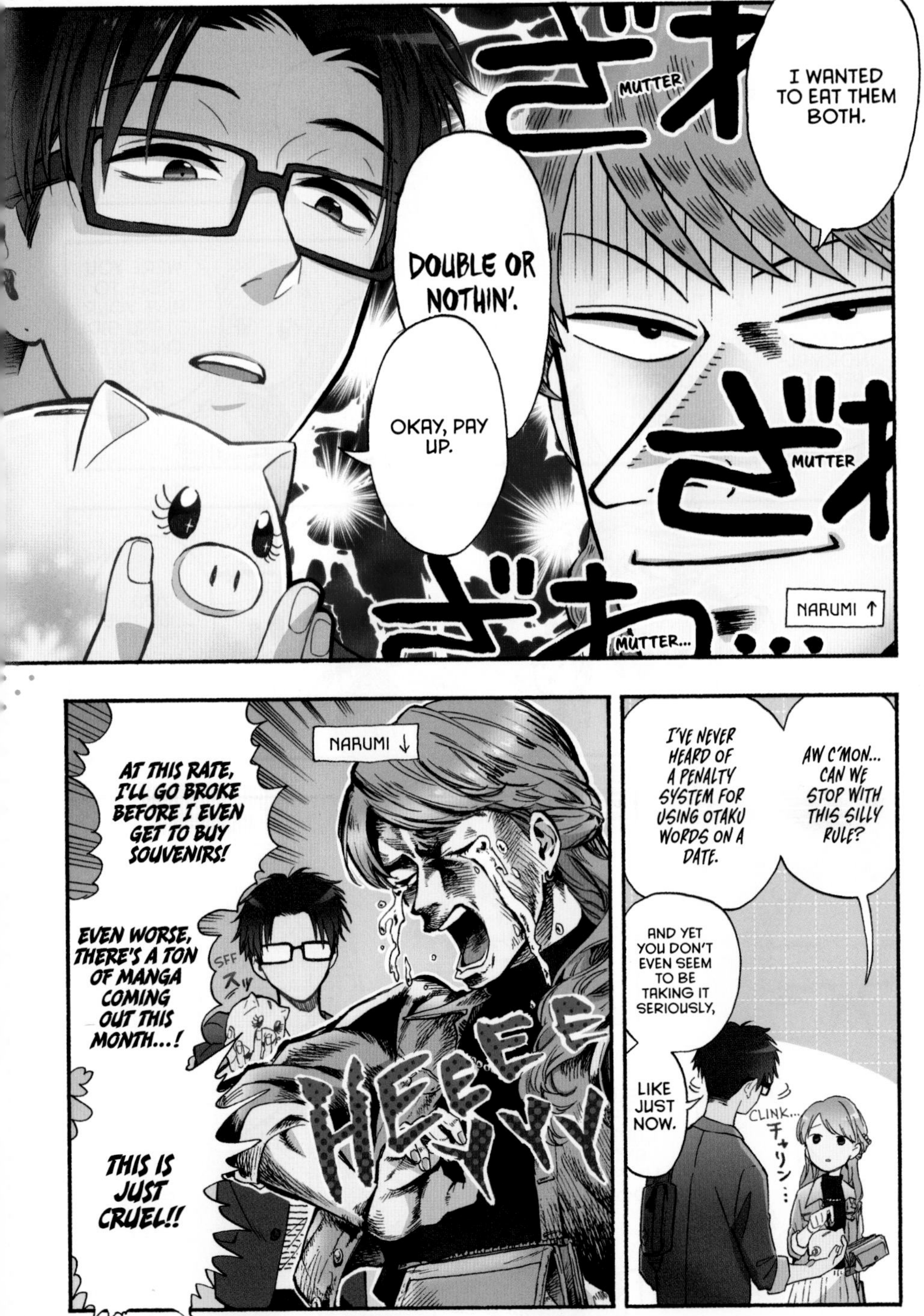
I WANTED TO EAT THEM BOTH.
MUTTER
DOUBLE OR NOTHIN'.
OKAY, PAY UP.
MUTTER
NARUMI ↑
MUTTER...
AW C'MON... CAN WE STOP WITH THIS SILLY RULE?
I'VE NEVER HEARD OF A PENALTY SYSTEM FOR USING OTAKU WORDS ON A DATE.
AND YET YOU DON'T EVEN SEEM TO BE TAKING IT SERIOUSLY,
LIKE JUST NOW.
CLINK...
チャリン…
NARUMI ↓
AT THIS RATE, I'LL GO BROKE BEFORE I EVEN GET TO BUY SOUVENIRS!
EVEN WORSE, THERE'S A TON OF MANGA COMING OUT THIS MONTH...!
HEEEEYY
SFF
スッ
THIS IS JUST CRUEL!!

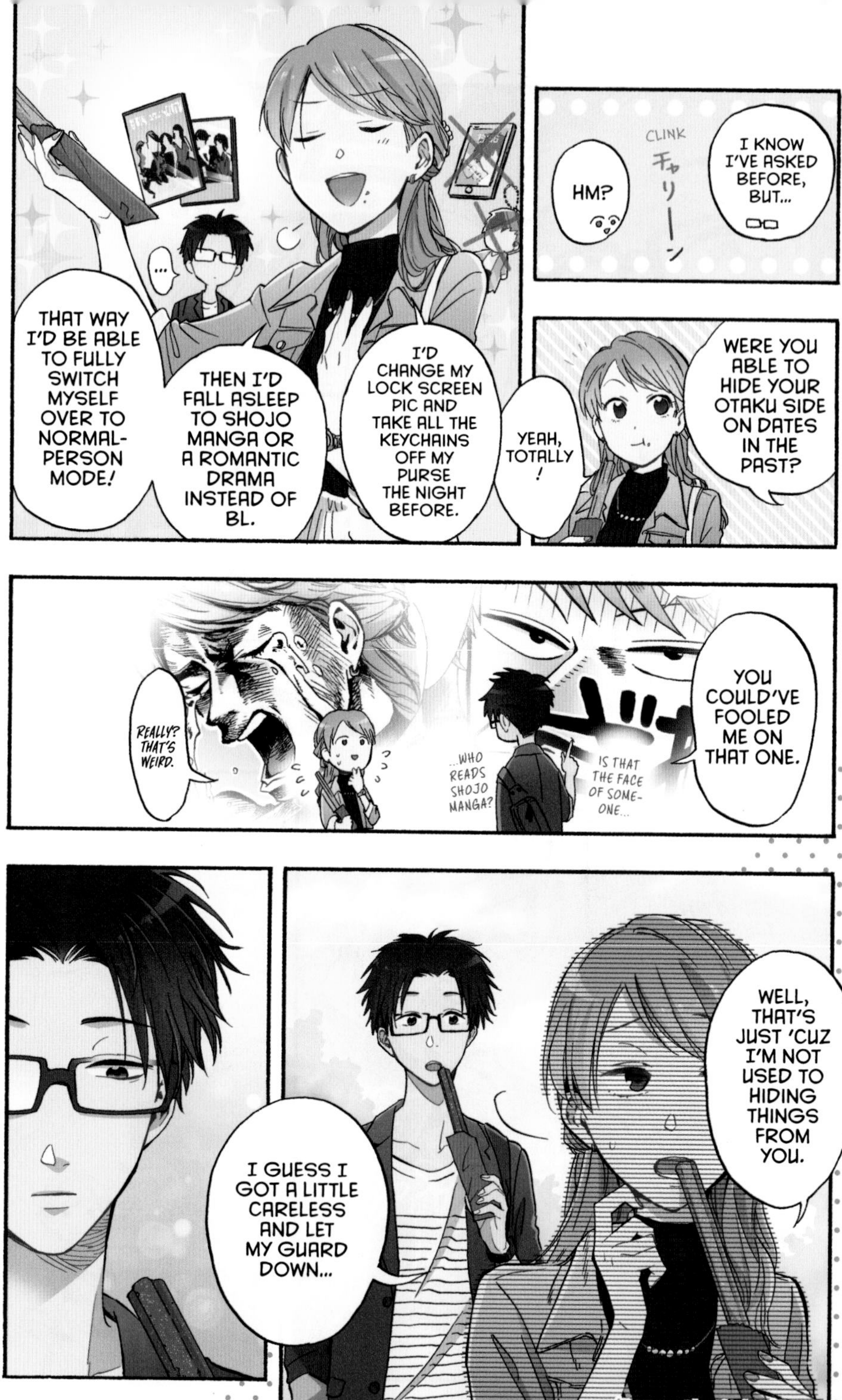
I KNOW I'VE ASKED BEFORE, BUT...
CLINK
チャリーン
HM?
WERE YOU ABLE TO HIDE YOUR OTAKU SIDE ON DATES IN THE PAST?
YEAH, TOTALLY!
I'D CHANGE MY LOCK SCREEN PIC AND TAKE ALL THE KEYCHAINS OFF MY PURSE THE NIGHT BEFORE.
THEN I'D FALL ASLEEP TO SHOJO MANGA OR A ROMANTIC DRAMA INSTEAD OF BL.
THAT WAY I'D BE ABLE TO FULLY SWITCH MYSELF OVER TO NORMAL-PERSON MODE!
...
YOU COULD'VE FOOLED ME ON THAT ONE.
IS THAT THE FACE OF SOME-ONE...
...WHO READS SHOJO MANGA?
REALLY? THAT'S WEIRD.
WELL, THAT'S JUST 'CUZ I'M NOT USED TO HIDING THINGS FROM YOU.
I GUESS I GOT A LITTLE CARELESS AND LET MY GUARD DOWN...

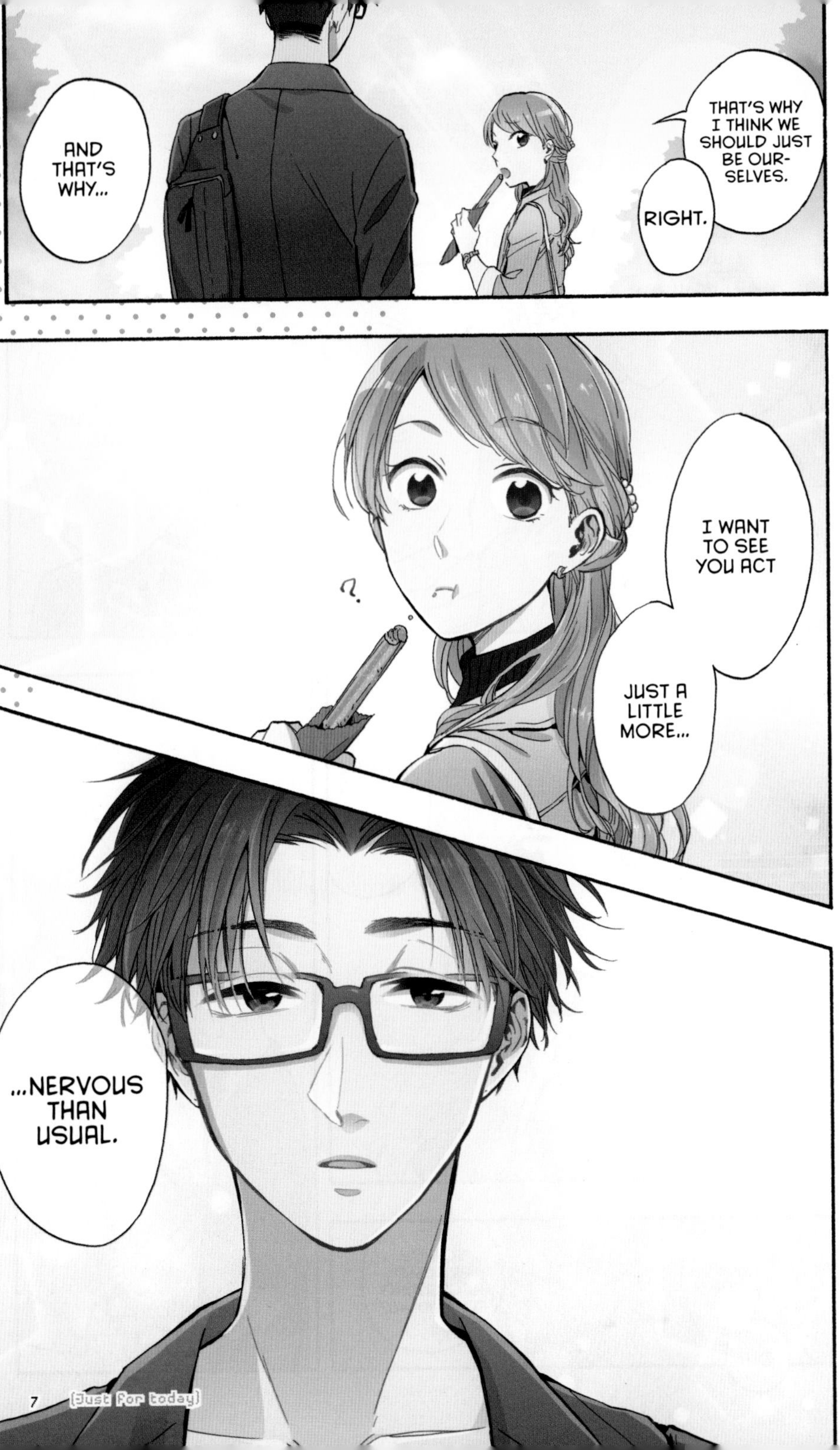
THAT'S WHY I THINK WE SHOULD JUST BE OUR-SELVES.
RIGHT.
AND THAT'S WHY...
I WANT TO SEE YOU ACT
JUST A LITTLE MORE...
...NERVOUS THAN USUAL.

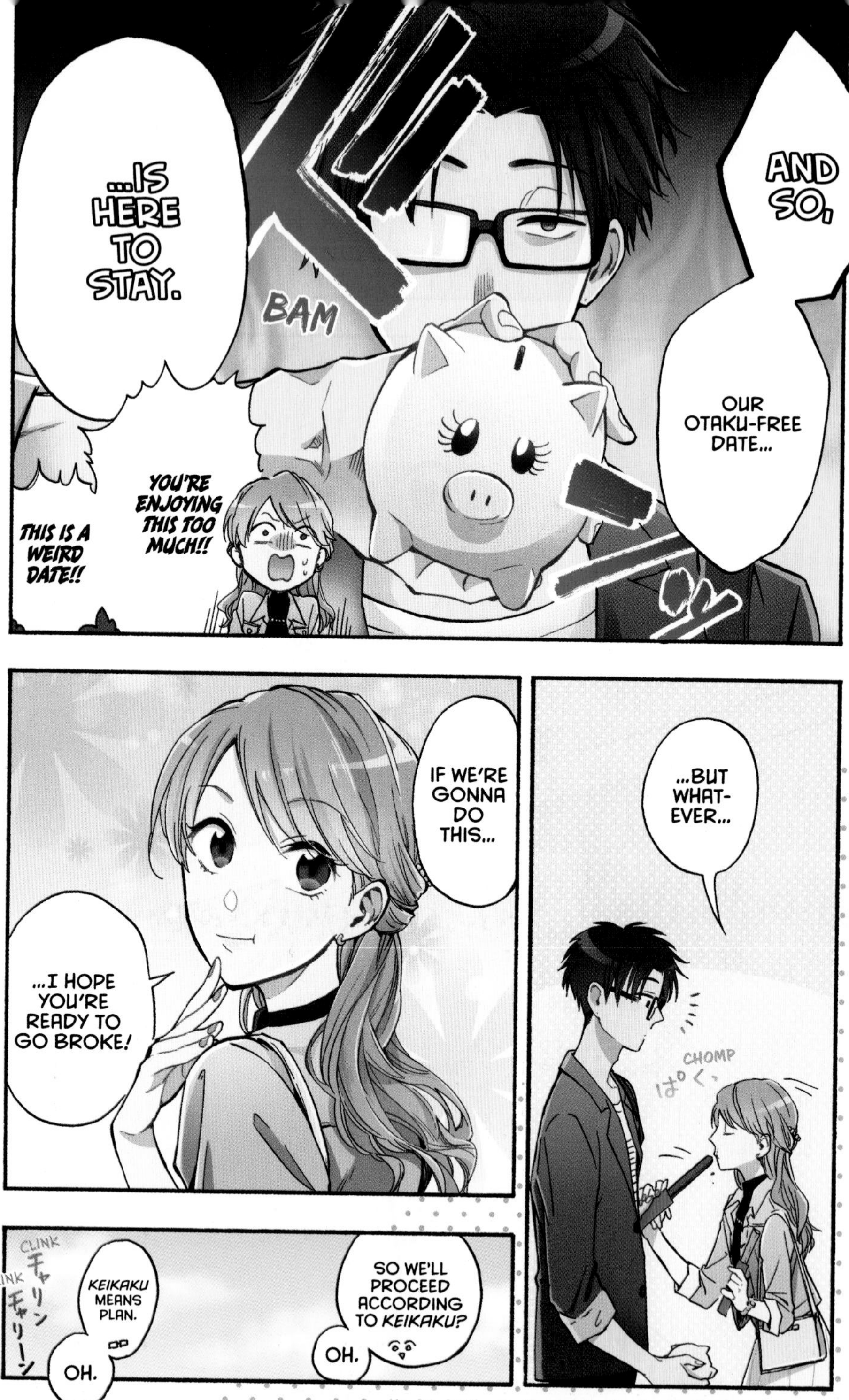
AND SO,
OUR OTAKU-FREE DATE...
...IS HERE TO STAY.
BAM
YOU'RE ENJOYING THIS TOO MUCH!!
THIS IS A WEIRD DATE!!
...BUT WHATEVER...
CHOMP
ぱく
IF WE'RE GONNA DO THIS...
...I HOPE YOU'RE READY TO GO BROKE!
SO WE'LL PROCEED ACCORDING TO KEIKAKU?
OH.
KEIKAKU MEANS PLAN.
OH.
CLINK
チャリン
CLINK
チャリーン

(In the throes of a date with strings attached)

To Be Continued...

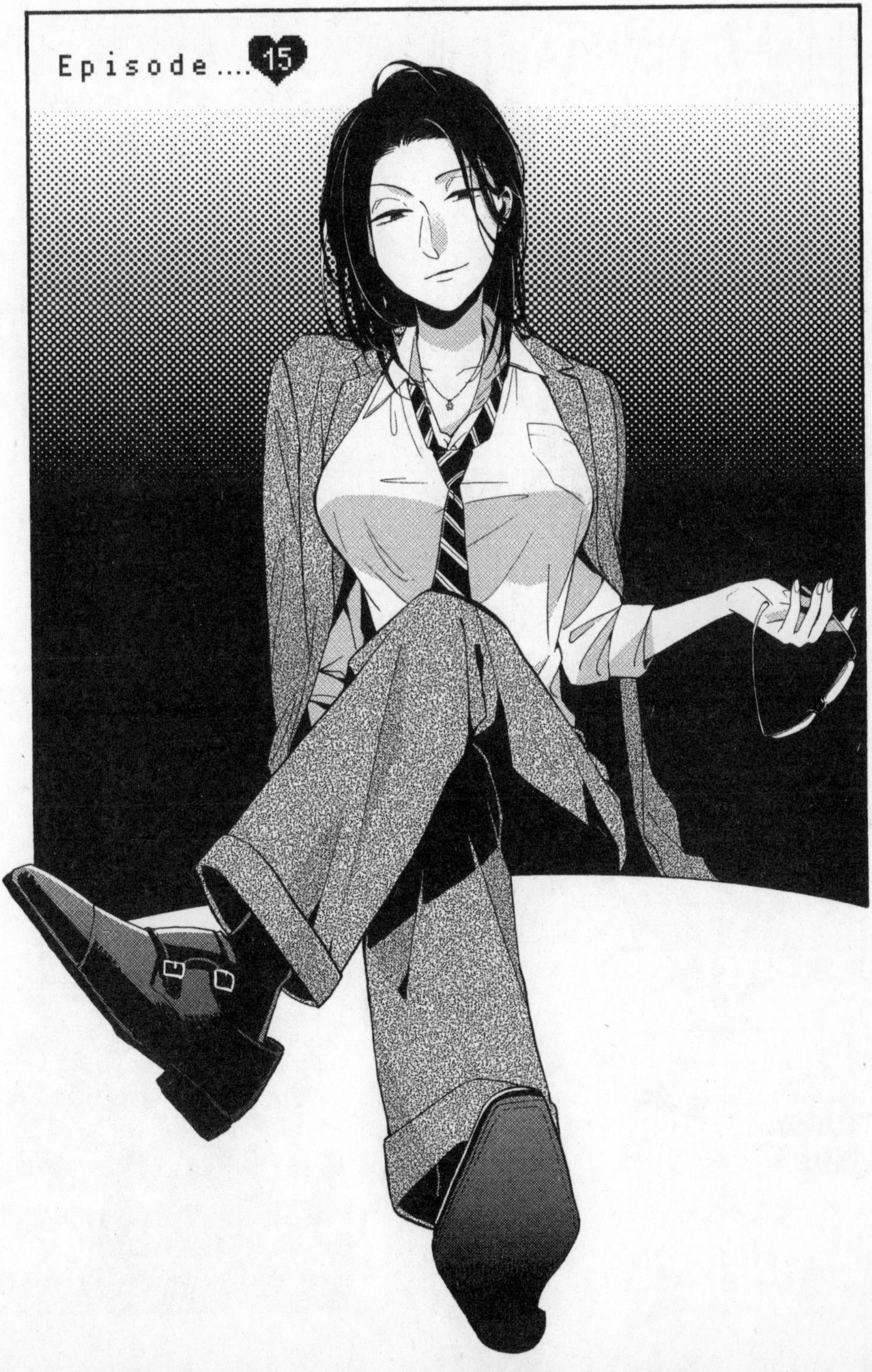
Episode.... 15

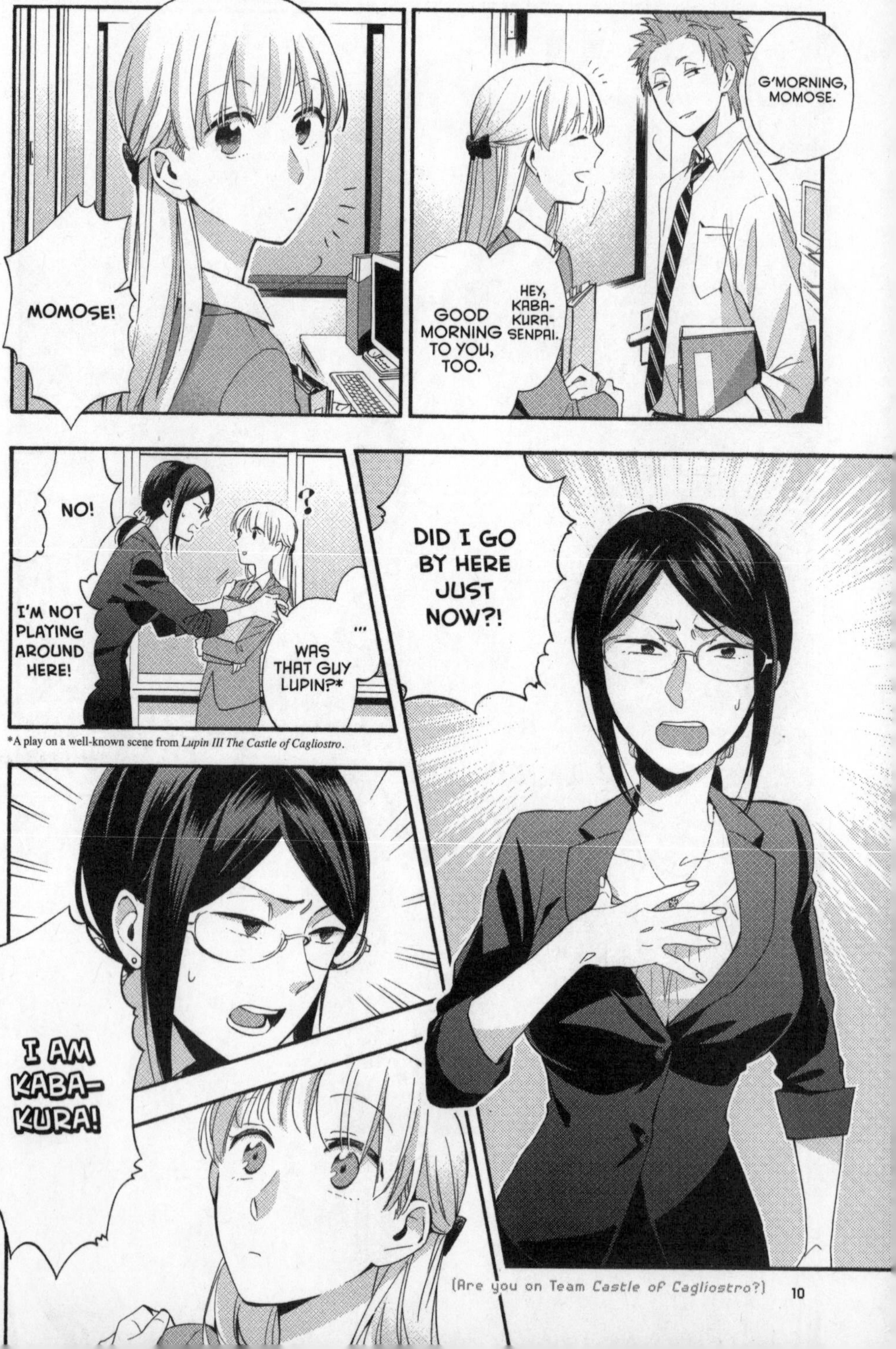
G'MORNING, MOMOSE.
HEY, KABA-KURA-SENPAI.
GOOD MORNING TO YOU, TOO.
MOMOSE!
DID I GO BY HERE JUST NOW?!
...
WAS THAT GUY LUPIN?*
NO!
I'M NOT PLAYING AROUND HERE!
I AM KABA-KURA!
(Are you on Team *Castle of Cagliostro*?)

*A play on a well-known scene from *Lupin III The Castle of Cagliostro*.

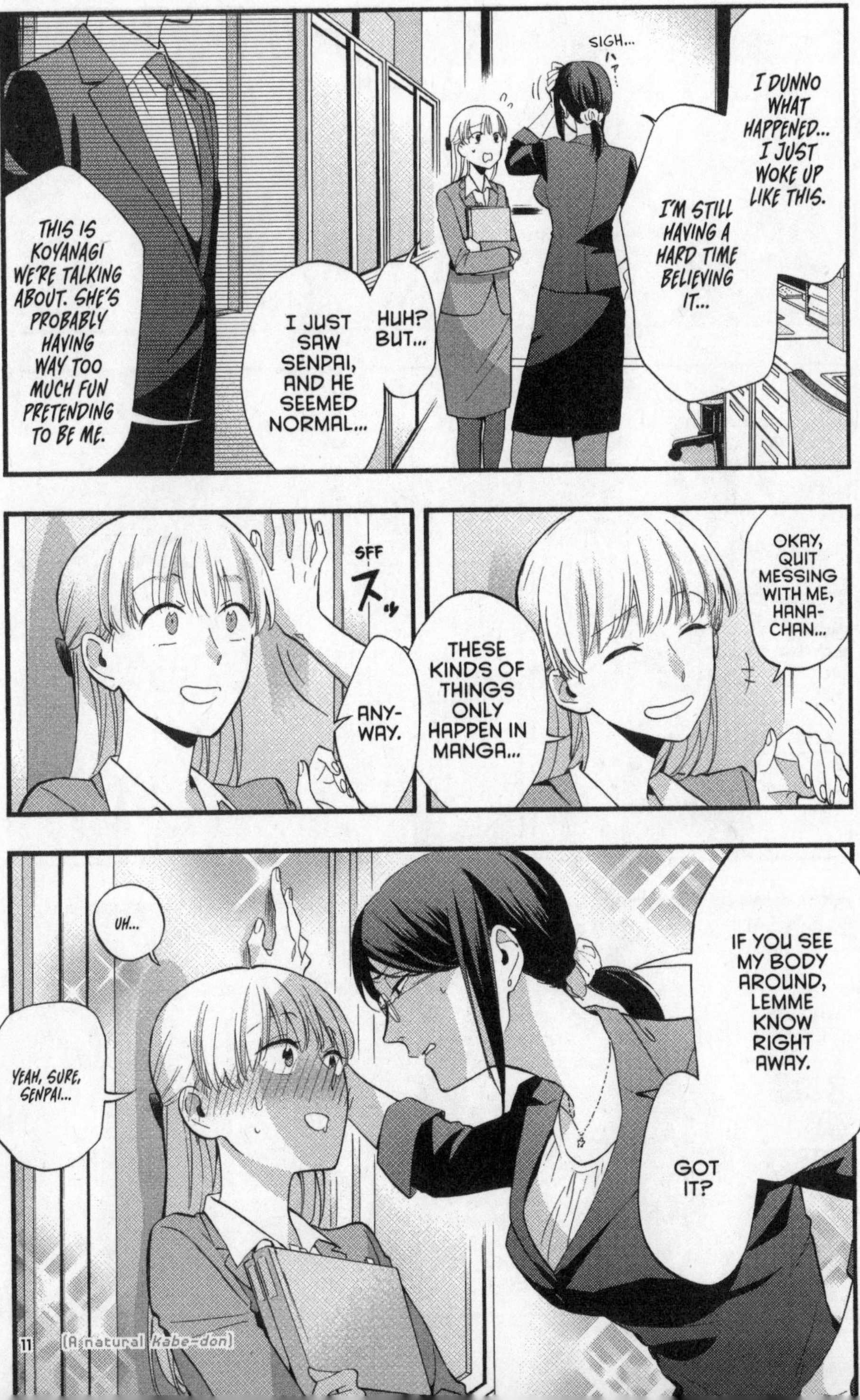
SIGH... ハァ...
I DUNNO WHAT HAPPENED... I JUST WOKE UP LIKE THIS.
I'M STILL HAVING A HARD TIME BELIEVING IT...
HUH? BUT...
I JUST SAW SENPAI, AND HE SEEMED NORMAL...
THIS IS KOYANAGI WE'RE TALKING ABOUT. SHE'S PROBABLY HAVING WAY TOO MUCH FUN PRETENDING TO BE ME.
OKAY, QUIT MESSING WITH ME, HANA-CHAN...
THESE KINDS OF THINGS ONLY HAPPEN IN MANGA...
SFF スッ
ANY-WAY.
IF YOU SEE MY BODY AROUND, LEMME KNOW RIGHT AWAY.
GOT IT?
UH...
YEAH, SURE, SENPAI...
(A natural kabe-don)

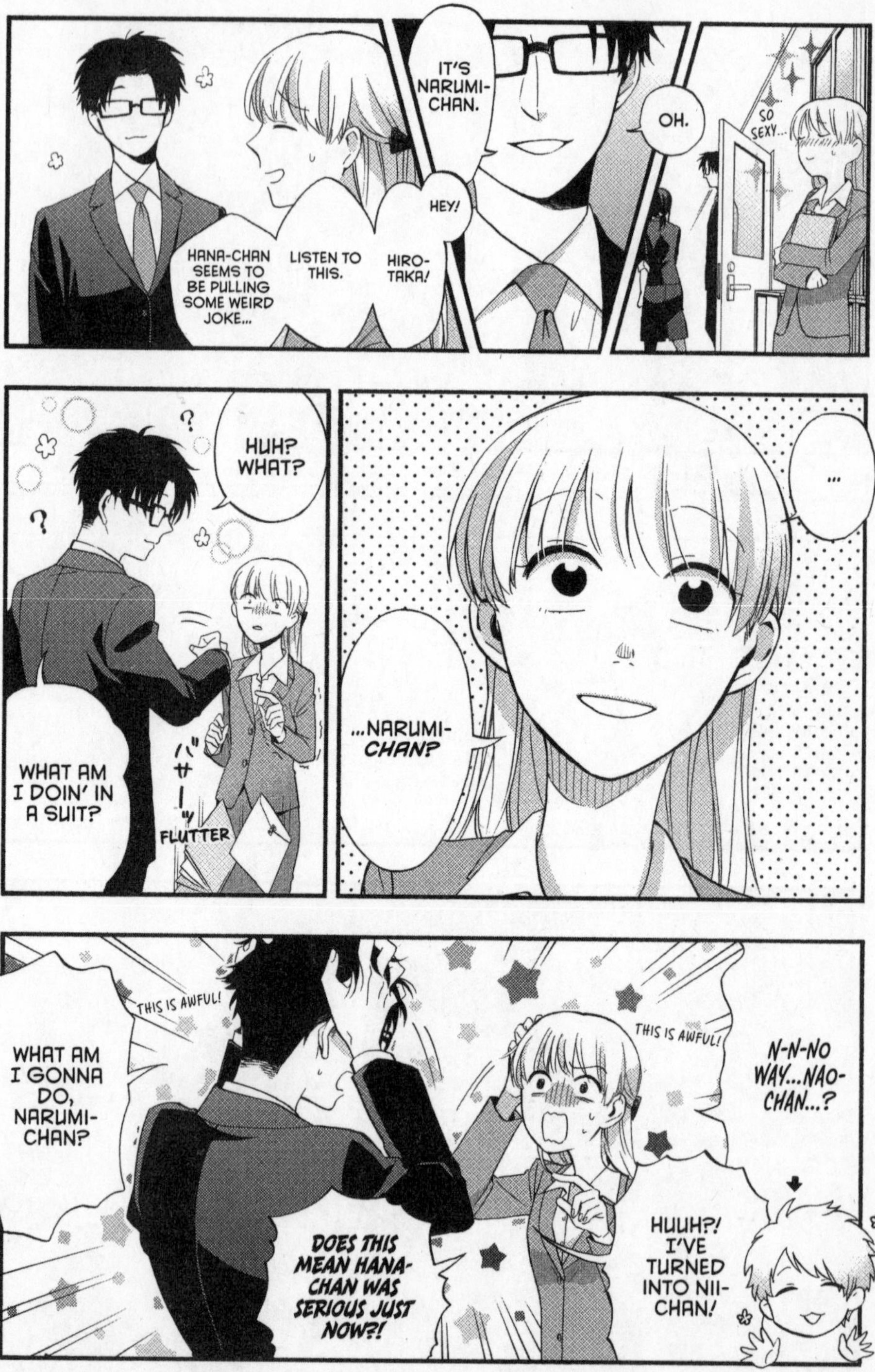
SO SEXY...
OH.
IT'S NARUMI-CHAN.
HEY!
HIRO-TAKA!
LISTEN TO THIS.
HANA-CHAN SEEMS TO BE PULLING SOME WEIRD JOKE...
...
...NARUMI-CHAN?
HUH? WHAT?
バサーッ
FLUTTER
WHAT AM I DOIN' IN A SUIT?
N-N-NO WAY...NAO-CHAN...?
THIS IS AWFUL!
HUUH?! I'VE TURNED INTO NII-CHAN!
THIS IS AWFUL!
DOES THIS MEAN HANA-CHAN WAS SERIOUS JUST NOW?!
WHAT AM I GONNA DO, NARUMI-CHAN?

(? ω ?)

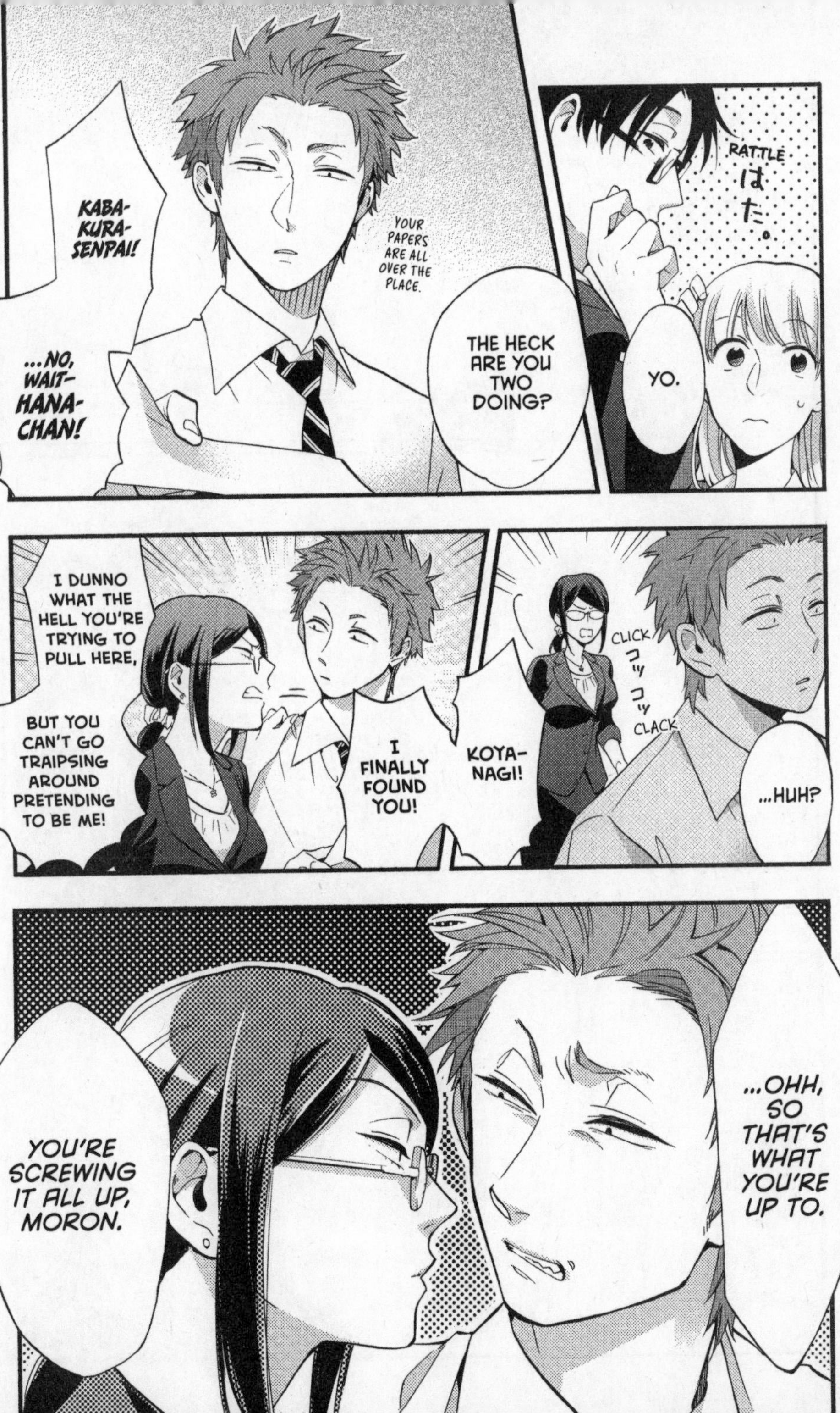
RATTLE
はた。
YO.
THE HECK ARE YOU TWO DOING?
YOUR PAPERS ARE ALL OVER THE PLACE.
KABA-KURA-SENPAI!
...NO, WAIT-HANA-CHAN!
...HUH?
CLICK
コツ
コツ
CLACK
KOYA-NAGI!
I FINALLY FOUND YOU!
I DUNNO WHAT THE HELL YOU'RE TRYING TO PULL HERE,
BUT YOU CAN'T GO TRAIPSING AROUND PRETENDING TO BE ME!
...OHH, SO THAT'S WHAT YOU'RE UP TO.
YOU'RE SCREWING IT ALL UP, MORON.

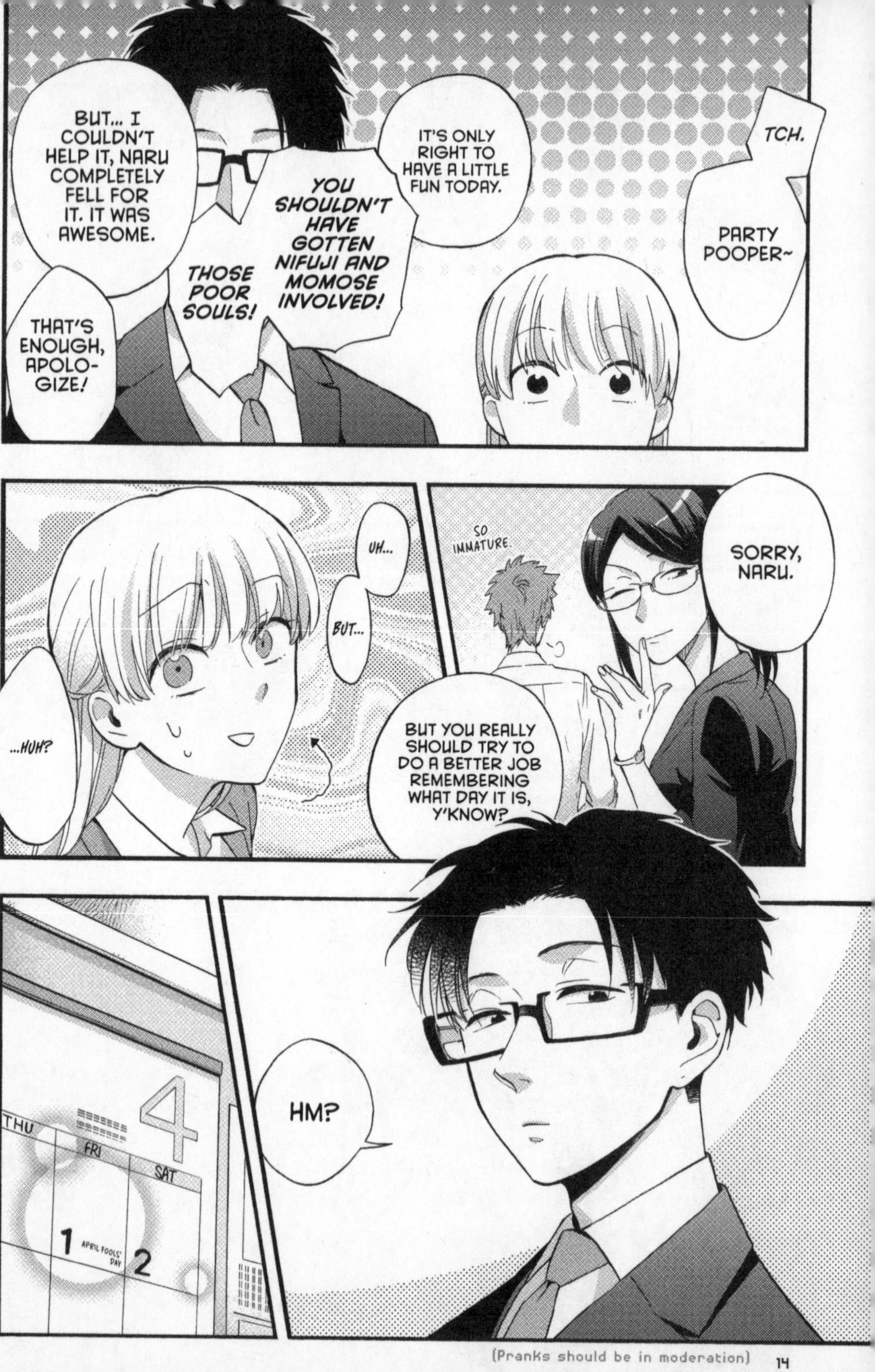
TCH.
PARTY POOPER~
IT'S ONLY RIGHT TO HAVE A LITTLE FUN TODAY.
YOU SHOULDN'T HAVE GOTTEN NIFUJI AND MOMOSE INVOLVED!
THOSE POOR SOULS!
BUT... I COULDN'T HELP IT, NARU COMPLETELY FELL FOR IT. IT WAS AWESOME.
THAT'S ENOUGH, APOLOGIZE!
SORRY, NARU.
SO IMMATURE.
BUT YOU REALLY SHOULD TRY TO DO A BETTER JOB REMEMBERING WHAT DAY IT IS, Y'KNOW?
UH...
BUT...
...HUH?
HM?
4
THU
FRI
SAT
1
APRIL FOOLS' DAY
2

(Pranks should be in moderation)

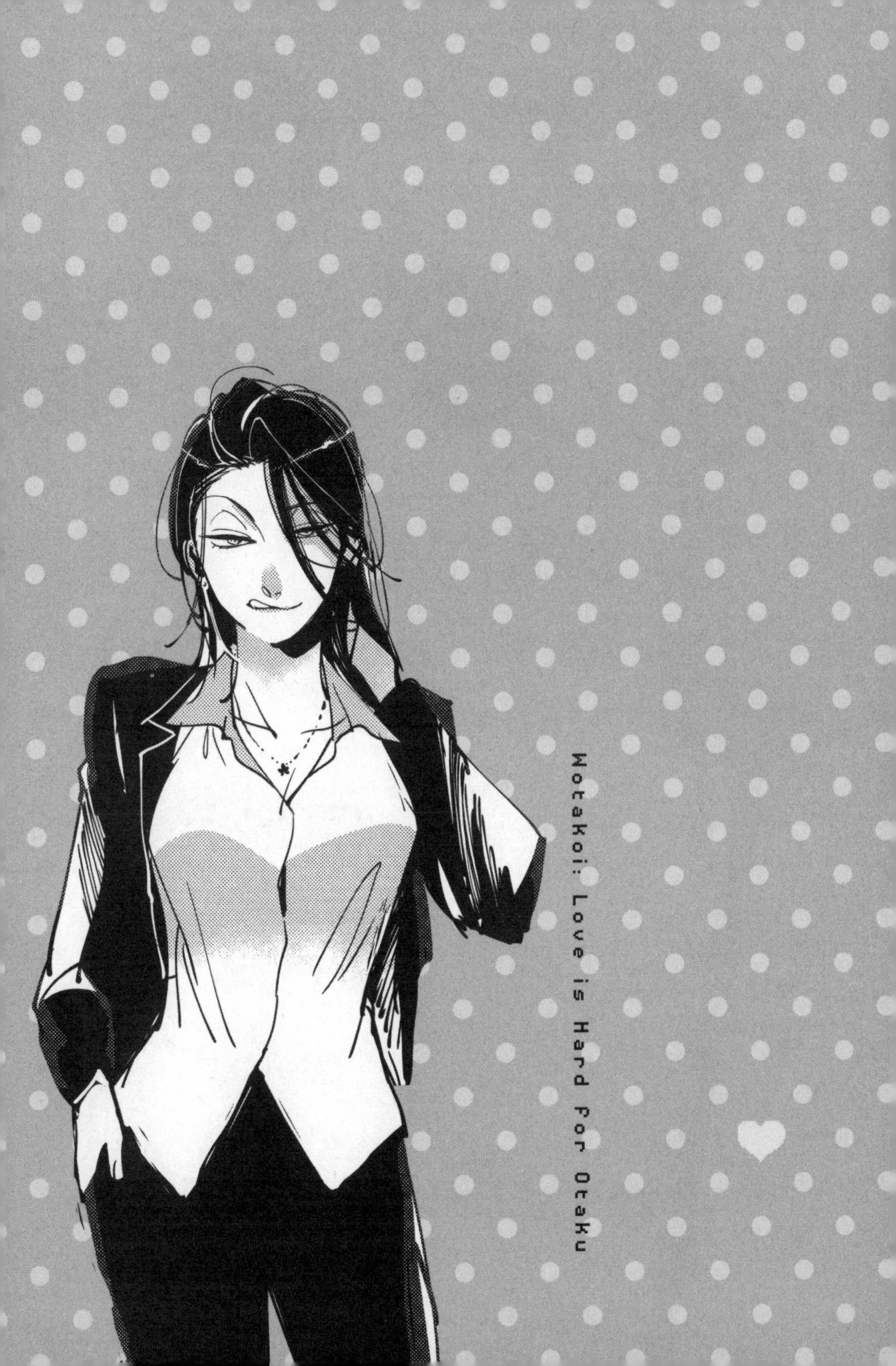
Wotakoi: Love is Hard for Otaku

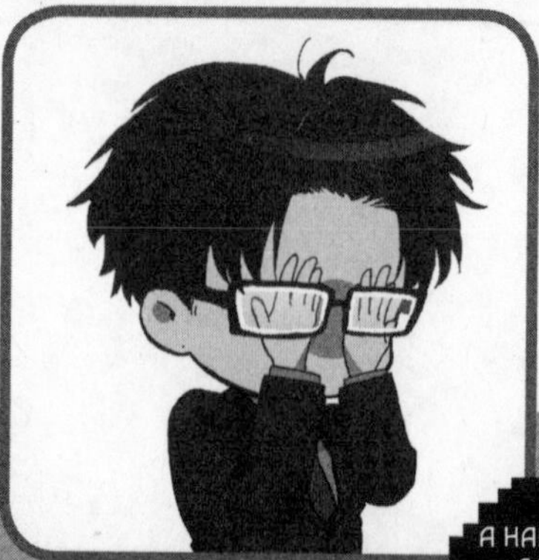

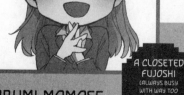

A HARDCORE GAMER
(HE'S GOOD AT PRETTY MUCH ALL TYPES OF VIDEO GAMES)

HIROTAKA NIFUJI

Frequently sends messages with just stamps and emoticons. He will faithfully return texts, but his response time varies. He's much more expressive when he's communicating electronically. He's a fairly fast typer on his smartphone, but even faster on a keyboard.

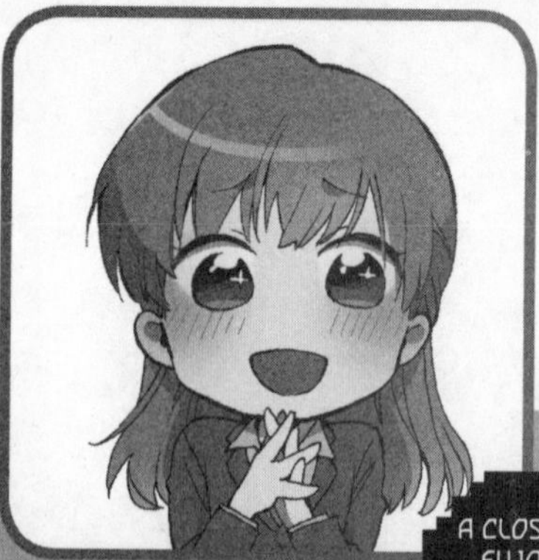

A CLOSETED FUJOSHI
(ALWAYS BUSY WITH WAY TOO MANY INTERESTS)

NARUMI MOMOSE

No matter when you text her, she'll read it in under a minute, and reply 10 seconds after that. She types just as quickly on her smartphone as she does on a normal keyboard.

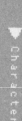

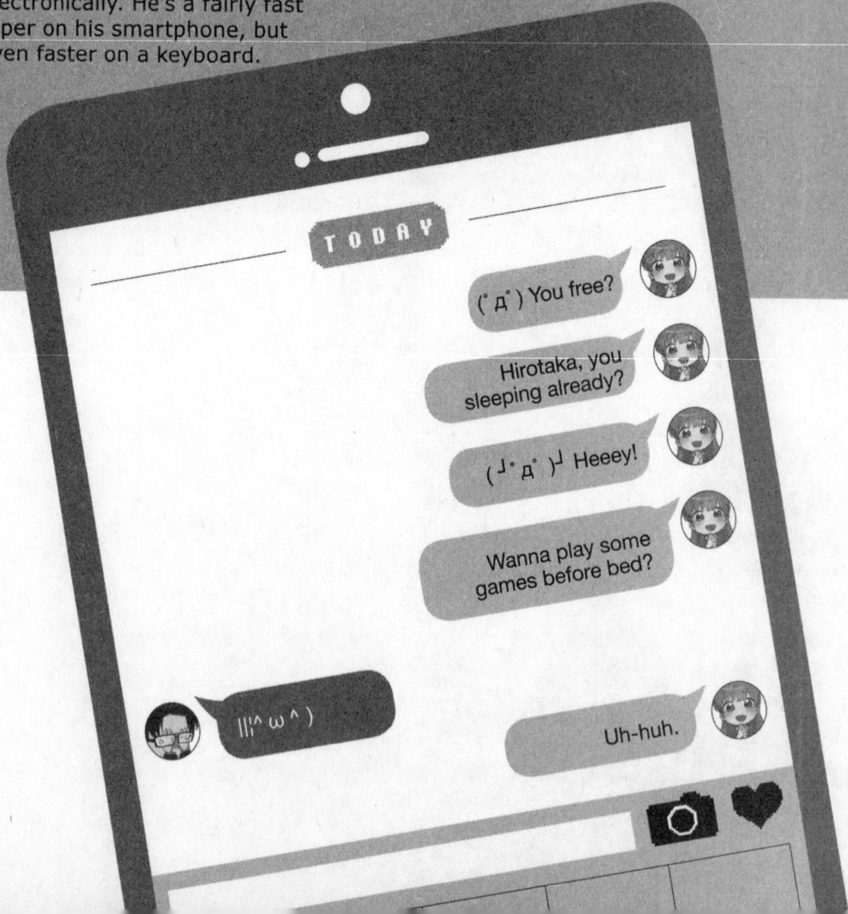
TODAY
(°д°) You free?
Hirotaka, you sleeping already?
(┘°д°)┘ Heeey!
Wanna play some games before bed?
||i^ω^)
Uh-huh.

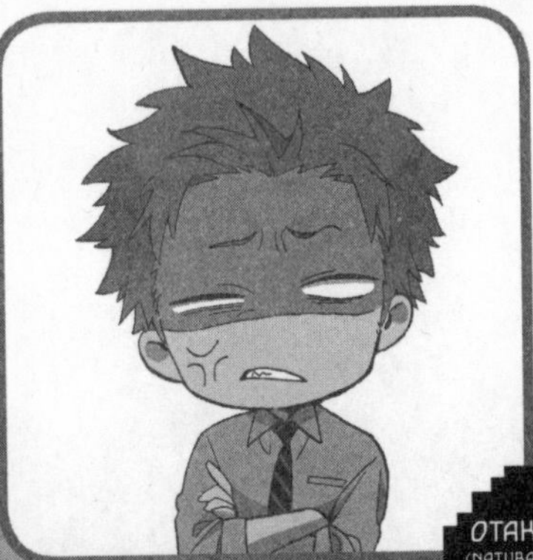

OTAKU LIGHT
(NATURALLY, HE GETS LURED IN BY COVERS WITH PRETTY GIRLS ON THEM)

TARO KABAKURA

SNS is about the only communication method he uses. He responds quickly but doesn't use flowery language, so his texts seem curt. He's never really gotten used to typing on a smartphone. He isn't exactly a slow typer, but because the others are abnormally quick he's the slowest of the four.

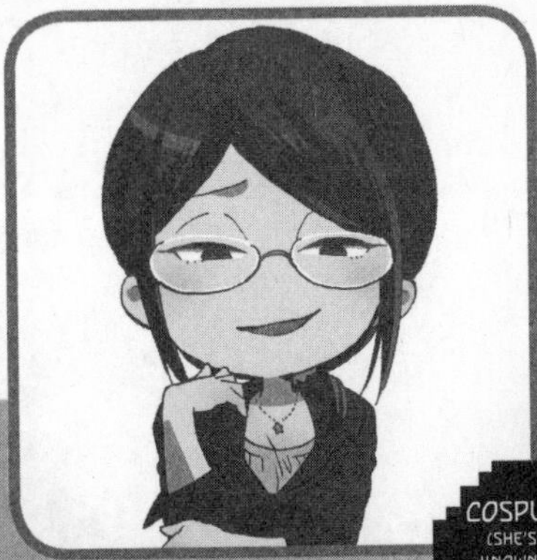

COSPLAYER
(SHE'S WELL-KNOWN IN THE SCENE FOR HER SKILL IN CROSSPLAY)

HANAKO KOYANAGI

Responds quickly to texts so long as she's not busy. She doesn't like to be curt, but she rarely uses emoticons (some might say *too* rarely) because she gets embarrassed. She's a self-taught typist so she has weird habits, but still types fairly quickly. She seems to have a bunch of online acquaintances.

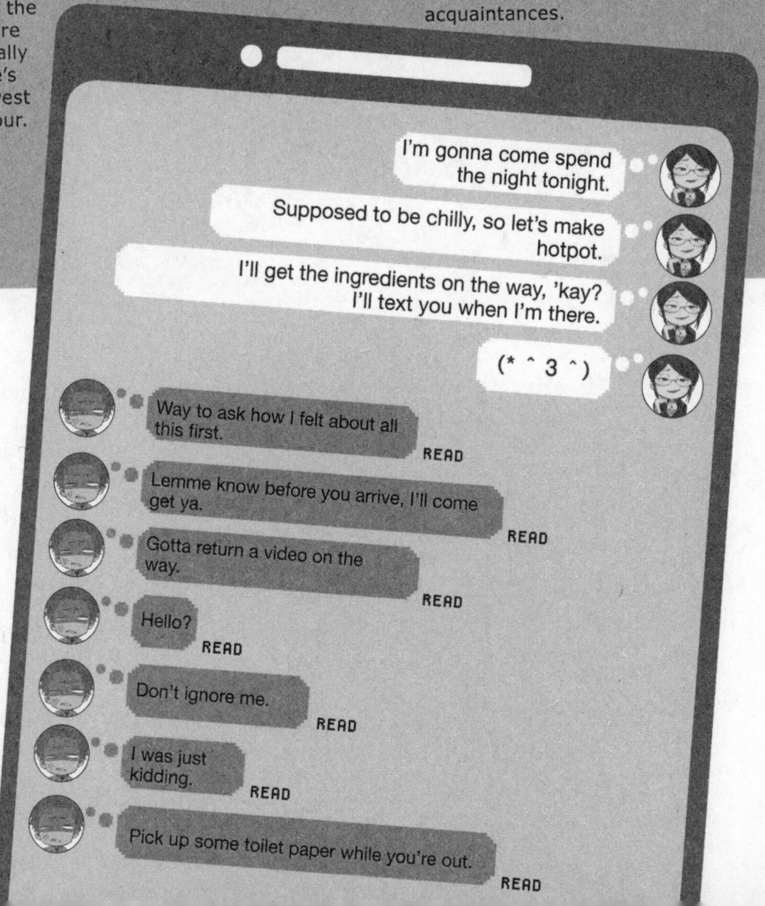
I'm gonna come spend the night tonight.
Supposed to be chilly, so let's make hotpot.
I'll get the ingredients on the way, 'kay? I'll text you when I'm there.
(* ^ 3 ^)
Way to ask how I felt about all this first.
READ
Lemme know before you arrive, I'll come get ya.
READ
Gotta return a video on the way.
READ
Hello?
READ
Don't ignore me.
READ
I was just kidding.
READ
Pick up some toilet paper while you're out.
READ

Wotakoi: Love is Hard for Otaku

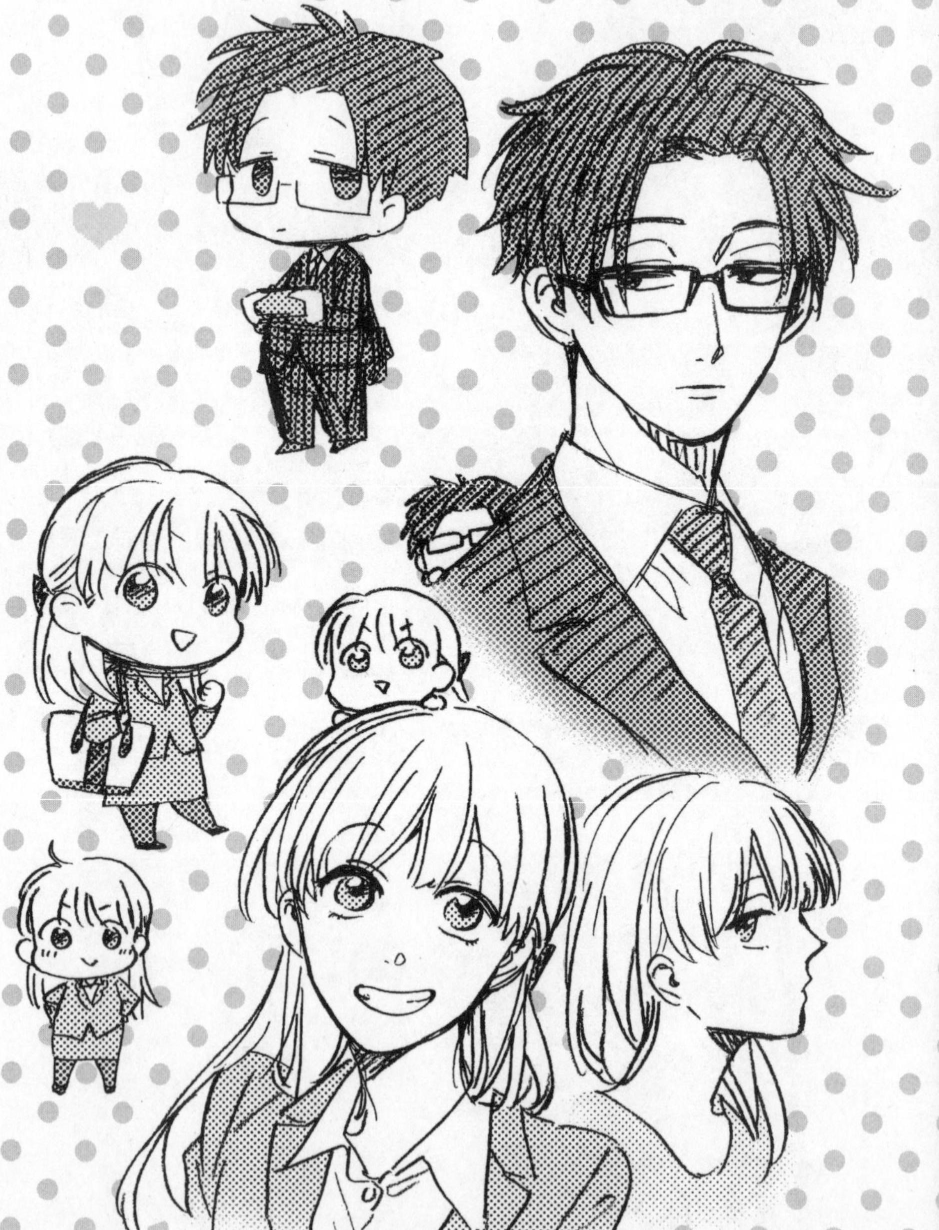

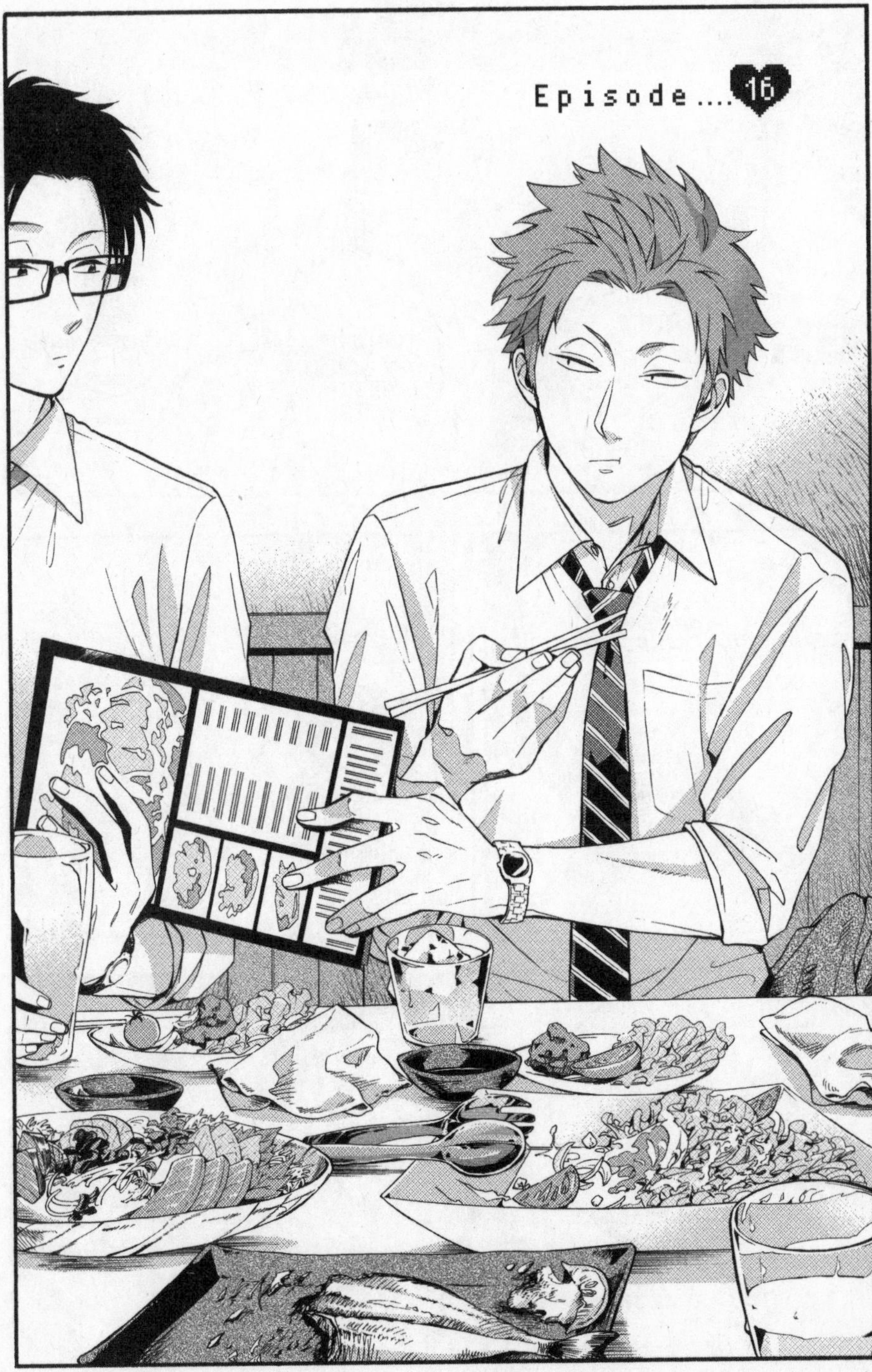
Episode....16

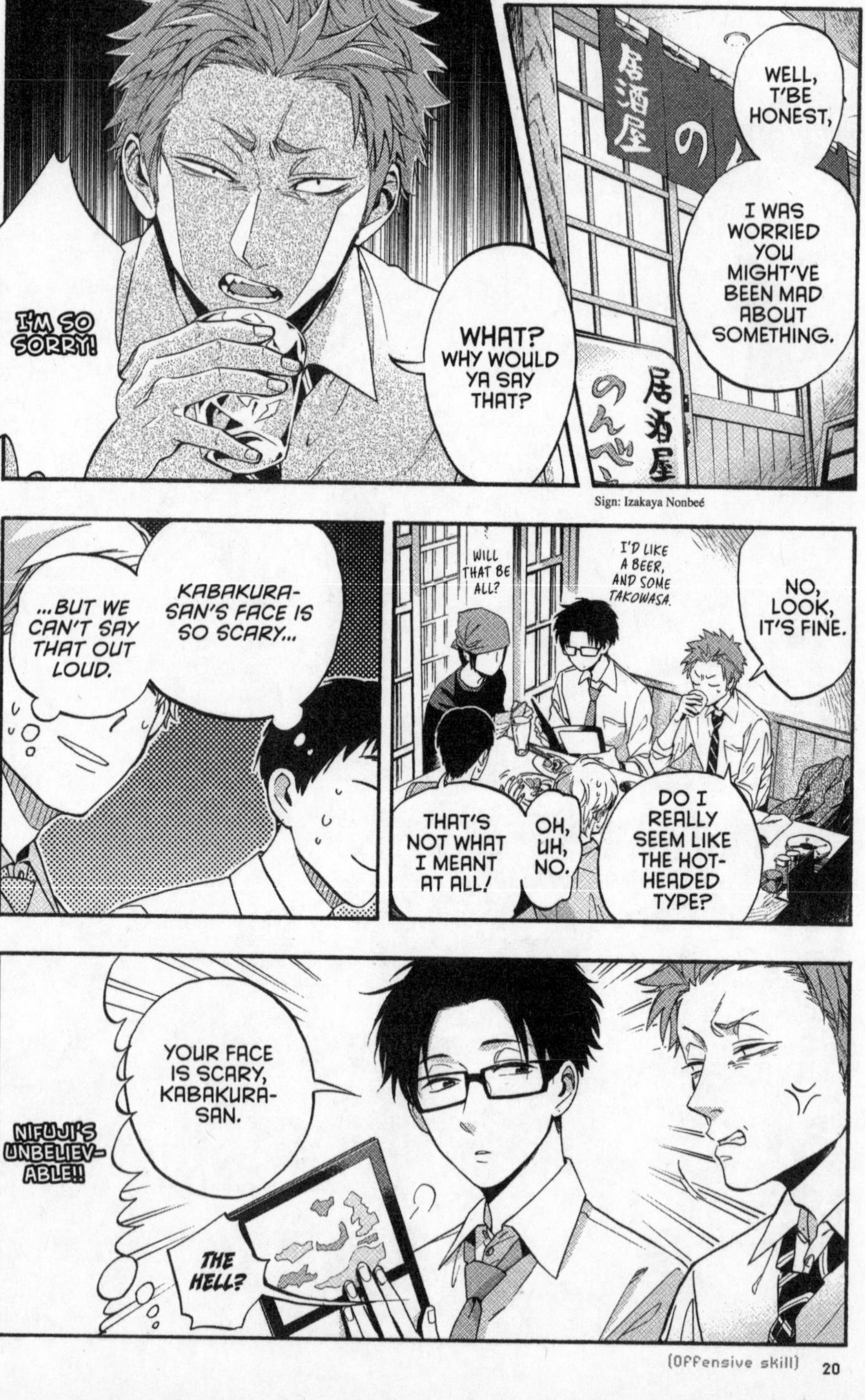
WELL, T'BE HONEST,
I WAS WORRIED YOU MIGHT'VE BEEN MAD ABOUT SOMETHING.
WHAT? WHY WOULD YA SAY THAT?
I'M SO SORRY!
NO, LOOK, IT'S FINE.
I'D LIKE A BEER, AND SOME TAKOWASA.
WILL THAT BE ALL?
DO I REALLY SEEM LIKE THE HOT-HEADED TYPE?
OH, UH, NO.
THAT'S NOT WHAT I MEANT AT ALL!
KABAKURA-SAN'S FACE IS SO SCARY...
...BUT WE CAN'T SAY THAT OUT LOUD.
YOUR FACE IS SCARY, KABAKURA-SAN.
NIFUJI'S UNBELIEV-ABLE!!
THE HELL?

Sign: Izakaya Nonbeé

(Offensive skill)

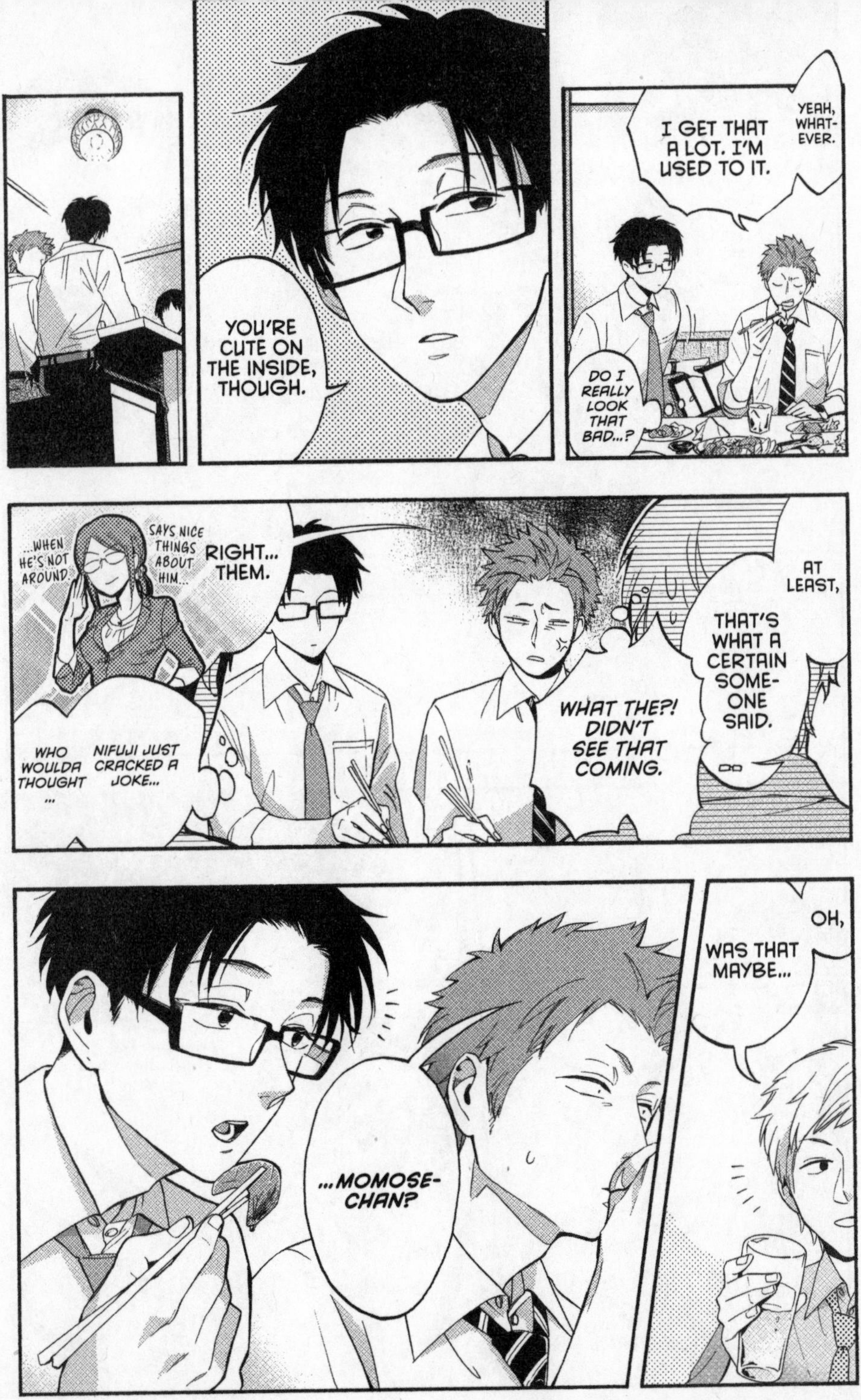
YEAH, WHAT-EVER.
I GET THAT A LOT. I'M USED TO IT.
DO I REALLY LOOK THAT BAD...?
YOU'RE CUTE ON THE INSIDE, THOUGH.
AT LEAST,
THAT'S WHAT A CERTAIN SOME-ONE SAID.
WHAT THE?! DIDN'T SEE THAT COMING.
RIGHT... THEM.
SAYS NICE THINGS ABOUT HIM...
...WHEN HE'S NOT AROUND.
NIFUJI JUST CRACKED A JOKE...
WHO WOULDA THOUGHT ...
OH,
WAS THAT MAYBE...
...MOMOSE-CHAN?

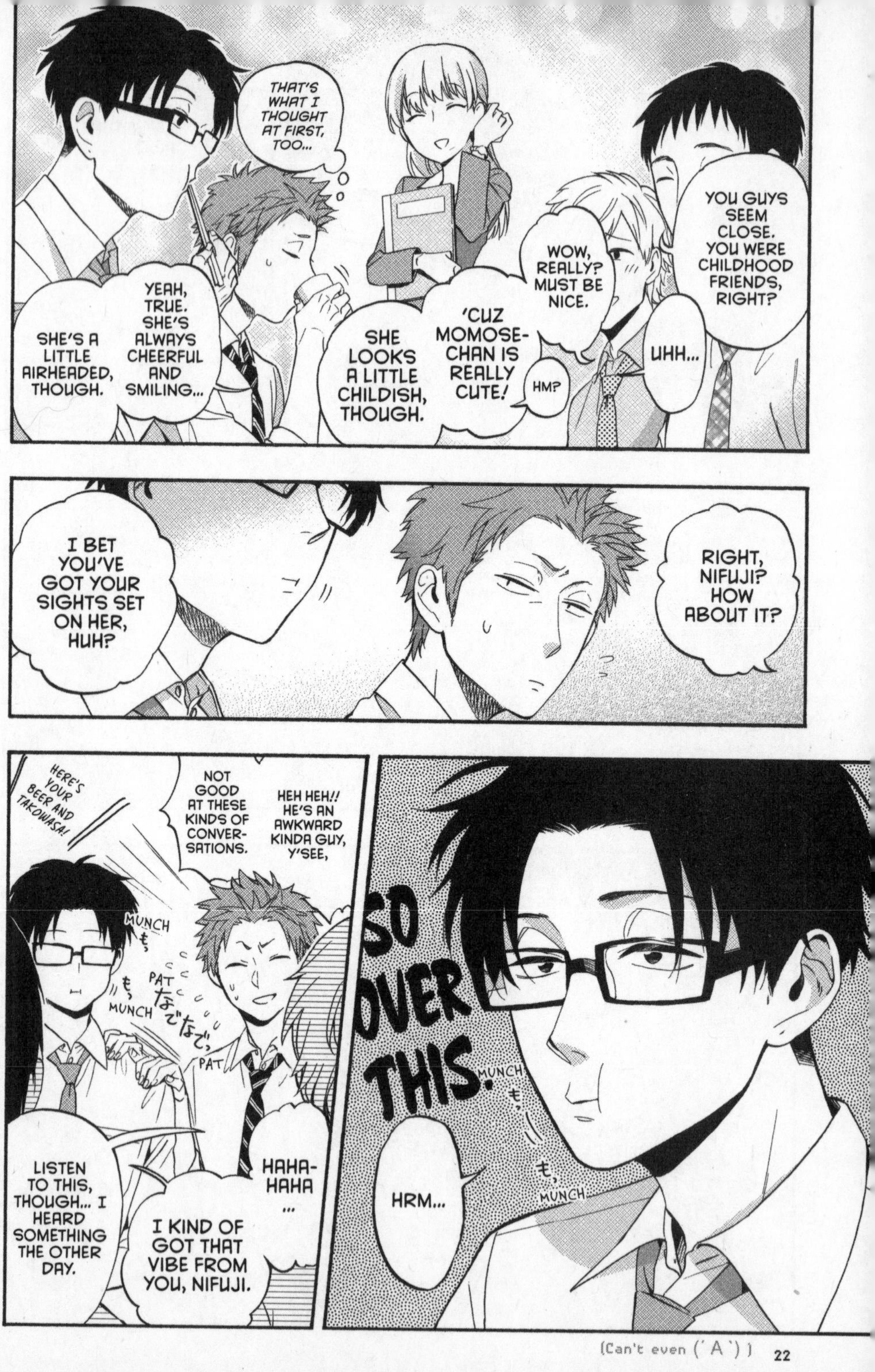
YOU GUYS SEEM CLOSE. YOU WERE CHILDHOOD FRIENDS, RIGHT?
UHH...
WOW, REALLY? MUST BE NICE.
HM?
'CUZ MOMOSE-CHAN IS REALLY CUTE!
SHE LOOKS A LITTLE CHILDISH, THOUGH.
THAT'S WHAT I THOUGHT AT FIRST, TOO...
YEAH, TRUE. SHE'S ALWAYS CHEERFUL AND SMILING...
SHE'S A LITTLE AIRHEADED, THOUGH.
RIGHT, NIFUJI? HOW ABOUT IT?
I BET YOU'VE GOT YOUR SIGHTS SET ON HER, HUH?
SO OVER THIS.
MUNCH も,
HRM...
も, MUNCH
HEH HEH!! HE'S AN AWKWARD KINDA GUY, Y'SEE,
NOT GOOD AT THESE KINDS OF CONVER-SATIONS.
HERE'S YOUR BEER AND TAKOWASA!
MUNCH も,
PAT なで
も, MUNCH
なで, PAT
HAHA-HAHA...
I KIND OF GOT THAT VIBE FROM YOU, NIFUJI.
LISTEN TO THIS, THOUGH... I HEARD SOMETHING THE OTHER DAY.

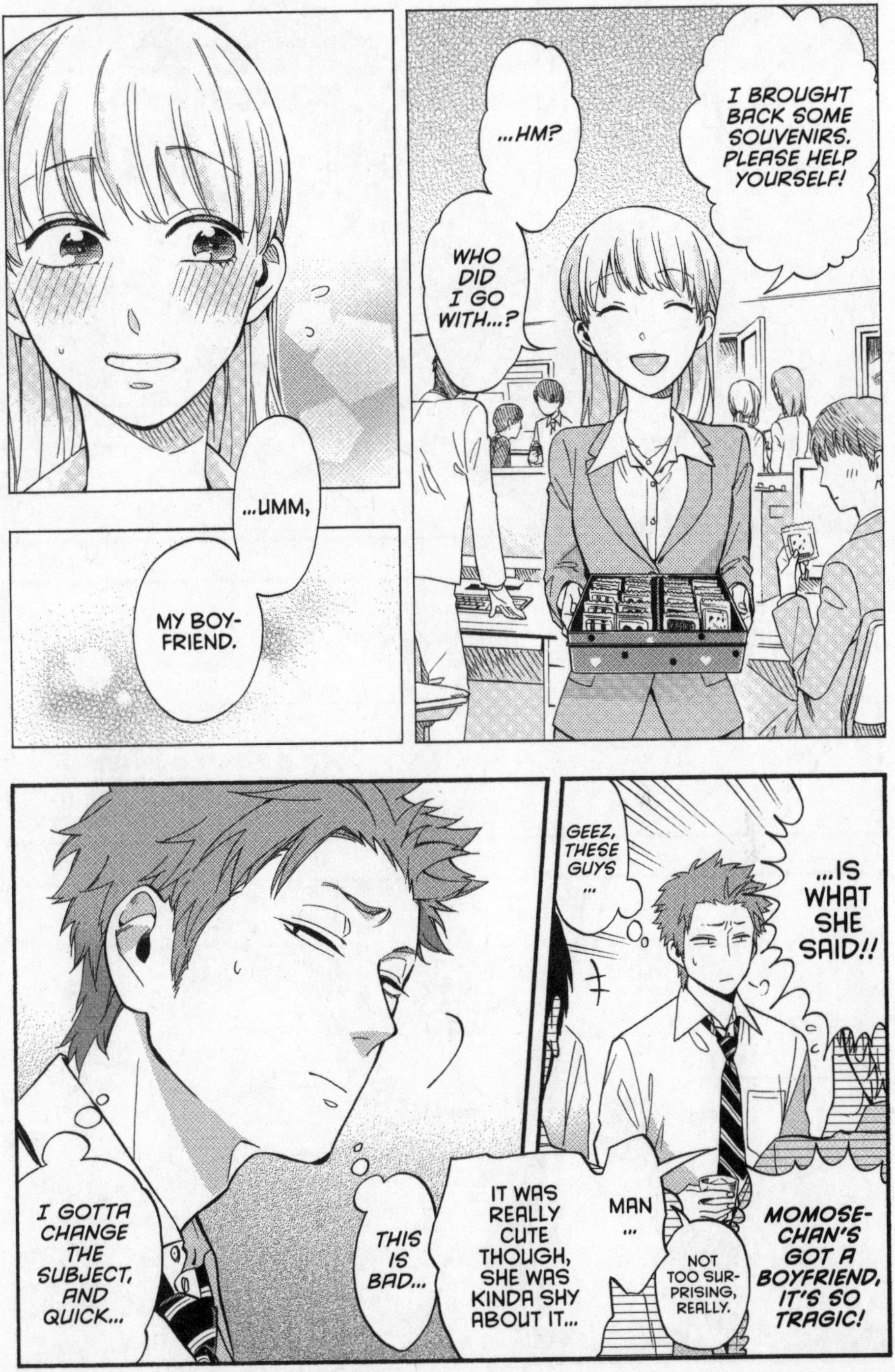
I BROUGHT BACK SOME SOUVENIRS. PLEASE HELP YOURSELF!
...HM?
WHO DID I GO WITH...?
...UMM,
MY BOY-FRIEND.
...IS WHAT SHE SAID!!
GEEZ, THESE GUYS ...
MOMOSE-CHAN'S GOT A BOYFRIEND, IT'S SO TRAGIC!
NOT TOO SUR-PRISING, REALLY.
MAN ...
IT WAS REALLY CUTE THOUGH, SHE WAS KINDA SHY ABOUT IT...
THIS IS BAD...
I GOTTA CHANGE THE SUBJECT, AND QUICK...

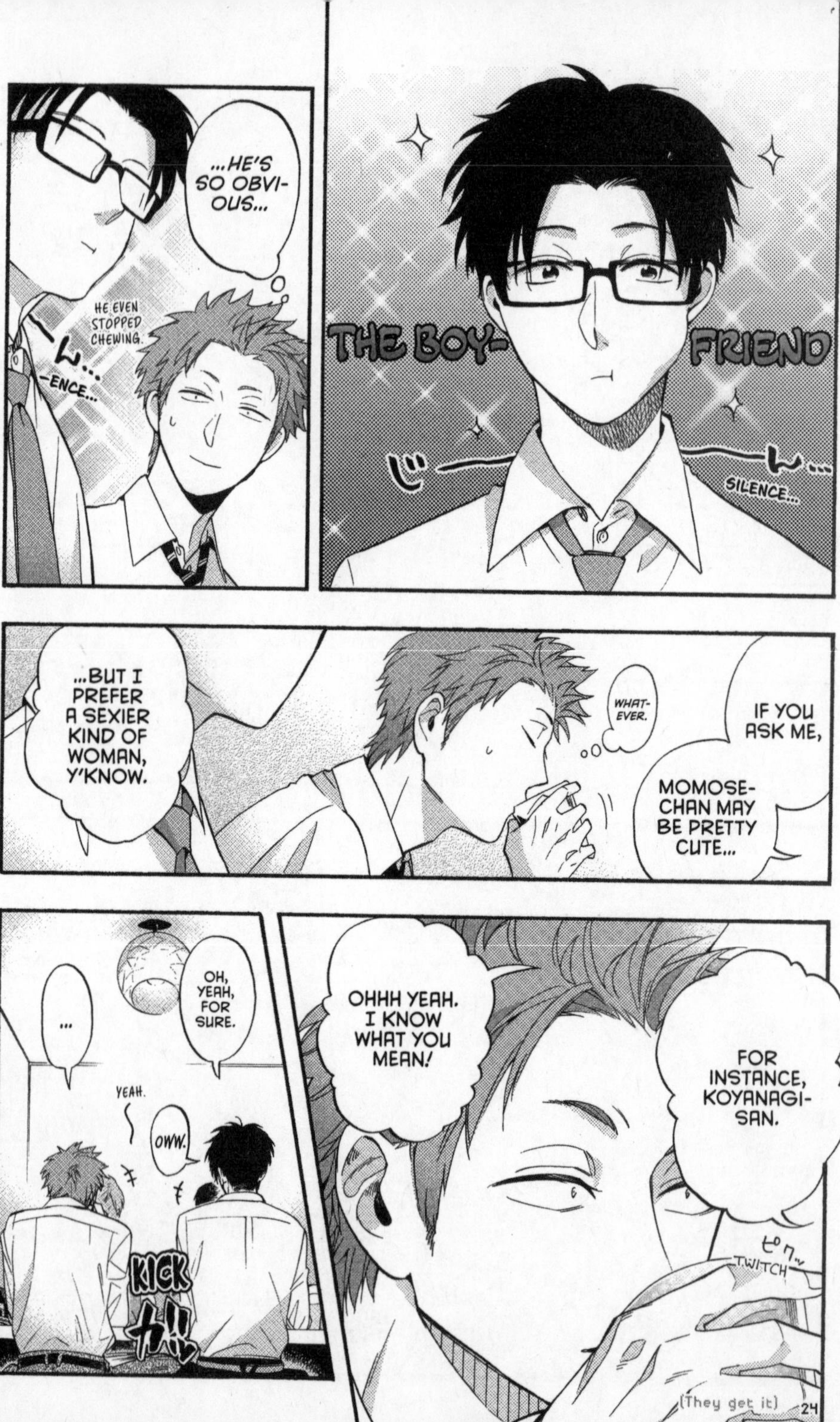
THE BOY-
FRIEND
じーーーーん...
SILENCE...
...HE'S SO OBVIOUS...
HE EVEN STOPPED CHEWING.
ーん...
—ENCE...
IF YOU ASK ME,
MOMOSE-CHAN MAY BE PRETTY CUTE...
WHAT-EVER.
...BUT I PREFER A SEXIER KIND OF WOMAN, Y'KNOW.
FOR INSTANCE, KOYANAGI-SAN.
OHHH YEAH. I KNOW WHAT YOU MEAN!
TWITCH
OH, YEAH, FOR SURE.
...
OWW.
YEAH.
KICK

(They get it)

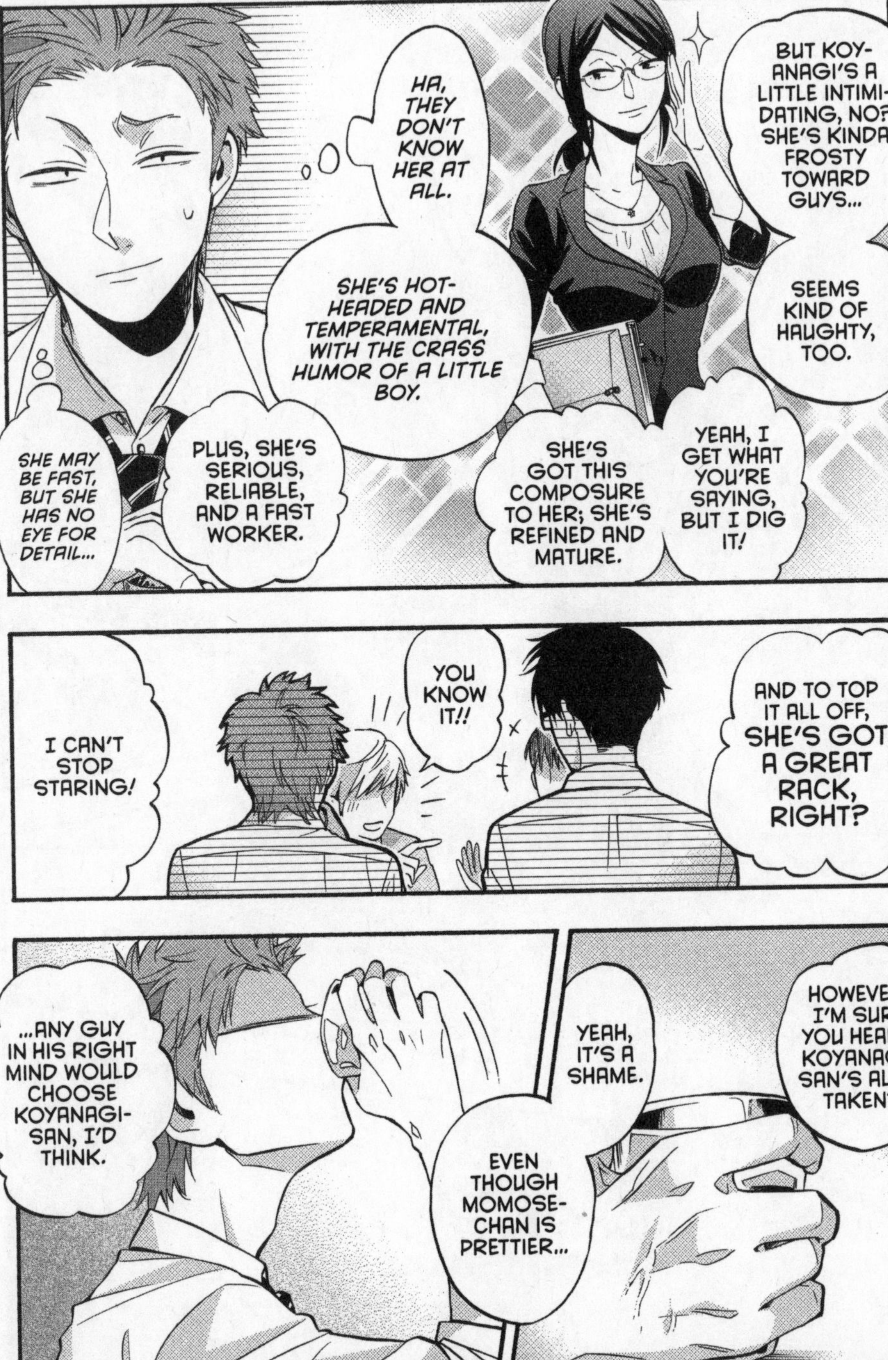
BUT KOY-ANAGI'S A LITTLE INTIMIDATING, NO? SHE'S KINDA FROSTY TOWARD GUYS...
SEEMS KIND OF HAUGHTY, TOO.
HA, THEY DON'T KNOW HER AT ALL.
SHE'S HOT-HEADED AND TEMPERAMENTAL, WITH THE CRASS HUMOR OF A LITTLE BOY.
YEAH, I GET WHAT YOU'RE SAYING, BUT I DIG IT!
SHE'S GOT THIS COMPOSURE TO HER; SHE'S REFINED AND MATURE.
PLUS, SHE'S SERIOUS, RELIABLE, AND A FAST WORKER.
SHE MAY BE FAST, BUT SHE HAS NO EYE FOR DETAIL...
AND TO TOP IT ALL OFF, SHE'S GOT A GREAT RACK, RIGHT?
YOU KNOW IT!!
I CAN'T STOP STARING!
HOWEVER, I'M SURE YOU HEARD KOYANAGI-SAN'S ALSO TAKEN?
YEAH, IT'S A SHAME.
EVEN THOUGH MOMOSE-CHAN IS PRETTIER...
...ANY GUY IN HIS RIGHT MIND WOULD CHOOSE KOYANAGI-SAN, I'D THINK.

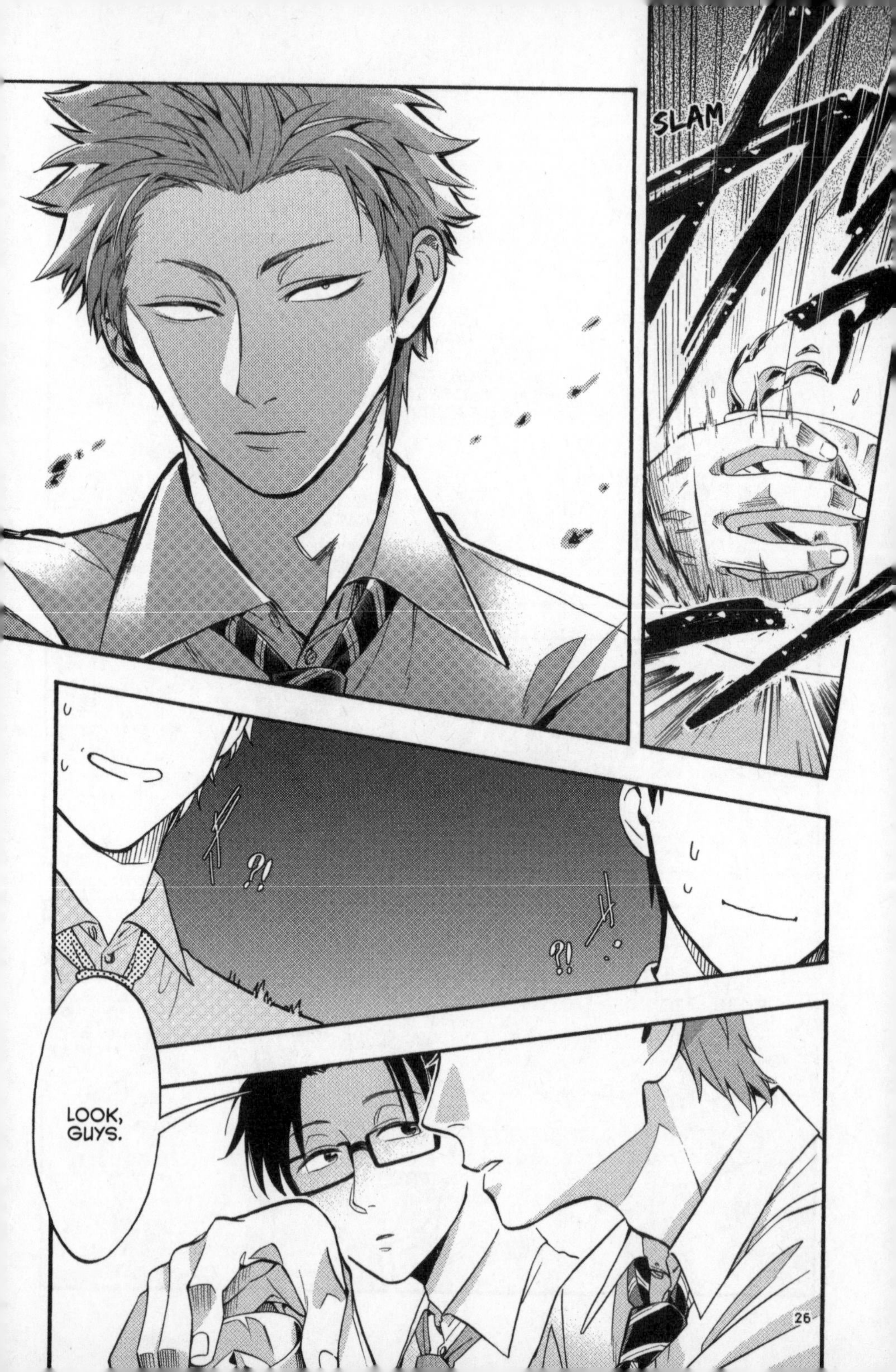
SLAM
?!
?!
LOOK, GUYS.

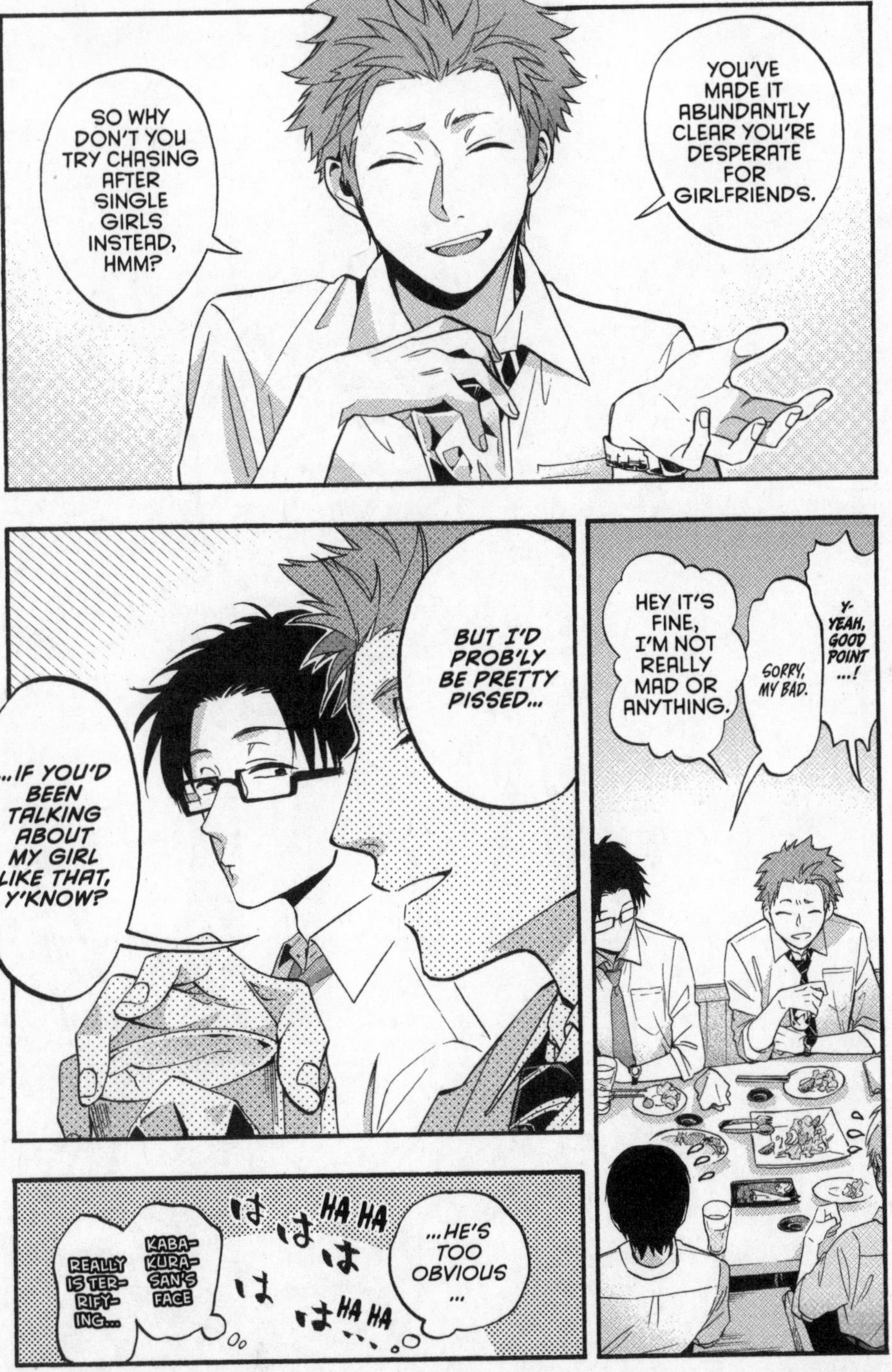
YOU'VE MADE IT ABUNDANTLY CLEAR YOU'RE DESPERATE FOR GIRLFRIENDS.
SO WHY DON'T YOU TRY CHASING AFTER SINGLE GIRLS INSTEAD, HMM?
Y-YEAH, GOOD POINT ...!
SORRY, MY BAD.
HEY IT'S FINE, I'M NOT REALLY MAD OR ANYTHING.
BUT I'D PROB'LY BE PRETTY PISSED...
...IF YOU'D BEEN TALKING ABOUT MY GIRL LIKE THAT, Y'KNOW?
はは
HA HA
...HE'S TOO OBVIOUS ...
はは
HA HA
KABA-KURA-SAN'S FACE
REALLY IS TER-RIFY-ING...

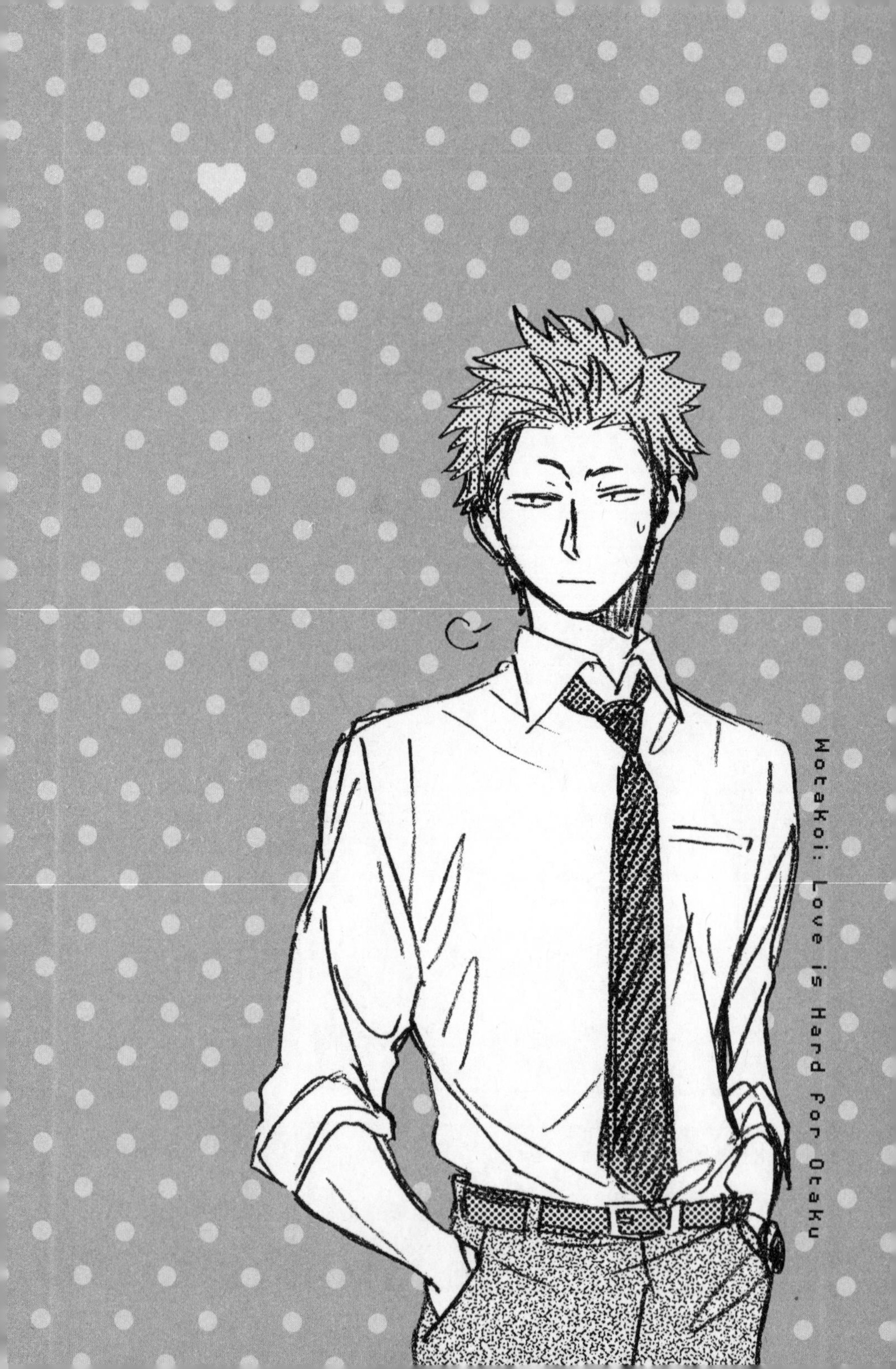
Wotakoi: Love is Hard for Otaku

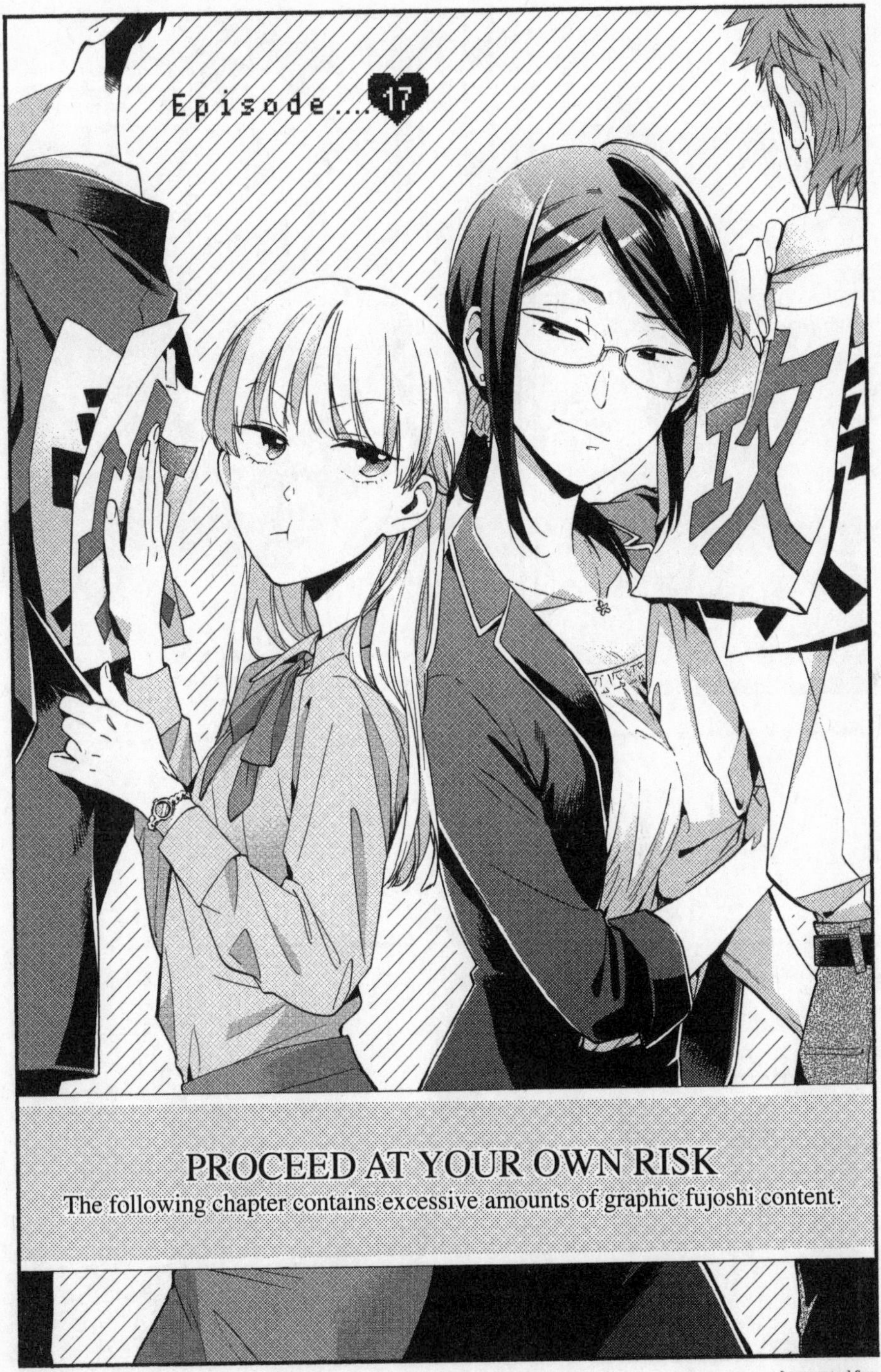
Episode.... 17
攻
PROCEED AT YOUR OWN RISK
The following chapter contains excessive amounts of graphic fujoshi content.

[paper on top] *Seme*
[paper on bottom] *Uke*

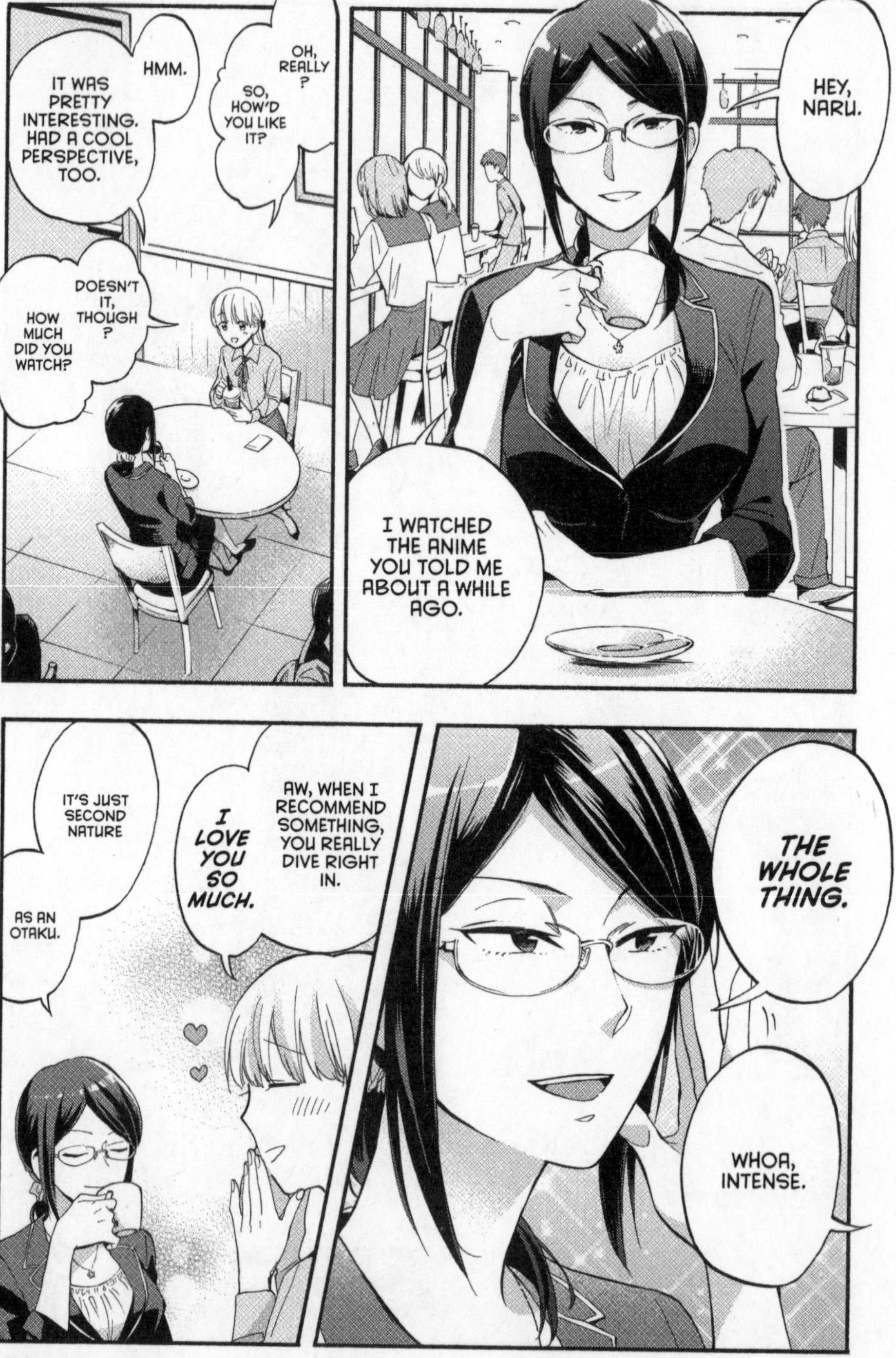
HEY, NARU.
I WATCHED THE ANIME YOU TOLD ME ABOUT A WHILE AGO.
OH, REALLY?
SO, HOW'D YOU LIKE IT?
HMM.
IT WAS PRETTY INTERESTING. HAD A COOL PERSPECTIVE, TOO.
DOESN'T IT, THOUGH?
HOW MUCH DID YOU WATCH?
THE WHOLE THING.
WHOA, INTENSE.
AW, WHEN I RECOMMEND SOMETHING, YOU REALLY DIVE RIGHT IN.
I LOVE YOU SO MUCH.
IT'S JUST SECOND NATURE
AS AN OTAKU.

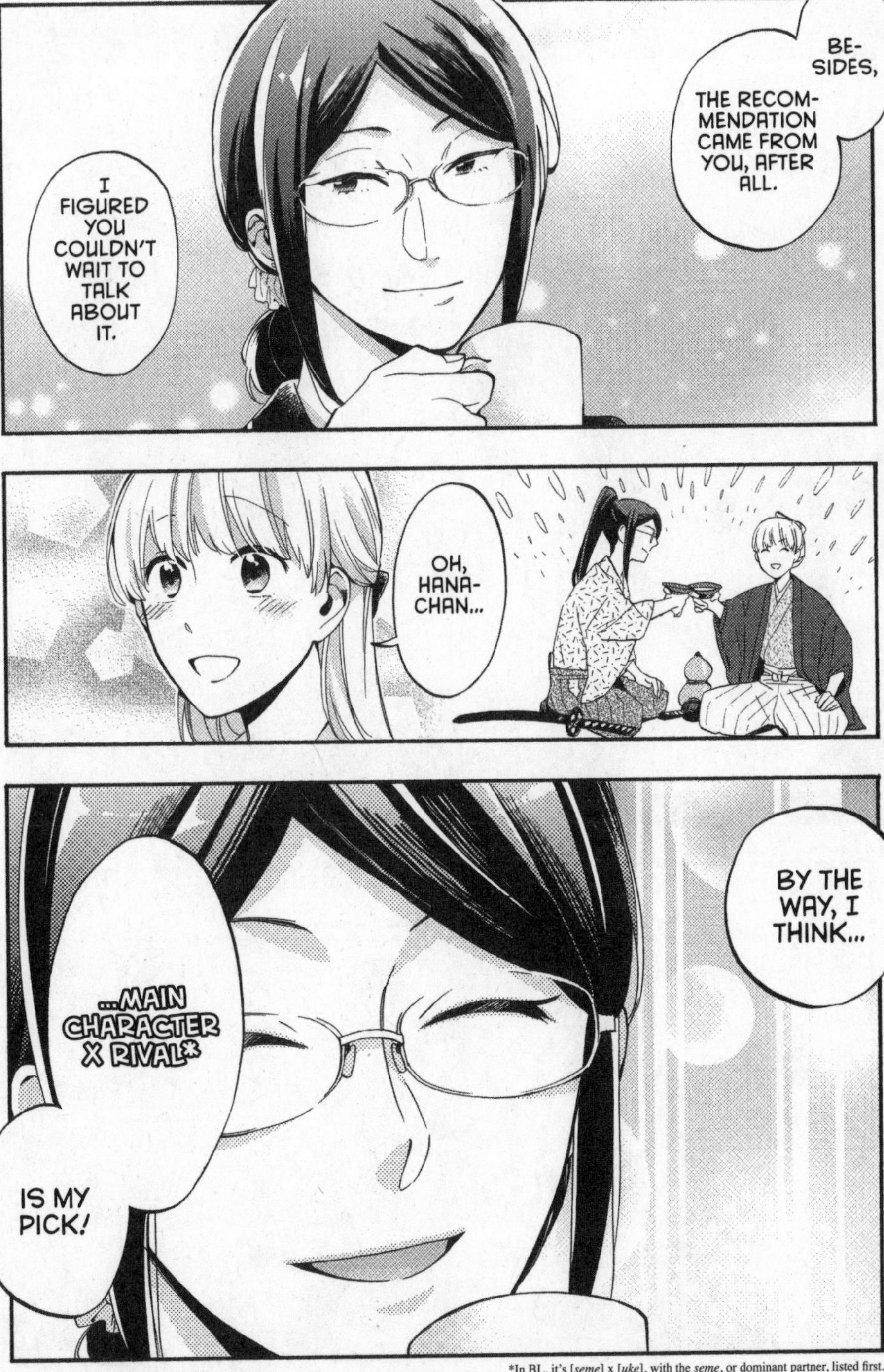
BE-SIDES, THE RECOMMENDATION CAME FROM YOU, AFTER ALL.
I FIGURED YOU COULDN'T WAIT TO TALK ABOUT IT.
OH, HANA-CHAN...
BY THE WAY, I THINK...
...MAIN CHARACTER X RIVAL*
IS MY PICK!

*In BL, it's [*seme*] x [*uke*], with the *seme*, or dominant partner, listed first.

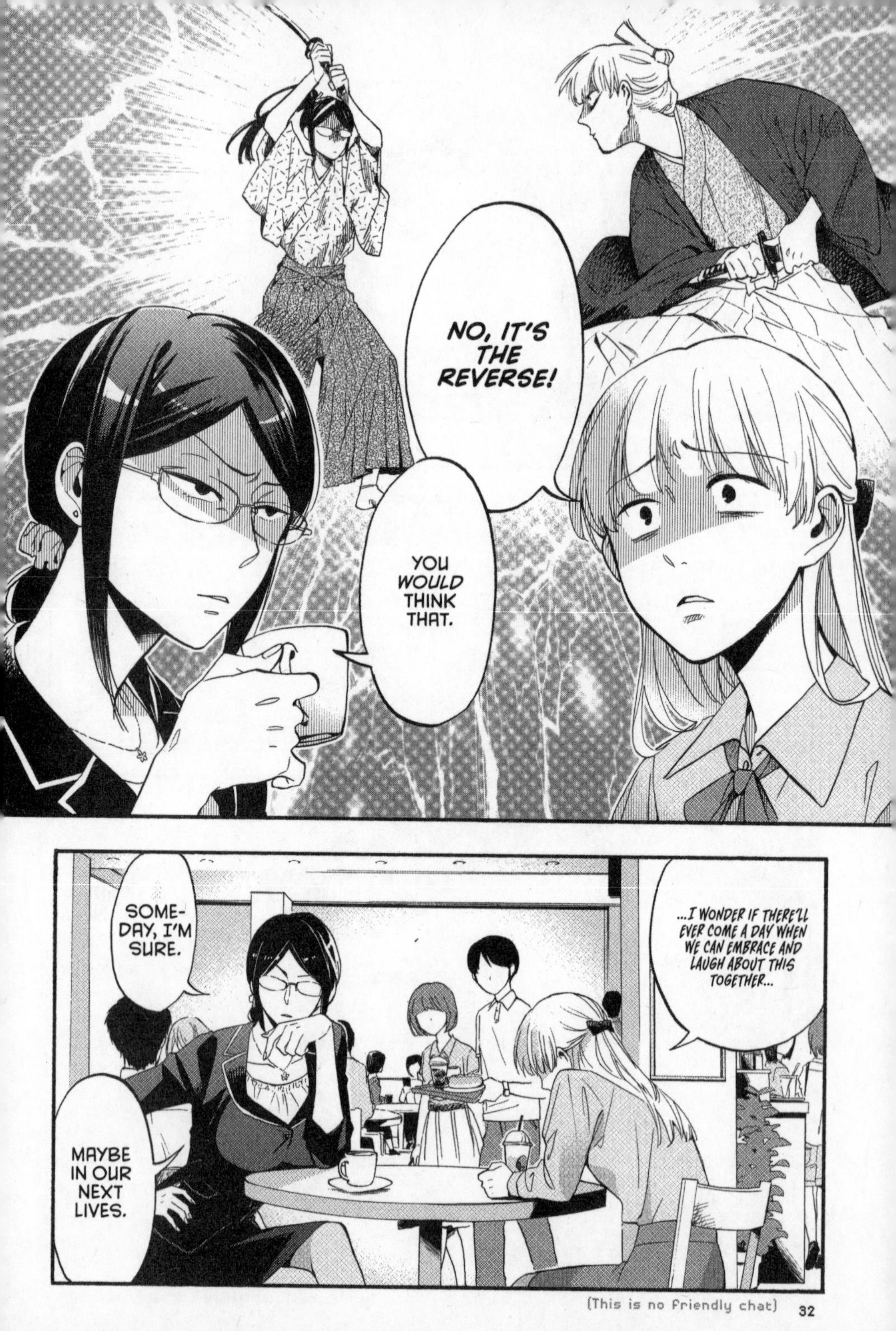
NO, IT'S THE REVERSE!
YOU WOULD THINK THAT.
...I WONDER IF THERE'LL EVER COME A DAY WHEN WE CAN EMBRACE AND LAUGH ABOUT THIS TOGETHER...
SOME-DAY, I'M SURE.
MAYBE IN OUR NEXT LIVES.

(This is no friendly chat)

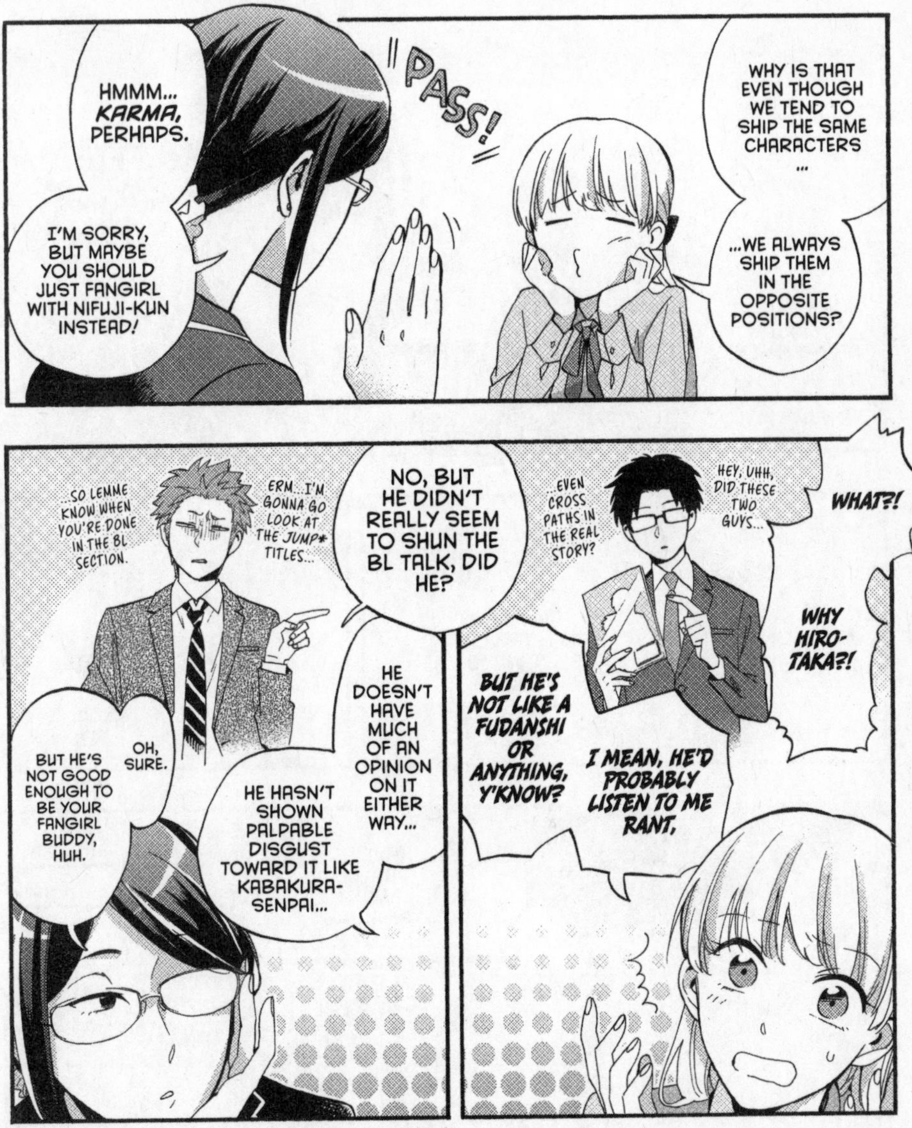
WHY IS THAT EVEN THOUGH WE TEND TO SHIP THE SAME CHARACTERS ...
...WE ALWAYS SHIP THEM IN THE OPPOSITE POSITIONS?
PASS!
HMMM... *KARMA,* PERHAPS.
I'M SORRY, BUT MAYBE YOU SHOULD JUST FANGIRL WITH NIFUJI-KUN INSTEAD!
WHAT?!
WHY HIRO-TAKA?!
HEY, UHH, DID THESE TWO GUYS...
...EVEN CROSS PATHS IN THE REAL STORY?
I MEAN, HE'D PROBABLY LISTEN TO ME RANT,
BUT HE'S NOT LIKE A FUDANSHI OR ANYTHING, Y'KNOW?
NO, BUT HE DIDN'T REALLY SEEM TO SHUN THE BL TALK, DID HE?
ERM...I'M GONNA GO LOOK AT THE *JUMP** TITLES...
...SO LEMME KNOW WHEN YOU'RE DONE IN THE BL SECTION.
HE DOESN'T HAVE MUCH OF AN OPINION ON IT EITHER WAY...
HE HASN'T SHOWN PALPABLE DISGUST TOWARD IT LIKE KABAKURA-SENPAI...
OH, SURE.
BUT HE'S NOT GOOD ENOUGH TO BE YOUR FANGIRL BUDDY, HUH.

**Shonen Jump*, a weekly *shonen* (young men's) manga magazine/brand.

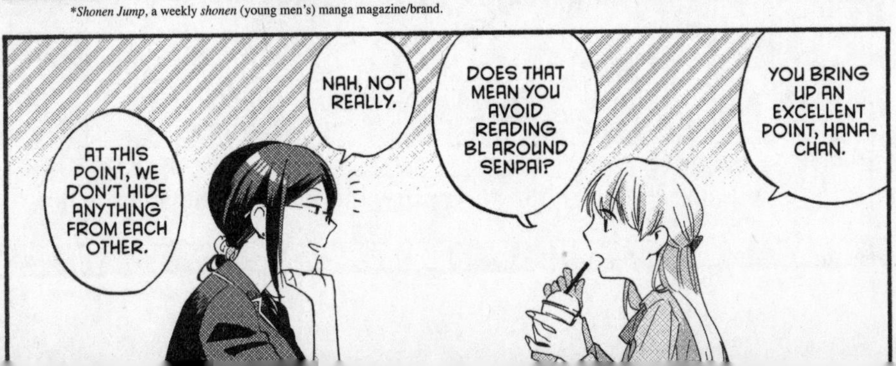
YOU BRING UP AN EXCELLENT POINT, HANA-CHAN.
DOES THAT MEAN YOU AVOID READING BL AROUND SENPAI?
NAH, NOT REALLY.
AT THIS POINT, WE DON'T HIDE ANYTHING FROM EACH OTHER.

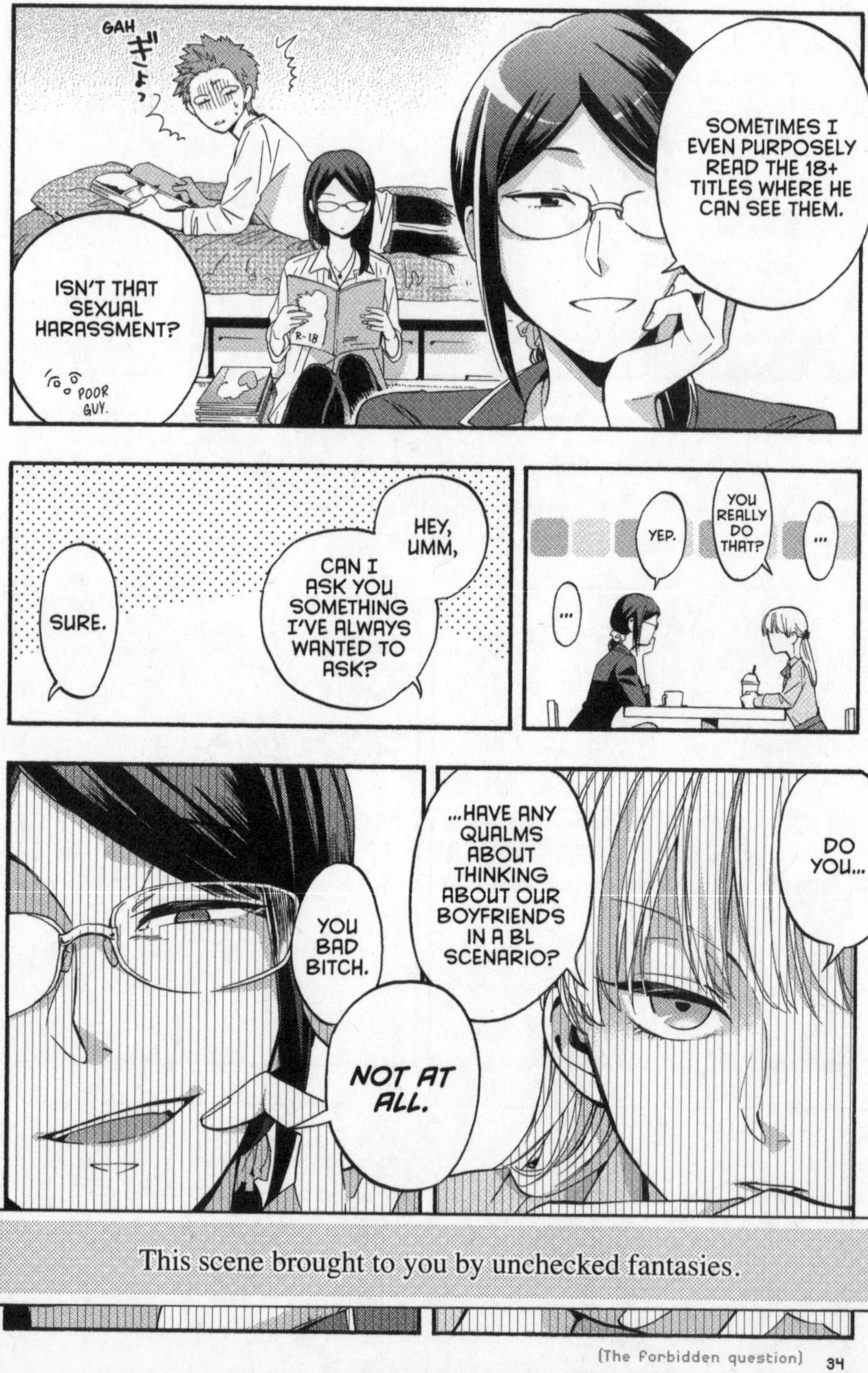
SOMETIMES I EVEN PURPOSELY READ THE 18+ TITLES WHERE HE CAN SEE THEM.
GAH
R-18
ISN'T THAT SEXUAL HARASSMENT?
POOR GUY.
...
YOU REALLY DO THAT?
YEP.
...
HEY, UMM, CAN I ASK YOU SOMETHING I'VE ALWAYS WANTED TO ASK?
SURE.
DO YOU...
...HAVE ANY QUALMS ABOUT THINKING ABOUT OUR BOYFRIENDS IN A BL SCENARIO?
NOT AT ALL.
YOU BAD BITCH.

This scene brought to you by unchecked fantasies.

(The Forbidden question)

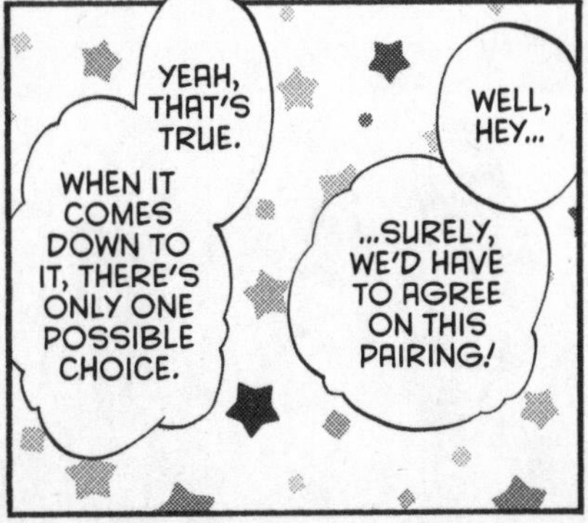

WELL, HEY...
...SURELY, WE'D HAVE TO AGREE ON THIS PAIRING!
YEAH, THAT'S TRUE.
WHEN IT COMES DOWN TO IT, THERE'S ONLY ONE POSSIBLE CHOICE.

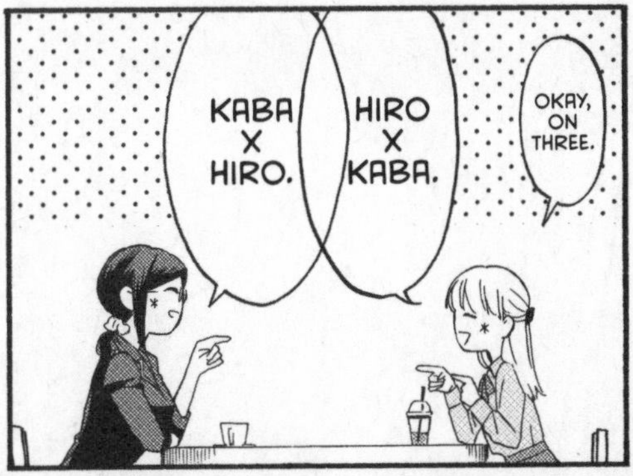

OKAY, ON THREE.
HIRO X KABA.
KABA X HIRO.

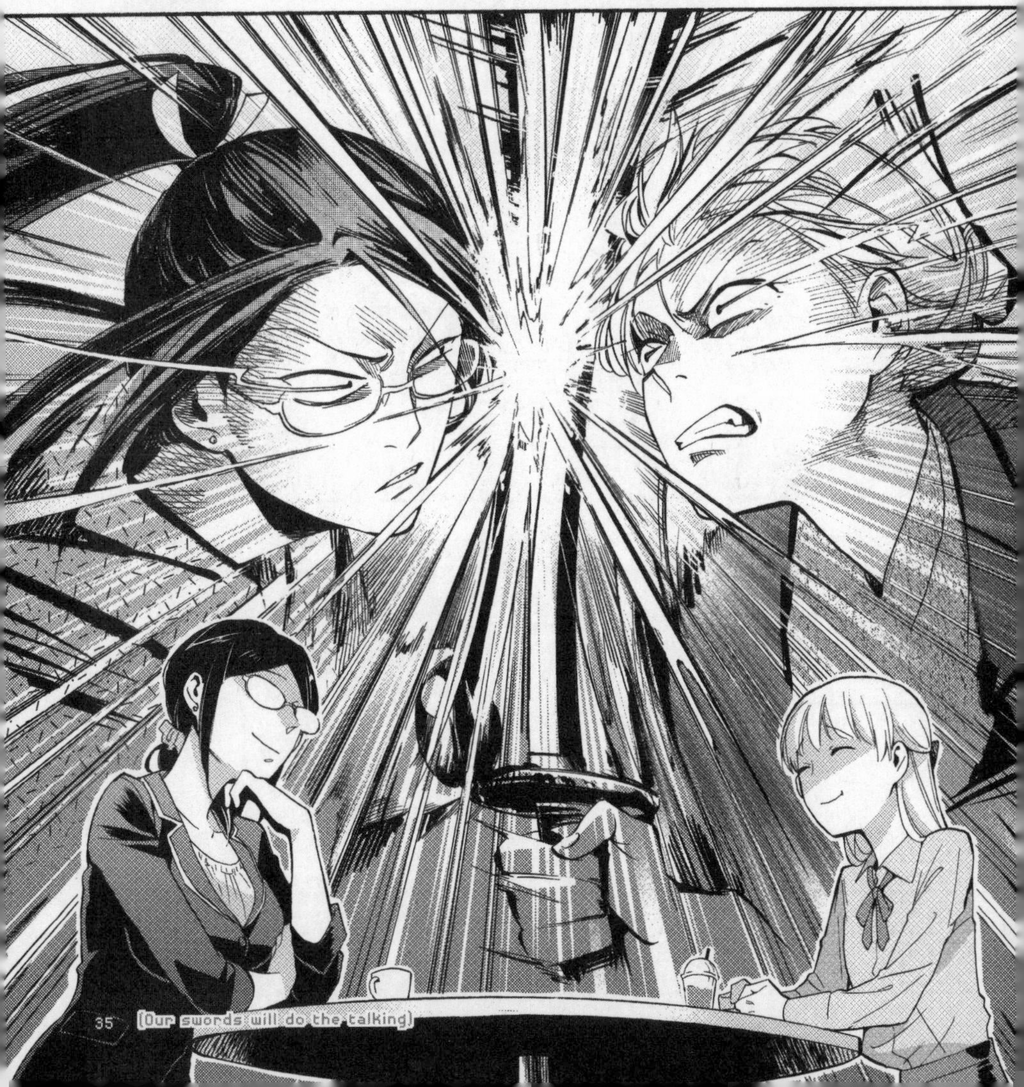

(Our swords will do the talking)

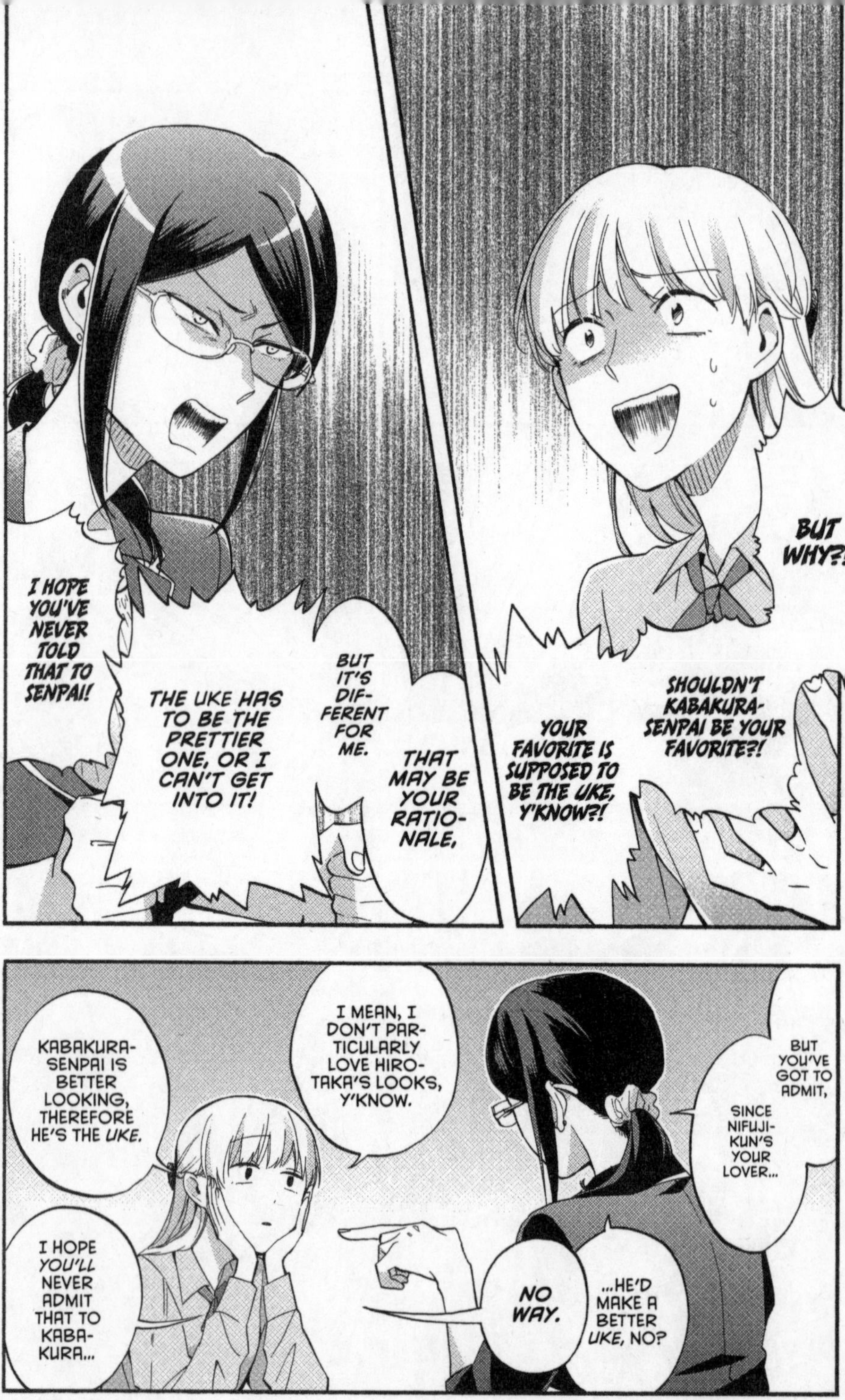
BUT WHY?!
SHOULDN'T KABAKURA-SENPAI BE YOUR FAVORITE?!
YOUR FAVORITE IS SUPPOSED TO BE THE UKE, Y'KNOW?!
THAT MAY BE YOUR RATIONALE,
BUT IT'S DIFFERENT FOR ME.
THE UKE HAS TO BE THE PRETTIER ONE, OR I CAN'T GET INTO IT!
I HOPE YOU'VE NEVER TOLD THAT TO SENPAI!
BUT YOU'VE GOT TO ADMIT, SINCE NIFUJI-KUN'S YOUR LOVER...
...HE'D MAKE A BETTER *UKE*, NO?
NO WAY.
I MEAN, I DON'T PARTICULARLY LOVE HIROTAKA'S LOOKS, Y'KNOW.
KABAKURA-SENPAI IS BETTER LOOKING, THEREFORE HE'S THE *UKE*.
I HOPE *YOU'LL* NEVER ADMIT THAT TO KABAKURA...

(Everyone has their own preferences)

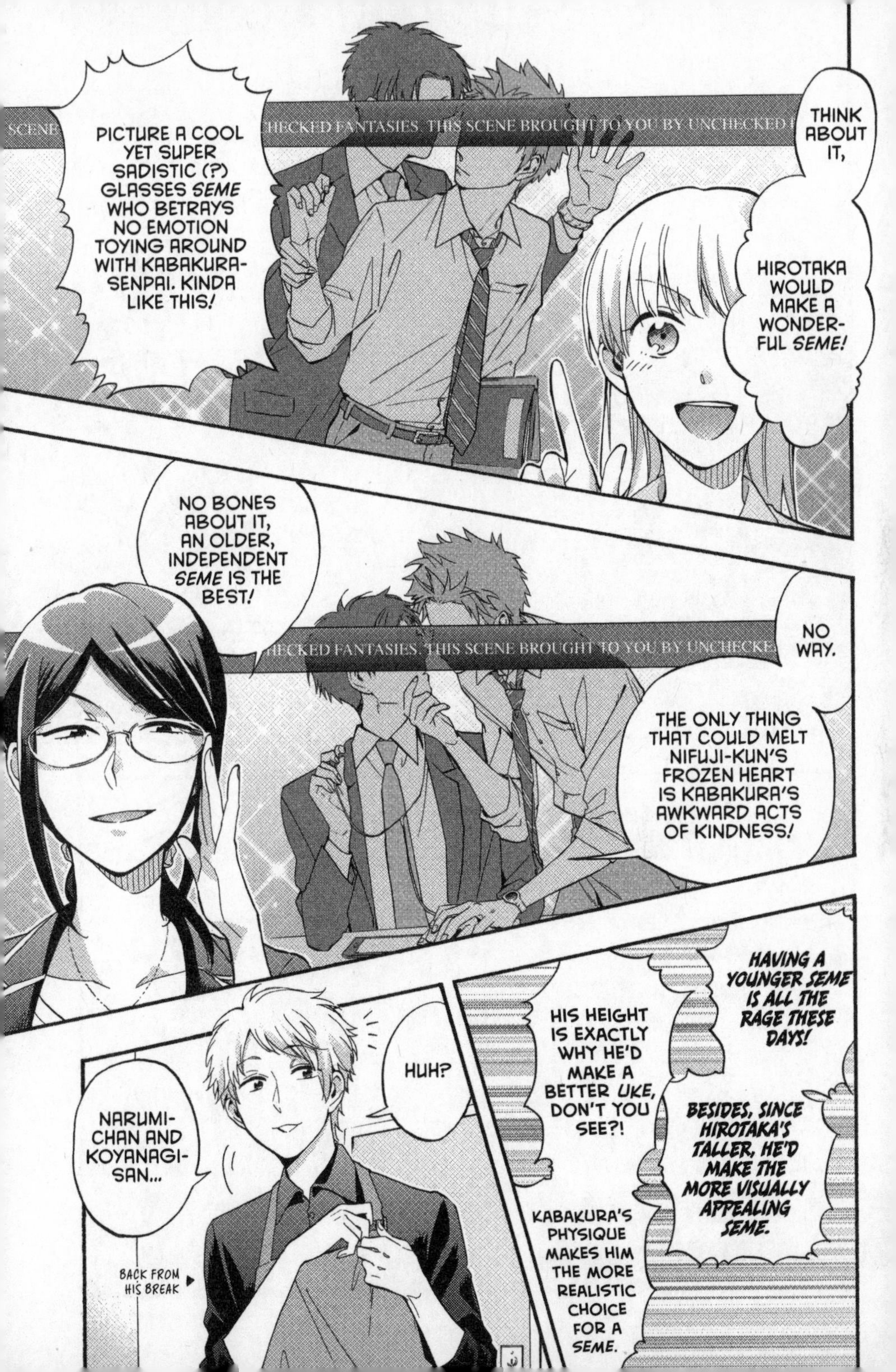
THINK ABOUT IT,
HIROTAKA WOULD MAKE A WONDERFUL SEME!
PICTURE A COOL YET SUPER SADISTIC (?) GLASSES SEME WHO BETRAYS NO EMOTION TOYING AROUND WITH KABAKURA-SENPAI. KINDA LIKE THIS!
THIS SCENE BROUGHT TO YOU BY
NO WAY.
THE ONLY THING THAT COULD MELT NIFUJI-KUN'S FROZEN HEART IS KABAKURA'S AWKWARD ACTS OF KINDNESS!
NO BONES ABOUT IT, AN OLDER, INDEPENDENT SEME IS THE BEST!
THIS SCENE BROUGHT TO YOU BY
HAVING A YOUNGER SEME IS ALL THE RAGE THESE DAYS!
BESIDES, SINCE HIROTAKA'S TALLER, HE'D MAKE THE MORE VISUALLY APPEALING SEME.
HIS HEIGHT IS EXACTLY WHY HE'D MAKE A BETTER UKE, DON'T YOU SEE?!
KABAKURA'S PHYSIQUE MAKES HIM THE MORE REALISTIC CHOICE FOR A SEME.
HUH?
NARUMI-CHAN AND KOYANAGI-SAN...
BACK FROM HIS BREAK

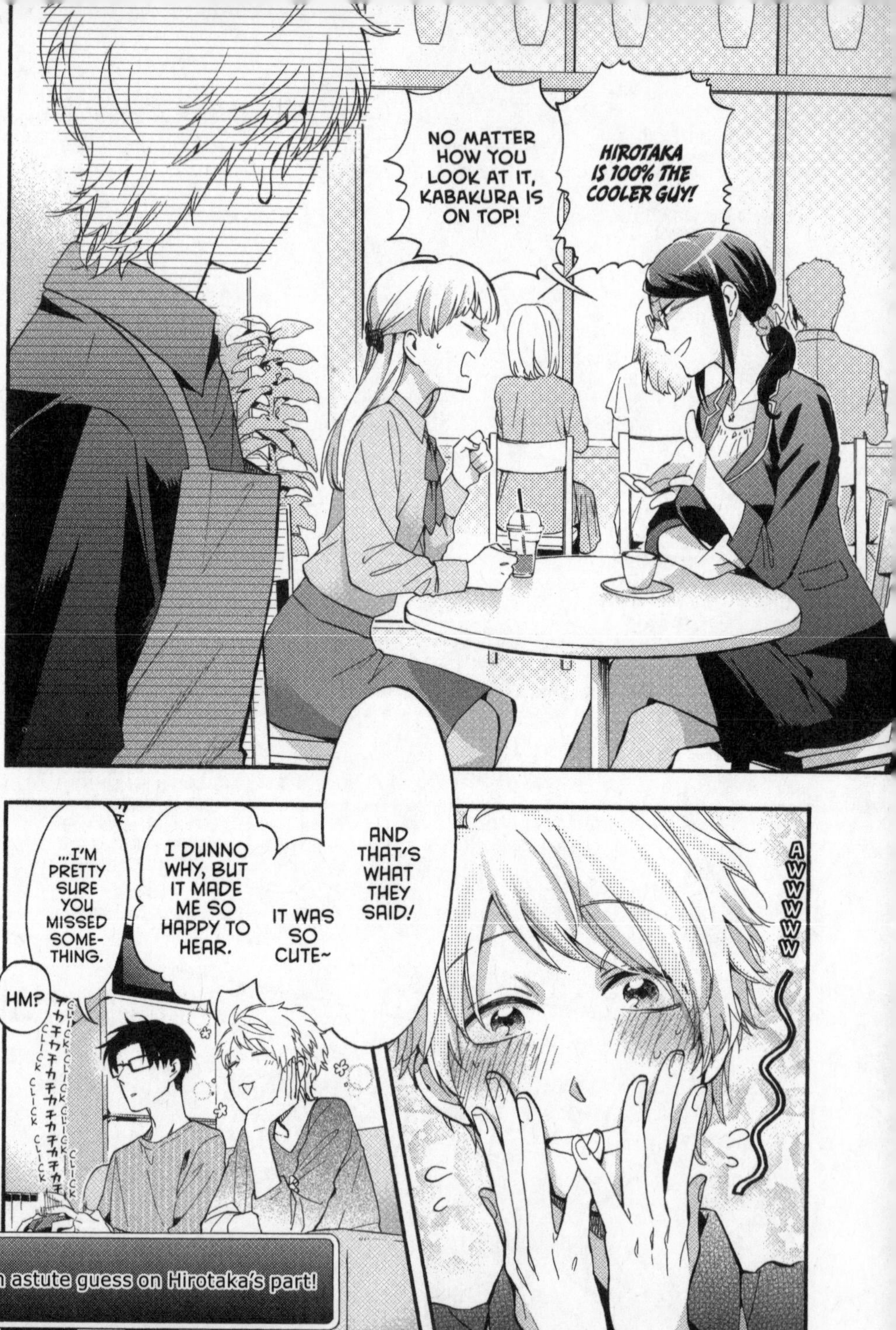
HIROTAKA IS 100% THE COOLER GUY!
NO MATTER HOW YOU LOOK AT IT, KABAKURA IS ON TOP!
AWWWWWW
AND THAT'S WHAT THEY SAID!
IT WAS SO CUTE~
I DUNNO WHY, BUT IT MADE ME SO HAPPY TO HEAR.
...I'M PRETTY SURE YOU MISSED SOMETHING.
HM?
CLICK CLICK CLICK CLICK
An astute guess on Hirotaka's part!

(Ignorance is bliss)

Wotakoi: Love is Hard for Otaku

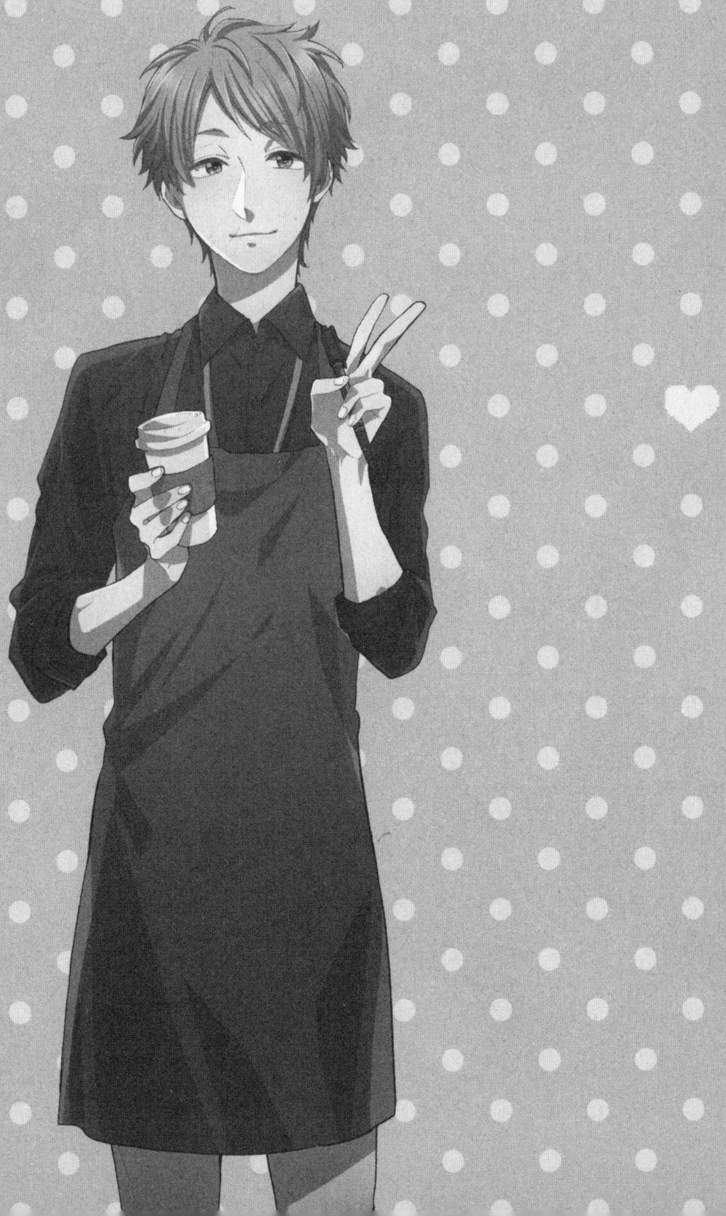

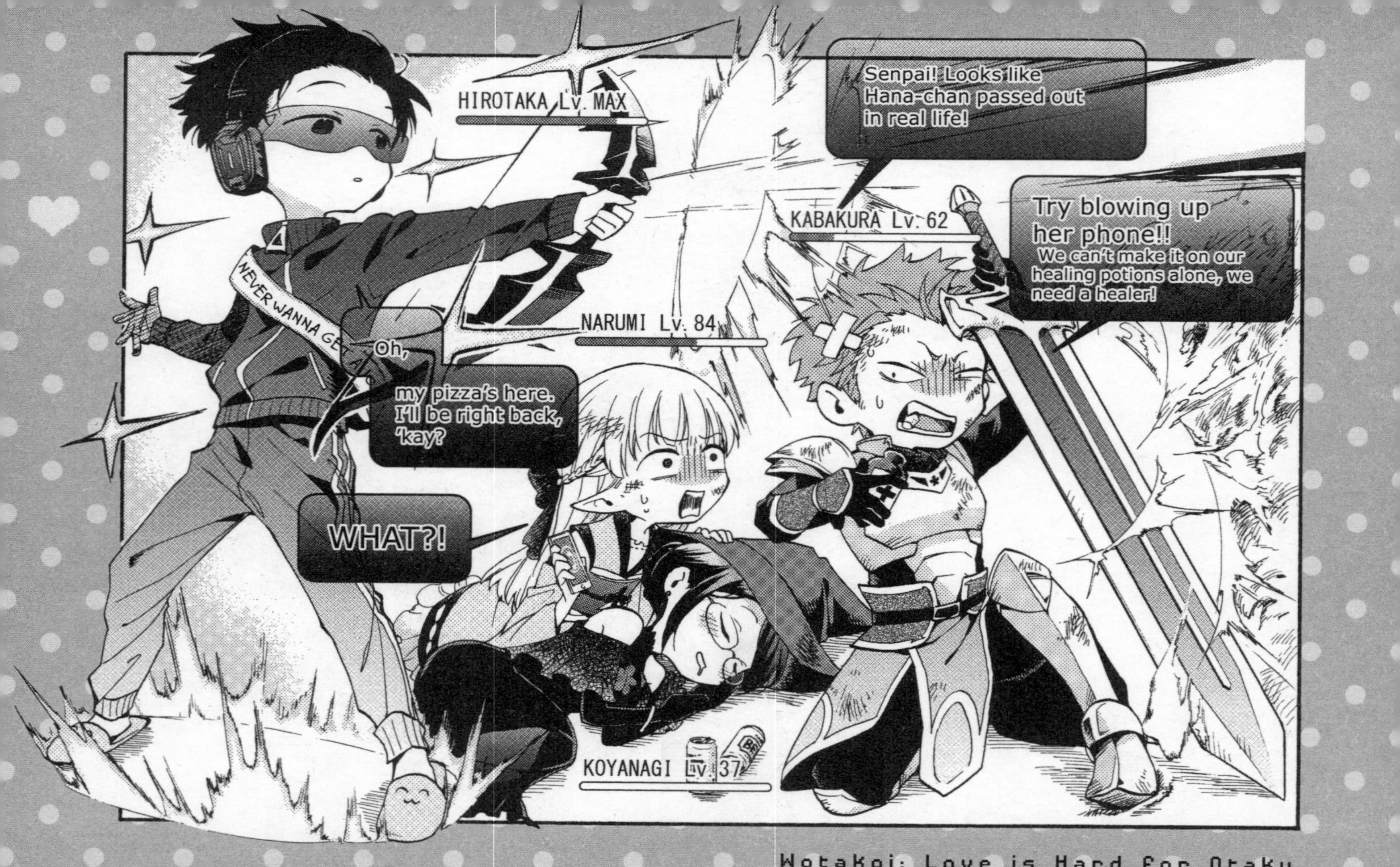
Senpai! Looks like Hana-chan passed out in real life!
Try blowing up her phone!! We can't make it on our healing potions alone, we need a healer!
KABAKURA Lv. 62
HIROTAKA Lv. MAX
NARUMI Lv. 84
KOYANAGI Lv. 37
NEVER WANNA GE
Oh, my pizza's here. I'll be right back, 'kay?
WHAT?!

Wotakoi: Love is Hard for Otaku

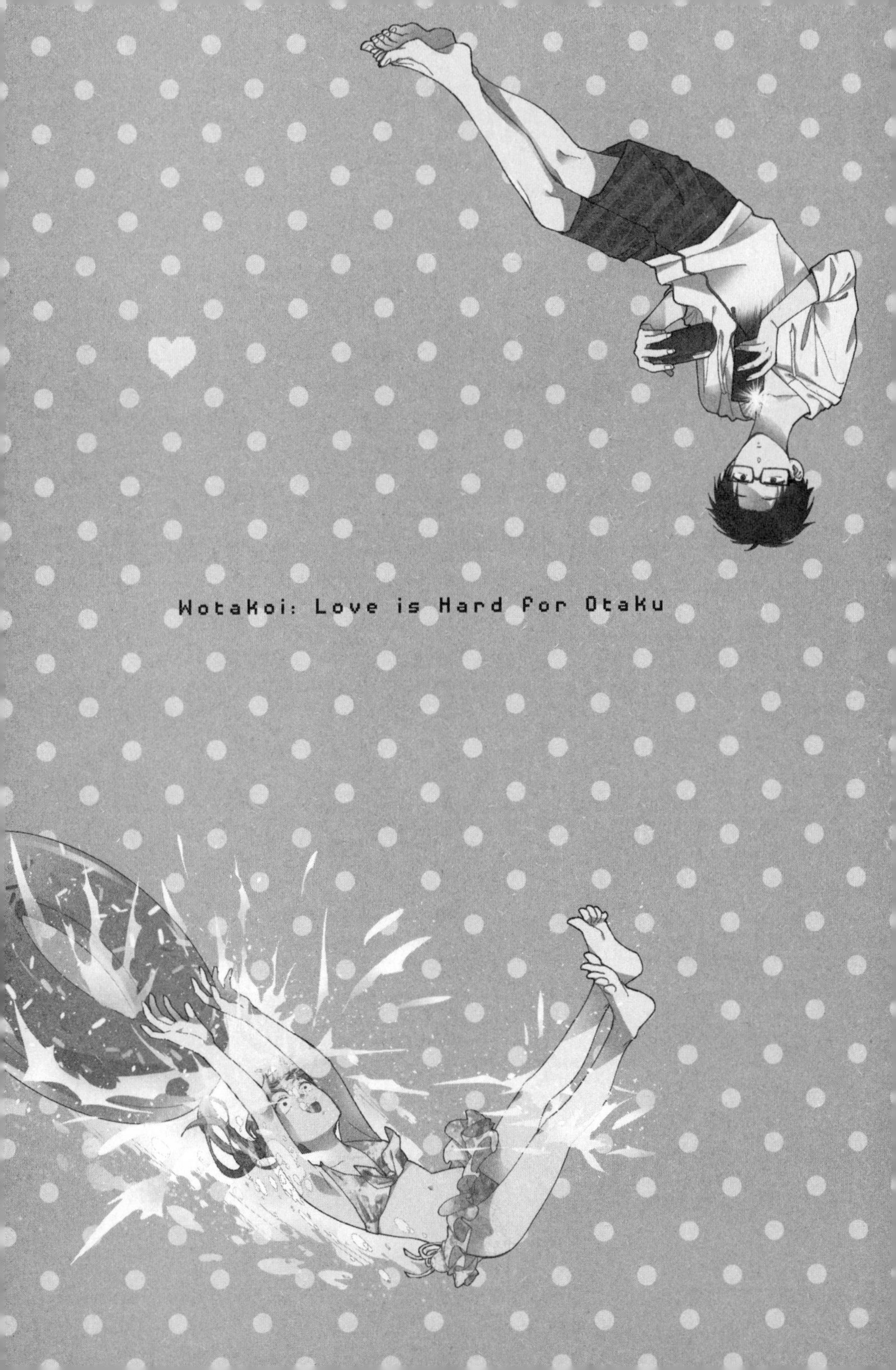
Wotakoi: Love is Hard for Otaku

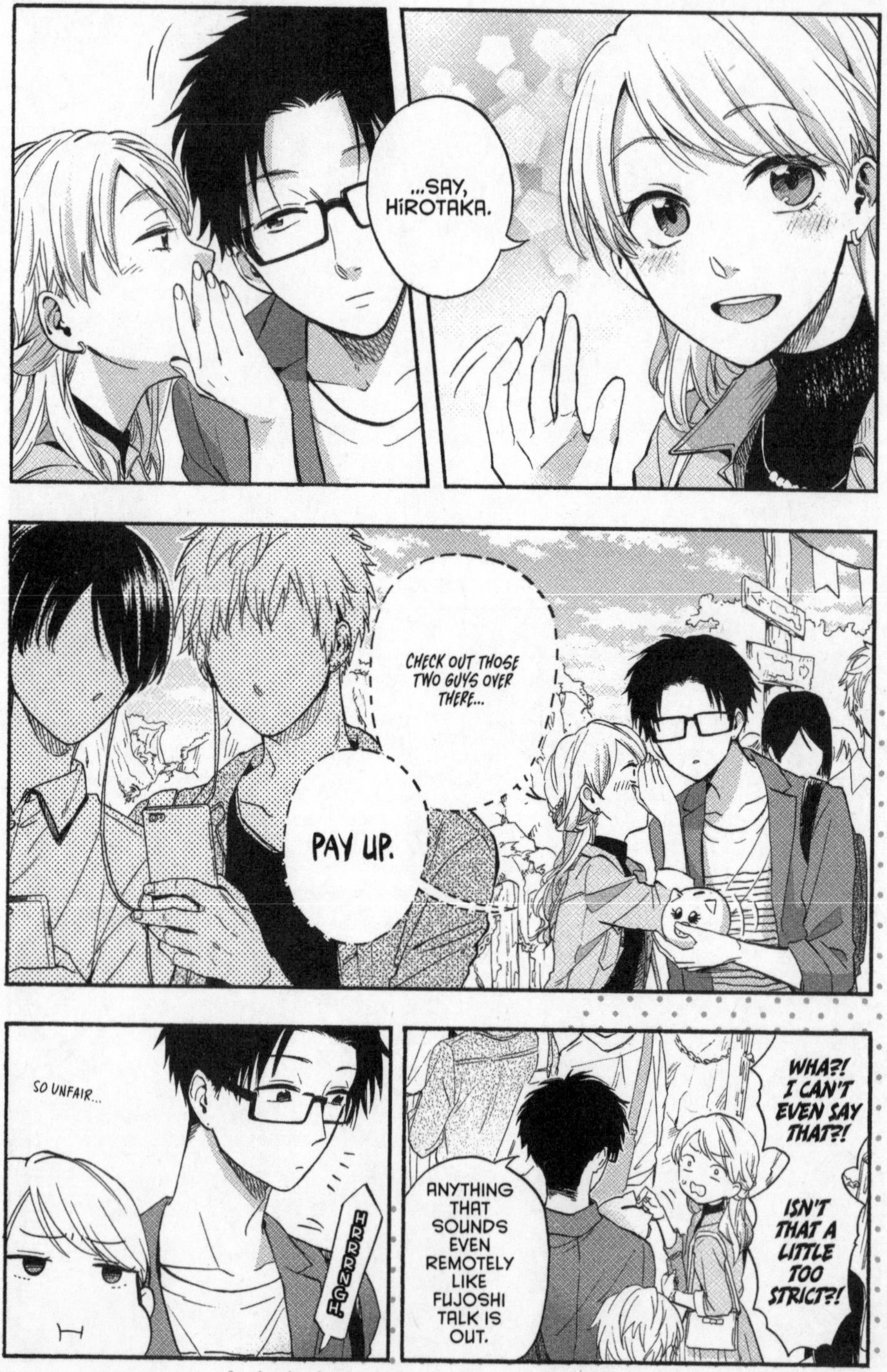
...SAY, HIROTAKA.
CHECK OUT THOSE TWO GUYS OVER THERE...
PAY UP.
WHA?! I CAN'T EVEN SAY THAT?!
ISN'T THAT A LITTLE TOO STRICT?!
ANYTHING THAT SOUNDS EVEN REMOTELY LIKE FUJOSHI TALK IS OUT.
SO UNFAIR...
HRRRNGH.

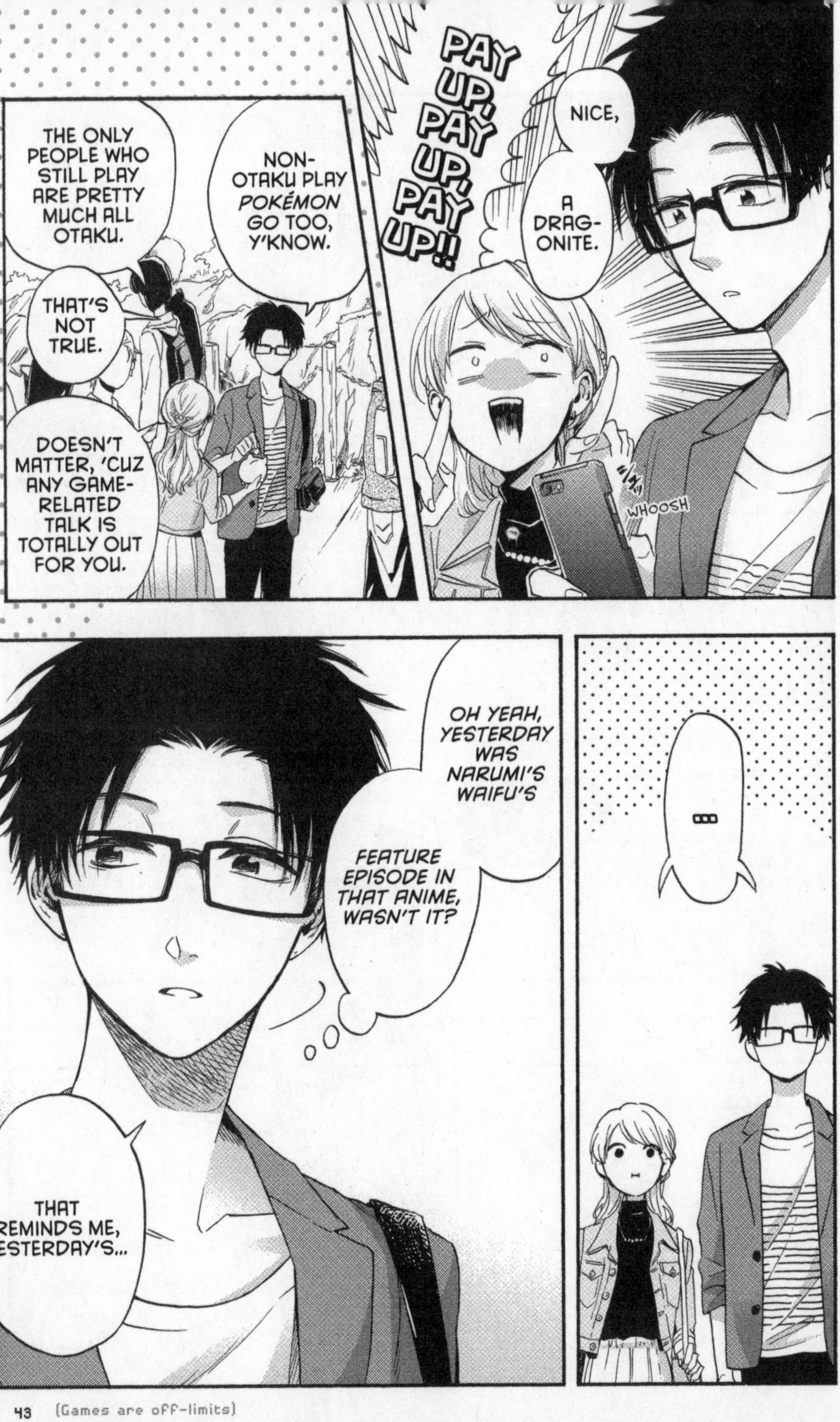
NICE,
A DRAGONITE.
PAY UP, PAY UP, PAY UP!!
WHOOSH
NON-OTAKU PLAY POKÉMON GO TOO, Y'KNOW.
THE ONLY PEOPLE WHO STILL PLAY ARE PRETTY MUCH ALL OTAKU.
THAT'S NOT TRUE.
DOESN'T MATTER, 'CUZ ANY GAME-RELATED TALK IS TOTALLY OUT FOR YOU.
...
OH YEAH, YESTERDAY WAS NARUMI'S WAIFU'S
FEATURE EPISODE IN THAT ANIME, WASN'T IT?
THAT REMINDS ME, YESTERDAY'S...

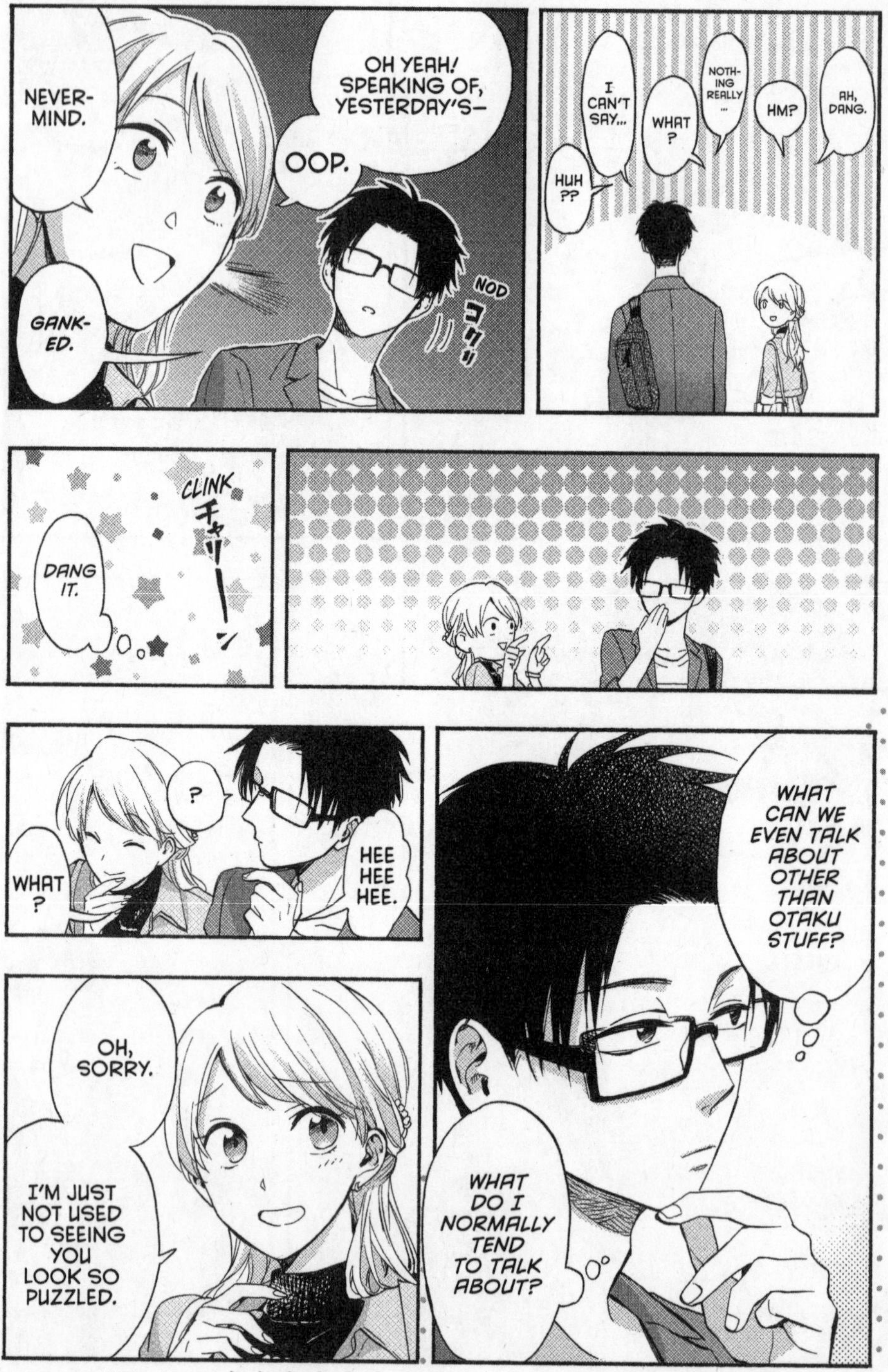
AH, DANG.
HM?
NOTHING REALLY...
WHAT?
I CAN'T SAY...
HUH??
OH YEAH! SPEAKING OF, YESTERDAY'S—
OOP.
NEVERMIND.
NOD
GANKED.
CLINK
DANG IT.
WHAT CAN WE EVEN TALK ABOUT OTHER THAN OTAKU STUFF?
WHAT DO I NORMALLY TEND TO TALK ABOUT?
?
HEE HEE HEE.
WHAT?
OH, SORRY.
I'M JUST NOT USED TO SEEING YOU LOOK SO PUZZLED.

(If you take that away, what's left?)

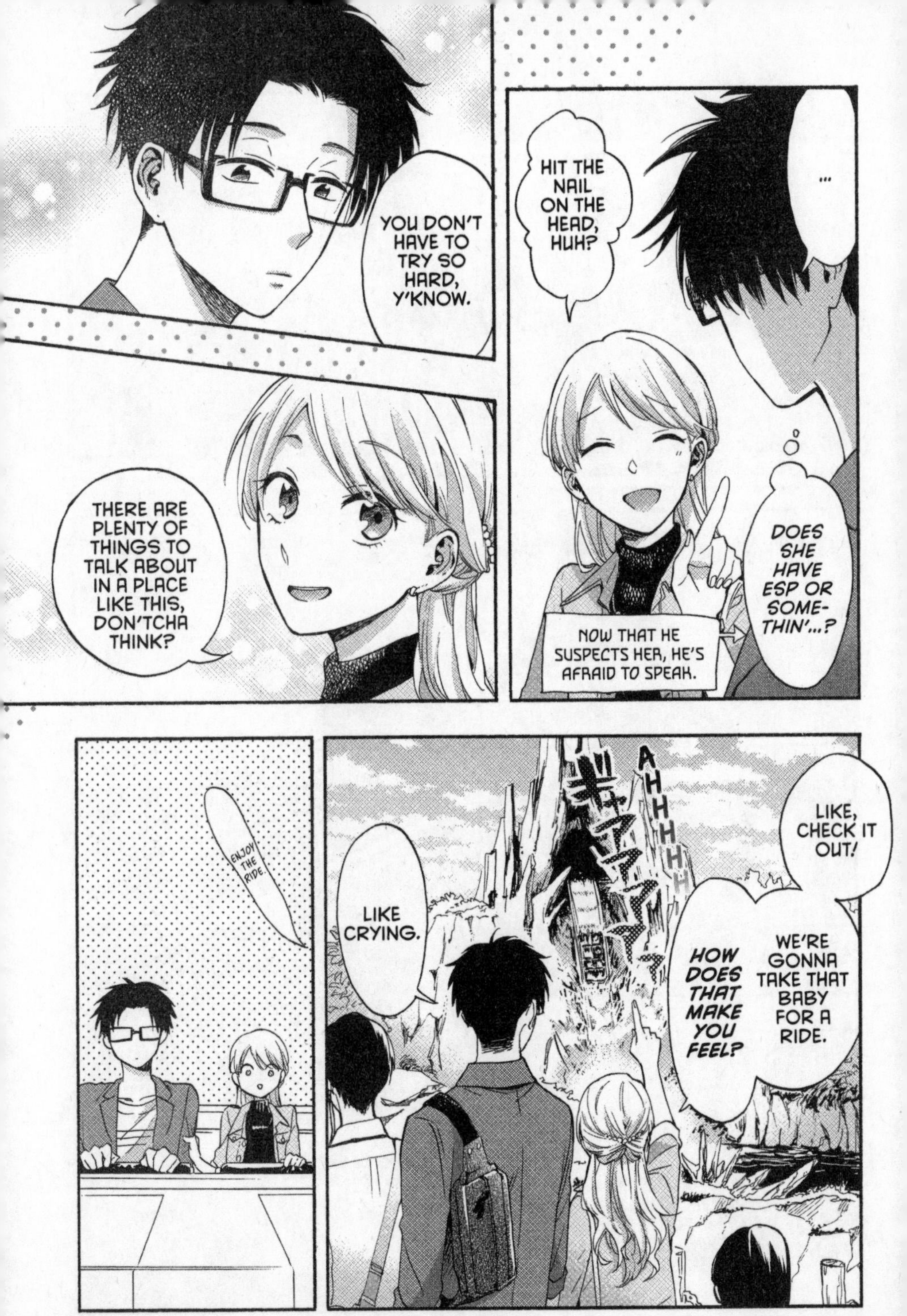
YOU DON'T HAVE TO TRY SO HARD, Y'KNOW.
...
HIT THE NAIL ON THE HEAD, HUH?
DOES SHE HAVE ESP OR SOME-THIN'...?
NOW THAT HE SUSPECTS HER, HE'S AFRAID TO SPEAK.
THERE ARE PLENTY OF THINGS TO TALK ABOUT IN A PLACE LIKE THIS, DON'TCHA THINK?
LIKE, CHECK IT OUT!
WE'RE GONNA TAKE THAT BABY FOR A RIDE.
AHHHHHH
HOW DOES THAT MAKE YOU FEEL?
LIKE CRYING.
ENJOY THE RIDE.

(Nothing like the feeling of despair as you ascend)

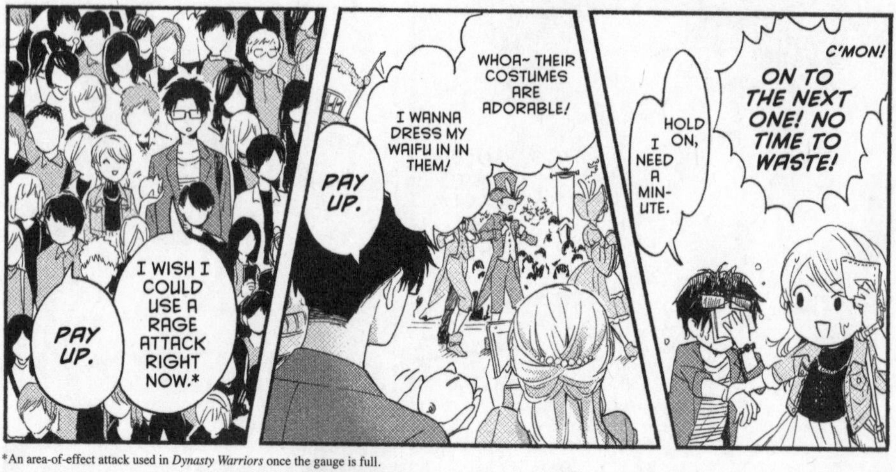
C'MON!
ON TO THE NEXT ONE! NO TIME TO WASTE!
HOLD ON, I NEED A MIN-UTE.
WHOA~ THEIR COSTUMES ARE ADORABLE!
I WANNA DRESS MY WAIFU IN IN THEM!
PAY UP.
I WISH I COULD USE A RAGE ATTACK RIGHT NOW.*
PAY UP.

*An area-of-effect attack used in *Dynasty Warriors* once the gauge is full.

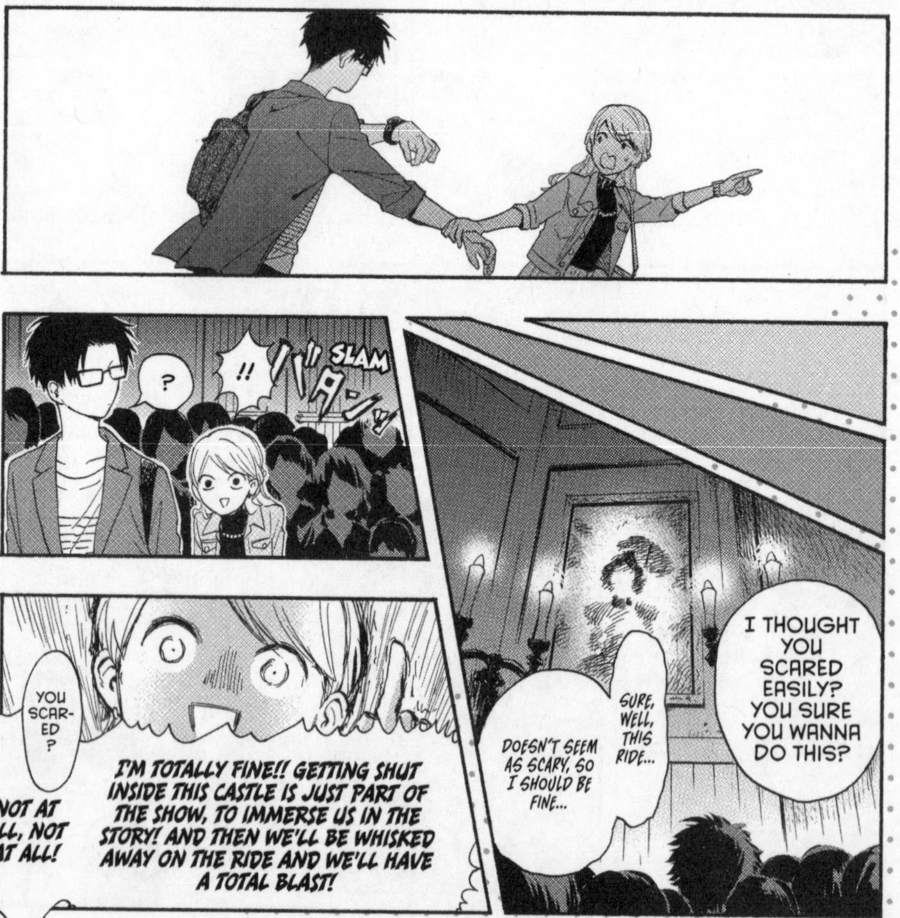
I THOUGHT YOU SCARED EASILY? YOU SURE YOU WANNA DO THIS?
SURE, WELL, THIS RIDE...
DOESN'T SEEM AS SCARY, SO I SHOULD BE FINE...
SLAM
!!
?
YOU SCAR-ED?
I'M TOTALLY FINE!! GETTING SHUT INSIDE THIS CASTLE IS JUST PART OF THE SHOW, TO IMMERSE US IN THE STORY! AND THEN WE'LL BE WHISKED AWAY ON THE RIDE AND WE'LL HAVE A TOTAL BLAST!
NOT AT ALL, NOT AT ALL!

(On the contrary, she gets talkative when she's worried)

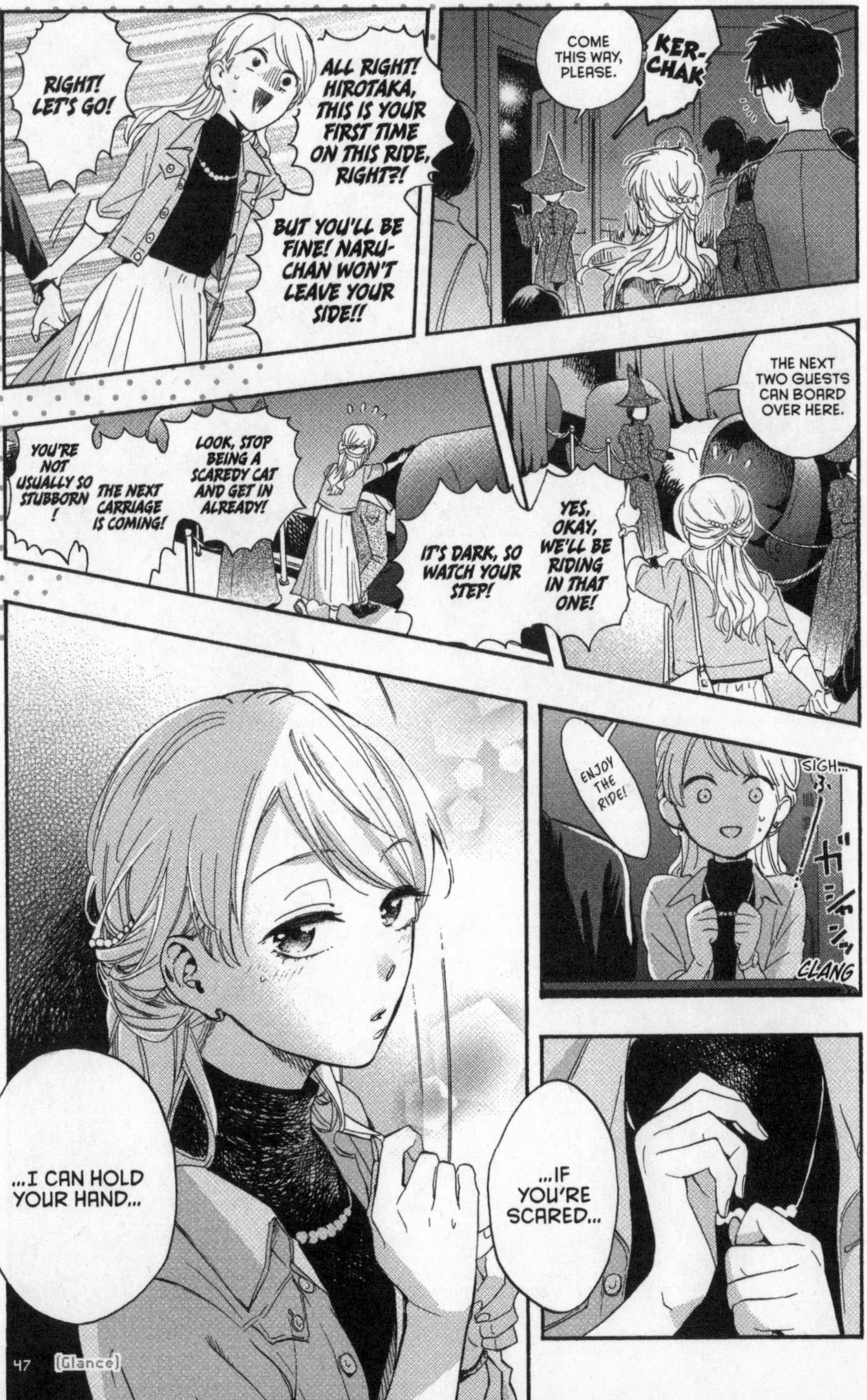
COME THIS WAY, PLEASE.
KER-CHAK
ALL RIGHT! HIROTAKA, THIS IS YOUR FIRST TIME ON THIS RIDE, RIGHT?!
RIGHT! LET'S GO!
BUT YOU'LL BE FINE! NARU-CHAN WON'T LEAVE YOUR SIDE!!
THE NEXT TWO GUESTS CAN BOARD OVER HERE.
YES, OKAY, WE'LL BE RIDING IN THAT ONE!
IT'S DARK, SO WATCH YOUR STEP!
LOOK, STOP BEING A SCAREDY CAT AND GET IN ALREADY!
THE NEXT CARRIAGE IS COMING!
YOU'RE NOT USUALLY SO STUBBORN!
ENJOY THE RIDE!
SIGH...
CLANG
...I CAN HOLD YOUR HAND...
...IF YOU'RE SCARED...

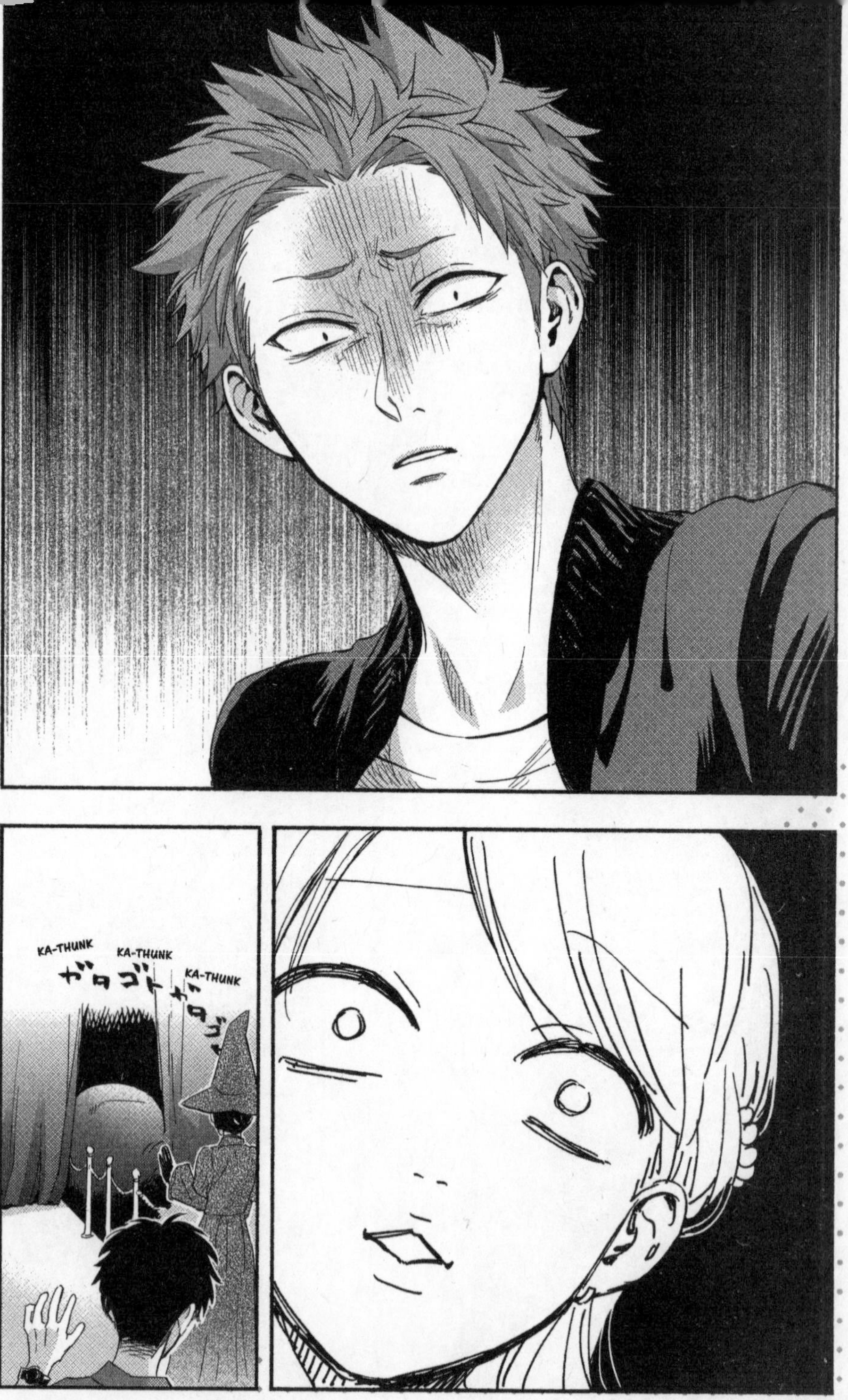
KA-THUNK
KA-THUNK
KA-THUNK

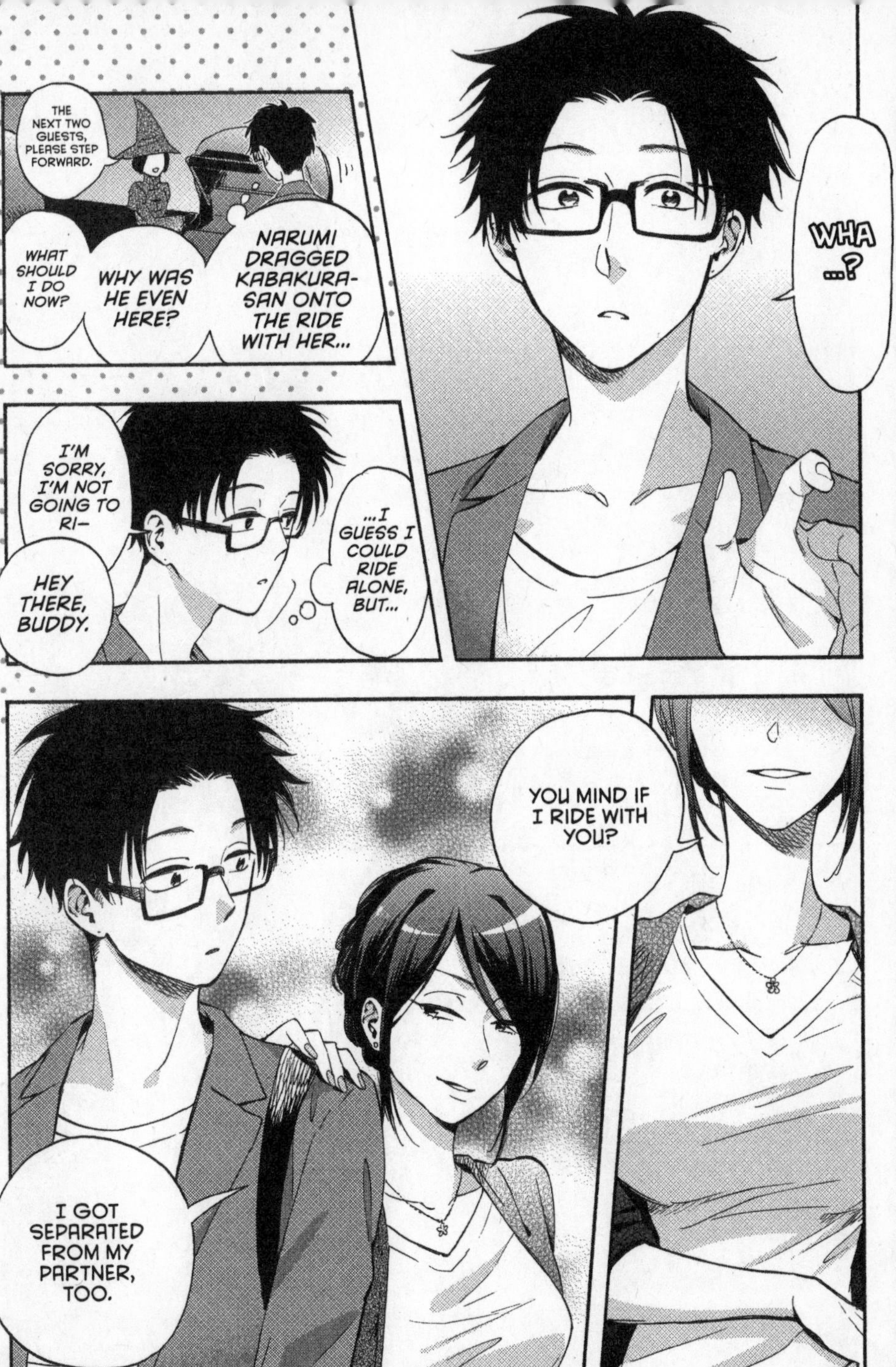
WHA ...?
THE NEXT TWO GUESTS, PLEASE STEP FORWARD.
NARUMI DRAGGED KABAKURA-SAN ONTO THE RIDE WITH HER...
WHY WAS HE EVEN HERE?
WHAT SHOULD I DO NOW?
...I GUESS I COULD RIDE ALONE, BUT...
I'M SORRY, I'M NOT GOING TO RI–
HEY THERE, BUDDY.
YOU MIND IF I RIDE WITH YOU?
I GOT SEPARATED FROM MY PARTNER, TOO.

(Party member change)
← To be continued...

Wotakoi: Love is Hard for Otaku

Episode....18

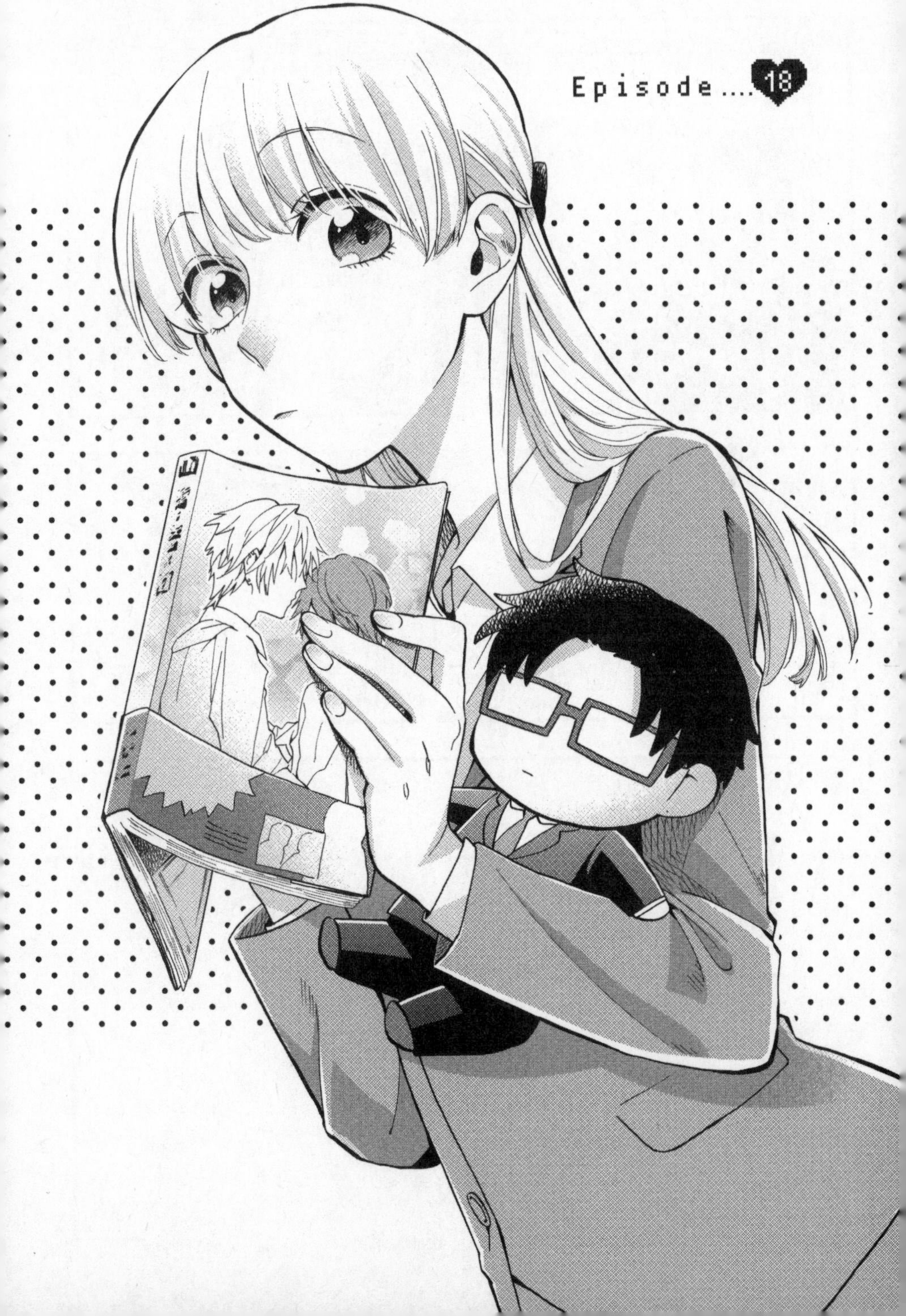

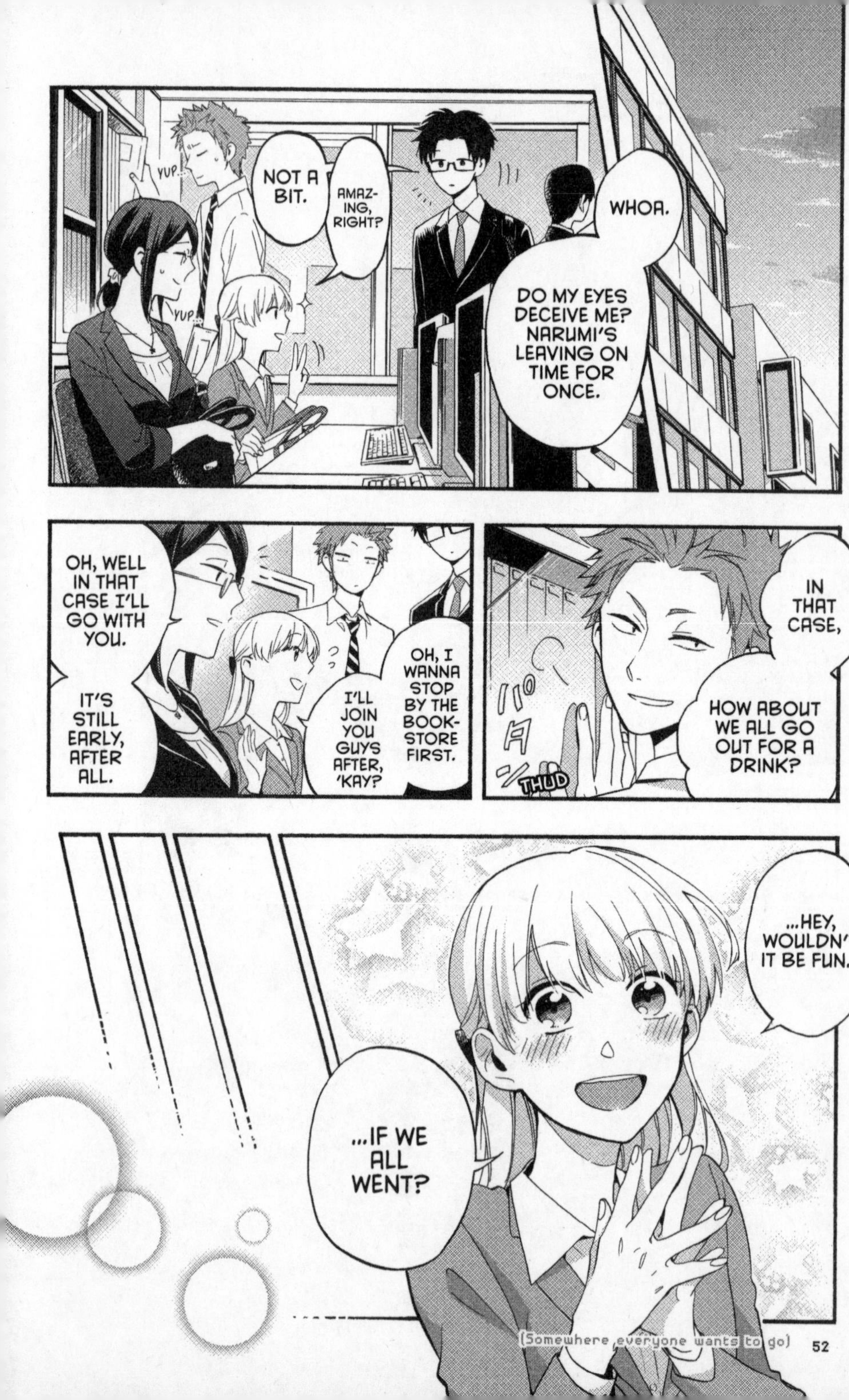
WHOA.
DO MY EYES DECEIVE ME? NARUMI'S LEAVING ON TIME FOR ONCE.
AMAZ-ING, RIGHT?
NOT A BIT.
YUP...
YUP...
IN THAT CASE,
HOW ABOUT WE ALL GO OUT FOR A DRINK?
THUD
OH, I WANNA STOP BY THE BOOK-STORE FIRST.
I'LL JOIN YOU GUYS AFTER, 'KAY?
OH, WELL IN THAT CASE I'LL GO WITH YOU.
IT'S STILL EARLY, AFTER ALL.
...HEY, WOULDN'T IT BE FUN...
...IF WE ALL WENT?

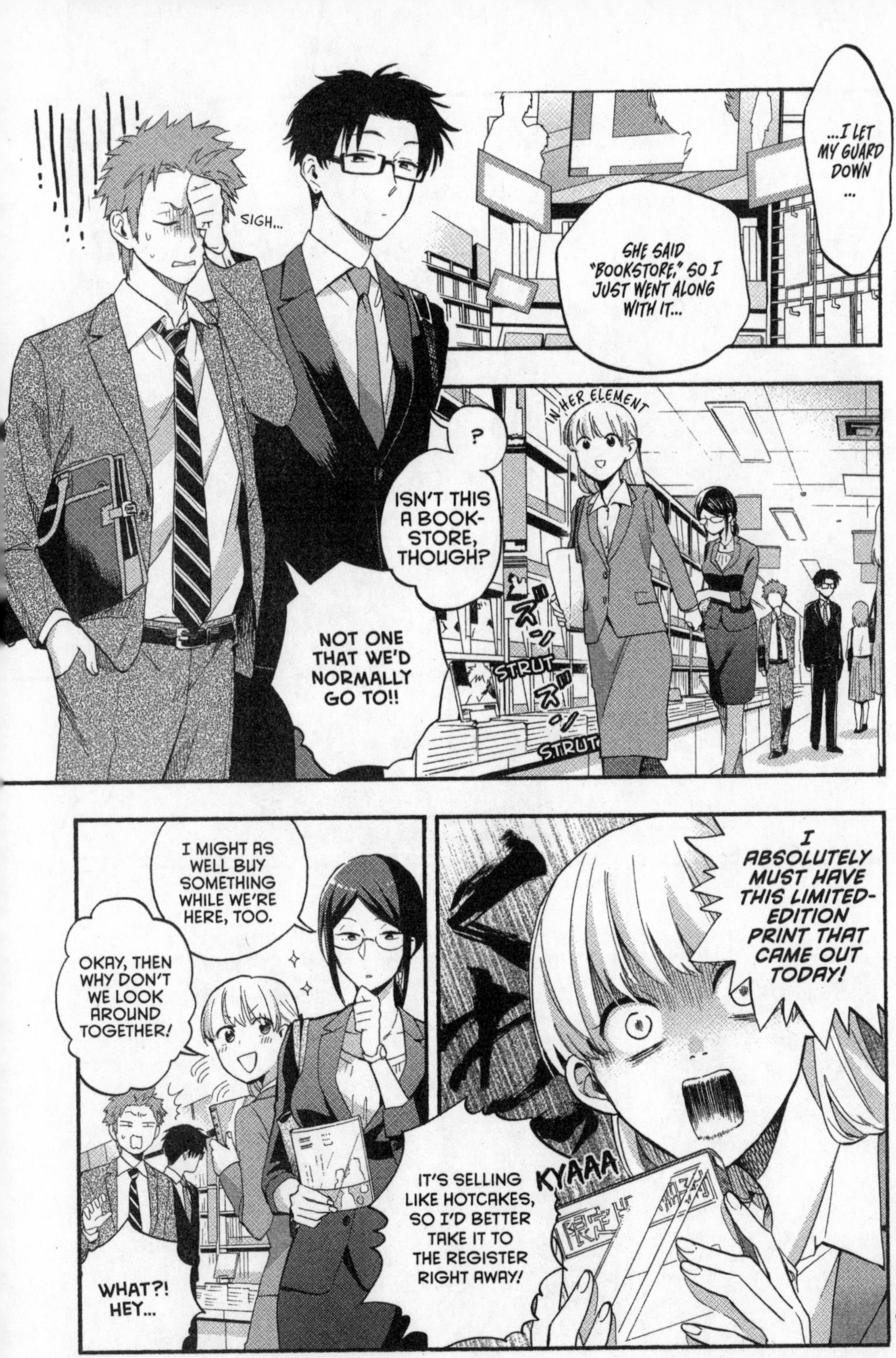

...I LET MY GUARD DOWN ...
SHE SAID "BOOKSTORE," SO I JUST WENT ALONG WITH IT...
IN HER ELEMENT
STRUT
STRUT
SIGH...
?
ISN'T THIS A BOOK-STORE, THOUGH?
NOT ONE THAT WE'D NORMALLY GO TO!!
I ABSOLUTELY MUST HAVE THIS LIMITED-EDITION PRINT THAT CAME OUT TODAY!
KYAAA
IT'S SELLING LIKE HOTCAKES, SO I'D BETTER TAKE IT TO THE REGISTER RIGHT AWAY!
I MIGHT AS WELL BUY SOMETHING WHILE WE'RE HERE, TOO.
OKAY, THEN WHY DON'T WE LOOK AROUND TOGETHER!
WHAT?! HEY...

Cover: Limited-Edition Magazine

(Naturally she got the in-store exclusives, too)

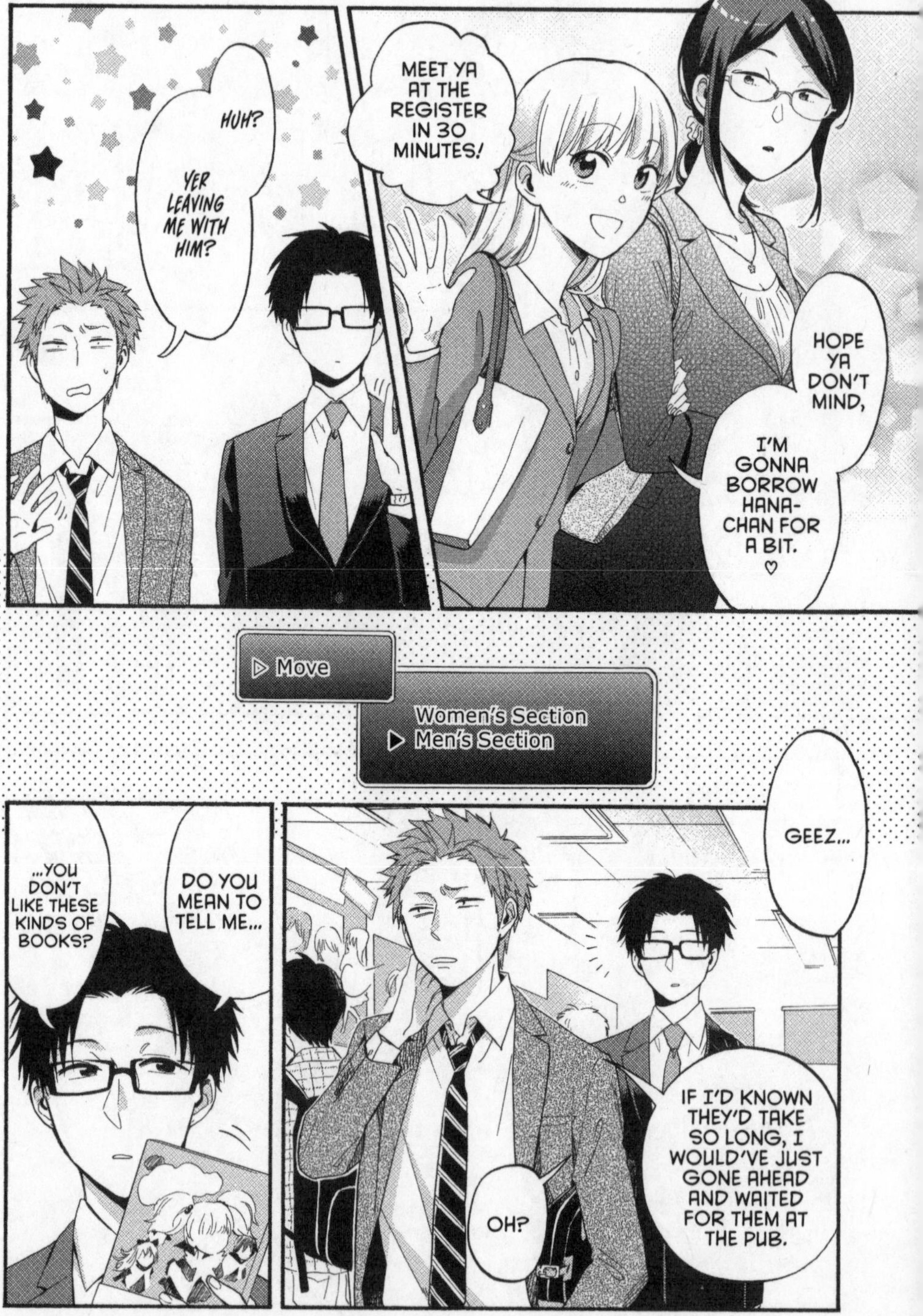
HOPE YA DON'T MIND, I'M GONNA BORROW HANA-CHAN FOR A BIT. ♡
MEET YA AT THE REGISTER IN 30 MINUTES!
HUH?
YER LEAVING ME WITH HIM?
▷ Move
Women's Section
▷ Men's Section
GEEZ...
IF I'D KNOWN THEY'D TAKE SO LONG, I WOULD'VE JUST GONE AHEAD AND WAITED FOR THEM AT THE PUB.
OH?
DO YOU MEAN TO TELL ME...
...YOU DON'T LIKE THESE KINDS OF BOOKS?

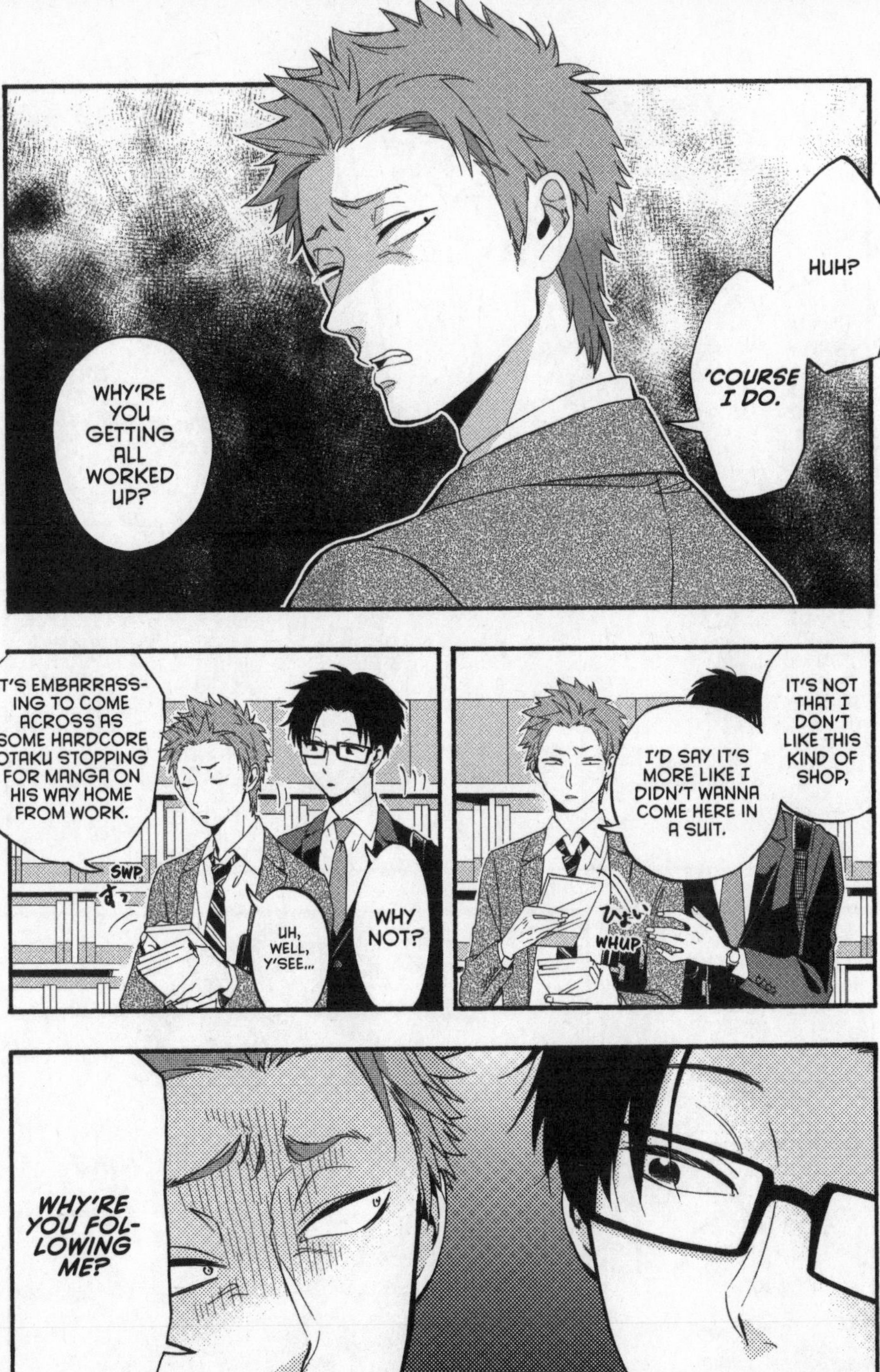
HUH?
'COURSE I DO.
WHY'RE YOU GETTING ALL WORKED UP?
IT'S NOT THAT I DON'T LIKE THIS KIND OF SHOP,
I'D SAY IT'S MORE LIKE I DIDN'T WANNA COME HERE IN A SUIT.
ひょい
WHUP
WHY NOT?
UH, WELL, Y'SEE...
IT'S EMBARRASSING TO COME ACROSS AS SOME HARDCORE OTAKU STOPPING FOR MANGA ON HIS WAY HOME FROM WORK.
SWP
すっ
WHY'RE YOU FOLLOWING ME?

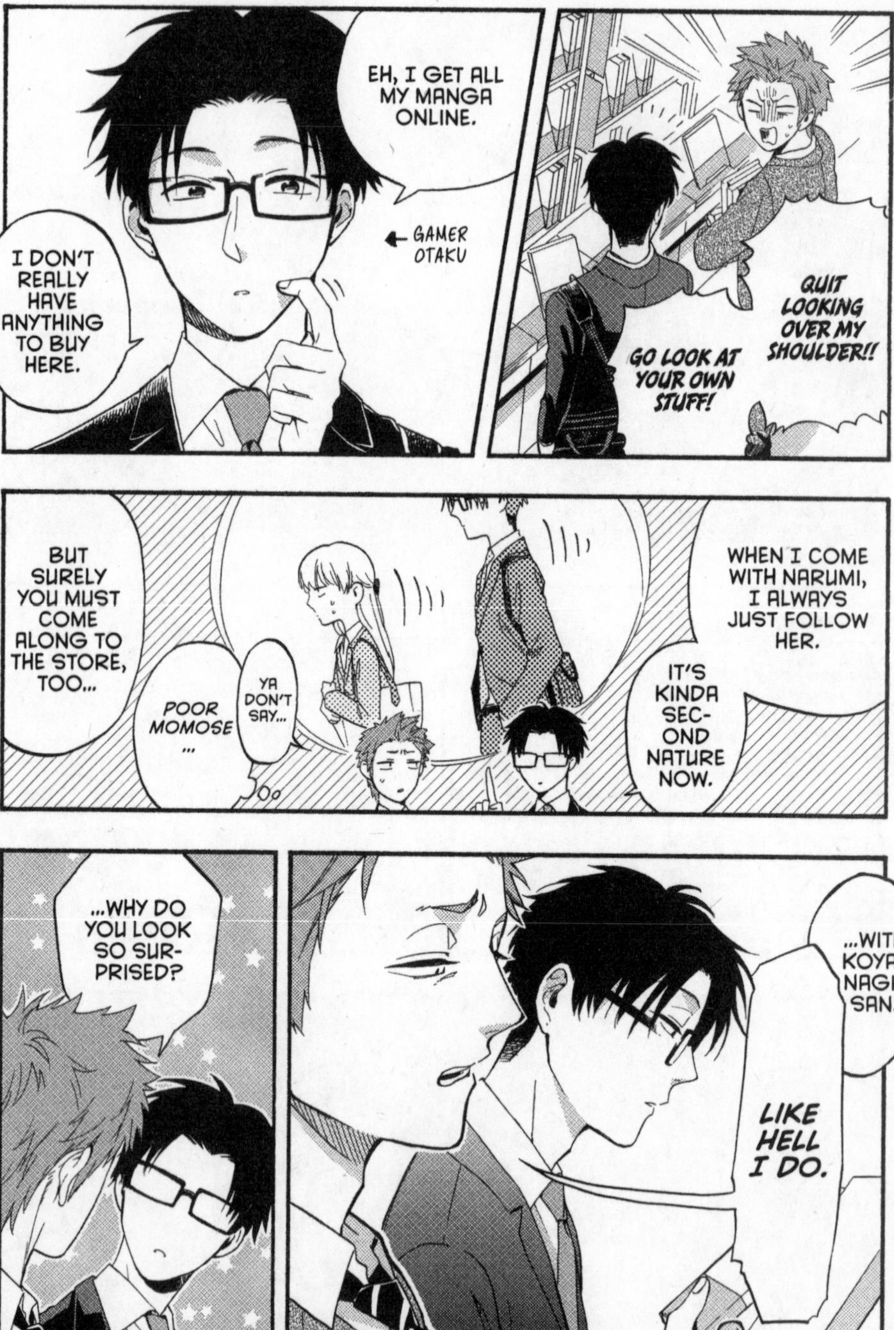
QUIT LOOKING OVER MY SHOULDER!!
GO LOOK AT YOUR OWN STUFF!
EH, I GET ALL MY MANGA ONLINE.
← GAMER OTAKU
I DON'T REALLY HAVE ANYTHING TO BUY HERE.
WHEN I COME WITH NARUMI, I ALWAYS JUST FOLLOW HER.
IT'S KINDA SEC-OND NATURE NOW.
YA DON'T SAY...
POOR MOMOSE ...
BUT SURELY YOU MUST COME ALONG TO THE STORE, TOO...
...WITH KOYA-NAGI-SAN.
LIKE HELL I DO.
...WHY DO YOU LOOK SO SUR-PRISED?

(No-Face?)

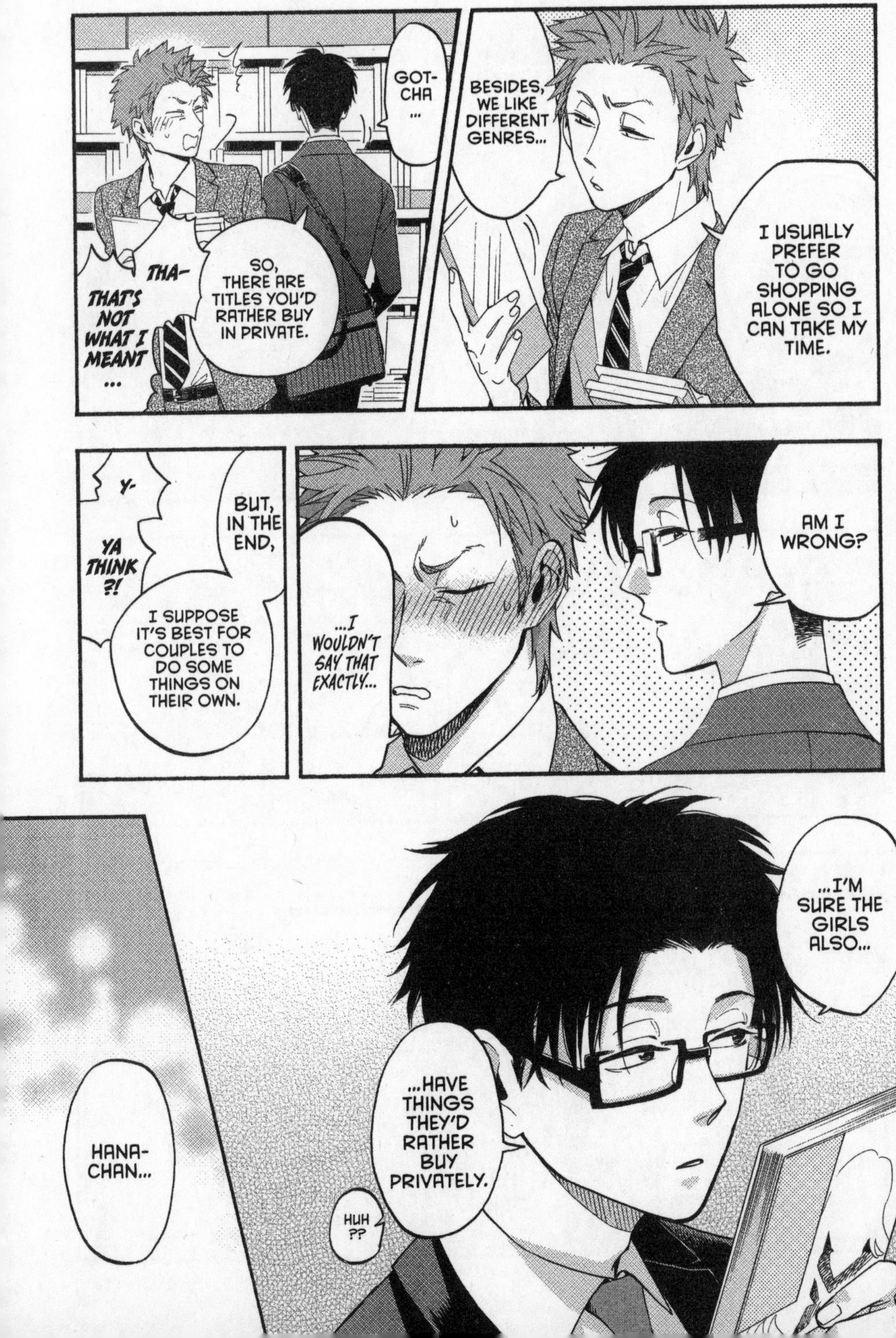

BESIDES, WE LIKE DIFFERENT GENRES...
I USUALLY PREFER TO GO SHOPPING ALONE SO I CAN TAKE MY TIME.
GOT-CHA ...
SO, THERE ARE TITLES YOU'D RATHER BUY IN PRIVATE.
THA-
THAT'S NOT WHAT I MEANT ...
AM I WRONG?
...I WOULDN'T SAY THAT EXACTLY...
BUT, IN THE END,
I SUPPOSE IT'S BEST FOR COUPLES TO DO SOME THINGS ON THEIR OWN.
Y-
YA THINK ?!
...I'M SURE THE GIRLS ALSO...
...HAVE THINGS THEY'D RATHER BUY PRIVATELY.
HUH ??
HANA-CHAN...

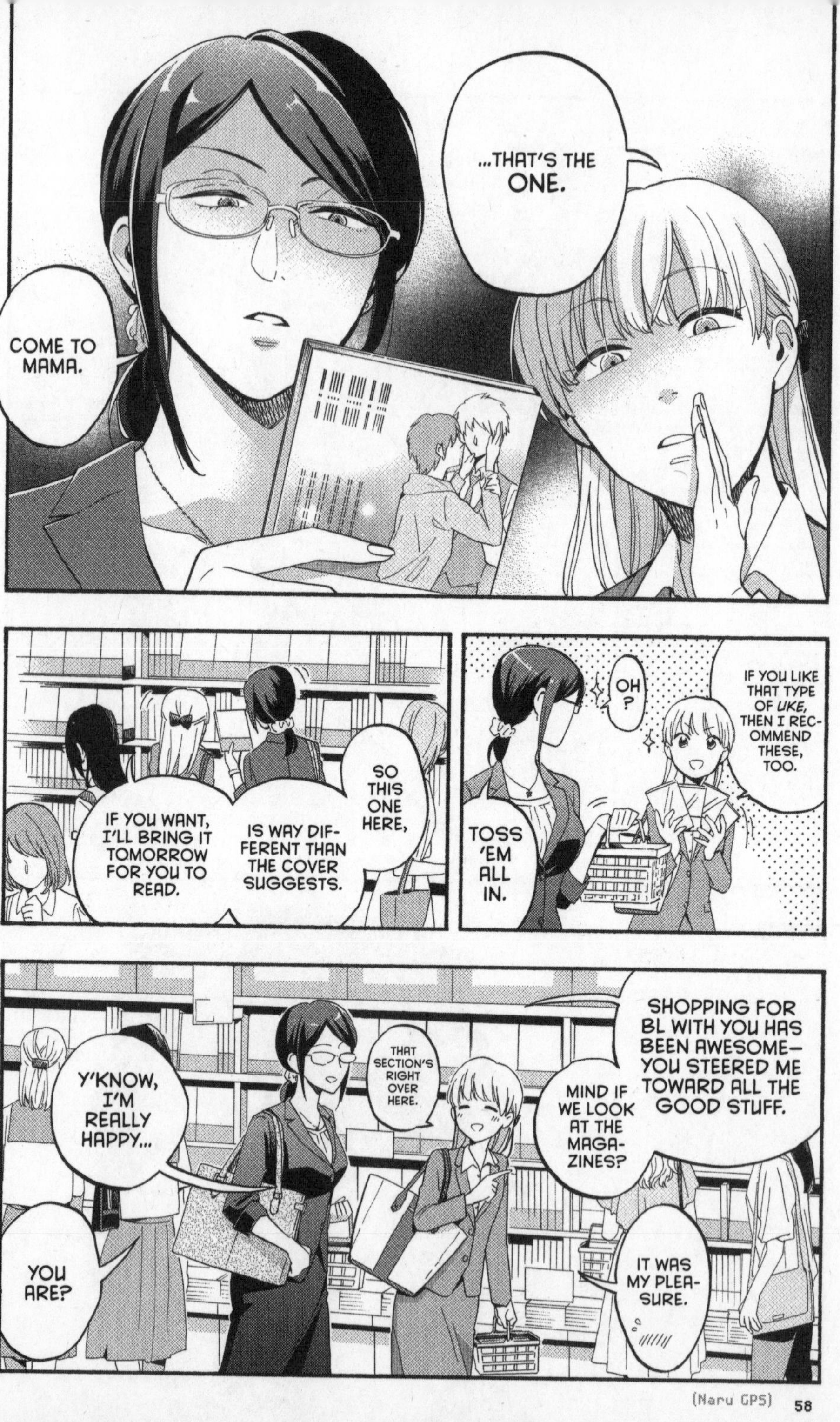
...THAT'S THE ONE.
COME TO MAMA.
IF YOU LIKE THAT TYPE OF *UKE*, THEN I RECOMMEND THESE, TOO.
OH?
TOSS 'EM ALL IN.
SO THIS ONE HERE,
IS WAY DIFFERENT THAN THE COVER SUGGESTS.
IF YOU WANT, I'LL BRING IT TOMORROW FOR YOU TO READ.
SHOPPING FOR BL WITH YOU HAS BEEN AWESOME—YOU STEERED ME TOWARD ALL THE GOOD STUFF.
IT WAS MY PLEASURE.
MIND IF WE LOOK AT THE MAGAZINES?
THAT SECTION'S RIGHT OVER HERE.
Y'KNOW, I'M REALLY HAPPY...
YOU ARE?

(Naru GPS)

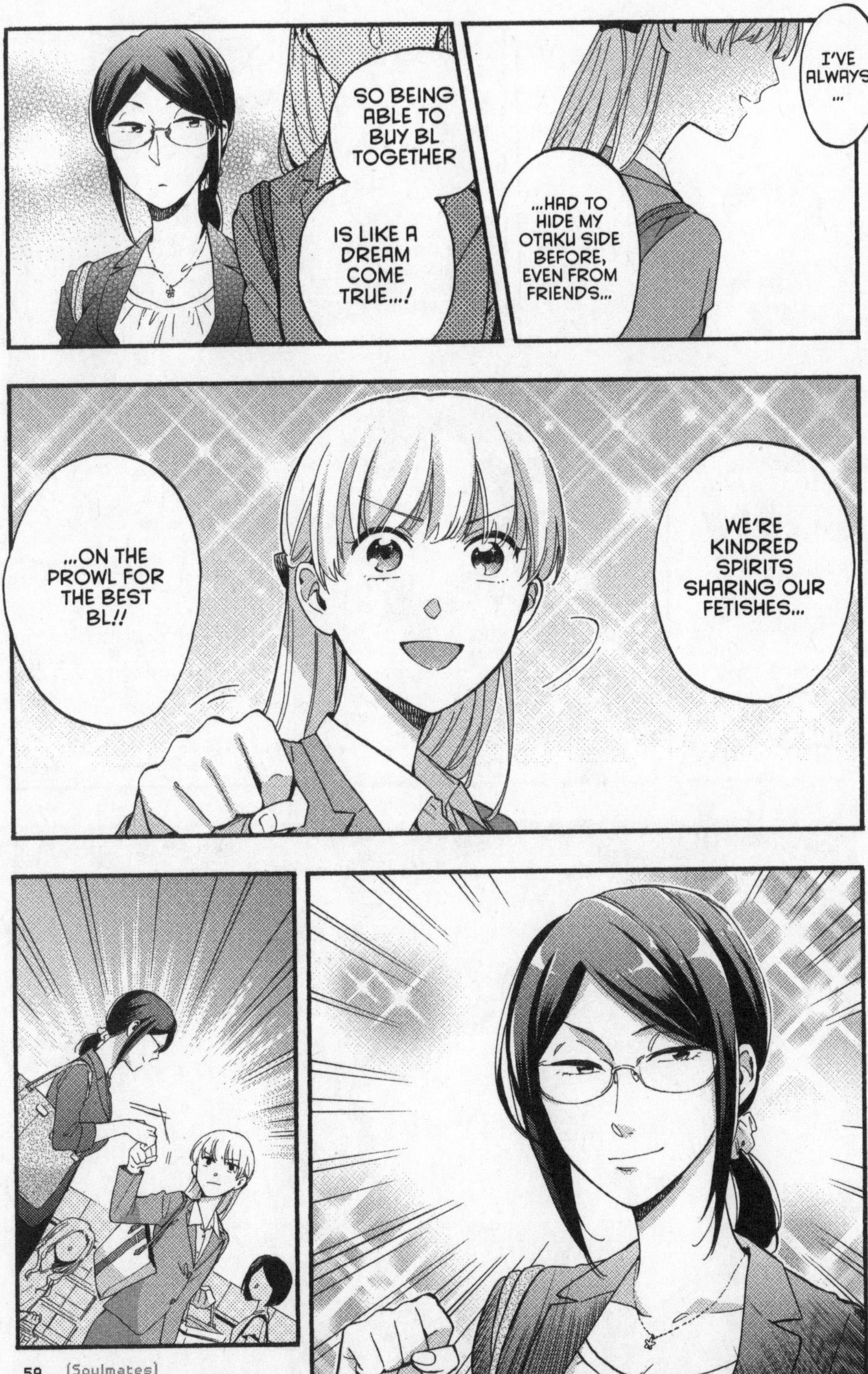
I'VE ALWAYS ...
...HAD TO HIDE MY OTAKU SIDE BEFORE, EVEN FROM FRIENDS...
SO BEING ABLE TO BUY BL TOGETHER
IS LIKE A DREAM COME TRUE...!
WE'RE KINDRED SPIRITS SHARING OUR FETISHES...
...ON THE PROWL FOR THE BEST BL!!

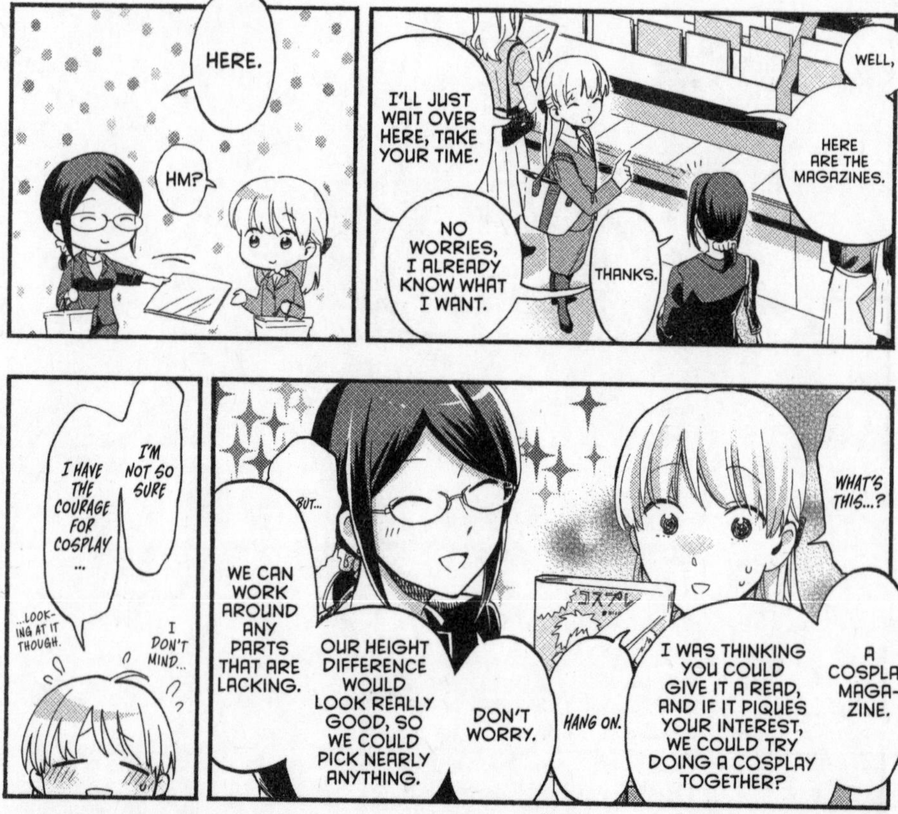
WELL,
HERE ARE THE MAGAZINES.
THANKS.
NO WORRIES, I ALREADY KNOW WHAT I WANT.
I'LL JUST WAIT OVER HERE, TAKE YOUR TIME.
HERE.
HM?
WHAT'S THIS...?
A COSPLAY MAGA-ZINE.
I WAS THINKING YOU COULD GIVE IT A READ, AND IF IT PIQUES YOUR INTEREST, WE COULD TRY DOING A COSPLAY TOGETHER?
HANG ON.
DON'T WORRY.
OUR HEIGHT DIFFERENCE WOULD LOOK REALLY GOOD, SO WE COULD PICK NEARLY ANYTHING.
WE CAN WORK AROUND ANY PARTS THAT ARE LACKING.
BUT...
I'M NOT SO SURE
I HAVE THE COURAGE FOR COSPLAY ...
I DON'T MIND...
...LOOKING AT IT THOUGH.

Title: Cosplay

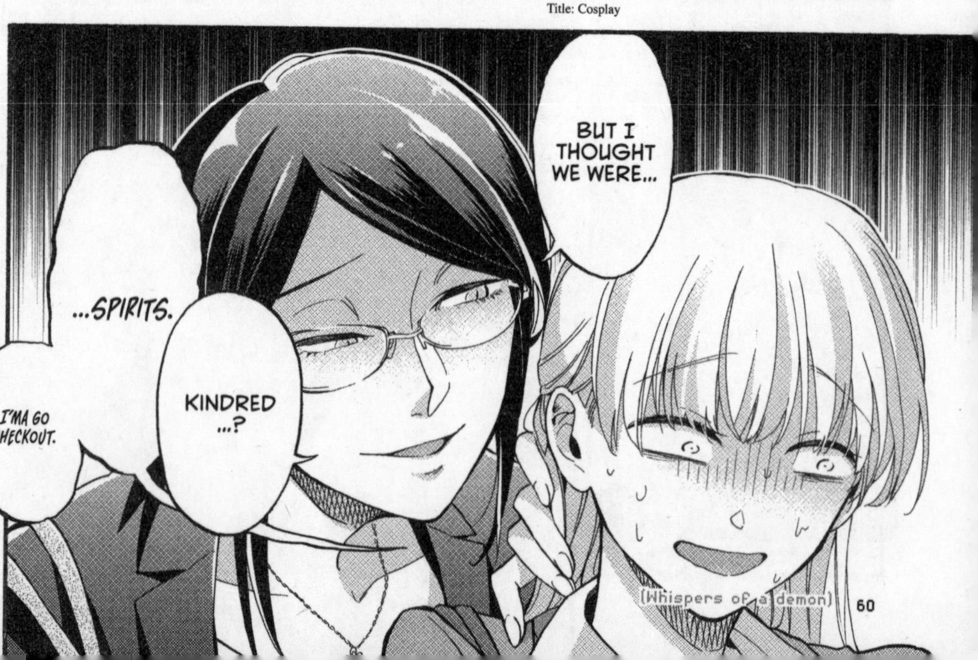
BUT I THOUGHT WE WERE...
KINDRED ...?
...SPIRITS.
I'MA GO CHECKOUT.
(Whispers of a demon)

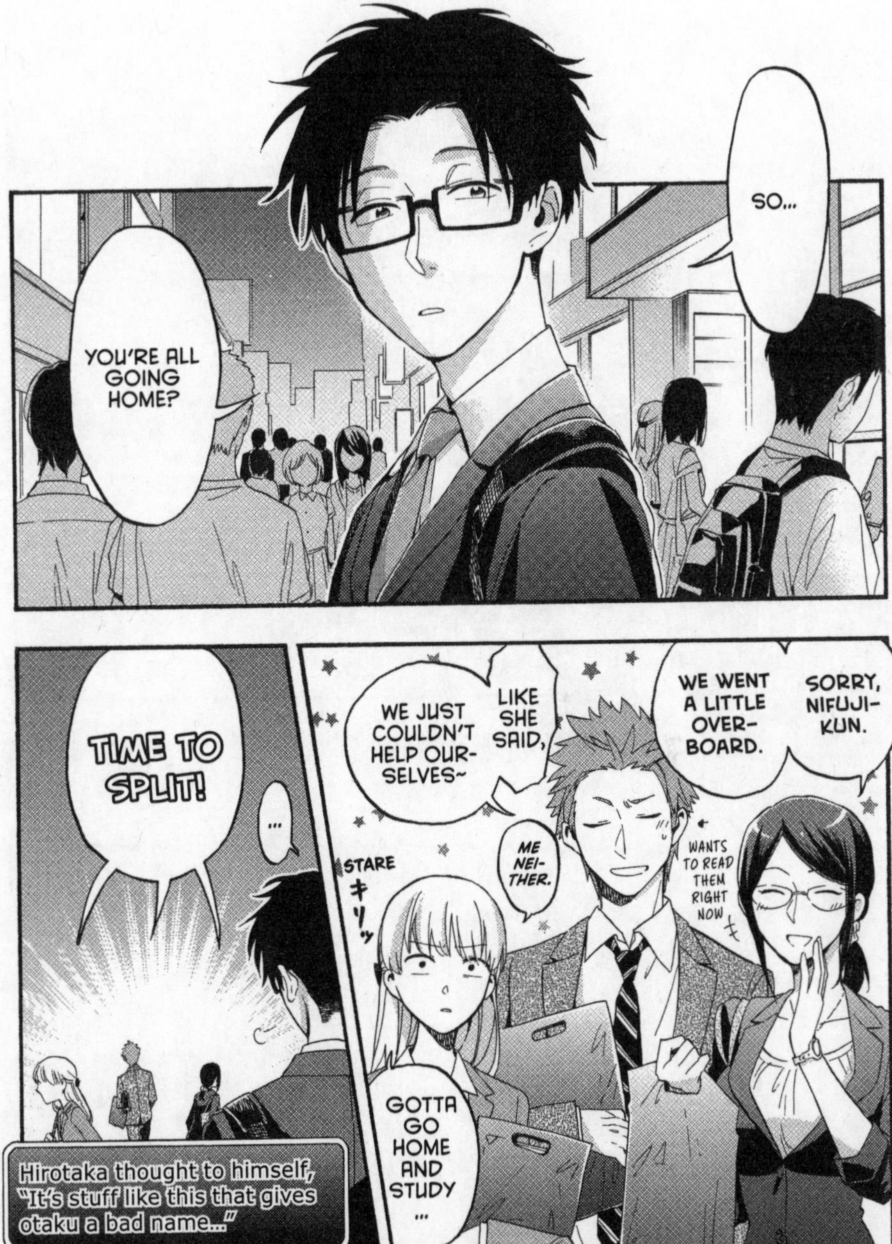
SO...
YOU'RE ALL GOING HOME?
SORRY, NIFUJI-KUN.
WE WENT A LITTLE OVER-BOARD.
LIKE SHE SAID,
WE JUST COULDN'T HELP OUR-SELVES~
WANTS TO READ THEM RIGHT NOW
ME NEITHER.
STARE
キリッ
GOTTA GO HOME AND STUDY ...
TIME TO SPLIT!
...
Hirotaka thought to himself, "It's stuff like this that gives otaku a bad name..."

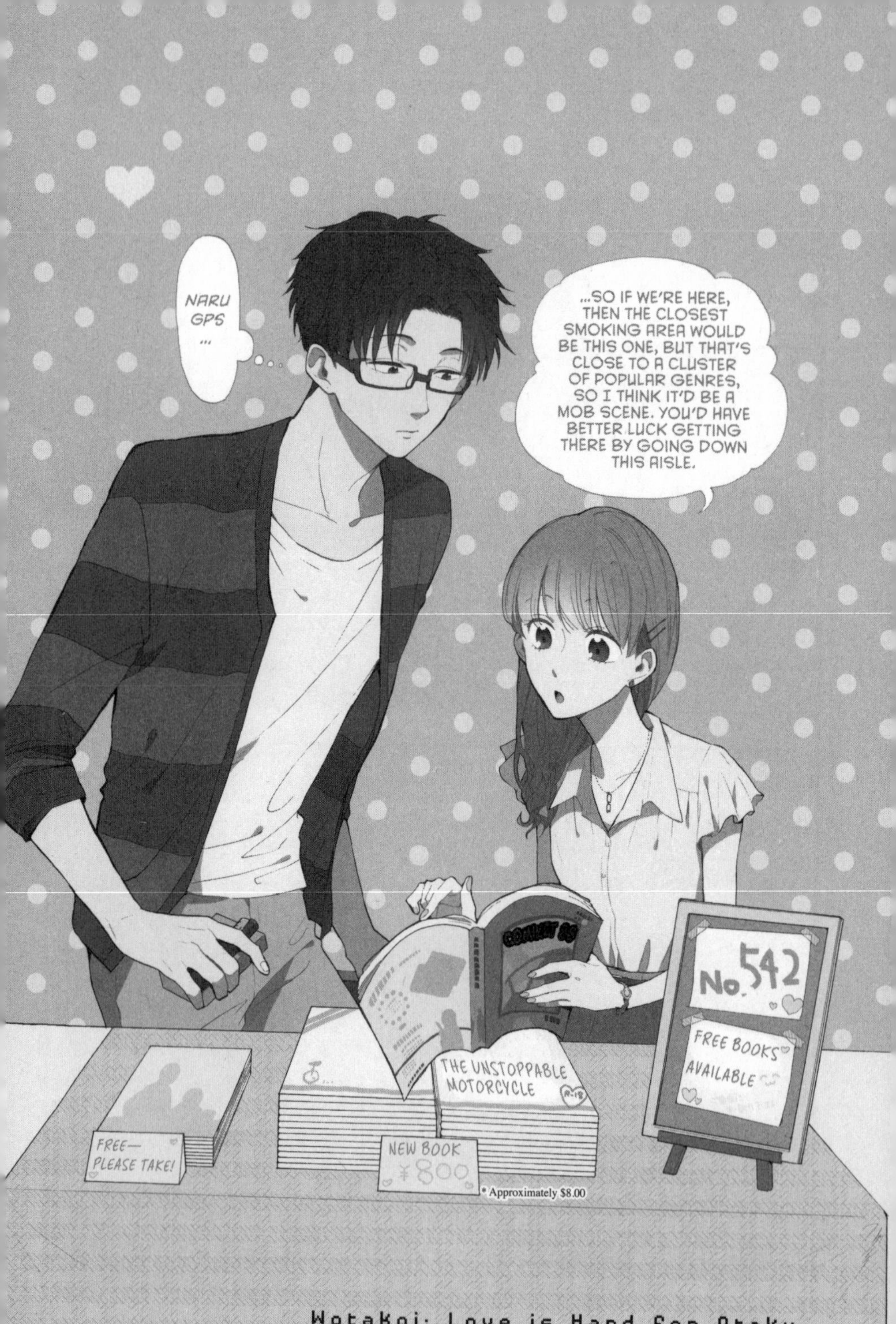
...SO IF WE'RE HERE, THEN THE CLOSEST SMOKING AREA WOULD BE THIS ONE, BUT THAT'S CLOSE TO A CLUSTER OF POPULAR GENRES, SO I THINK IT'D BE A MOB SCENE. YOU'D HAVE BETTER LUCK GETTING THERE BY GOING DOWN THIS AISLE.
NARU GPS ...
No. 542
FREE BOOKS AVAILABLE
THE UNSTOPPABLE MOTORCYCLE
NEW BOOK ¥800
FREE— PLEASE TAKE!
* Approximately $8.00

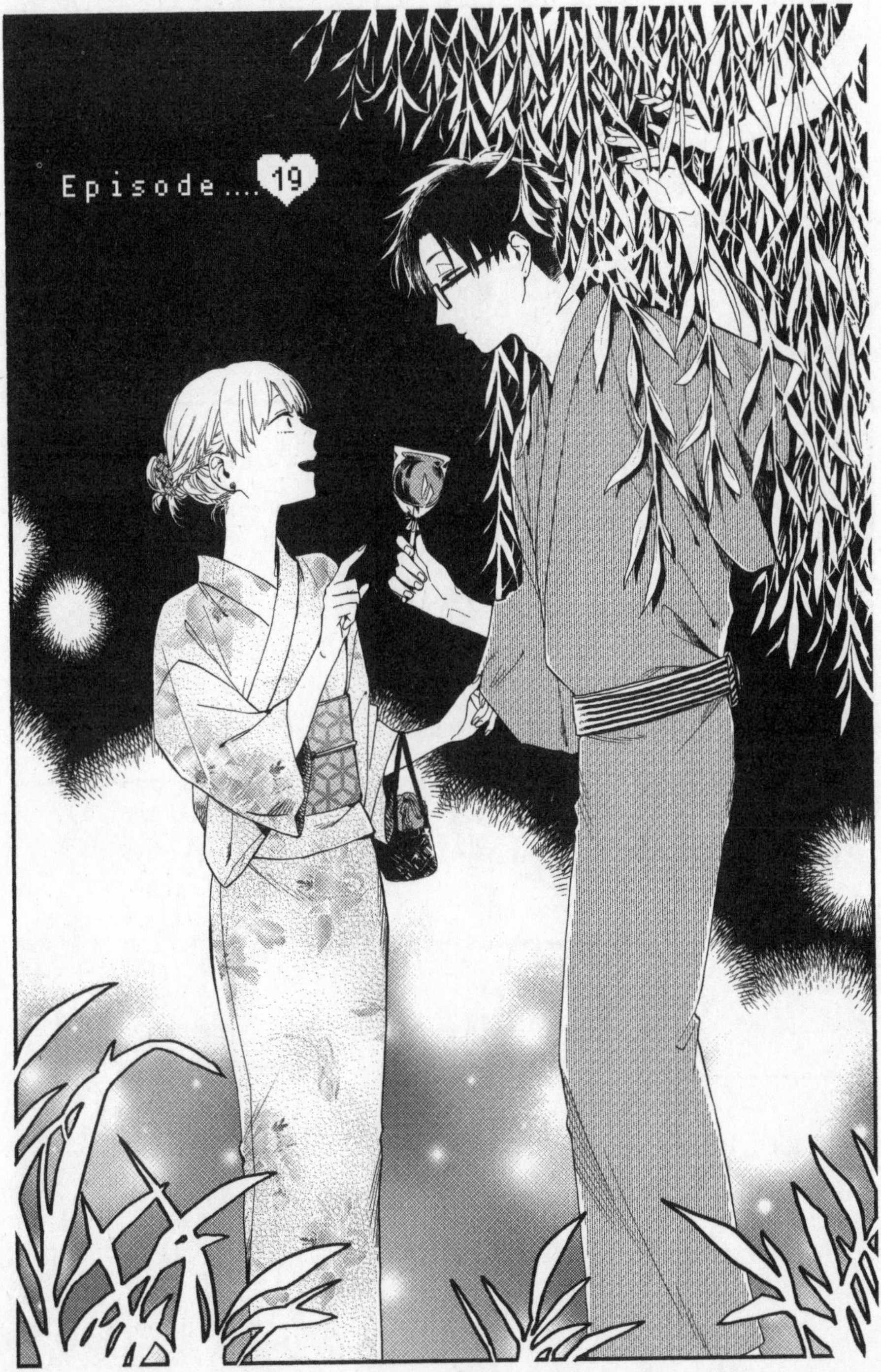
Episode.... 19

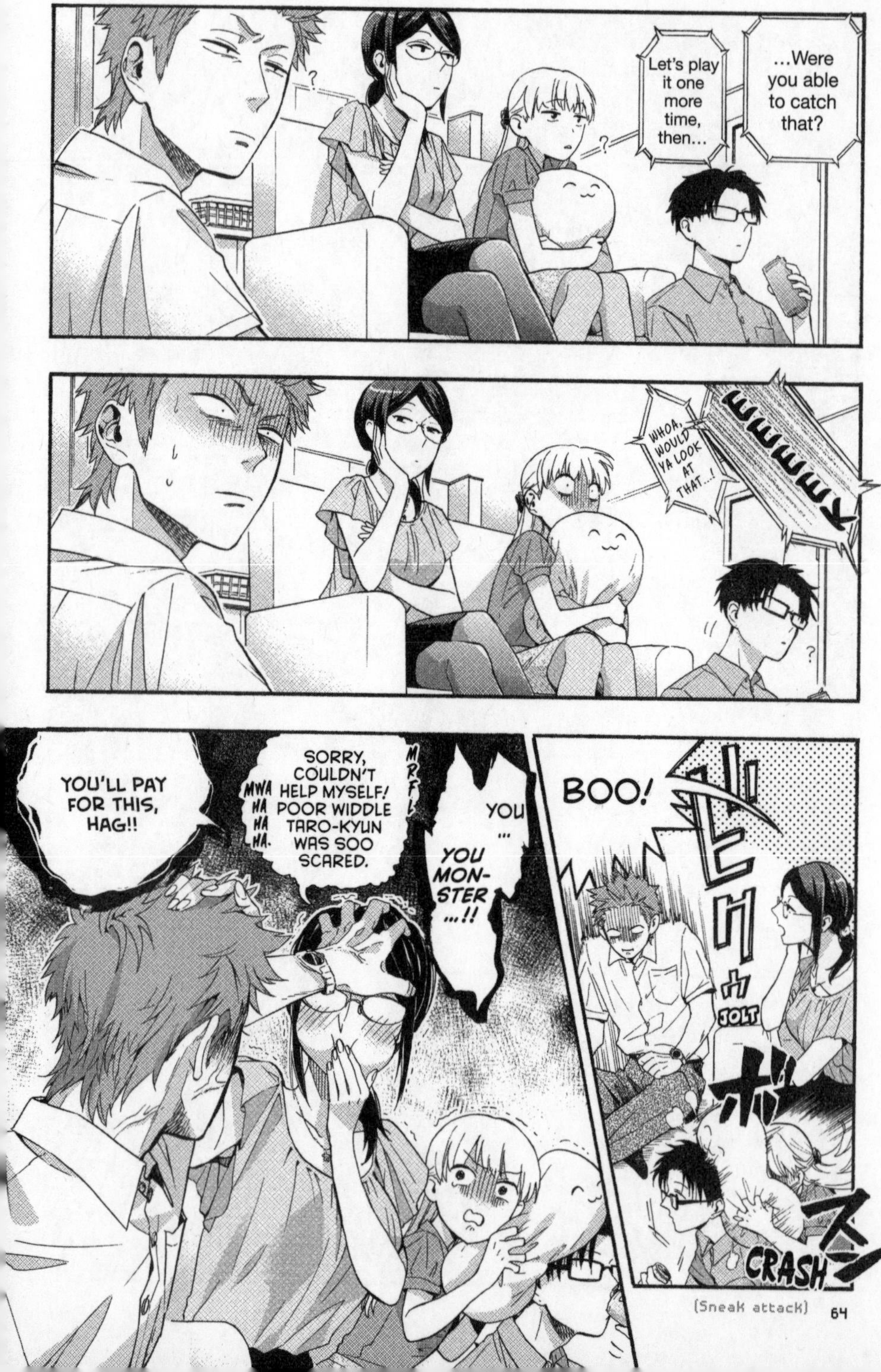
...Were you able to catch that?
Let's play it one more time, then...
EEEEEK
WHOA, WOULD YA LOOK AT THAT...!
BOO!
JOLT
CRASH
YOU ...
YOU MONSTER ...!!
MRFL
SORRY, COULDN'T HELP MYSELF! POOR WIDDLE TARO-KYUN WAS SOO SCARED.
MWA HA HA HA.
YOU'LL PAY FOR THIS, HAG!!

(Sneak attack)

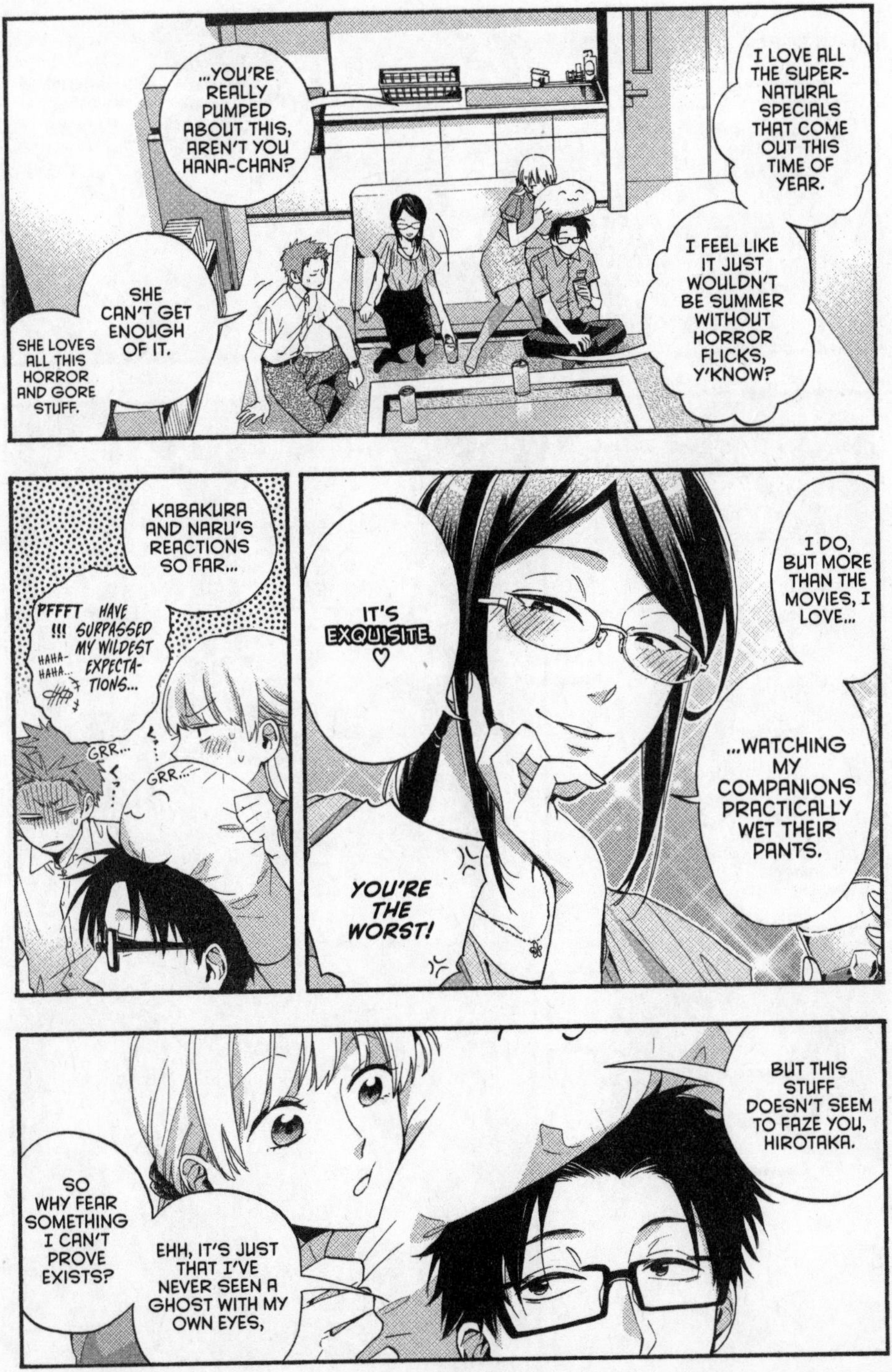
I LOVE ALL THE SUPERNATURAL SPECIALS THAT COME OUT THIS TIME OF YEAR.
I FEEL LIKE IT JUST WOULDN'T BE SUMMER WITHOUT HORROR FLICKS, Y'KNOW?
...YOU'RE REALLY PUMPED ABOUT THIS, AREN'T YOU HANA-CHAN?
SHE CAN'T GET ENOUGH OF IT.
SHE LOVES ALL THIS HORROR AND GORE STUFF.
I DO, BUT MORE THAN THE MOVIES, I LOVE...
...WATCHING MY COMPANIONS PRACTICALLY WET THEIR PANTS.
IT'S EXQUISITE. ♥
YOU'RE THE WORST!
KABAKURA AND NARU'S REACTIONS SO FAR...
HAVE SURPASSED MY WILDEST EXPECTATIONS...
PFFFT!!!
HAHA-HAHA...
GRR...
GRR...
BUT THIS STUFF DOESN'T SEEM TO FAZE YOU, HIROTAKA.
EHH, IT'S JUST THAT I'VE NEVER SEEN A GHOST WITH MY OWN EYES,
SO WHY FEAR SOMETHING I CAN'T PROVE EXISTS?

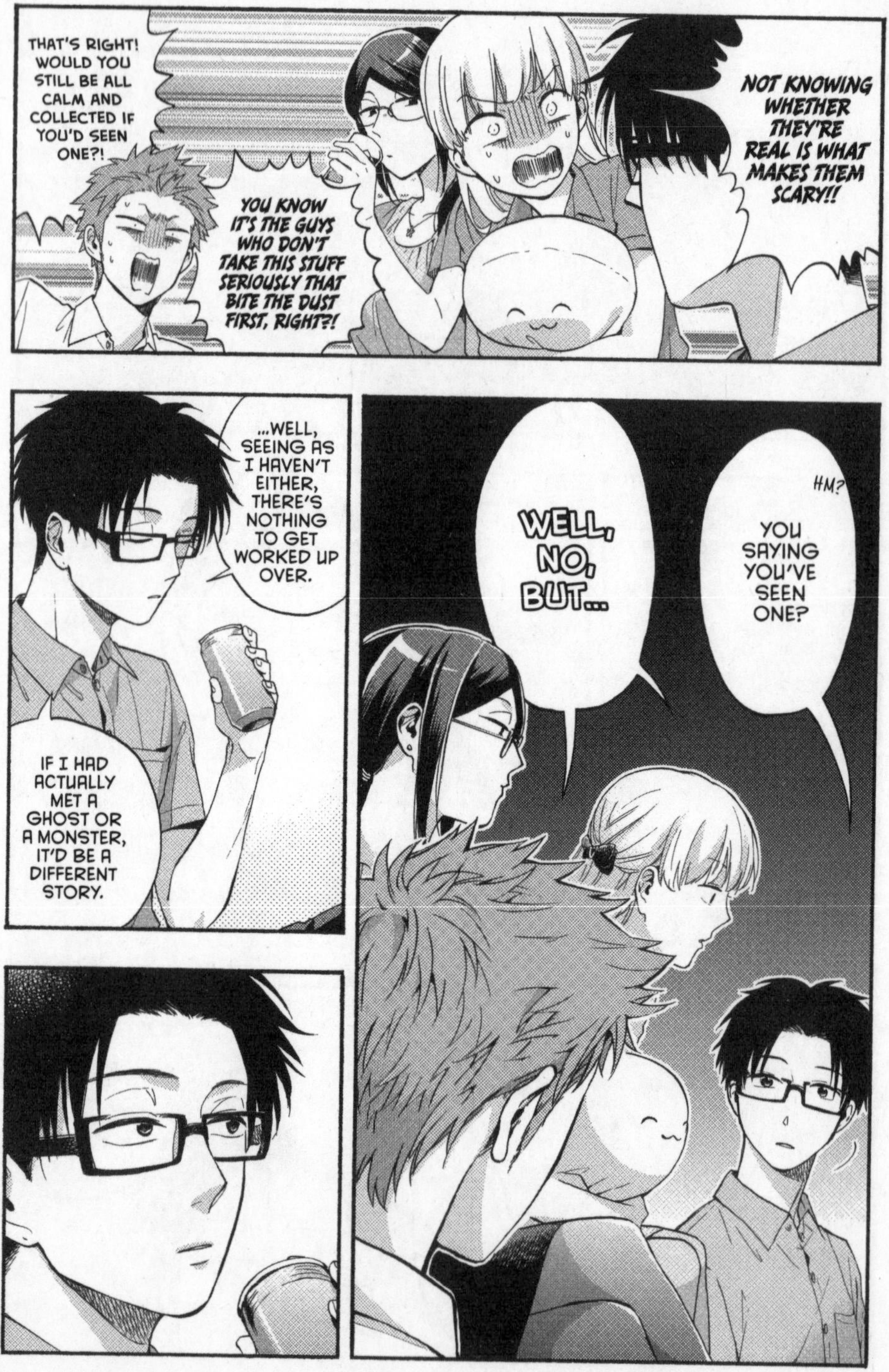

NOT KNOWING WHETHER THEY'RE REAL IS WHAT MAKES THEM SCARY!!
YOU KNOW IT'S THE GUYS WHO DON'T TAKE THIS STUFF SERIOUSLY THAT BITE THE DUST FIRST, RIGHT?!
THAT'S RIGHT! WOULD YOU STILL BE ALL CALM AND COLLECTED IF YOU'D SEEN ONE?!
...WELL, SEEING AS I HAVEN'T EITHER, THERE'S NOTHING TO GET WORKED UP OVER.
IF I HAD ACTUALLY MET A GHOST OR A MONSTER, IT'D BE A DIFFERENT STORY.
HM?
YOU SAYING YOU'VE SEEN ONE?
WELL, NO, BUT...

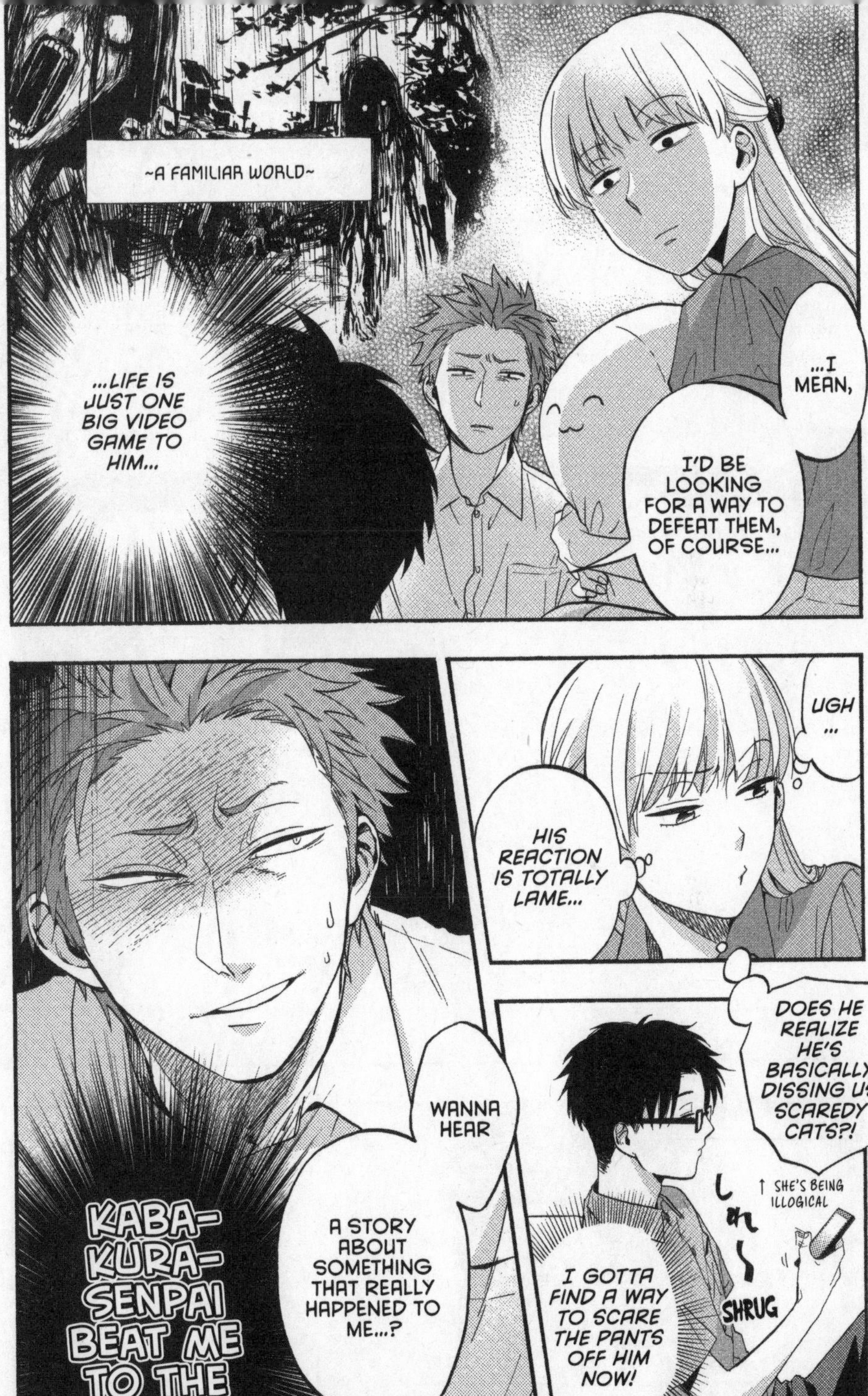
...I MEAN,
I'D BE LOOKING FOR A WAY TO DEFEAT THEM, OF COURSE...
~A FAMILIAR WORLD~
...LIFE IS JUST ONE BIG VIDEO GAME TO HIM...
UGH ...
HIS REACTION IS TOTALLY LAME...
DOES HE REALIZE HE'S BASICALLY DISSING US SCAREDY CATS?!
↑ SHE'S BEING ILLOGICAL
しれ～
SHRUG
I GOTTA FIND A WAY TO SCARE THE PANTS OFF HIM NOW!
WANNA HEAR
A STORY ABOUT SOMETHING THAT REALLY HAPPENED TO ME...?
KABA-KURA-SENPAI BEAT ME TO THE PUNCH!!

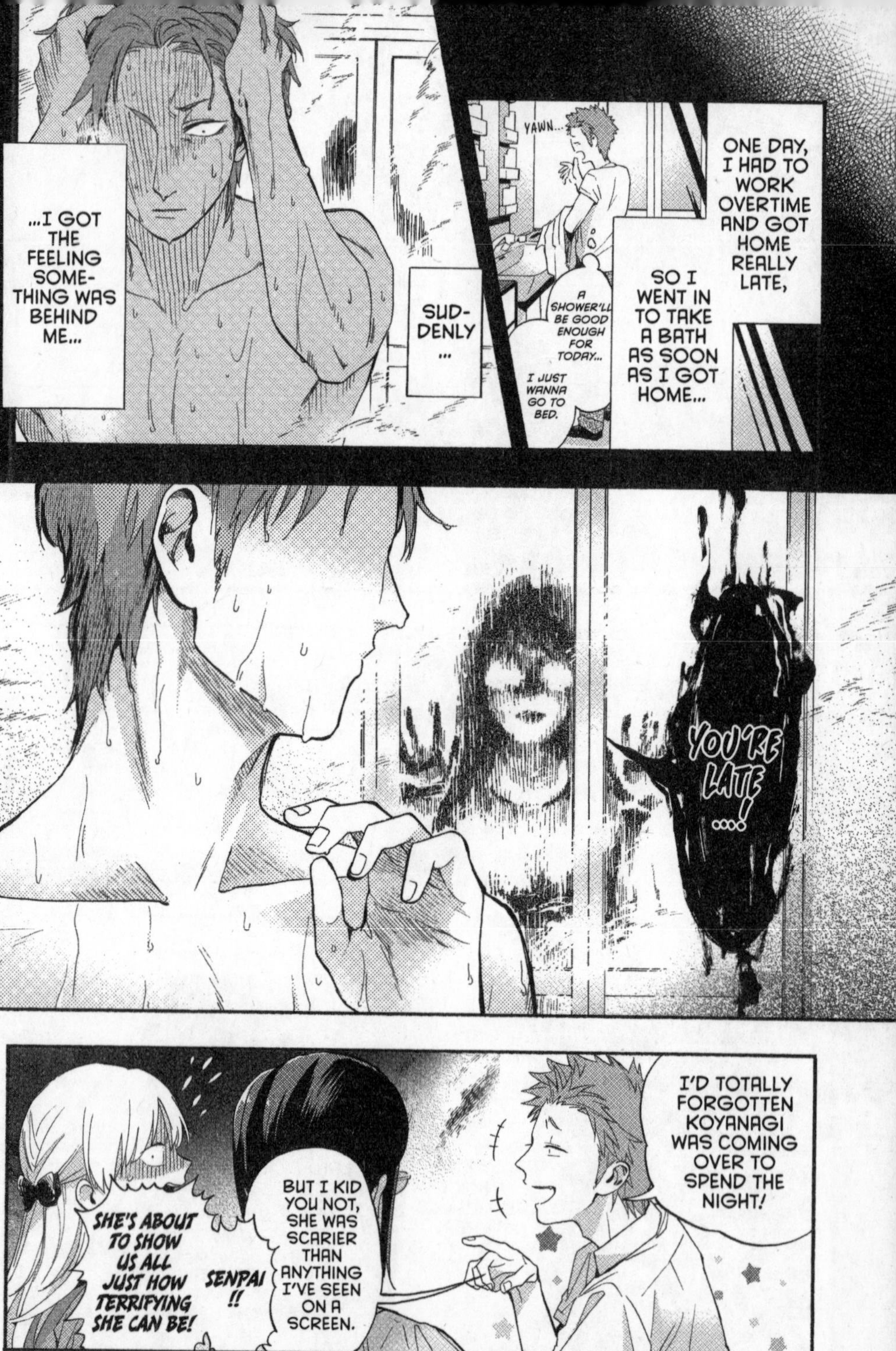
ONE DAY, I HAD TO WORK OVERTIME AND GOT HOME REALLY LATE,
YAWN...
SO I WENT IN TO TAKE A BATH AS SOON AS I GOT HOME...
A SHOWER'LL BE GOOD ENOUGH FOR TODAY...
I JUST WANNA GO TO BED.
SUD-DENLY ...
...I GOT THE FEELING SOME-THING WAS BEHIND ME...
YOU'RE LATE ...!
I'D TOTALLY FORGOTTEN KOYANAGI WAS COMING OVER TO SPEND THE NIGHT!
BUT I KID YOU NOT, SHE WAS SCARIER THAN ANYTHING I'VE SEEN ON A SCREEN.
SENPAI !!
SHE'S ABOUT TO SHOW US ALL JUST HOW TERRIFYING SHE CAN BE!

(Clear and present horror)

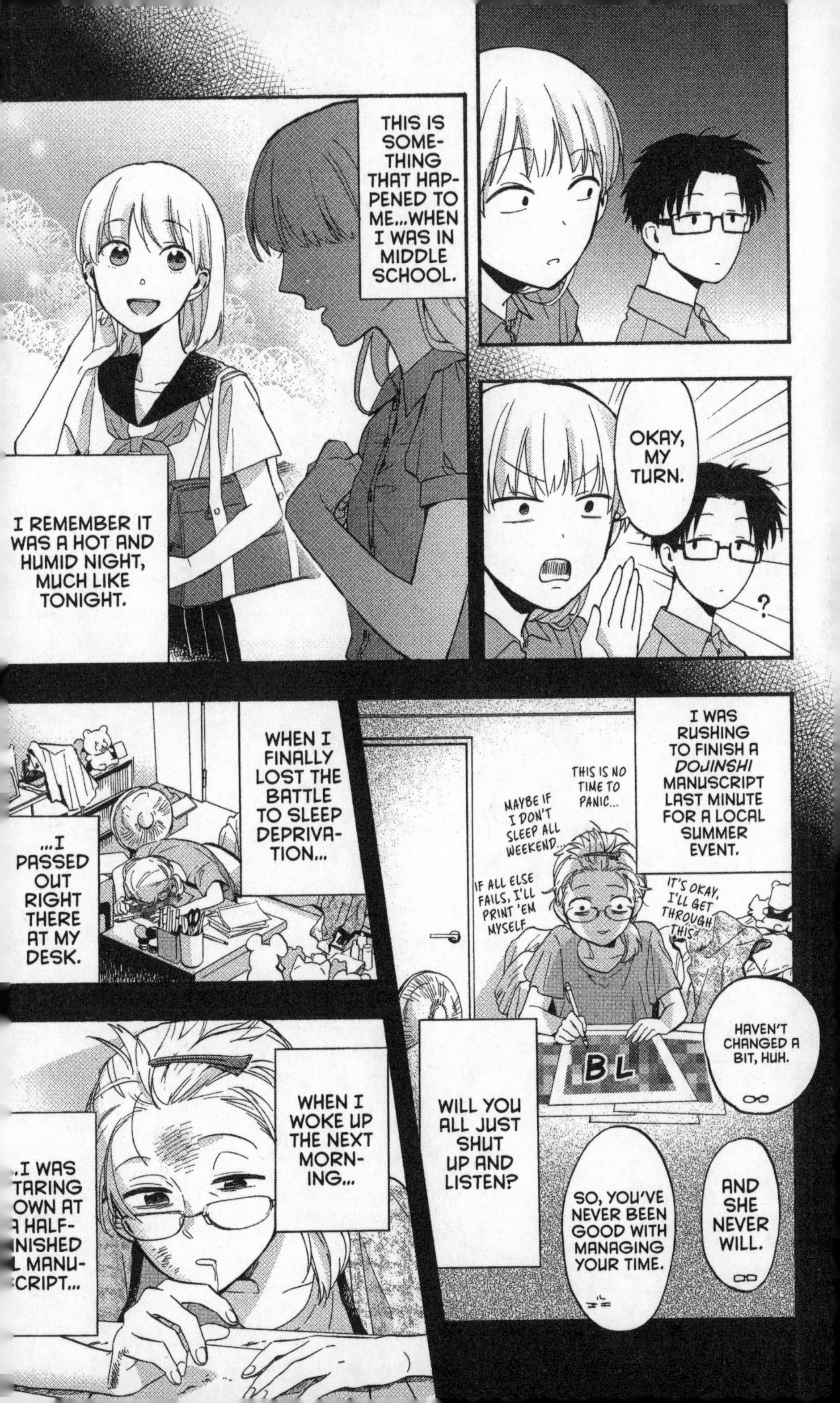
OKAY, MY TURN.
THIS IS SOMETHING THAT HAPPENED TO ME...WHEN I WAS IN MIDDLE SCHOOL.
I REMEMBER IT WAS A HOT AND HUMID NIGHT, MUCH LIKE TONIGHT.
I WAS RUSHING TO FINISH A *DOJINSHI* MANUSCRIPT LAST MINUTE FOR A LOCAL SUMMER EVENT.
THIS IS NO TIME TO PANIC...
MAYBE IF I DON'T SLEEP ALL WEEKEND...
IT'S OKAY, I'LL GET THROUGH THIS.
IF ALL ELSE FAILS, I'LL PRINT 'EM MYSELF
BL
HAVEN'T CHANGED A BIT, HUH.
SO, YOU'VE NEVER BEEN GOOD WITH MANAGING YOUR TIME.
AND SHE NEVER WILL.
WILL YOU ALL JUST SHUT UP AND LISTEN?
WHEN I FINALLY LOST THE BATTLE TO SLEEP DEPRIVATION...
...I PASSED OUT RIGHT THERE AT MY DESK.
WHEN I WOKE UP THE NEXT MORNING...
..I WAS TARING OWN AT A HALF-INISHED L MANU-SCRIPT...

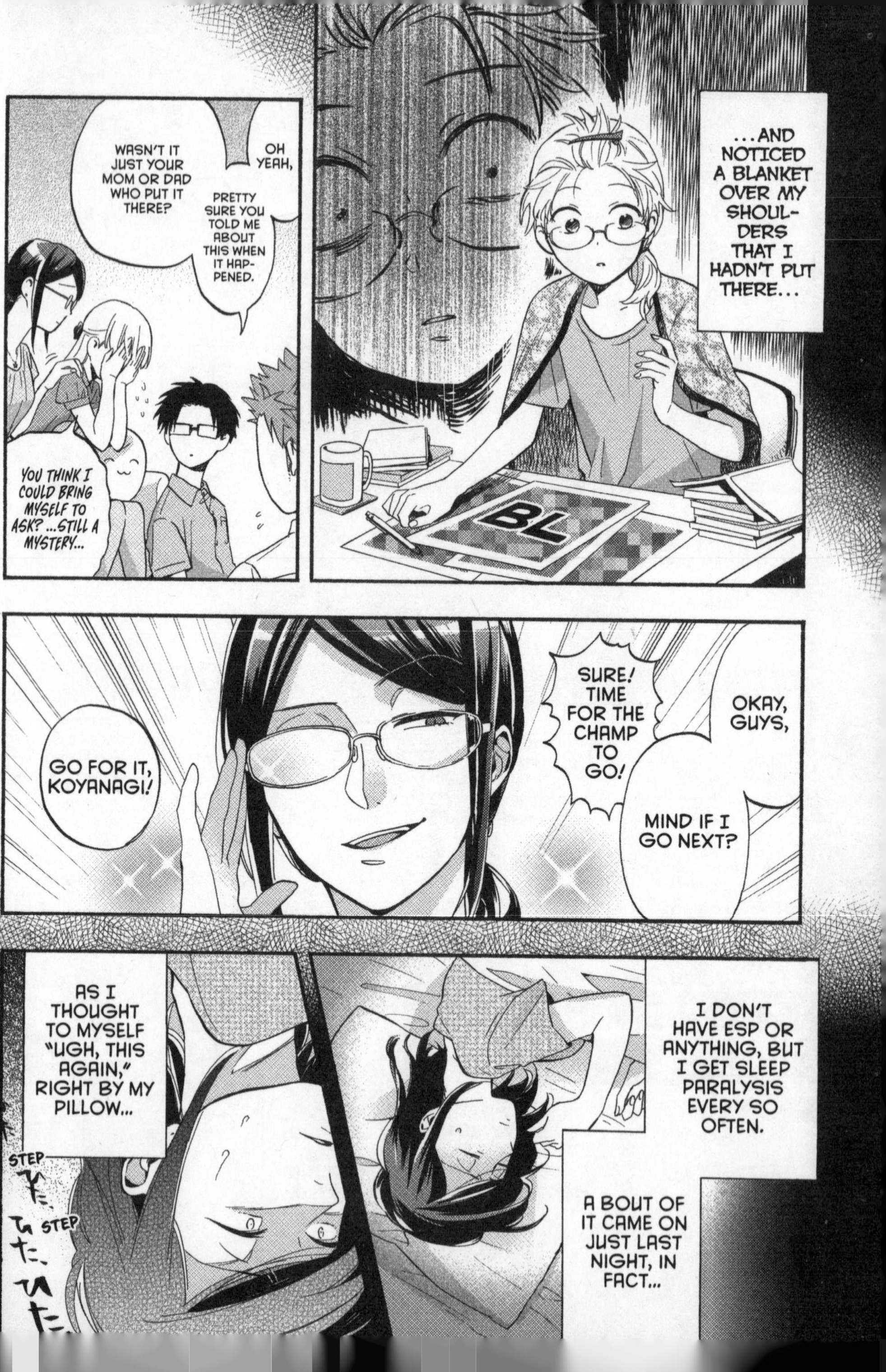
...AND NOTICED A BLANKET OVER MY SHOUL-DERS THAT I HADN'T PUT THERE...
OH YEAH,
PRETTY SURE YOU TOLD ME ABOUT THIS WHEN IT HAP-PENED.
WASN'T IT JUST YOUR MOM OR DAD WHO PUT IT THERE?
YOU THINK I COULD BRING MYSELF TO ASK? ...STILL A MYSTERY...
BL
OKAY, GUYS,
MIND IF I GO NEXT?
SURE! TIME FOR THE CHAMP TO GO!
GO FOR IT, KOYANAGI!
I DON'T HAVE ESP OR ANYTHING, BUT I GET SLEEP PARALYSIS EVERY SO OFTEN.
A BOUT OF IT CAME ON JUST LAST NIGHT, IN FACT...
AS I THOUGHT TO MYSELF "UGH, THIS AGAIN," RIGHT BY MY PILLOW...
STEP
STEP

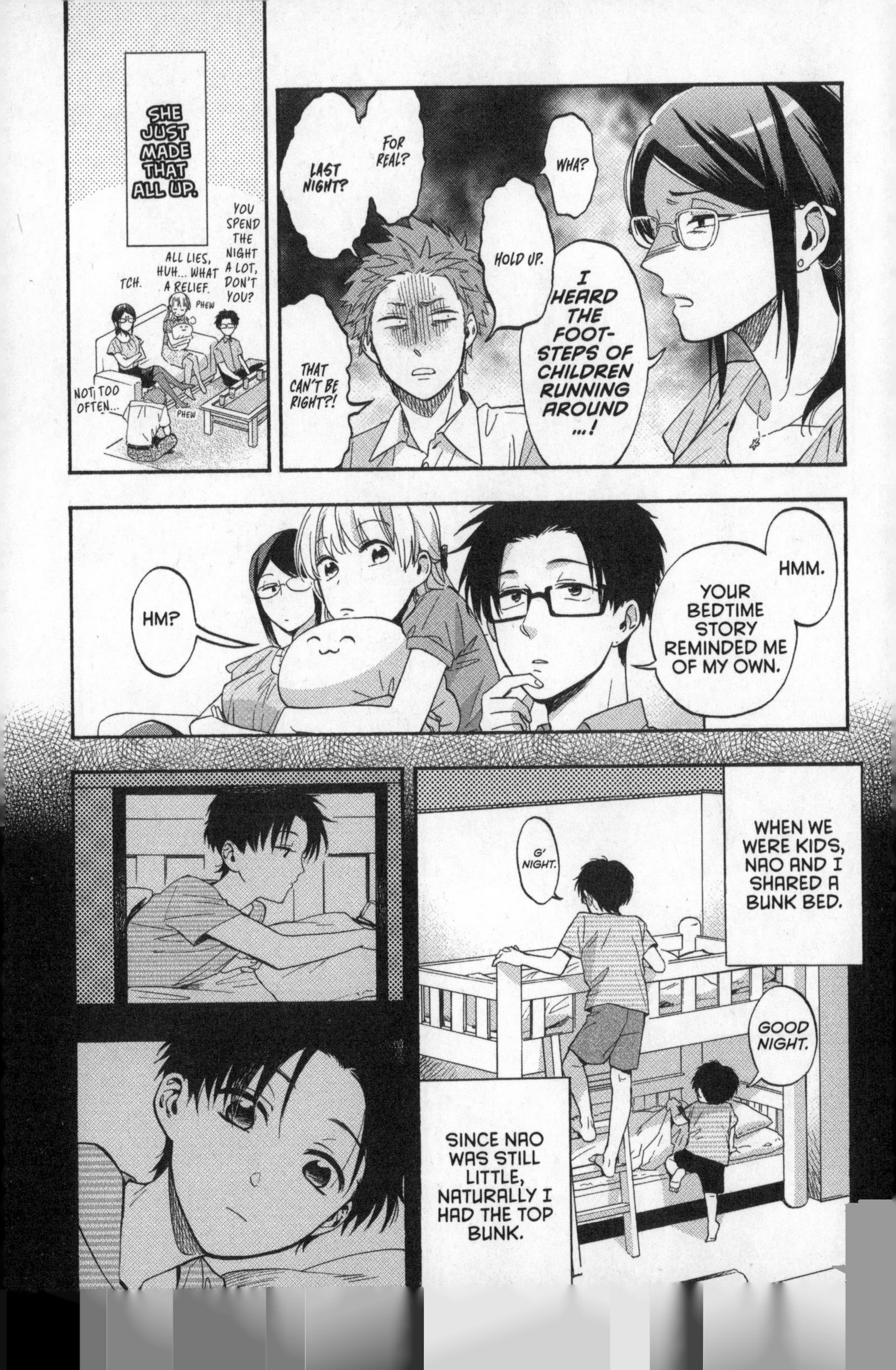
WHA?
I HEARD THE FOOT-STEPS OF CHILDREN RUNNING AROUND ...!
HOLD UP.
FOR REAL?
LAST NIGHT?
THAT CAN'T BE RIGHT?!
SHE JUST MADE THAT ALL UP.
YOU SPEND THE NIGHT A LOT, DON'T YOU?
ALL LIES, HUH... WHAT A RELIEF.
PHEW
TCH.
NOT TOO OFTEN...
PHEW
HMM.
YOUR BEDTIME STORY REMINDED ME OF MY OWN.
HM?
WHEN WE WERE KIDS, NAO AND I SHARED A BUNK BED.
G' NIGHT.
GOOD NIGHT.
SINCE NAO WAS STILL LITTLE, NATURALLY I HAD THE TOP BUNK.

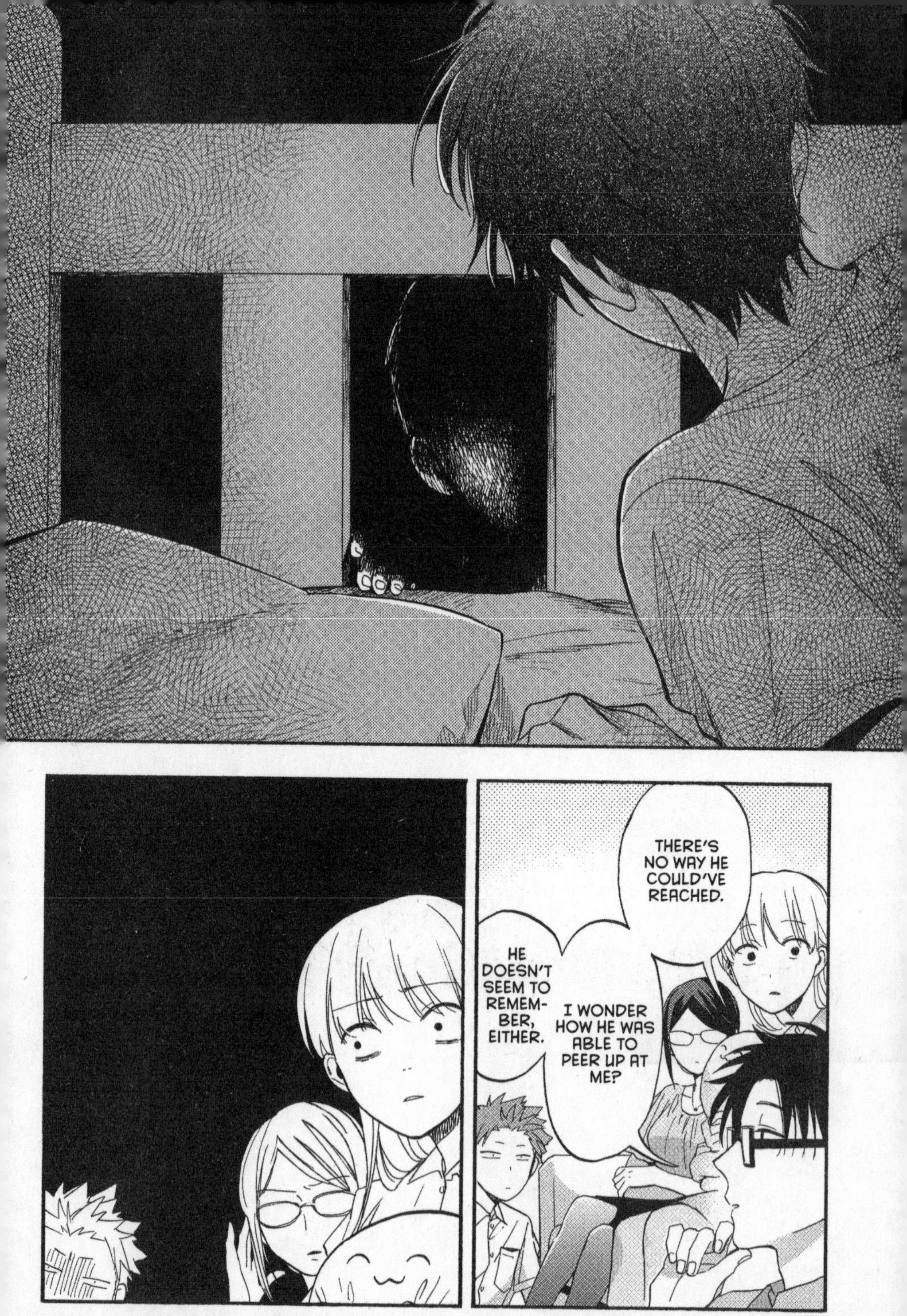
THERE'S NO WAY HE COULD'VE REACHED.
I WONDER HOW HE WAS ABLE TO PEER UP AT ME?
HE DOESN'T SEEM TO REMEM-BER, EITHER.

(It can happen anywhere)

Wotakoi: Love is Hard for Otaku

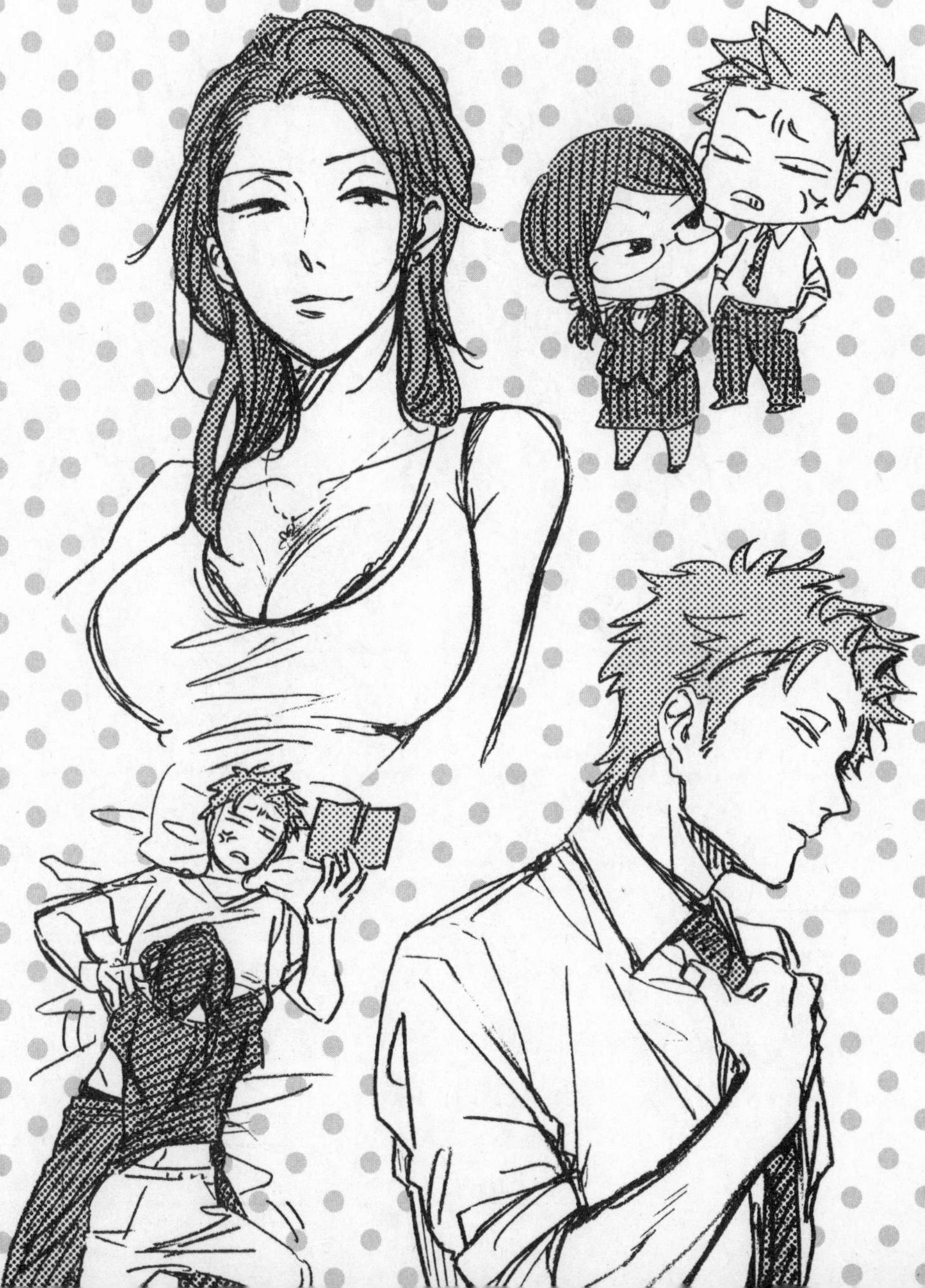

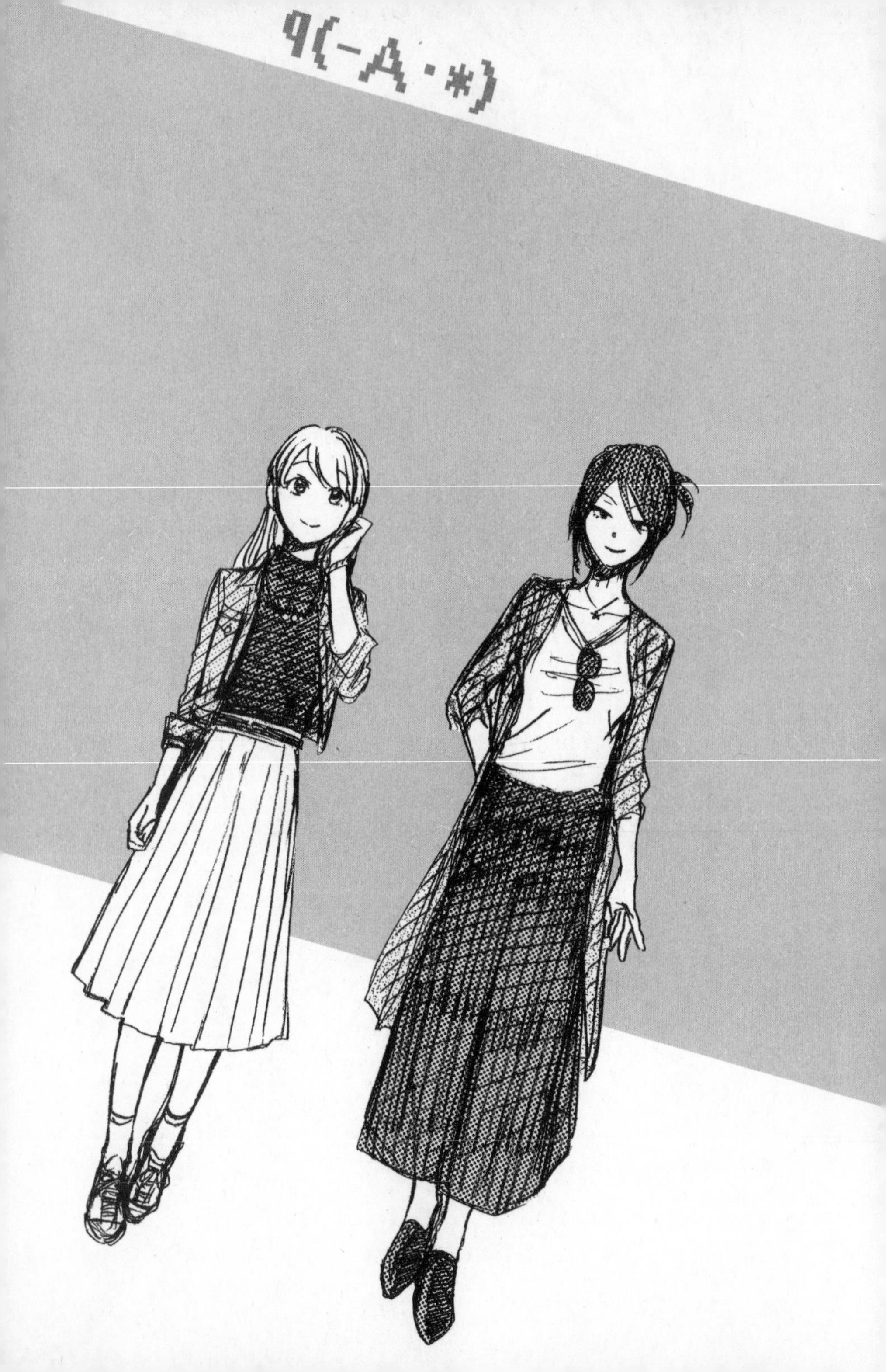
٩(-Д・*)

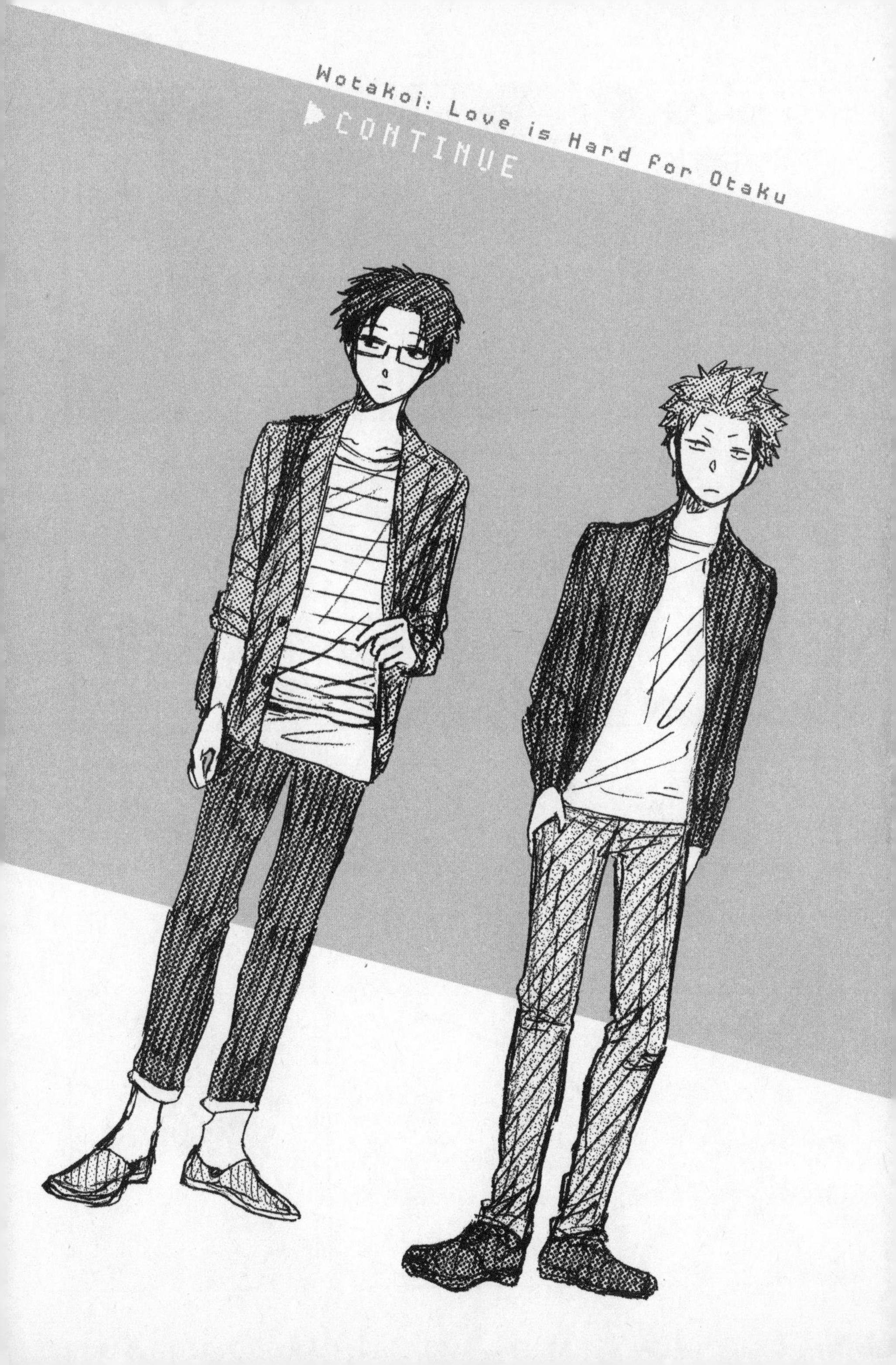
Wotakoi: Love is Hard for Otaku
CONTINUE

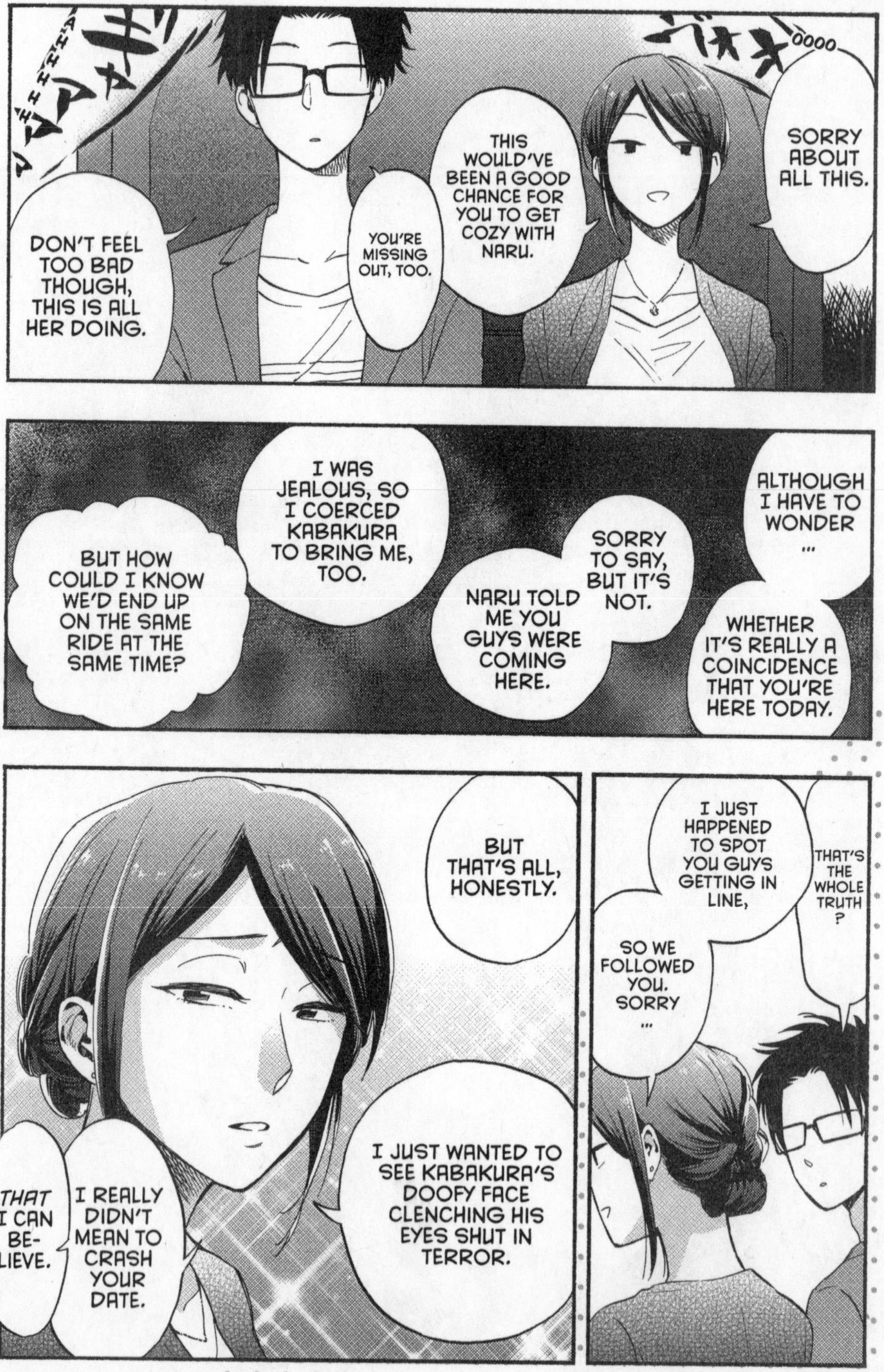
OOOO
SORRY ABOUT ALL THIS.
THIS WOULD'VE BEEN A GOOD CHANCE FOR YOU TO GET COZY WITH NARU.
YOU'RE MISSING OUT, TOO.
DON'T FEEL TOO BAD THOUGH, THIS IS ALL HER DOING.
ALTHOUGH I HAVE TO WONDER ...
WHETHER IT'S REALLY A COINCIDENCE THAT YOU'RE HERE TODAY.
SORRY TO SAY, BUT IT'S NOT.
NARU TOLD ME YOU GUYS WERE COMING HERE.
I WAS JEALOUS, SO I COERCED KABAKURA TO BRING ME, TOO.
BUT HOW COULD I KNOW WE'D END UP ON THE SAME RIDE AT THE SAME TIME?
THAT'S THE WHOLE TRUTH?
I JUST HAPPENED TO SPOT YOU GUYS GETTING IN LINE,
SO WE FOLLOWED YOU. SORRY ...
BUT THAT'S ALL, HONESTLY.
I JUST WANTED TO SEE KABAKURA'S DOOFY FACE CLENCHING HIS EYES SHUT IN TERROR.
I REALLY DIDN'T MEAN TO CRASH YOUR DATE.
THAT I CAN BE-LIEVE.

(She really gets off on this)

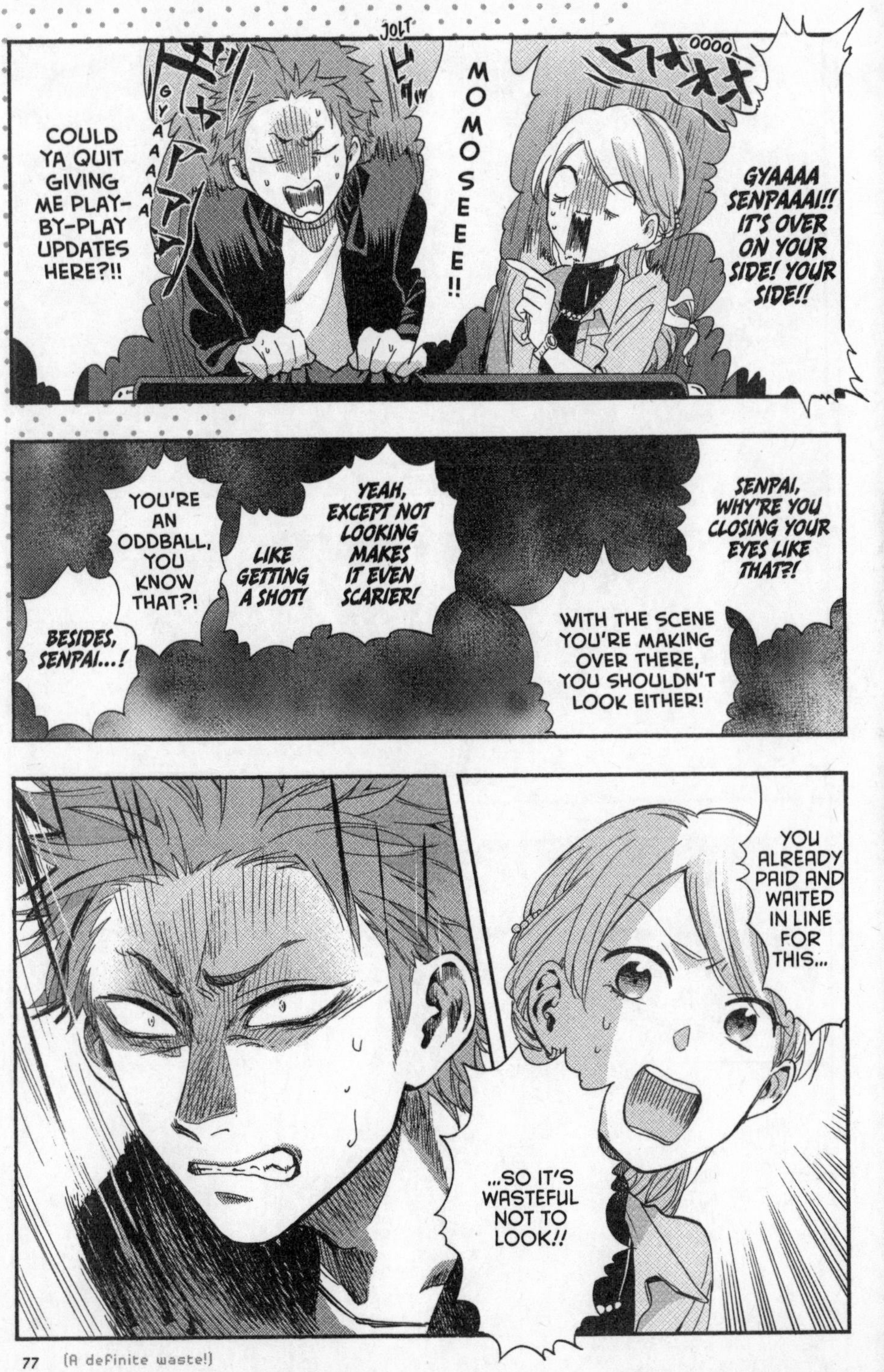
OOOO
GYAAAA SENPAAAI!! IT'S OVER ON YOUR SIDE! YOUR SIDE!!
MOMOSEEE!!
JOLT
GYAAAAAA
COULD YA QUIT GIVING ME PLAY-BY-PLAY UPDATES HERE?!!
SENPAI, WHY'RE YOU CLOSING YOUR EYES LIKE THAT?!
WITH THE SCENE YOU'RE MAKING OVER THERE, YOU SHOULDN'T LOOK EITHER!
YEAH, EXCEPT NOT LOOKING MAKES IT EVEN SCARIER!
LIKE GETTING A SHOT!
YOU'RE AN ODDBALL, YOU KNOW THAT?!
BESIDES, SENPAI...!
YOU ALREADY PAID AND WAITED IN LINE FOR THIS...
...SO IT'S WASTEFUL NOT TO LOOK!!

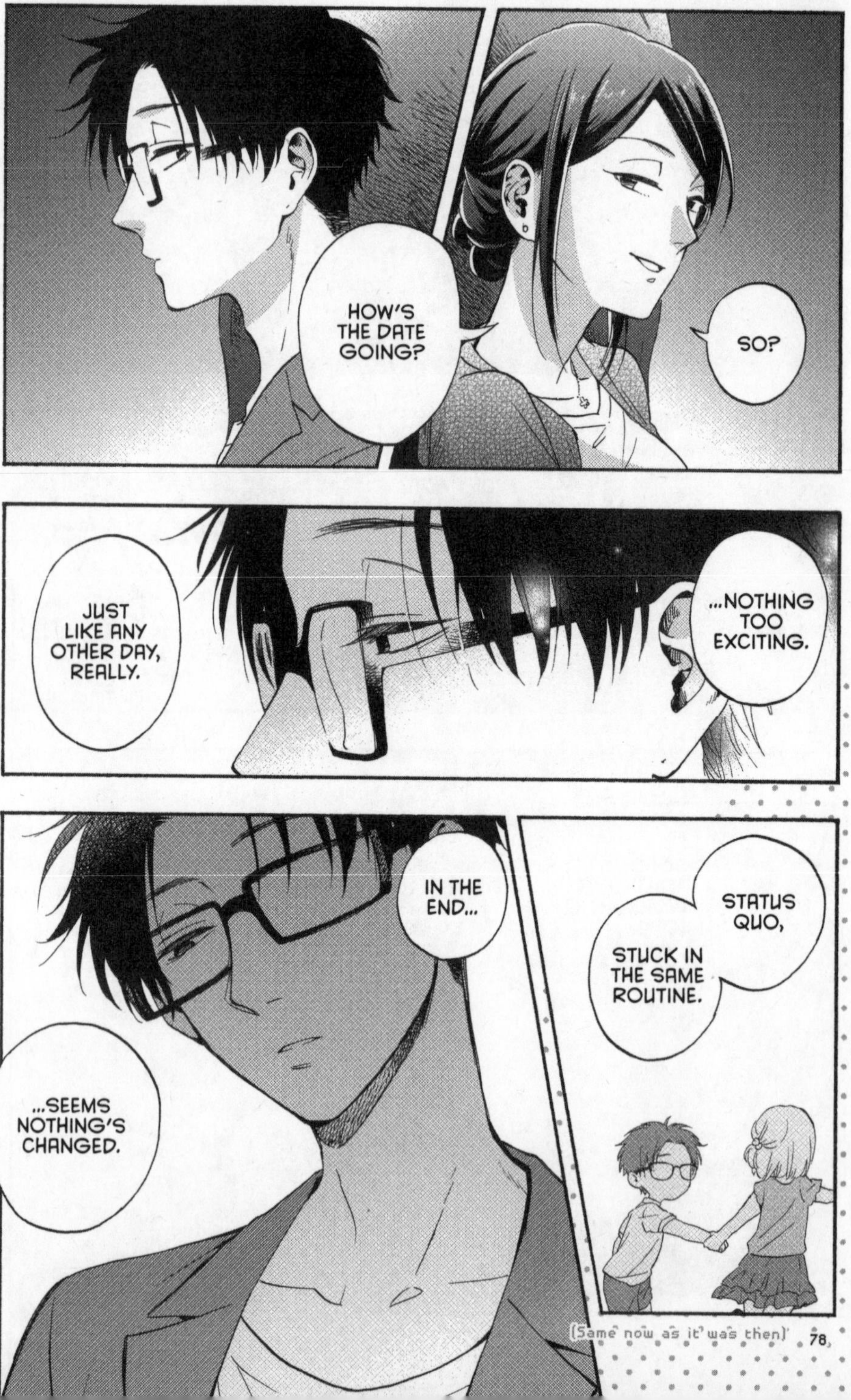
SO?
HOW'S THE DATE GOING?
...NOTHING TOO EXCITING.
JUST LIKE ANY OTHER DAY, REALLY.
STATUS QUO,
STUCK IN THE SAME ROUTINE.
IN THE END...
...SEEMS NOTHING'S CHANGED.

(Same now as it was then)

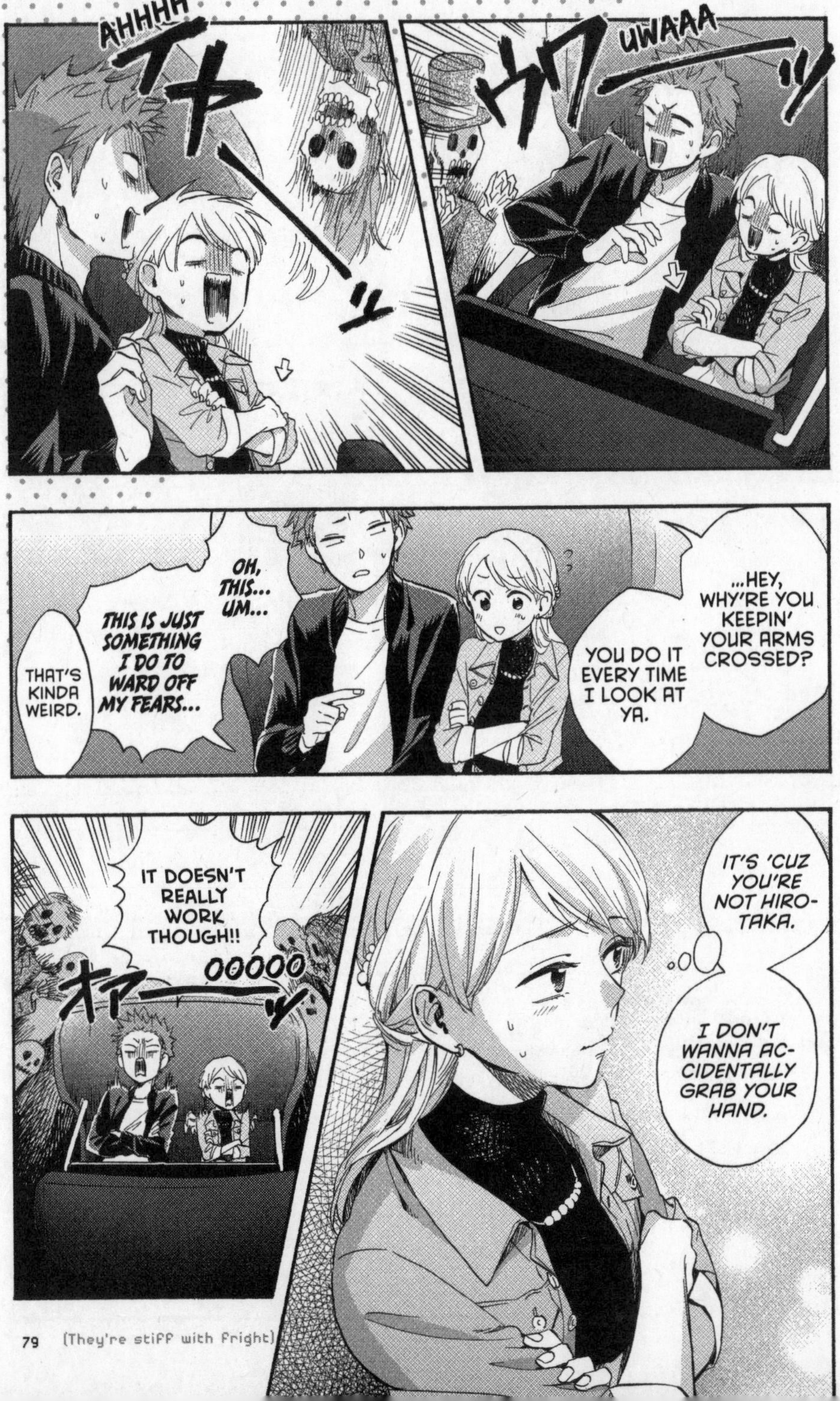
UWAAA
AHHHH
...HEY, WHY'RE YOU KEEPIN' YOUR ARMS CROSSED?
YOU DO IT EVERY TIME I LOOK AT YA.
OH, THIS... UM...
THIS IS JUST SOMETHING I DO TO WARD OFF MY FEARS...
THAT'S KINDA WEIRD.
IT'S 'CUZ YOU'RE NOT HIRO-TAKA.
I DON'T WANNA AC-CIDENTALLY GRAB YOUR HAND.
IT DOESN'T REALLY WORK THOUGH!!
OOOOO

(They're stiff with fright)

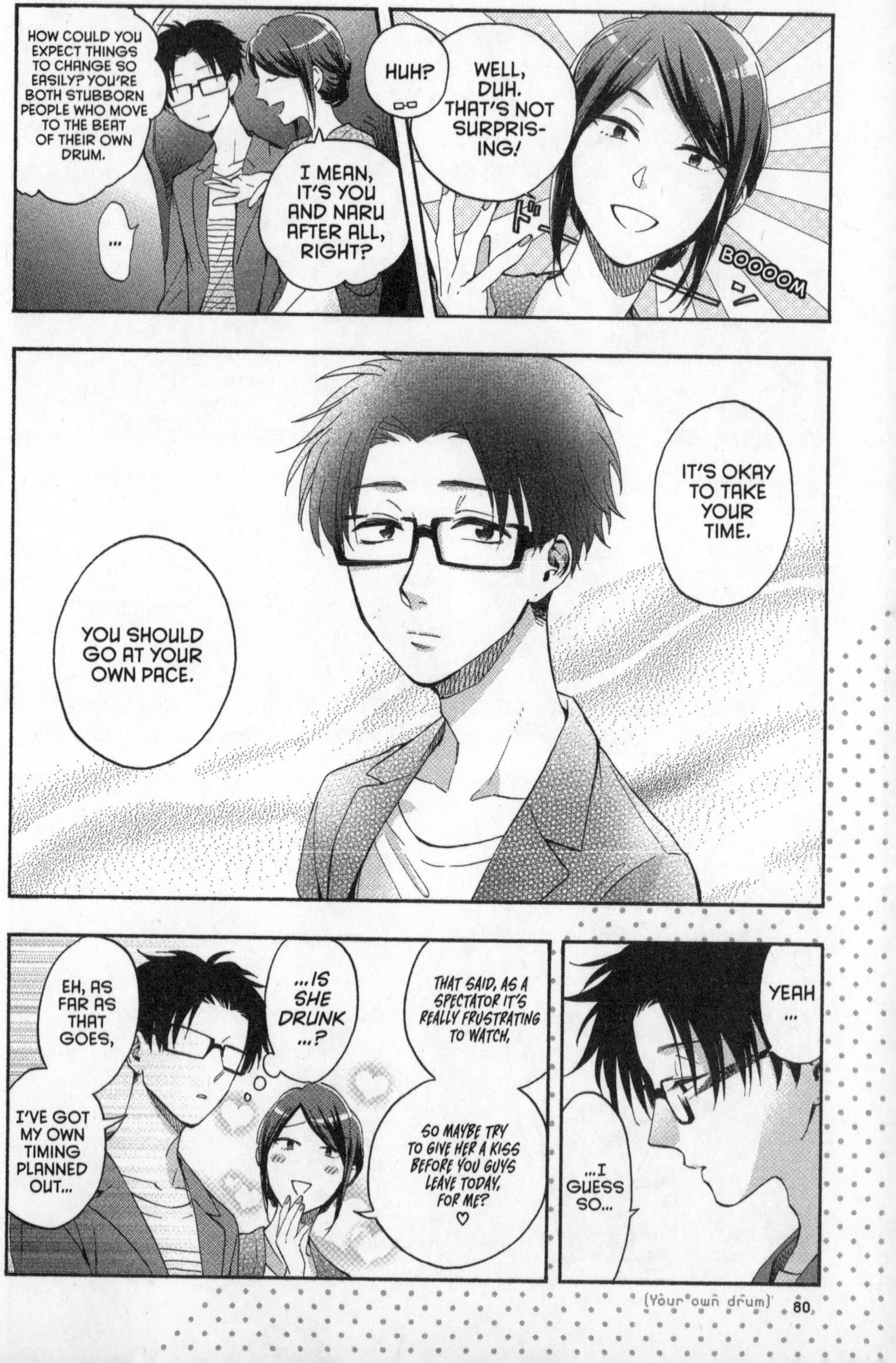
WELL, DUH. THAT'S NOT SURPRIS-ING!
HUH?
BOOOOM
I MEAN, IT'S YOU AND NARU AFTER ALL, RIGHT?
HOW COULD YOU EXPECT THINGS TO CHANGE SO EASILY? YOU'RE BOTH STUBBORN PEOPLE WHO MOVE TO THE BEAT OF THEIR OWN DRUM.
...
IT'S OKAY TO TAKE YOUR TIME.
YOU SHOULD GO AT YOUR OWN PACE.
YEAH ...
...I GUESS SO...
THAT SAID, AS A SPECTATOR IT'S REALLY FRUSTRATING TO WATCH,
...IS SHE DRUNK ...?
EH, AS FAR AS THAT GOES,
SO MAYBE TRY TO GIVE HER A KISS BEFORE YOU GUYS LEAVE TODAY, FOR ME? ♡
I'VE GOT MY OWN TIMING PLANNED OUT...

(Your own drum)

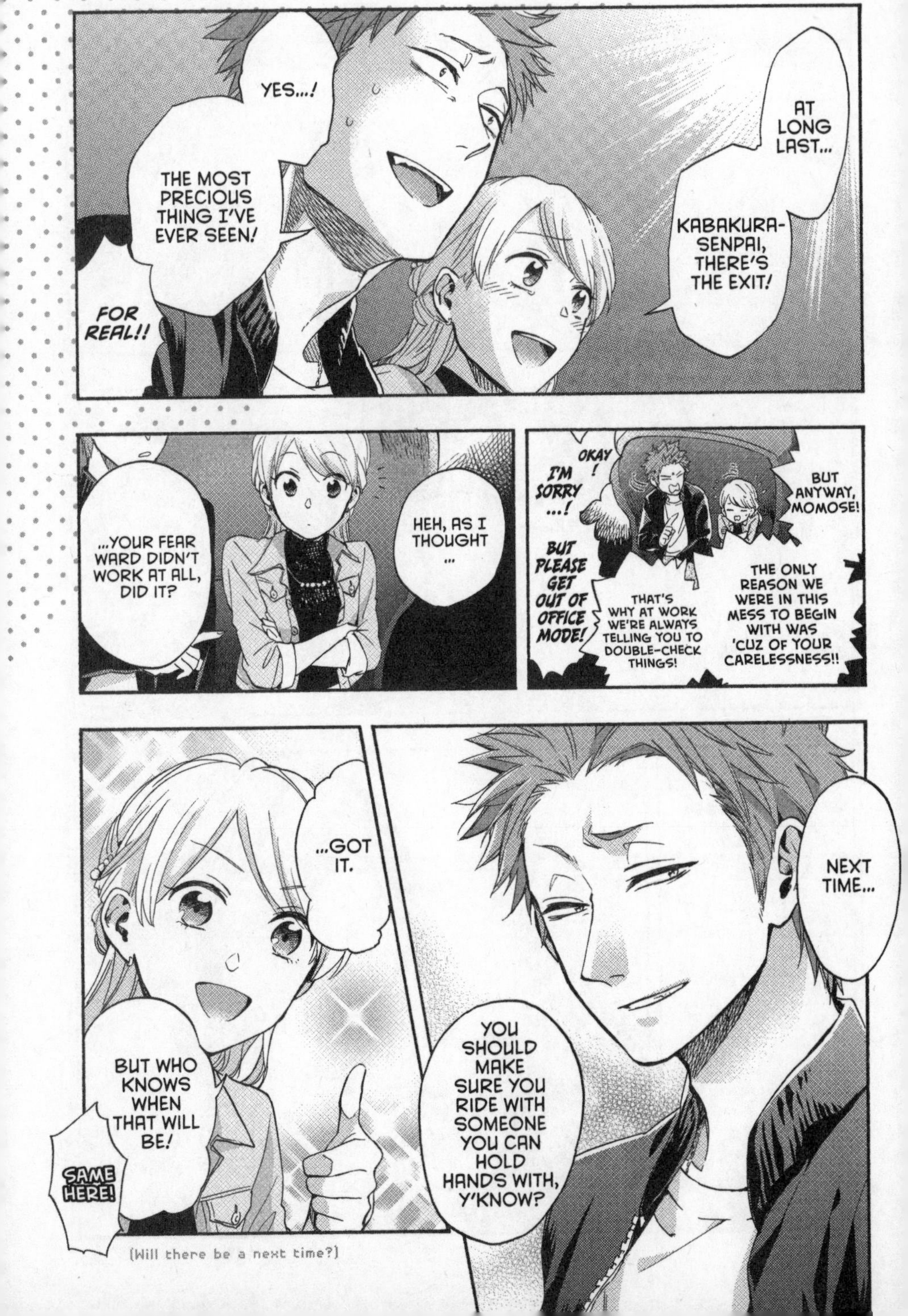
AT LONG LAST...
KABAKURA-SENPAI, THERE'S THE EXIT!
YES...!
THE MOST PRECIOUS THING I'VE EVER SEEN!
FOR REAL!!
BUT ANYWAY, MOMOSE!
THE ONLY REASON WE WERE IN THIS MESS TO BEGIN WITH WAS 'CUZ OF YOUR CARELESSNESS!!
THAT'S WHY AT WORK WE'RE ALWAYS TELLING YOU TO DOUBLE-CHECK THINGS!
OKAY!
I'M SORRY...!
BUT PLEASE GET OUT OF OFFICE MODE!
HEH, AS I THOUGHT...
...YOUR FEAR WARD DIDN'T WORK AT ALL, DID IT?
NEXT TIME...
YOU SHOULD MAKE SURE YOU RIDE WITH SOMEONE YOU CAN HOLD HANDS WITH, Y'KNOW?
...GOT IT.
BUT WHO KNOWS WHEN THAT WILL BE!
SAME HERE!

[Will there be a next time?]

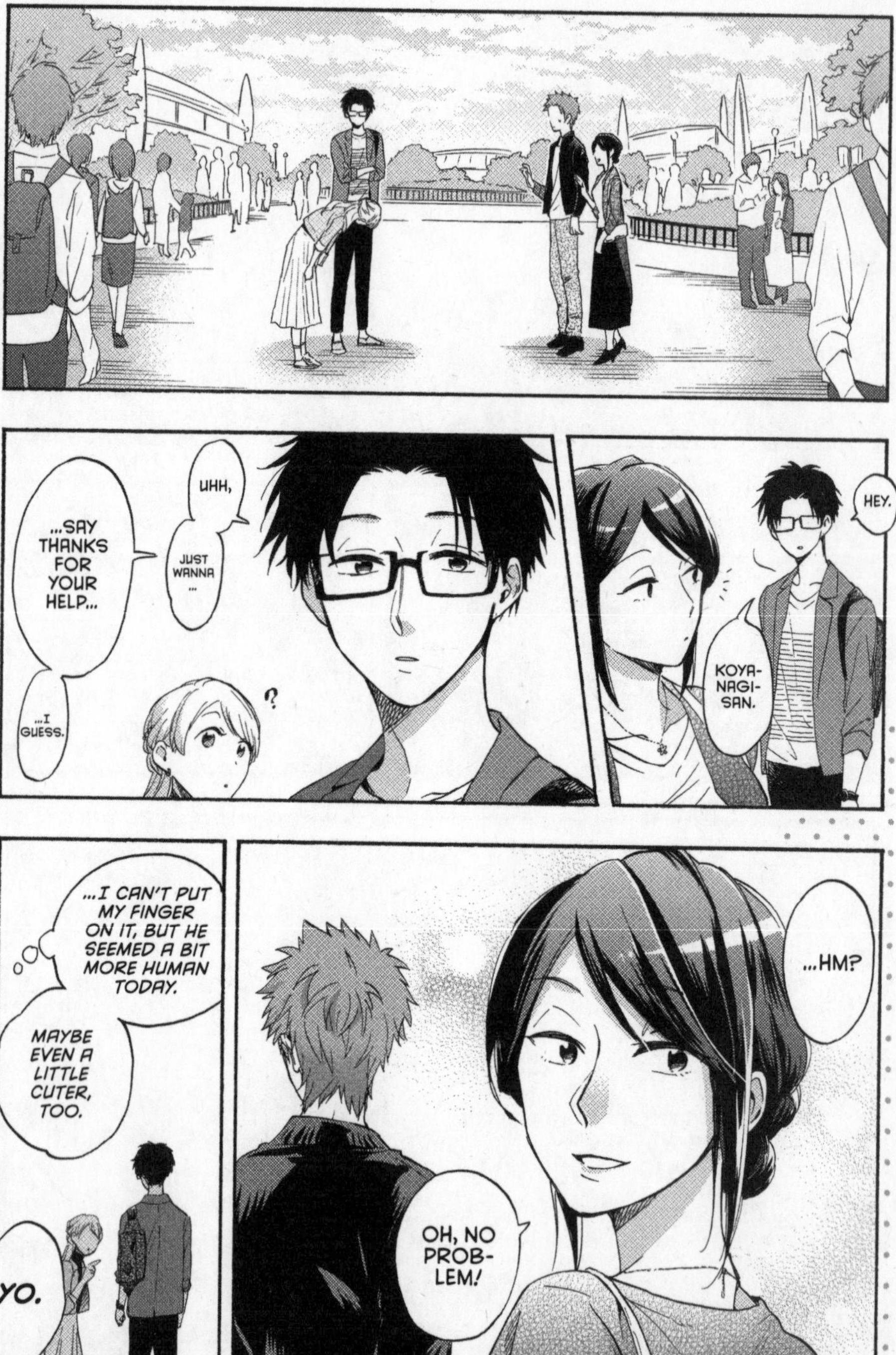
HEY.
KOYA-NAGI-SAN.
UHH,
JUST WANNA ...
...SAY THANKS FOR YOUR HELP...
...I GUESS.
?
...HM?
OH, NO PROB-LEM!
...I CAN'T PUT MY FINGER ON IT, BUT HE SEEMED A BIT MORE HUMAN TODAY.
MAYBE EVEN A LITTLE CUTER, TOO.
YO.

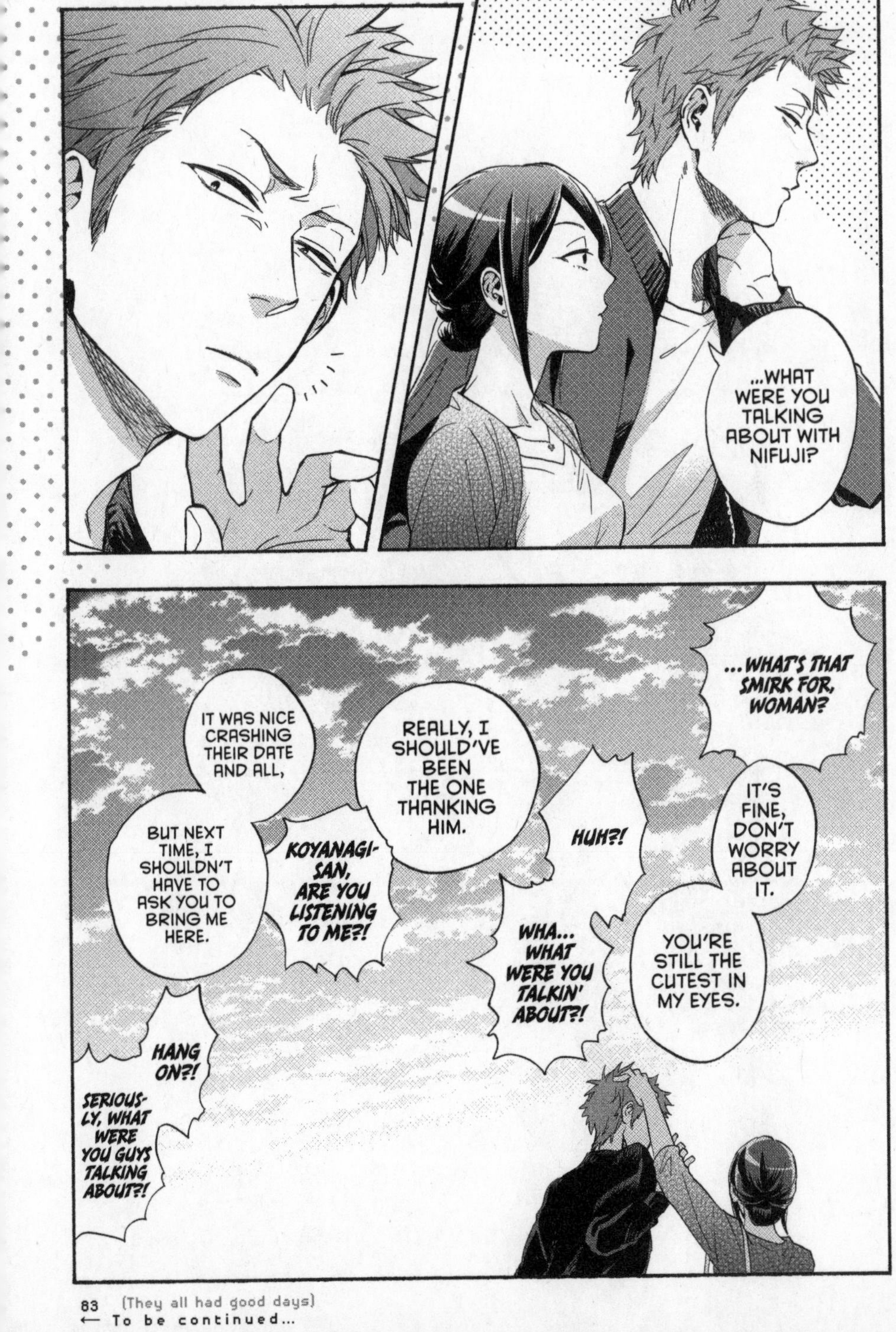
...WHAT WERE YOU TALKING ABOUT WITH NIFUJI?
...WHAT'S THAT SMIRK FOR, WOMAN?
IT'S FINE, DON'T WORRY ABOUT IT.
YOU'RE STILL THE CUTEST IN MY EYES.
HUH?!
WHA... WHAT WERE YOU TALKIN' ABOUT?!
REALLY, I SHOULD'VE BEEN THE ONE THANKING HIM.
KOYANAGI-SAN, ARE YOU LISTENING TO ME?!
IT WAS NICE CRASHING THEIR DATE AND ALL,
BUT NEXT TIME, I SHOULDN'T HAVE TO ASK YOU TO BRING ME HERE.
HANG ON?!
SERIOUS-LY, WHAT WERE YOU GUYS TALKING ABOUT?!

 (They all had good days)
← To be continued...

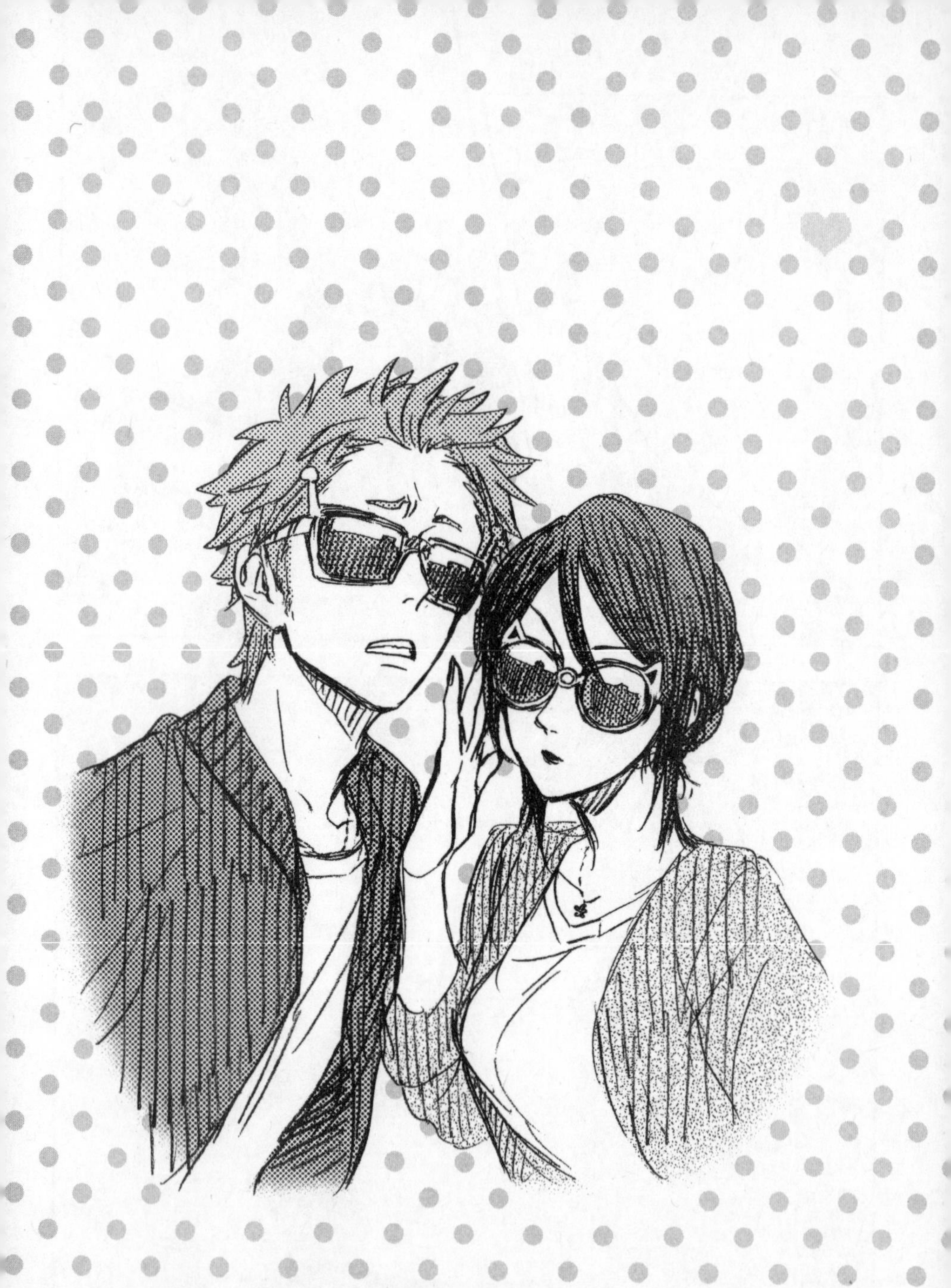

Wotakoi: Love is Hard for Otaku

Episode.... 20

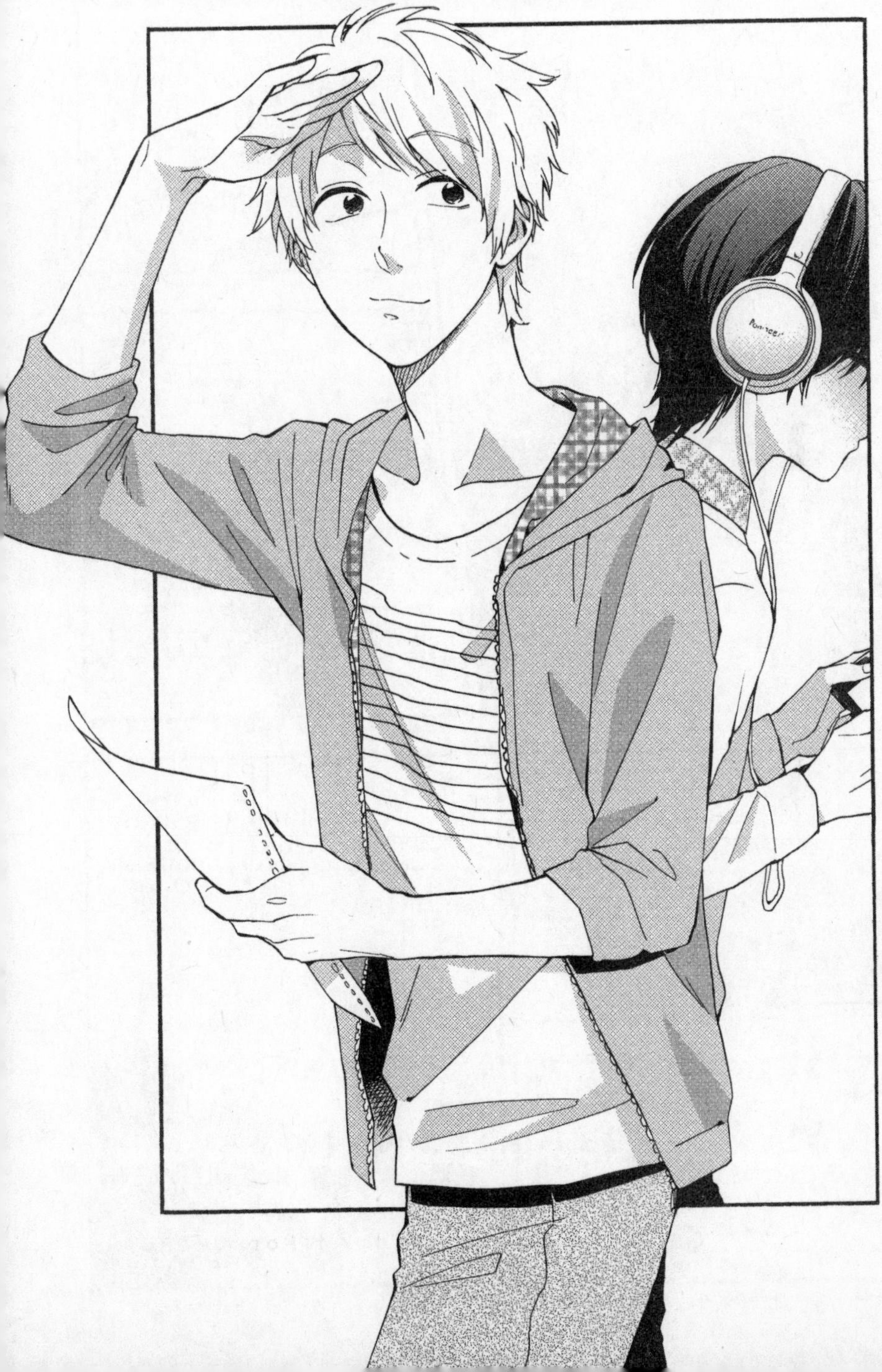

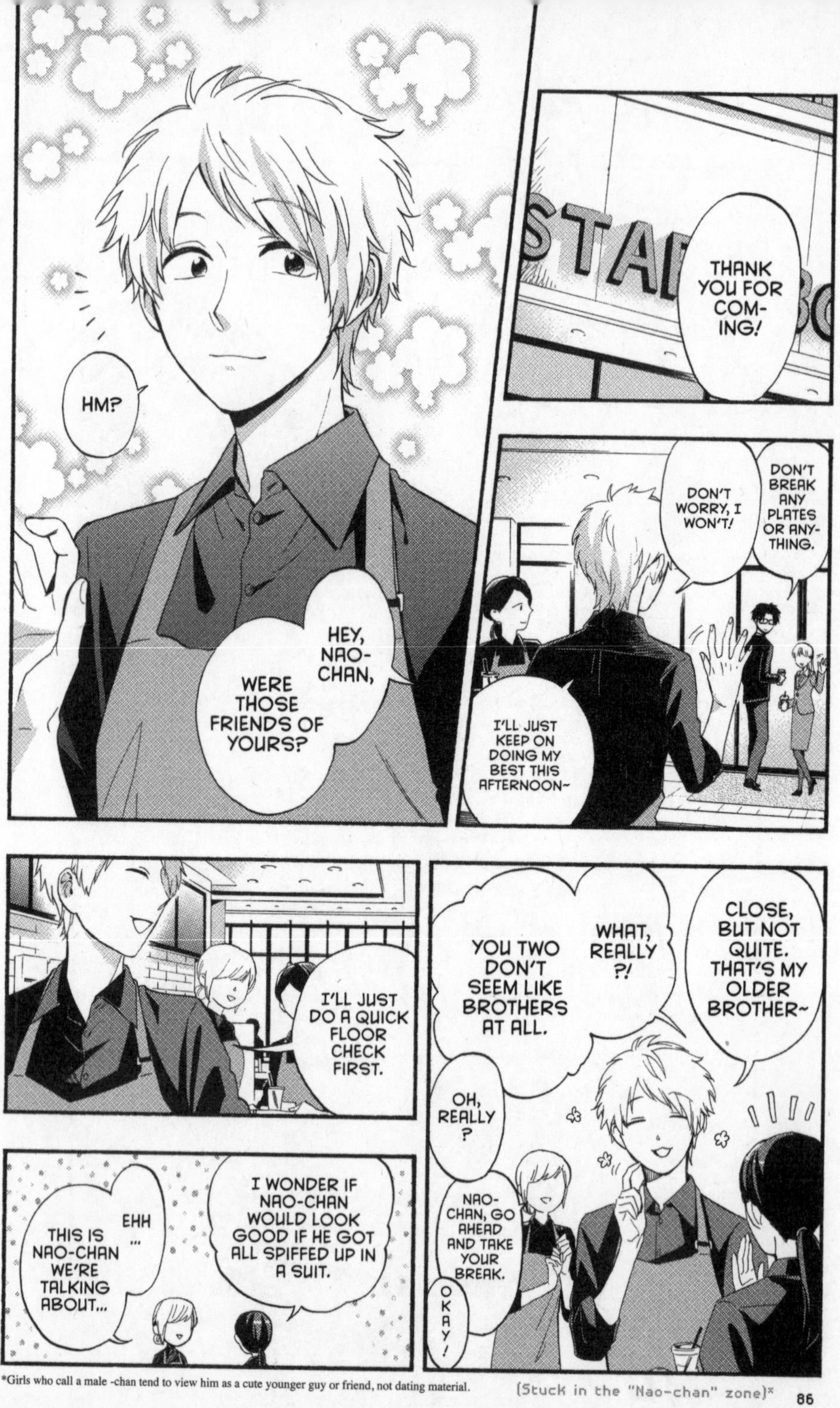
THANK YOU FOR COMING!
DON'T BREAK ANY PLATES OR ANYTHING.
DON'T WORRY, I WON'T!
I'LL JUST KEEP ON DOING MY BEST THIS AFTERNOON~
HEY, NAO-CHAN, WERE THOSE FRIENDS OF YOURS?
HM?
CLOSE, BUT NOT QUITE. THAT'S MY OLDER BROTHER~
WHAT, REALLY?!
YOU TWO DON'T SEEM LIKE BROTHERS AT ALL.
OH, REALLY?
NAO-CHAN, GO AHEAD AND TAKE YOUR BREAK.
OKAY!
I'LL JUST DO A QUICK FLOOR CHECK FIRST.
I WONDER IF NAO-CHAN WOULD LOOK GOOD IF HE GOT ALL SPIFFED UP IN A SUIT.
EHH...
THIS IS NAO-CHAN WE'RE TALKING ABOUT...

*Girls who call a male -chan tend to view him as a cute younger guy or friend, not dating material.

(Stuck in the "Nao-chan" zone)*

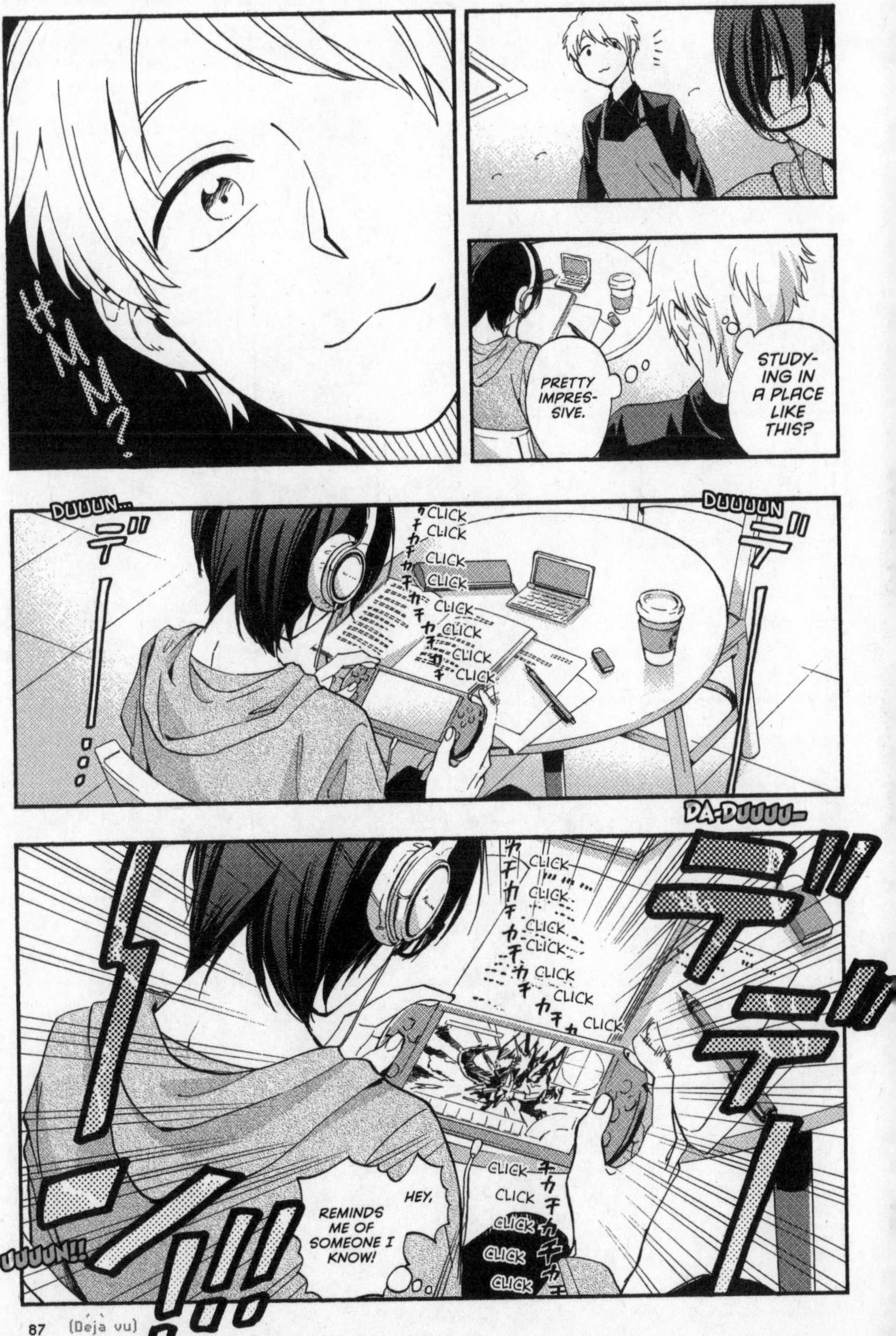
STUDYING IN A PLACE LIKE THIS?
PRETTY IMPRESSIVE.
HMM?
DUUUUN
DUUUN...
CLICK CLICK CLICK CLICK CLICK CLICK CLICK CLICK
DA-DUUUU-
CLICK CLICK CLICK CLICK CLICK CLICK CLICK
CLICK CLICK CLICK CLICK CLICK
HEY, REMINDS ME OF SOMEONE I KNOW!
-UUUUN!!

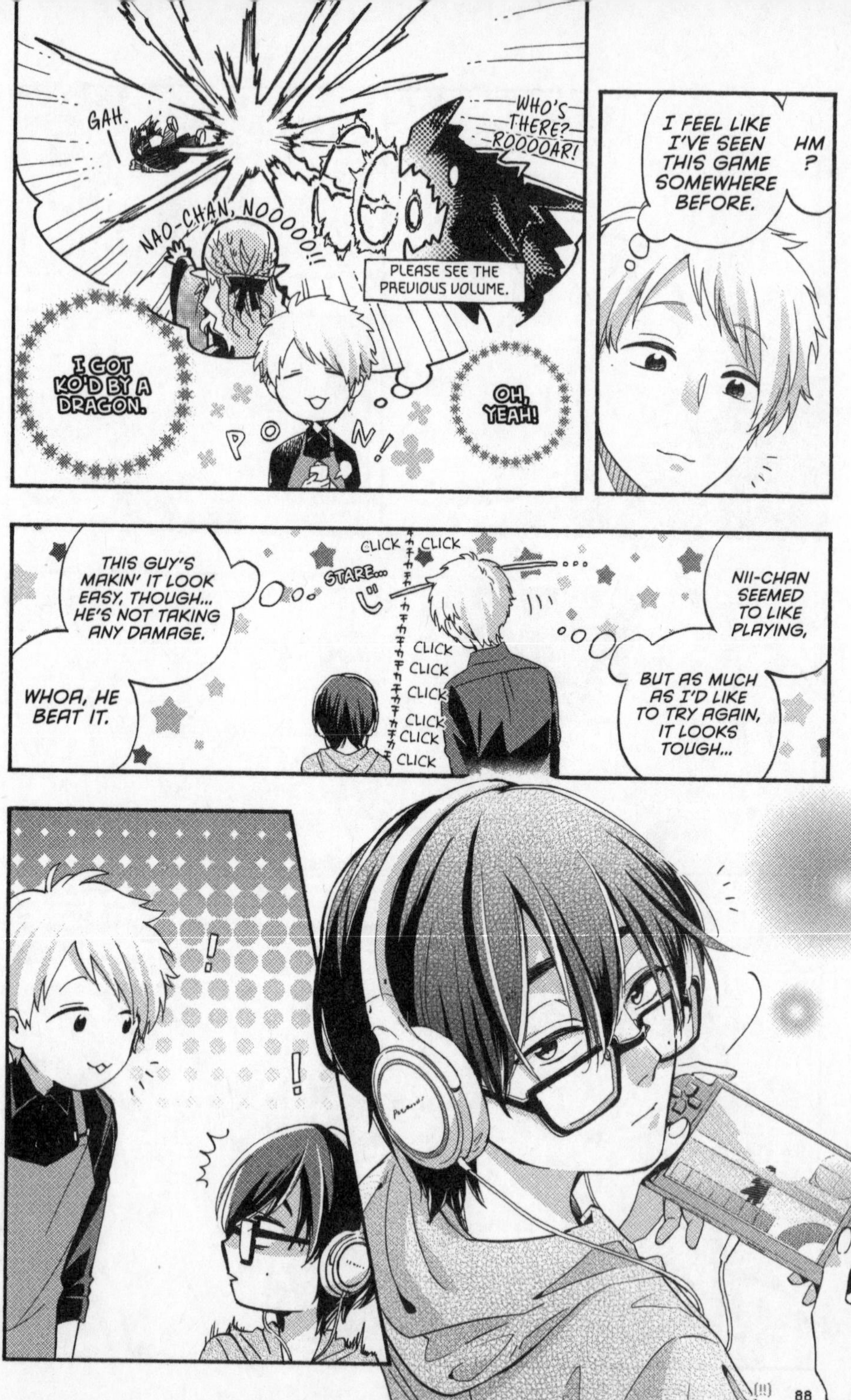

I FEEL LIKE I'VE SEEN THIS GAME SOMEWHERE BEFORE.
HM?
WHO'S THERE? ROOOOAR!
GAH.
NAO-CHAN, NOOOOO!!
PLEASE SEE THE PREVIOUS VOLUME.
OH, YEAH!
I GOT KO'D BY A DRAGON.
PON!
NII-CHAN SEEMED TO LIKE PLAYING,
BUT AS MUCH AS I'D LIKE TO TRY AGAIN, IT LOOKS TOUGH...
...
CLICK CLICK
STARE...
CLICK CLICK CLICK CLICK CLICK CLICK
THIS GUY'S MAKIN' IT LOOK EASY, THOUGH... HE'S NOT TAKING ANY DAMAGE.
WHOA, HE BEAT IT.
!
!
(!!)

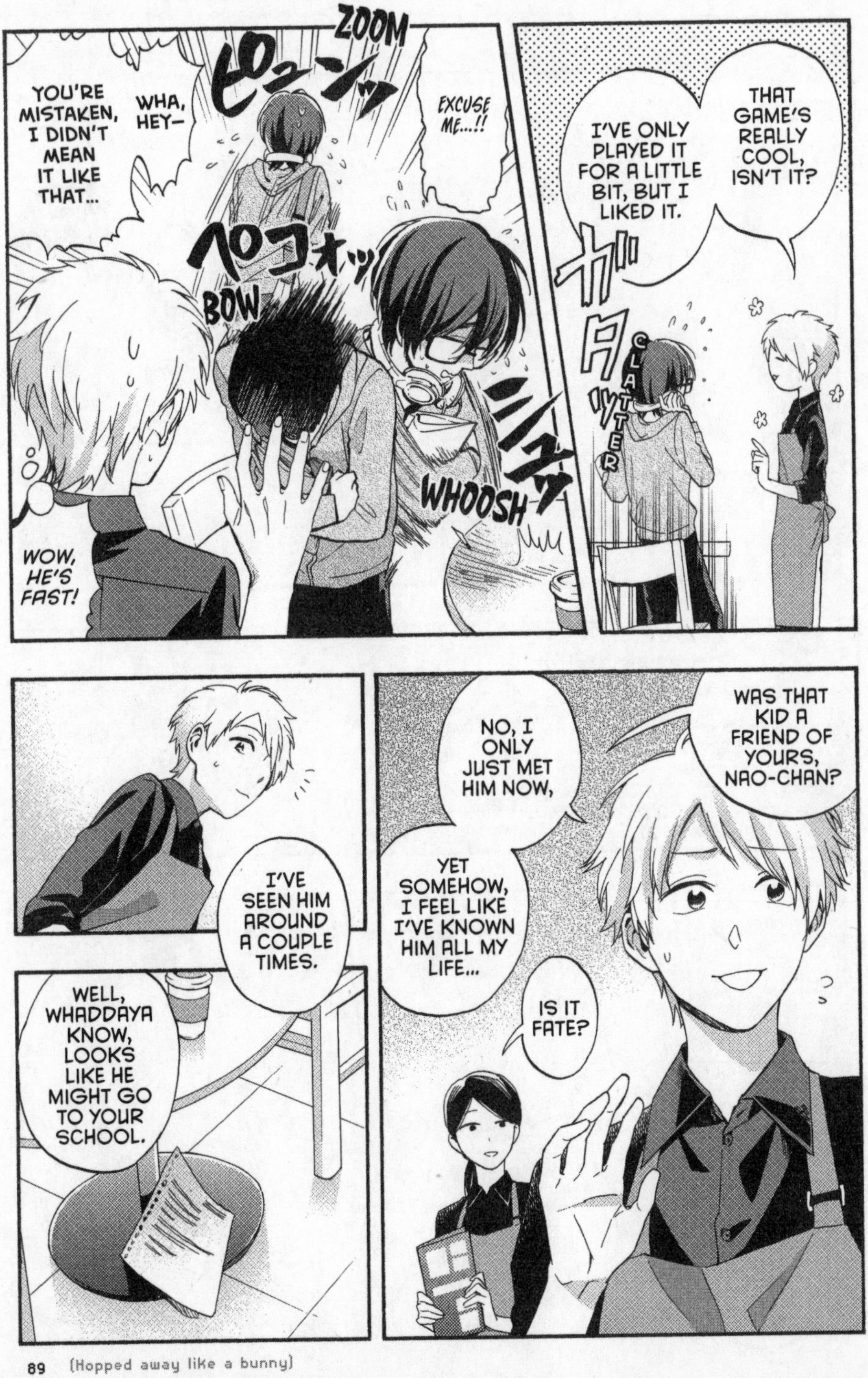
THAT GAME'S REALLY COOL, ISN'T IT?
I'VE ONLY PLAYED IT FOR A LITTLE BIT, BUT I LIKED IT.
ガタッ
CLATTER
EXCUSE ME...!!
ピューッ
ZOOM
WHA, HEY—
YOU'RE MISTAKEN, I DIDN'T MEAN IT LIKE THAT...
ペコォッ
BOW
シュッ
WHOOSH
WOW, HE'S FAST!
WAS THAT KID A FRIEND OF YOURS, NAO-CHAN?
NO, I ONLY JUST MET HIM NOW,
YET SOMEHOW, I FEEL LIKE I'VE KNOWN HIM ALL MY LIFE...
IS IT FATE?
I'VE SEEN HIM AROUND A COUPLE TIMES.
WELL, WHADDAYA KNOW, LOOKS LIKE HE MIGHT GO TO YOUR SCHOOL.

 (Hopped away like a bunny)

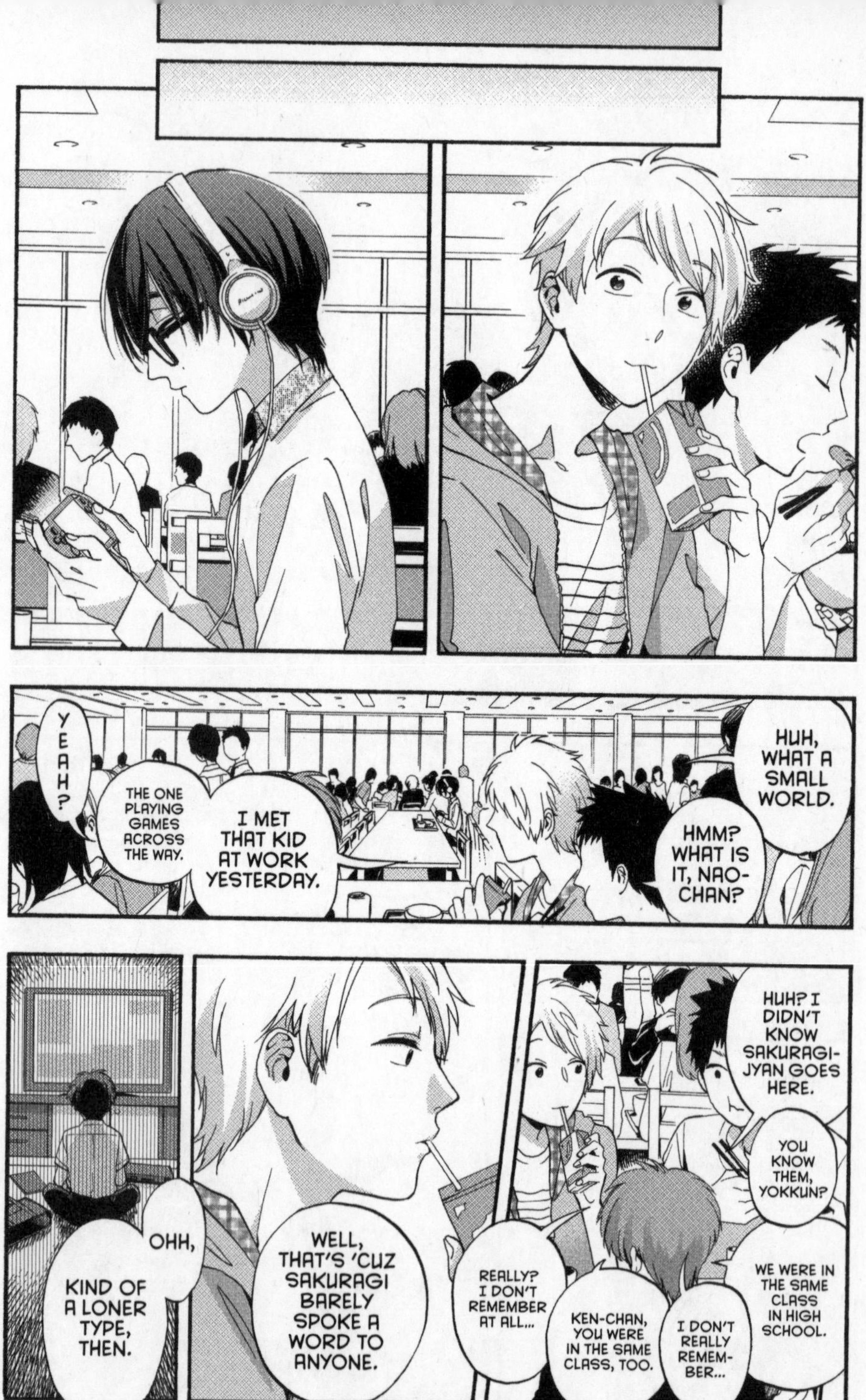
HUH, WHAT A SMALL WORLD.
HMM? WHAT IS IT, NAO-CHAN?
I MET THAT KID AT WORK YESTERDAY.
THE ONE PLAYING GAMES ACROSS THE WAY.
YEAH?
HUH? I DIDN'T KNOW SAKURAGI-JYAN GOES HERE.
YOU KNOW THEM, YOKKUN?
WE WERE IN THE SAME CLASS IN HIGH SCHOOL.
I DON'T REALLY REMEMBER...
KEN-CHAN, YOU WERE IN THE SAME CLASS, TOO.
REALLY? I DON'T REMEMBER AT ALL...
WELL, THAT'S 'CUZ SAKURAGI BARELY SPOKE A WORD TO ANYONE.
OHH, KIND OF A LONER TYPE, THEN.

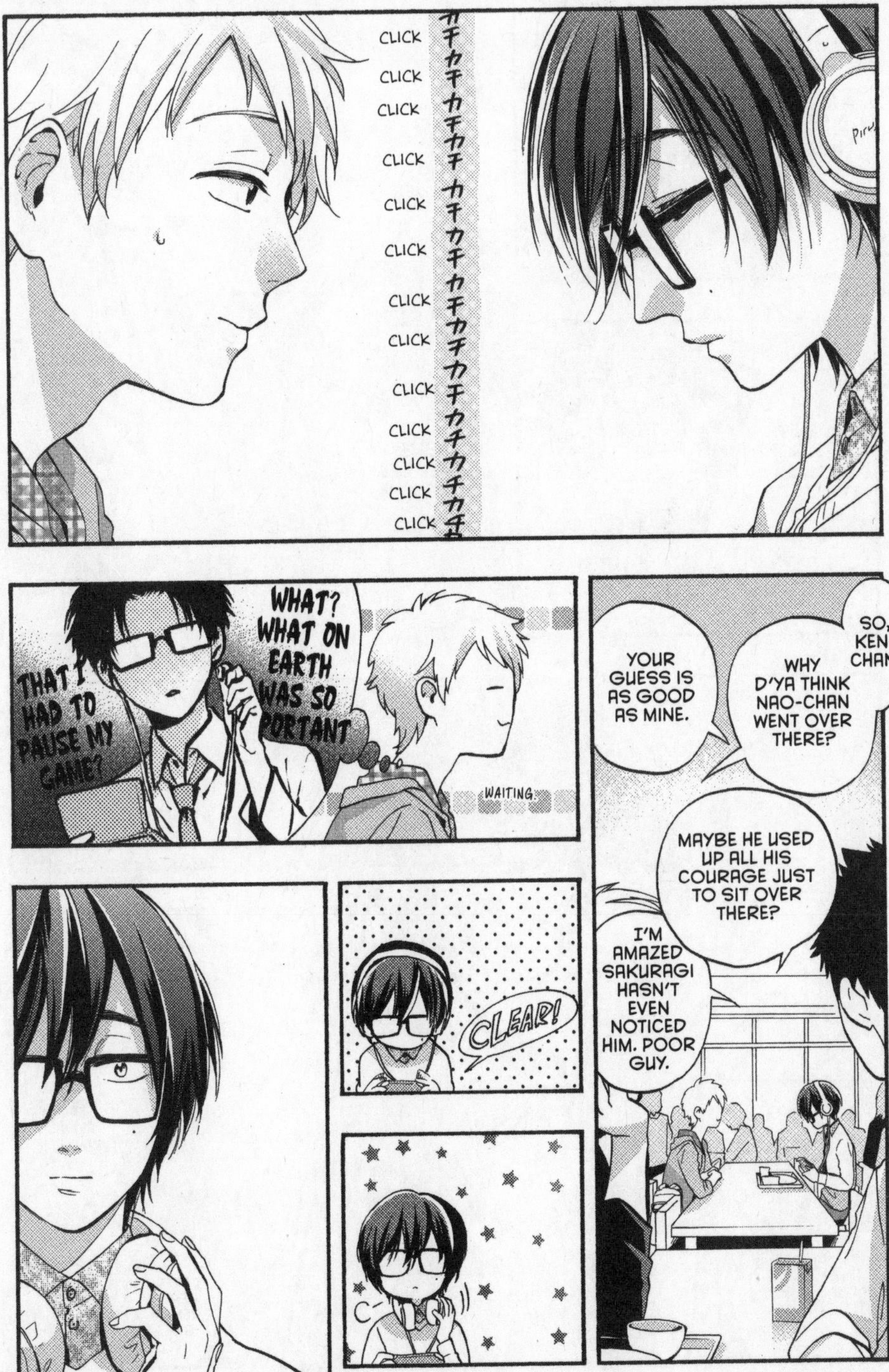
CLICK
CLICK
CLICK
CLICK
CLICK
CLICK
CLICK
CLICK
CLICK
CLICK
CLICK
CLICK
CLICK
SO, KEN-CHAN, WHY D'YA THINK NAO-CHAN WENT OVER THERE?
YOUR GUESS IS AS GOOD AS MINE.
MAYBE HE USED UP ALL HIS COURAGE JUST TO SIT OVER THERE?
I'M AMAZED SAKURAGI HASN'T EVEN NOTICED HIM. POOR GUY.
WHAT? WHAT ON EARTH WAS SO PORTANT
THAT I HAD TO PAUSE MY GAME?
WAITING.
CLEAR!

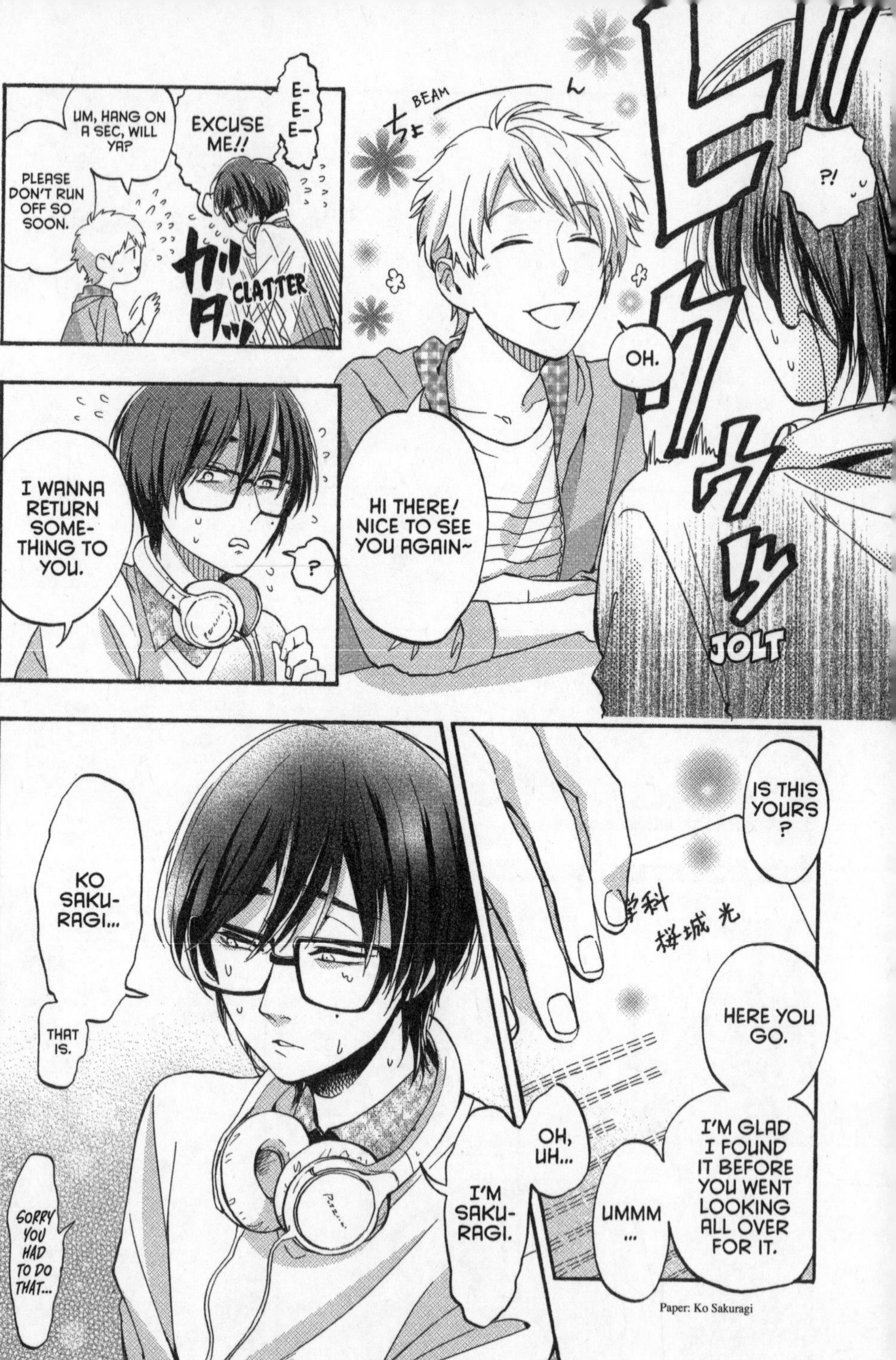
?!
JOLT
BEAM
OH.
HI THERE! NICE TO SEE YOU AGAIN~
EXCUSE ME!!
E-E-E—
UM, HANG ON A SEC, WILL YA?
PLEASE DON'T RUN OFF SO SOON.
CLATTER
?
I WANNA RETURN SOME-THING TO YOU.
IS THIS YOURS?
桜城光
HERE YOU GO.
I'M GLAD I FOUND IT BEFORE YOU WENT LOOKING ALL OVER FOR IT.
UMMM...
OH, UH...
I'M SAKU-RAGI.
KO SAKU-RAGI...
THAT IS.
SORRY YOU HAD TO DO THAT...
Paper: Ko Sakuragi

(Escape: Failed)

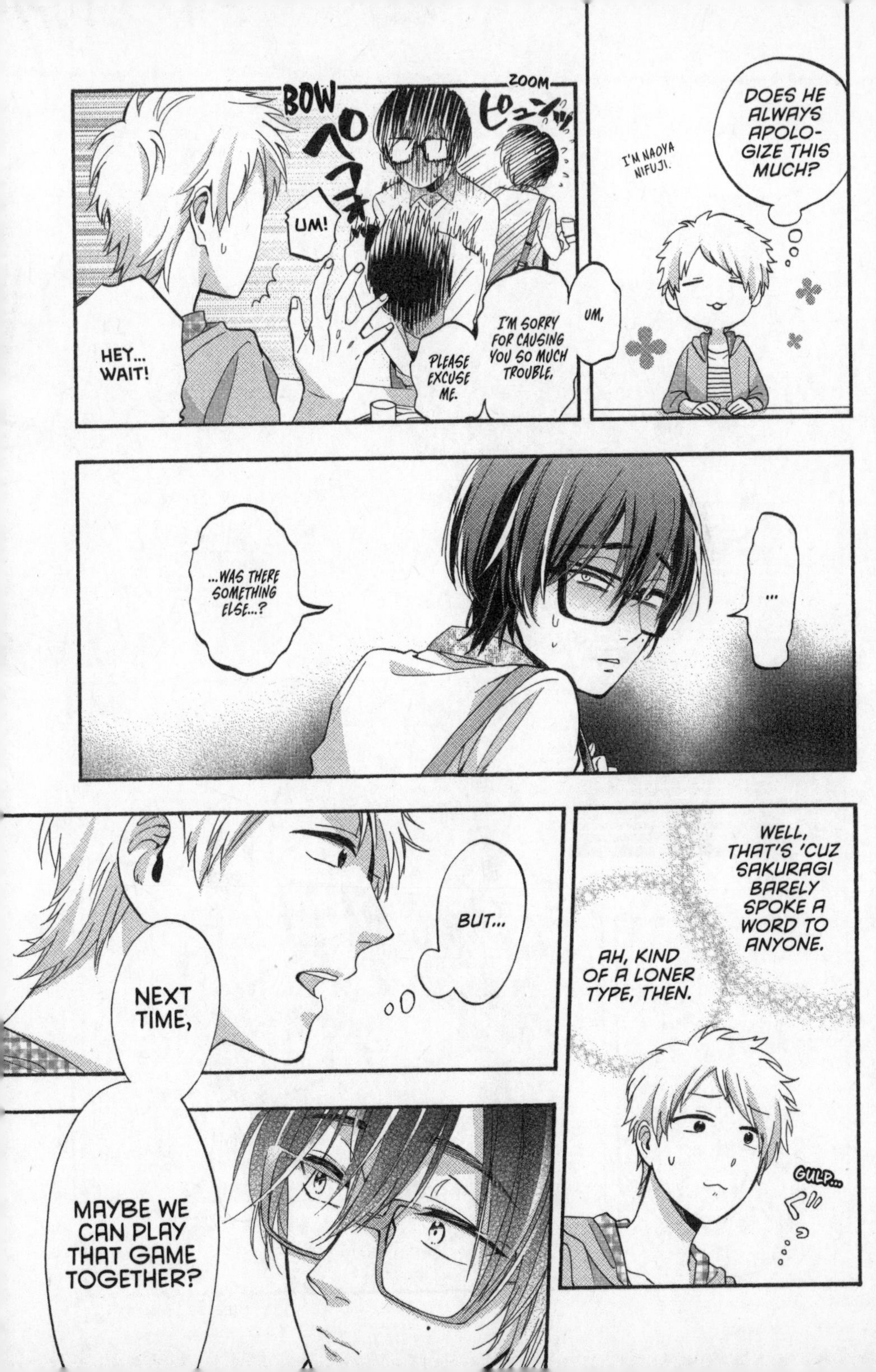
DOES HE ALWAYS APOLOGIZE THIS MUCH?
I'M NAOYA NIFUJI.
ZOOM
BOW
UM,
I'M SORRY FOR CAUSING YOU SO MUCH TROUBLE,
PLEASE EXCUSE ME.
UM!
HEY... WAIT!
...
...WAS THERE SOMETHING ELSE...?
WELL, THAT'S 'CUZ SAKURAGI BARELY SPOKE A WORD TO ANYONE.
AH, KIND OF A LONER TYPE, THEN.
GULP...
BUT...
NEXT TIME,
MAYBE WE CAN PLAY THAT GAME TOGETHER?

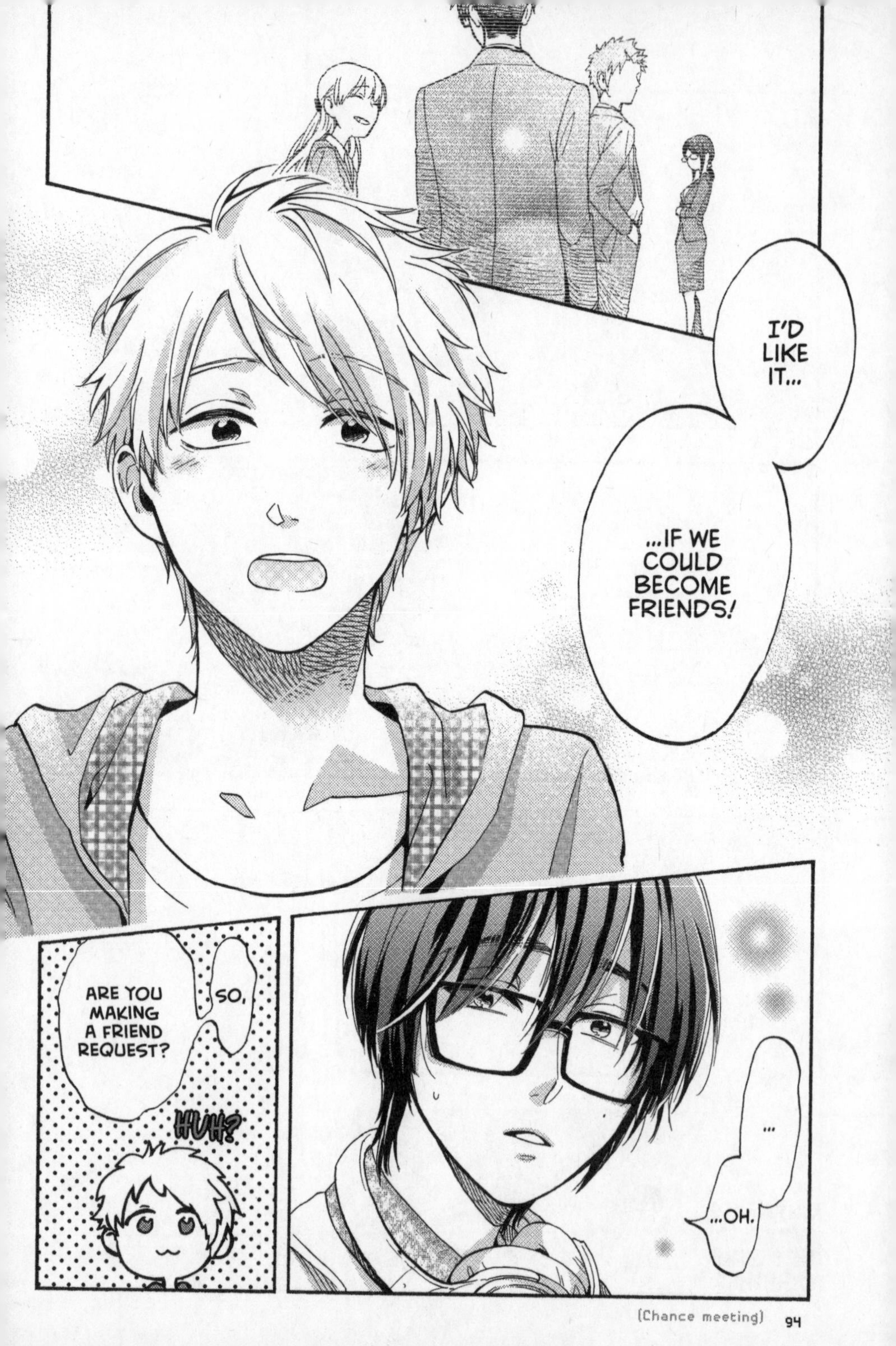
I'D LIKE IT...
...IF WE COULD BECOME FRIENDS!
...
...OH.
SO,
ARE YOU MAKING A FRIEND REQUEST?
HUH?

(Chance meeting)

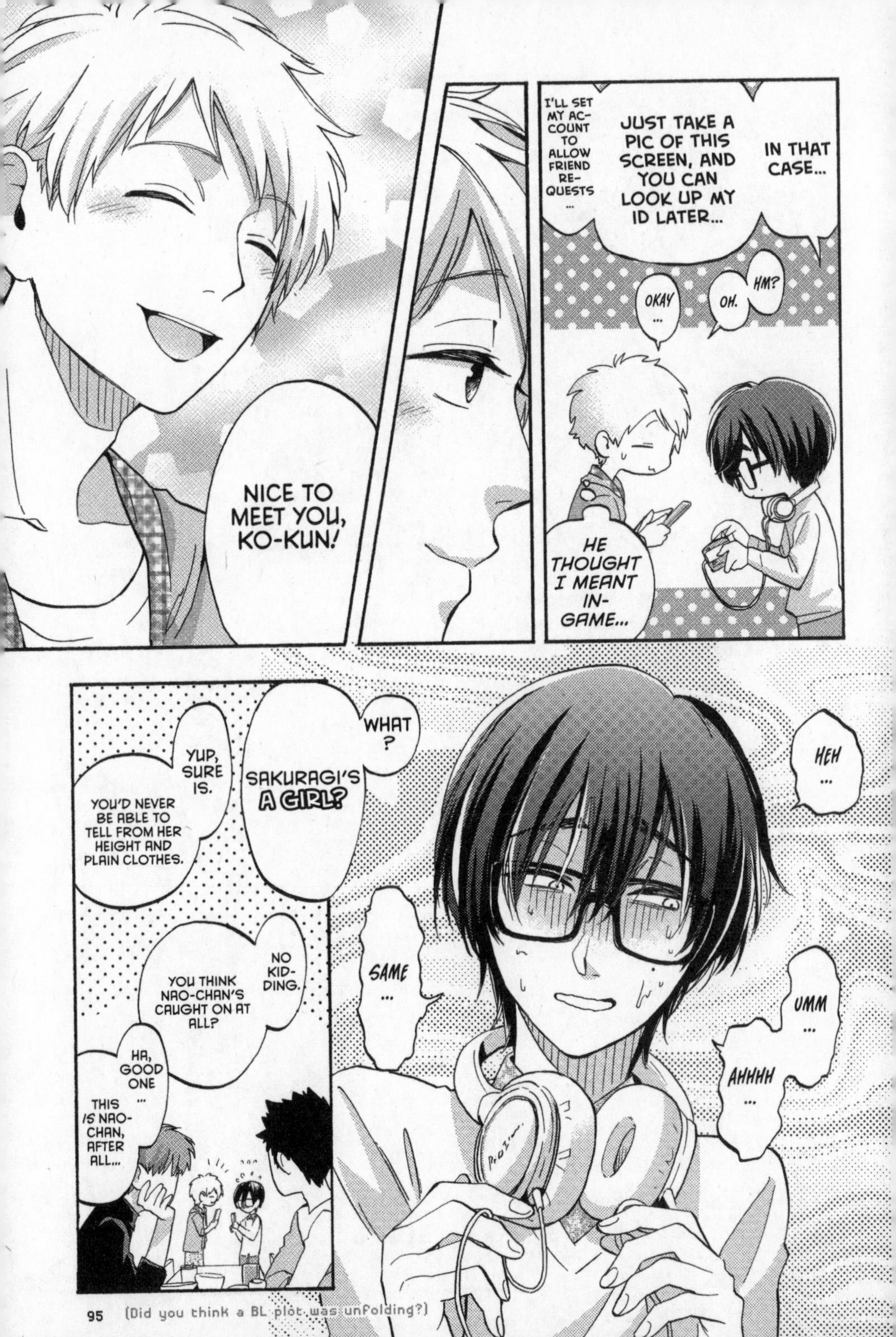
IN THAT CASE...
JUST TAKE A PIC OF THIS SCREEN, AND YOU CAN LOOK UP MY ID LATER...
I'LL SET MY AC-COUNT TO ALLOW FRIEND RE-QUESTS...
HM?
OH.
OKAY...
HE THOUGHT I MEANT IN-GAME...
NICE TO MEET YOU, KO-KUN!
HEH...
UMM...
AHHHH...
SAME...
WHAT?
SAKURAGI'S A GIRL?
YUP, SURE IS.
YOU'D NEVER BE ABLE TO TELL FROM HER HEIGHT AND PLAIN CLOTHES.
NO KID-DING.
YOU THINK NAO-CHAN'S CAUGHT ON AT ALL?
HA, GOOD ONE...
THIS *IS* NAO-CHAN, AFTER ALL...

 (Did you think a BL plot was unfolding?)

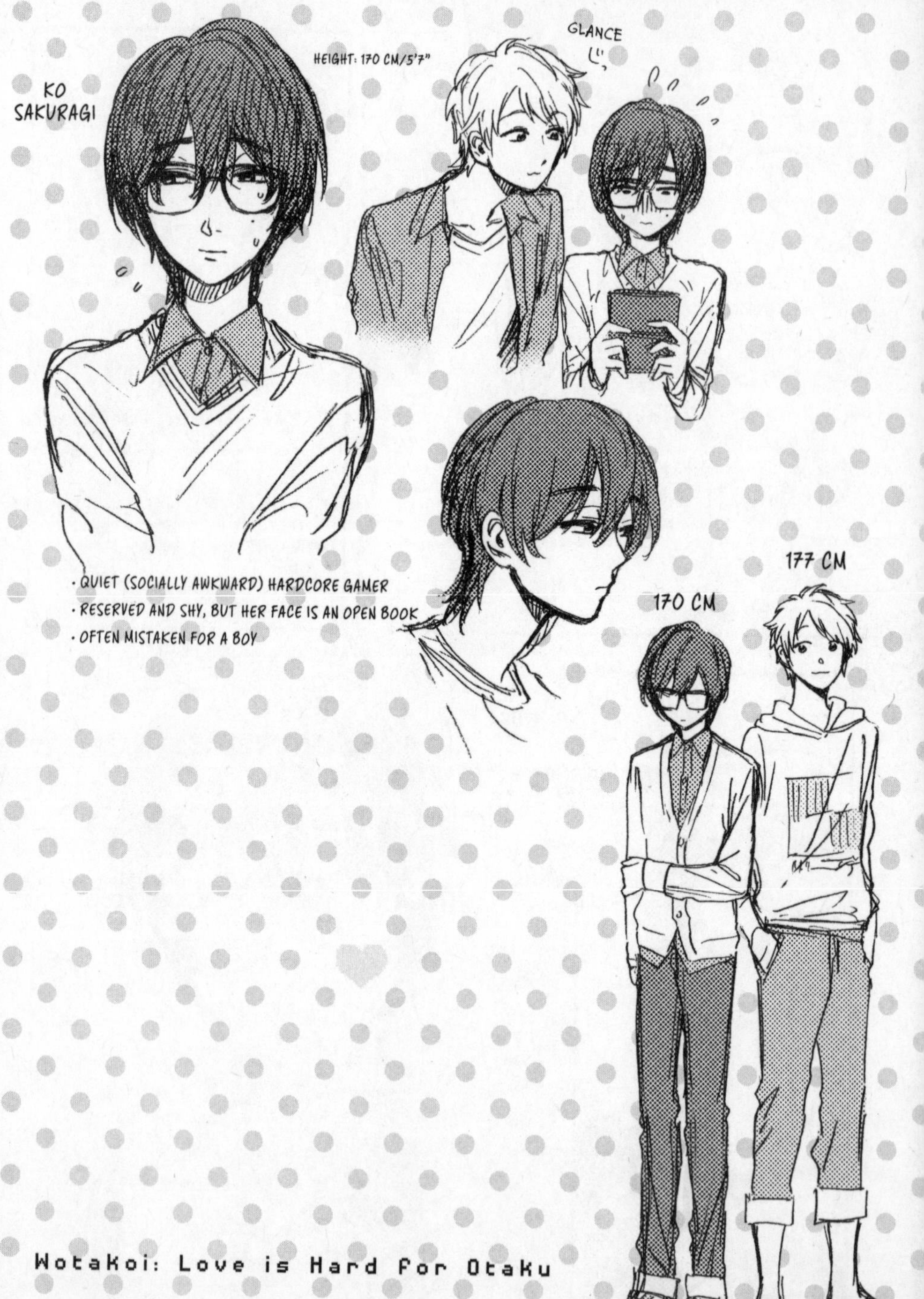
KO SAKURAGI
HEIGHT: 170 CM/5'7"
GLANCE
• QUIET (SOCIALLY AWKWARD) HARDCORE GAMER
• RESERVED AND SHY, BUT HER FACE IS AN OPEN BOOK
• OFTEN MISTAKEN FOR A BOY
177 CM
170 CM
Wotakoi: Love is Hard for Otaku

Episode.... 21

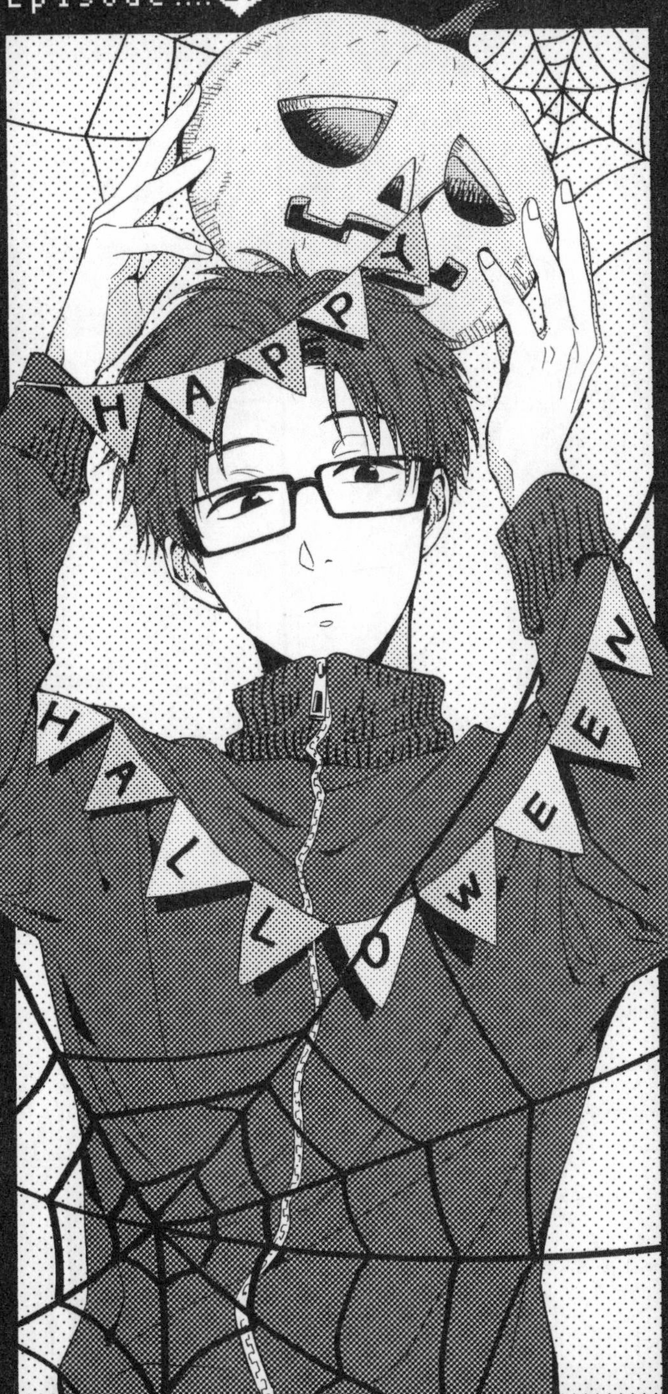
HAPPY
HALLOWEEN

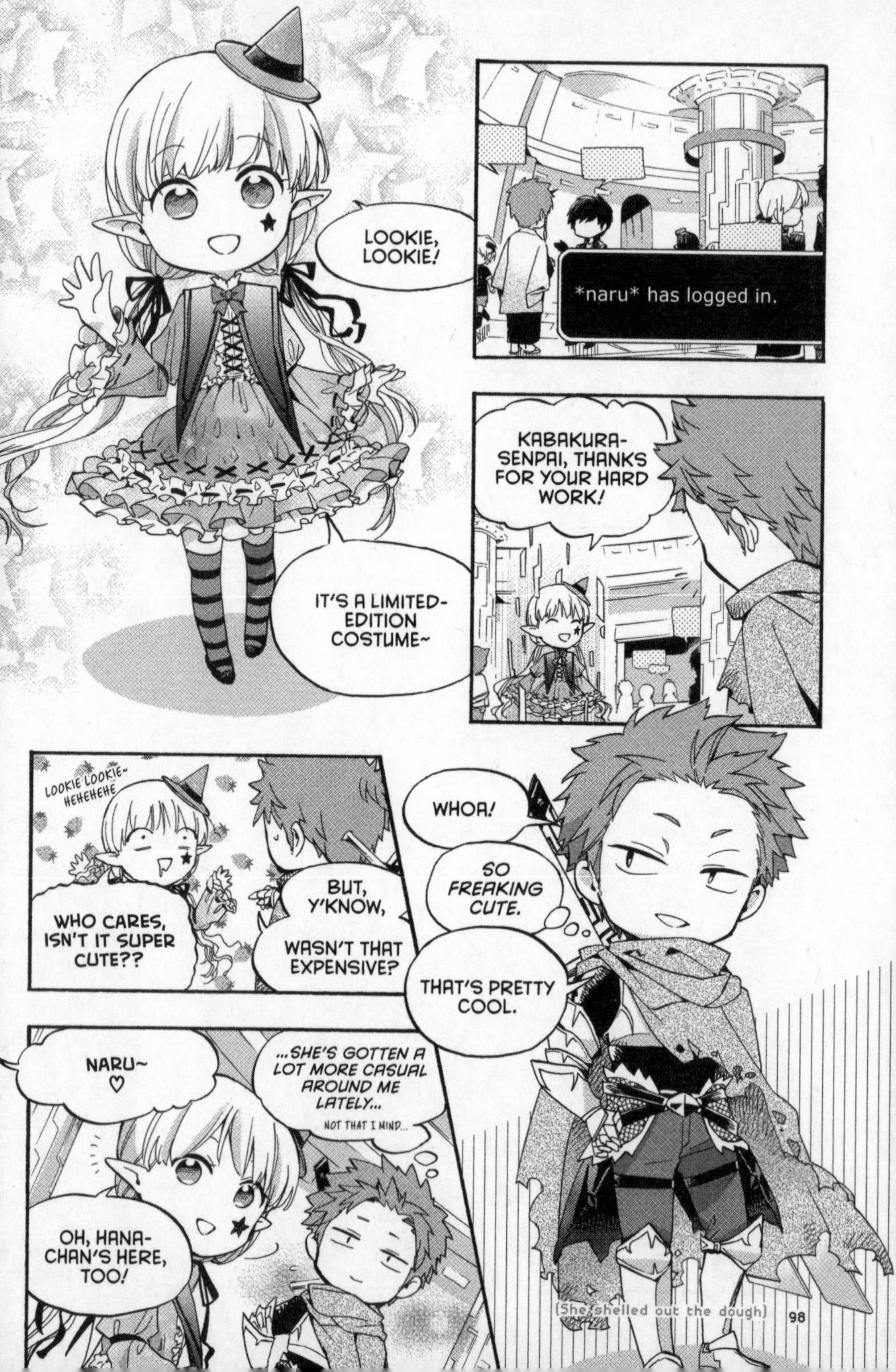
naru has logged in.
KABAKURA-SENPAI, THANKS FOR YOUR HARD WORK!
LOOKIE, LOOKIE!
IT'S A LIMITED-EDITION COSTUME~
WHOA!
SO FREAKING CUTE.
THAT'S PRETTY COOL.
BUT, Y'KNOW,
WASN'T THAT EXPENSIVE?
LOOKIE LOOKIE~ HEHEHEHE
WHO CARES, ISN'T IT SUPER CUTE??
...SHE'S GOTTEN A LOT MORE CASUAL AROUND ME LATELY...
NOT THAT I MIND...
NARU~ ♡
OH, HANA-CHAN'S HERE, TOO!
(She shelled out the dough)

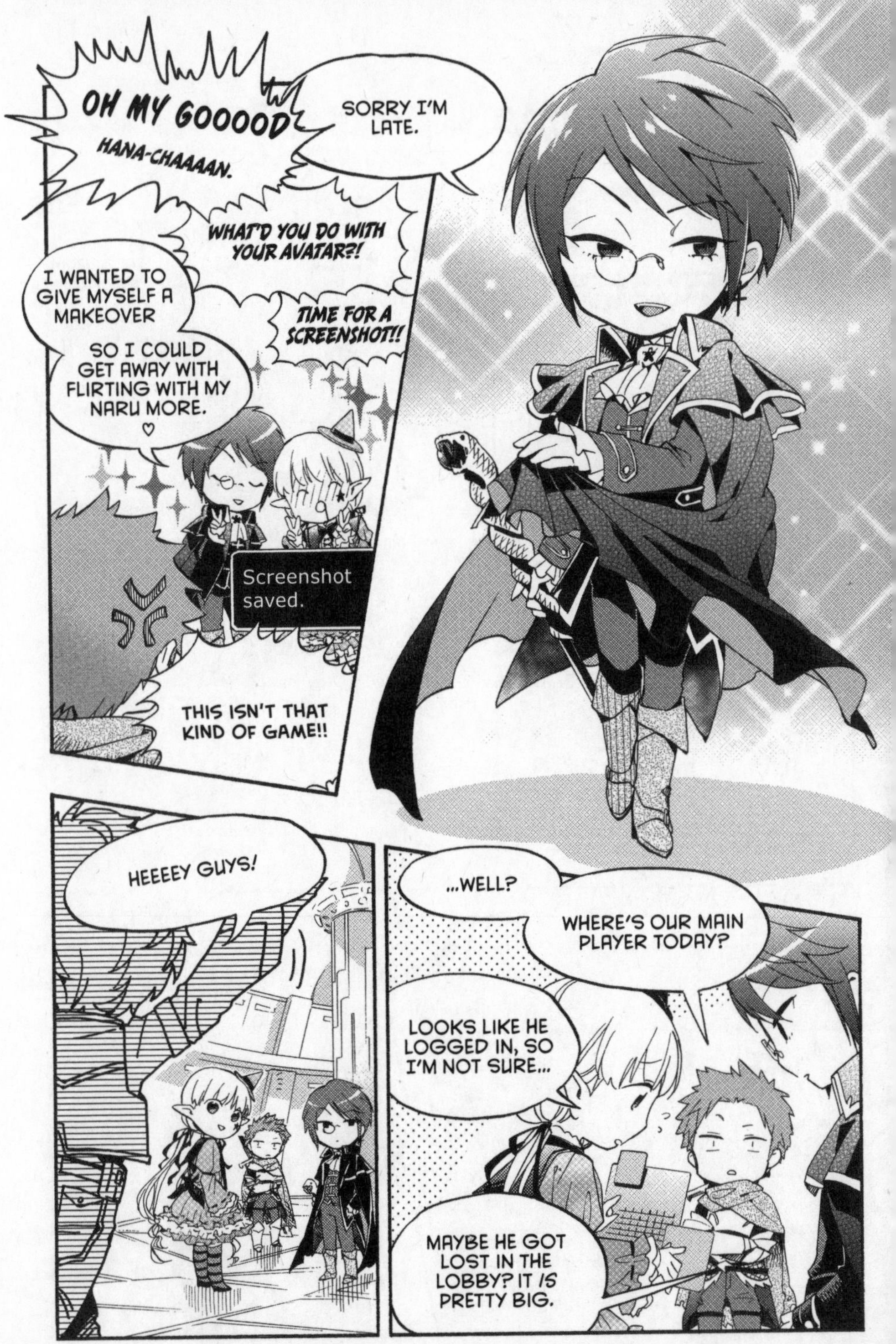
SORRY I'M LATE.
OH MY GOOOOD HANA-CHAAAAN.
WHAT'D YOU DO WITH YOUR AVATAR?!
I WANTED TO GIVE MYSELF A MAKEOVER
SO I COULD GET AWAY WITH FLIRTING WITH MY NARU MORE. ♡
TIME FOR A SCREENSHOT!!
Screenshot saved.
THIS ISN'T THAT KIND OF GAME!!
...WELL?
WHERE'S OUR MAIN PLAYER TODAY?
LOOKS LIKE HE LOGGED IN, SO I'M NOT SURE...
MAYBE HE GOT LOST IN THE LOBBY? IT *IS* PRETTY BIG.
HEEEEY GUYS!

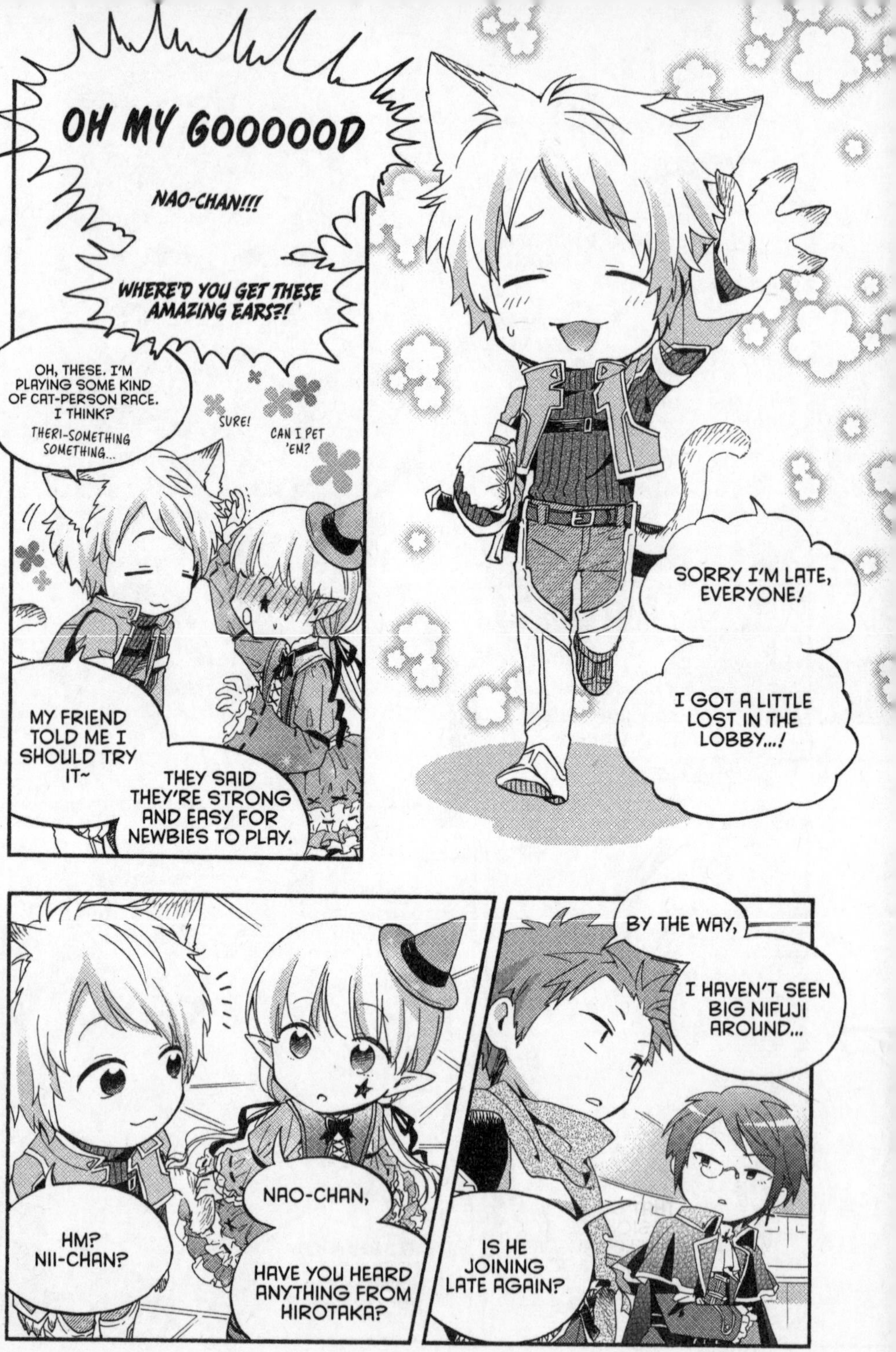
SORRY I'M LATE, EVERYONE!
I GOT A LITTLE LOST IN THE LOBBY...!
OH MY GOOOOOD
NAO-CHAN!!!
WHERE'D YOU GET THESE AMAZING EARS?!
CAN I PET 'EM?
SURE!
OH, THESE. I'M PLAYING SOME KIND OF CAT-PERSON RACE. I THINK?
THERI-SOMETHING SOMETHING...
MY FRIEND TOLD ME I SHOULD TRY IT~
THEY SAID THEY'RE STRONG AND EASY FOR NEWBIES TO PLAY.
BY THE WAY,
I HAVEN'T SEEN BIG NIFUJI AROUND...
IS HE JOINING LATE AGAIN?
NAO-CHAN,
HAVE YOU HEARD ANYTHING FROM HIROTAKA?
HM? NII-CHAN?

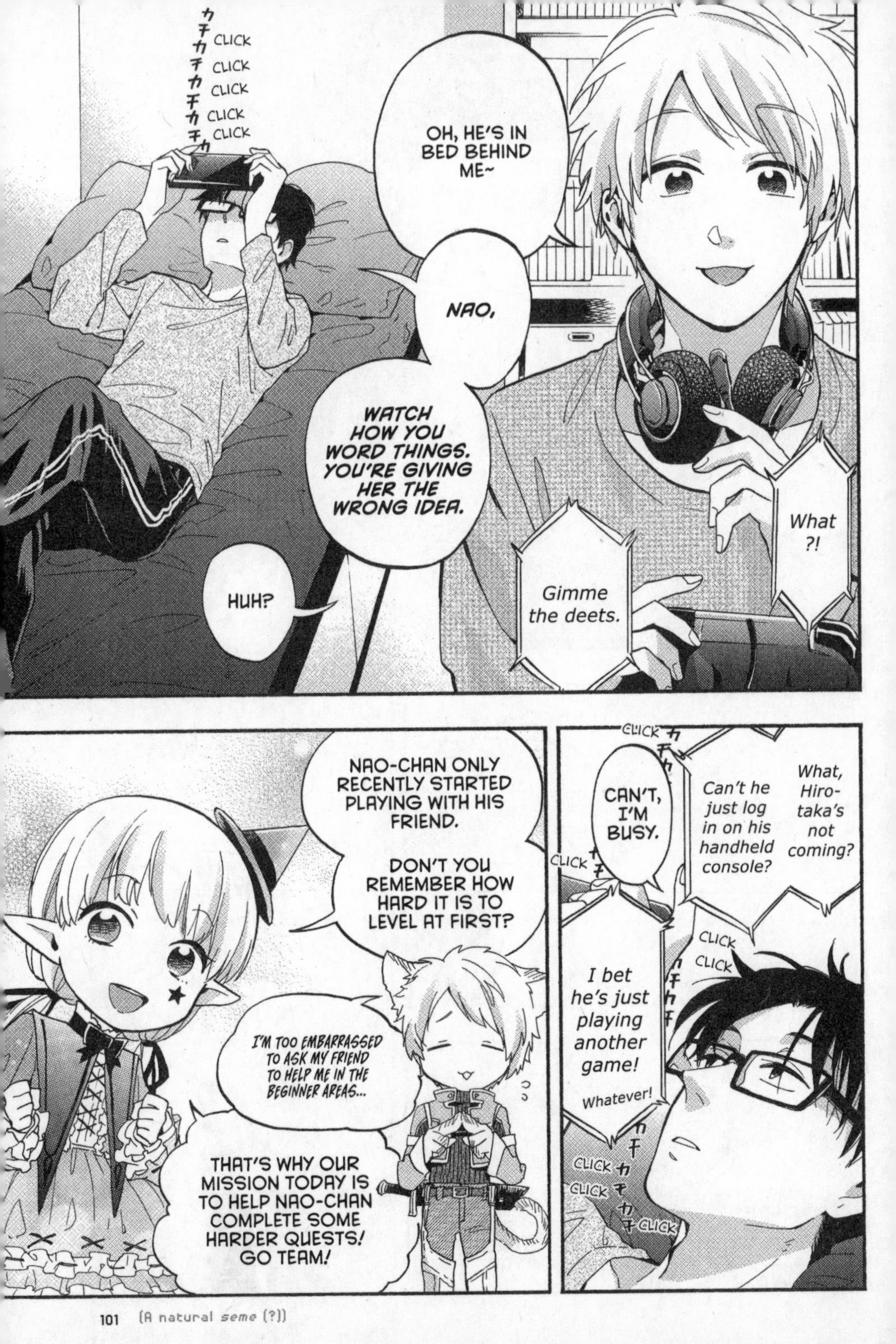
OH, HE'S IN BED BEHIND ME~
NAO,
WATCH HOW YOU WORD THINGS. YOU'RE GIVING HER THE WRONG IDEA.
What ?!
Gimme the deets.
HUH?
カチカチカチカチカチカ
CLICK CLICK CLICK CLICK CLICK
What, Hiro-taka's not coming?
Can't he just log in on his handheld console?
CAN'T, I'M BUSY.
CLICK カチカ
CLICK カチ
CLICK CLICK カチカチ
I bet he's just playing another game!
Whatever!
CLICK CLICK CLICK カチカチ
NAO-CHAN ONLY RECENTLY STARTED PLAYING WITH HIS FRIEND.
DON'T YOU REMEMBER HOW HARD IT IS TO LEVEL AT FIRST?
I'M TOO EMBARRASSED TO ASK MY FRIEND TO HELP ME IN THE BEGINNER AREAS...
THAT'S WHY OUR MISSION TODAY IS TO HELP NAO-CHAN COMPLETE SOME HARDER QUESTS! GO TEAM!

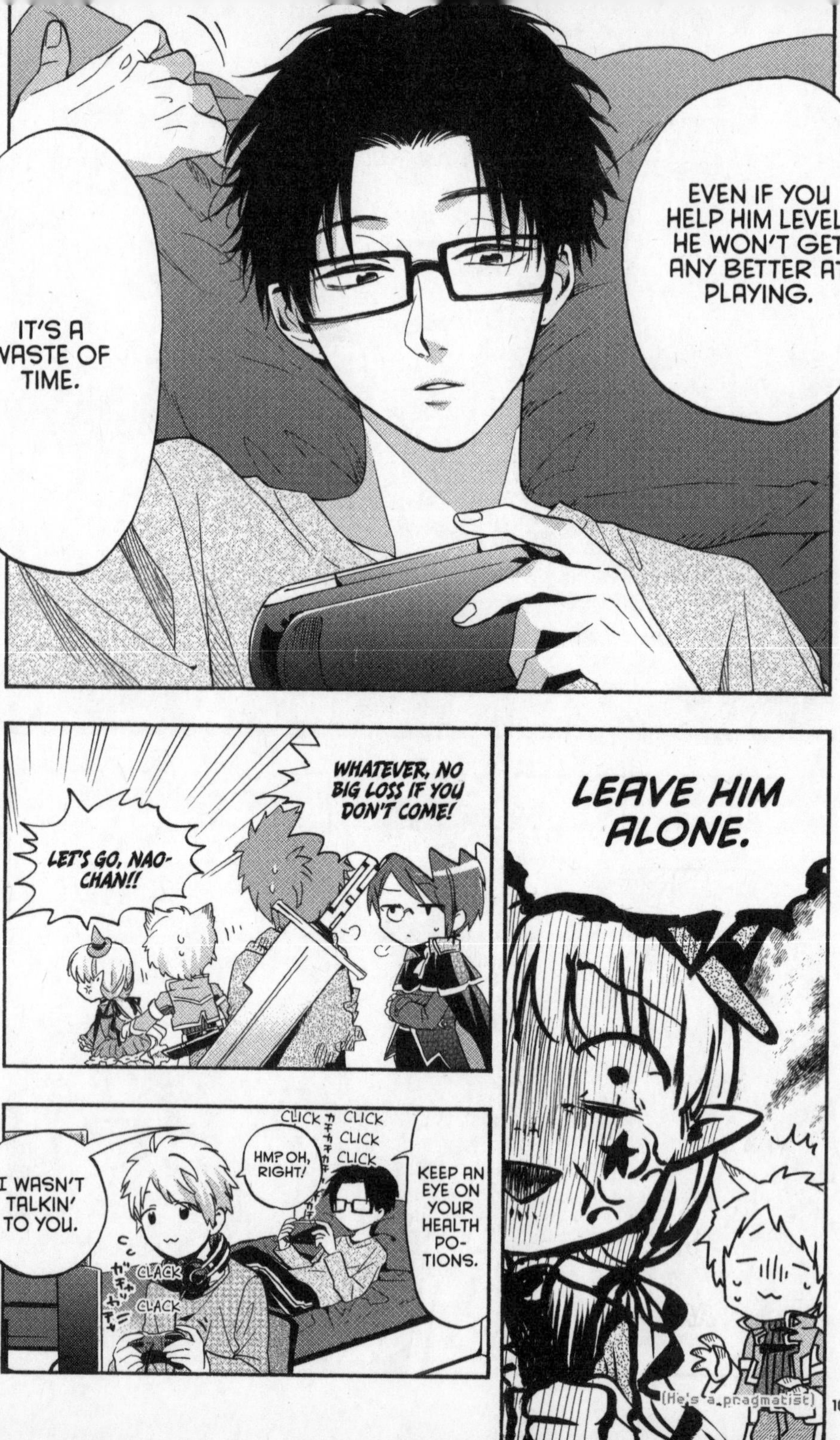
EVEN IF YOU HELP HIM LEVEL, HE WON'T GET ANY BETTER AT PLAYING.
IT'S A WASTE OF TIME.
LEAVE HIM ALONE.
(He's a pragmatist)
WHATEVER, NO BIG LOSS IF YOU DON'T COME!
LET'S GO, NAO-CHAN!!
KEEP AN EYE ON YOUR HEALTH POTIONS.
CLICK CLICK CLICK CLICK
HM? OH, RIGHT!
I WASN'T TALKIN' TO YOU.
CLACK
CLACK

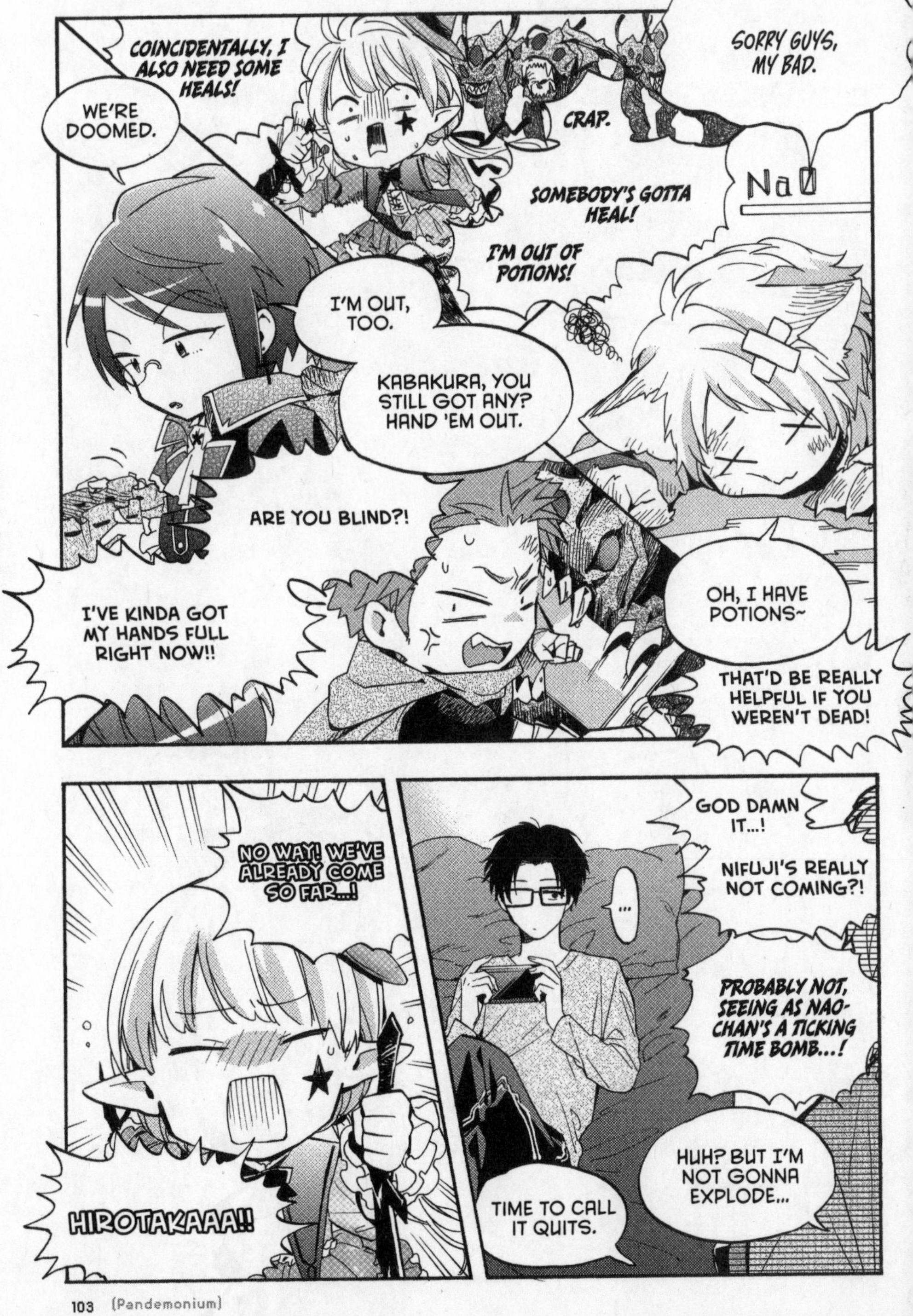
SORRY GUYS, MY BAD.
NaO
CRAP.
COINCIDENTALLY, I ALSO NEED SOME HEALS!
WE'RE DOOMED.
SOMEBODY'S GOTTA HEAL!
I'M OUT OF POTIONS!
I'M OUT, TOO.
KABAKURA, YOU STILL GOT ANY? HAND 'EM OUT.
OH, I HAVE POTIONS~
THAT'D BE REALLY HELPFUL IF YOU WEREN'T DEAD!
ARE YOU BLIND?!
I'VE KINDA GOT MY HANDS FULL RIGHT NOW!!
GOD DAMN IT...!
NIFUJI'S REALLY NOT COMING?!
PROBABLY NOT, SEEING AS NAO-CHAN'S A TICKING TIME BOMB...!
...
HUH? BUT I'M NOT GONNA EXPLODE...
TIME TO CALL IT QUITS.
NO WAY! WE'VE ALREADY COME SO FAR...!
HIROTAKAAA!!

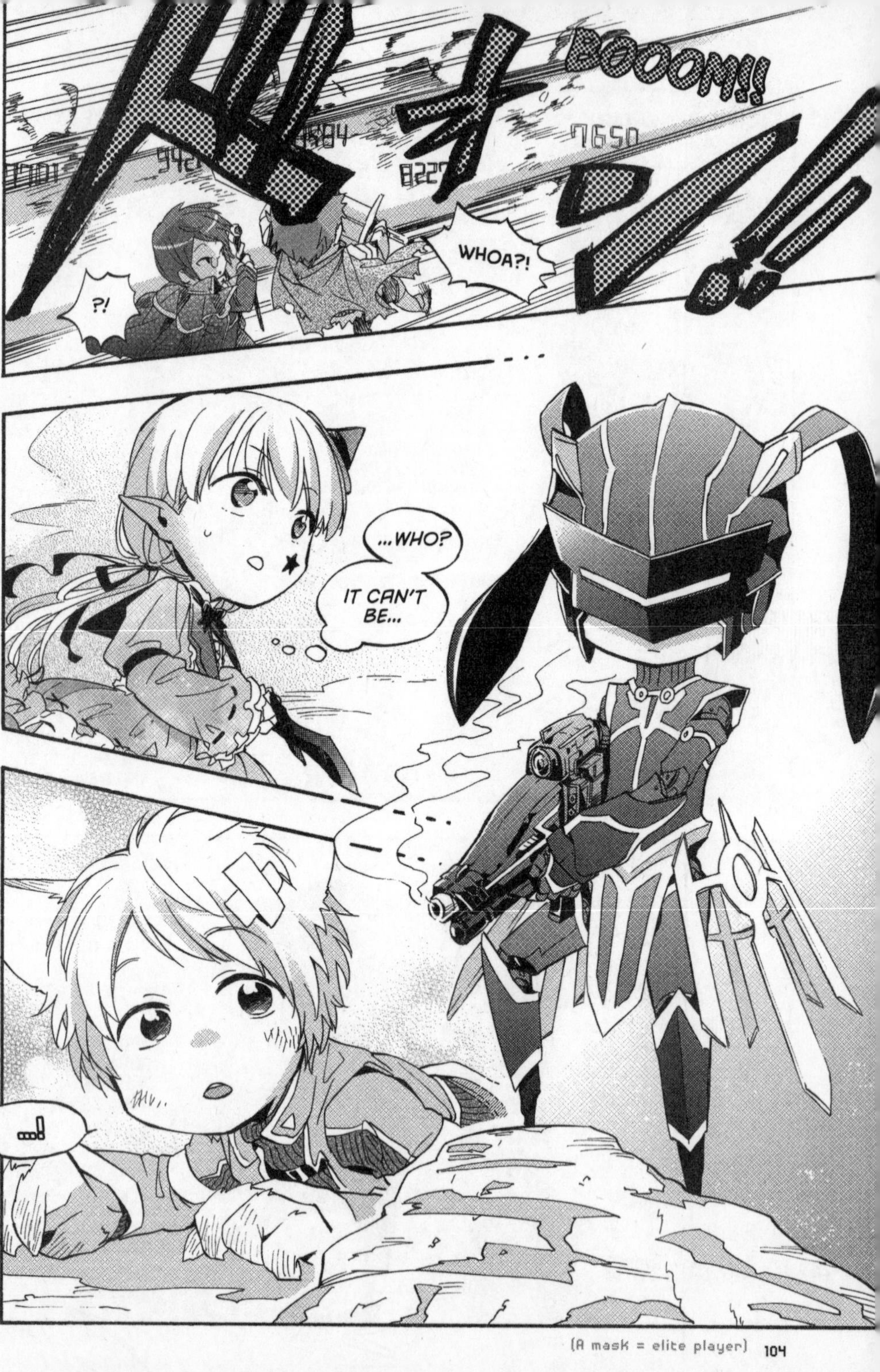
BOOOM!!
WHOA?!
?!
...WHO?
IT CAN'T BE...
...!

(A mask = elite player)

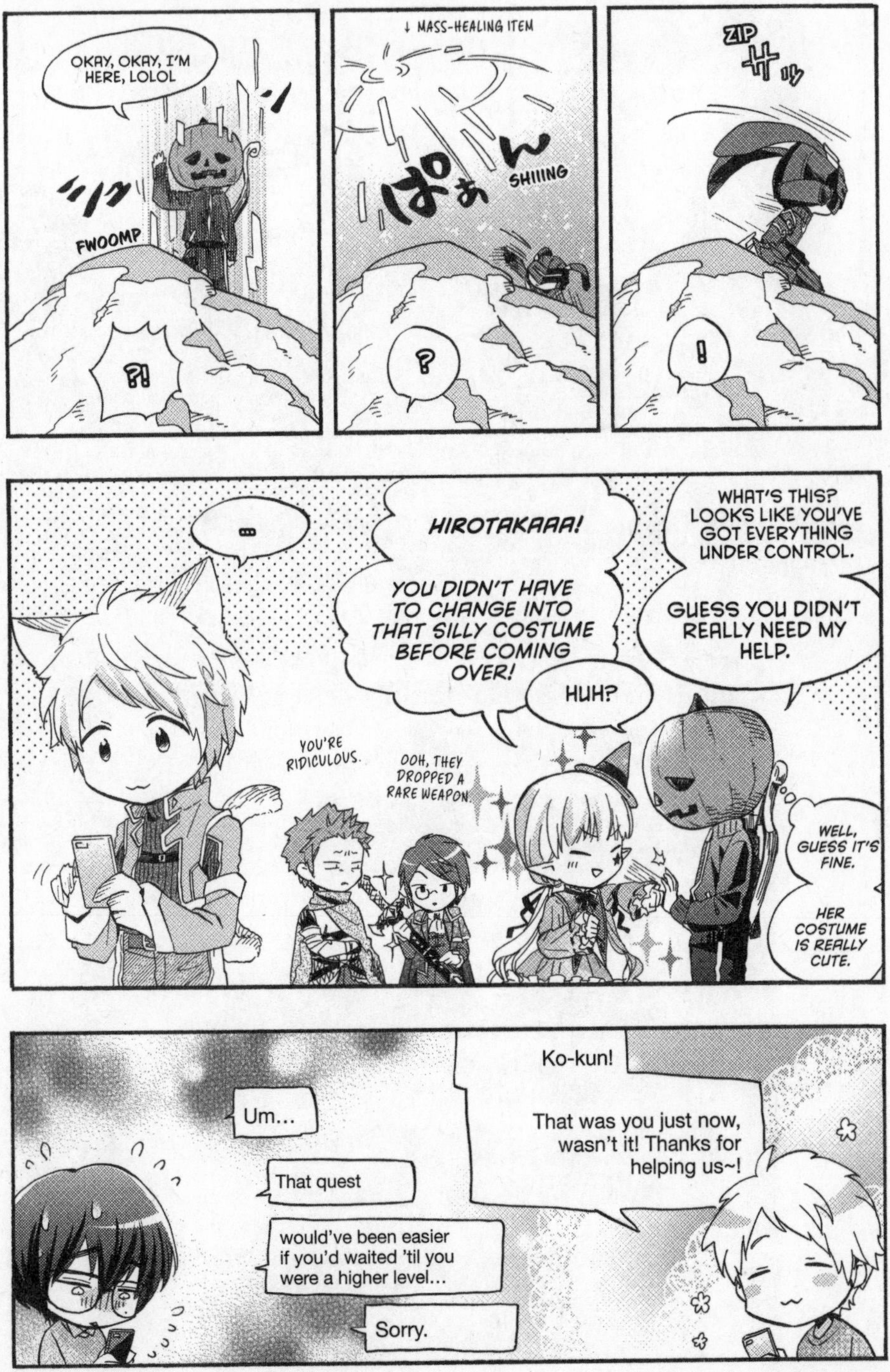
ZIP
!
↓ MASS-HEALING ITEM
SHIIING
?
OKAY, OKAY, I'M HERE, LOLOL
FWOOMP
?!
WHAT'S THIS? LOOKS LIKE YOU'VE GOT EVERYTHING UNDER CONTROL.
GUESS YOU DIDN'T REALLY NEED MY HELP.
HIROTAKAAA!
YOU DIDN'T HAVE TO CHANGE INTO THAT SILLY COSTUME BEFORE COMING OVER!
...
HUH?
WELL, GUESS IT'S FINE.
HER COSTUME IS REALLY CUTE.
OOH, THEY DROPPED A RARE WEAPON.
YOU'RE RIDICULOUS.
Ko-kun!
That was you just now, wasn't it! Thanks for helping us~!
Um...
That quest
would've been easier if you'd waited 'til you were a higher level...
Sorry.

 (She dashed away like a startled bunny)

HIROTAKA'S LITTLE BROTHER
(NON-OTAKU—TERRIBLE AT GAMES)

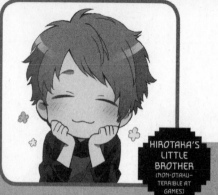

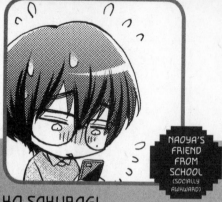

NAOYA NIFUJI

As much of a non-otaku as one can get. He doesn't have a clue about otaku slang or trends, and is a bit of an airhead. Provided it's before 10 p.m. (his bedtime), there's a high chance he'll respond quickly to texts, though not quite as quickly as Narumi. He's tried a few games and smartphone apps his friends have told him about, but he's awful at them all. (At least he has fun.) Not surprisingly, he can only type with his index fingers, and has to look at the keyboard while he types.

NAOYA'S FRIEND FROM SCHOOL
(SOCIALLY AWKWARD)

KO SAKURAGI

She gets fully absorbed in her games, much like another certain someone. Doesn't use social media. Super slow typer on her smartphone. She replies to everything in one go, so her messages tend to be huge blocks of text. She's slow to respond because she tends to labor over every word, writing, deleting, and rewriting until it's perfect. "I'm sorry" and "Excuse me" pop up in her predictive text box the most. She gets so anxious texting and talking on the phone she feels like she's gonna have a heart attack.

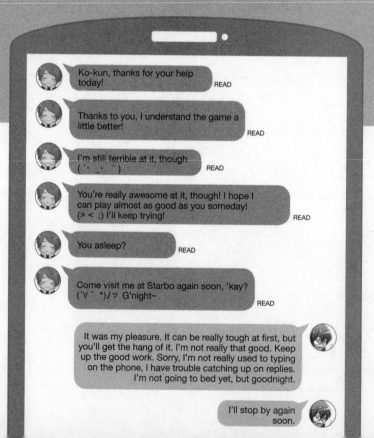

Ko-kun, thanks for your help today! READ

Thanks to you, I understand the game a little better! READ

I'm still terrible at it, though (´・_・`) READ

You're really awesome at it, though! I hope I can play almost as good as you someday! (> < ;) I'll keep trying! READ

You asleep? READ

Come visit me at Starbo again soon, 'kay? (´∀` *)ノシ G'night~ READ

It was my pleasure. It can be really tough at first, but you'll get the hang of it. I'm not really that good. Keep up the good work. Sorry, I'm not really used to typing on the phone, I have trouble catching up on replies. I'm not going to bed yet, but goodnight.

I'll stop by again soon.

Wotakoi: Love is Hard for Otaku

CAN YOU BELIEVE IT?

WHEN I LOOKED OVER, HE HAD HIS EYES SQUEEZED SHUT!

HE'S MORE OF A SCAREDY CAT THAN HE LETS ON.

BUT I GUESS I DON'T HAVE MUCH ROOM TO TALK, HUH~

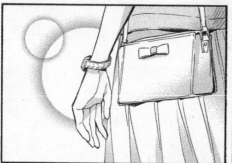

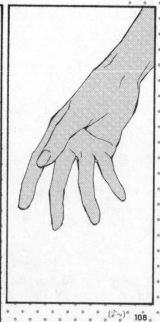

(♪~)°

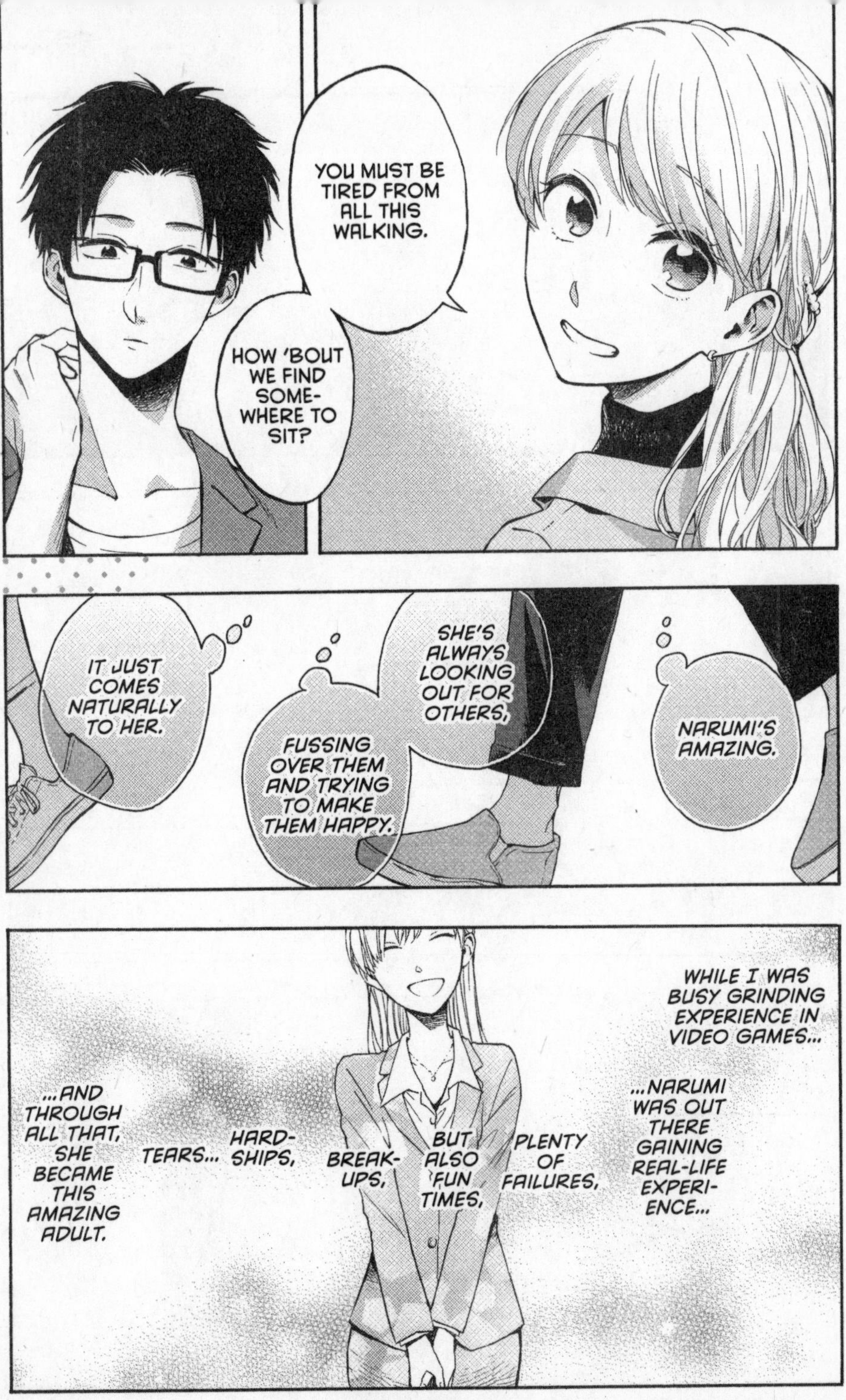
YOU MUST BE TIRED FROM ALL THIS WALKING.
HOW 'BOUT WE FIND SOME-WHERE TO SIT?
NARUMI'S AMAZING.
SHE'S ALWAYS LOOKING OUT FOR OTHERS,
FUSSING OVER THEM AND TRYING TO MAKE THEM HAPPY.
IT JUST COMES NATURALLY TO HER.
WHILE I WAS BUSY GRINDING EXPERIENCE IN VIDEO GAMES...
...NARUMI WAS OUT THERE GAINING REAL-LIFE EXPERI-ENCE...
PLENTY OF FAILURES,
BUT ALSO FUN TIMES,
BREAK-UPS,
HARD-SHIPS,
TEARS...
...AND THROUGH ALL THAT, SHE BECAME THIS AMAZING ADULT.

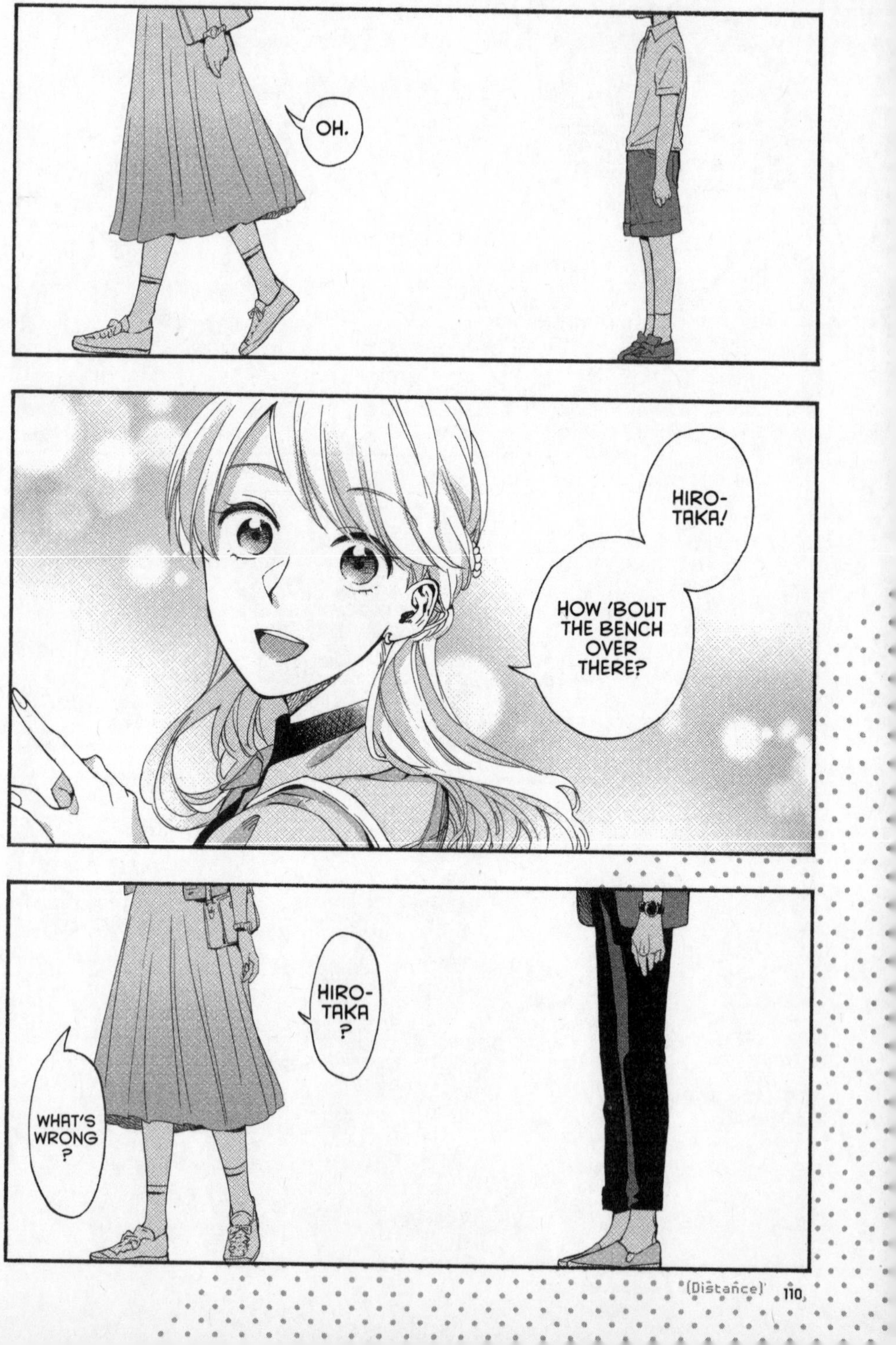
OH.
HIRO-TAKA!
HOW 'BOUT THE BENCH OVER THERE?
HIRO-TAKA?
WHAT'S WRONG?

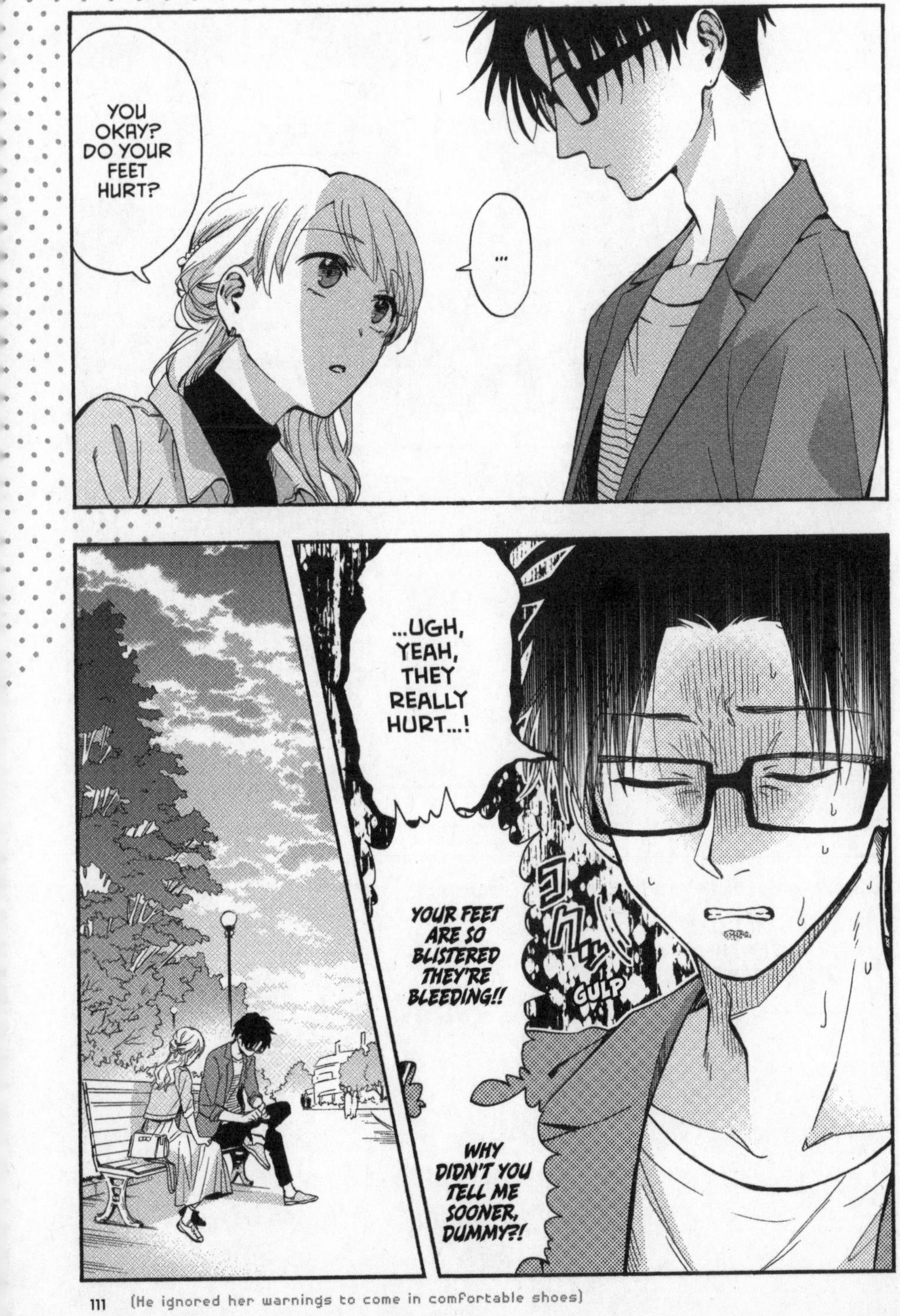
...
YOU OKAY? DO YOUR FEET HURT?
...UGH, YEAH, THEY REALLY HURT...!
GULP
YOUR FEET ARE SO BLISTERED THEY'RE BLEEDING!!
WHY DIDN'T YOU TELL ME SOONER, DUMMY?!

(He ignored her warnings to come in comfortable shoes)

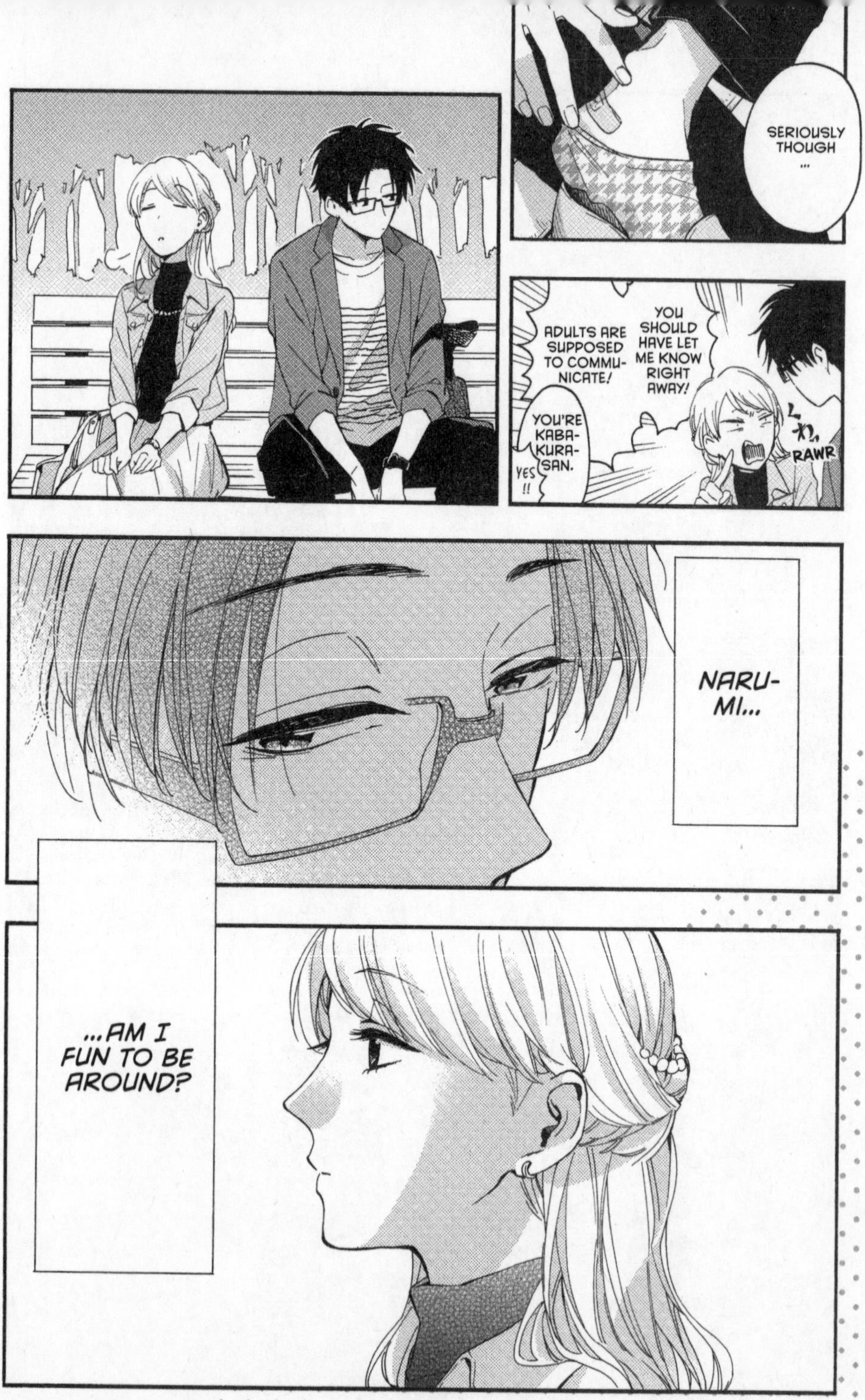

SERIOUSLY THOUGH ...
RAWR
YOU SHOULD HAVE LET ME KNOW RIGHT AWAY!
ADULTS ARE SUPPOSED TO COMMUNICATE!
YOU'RE KABAKURA-SAN.
YES !!
NARUMI...
...AM I FUN TO BE AROUND?

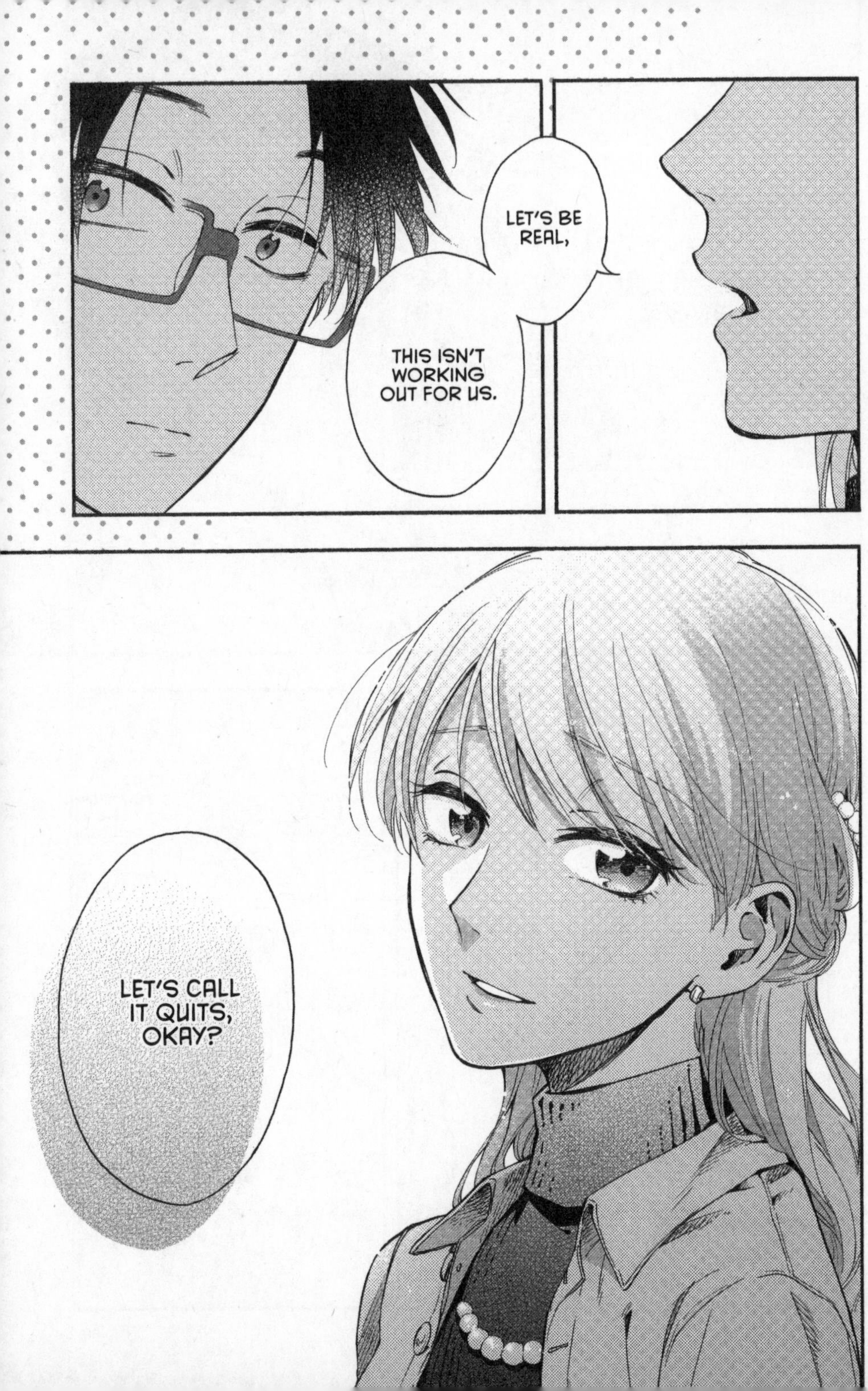
LET'S BE REAL,
THIS ISN'T WORKING OUT FOR US.
LET'S CALL IT QUITS, OKAY?

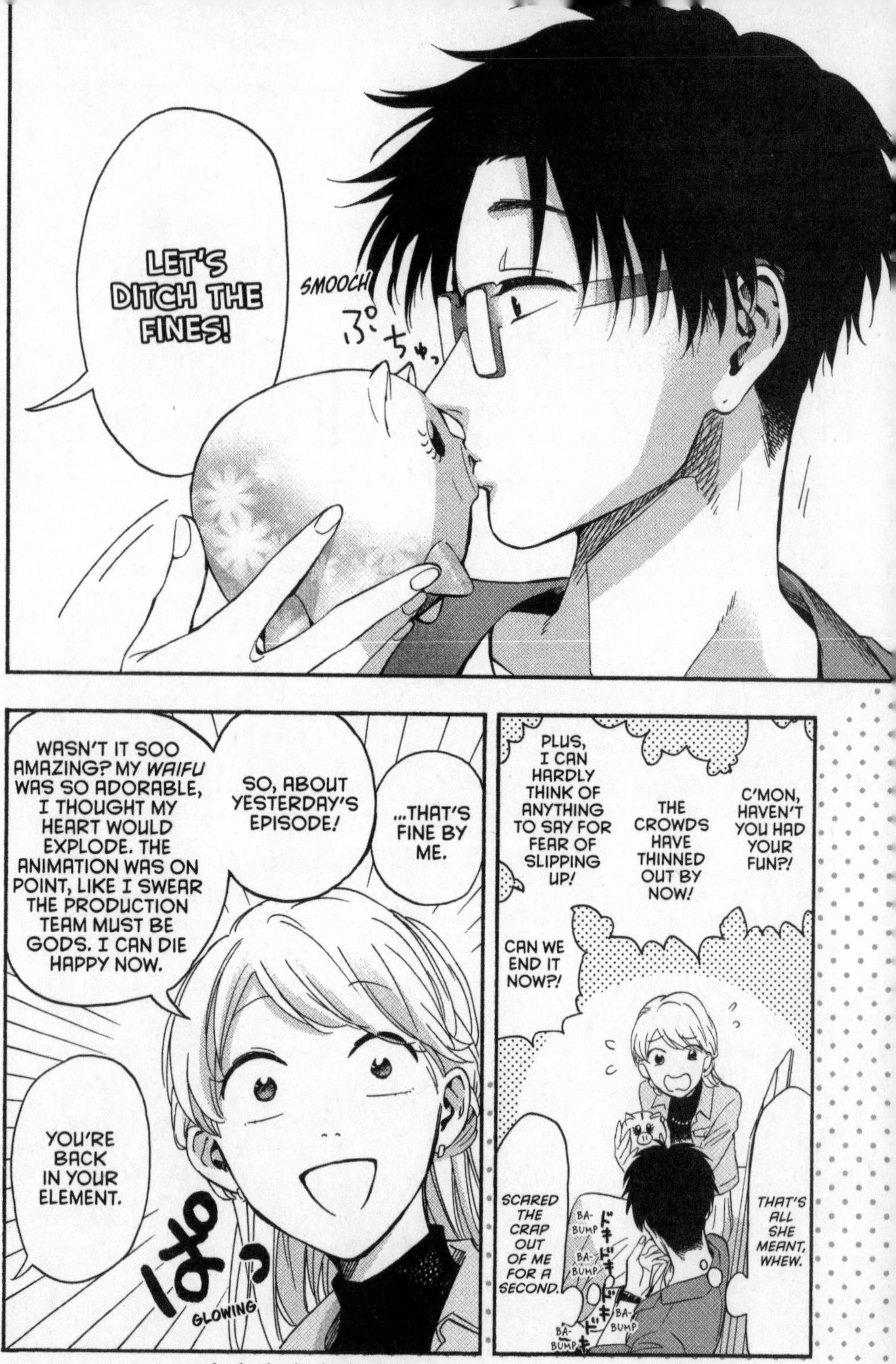
LET'S DITCH THE FINES!
SMOOCH
ぷちゅっ
C'MON, HAVEN'T YOU HAD YOUR FUN?!
THE CROWDS HAVE THINNED OUT BY NOW!
PLUS, I CAN HARDLY THINK OF ANYTHING TO SAY FOR FEAR OF SLIPPING UP!
CAN WE END IT NOW?!
THAT'S ALL SHE MEANT, WHEW.
BA-BUMP BA-BUMP BA-BUMP BA-BUMP
ドキドキドキドキ
SCARED THE CRAP OUT OF ME FOR A SECOND.
...THAT'S FINE BY ME.
SO, ABOUT YESTERDAY'S EPISODE!
WASN'T IT SOO AMAZING? MY *WAIFU* WAS SO ADORABLE, I THOUGHT MY HEART WOULD EXPLODE. THE ANIMATION WAS ON POINT, LIKE I SWEAR THE PRODUCTION TEAM MUST BE GODS. I CAN DIE HAPPY NOW.
YOU'RE BACK IN YOUR ELEMENT.
ぱっ
GLOWING

(Her true colors)

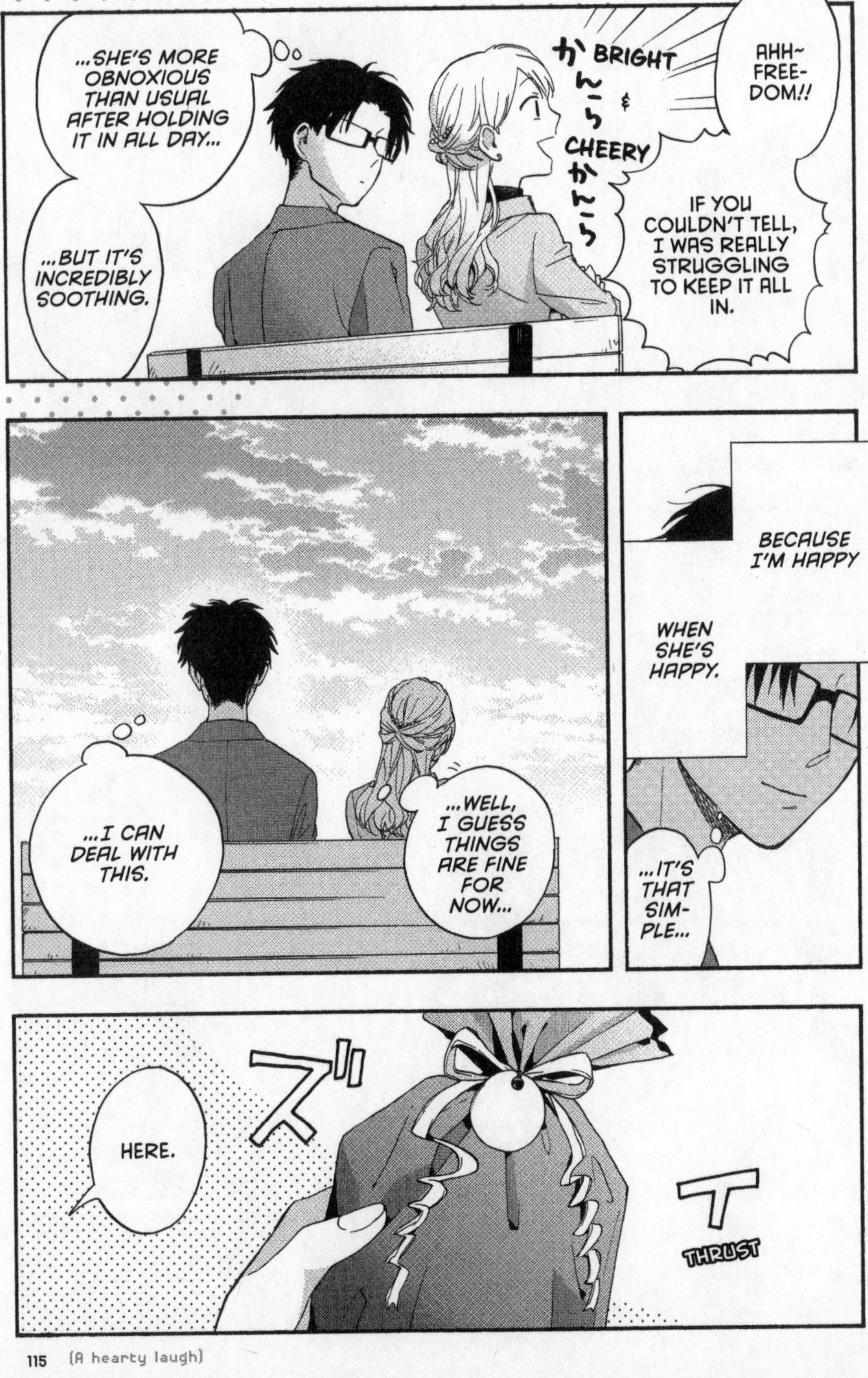
AHH~ FREE-DOM!!
IF YOU COULDN'T TELL, I WAS REALLY STRUGGLING TO KEEP IT ALL IN.
かんら BRIGHT & CHEERY かんら
...SHE'S MORE OBNOXIOUS THAN USUAL AFTER HOLDING IT IN ALL DAY...
...BUT IT'S INCREDIBLY SOOTHING.
BECAUSE I'M HAPPY
WHEN SHE'S HAPPY.
...IT'S THAT SIMPLE...
...WELL, I GUESS THINGS ARE FINE FOR NOW...
...I CAN DEAL WITH THIS.
ズイ THRUST
HERE.

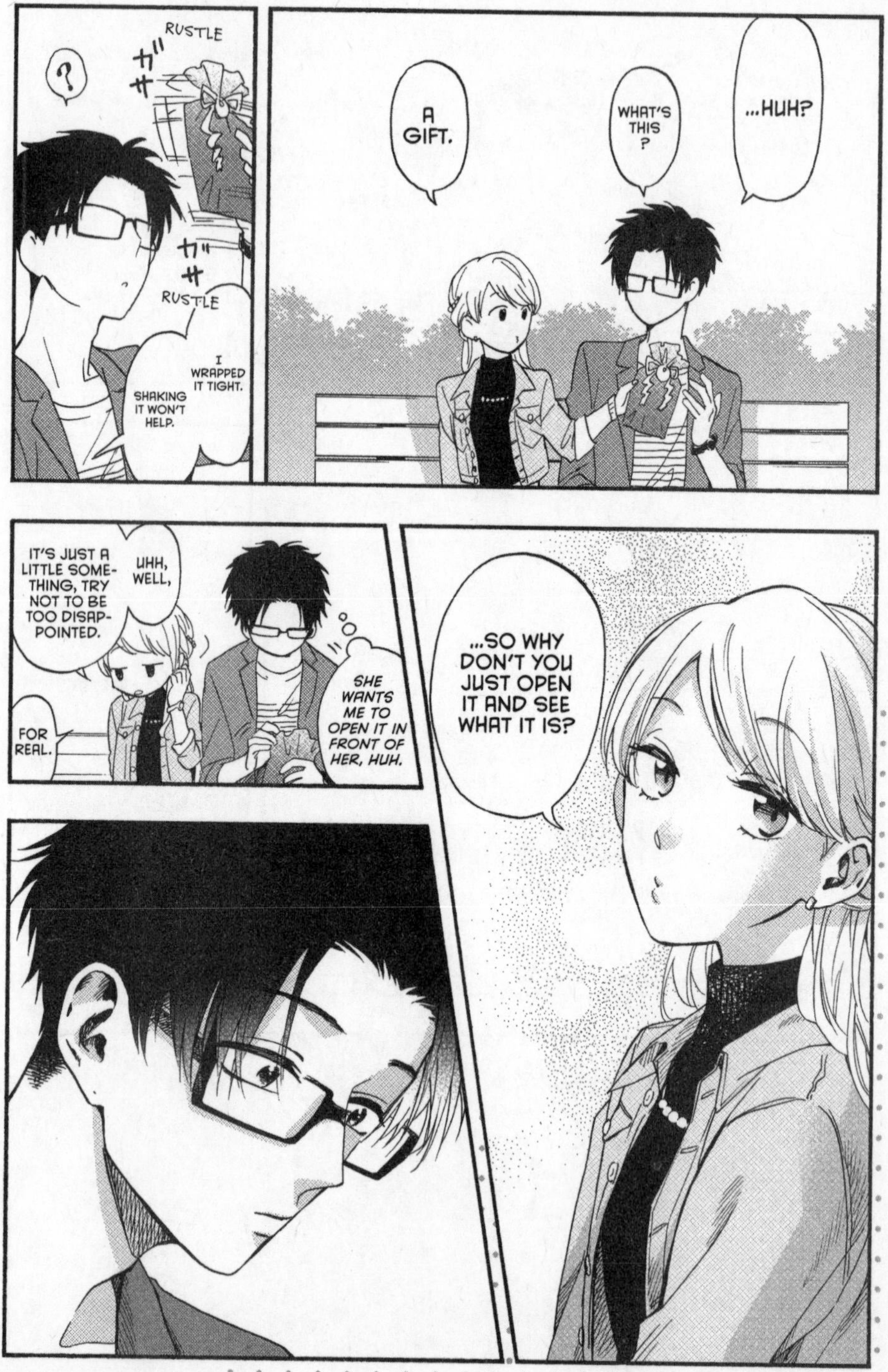
...HUH?
WHAT'S THIS ?
A GIFT.
?
RUSTLE
ガサ
ガサ
RUSTLE
I WRAPPED IT TIGHT.
SHAKING IT WON'T HELP.
...SO WHY DON'T YOU JUST OPEN IT AND SEE WHAT IT IS?
UHH, WELL,
IT'S JUST A LITTLE SOMETHING, TRY NOT TO BE TOO DISAPPOINTED.
SHE WANTS ME TO OPEN IT IN FRONT OF HER, HUH.
FOR REAL.

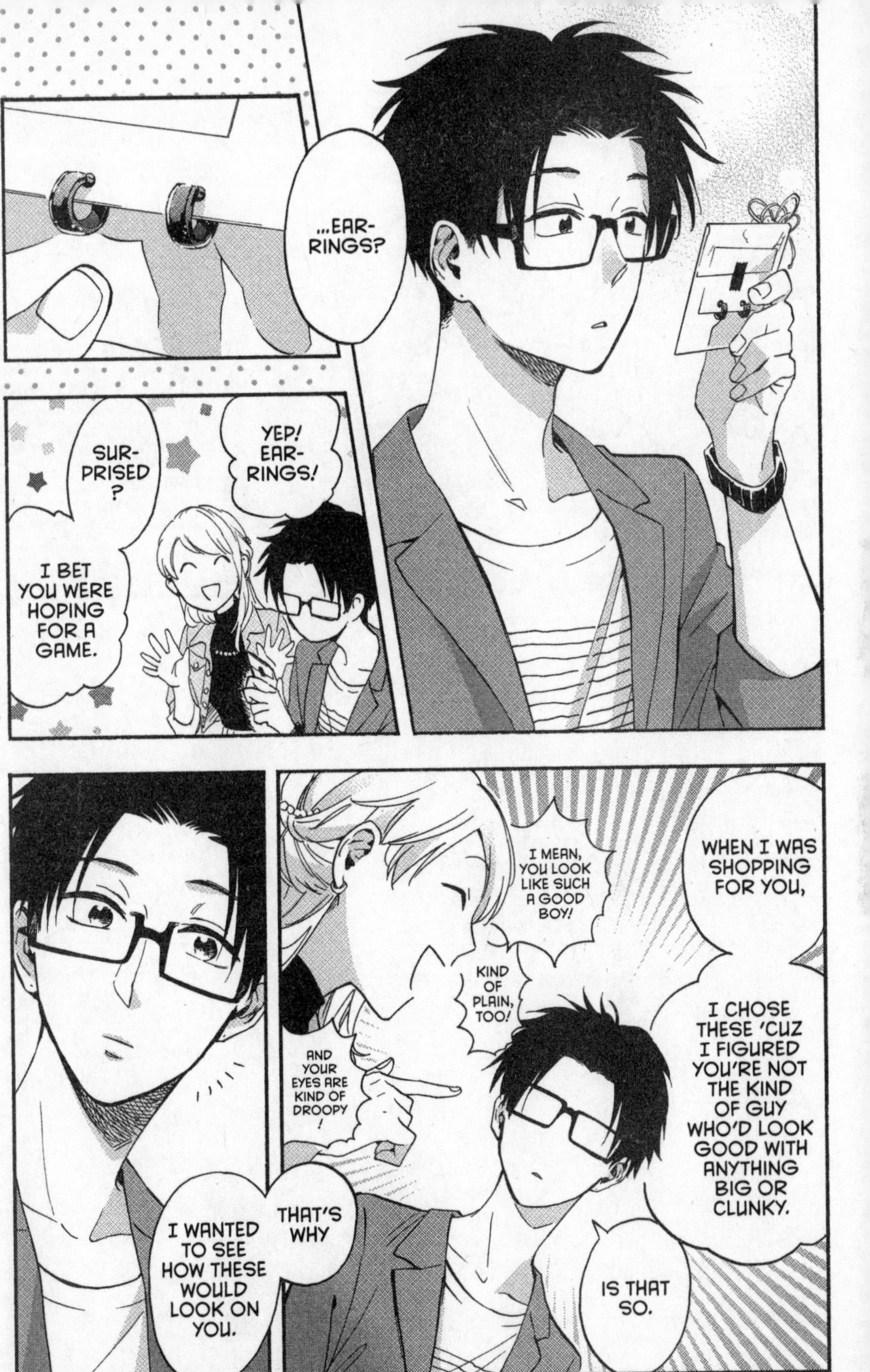
...EAR-RINGS?
YEP! EAR-RINGS!
SUR-PRISED?
I BET YOU WERE HOPING FOR A GAME.
WHEN I WAS SHOPPING FOR YOU,
I CHOSE THESE 'CUZ I FIGURED YOU'RE NOT THE KIND OF GUY WHO'D LOOK GOOD WITH ANYTHING BIG OR CLUNKY.
I MEAN, YOU LOOK LIKE SUCH A GOOD BOY!
KIND OF PLAIN, TOO!
AND YOUR EYES ARE KIND OF DROOPY!
IS THAT SO.
THAT'S WHY
I WANTED TO SEE HOW THESE WOULD LOOK ON YOU.

 (She doesn't pull punches)

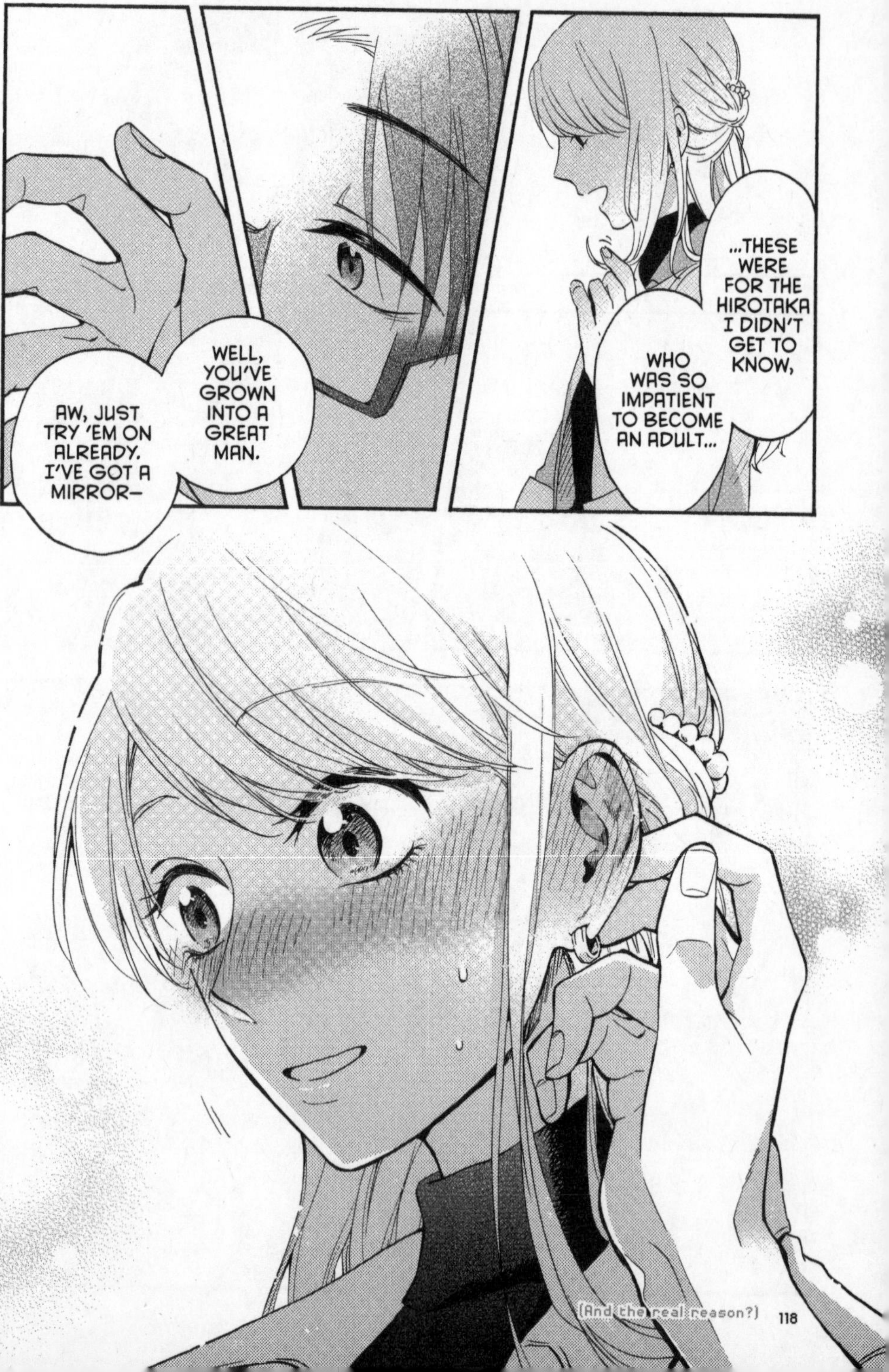
...THESE WERE FOR THE HIROTAKA I DIDN'T GET TO KNOW,
WHO WAS SO IMPATIENT TO BECOME AN ADULT...
WELL, YOU'VE GROWN INTO A GREAT MAN.
AW, JUST TRY 'EM ON ALREADY. I'VE GOT A MIRROR—

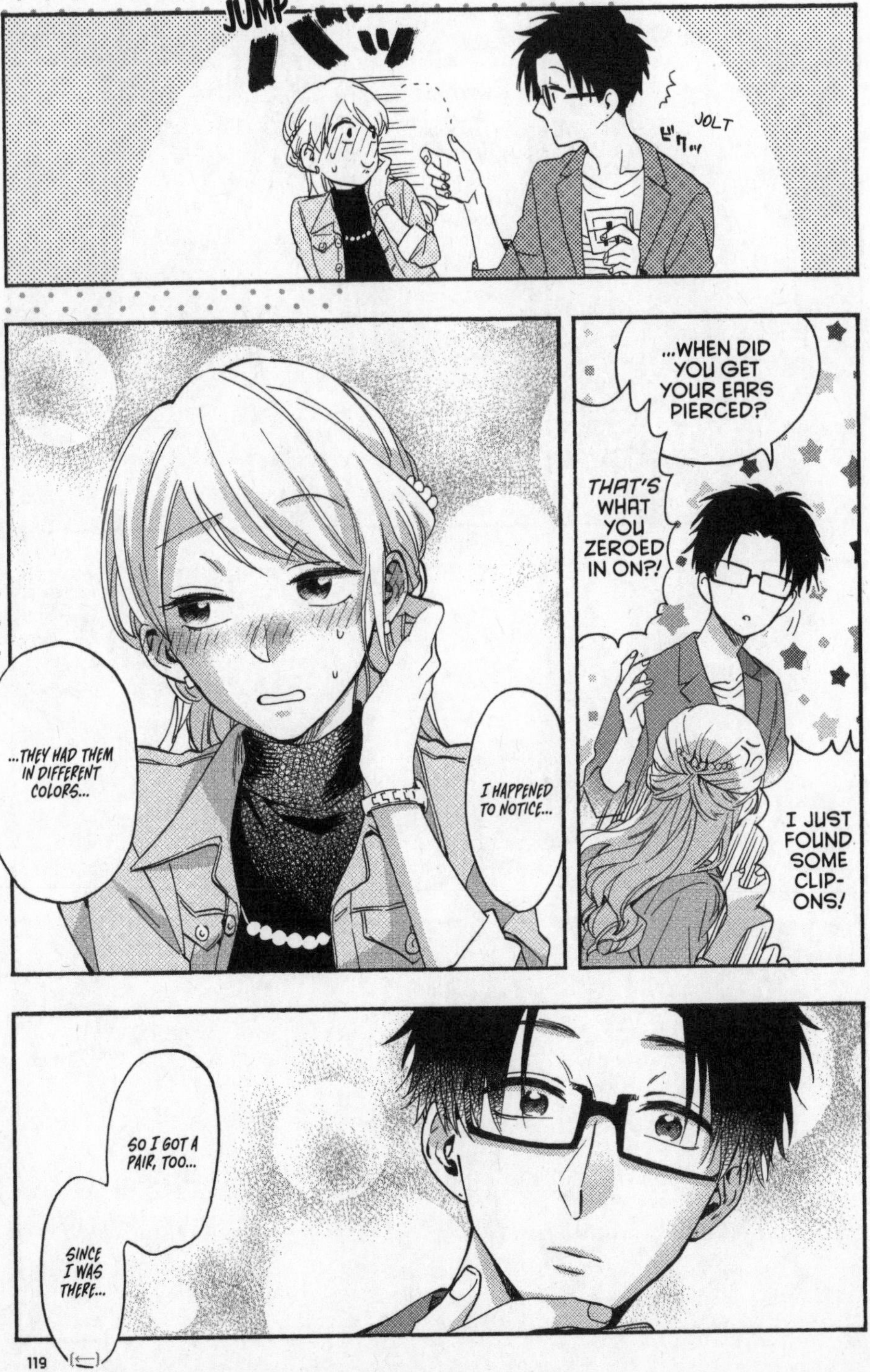

JUMP
バッ
JOLT
ビクッ
...WHEN DID YOU GET YOUR EARS PIERCED?
THAT'S WHAT YOU ZEROED IN ON?!
I JUST FOUND SOME CLIP-ONS!
I HAPPENED TO NOTICE...
...THEY HAD THEM IN DIFFERENT COLORS...
SO I GOT A PAIR, TOO...
SINCE I WAS THERE...

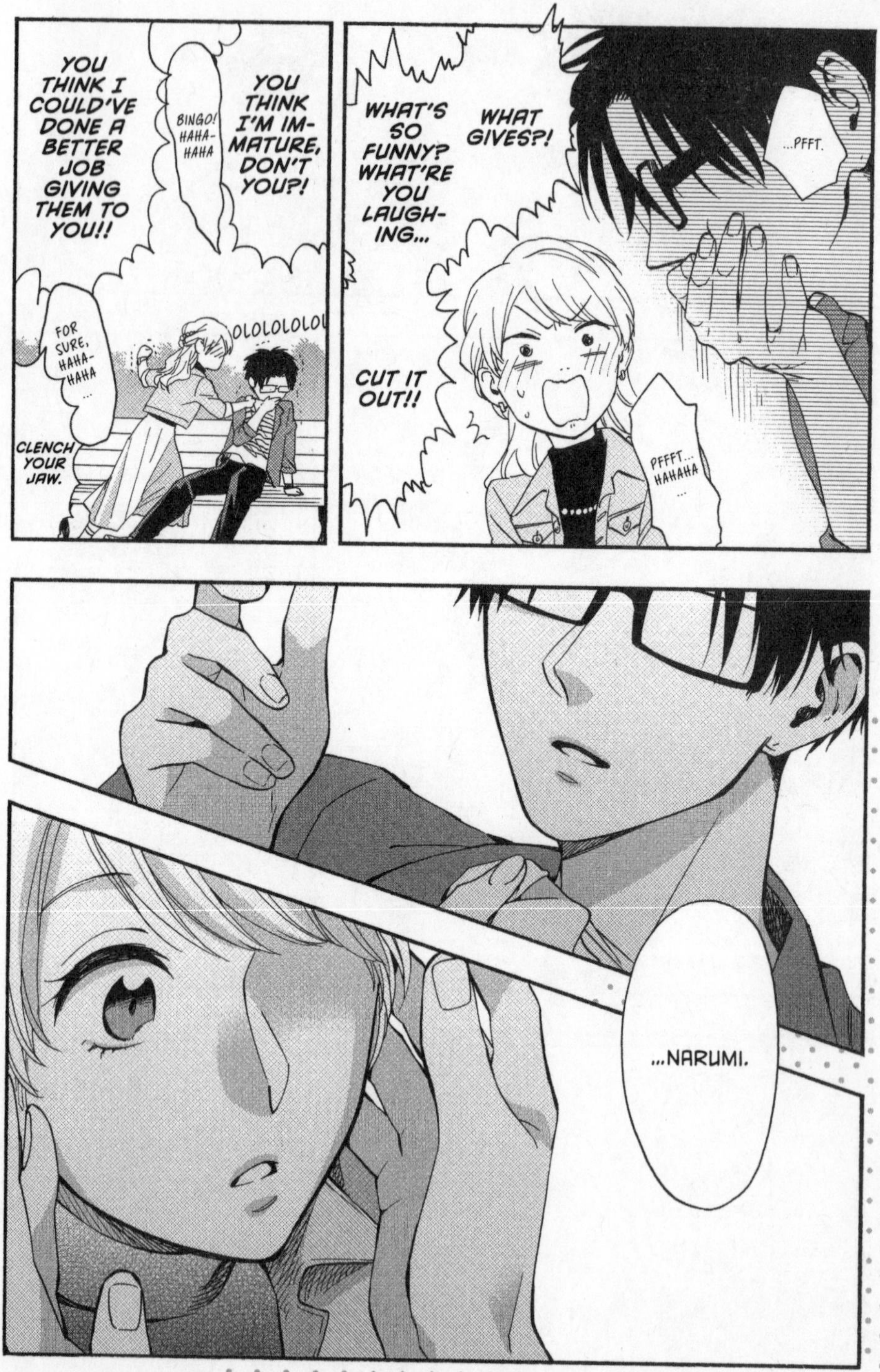
...PFFT.
WHAT GIVES?!
WHAT'S SO FUNNY? WHAT'RE YOU LAUGHING...
PFFFT... HAHAHA ...
CUT IT OUT!!
YOU THINK I'M IMMATURE, DON'T YOU?!
BINGO! HAHA-HAHA
YOU THINK I COULD'VE DONE A BETTER JOB GIVING THEM TO YOU!!
OLOLOLOLOL
FOR SURE, HAHA-HAHA ...
CLENCH YOUR JAW.
...NARUMI.

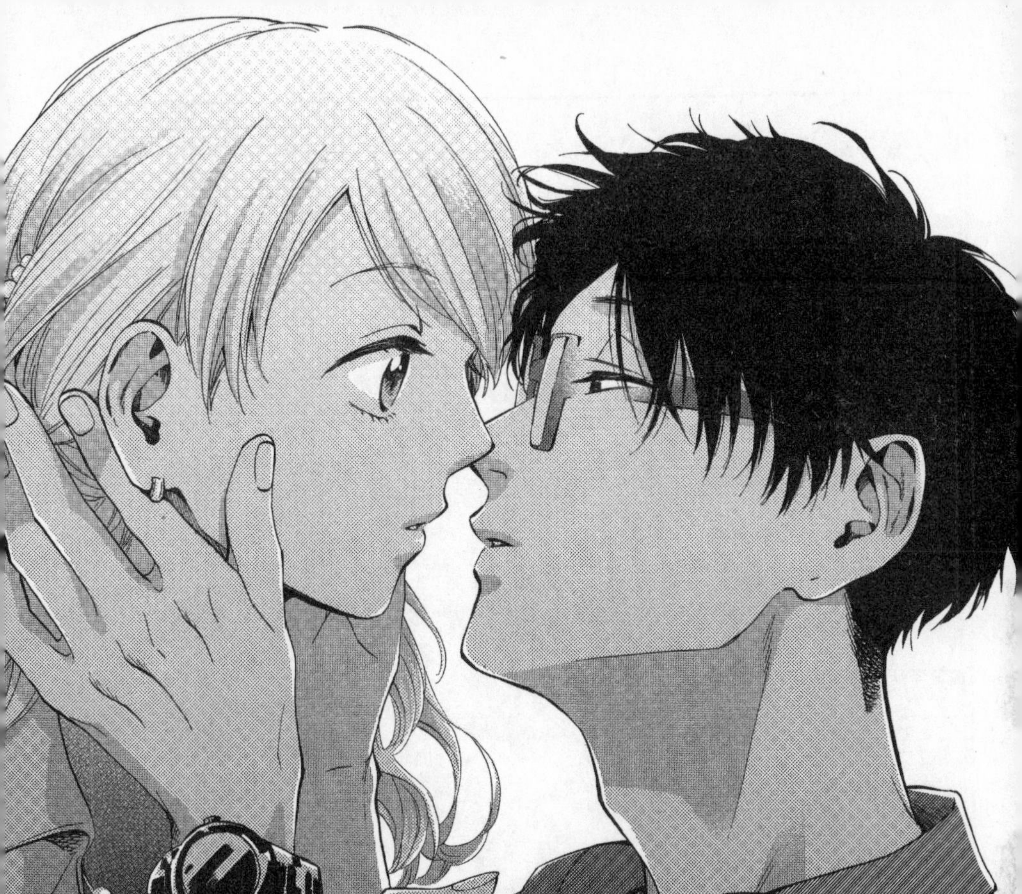
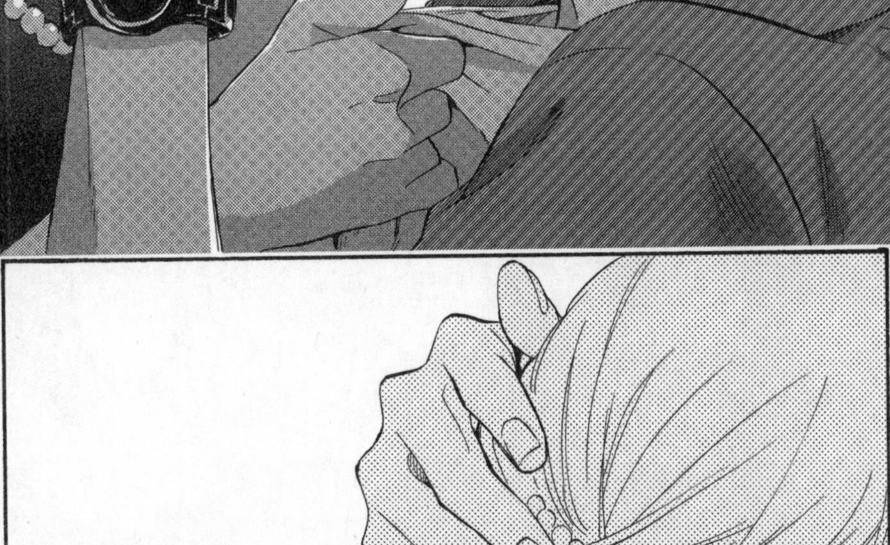

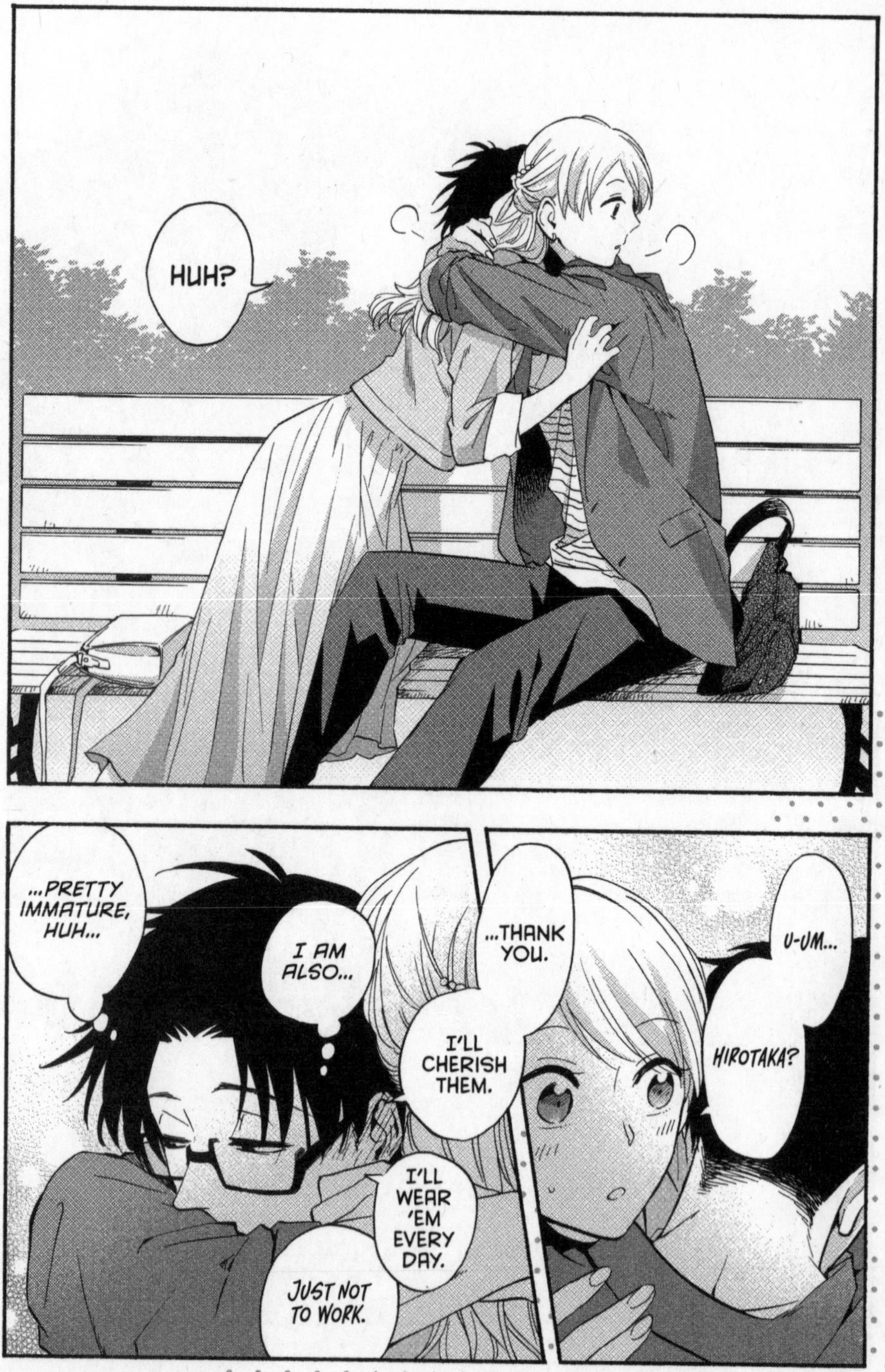
HUH?
U-UM...
HIROTAKA?
...THANK YOU.
I AM ALSO...
...PRETTY IMMATURE, HUH...
I'LL CHERISH THEM.
I'LL WEAR 'EM EVERY DAY.
JUST NOT TO WORK.

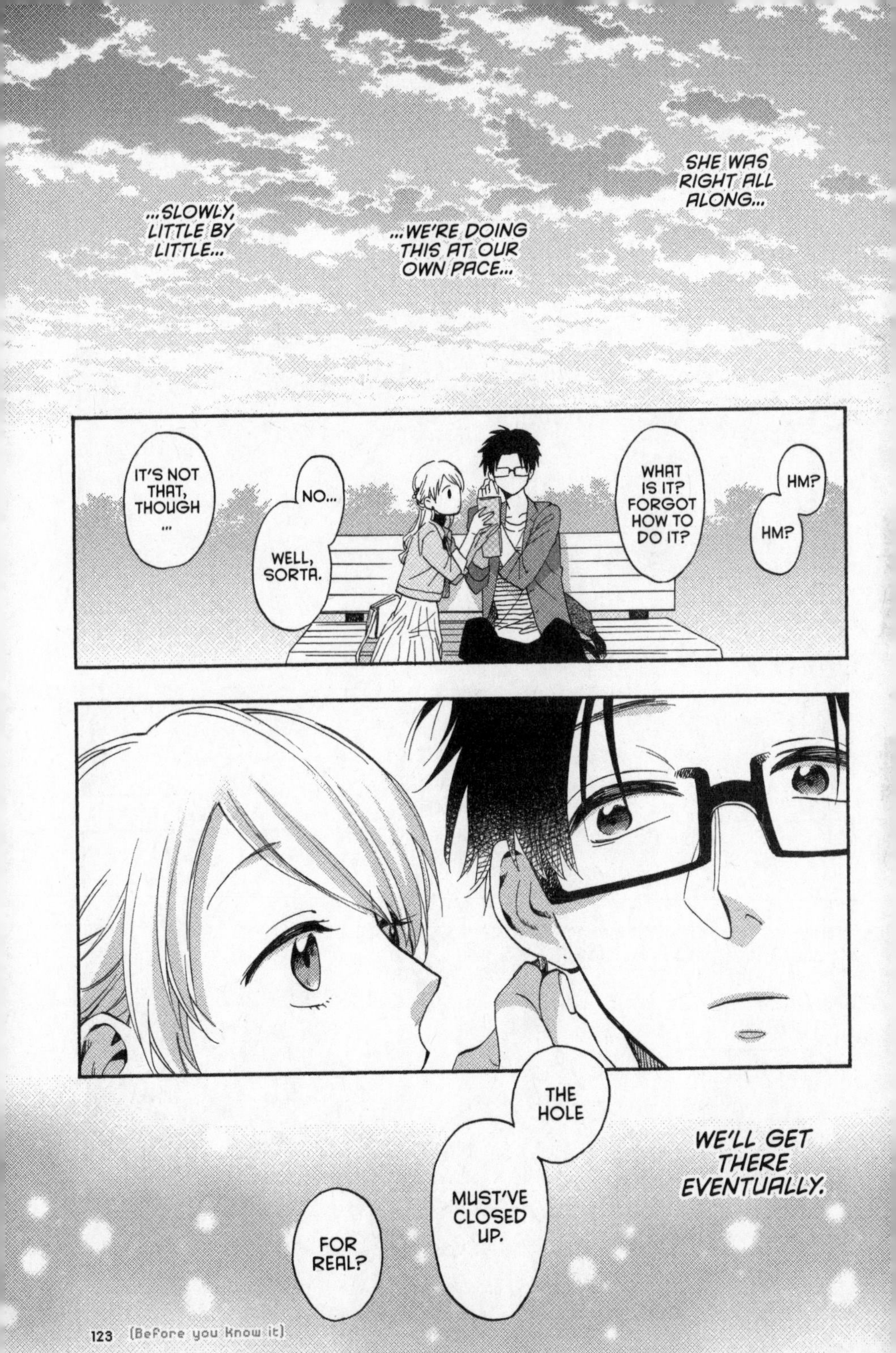
SHE WAS RIGHT ALL ALONG...
...WE'RE DOING THIS AT OUR OWN PACE...
...SLOWLY, LITTLE BY LITTLE...
HM?
HM?
WHAT IS IT? FORGOT HOW TO DO IT?
NO...
WELL, SORTA.
IT'S NOT THAT, THOUGH ...
THE HOLE
MUST'VE CLOSED UP.
FOR REAL?
WE'LL GET THERE EVENTUALLY.

Wotakoi: Love is Hard for Otaku

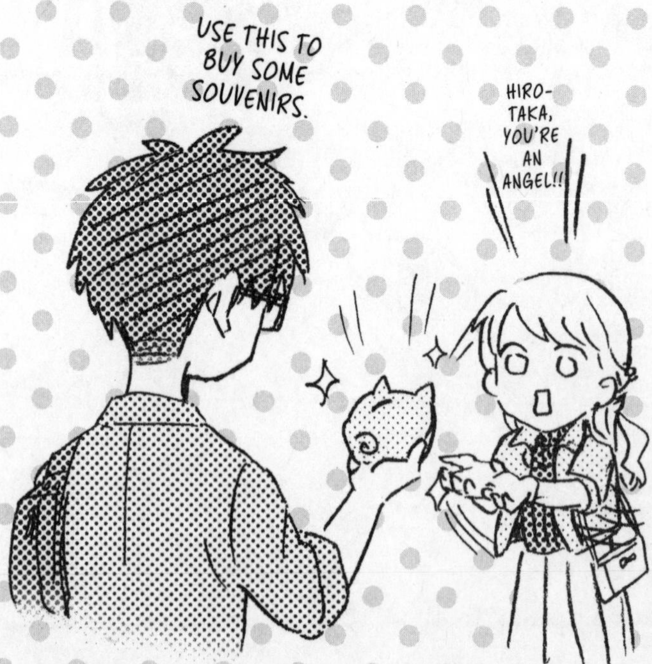
USE THIS TO BUY SOME SOUVENIRS.
HIRO-TAKA, YOU'RE AN ANGEL!!

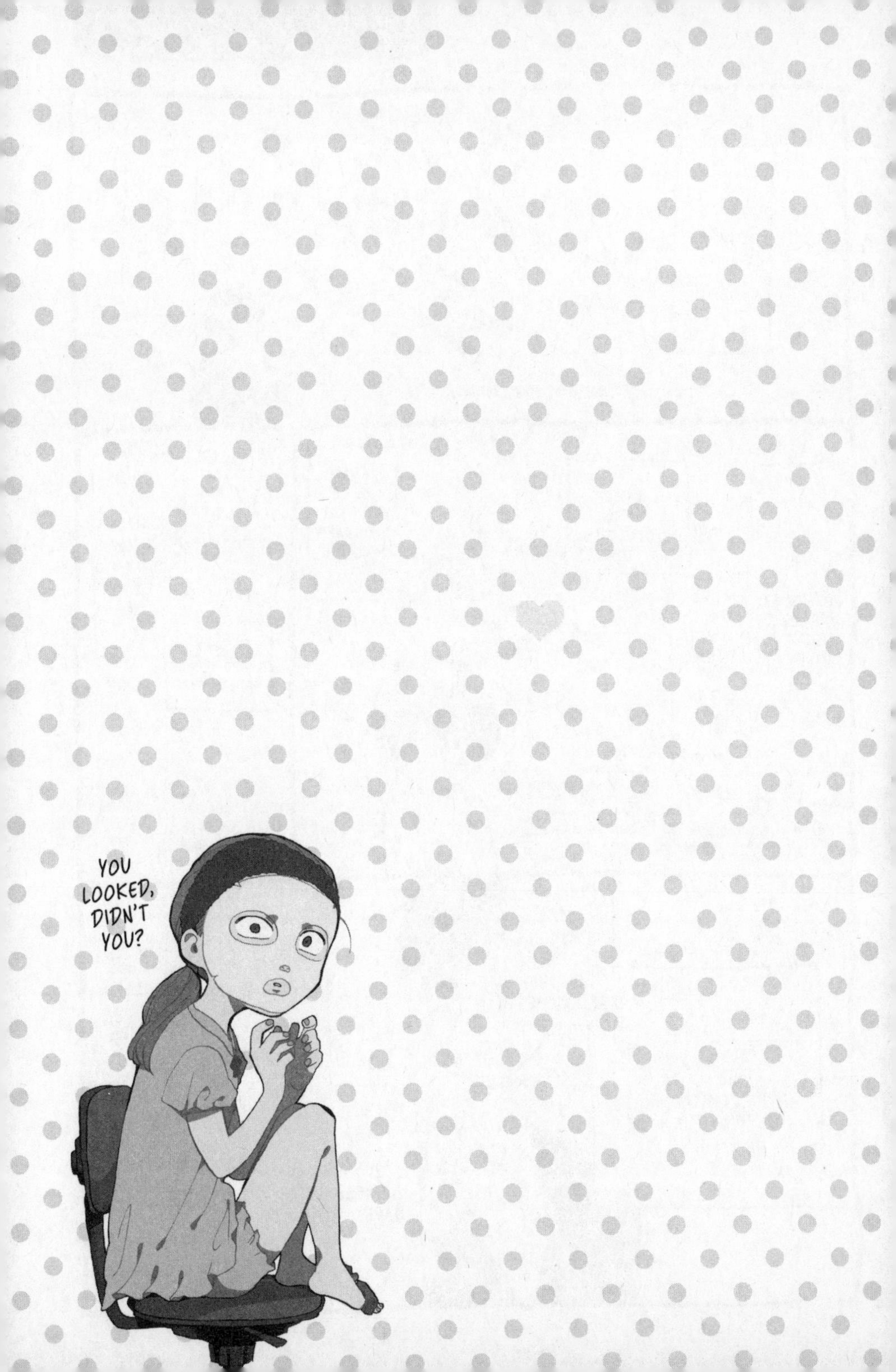
YOU LOOKED, DIDN'T YOU?

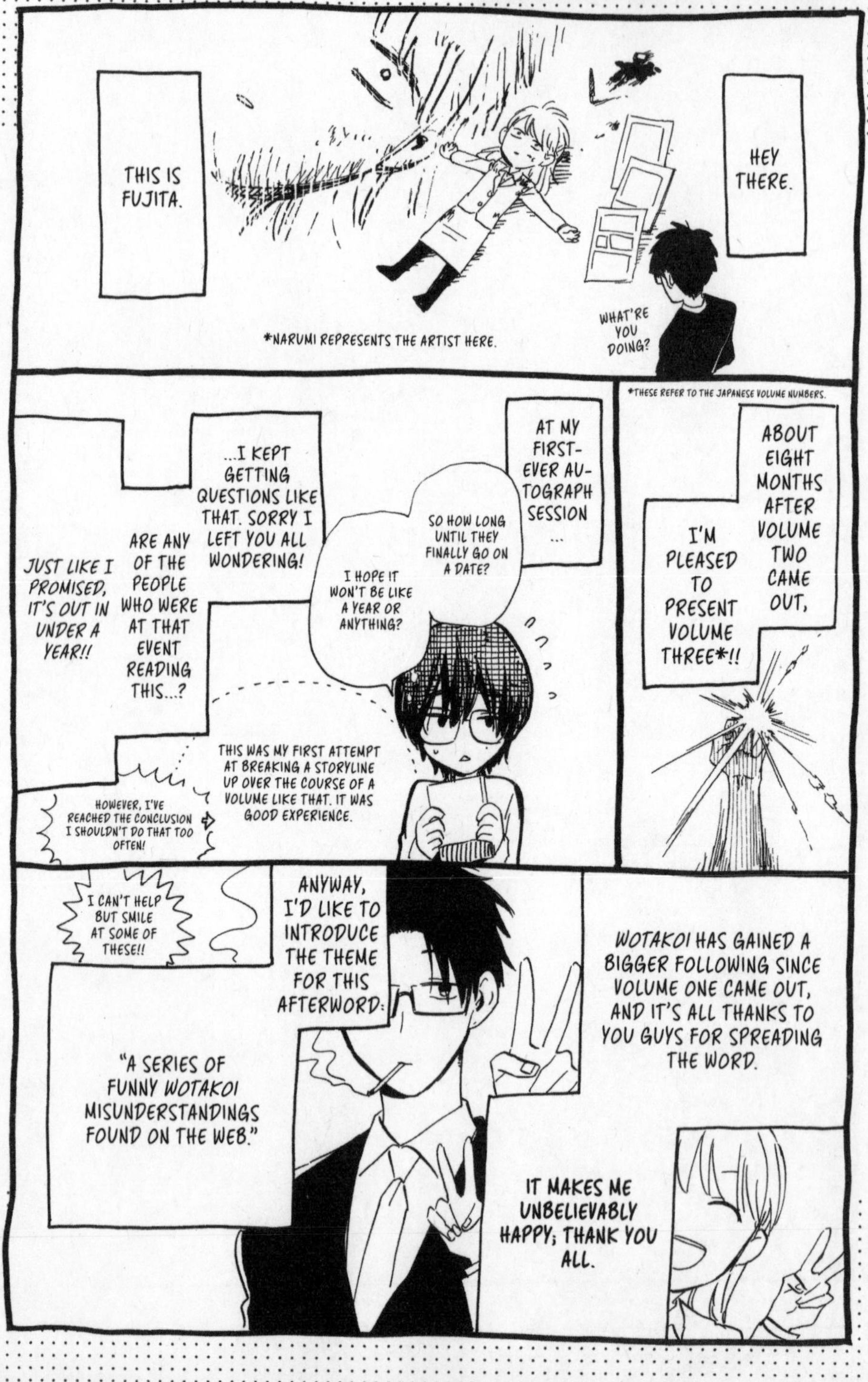
HEY THERE.
WHAT'RE YOU DOING?
THIS IS FUJITA.
*NARUMI REPRESENTS THE ARTIST HERE.
*THESE REFER TO THE JAPANESE VOLUME NUMBERS.
ABOUT EIGHT MONTHS AFTER VOLUME TWO CAME OUT,
I'M PLEASED TO PRESENT VOLUME THREE*!!
AT MY FIRST-EVER AUTOGRAPH SESSION...
SO HOW LONG UNTIL THEY FINALLY GO ON A DATE?
I HOPE IT WON'T BE LIKE A YEAR OR ANYTHING?
...I KEPT GETTING QUESTIONS LIKE THAT. SORRY I LEFT YOU ALL WONDERING!
ARE ANY OF THE PEOPLE WHO WERE AT THAT EVENT READING THIS...?
JUST LIKE I PROMISED, IT'S OUT IN UNDER A YEAR!!
THIS WAS MY FIRST ATTEMPT AT BREAKING A STORYLINE UP OVER THE COURSE OF A VOLUME LIKE THAT. IT WAS GOOD EXPERIENCE.
HOWEVER, I'VE REACHED THE CONCLUSION I SHOULDN'T DO THAT TOO OFTEN!
WOTAKOI HAS GAINED A BIGGER FOLLOWING SINCE VOLUME ONE CAME OUT, AND IT'S ALL THANKS TO YOU GUYS FOR SPREADING THE WORD.
IT MAKES ME UNBELIEVABLY HAPPY; THANK YOU ALL.
ANYWAY, I'D LIKE TO INTRODUCE THE THEME FOR THIS AFTERWORD:
I CAN'T HELP BUT SMILE AT SOME OF THESE!!
"A SERIES OF FUNNY WOTAKOI MISUNDERSTANDINGS FOUND ON THE WEB."

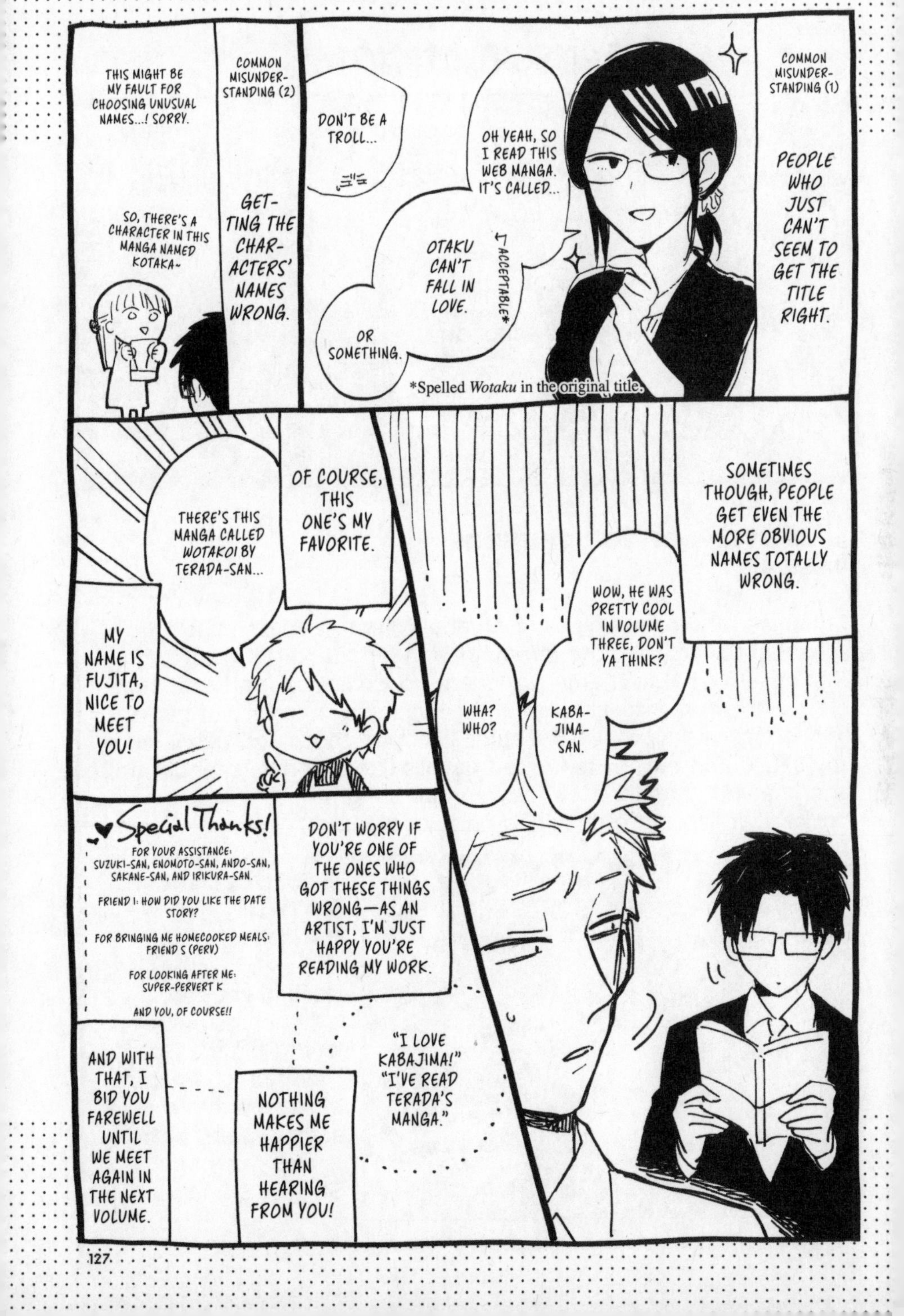
COMMON MISUNDER-STANDING (1)
PEOPLE WHO JUST CAN'T SEEM TO GET THE TITLE RIGHT.
OH YEAH, SO I READ THIS WEB MANGA. IT'S CALLED...
OTAKU CAN'T FALL IN LOVE.
OR SOMETHING.
ACCEPTABLE*
DON'T BE A TROLL...
*Spelled *Wotaku* in the original title.
COMMON MISUNDER-STANDING (2)
GET-TING THE CHAR-ACTERS' NAMES WRONG.
THIS MIGHT BE MY FAULT FOR CHOOSING UNUSUAL NAMES...! SORRY.
SO, THERE'S A CHARACTER IN THIS MANGA NAMED KOTAKA~
SOMETIMES THOUGH, PEOPLE GET EVEN THE MORE OBVIOUS NAMES TOTALLY WRONG.
WOW, HE WAS PRETTY COOL IN VOLUME THREE, DON'T YA THINK?
WHA? WHO?
KABA-JIMA-SAN.
OF COURSE, THIS ONE'S MY FAVORITE.
THERE'S THIS MANGA CALLED WOTAKOI BY TERADA-SAN...
MY NAME IS FUJITA, NICE TO MEET YOU!
DON'T WORRY IF YOU'RE ONE OF THE ONES WHO GOT THESE THINGS WRONG—AS AN ARTIST, I'M JUST HAPPY YOU'RE READING MY WORK.
Special Thanks!
FOR YOUR ASSISTANCE: SUZUKI-SAN, ENOMOTO-SAN, ANDO-SAN, SAKANE-SAN, AND IRIKURA-SAN.
FRIEND I: HOW DID YOU LIKE THE DATE STORY?
FOR BRINGING ME HOMECOOKED MEALS: FRIEND S (PERV)
FOR LOOKING AFTER ME: SUPER-PERVERT K
AND YOU, OF COURSE!!
"I LOVE KABAJIMA!" "I'VE READ TERADA'S MANGA."
NOTHING MAKES ME HAPPIER THAN HEARING FROM YOU!
AND WITH THAT, I BID YOU FAREWELL UNTIL WE MEET AGAIN IN THE NEXT VOLUME.

TRANSLATION NOTES

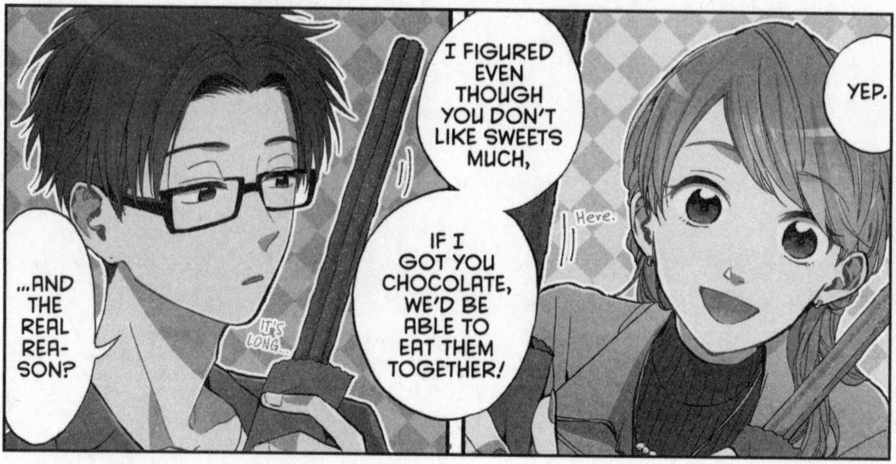
YEP.
Here.
I FIGURED EVEN THOUGH YOU DON'T LIKE SWEETS MUCH,
IF I GOT YOU CHOCOLATE, WE'D BE ABLE TO EAT THEM TOGETHER!
IT'S LONG...
...AND THE REAL REA-SON?

▲ LIMITED-EDITION CHURROS, PAGE 4

Japanese food companies are all about limited-edition and seasonal flavors, like the infamous and infinite varieties of Japanese Kit-Kats. Theme parks are no exception, and a certain mouse-themed amusement center has its own variety of park-only popcorn flavors, with staples like milk chocolate, curry, and soy sauce and butter, to limited flavors like coconut, cappuccino, and jalapeño and cheese. They can be bought in collectable buckets, which are redesigned on a yearly basis.

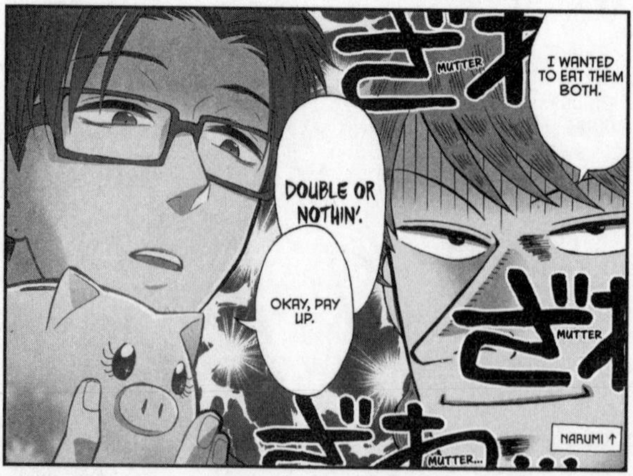
I WANTED TO EAT THEM BOTH.
ざわ
MUTTER
DOUBLE OR NOTHIN'.
OKAY, PAY UP.
ざわ
MUTTER
NARUMI ↑
ざわ…
MUTTER...

◀ DOUBLE OR NOTHIN', PAGE 5

Narumi is quoting a signature phrase from Shigeru Akagi, the main character of manga and anime series *Akagi*. Narumi is also drawn in Shigeru's image.

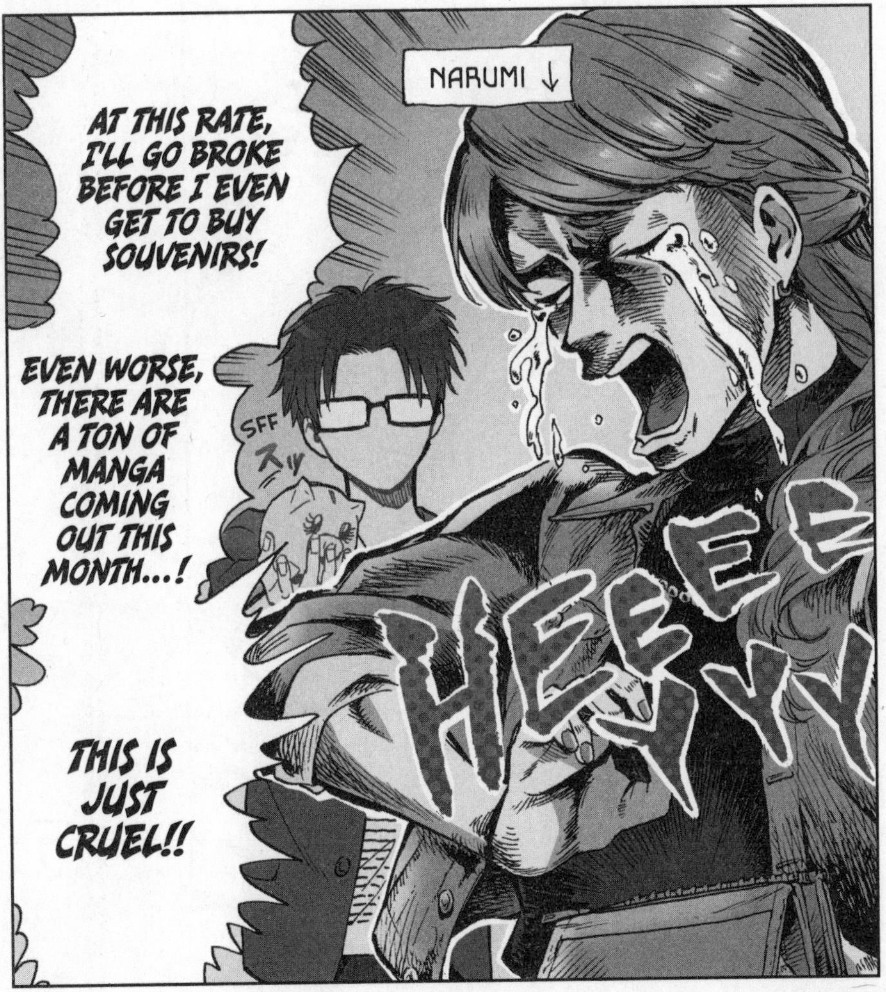
NARUMI ↓
AT THIS RATE, I'LL GO BROKE BEFORE I EVEN GET TO BUY SOUVENIRS!
EVEN WORSE, THERE ARE A TON OF MANGA COMING OUT THIS MONTH...!
THIS IS JUST CRUEL!!
SFF
スッ

▲ HEYYYY,
PAGE 5

This line is from a chapter of the manga *JoJo's Bizarre Adventure*. Narumi is also drawn in the manga's style.

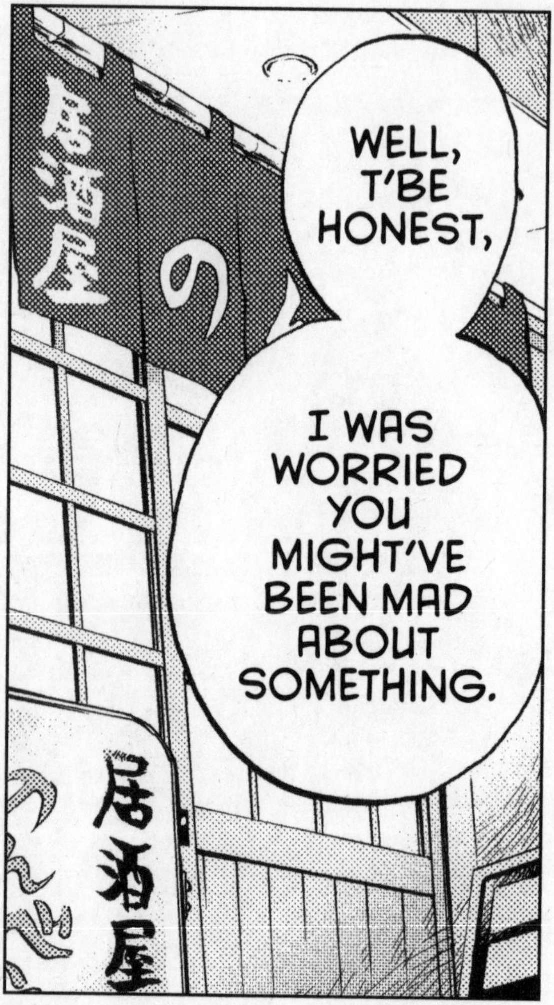
WELL, T'BE HONEST,
I WAS WORRIED YOU MIGHT'VE BEEN MAD ABOUT SOMETHING.
居酒屋の
居酒屋

▲ IZAKAYA, PAGE 20

A style of casual Japanese pub that is popular for after-work social drinking. In addition to alcohol, they also serve small plates of bar food that parties typically share together, similar to a tapas bar. Dishes tend to be ordered one or two at a time instead of all at once, so the pace is much slower than a typical Western pub or tavern.

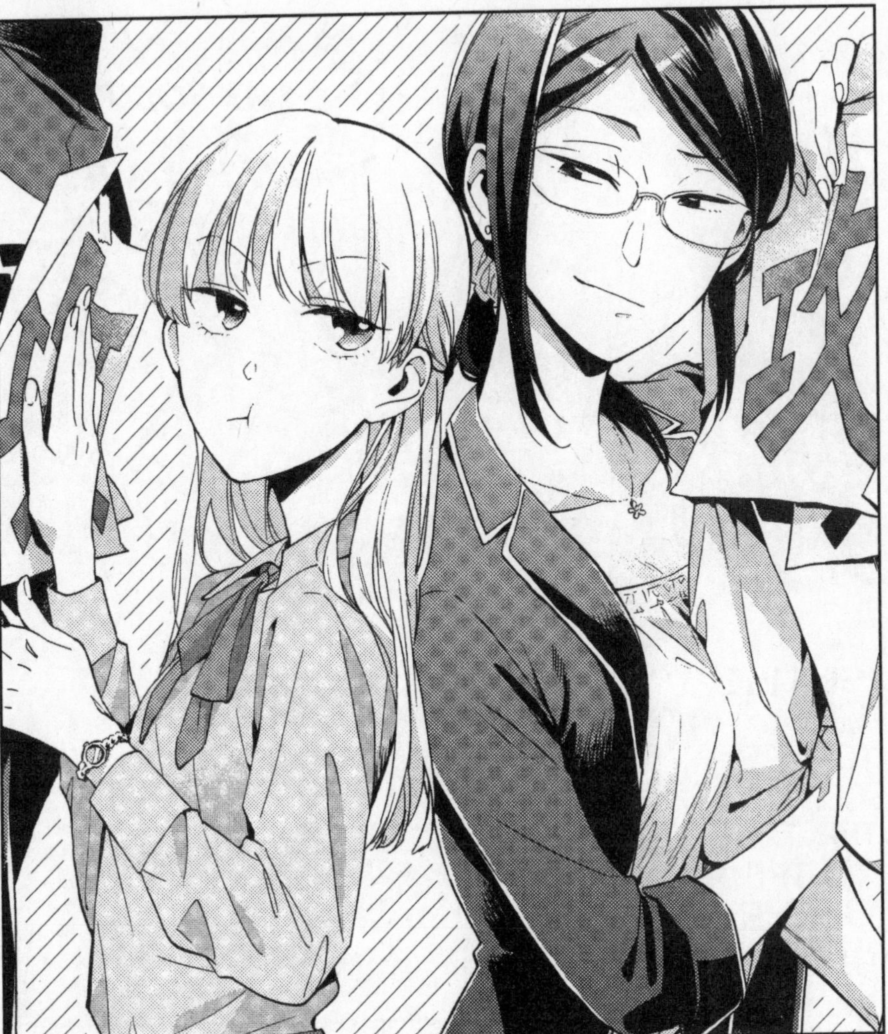
攻

▲ *SEME/UKE*,
PAGE 29

As mentioned in the last volume, *seme* and *uke* refer to respective roles in a BL pairing. The *seme* (short for *semeru*, "to chase") is the dominant partner, and the *uke* (short for *ukeru*, "to receive") is the submissive partner. When talking about a pairing or a ship, the name that comes first denotes the dominant partner and the latter signifies the submissive partner.

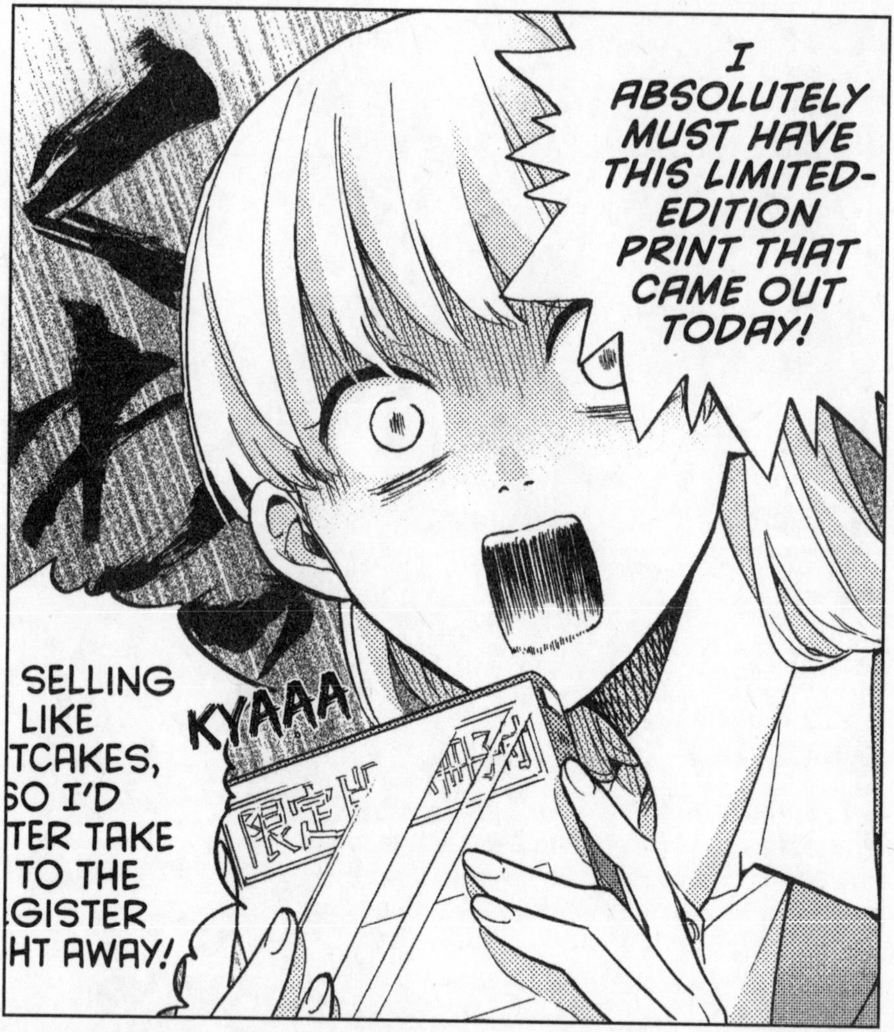
I ABSOLUTELY MUST HAVE THIS LIMITED-EDITION PRINT THAT CAME OUT TODAY!
KYAAA
SELLING LIKE TCAKES, SO I'D TER TAKE TO THE GISTER HT AWAY!

▲ LIMITED-EDITION MAGAZINE, PAGE 53

In Japan, manga usually comes out chapter by chapter in multi-series magazine collections that are published on a weekly or monthly basis. These magazines may include full-size color pages, and may be bundled with special collectibles not available anywhere else. And once they're gone, they're gone—thus Narumi's urgency!

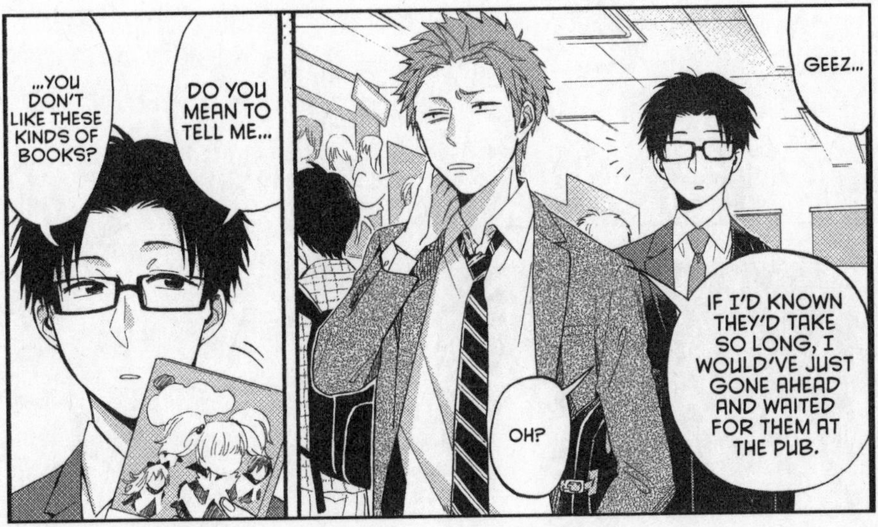
GEEZ...
IF I'D KNOWN THEY'D TAKE SO LONG, I WOULD'VE JUST GONE AHEAD AND WAITED FOR THEM AT THE PUB.
OH?
DO YOU MEAN TO TELL ME...
...YOU DON'T LIKE THESE KINDS OF BOOKS?

(Yuri Yurara)

**▲ YURI YURARA,
PAGE 54**

An abbreviation of "*Yuriyurarararayuruyuri Daijiken*" ("The Great *YuriYurararaYuruYuri* Incident"), this is the opening theme song for the anime *Yuru Yuri,* which originated as a manga. This slice-of-life series features a group of female friends in middle school who form an Amusement Club. Several of the main characters have crushes on each other, and so the series has *yuri* leanings much as the title suggests.

**NO-FACE,
PAGE 56**

No-Face is one of the main characters of the Hayao Miyazaki anime film *Spirited Away*—a shadowy masked figure, who happens to look very similar to a shocked Hirotaka.

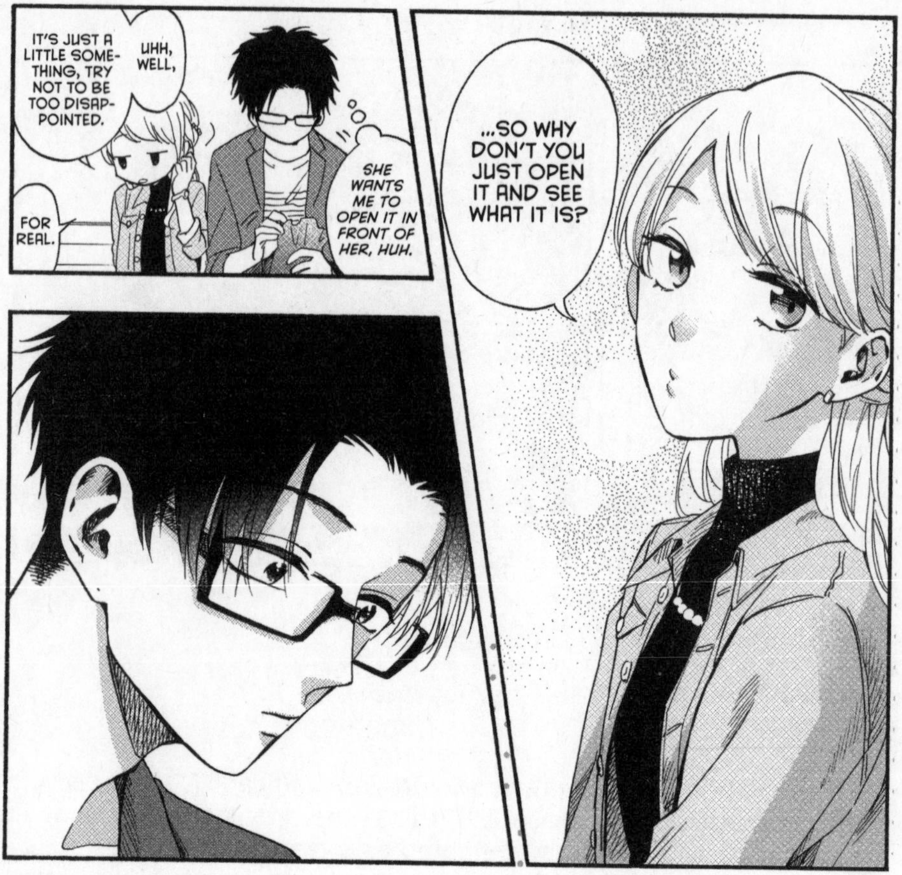
...SO WHY DON'T YOU JUST OPEN IT AND SEE WHAT IT IS?
UHH, WELL,
IT'S JUST A LITTLE SOME-THING, TRY NOT TO BE TOO DISAP-POINTED.
SHE WANTS ME TO OPEN IT IN FRONT OF HER, HUH.
FOR REAL.

(Is it a New Year's gift?)

▲ NEW YEAR'S GIFT, PAGE 116

New Year's Day is a major holiday in Japan, and it is customary for parents and other relatives to give children money inside decorated paper envelopes. The more ornate envelopes look similar to the way Narumi wrapped Hirotaka's gift.

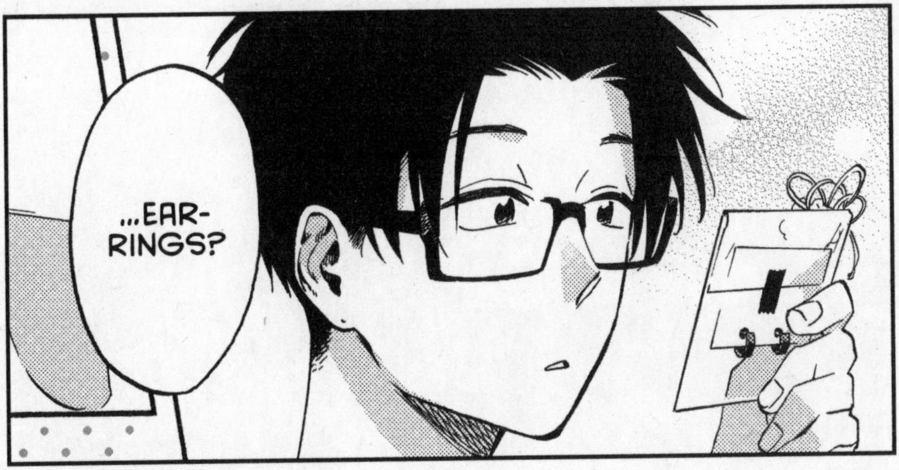
...EAR-
RINGS?

▲ COUPLE EARRINGS, PAGE 117

Couples matching portions or all of their outfits to each other is a trend in Japan, and the *Wotakoi* couples are no exception. Earrings are not as common as necklaces (as Hanako and Taro have), but are a sign from Narumi that she'd like to show some outward solidarity with Hirotaka. It's also not uncommon to buy and wear matching accessories on theme park dates, as seen on both couples: Narumi and Hirotaka on page 50, and Hanako and Taro on page 84.

WOTAKOI:

LOVE IS HARD FOR OTAKU

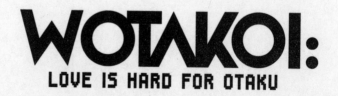

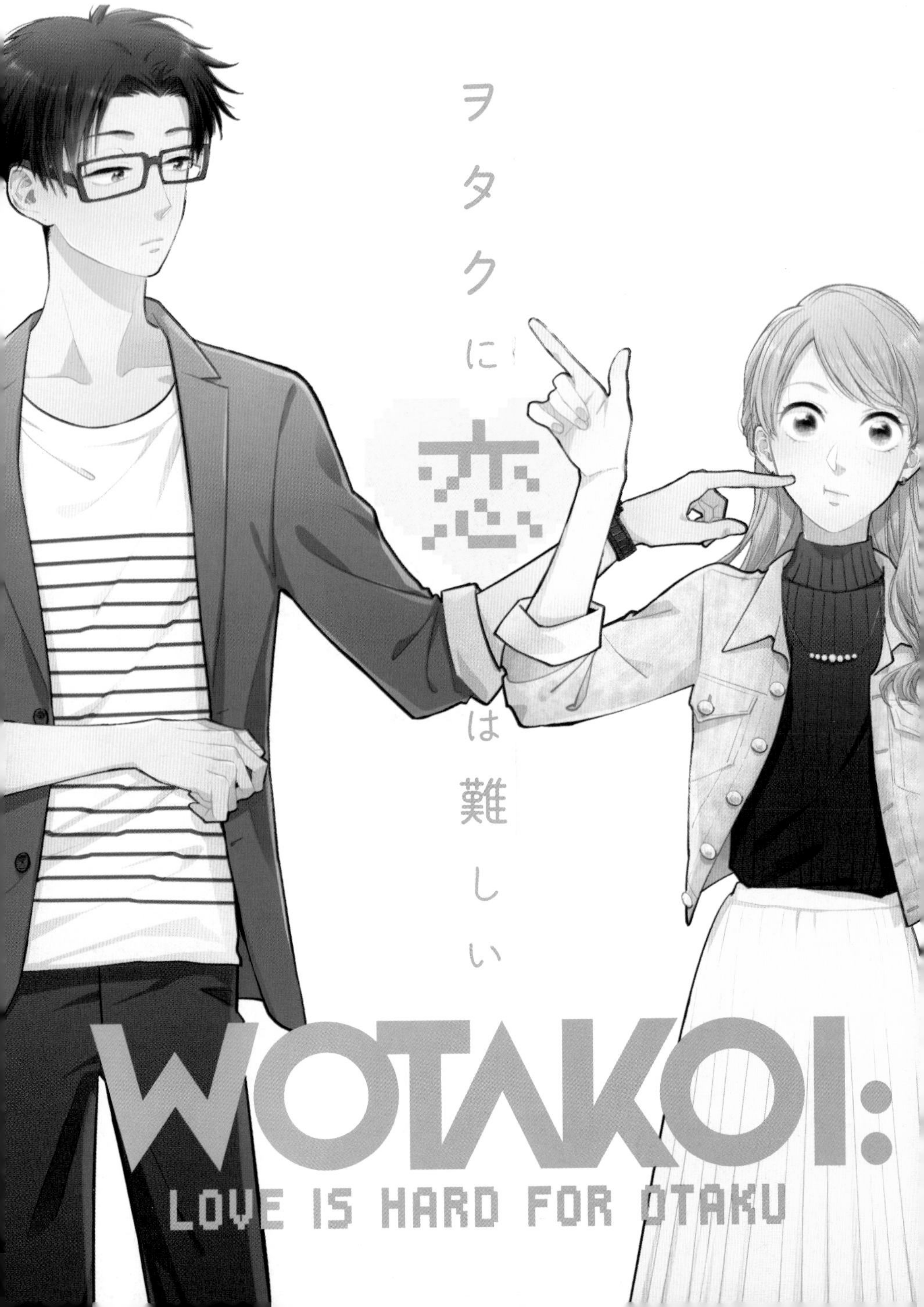
ヲタクに恋は難しい
WOTAKOI:
LOVE IS HARD FOR OTAKU

WOTAKOI:
LOVE IS HARD FOR OTAKU

FUJITA

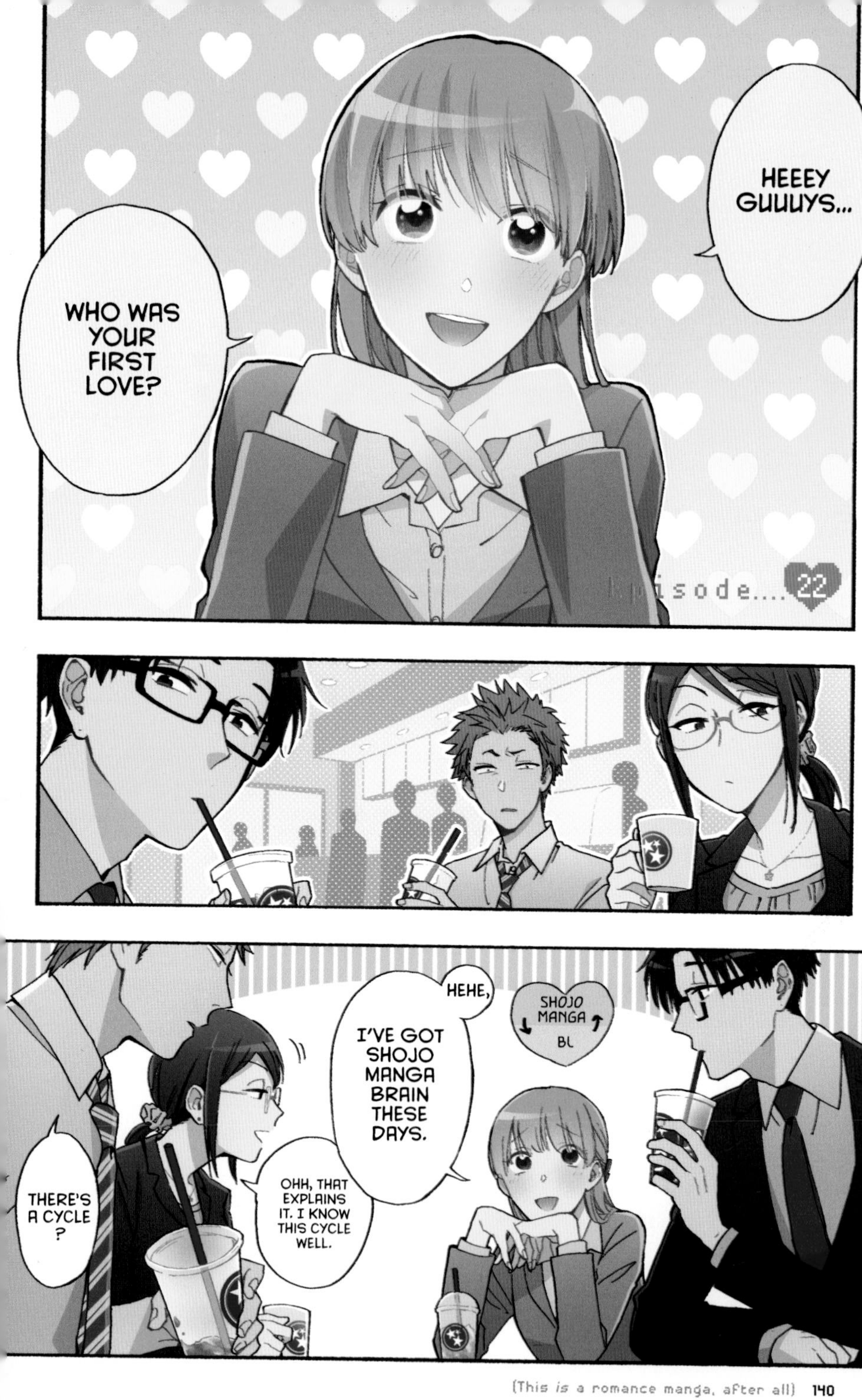
HEEEY GUUUYS...
WHO WAS YOUR FIRST LOVE?
Episode.... 22
SHOJO MANGA BL
HEHE,
I'VE GOT SHOJO MANGA BRAIN THESE DAYS.
OHH, THAT EXPLAINS IT. I KNOW THIS CYCLE WELL.
THERE'S A CYCLE ?

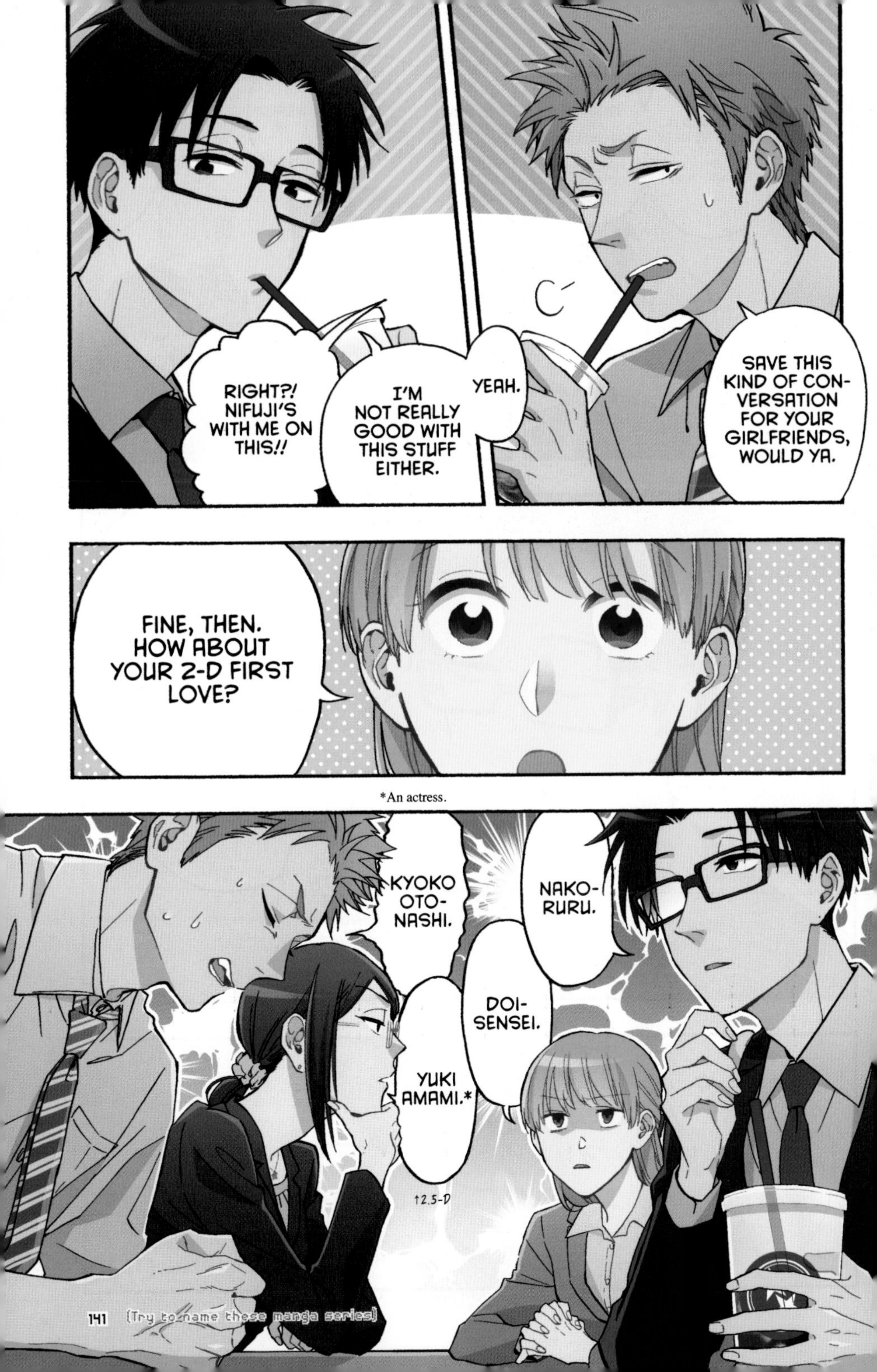
SAVE THIS KIND OF CON-VERSATION FOR YOUR GIRLFRIENDS, WOULD YA.
YEAH.
I'M NOT REALLY GOOD WITH THIS STUFF EITHER.
RIGHT?! NIFUJI'S WITH ME ON THIS!!
FINE, THEN. HOW ABOUT YOUR 2-D FIRST LOVE?
NAKO-RURU.
KYOKO OTO-NASHI.
DOI-SENSEI.
YUKI AMAMI.*
↑2.5-D

*An actress.

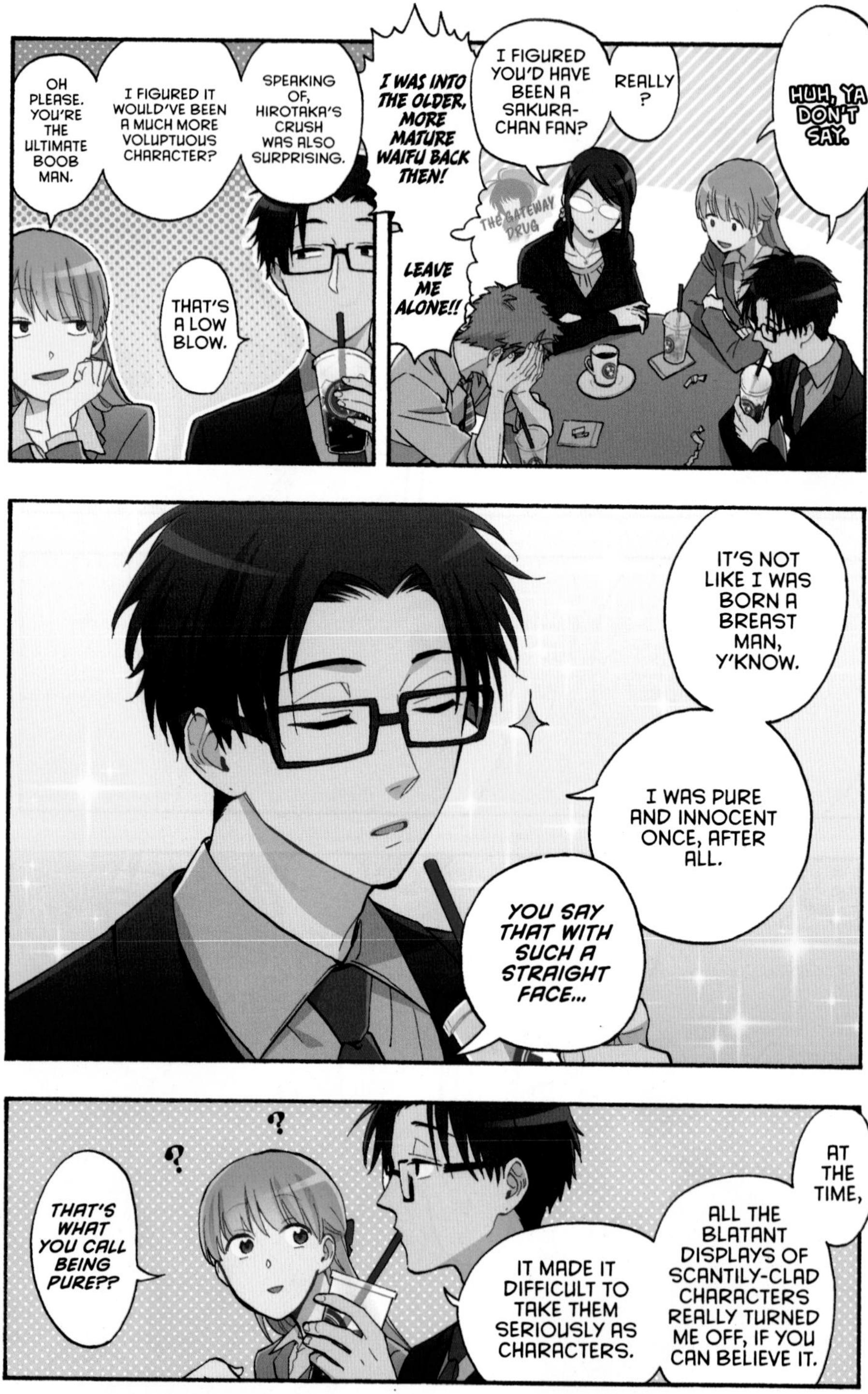
HUH, YA DON'T SAY.
REALLY?
I FIGURED YOU'D HAVE BEEN A SAKURA-CHAN FAN?
I WAS INTO THE OLDER, MORE MATURE WAIFU BACK THEN!
THE GATEWAY DRUG
LEAVE ME ALONE!!
SPEAKING OF, HIROTAKA'S CRUSH WAS ALSO SURPRISING.
I FIGURED IT WOULD'VE BEEN A MUCH MORE VOLUPTUOUS CHARACTER?
OH PLEASE. YOU'RE THE ULTIMATE BOOB MAN.
THAT'S A LOW BLOW.
IT'S NOT LIKE I WAS BORN A BREAST MAN, Y'KNOW.
I WAS PURE AND INNOCENT ONCE, AFTER ALL.
YOU SAY THAT WITH SUCH A STRAIGHT FACE...
AT THE TIME,
ALL THE BLATANT DISPLAYS OF SCANTILY-CLAD CHARACTERS REALLY TURNED ME OFF, IF YOU CAN BELIEVE IT.
IT MADE IT DIFFICULT TO TAKE THEM SERIOUSLY AS CHARACTERS.
THAT'S WHAT YOU CALL BEING PURE??

(The worries of an adolescent boy)

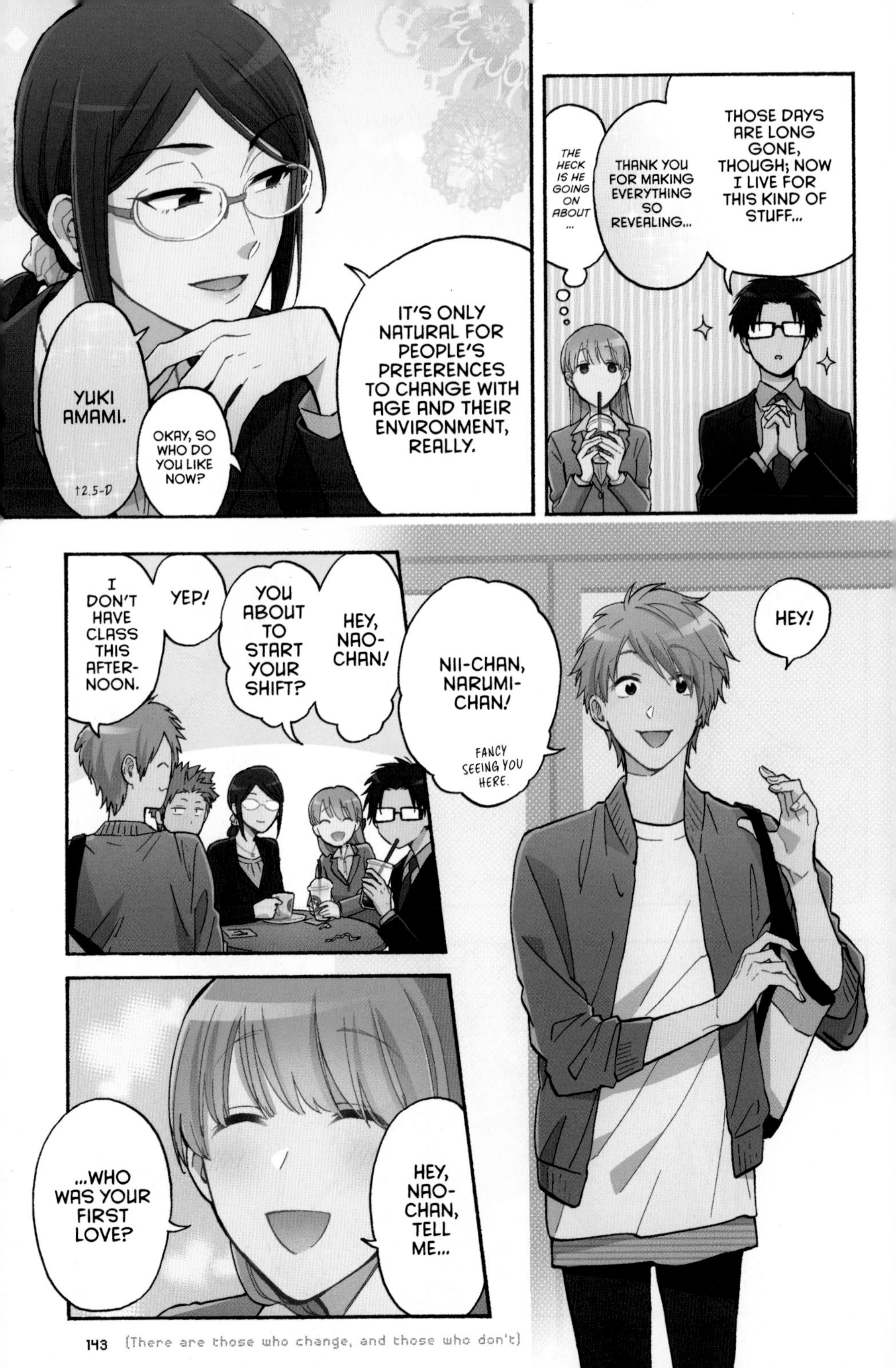
THOSE DAYS ARE LONG GONE, THOUGH; NOW I LIVE FOR THIS KIND OF STUFF...
THANK YOU FOR MAKING EVERYTHING SO REVEALING...
THE HECK IS HE GOING ON ABOUT...
IT'S ONLY NATURAL FOR PEOPLE'S PREFERENCES TO CHANGE WITH AGE AND THEIR ENVIRONMENT, REALLY.
OKAY, SO WHO DO YOU LIKE NOW?
YUKI AMAMI.
↑2.5-D
HEY!
NII-CHAN, NARUMI-CHAN!
FANCY SEEING YOU HERE.
HEY, NAO-CHAN!
YOU ABOUT TO START YOUR SHIFT?
YEP!
I DON'T HAVE CLASS THIS AFTERNOON.
HEY, NAO-CHAN, TELL ME...
...WHO WAS YOUR FIRST LOVE?

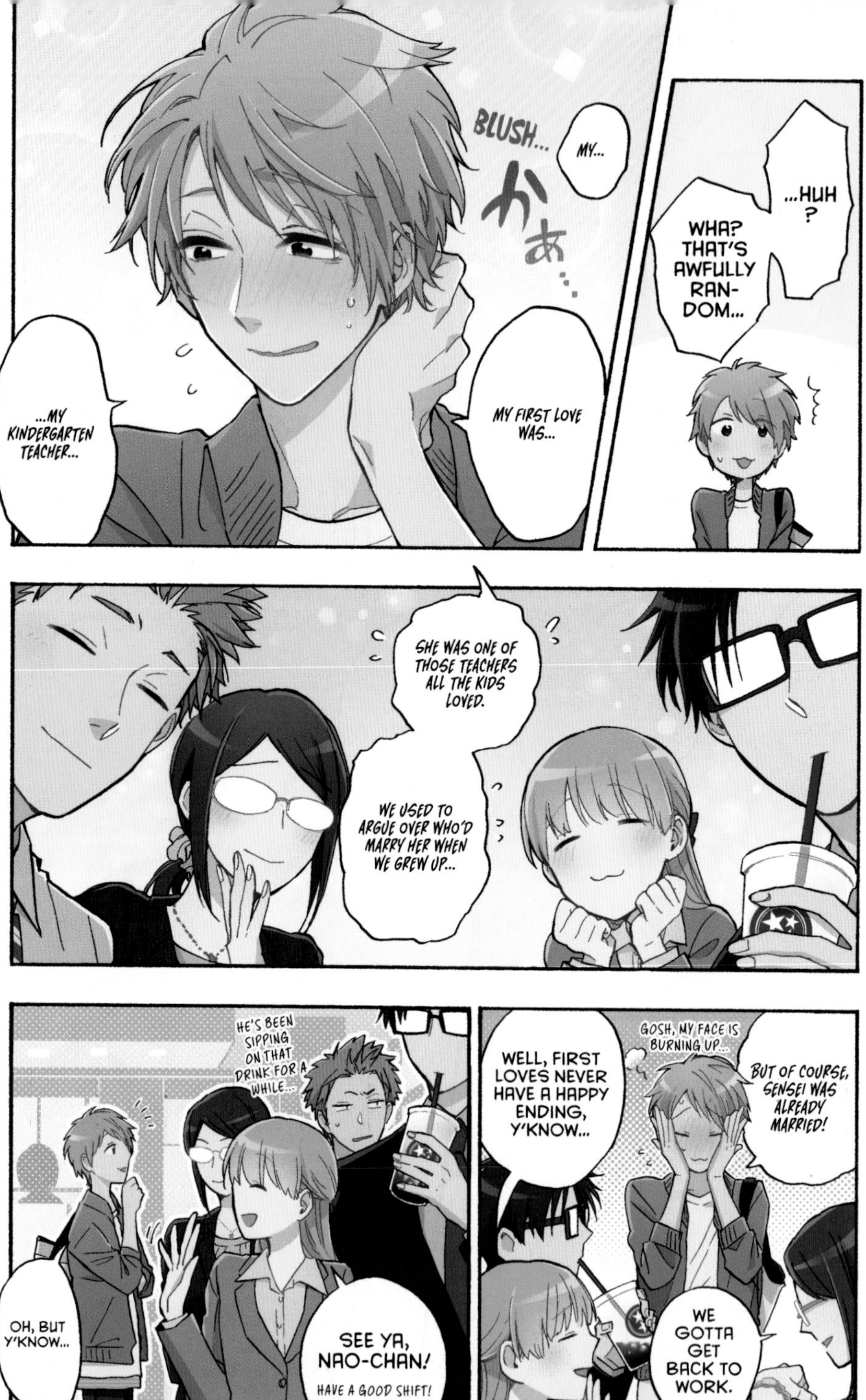
...HUH ?
WHA? THAT'S AWFULLY RAN- DOM...
MY...
BLUSH...
かぁ...
MY FIRST LOVE WAS...
...MY KINDERGARTEN TEACHER...
SHE WAS ONE OF THOSE TEACHERS ALL THE KIDS LOVED.
WE USED TO ARGUE OVER WHO'D MARRY HER WHEN WE GREW UP...
BUT OF COURSE, SENSEI WAS ALREADY MARRIED!
GOSH, MY FACE IS BURNING UP...
WELL, FIRST LOVES NEVER HAVE A HAPPY ENDING, Y'KNOW...
WE GOTTA GET BACK TO WORK.
HE'S BEEN SIPPING ON THAT DRINK FOR A WHILE...
SEE YA, NAO-CHAN!
HAVE A GOOD SHIFT!
OH, BUT Y'KNOW...

(Even Kabakura-senpai smiled)

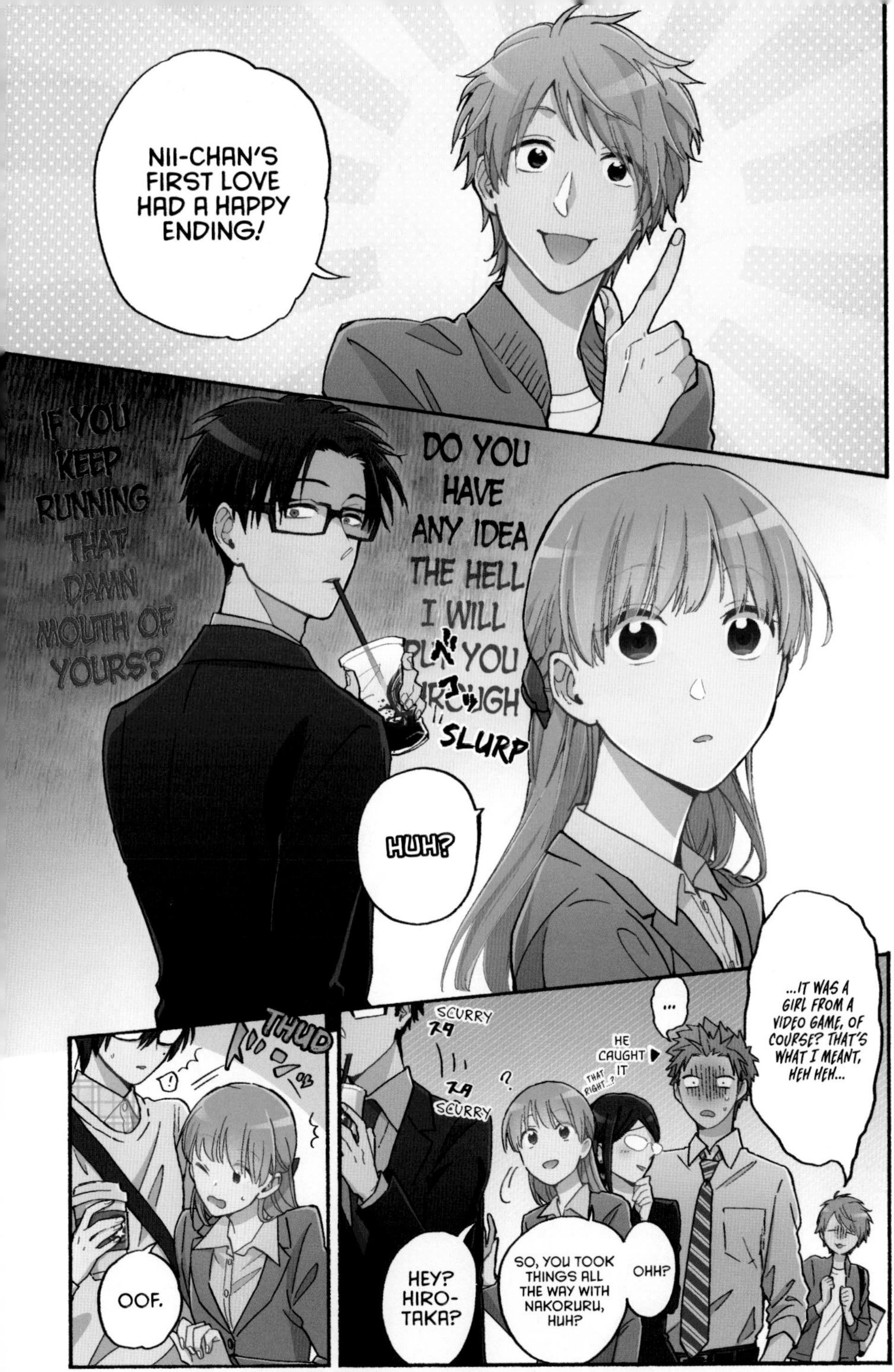
NII-CHAN'S FIRST LOVE HAD A HAPPY ENDING!
DO YOU HAVE ANY IDEA THE HELL I WILL PUT YOU THROUGH
IF YOU KEEP RUNNING THAT DAMN MOUTH OF YOURS?
SLURP
HUH?
...IT WAS A GIRL FROM A VIDEO GAME, OF COURSE? THAT'S WHAT I MEANT, HEH HEH...
...
HE CAUGHT IT
THAT RIGHT...?
OHH?
SO, YOU TOOK THINGS ALL THE WAY WITH NAKORURU, HUH?
?
SCURRY
SCURRY
HEY? HIRO-TAKA?
THUD
!
OOF.

 (Kabakura-senpai is shook, too)

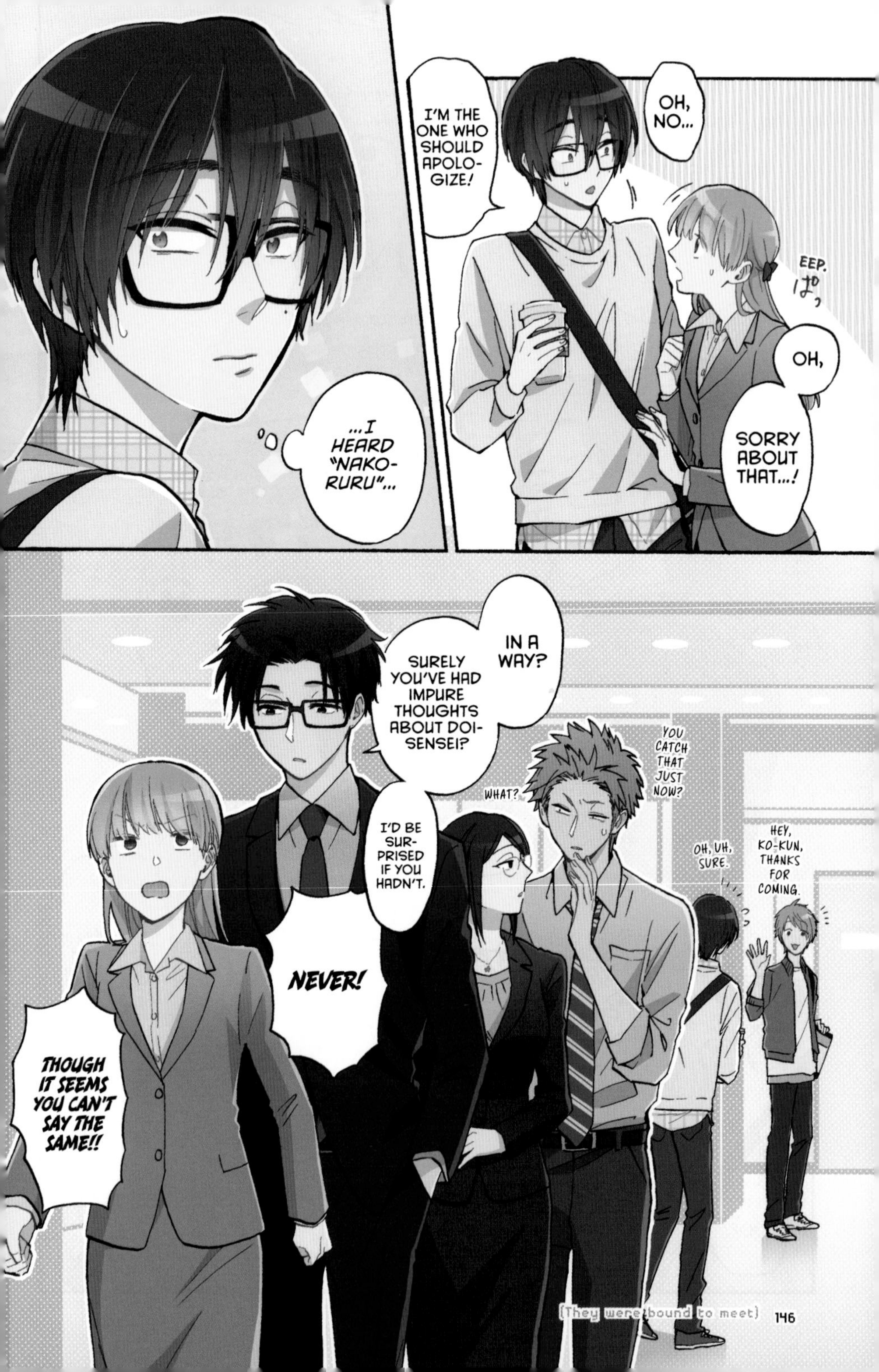
EEP.
ぱ
OH, SORRY ABOUT THAT...!
OH, NO...
I'M THE ONE WHO SHOULD APOLOGIZE!
...I HEARD "NAKORURU"...
HEY, KO-KUN, THANKS FOR COMING.
OH, UH, SURE.
YOU CATCH THAT JUST NOW?
WHAT?
IN A WAY?
SURELY YOU'VE HAD IMPURE THOUGHTS ABOUT DOI-SENSEI?
I'D BE SURPRISED IF YOU HADN'T.
NEVER!
THOUGH IT SEEMS YOU CAN'T SAY THE SAME!!
(They were bound to meet)

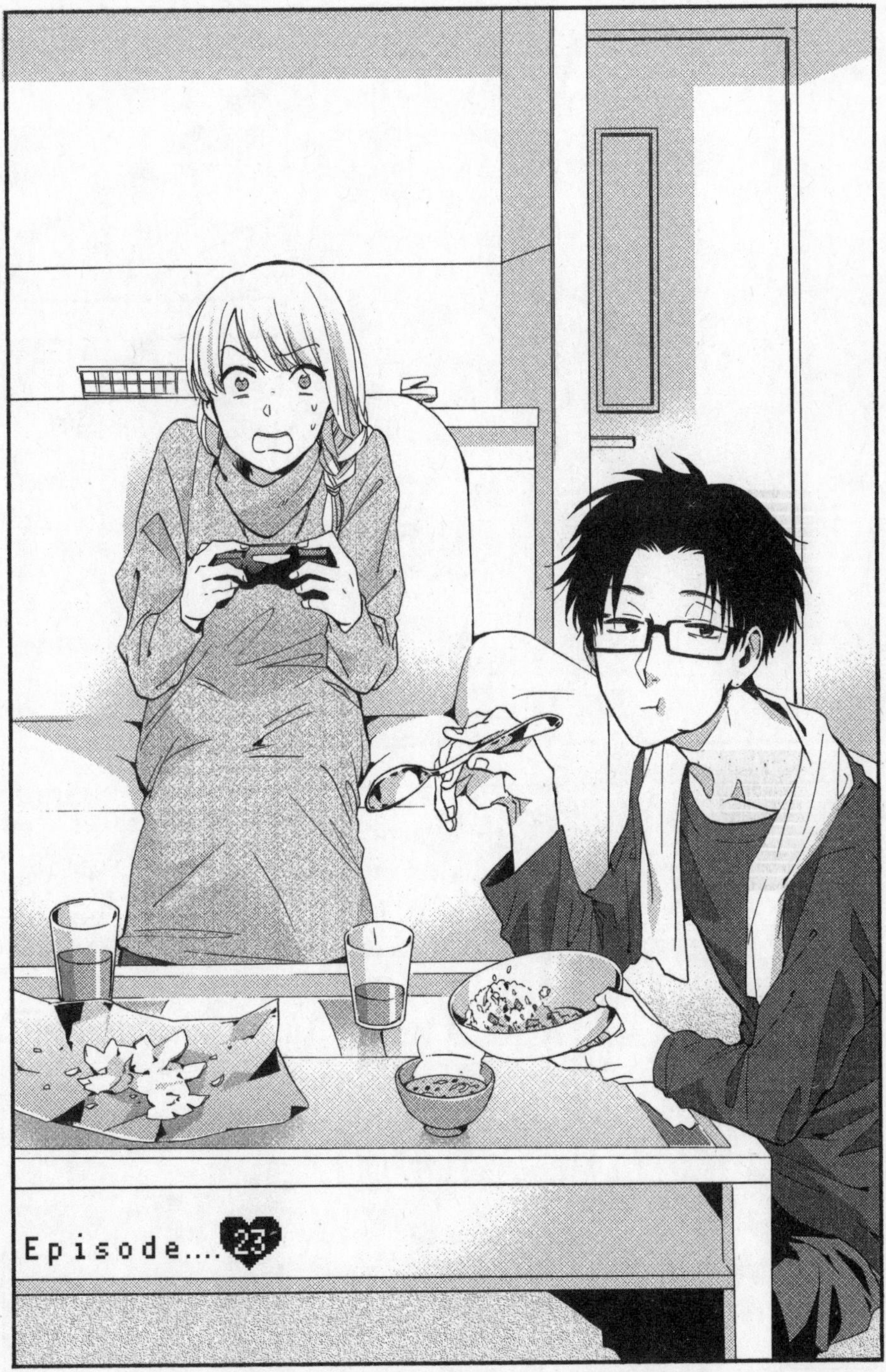
Episode....23

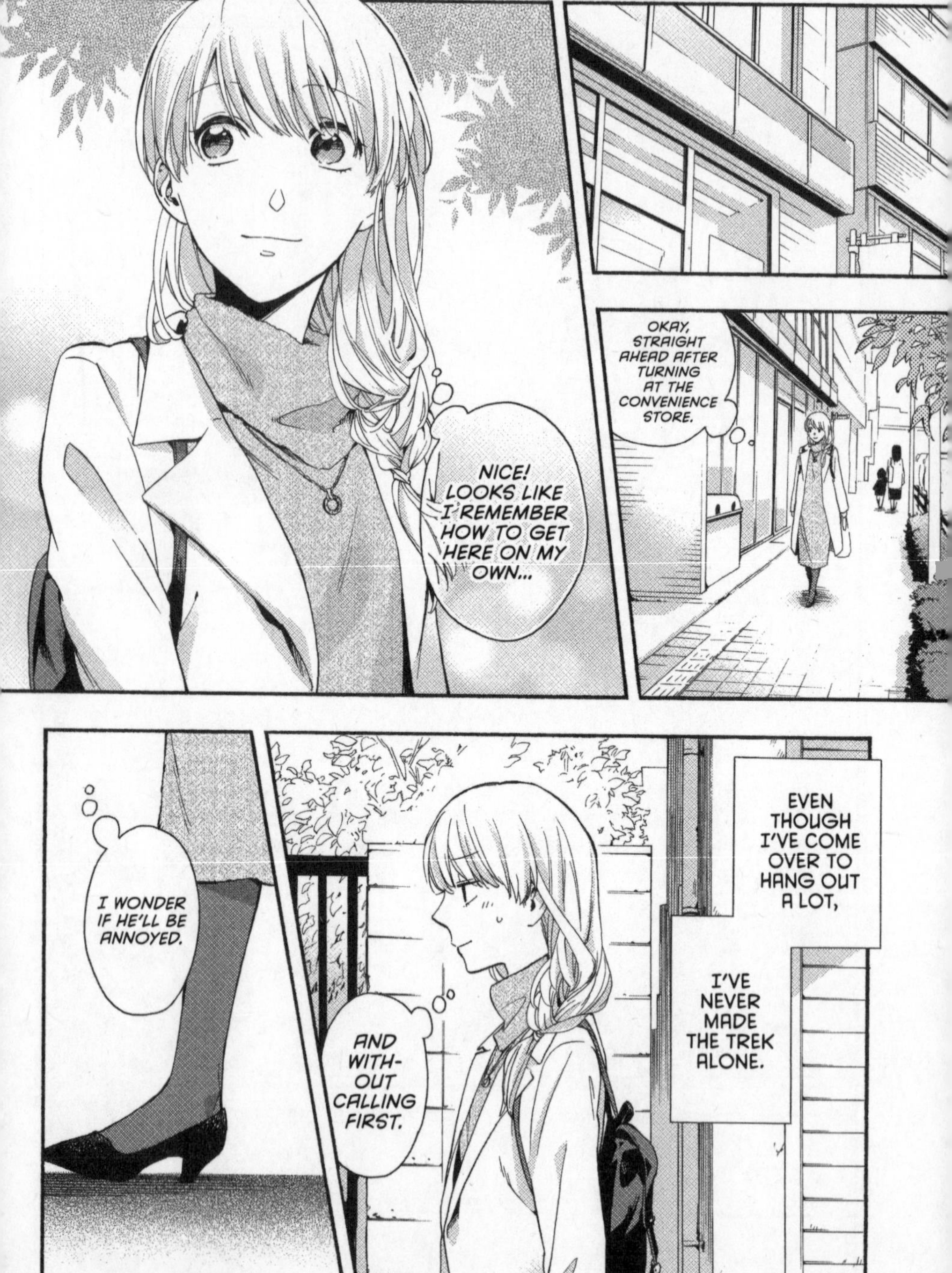
OKAY, STRAIGHT AHEAD AFTER TURNING AT THE CONVENIENCE STORE.
NICE! LOOKS LIKE I REMEMBER HOW TO GET HERE ON MY OWN...
EVEN THOUGH I'VE COME OVER TO HANG OUT A LOT,
I'VE NEVER MADE THE TREK ALONE.
AND WITH-OUT CALLING FIRST.
I WONDER IF HE'LL BE ANNOYED.

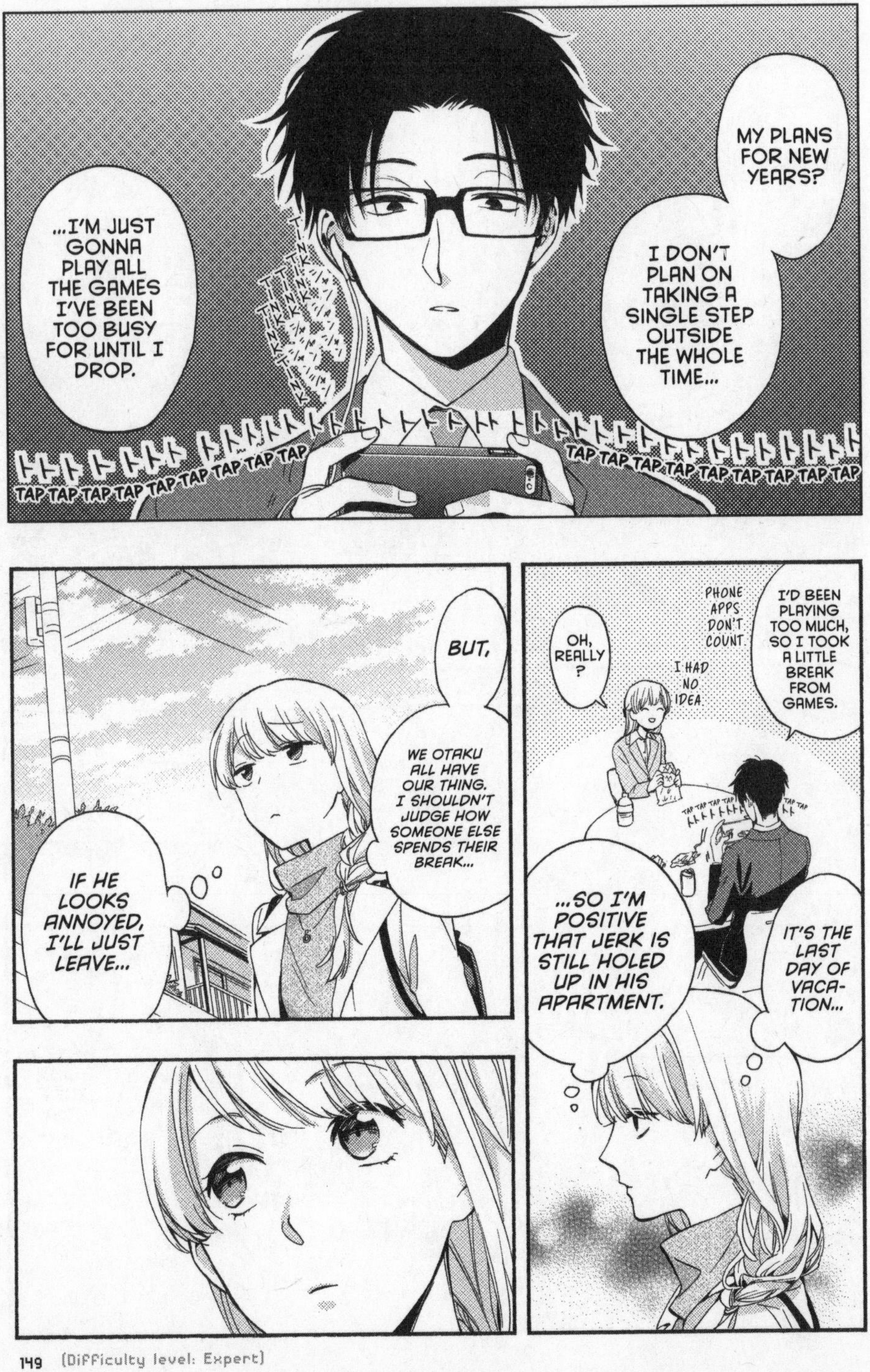
MY PLANS FOR NEW YEARS?
I DON'T PLAN ON TAKING A SINGLE STEP OUTSIDE THE WHOLE TIME...
...I'M JUST GONNA PLAY ALL THE GAMES I'VE BEEN TOO BUSY FOR UNTIL I DROP.
TINK TINK TINK TINK
TAP TAP TAP TAP TAP TAP TAP TAP TAP
TAP TAP TAP TAP TAP TAP TAP TAP TAP
I'D BEEN PLAYING TOO MUCH, SO I TOOK A LITTLE BREAK FROM GAMES.
PHONE APPS DON'T COUNT.
OH, REALLY?
I HAD NO IDEA.
TAP TAP
TAP TAP TAP TAP
IT'S THE LAST DAY OF VACATION...
...SO I'M POSITIVE THAT JERK IS STILL HOLED UP IN HIS APARTMENT.
BUT,
WE OTAKU ALL HAVE OUR THING. I SHOULDN'T JUDGE HOW SOMEONE ELSE SPENDS THEIR BREAK...
IF HE LOOKS ANNOYED, I'LL JUST LEAVE...

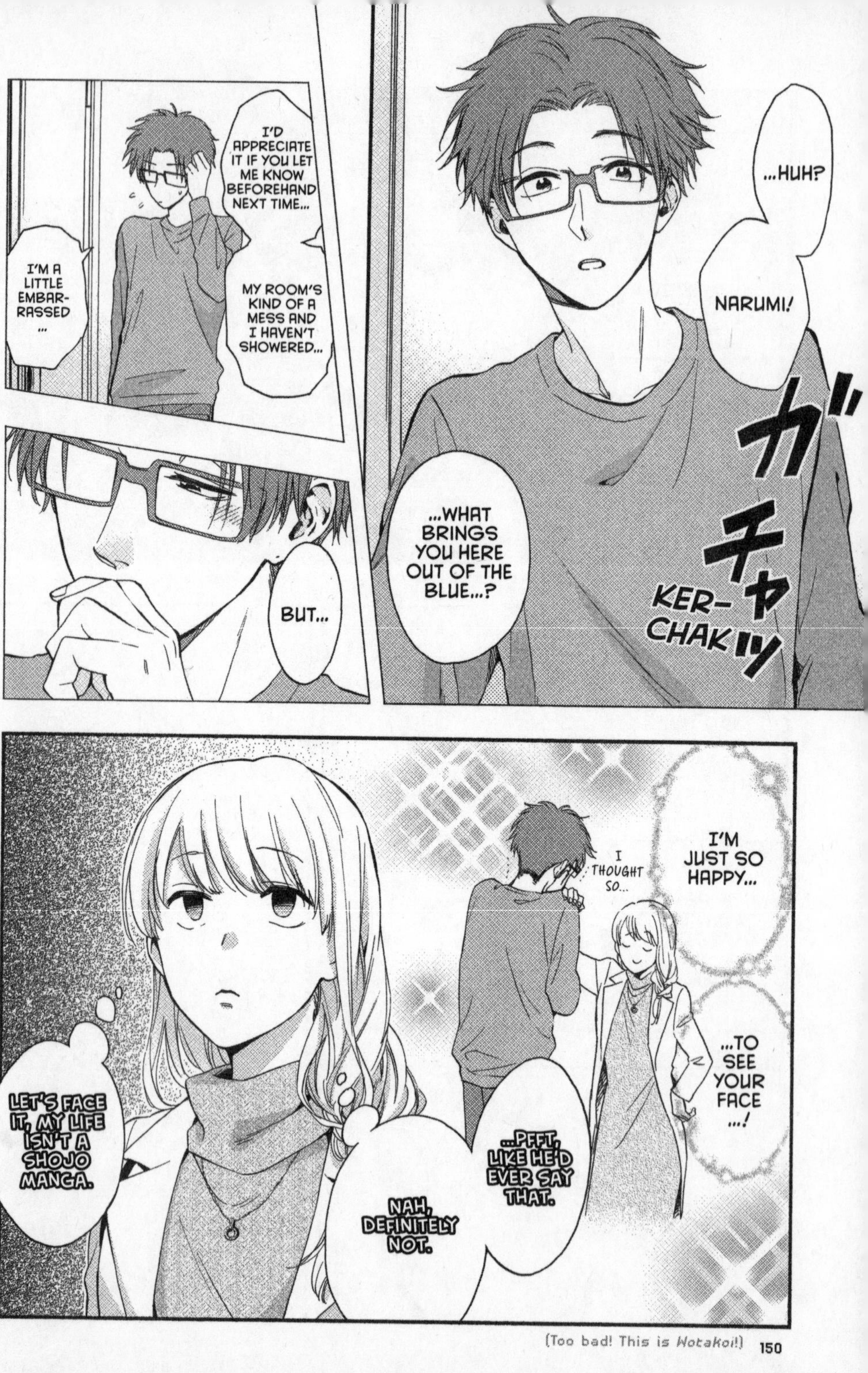

...HUH?
NARUMI!
ガチャッ
KER-CHAK
...WHAT BRINGS YOU HERE OUT OF THE BLUE...?
I'D APPRECIATE IT IF YOU LET ME KNOW BEFOREHAND NEXT TIME...
MY ROOM'S KIND OF A MESS AND I HAVEN'T SHOWERED...
I'M A LITTLE EMBARRASSED...
BUT...
I'M JUST SO HAPPY...
...TO SEE YOUR FACE...!
I THOUGHT SO...
...PFFT, LIKE HE'D EVER SAY THAT.
NAH, DEFINITELY NOT.
LET'S FACE IT, MY LIFE ISN'T A SHOJO MANGA.

(Too bad! This is *Wotakoi*!)

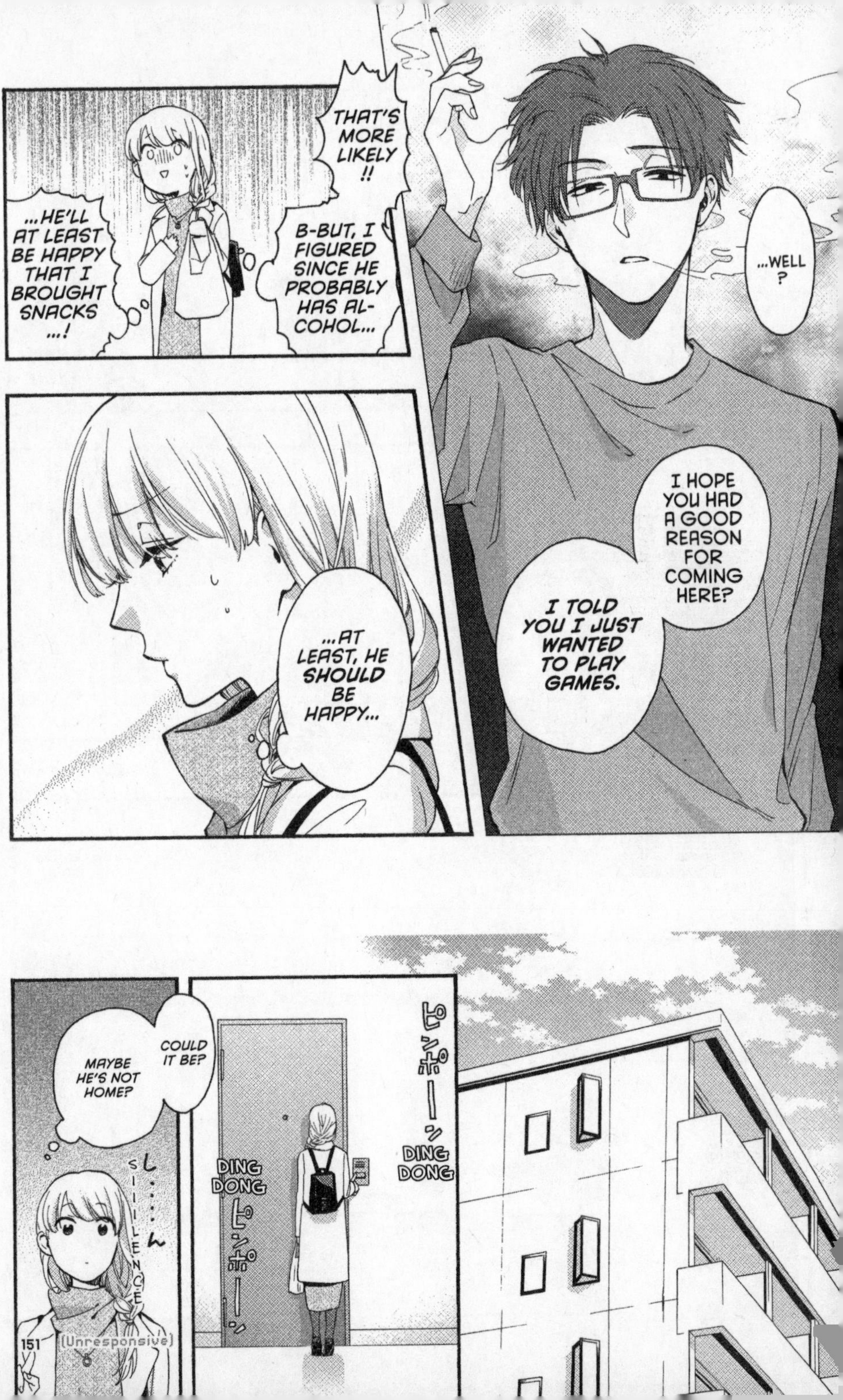
...WELL?
I HOPE YOU HAD A GOOD REASON FOR COMING HERE?
I TOLD YOU I JUST WANTED TO PLAY GAMES.
THAT'S MORE LIKELY!!
B-BUT, I FIGURED SINCE HE PROBABLY HAS AL-COHOL...
...HE'LL AT LEAST BE HAPPY THAT I BROUGHT SNACKS...!
...AT LEAST, HE SHOULD BE HAPPY...
ピンポーン
DING DONG
ピンポーン
DING DONG
COULD IT BE?
MAYBE HE'S NOT HOME?
し・・・ん
SIIILENCE
(Unresponsive)

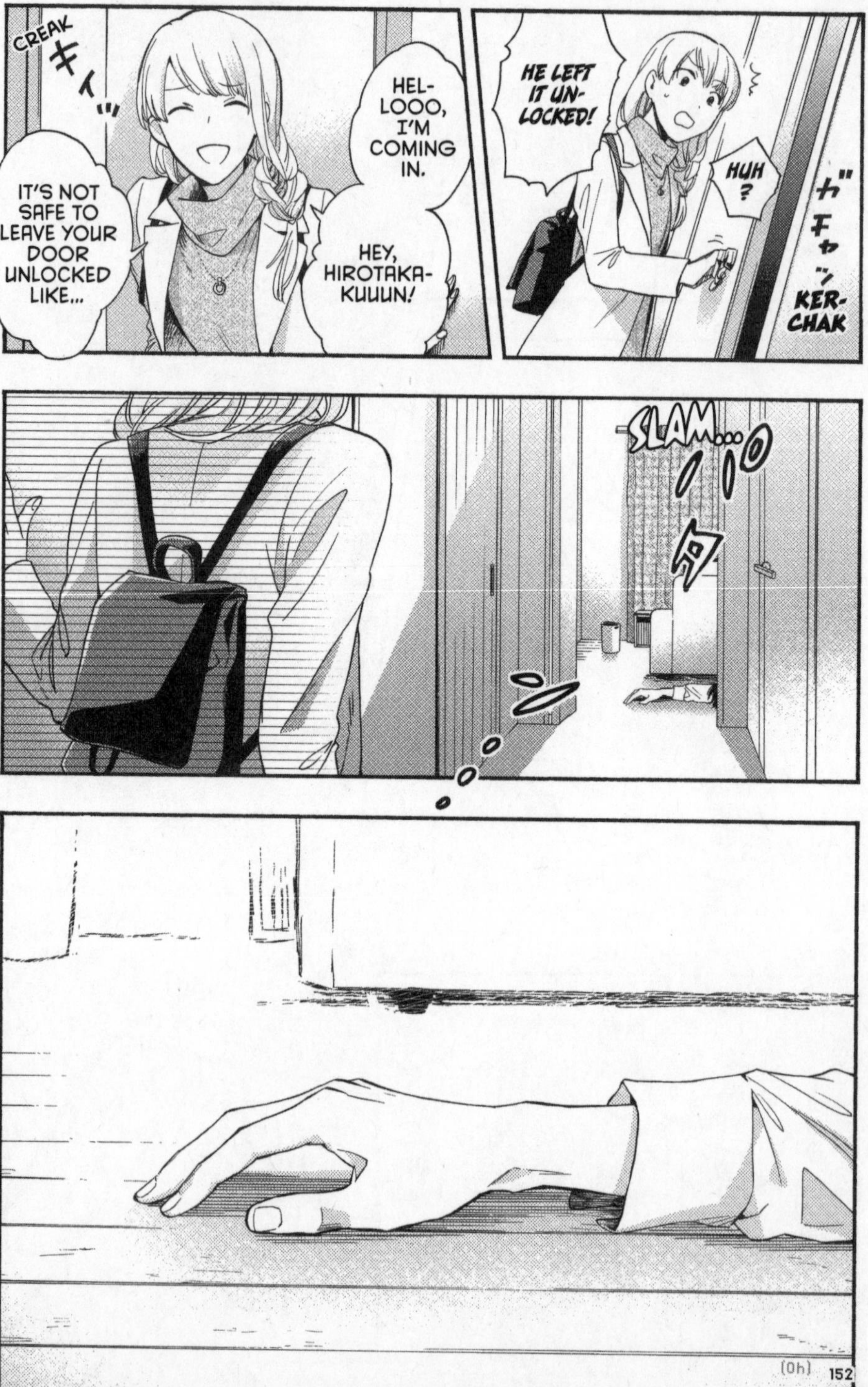
HE LEFT IT UN-LOCKED!
HUH?
ガチャッ
KER-CHAK
HEL-LOOO, I'M COMING IN.
HEY, HIROTAKA-KUUUN!
CREAK
キィッ
IT'S NOT SAFE TO LEAVE YOUR DOOR UNLOCKED LIKE...
SLAM...

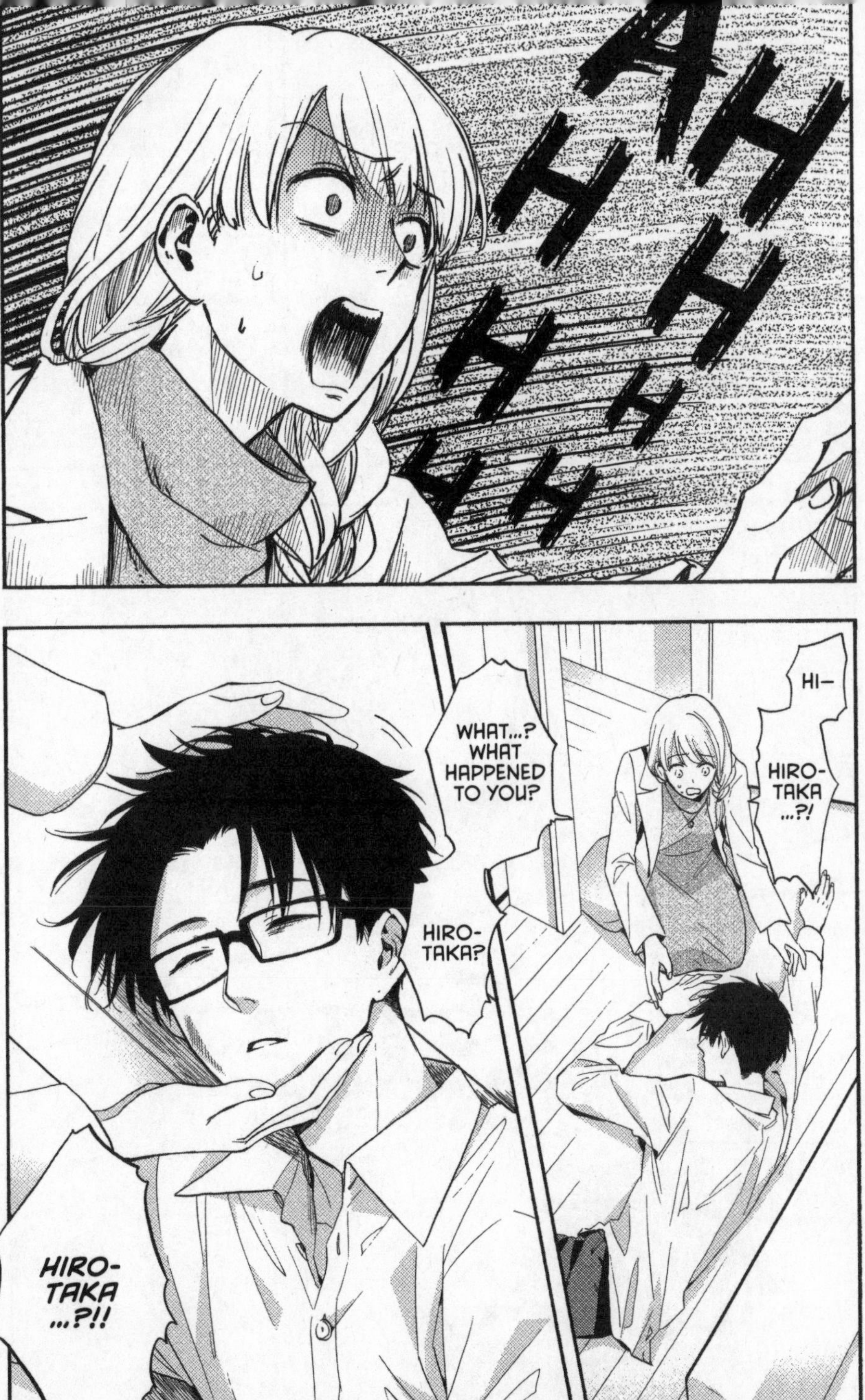
AHHHHH
HI—
HIRO-TAKA ...?!
WHAT...? WHAT HAPPENED TO YOU?
HIRO-TAKA?
HIRO-TAKA ...?!!

 (He's still breathing)

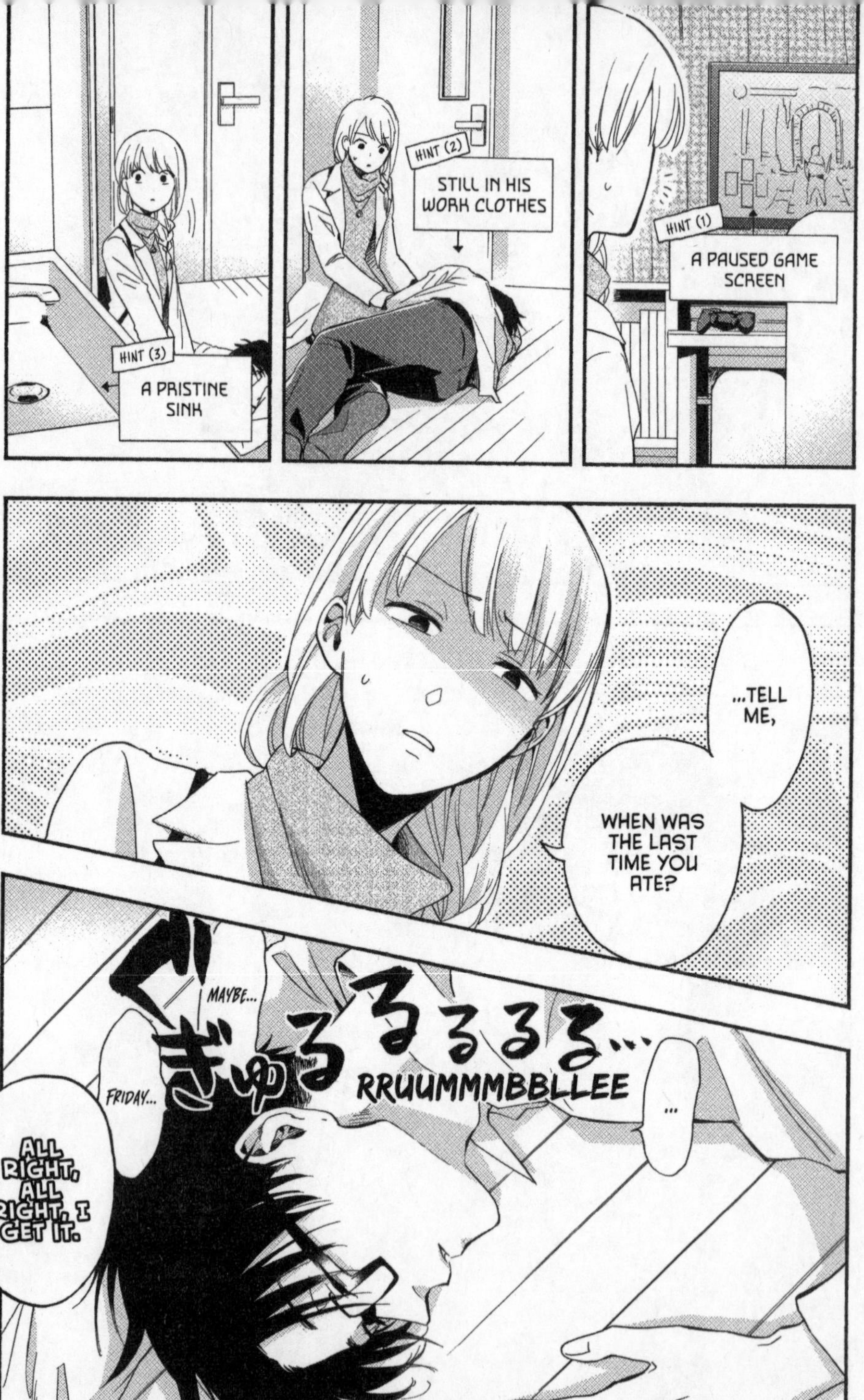
HINT (1)
A PAUSED GAME SCREEN
HINT (2)
STILL IN HIS WORK CLOTHES
HINT (3)
A PRISTINE SINK
...TELL ME,
WHEN WAS THE LAST TIME YOU ATE?
...
ぎゅるるるるるる…
RRUUMMMBBLLEE
MAYBE...
FRIDAY...
ALL RIGHT, ALL RIGHT, I GET IT.

(He sacrificed too much of his humanity)

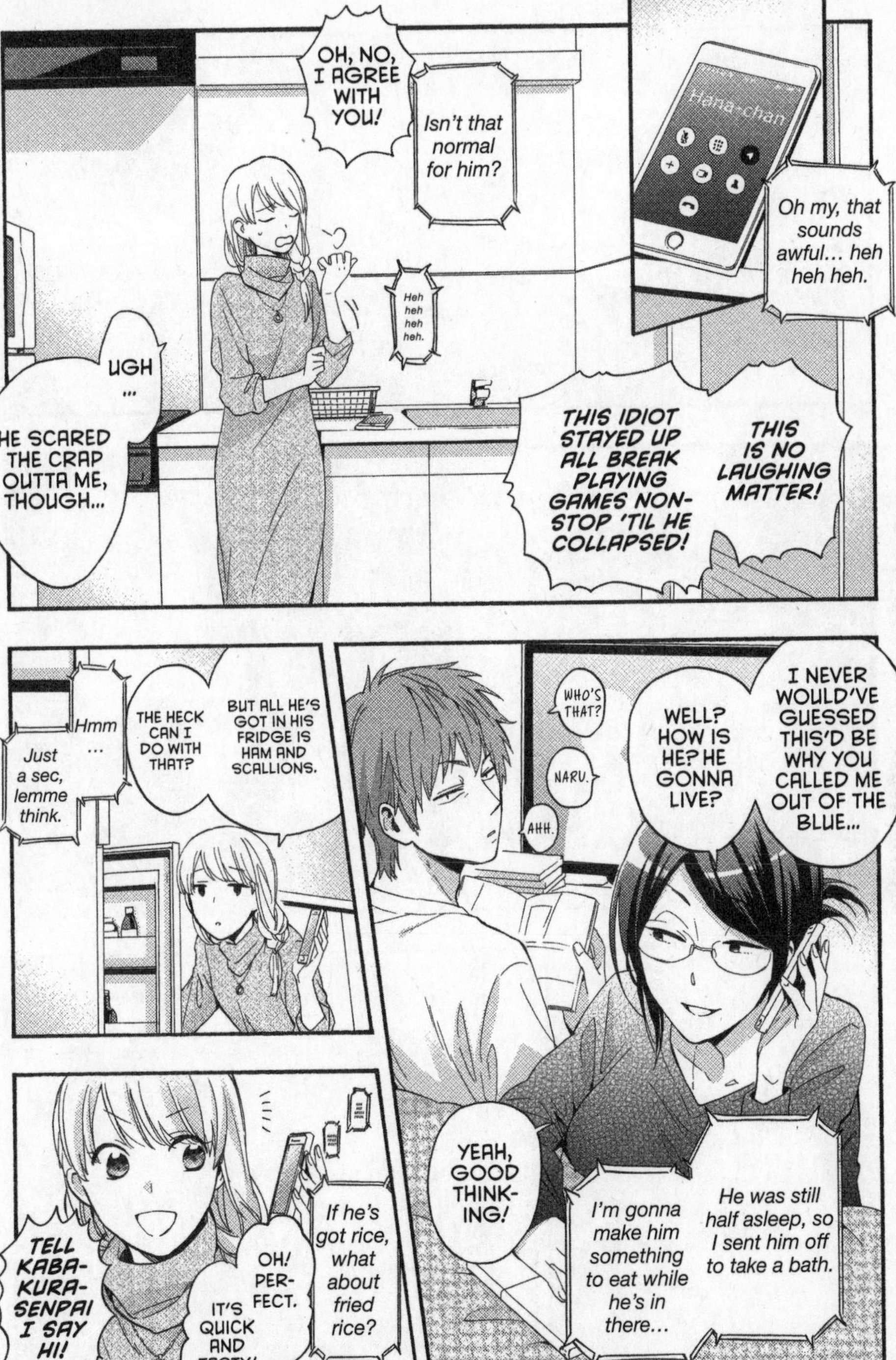
Oh my, that sounds awful… heh heh heh.
Isn't that normal for him?
OH, NO, I AGREE WITH YOU!
Heh heh heh heh.
THIS IS NO LAUGHING MATTER!
THIS IDIOT STAYED UP ALL BREAK PLAYING GAMES NON-STOP 'TIL HE COLLAPSED!
UGH… HE SCARED THE CRAP OUTTA ME, THOUGH…
I NEVER WOULD'VE GUESSED THIS'D BE WHY YOU CALLED ME OUT OF THE BLUE…
WELL? HOW IS HE? HE GONNA LIVE?
WHO'S THAT?
NARU.
AHH.
He was still half asleep, so I sent him off to take a bath.
I'm gonna make him something to eat while he's in there…
YEAH, GOOD THINKING!
BUT ALL HE'S GOT IN HIS FRIDGE IS HAM AND SCALLIONS.
THE HECK CAN I DO WITH THAT?
Hmm…
Just a sec, lemme think.
If he's got rice, what about fried rice?
OH! PERFECT.
IT'S QUICK AND TASTY!
TELL KABAKURA-SENPAI I SAY HI!

 (She just assumed he was there)

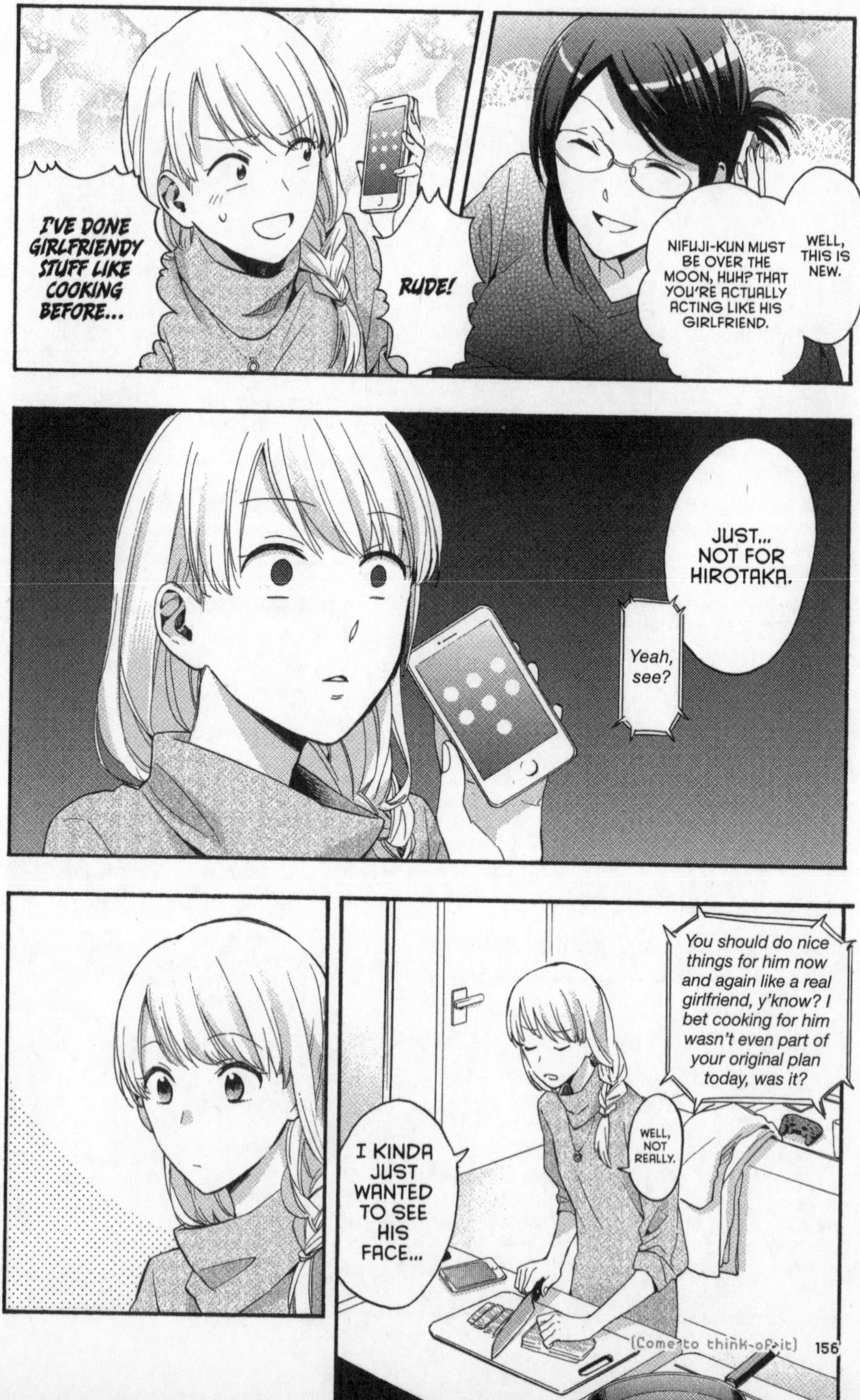
WELL, THIS IS NEW.
NIFUJI-KUN MUST BE OVER THE MOON, HUH? THAT YOU'RE ACTUALLY ACTING LIKE HIS GIRLFRIEND.
RUDE!
I'VE DONE GIRLFRIENDY STUFF LIKE COOKING BEFORE...
JUST... NOT FOR HIROTAKA.
Yeah, see?
You should do nice things for him now and again like a real girlfriend, y'know? I bet cooking for him wasn't even part of your original plan today, was it?
WELL, NOT REALLY.
I KINDA JUST WANTED TO SEE HIS FACE...
[Come to think of it]

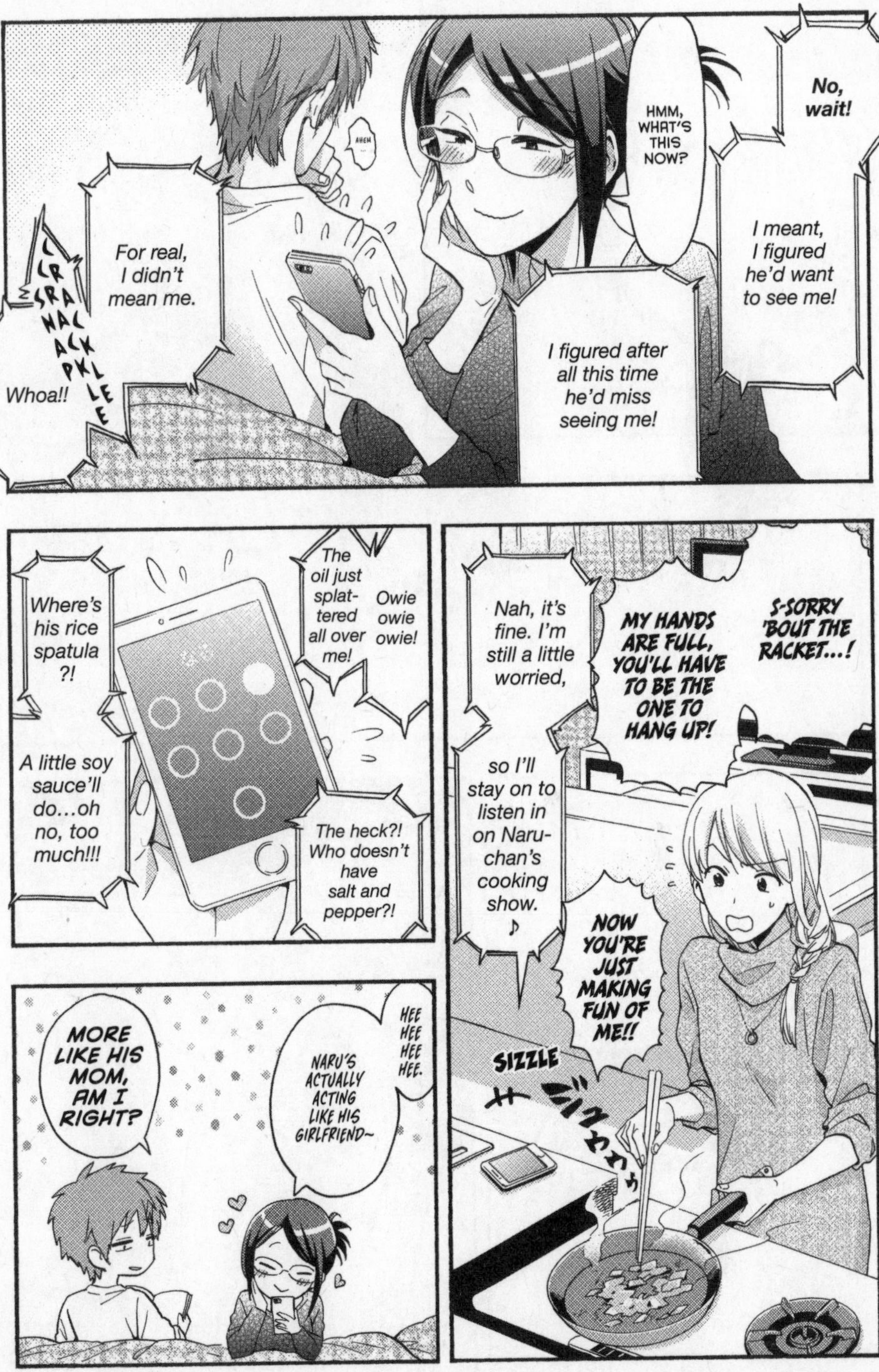
No, wait!
I meant, I figured he'd want to see me!
HMM, WHAT'S THIS NOW?
I figured after all this time he'd miss seeing me!
AHEM
For real, I didn't mean me.
Whoa!!
S-SORRY 'BOUT THE RACKET...!
MY HANDS ARE FULL, YOU'LL HAVE TO BE THE ONE TO HANG UP!
Nah, it's fine. I'm still a little worried,
so I'll stay on to listen in on Naru-chan's cooking show. ♪
NOW YOU'RE JUST MAKING FUN OF ME!!
SIZZLE
Owie owie owie!
The oil just splattered all over me!
Where's his rice spatula?!
The heck?! Who doesn't have salt and pepper?!
A little soy sauce'll do...oh no, too much!!!
HEE HEE HEE HEE.
NARU'S ACTUALLY ACTING LIKE HIS GIRLFRIEND~
MORE LIKE HIS MOM, AM I RIGHT?

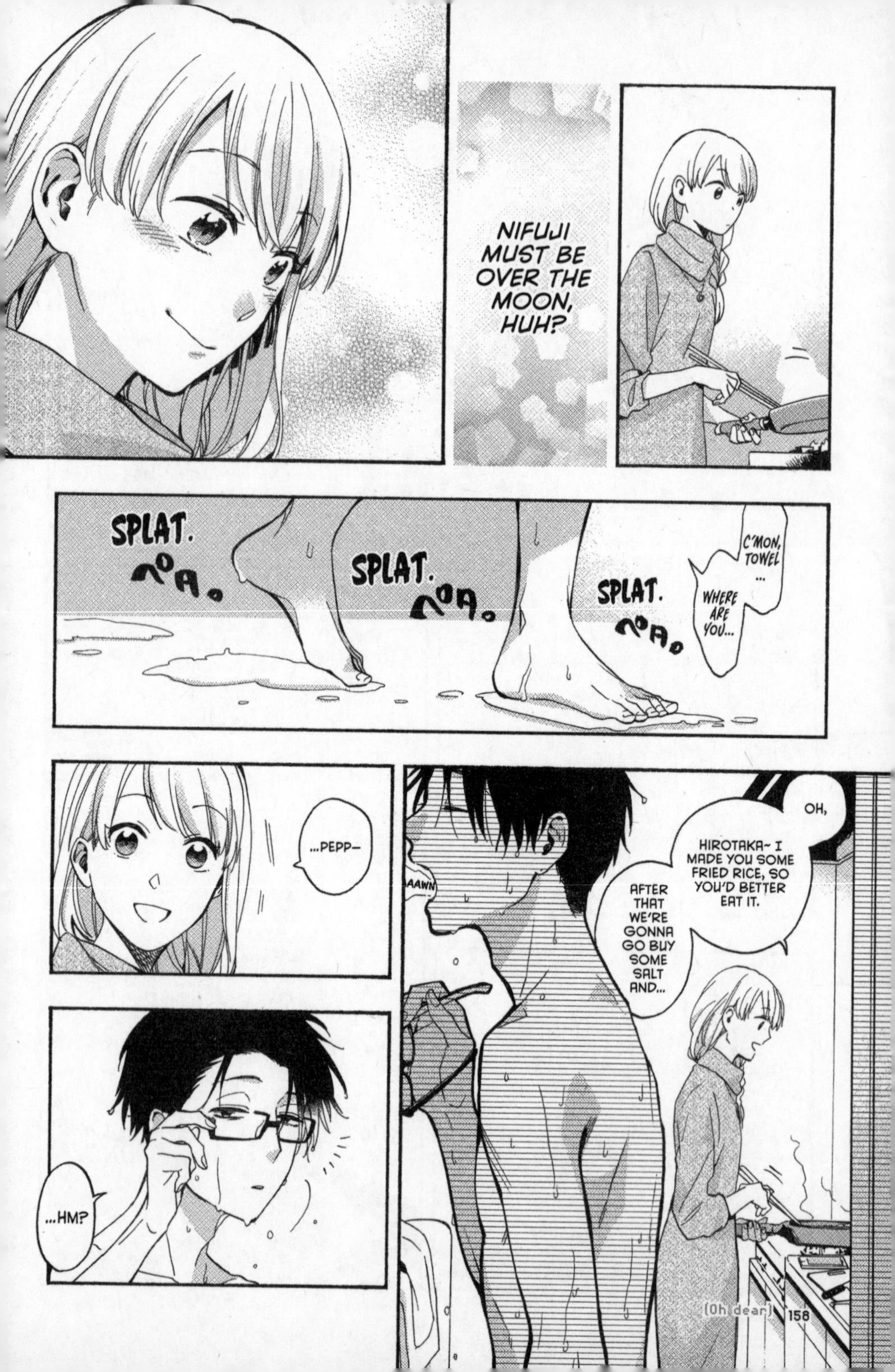
NIFUJI MUST BE OVER THE MOON, HUH?
C'MON, TOWEL ... WHERE ARE YOU...
SPLAT.
ペタ。
SPLAT.
ペタ。
SPLAT.
ペタ。
OH, HIROTAKA~ I MADE YOU SOME FRIED RICE, SO YOU'D BETTER EAT IT.
AFTER THAT WE'RE GONNA GO BUY SOME SALT AND...
...PEPP—
AAWN
...HM?
(Oh dear)

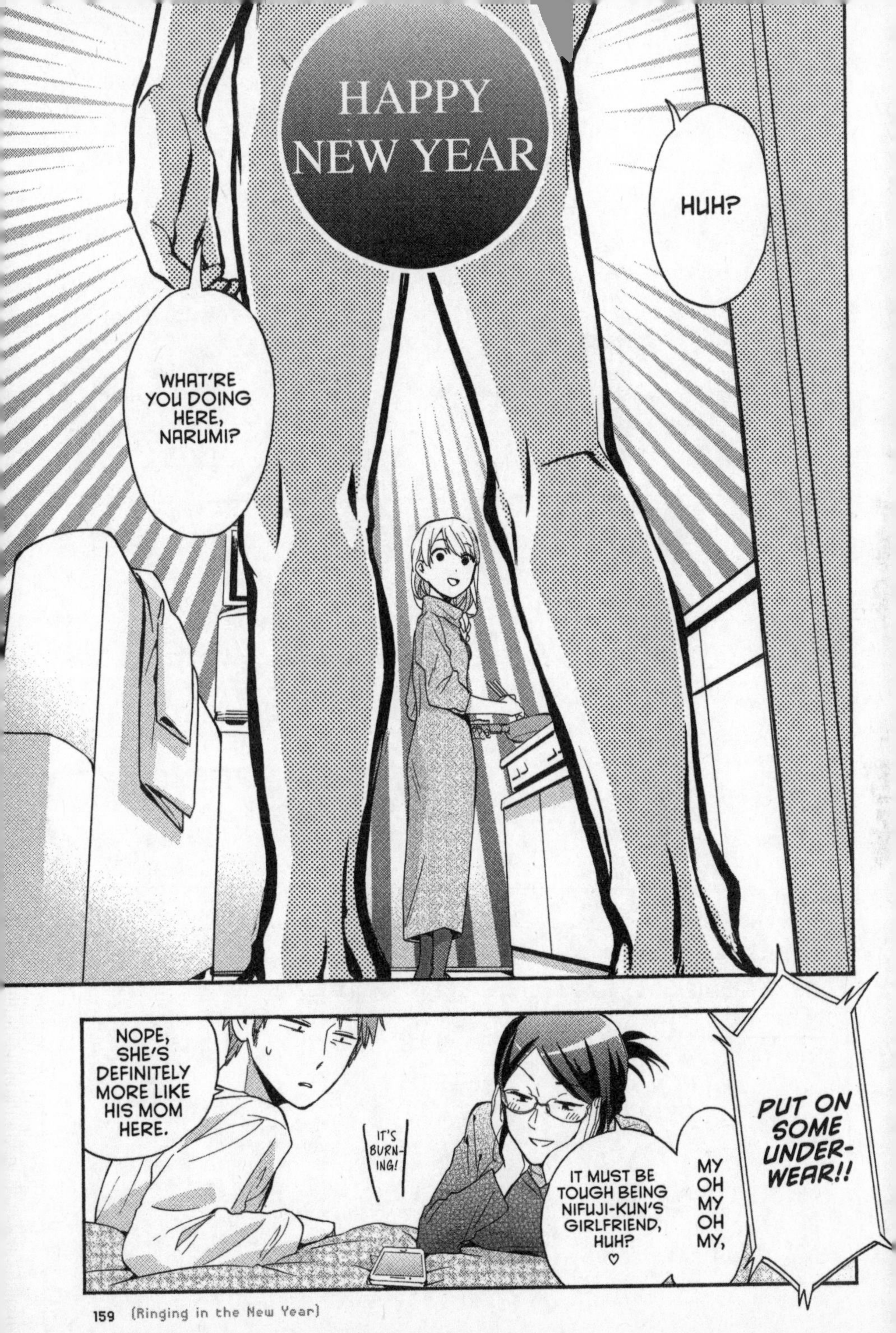
HAPPY NEW YEAR
HUH?
WHAT'RE YOU DOING HERE, NARUMI?
PUT ON SOME UNDER-WEAR!!
MY OH MY OH MY,
IT MUST BE TOUGH BEING NIFUJI-KUN'S GIRLFRIEND, HUH? ♡
IT'S BURN-ING!
NOPE, SHE'S DEFINITELY MORE LIKE HIS MOM HERE.

CHARACTERS

桃瀬成海 Narumi Momose

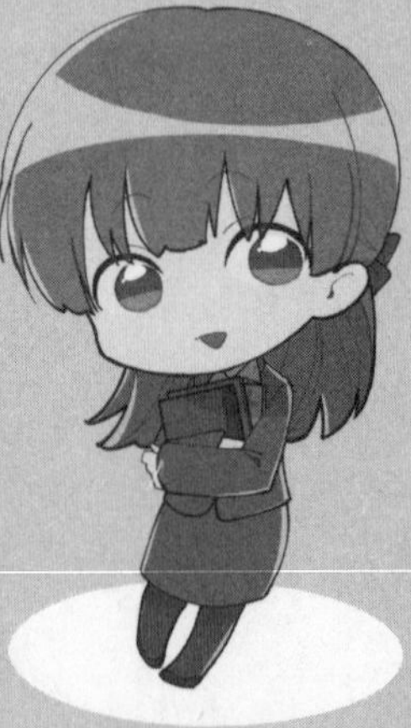

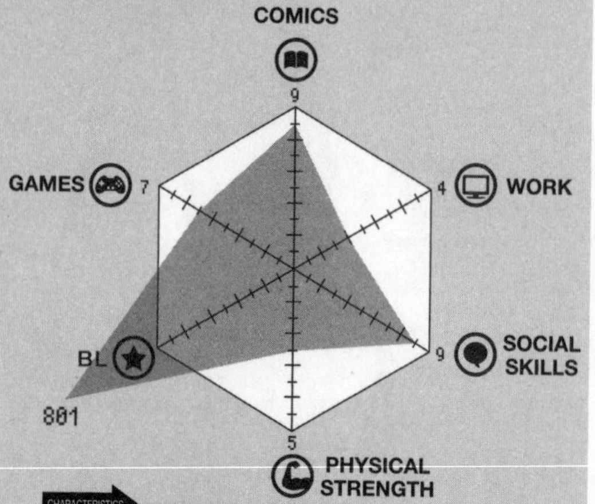
COMICS
9
WORK
4
SOCIAL SKILLS
9
PHYSICAL STRENGTH
5
BL
801
GAMES
7

CHARACTERISTICS

A well-rounded (stealth) fujoshi. She eats, sleeps, and breathes romance. She has an impulsive personality, and often acts before she thinks.

二藤宏嵩 Hirotaka Nifuji

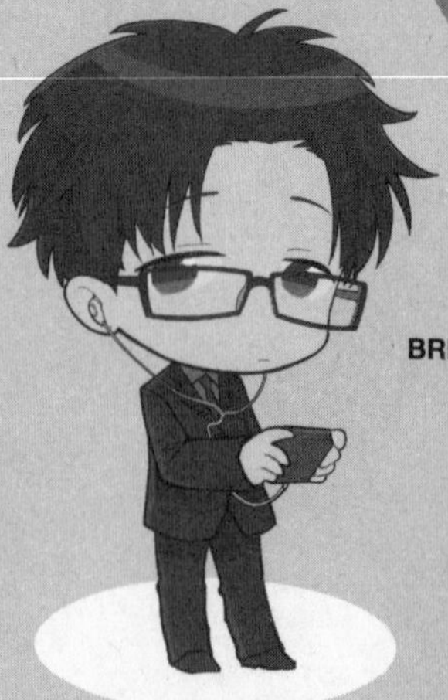

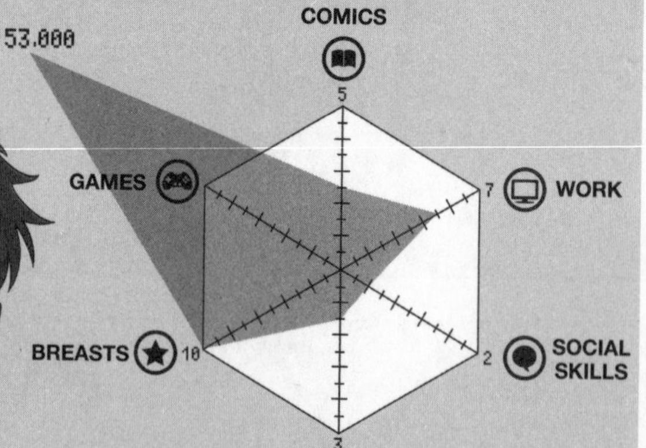
COMICS
5
WORK
7
SOCIAL SKILLS
2
PHYSICAL STRENGTH
3
BREASTS
10
GAMES
53,000

CHARACTERISTICS

Playing games boosts his energy reserves. No games, no life. He doesn't have trouble communicating, he just has no interest in other people.

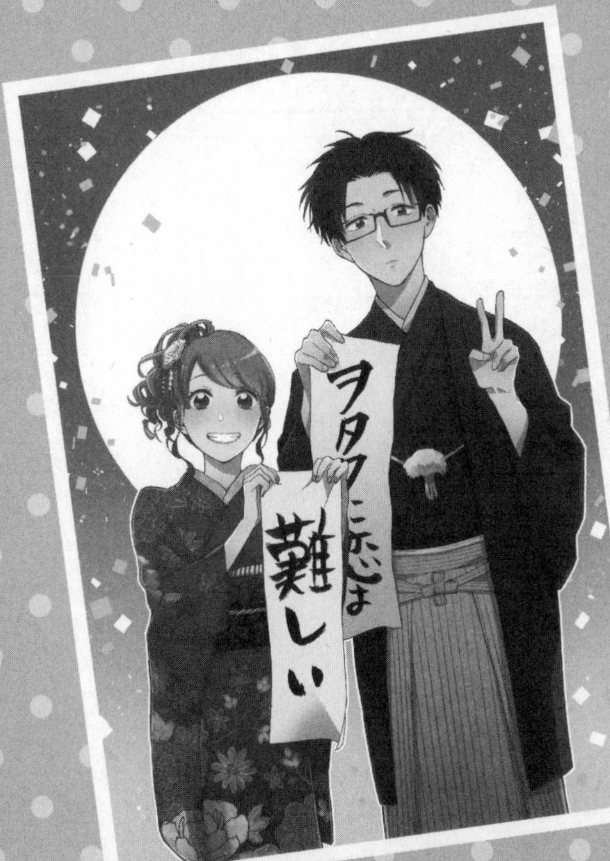
ヲタクに恋は難しい

Wotakoi: Love is Hard for Otaku

Episode....24

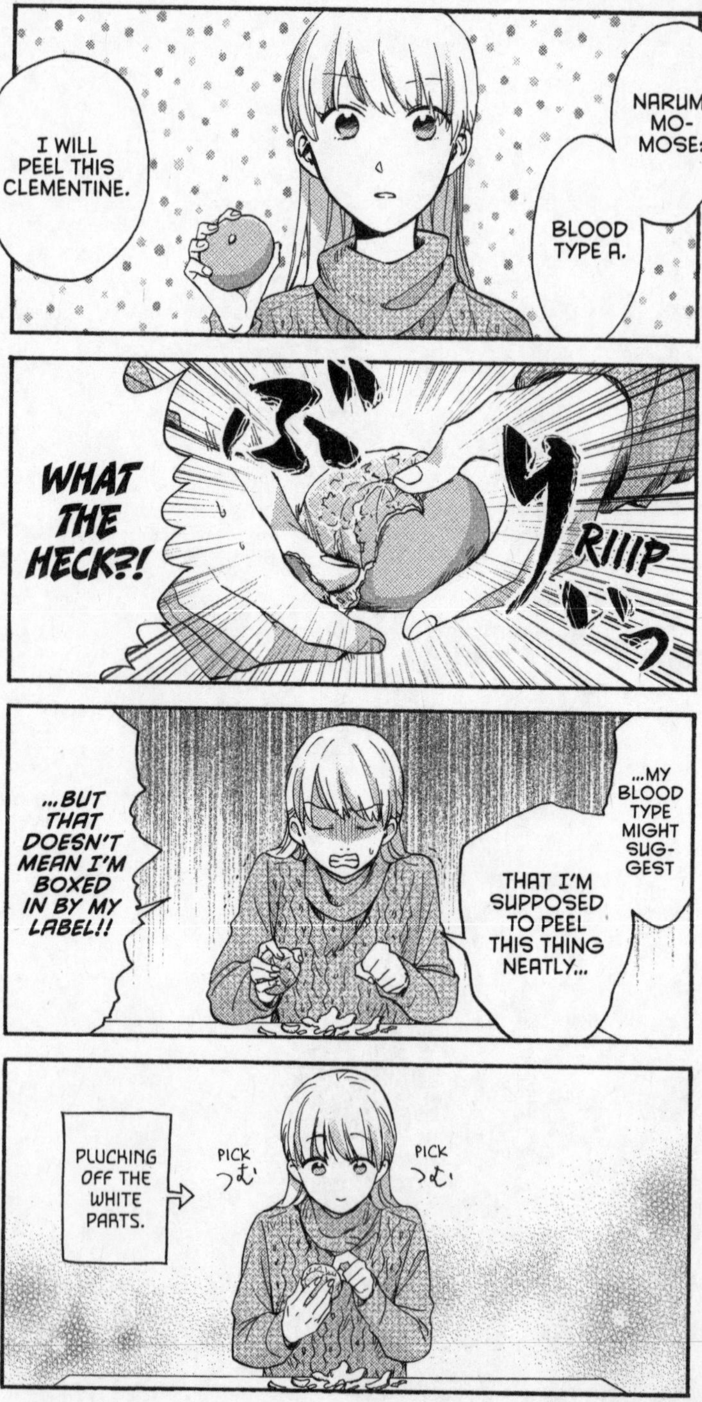
NARUMI MOMOSE:
BLOOD TYPE A.
I WILL PEEL THIS CLEMENTINE.
RIIIP
WHAT THE HECK?!
...MY BLOOD TYPE MIGHT SUGGEST
THAT I'M SUPPOSED TO PEEL THIS THING NEATLY...
...BUT THAT DOESN'T MEAN I'M BOXED IN BY MY LABEL!!
PICK
つむ
PICK
つむ
PLUCKING OFF THE WHITE PARTS.

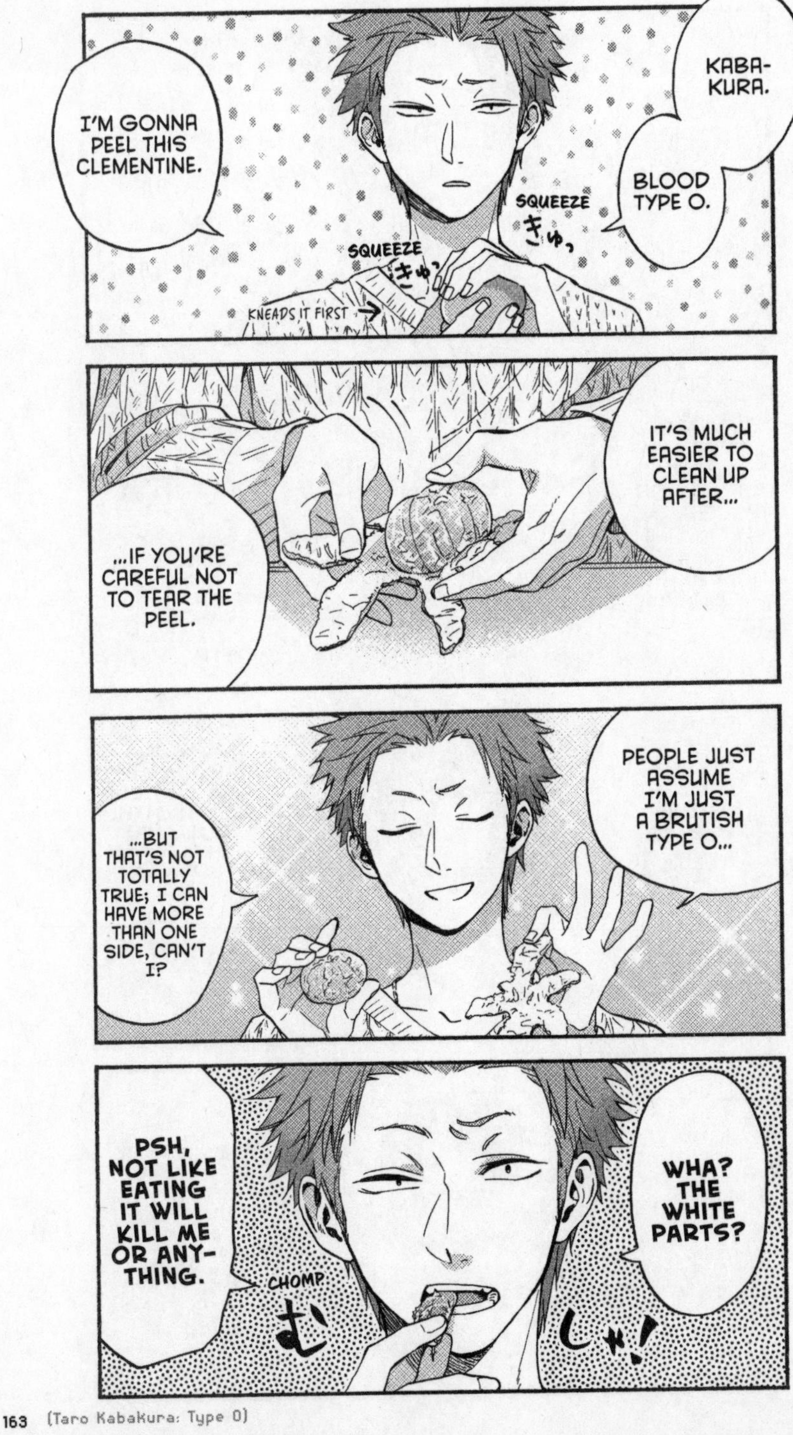
KABA-KURA.
BLOOD TYPE O.
SQUEEZE
きゅっ
I'M GONNA PEEL THIS CLEMENTINE.
SQUEEZE
きゅっ
KNEADS IT FIRST
IT'S MUCH EASIER TO CLEAN UP AFTER...
...IF YOU'RE CAREFUL NOT TO TEAR THE PEEL.
PEOPLE JUST ASSUME I'M JUST A BRUTISH TYPE O...
...BUT THAT'S NOT TOTALLY TRUE; I CAN HAVE MORE THAN ONE SIDE, CAN'T I?
WHA? THE WHITE PARTS?
PSH, NOT LIKE EATING IT WILL KILL ME OR ANY-THING.
CHOMP
むしゃ!

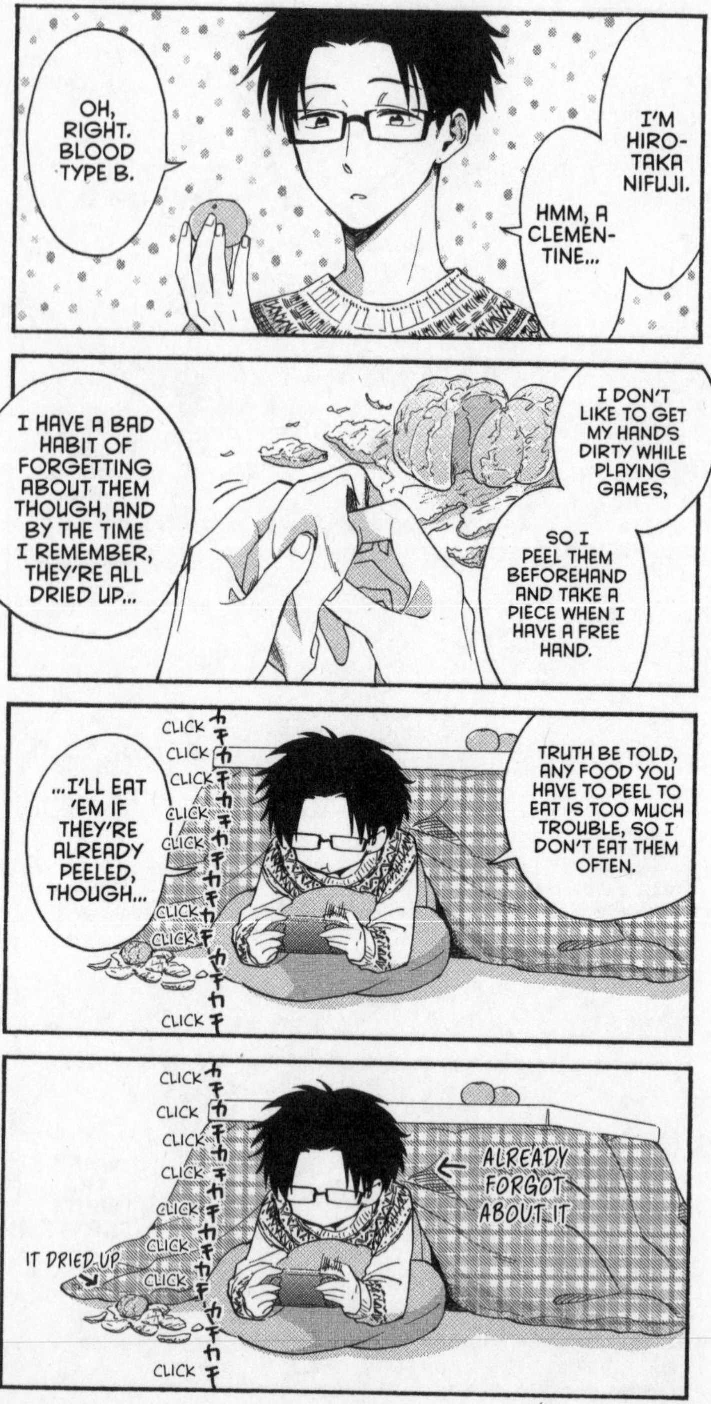
I'M HIRO-TAKA NIFUJI.
HMM, A CLEMEN-TINE...
OH, RIGHT. BLOOD TYPE B.
I DON'T LIKE TO GET MY HANDS DIRTY WHILE PLAYING GAMES,
SO I PEEL THEM BEFOREHAND AND TAKE A PIECE WHEN I HAVE A FREE HAND.
I HAVE A BAD HABIT OF FORGETTING ABOUT THEM THOUGH, AND BY THE TIME I REMEMBER, THEY'RE ALL DRIED UP...
TRUTH BE TOLD, ANY FOOD YOU HAVE TO PEEL TO EAT IS TOO MUCH TROUBLE, SO I DON'T EAT THEM OFTEN.
CLICK
CLICK
CLICK
CLICK
CLICK
CLICK
CLICK
CLICK
...I'LL EAT 'EM IF THEY'RE ALREADY PEELED, THOUGH...
ALREADY FORGOT ABOUT IT
CLICK
CLICK
CLICK
CLICK
CLICK
CLICK
CLICK
CLICK
IT DRIED UP

(Hirotaka Nifuji: Type B)

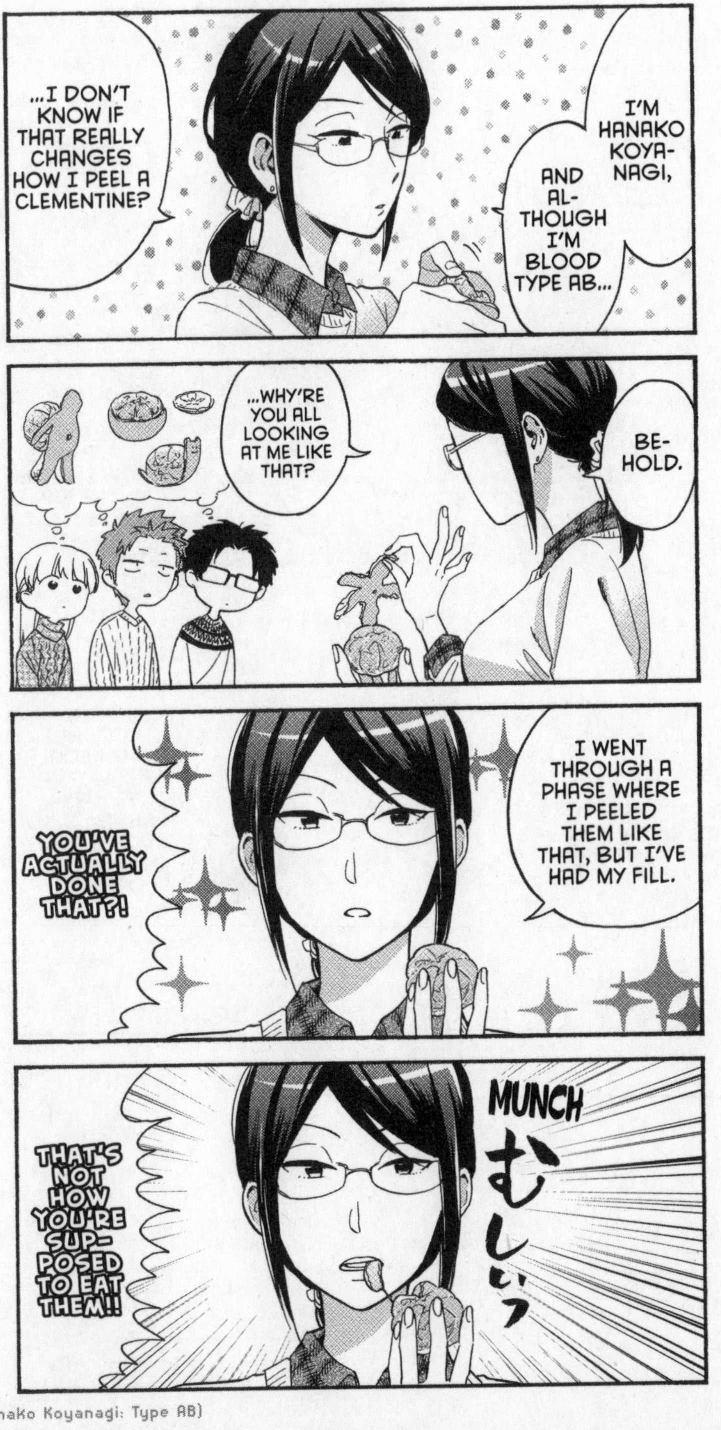
I'M HANAKO KOYA-NAGI,
AND AL-THOUGH I'M BLOOD TYPE AB...
...I DON'T KNOW IF THAT REALLY CHANGES HOW I PEEL A CLEMENTINE?
BE-HOLD.
...WHY'RE YOU ALL LOOKING AT ME LIKE THAT?
I WENT THROUGH A PHASE WHERE I PEELED THEM LIKE THAT, BUT I'VE HAD MY FILL.
YOU'VE ACTUALLY DONE THAT?!
MUNCH
むしっ
THAT'S NOT HOW YOU'RE SUP-POSED TO EAT THEM!!

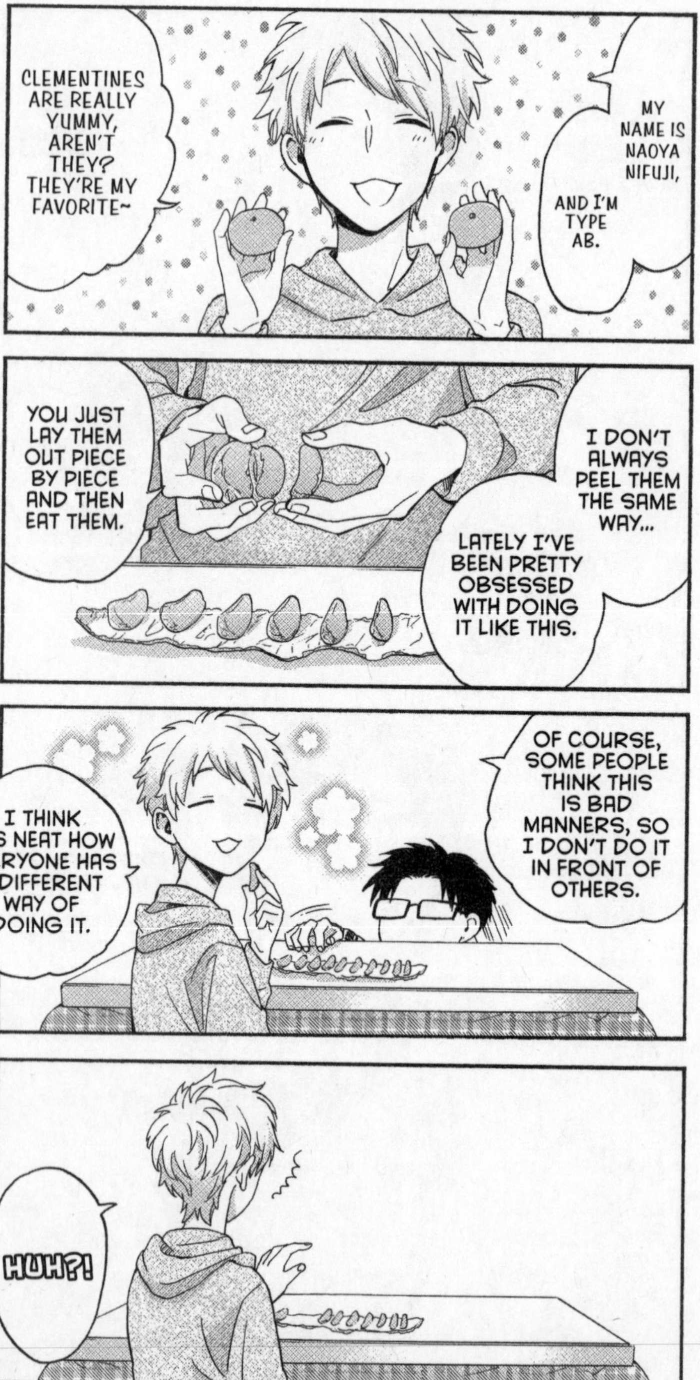
MY NAME IS NAOYA NIFUJI,
AND I'M TYPE AB.
CLEMENTINES ARE REALLY YUMMY, AREN'T THEY? THEY'RE MY FAVORITE~
I DON'T ALWAYS PEEL THEM THE SAME WAY...
LATELY I'VE BEEN PRETTY OBSESSED WITH DOING IT LIKE THIS.
YOU JUST LAY THEM OUT PIECE BY PIECE AND THEN EAT THEM.
OF COURSE, SOME PEOPLE THINK THIS IS BAD MANNERS, SO I DON'T DO IT IN FRONT OF OTHERS.
I THINK IT'S NEAT HOW EVERYONE HAS A DIFFERENT WAY OF DOING IT.
HUH?!

(Naoya Nifuji: Type AB)

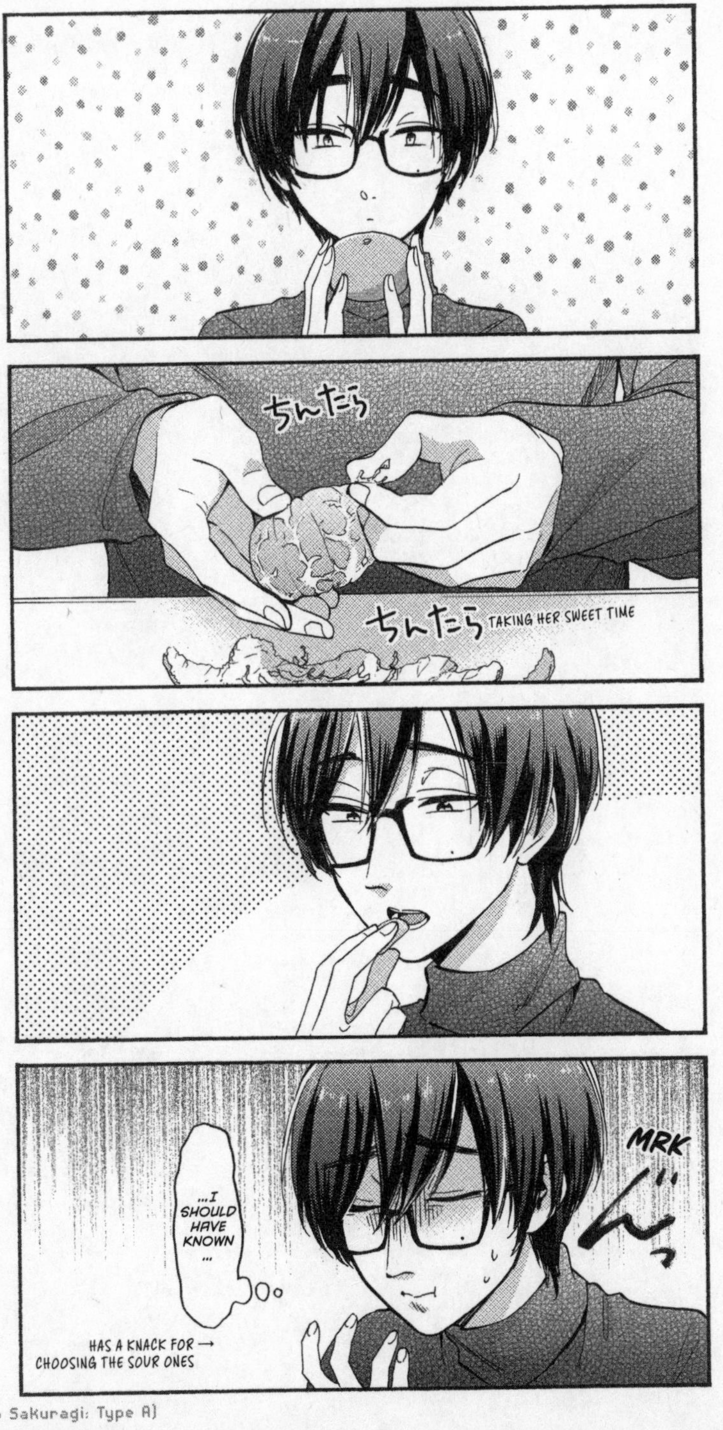
ちんたら
ちんたら TAKING HER SWEET TIME
MRK
...I SHOULD HAVE KNOWN ...
HAS A KNACK FOR → CHOOSING THE SOUR ONES

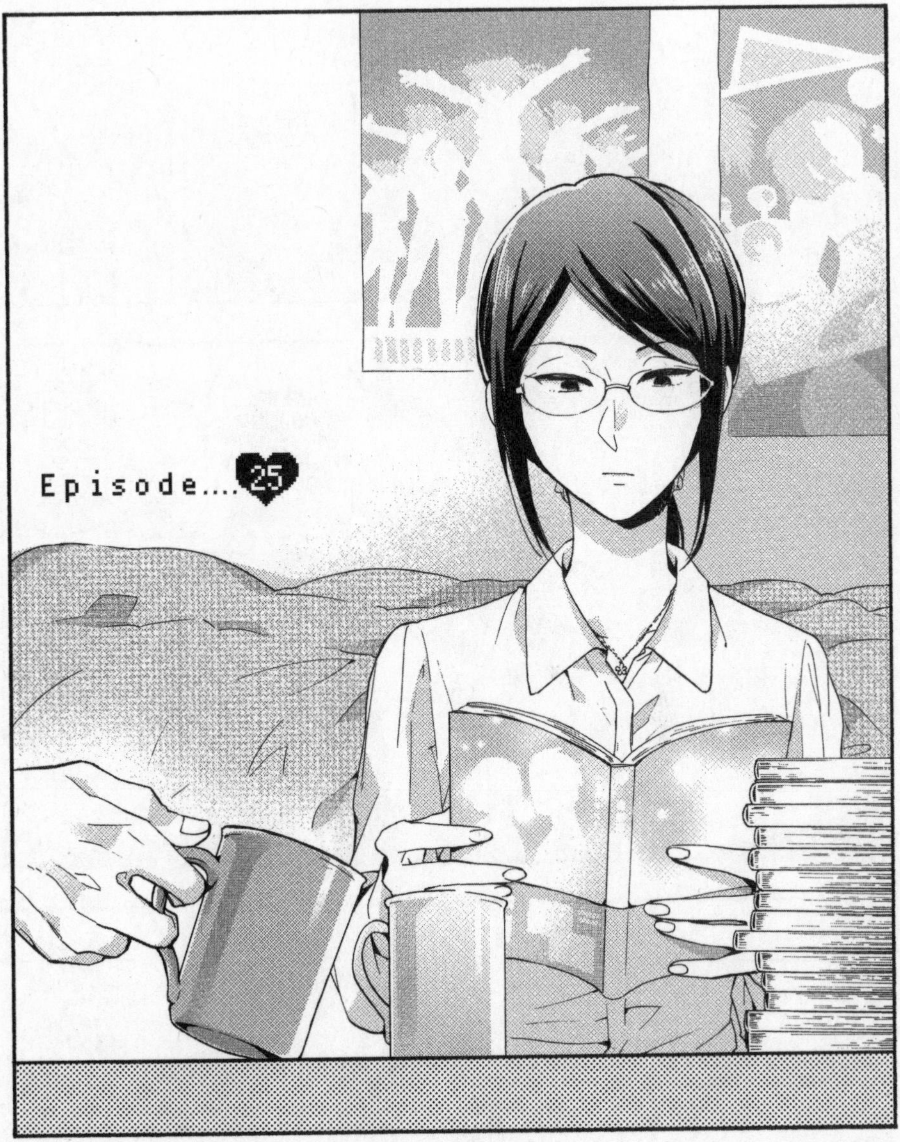
Episode....25

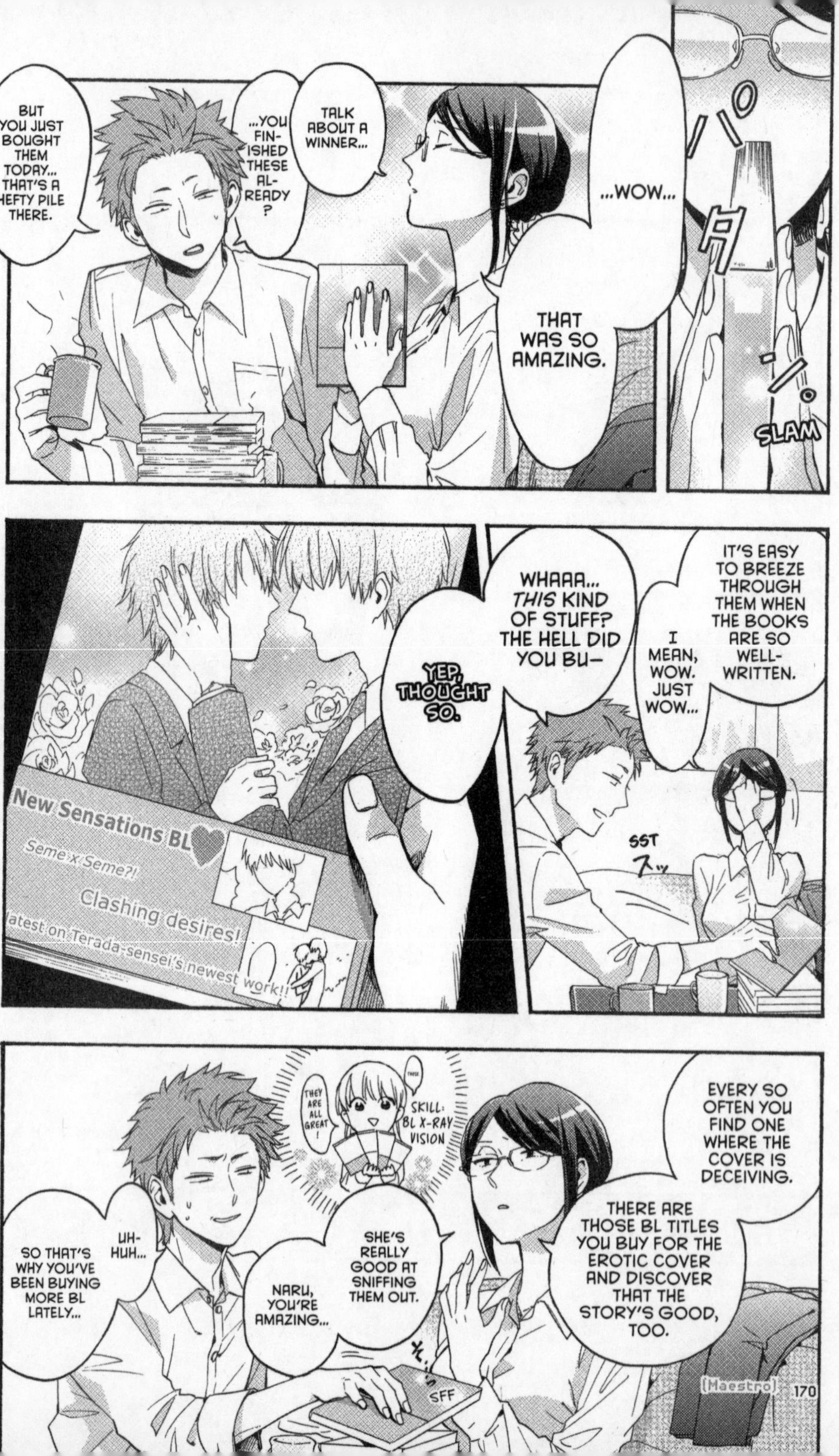
パ
タ
ー
ン
SLAM
...WOW...
THAT WAS SO AMAZING.
TALK ABOUT A WINNER...
...YOU FINISHED THESE ALREADY?
BUT YOU JUST BOUGHT THEM TODAY... THAT'S A HEFTY PILE THERE.
IT'S EASY TO BREEZE THROUGH THEM WHEN THE BOOKS ARE SO WELL-WRITTEN.
I MEAN, WOW. JUST WOW...
WHAAA... *THIS* KIND OF STUFF? THE HELL DID YOU BU—
SST
スッ
YEP, THOUGHT SO.
New Sensations BL
Seme x Seme?!
Clashing desires!
latest on Terada-sensei's newest work!!
EVERY SO OFTEN YOU FIND ONE WHERE THE COVER IS DECEIVING.
THERE ARE THOSE BL TITLES YOU BUY FOR THE EROTIC COVER AND DISCOVER THAT THE STORY'S GOOD, TOO.
THESE.
SKILL: BL X-RAY VISION
THEY ARE ALL GREAT!
SHE'S REALLY GOOD AT SNIFFING THEM OUT.
NARU, YOU'RE AMAZING...
UH-HUH...
SO THAT'S WHY YOU'VE BEEN BUYING MORE BL LATELY...
SFF
[Maestro]

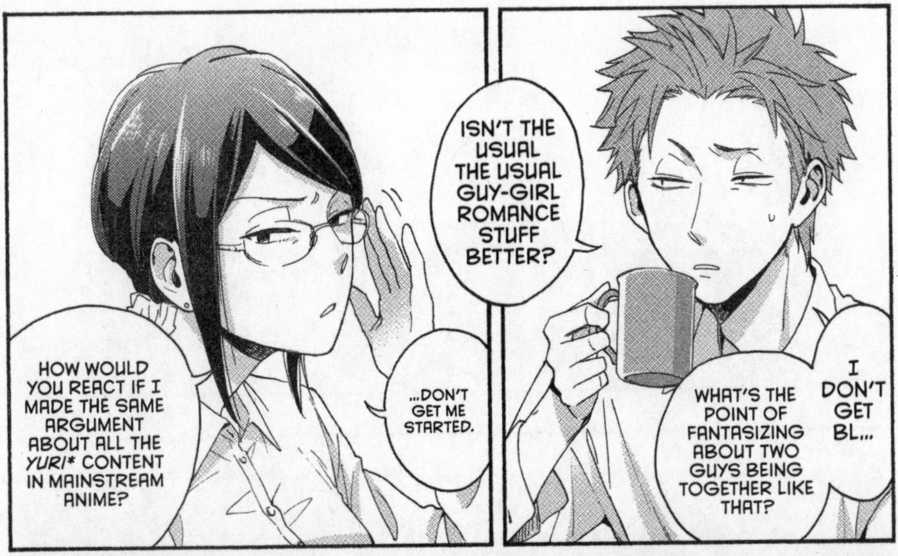
I DON'T GET BL...
WHAT'S THE POINT OF FANTASIZING ABOUT TWO GUYS BEING TOGETHER LIKE THAT?
ISN'T THE USUAL THE USUAL GUY-GIRL ROMANCE STUFF BETTER?
...DON'T GET ME STARTED.
HOW WOULD YOU REACT IF I MADE THE SAME ARGUMENT ABOUT ALL THE *YURI** CONTENT IN MAINSTREAM ANIME?

*Female-to-female romance.

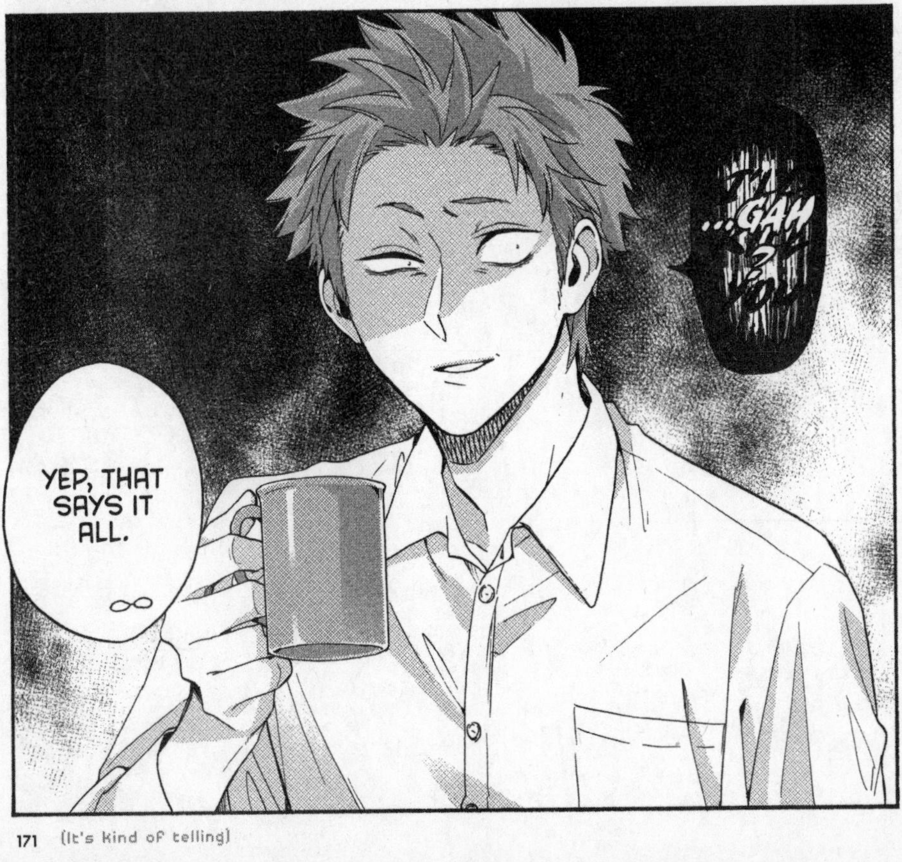
...GAH?!
YEP, THAT SAYS IT ALL.

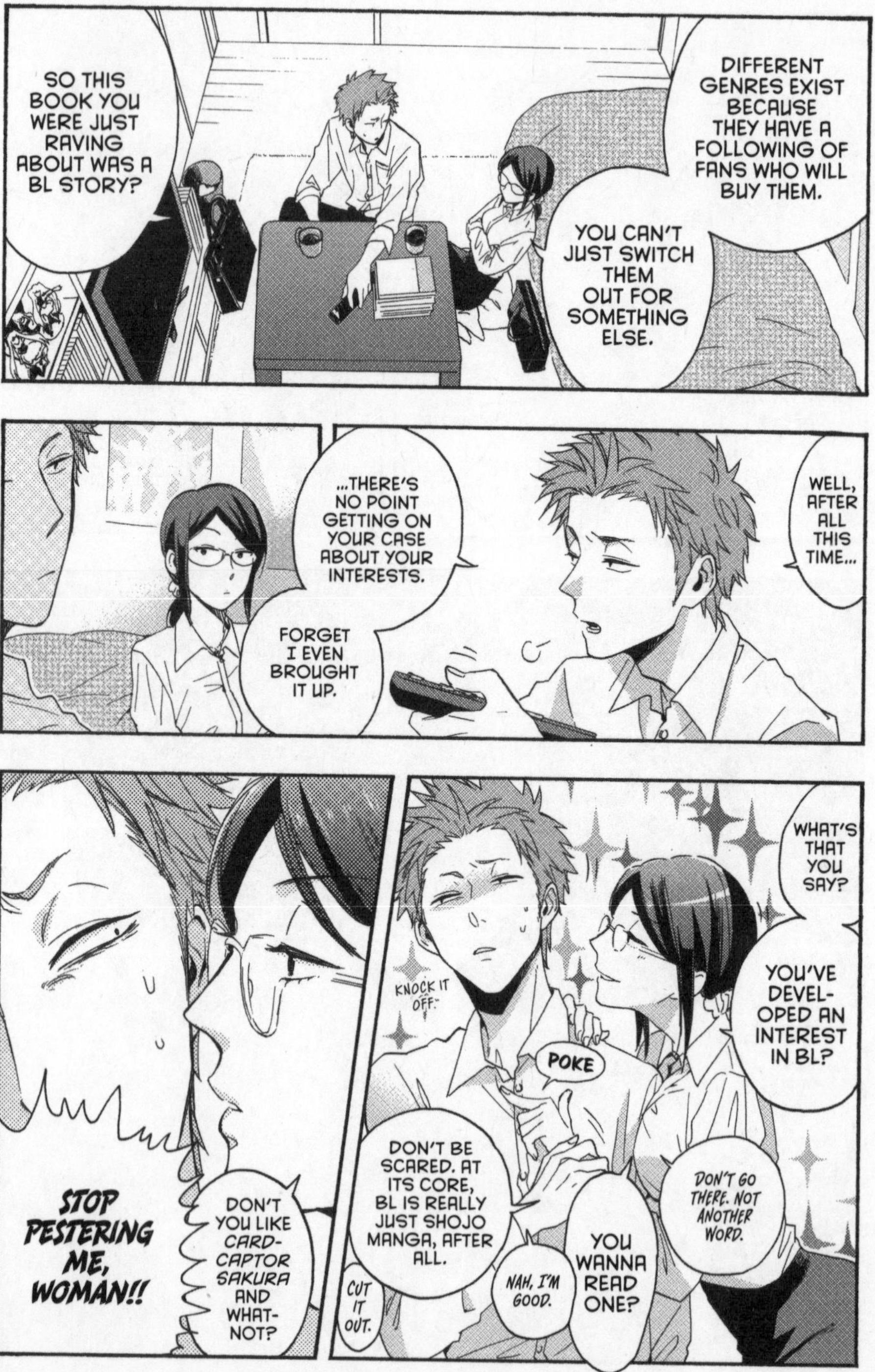
SO THIS BOOK YOU WERE JUST RAVING ABOUT WAS A BL STORY?
DIFFERENT GENRES EXIST BECAUSE THEY HAVE A FOLLOWING OF FANS WHO WILL BUY THEM.
YOU CAN'T JUST SWITCH THEM OUT FOR SOMETHING ELSE.
WELL, AFTER ALL THIS TIME...
...THERE'S NO POINT GETTING ON YOUR CASE ABOUT YOUR INTERESTS.
FORGET I EVEN BROUGHT IT UP.
WHAT'S THAT YOU SAY?
YOU'VE DEVEL-OPED AN INTEREST IN BL?
KNOCK IT OFF.
POKE
DON'T GO THERE. NOT ANOTHER WORD.
DON'T BE SCARED. AT ITS CORE, BL IS REALLY JUST SHOJO MANGA, AFTER ALL.
YOU WANNA READ ONE?
NAH, I'M GOOD.
CUT IT OUT.
DON'T YOU LIKE CARD-CAPTOR SAKURA AND WHAT-NOT?
STOP PESTERING ME, WOMAN!!

(Congratulations on *Clear Card*.)

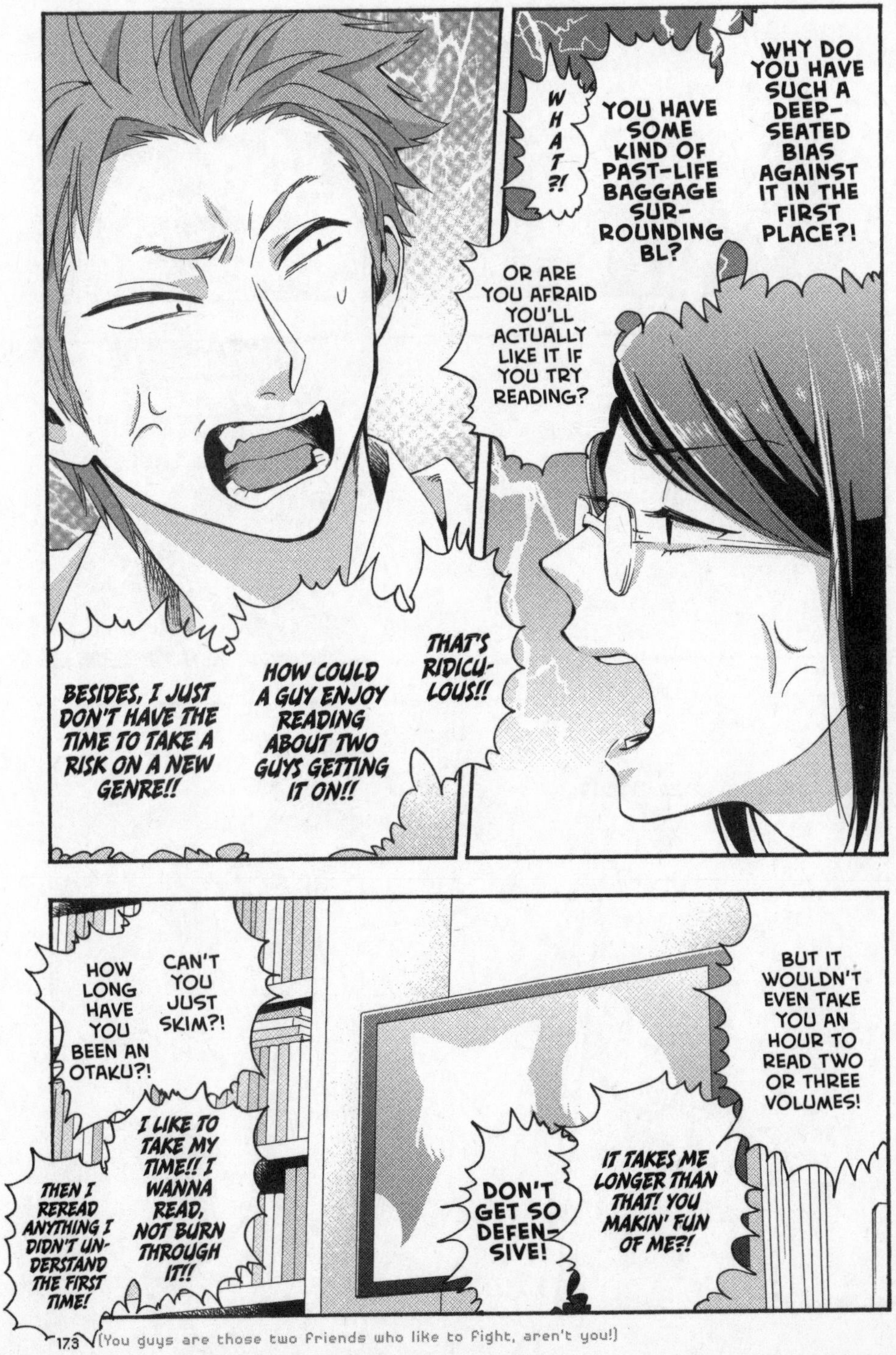
WHY DO YOU HAVE SUCH A DEEP-SEATED BIAS AGAINST IT IN THE FIRST PLACE?!
YOU HAVE SOME KIND OF PAST-LIFE BAGGAGE SUR-ROUNDING BL?
WHAT?!
OR ARE YOU AFRAID YOU'LL ACTUALLY LIKE IT IF YOU TRY READING?
THAT'S RIDICU-LOUS!!
HOW COULD A GUY ENJOY READING ABOUT TWO GUYS GETTING IT ON!!
BESIDES, I JUST DON'T HAVE THE TIME TO TAKE A RISK ON A NEW GENRE!!
BUT IT WOULDN'T EVEN TAKE YOU AN HOUR TO READ TWO OR THREE VOLUMES!
IT TAKES ME LONGER THAN THAT! YOU MAKIN' FUN OF ME?!
DON'T GET SO DEFEN-SIVE!
CAN'T YOU JUST SKIM?!
HOW LONG HAVE YOU BEEN AN OTAKU?!
I LIKE TO TAKE MY TIME!! I WANNA READ, NOT BURN THROUGH IT!!
THEN I REREAD ANYTHING I DIDN'T UN-DERSTAND THE FIRST TIME!

 (You guys are those two friends who like to fight, aren't you!)

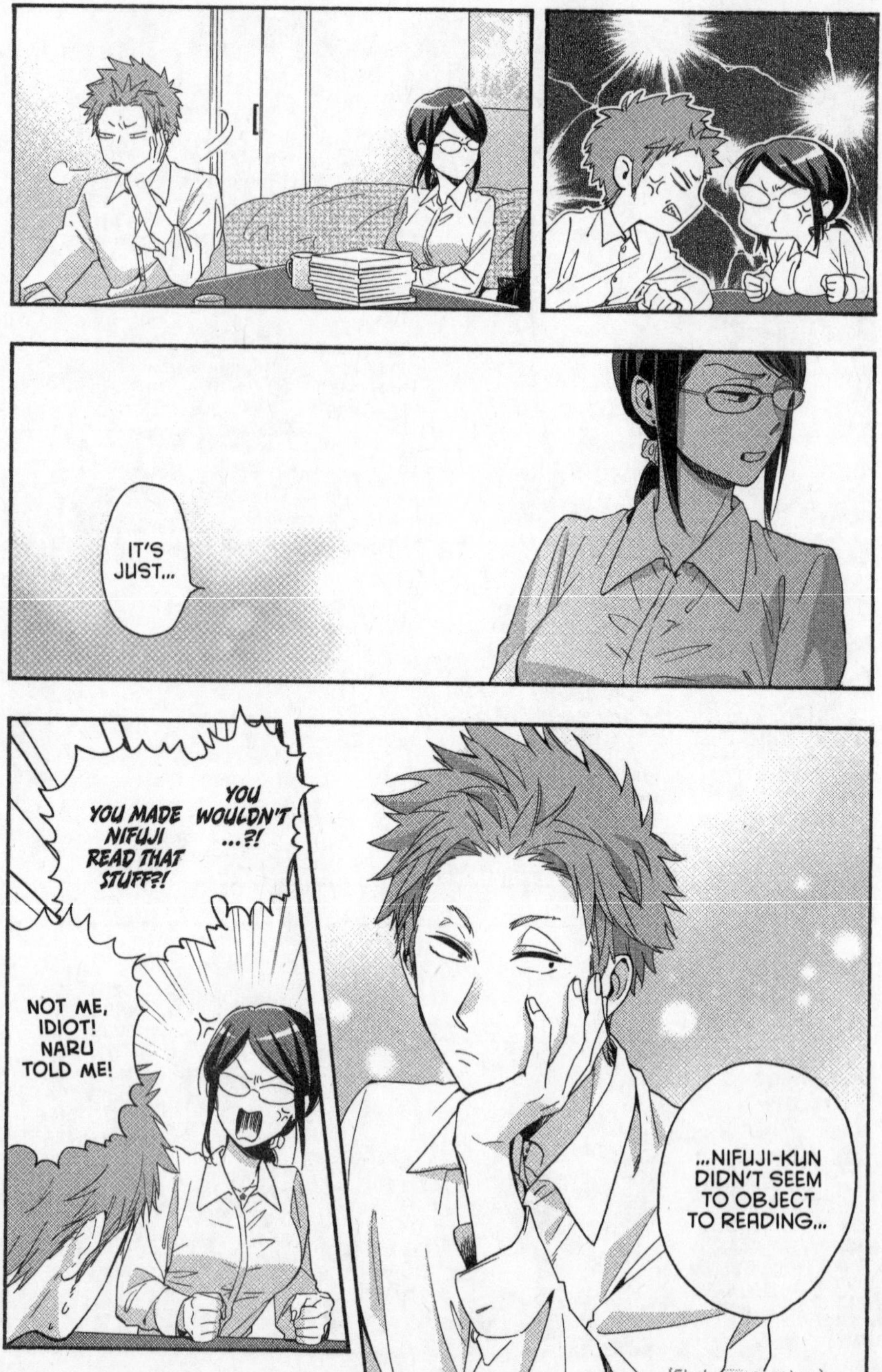
IT'S JUST...
...NIFUJI-KUN DIDN'T SEEM TO OBJECT TO READING...
YOU WOULDN'T ...?!
YOU MADE NIFUJI READ THAT STUFF?!
NOT ME, IDIOT! NARU TOLD ME!
(She's protective.)

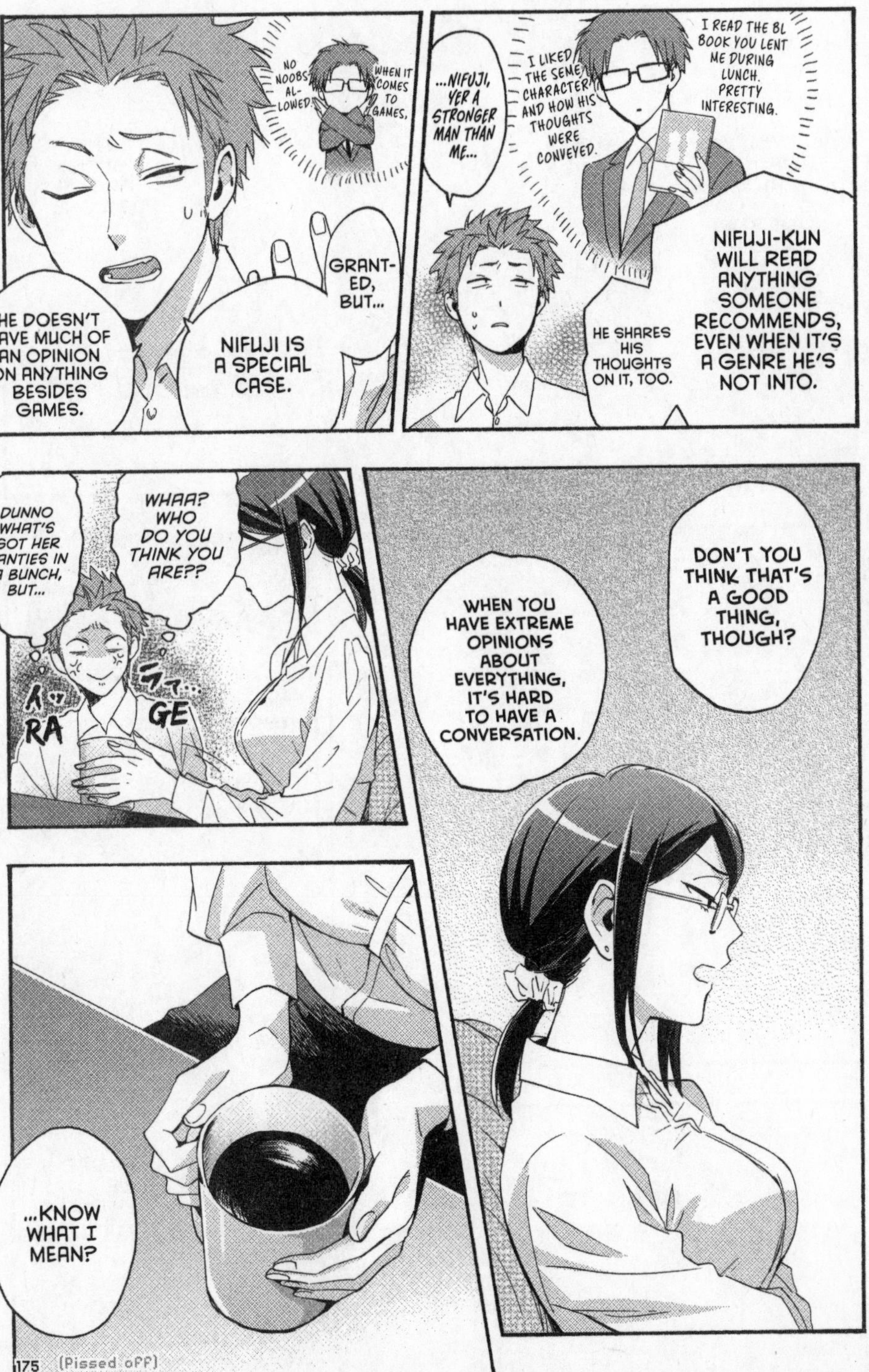
I READ THE BL BOOK YOU LENT ME DURING LUNCH. PRETTY INTERESTING.
I LIKED THE SEME CHARACTER AND HOW HIS THOUGHTS WERE CONVEYED.
...NIFUJI, YER A STRONGER MAN THAN ME...
NIFUJI-KUN WILL READ ANYTHING SOMEONE RECOMMENDS, EVEN WHEN IT'S A GENRE HE'S NOT INTO.
HE SHARES HIS THOUGHTS ON IT, TOO.
WHEN IT COMES TO GAMES,
NO NOOBS ALLOWED.
GRANTED, BUT...
NIFUJI IS A SPECIAL CASE.
HE DOESN'T HAVE MUCH OF AN OPINION ON ANYTHING BESIDES GAMES.
DON'T YOU THINK THAT'S A GOOD THING, THOUGH?
WHEN YOU HAVE EXTREME OPINIONS ABOUT EVERYTHING, IT'S HARD TO HAVE A CONVERSATION.
WHAA? WHO DO YOU THINK YOU ARE??
DUNNO WHAT'S GOT HER PANTIES IN A BUNCH, BUT...
RA
GE
...KNOW WHAT I MEAN?

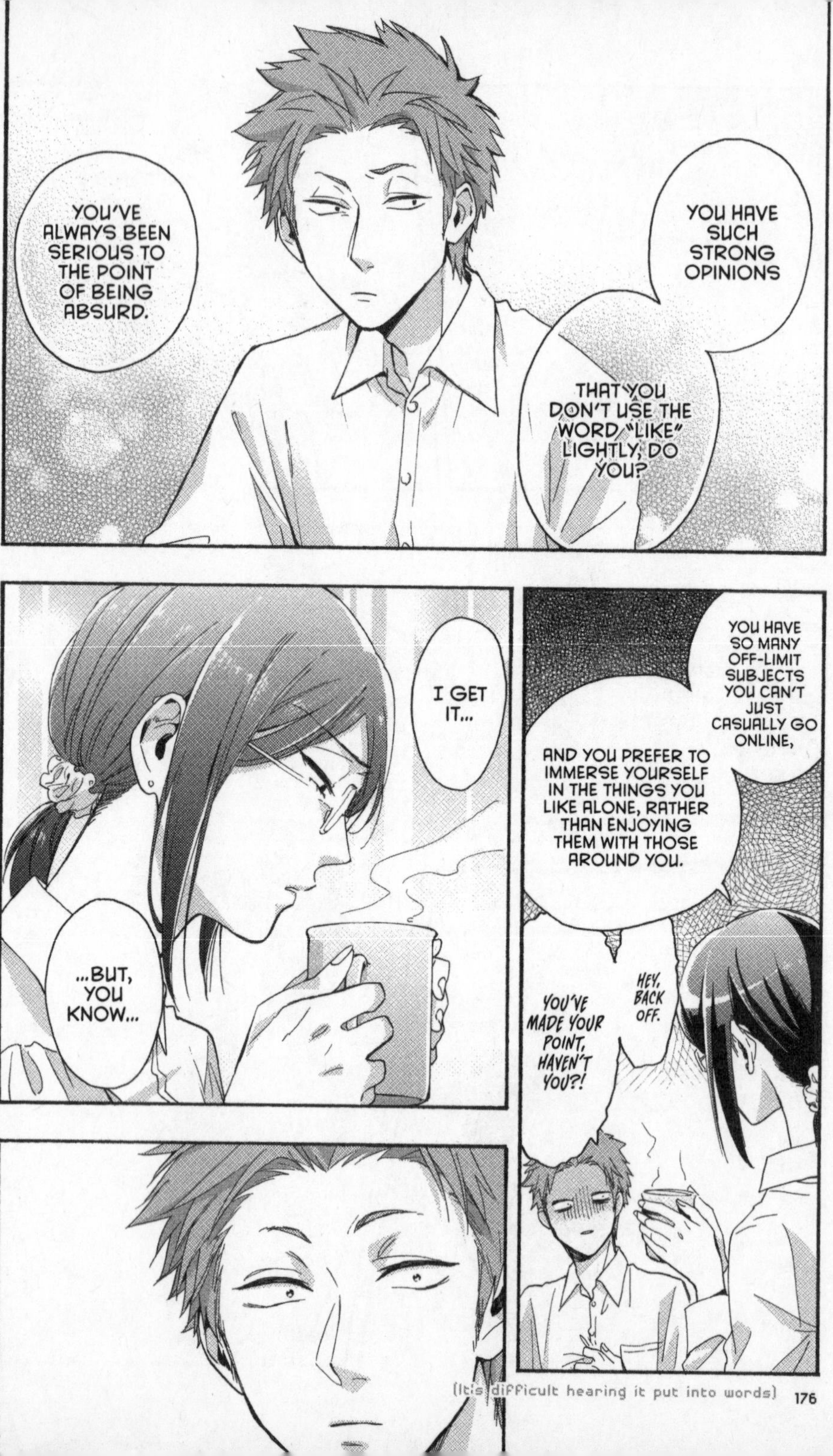
YOU HAVE SUCH STRONG OPINIONS
THAT YOU DON'T USE THE WORD "LIKE" LIGHTLY, DO YOU?
YOU'VE ALWAYS BEEN SERIOUS TO THE POINT OF BEING ABSURD.
YOU HAVE SO MANY OFF-LIMIT SUBJECTS YOU CAN'T JUST CASUALLY GO ONLINE,
AND YOU PREFER TO IMMERSE YOURSELF IN THE THINGS YOU LIKE ALONE, RATHER THAN ENJOYING THEM WITH THOSE AROUND YOU.
HEY, BACK OFF.
YOU'VE MADE YOUR POINT, HAVEN'T YOU?!
I GET IT...
...BUT, YOU KNOW...

(It's difficult hearing it put into words)

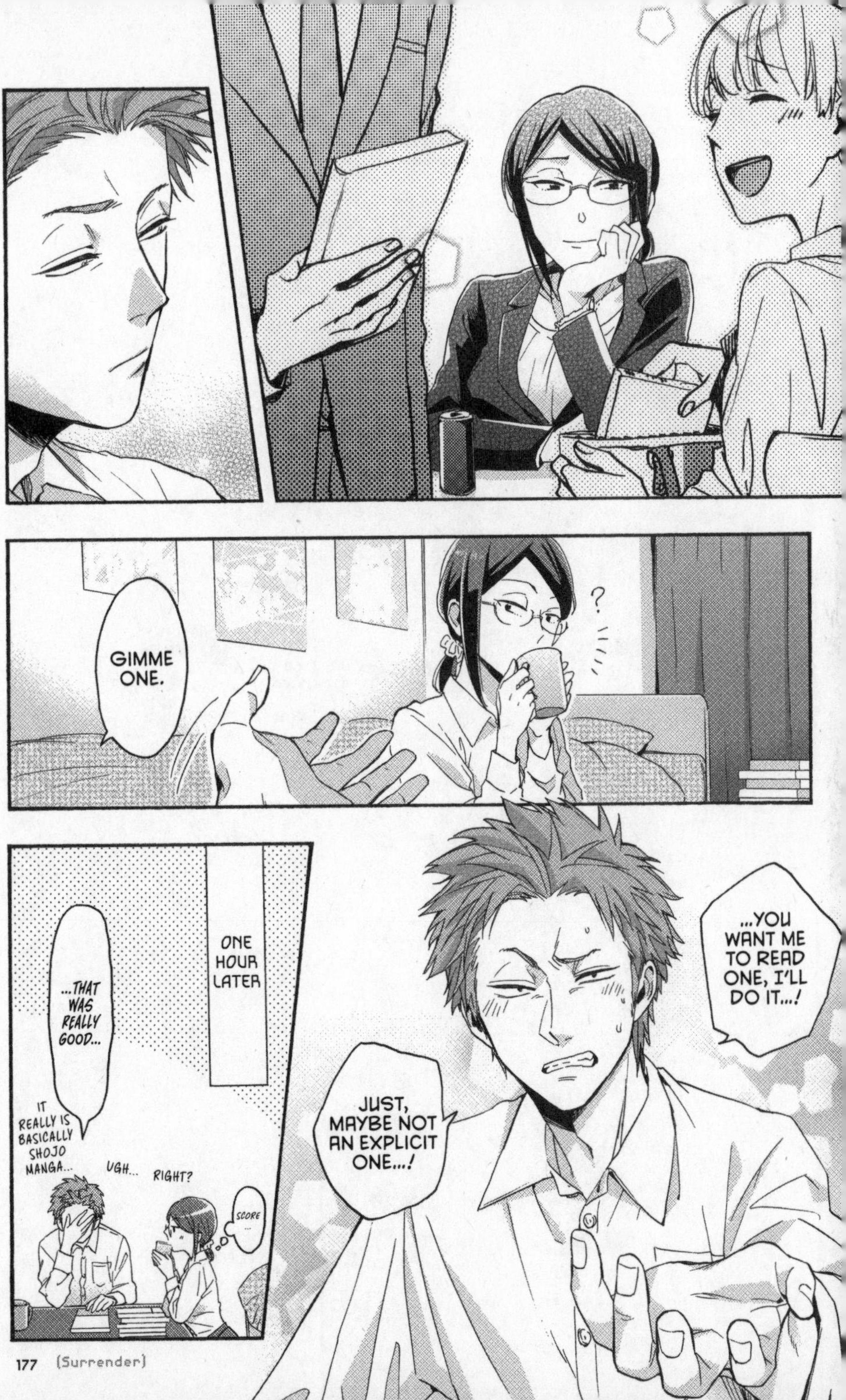
GIMME ONE.
?
...YOU WANT ME TO READ ONE, I'LL DO IT...!
JUST, MAYBE NOT AN EXPLICIT ONE...!
ONE HOUR LATER
...THAT WAS REALLY GOOD...
IT REALLY IS BASICALLY SHOJO MANGA...
UGH...
RIGHT?
SCORE...

CHARACTERS

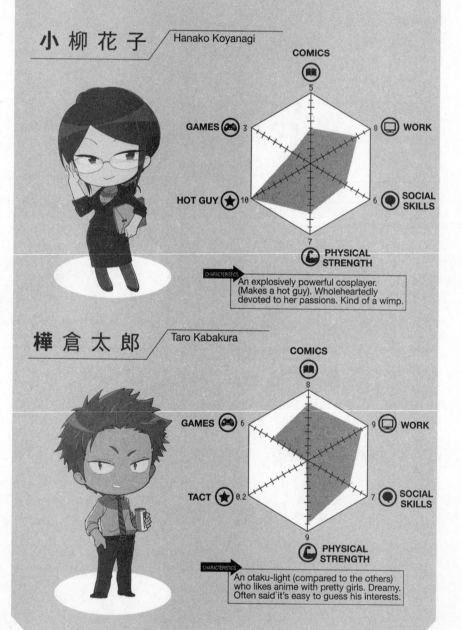

小柳花子 Hanako Koyanagi

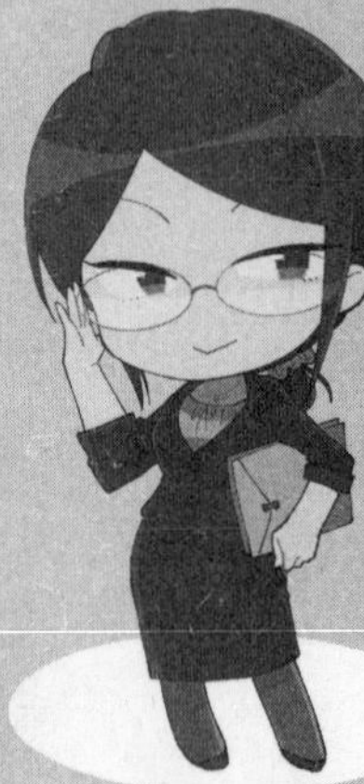

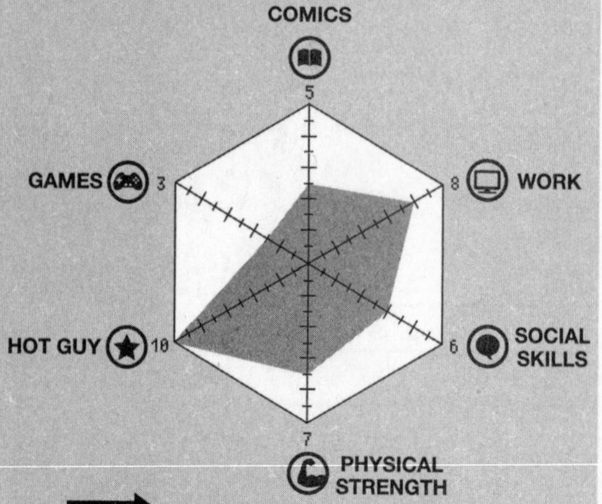
COMICS
5
GAMES
3
WORK
8
HOT GUY
10
SOCIAL SKILLS
6
PHYSICAL STRENGTH
7

CHARACTERISTICS

An explosively powerful cosplayer. (Makes a hot guy). Wholeheartedly devoted to her passions. Kind of a wimp.

樺倉太郎 Taro Kabakura

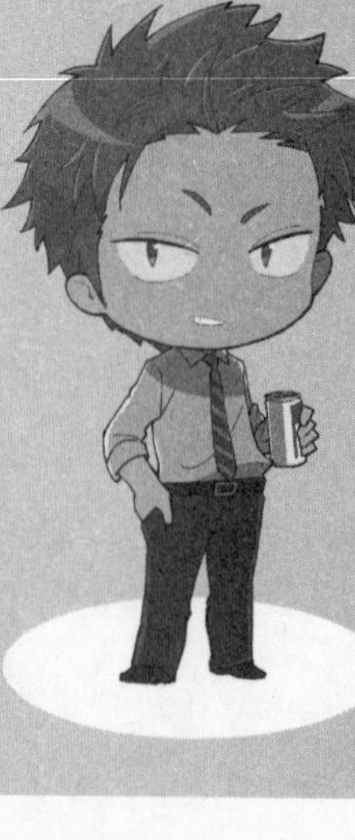

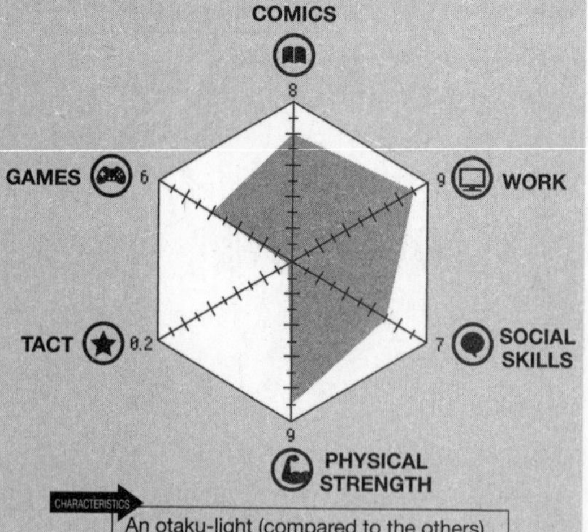
COMICS
8
GAMES
6
WORK
9
TACT
0.2
SOCIAL SKILLS
7
PHYSICAL STRENGTH
9

CHARACTERISTICS

An otaku-light (compared to the others) who likes anime with pretty girls. Dreamy. Often said it's easy to guess his interests.

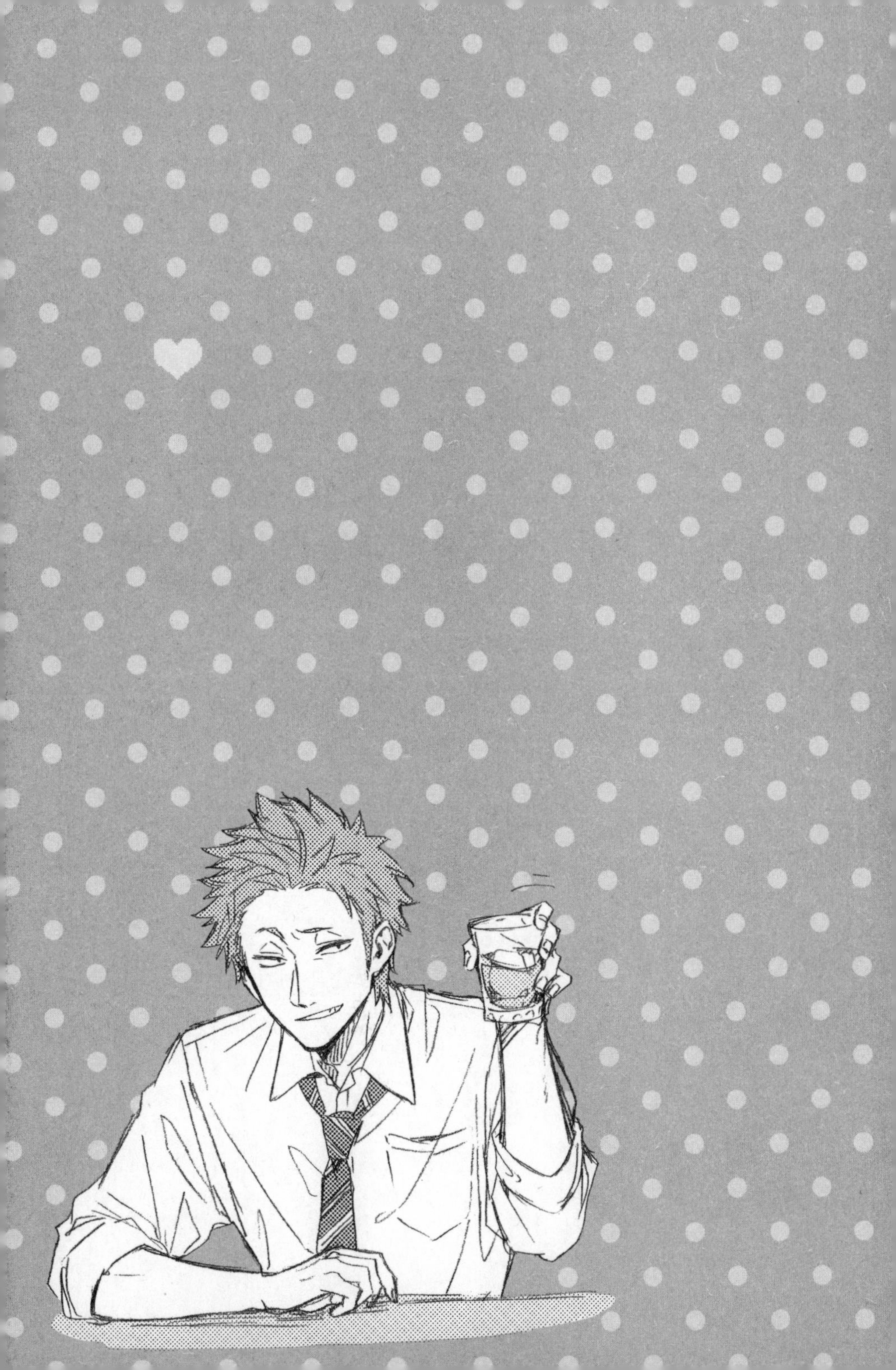

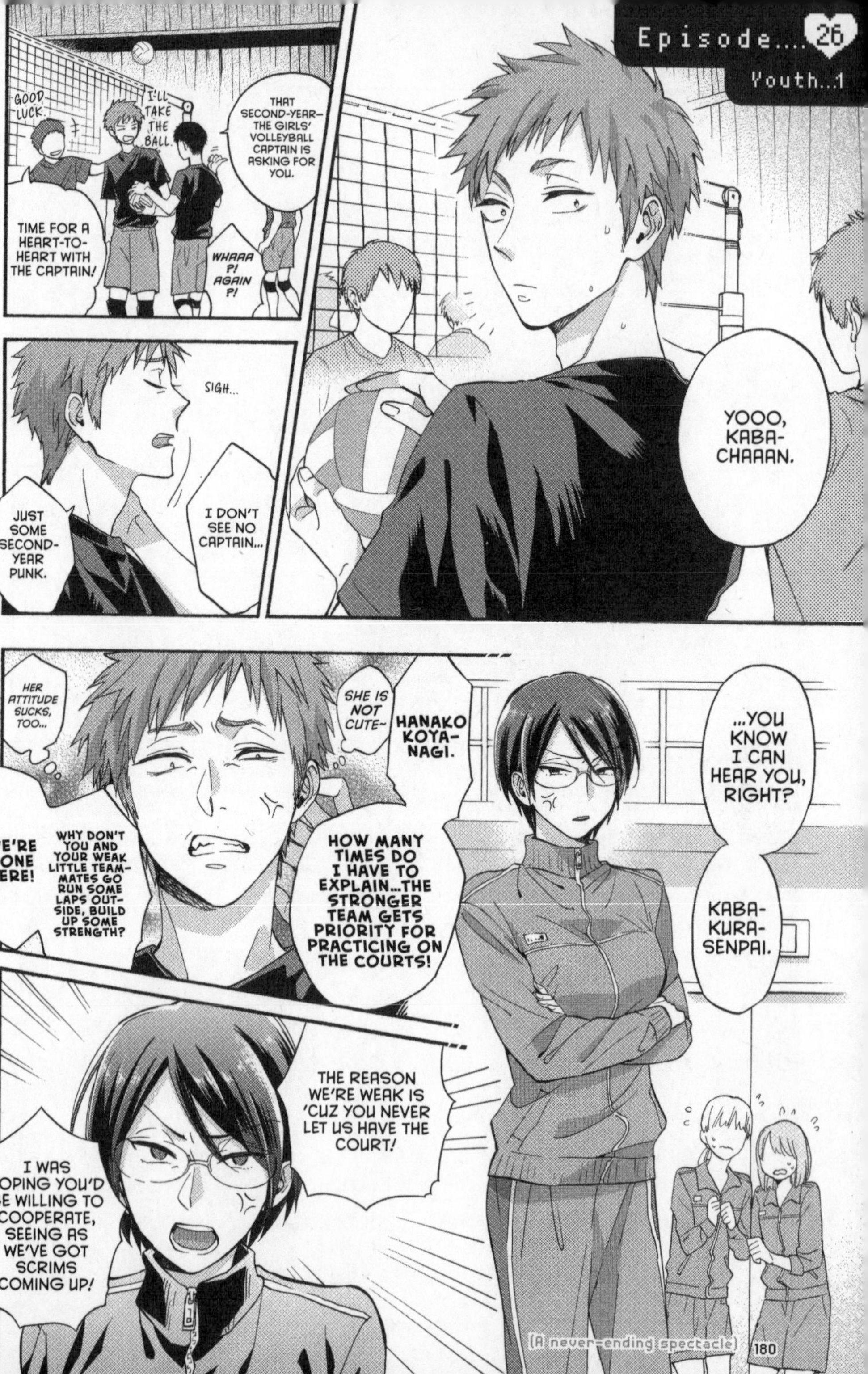
Episode....26
Youth...1
YOOO, KABA-CHAAAN.
THAT SECOND-YEAR— THE GIRLS' VOLLEYBALL CAPTAIN IS ASKING FOR YOU.
I'LL TAKE THE BALL.
GOOD LUCK.
WHAAAP! AGAIN P!
TIME FOR A HEART-TO-HEART WITH THE CAPTAIN!
SIGH...
I DON'T SEE NO CAPTAIN...
JUST SOME SECOND-YEAR PUNK.
...YOU KNOW I CAN HEAR YOU, RIGHT?
KABA-KURA-SENPAI.
HANAKO KOYA-NAGI.
SHE IS NOT CUTE~
HER ATTITUDE SUCKS, TOO...
HOW MANY TIMES DO I HAVE TO EXPLAIN...THE STRONGER TEAM GETS PRIORITY FOR PRACTICING ON THE COURTS!
WHY DON'T YOU AND YOUR WEAK LITTLE TEAM-MATES GO RUN SOME LAPS OUT-SIDE, BUILD UP SOME STRENGTH?
WE'RE DONE HERE!
THE REASON WE'RE WEAK IS 'CUZ YOU NEVER LET US HAVE THE COURT!
I WAS HOPING YOU'D BE WILLING TO COOPERATE, SEEING AS WE'VE GOT SCRIMS COMING UP!

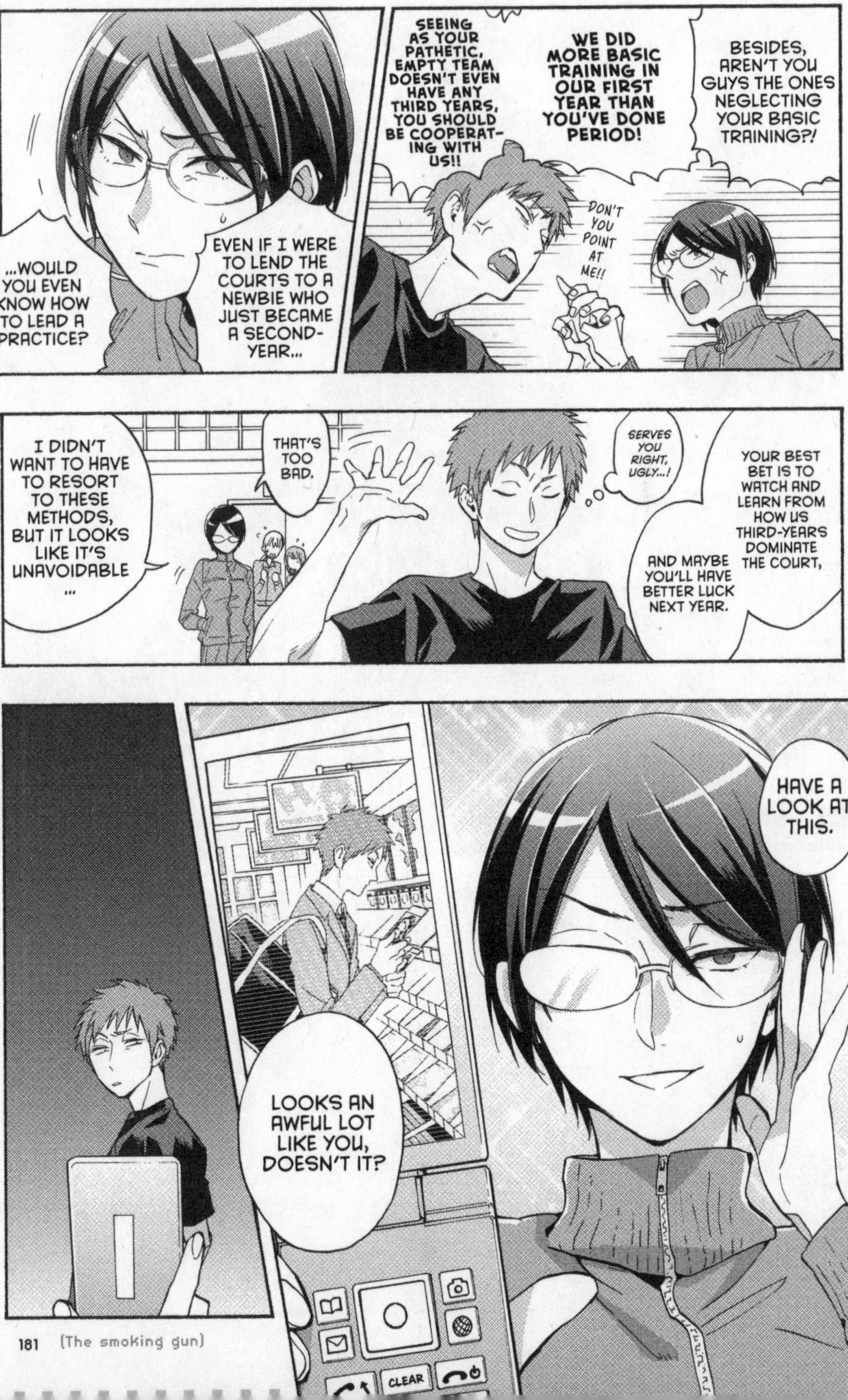
BESIDES, AREN'T YOU GUYS THE ONES NEGLECTING YOUR BASIC TRAINING?!
WE DID MORE BASIC TRAINING IN OUR FIRST YEAR THAN YOU'VE DONE PERIOD!
SEEING AS YOUR PATHETIC, EMPTY TEAM DOESN'T EVEN HAVE ANY THIRD YEARS, YOU SHOULD BE COOPERATING WITH US!!
DON'T YOU POINT AT ME!!
EVEN IF I WERE TO LEND THE COURTS TO A NEWBIE WHO JUST BECAME A SECOND-YEAR...
...WOULD YOU EVEN KNOW HOW TO LEAD A PRACTICE?
YOUR BEST BET IS TO WATCH AND LEARN FROM HOW US THIRD-YEARS DOMINATE THE COURT,
AND MAYBE YOU'LL HAVE BETTER LUCK NEXT YEAR.
SERVES YOU RIGHT, UGLY...!
THAT'S TOO BAD.
I DIDN'T WANT TO HAVE TO RESORT TO THESE METHODS, BUT IT LOOKS LIKE IT'S UNAVOIDABLE ...
HAVE A LOOK AT THIS.
LOOKS AN AWFUL LOT LIKE YOU, DOESN'T IT?
CLEAR

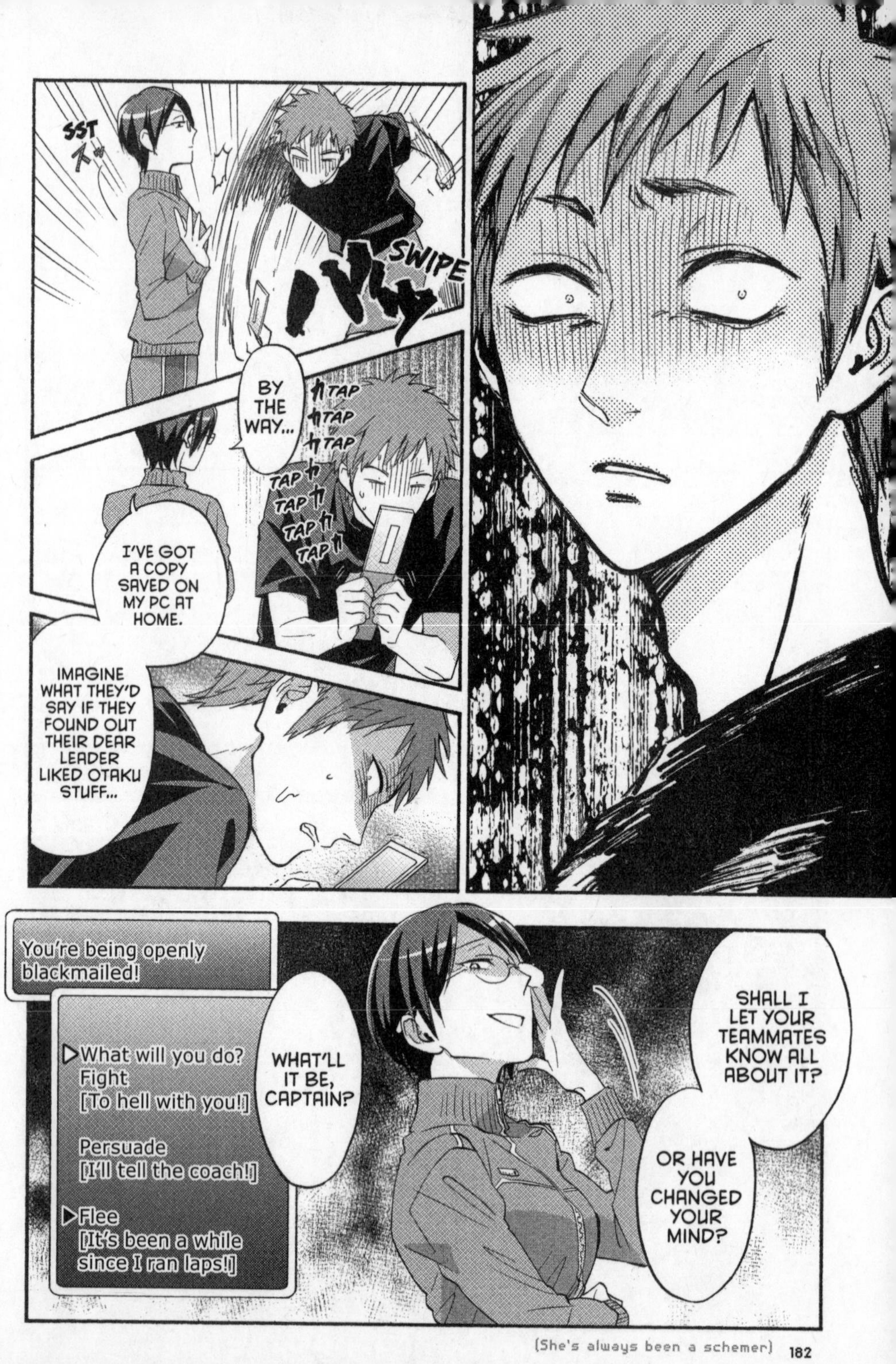
SST
SWIPE
BY THE WAY...
TAP TAP TAP TAP TAP TAP TAP
I'VE GOT A COPY SAVED ON MY PC AT HOME.
IMAGINE WHAT THEY'D SAY IF THEY FOUND OUT THEIR DEAR LEADER LIKED OTAKU STUFF...
SHALL I LET YOUR TEAMMATES KNOW ALL ABOUT IT?
OR HAVE YOU CHANGED YOUR MIND?
WHAT'LL IT BE, CAPTAIN?
You're being openly blackmailed!
▷What will you do?
Fight
[To hell with you!]
Persuade
[I'll tell the coach!]
▷Flee
[It's been a while since I ran laps!]

(She's always been a schemer)

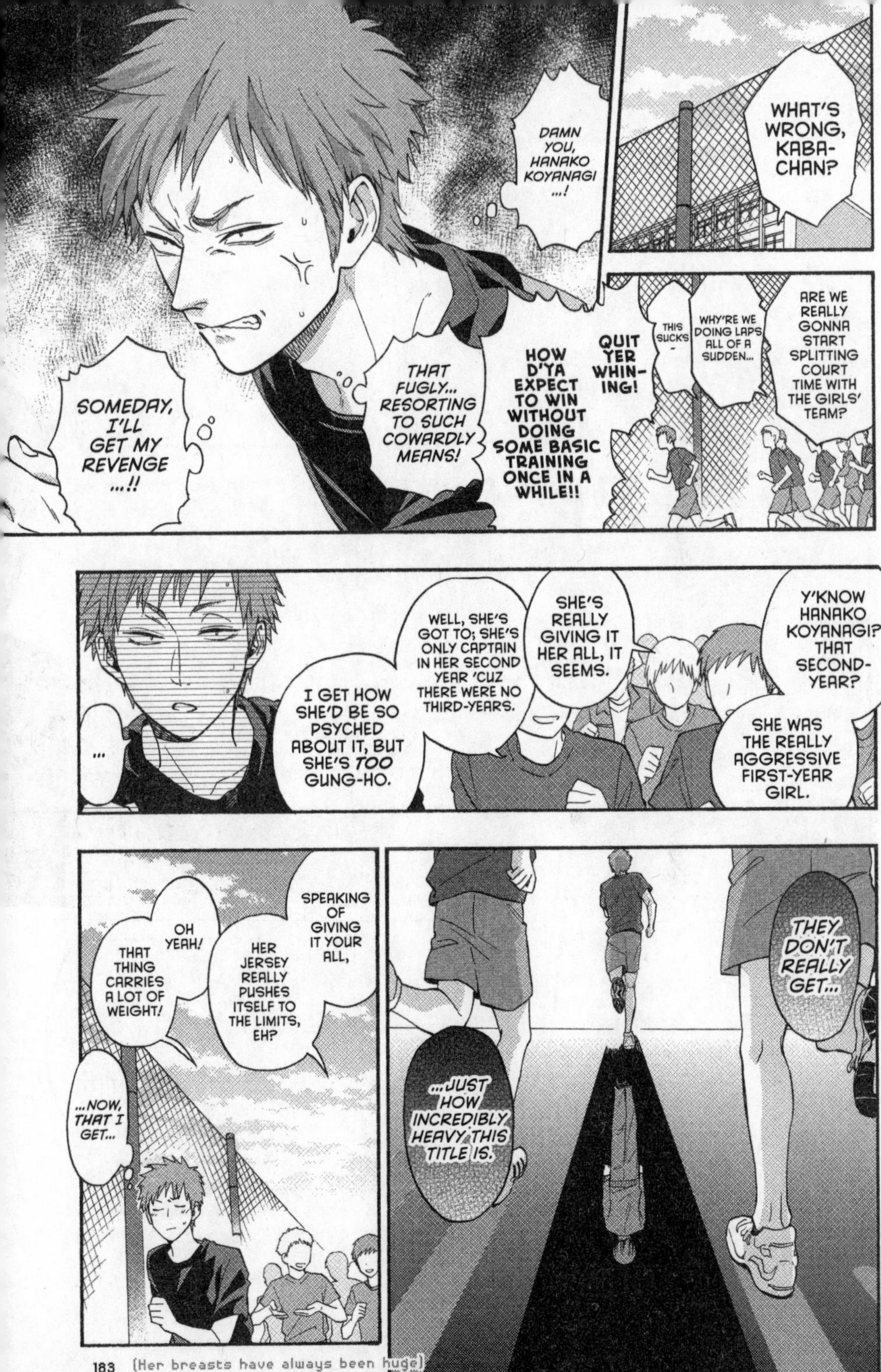
WHAT'S WRONG, KABA-CHAN?
ARE WE REALLY GONNA START SPLITTING COURT TIME WITH THE GIRLS' TEAM?
WHY'RE WE DOING LAPS ALL OF A SUDDEN...
THIS SUCKS~
QUIT YER WHINING!
HOW D'YA EXPECT TO WIN WITHOUT DOING SOME BASIC TRAINING ONCE IN A WHILE!!
DAMN YOU, HANAKO KOYANAGI ...!
THAT FUGLY... RESORTING TO SUCH COWARDLY MEANS!
SOMEDAY, I'LL GET MY REVENGE ...!!
Y'KNOW HANAKO KOYANAGI? THAT SECOND-YEAR?
SHE WAS THE REALLY AGGRESSIVE FIRST-YEAR GIRL.
SHE'S REALLY GIVING IT HER ALL, IT SEEMS.
WELL, SHE'S GOT TO; SHE'S ONLY CAPTAIN IN HER SECOND YEAR 'CUZ THERE WERE NO THIRD-YEARS.
I GET HOW SHE'D BE SO PSYCHED ABOUT IT, BUT SHE'S TOO GUNG-HO.
...
THEY DON'T REALLY GET...
...JUST HOW INCREDIBLY HEAVY THIS TITLE IS.
SPEAKING OF GIVING IT YOUR ALL,
HER JERSEY REALLY PUSHES ITSELF TO THE LIMITS, EH?
OH YEAH! THAT THING CARRIES A LOT OF WEIGHT!
...NOW, THAT I GET...

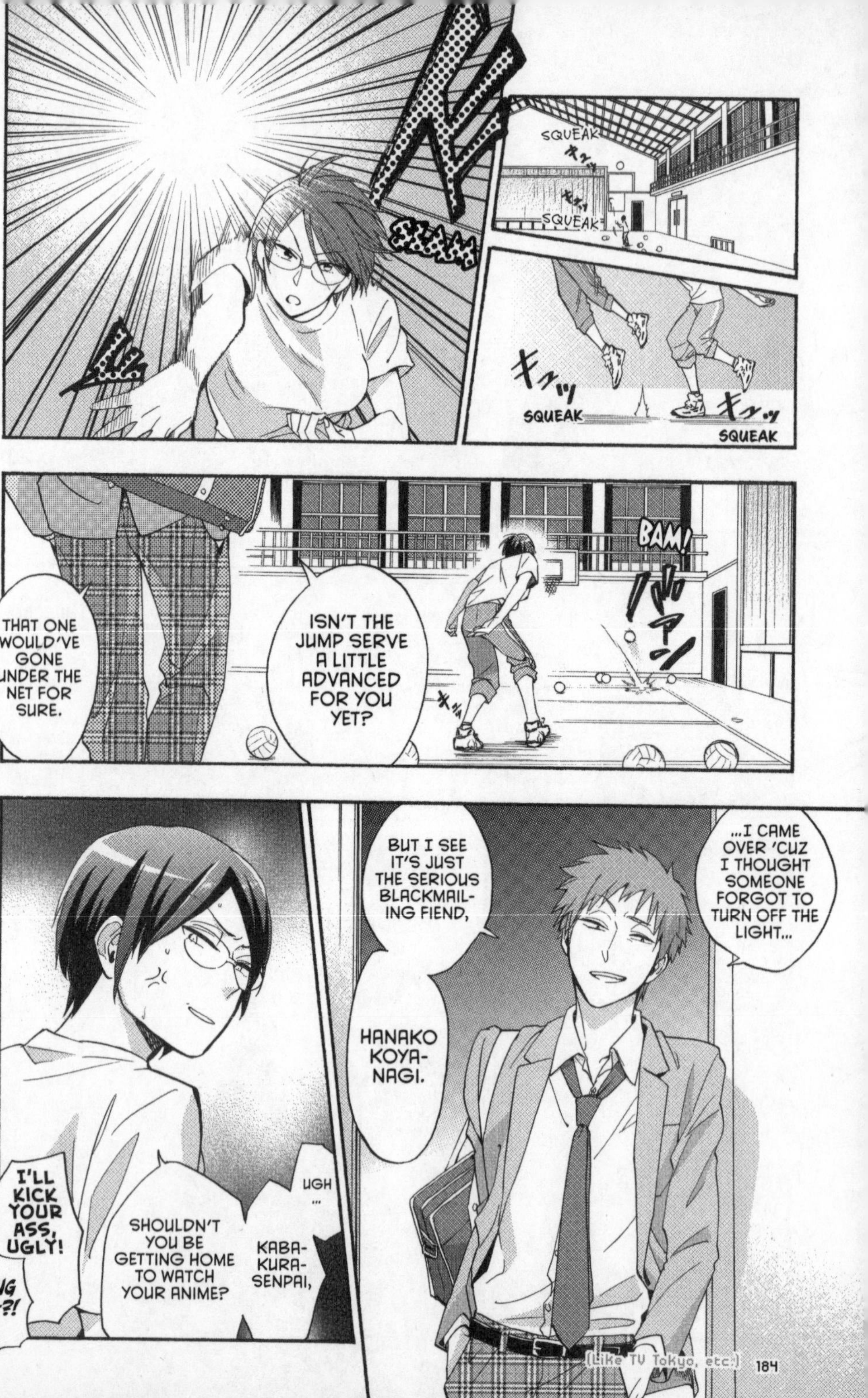
SQUEAK
SQUEAK
SQUEAK
SQUEAK
BAM!
ISN'T THE JUMP SERVE A LITTLE ADVANCED FOR YOU YET?
THAT ONE WOULD'VE GONE UNDER THE NET FOR SURE.
...I CAME OVER 'CUZ I THOUGHT SOMEONE FORGOT TO TURN OFF THE LIGHT...
BUT I SEE IT'S JUST THE SERIOUS BLACKMAIL-ING FIEND,
HANAKO KOYA-NAGI.
UGH ...
KABA-KURA-SENPAI,
SHOULDN'T YOU BE GETTING HOME TO WATCH YOUR ANIME?
I'LL KICK YOUR ASS, UGLY!
UG-?!

(Like TV Tokyo, etc.)

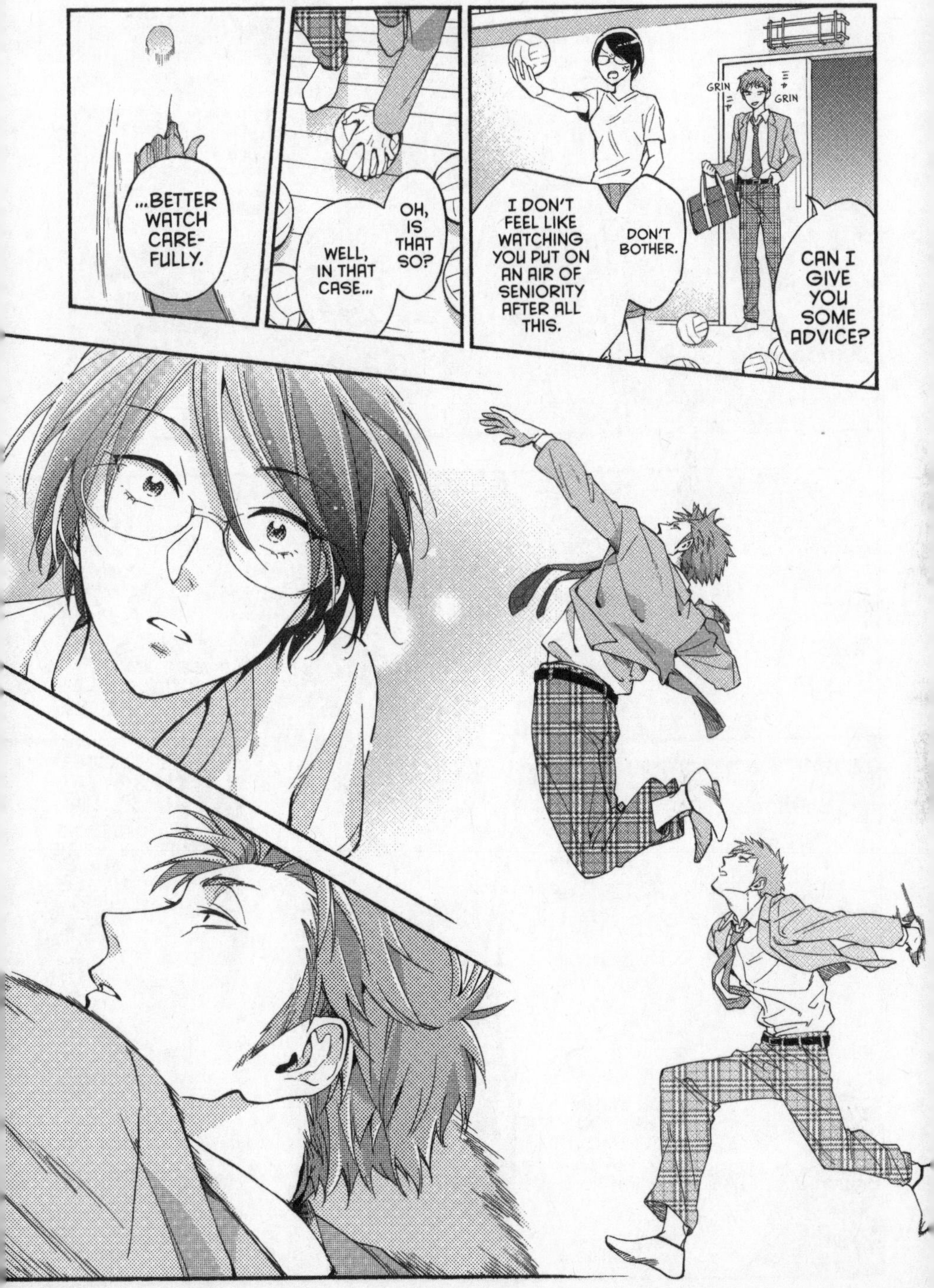
GRIN GRIN
CAN I GIVE YOU SOME ADVICE?
DON'T BOTHER.
I DON'T FEEL LIKE WATCHING YOU PUT ON AN AIR OF SENIORITY AFTER ALL THIS.
OH, IS THAT SO?
WELL, IN THAT CASE...
...BETTER WATCH CAREFULLY.

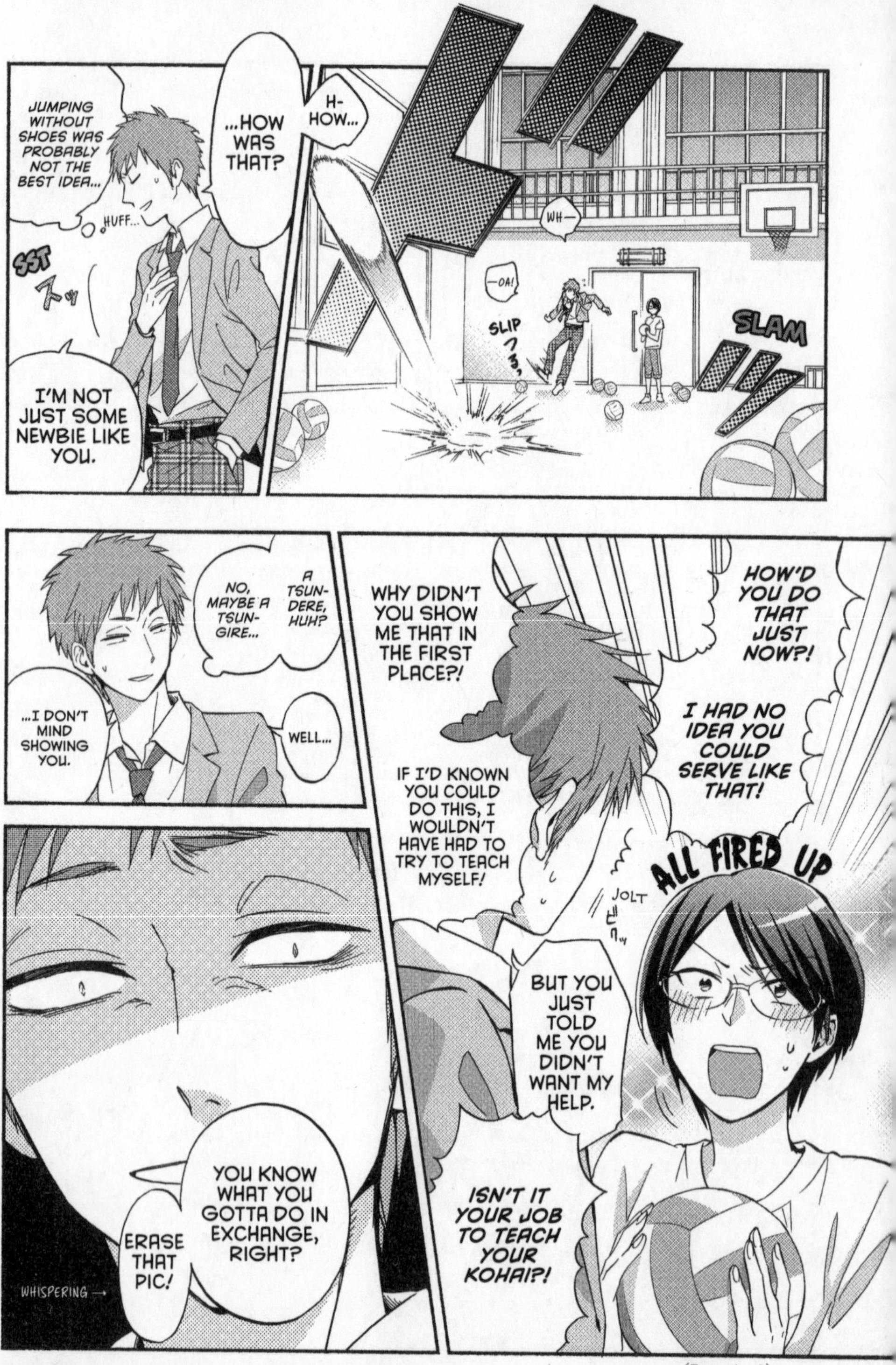
H-HOW...
...HOW WAS THAT?
WH—
—OA!
SLAM
SLIP
JUMPING WITHOUT SHOES WAS PROBABLY NOT THE BEST IDEA...
HUFF...
SST
I'M NOT JUST SOME NEWBIE LIKE YOU.
HOW'D YOU DO THAT JUST NOW?!
WHY DIDN'T YOU SHOW ME THAT IN THE FIRST PLACE?!
I HAD NO IDEA YOU COULD SERVE LIKE THAT!
IF I'D KNOWN YOU COULD DO THIS, I WOULDN'T HAVE HAD TO TRY TO TEACH MYSELF!
ALL FIRED UP
JOLT
BUT YOU JUST TOLD ME YOU DIDN'T WANT MY HELP.
ISN'T IT YOUR JOB TO TEACH YOUR KOHAI?!
A TSUNDERE, HUH?
NO, MAYBE A TSUNGIRE...
WELL...
...I DON'T MIND SHOWING YOU.
YOU KNOW WHAT YOU GOTTA DO IN EXCHANGE, RIGHT?
ERASE THAT PIC!
WHISPERING →

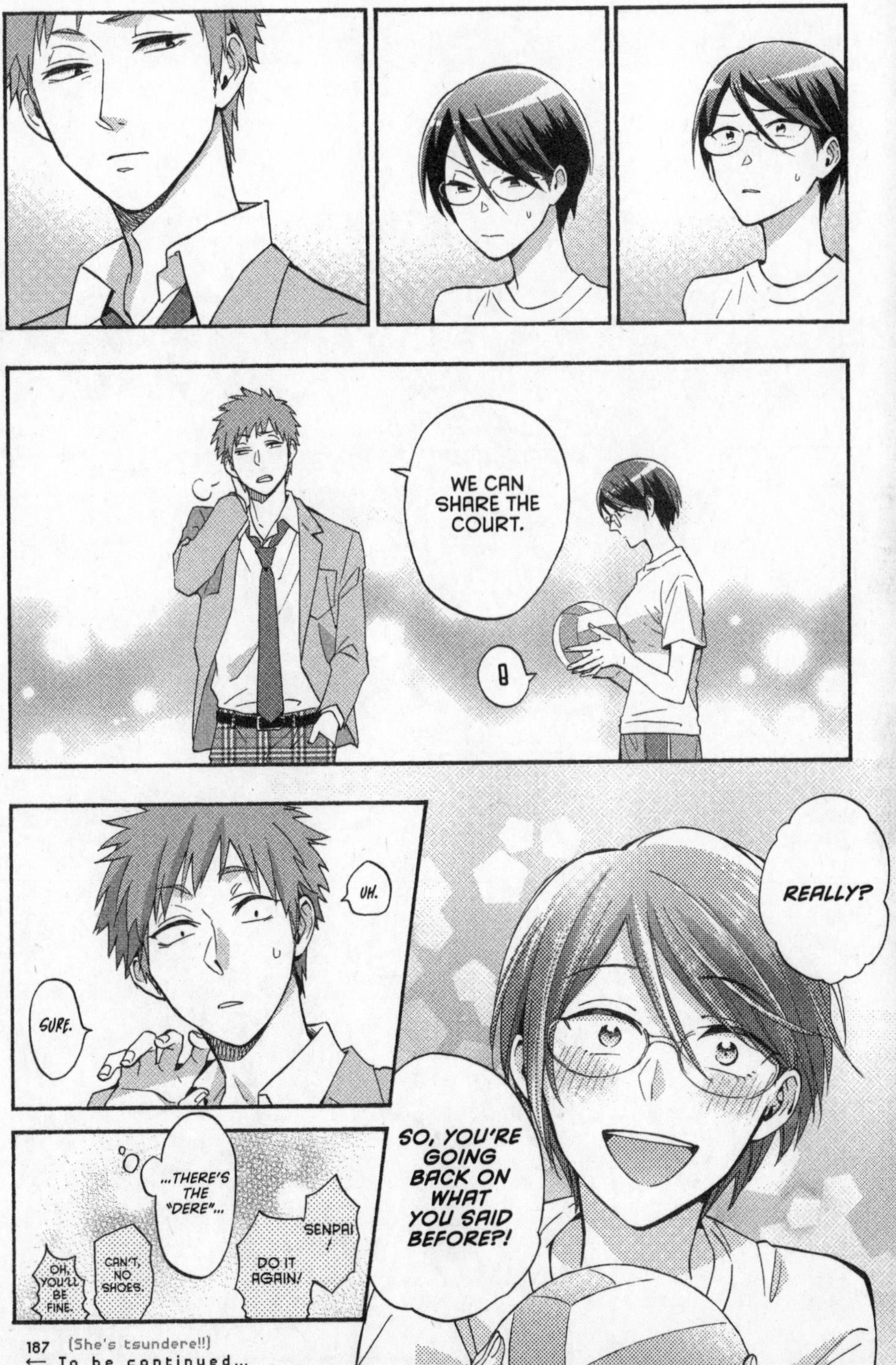
WE CAN SHARE THE COURT.
!
REALLY?
SO, YOU'RE GOING BACK ON WHAT YOU SAID BEFORE?!
UH.
SURE.
...THERE'S THE "DERE"...
SENPAI!
DO IT AGAIN!
CAN'T, NO SHOES.
OH, YOU'LL BE FINE.

(She's tsundere!!)

← To be continued...

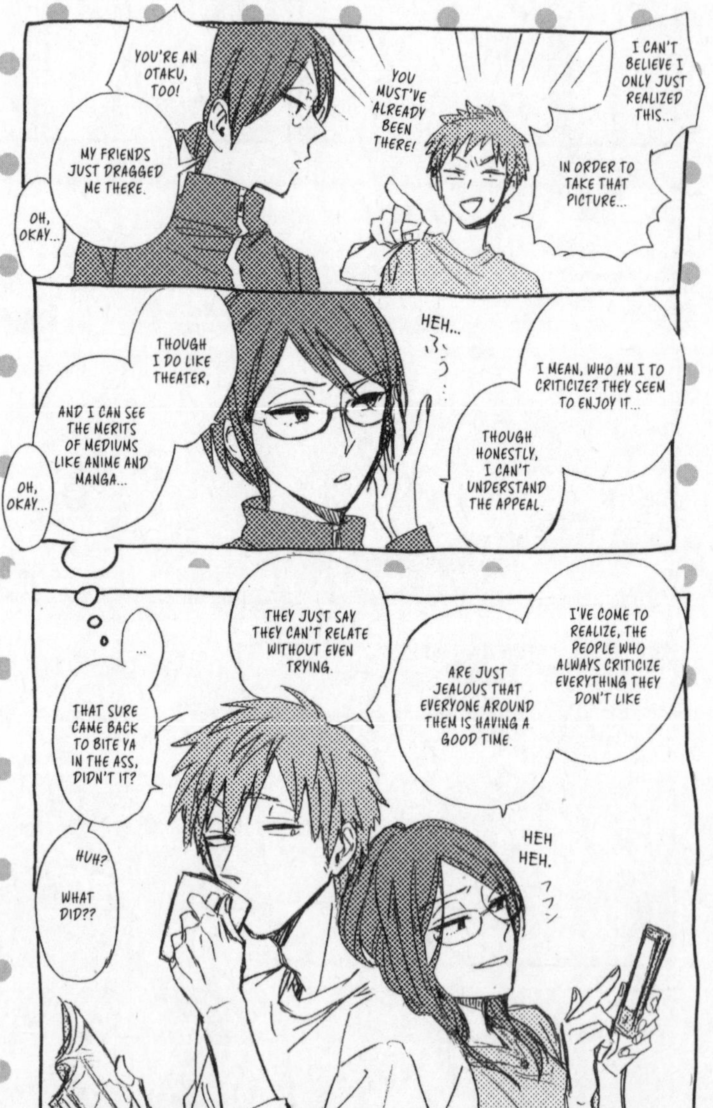
I CAN'T BELIEVE I ONLY JUST REALIZED THIS...
IN ORDER TO TAKE THAT PICTURE...
YOU MUST'VE ALREADY BEEN THERE!
YOU'RE AN OTAKU, TOO!
MY FRIENDS JUST DRAGGED ME THERE.
OH, OKAY...
HEH...
ふぅ
I MEAN, WHO AM I TO CRITICIZE? THEY SEEM TO ENJOY IT...
THOUGH HONESTLY, I CAN'T UNDERSTAND THE APPEAL.
THOUGH I DO LIKE THEATER,
AND I CAN SEE THE MERITS OF MEDIUMS LIKE ANIME AND MANGA...
OH, OKAY...
I'VE COME TO REALIZE, THE PEOPLE WHO ALWAYS CRITICIZE EVERYTHING THEY DON'T LIKE
ARE JUST JEALOUS THAT EVERYONE AROUND THEM IS HAVING A GOOD TIME.
THEY JUST SAY THEY CAN'T RELATE WITHOUT EVEN TRYING.
HEH HEH.
フフン
...
THAT SURE CAME BACK TO BITE YA IN THE ASS, DIDN'T IT?
HUH?
WHAT DID??

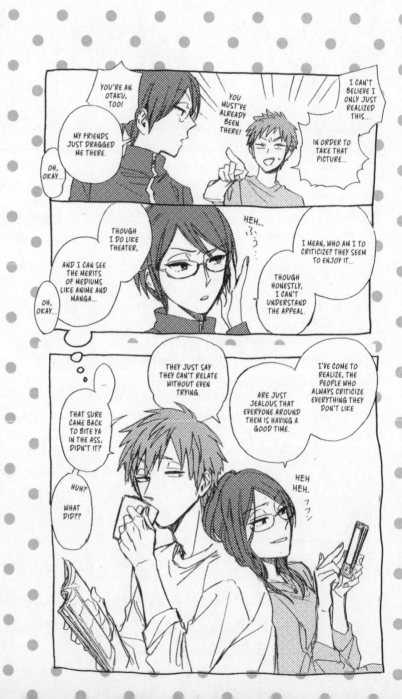

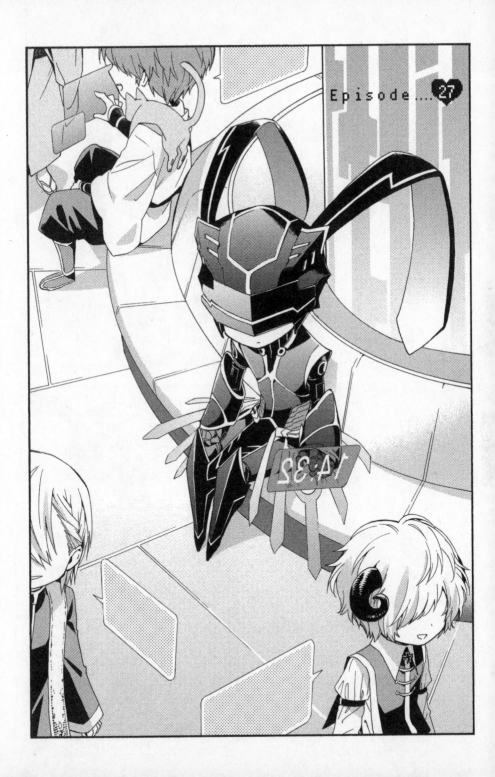

Episode....27

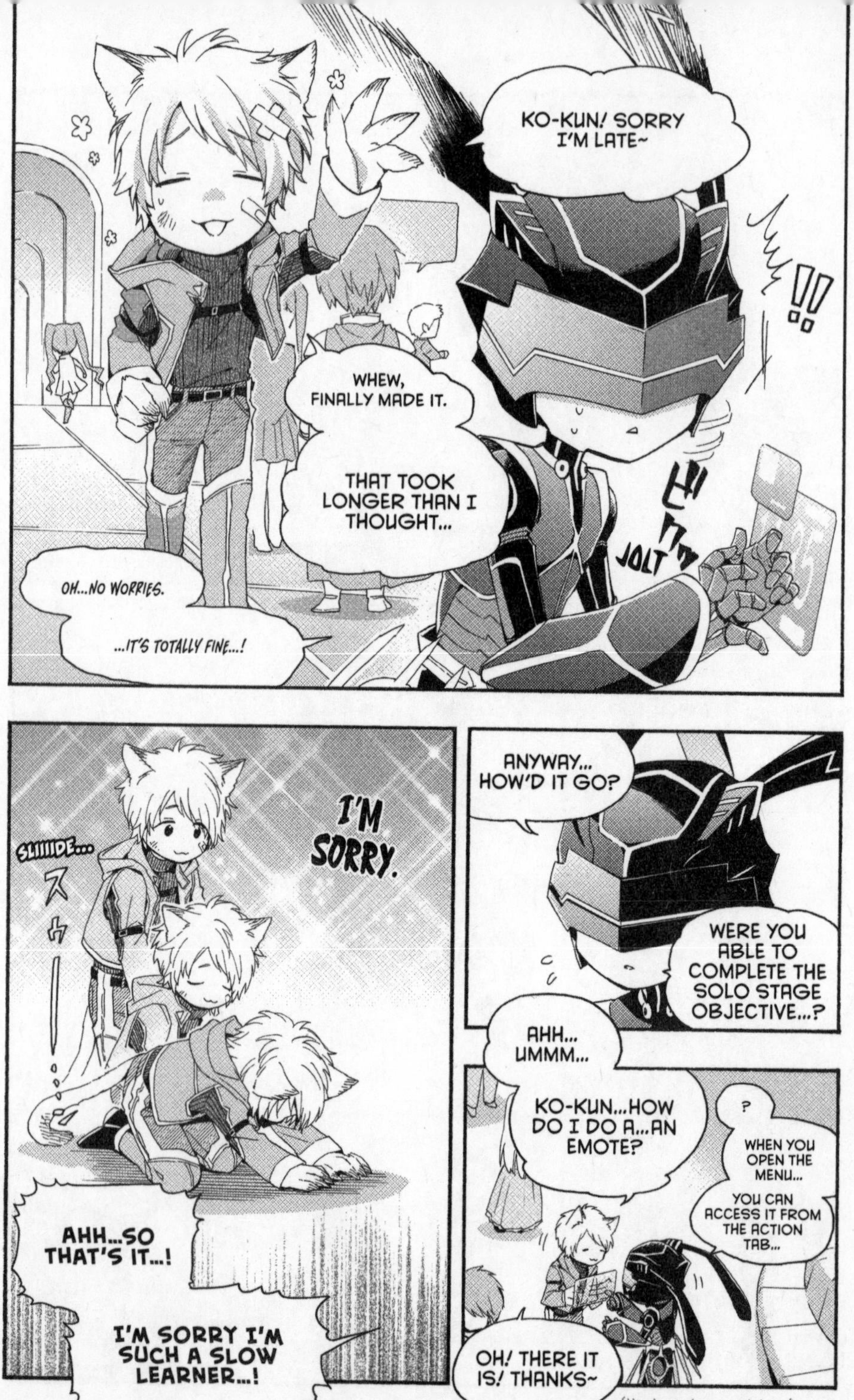
KO-KUN! SORRY I'M LATE~
!!
WHEW, FINALLY MADE IT.
THAT TOOK LONGER THAN I THOUGHT...
ビクッ
JOLT
OH...NO WORRIES.
...IT'S TOTALLY FINE...!
ANYWAY... HOW'D IT GO?
WERE YOU ABLE TO COMPLETE THE SOLO STAGE OBJECTIVE...?
AHH... UMMM...
KO-KUN...HOW DO I DO A...AN EMOTE?
?
WHEN YOU OPEN THE MENU...
YOU CAN ACCESS IT FROM THE ACTION TAB...
OH! THERE IT IS! THANKS~
I'M SORRY.
SLIIIIDE...
スゥー
AHH...SO THAT'S IT...!
I'M SORRY I'M SUCH A SLOW LEARNER...!

(He just learned how)

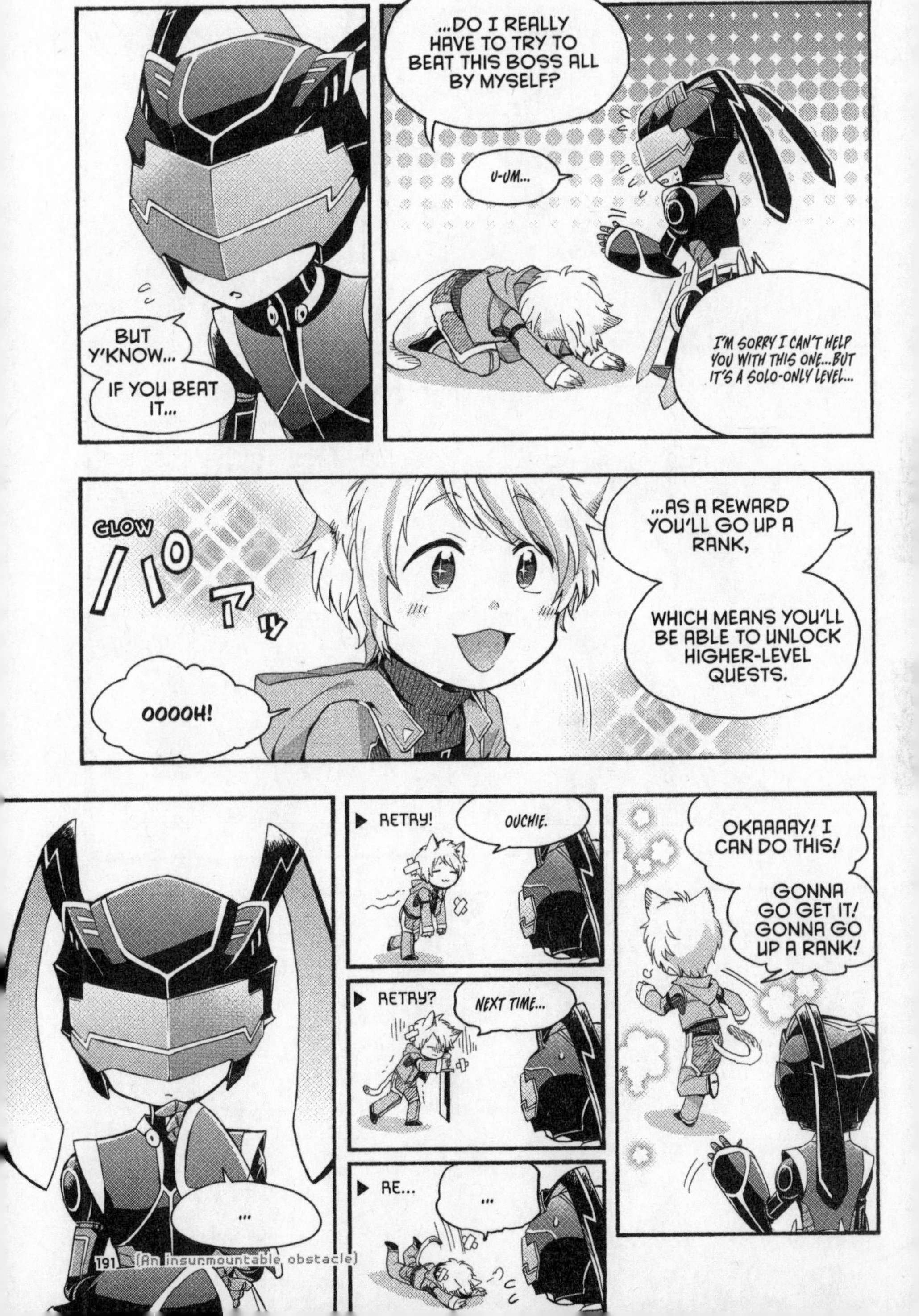
...DO I REALLY HAVE TO TRY TO BEAT THIS BOSS ALL BY MYSELF?
U-UM...
I'M SORRY I CAN'T HELP YOU WITH THIS ONE...BUT IT'S A SOLO-ONLY LEVEL...
BUT Y'KNOW...
IF YOU BEAT IT...
...AS A REWARD YOU'LL GO UP A RANK,
WHICH MEANS YOU'LL BE ABLE TO UNLOCK HIGHER-LEVEL QUESTS.
GLOW
OOOOH!
OKAAAAY! I CAN DO THIS!
GONNA GO GET IT! GONNA GO UP A RANK!
RETRY!
OUCHIE.
RETRY?
NEXT TIME...
RE...
...
...
(An insurmountable obstacle)

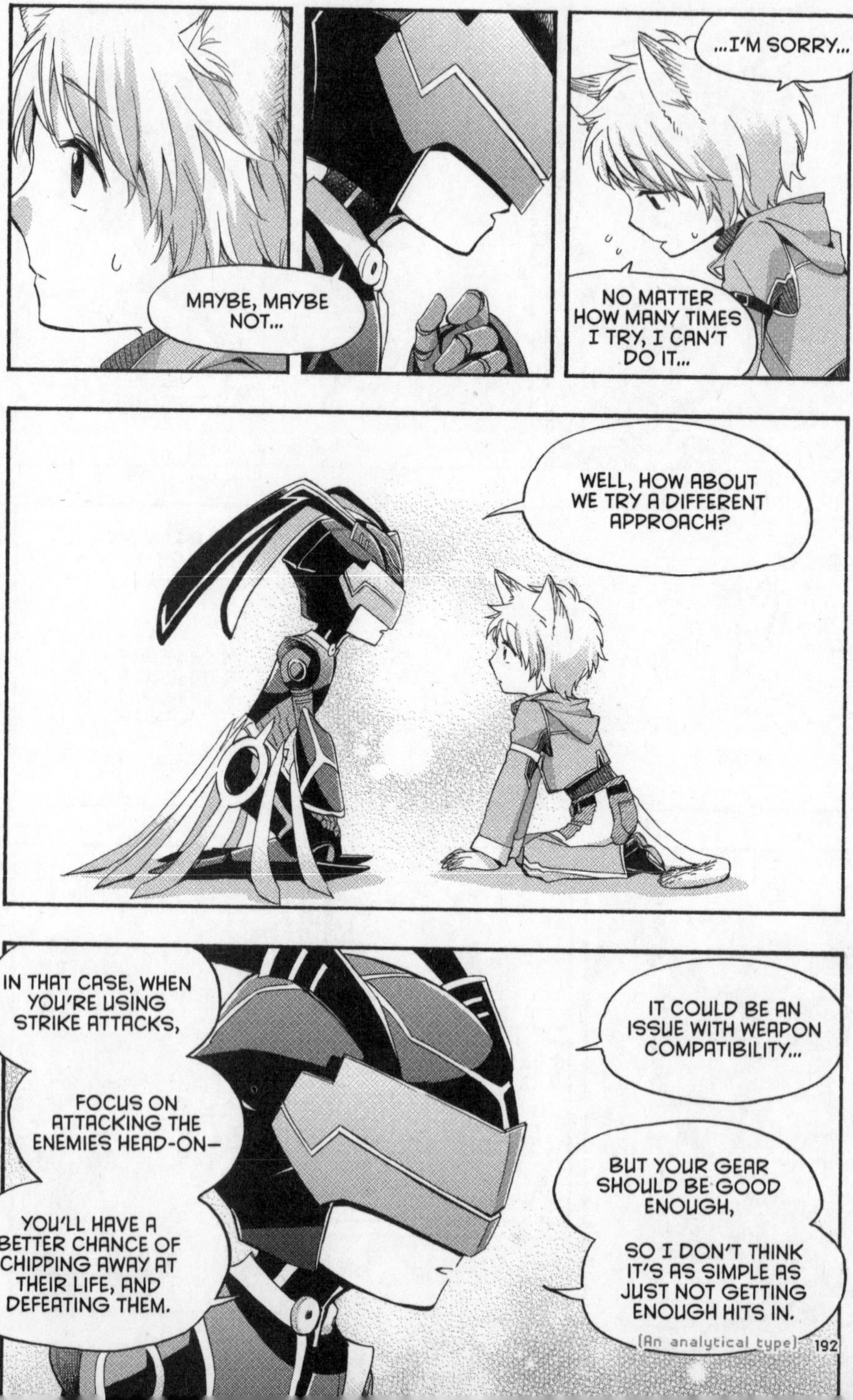
...I'M SORRY...
NO MATTER HOW MANY TIMES I TRY, I CAN'T DO IT...
MAYBE, MAYBE NOT...
WELL, HOW ABOUT WE TRY A DIFFERENT APPROACH?
IT COULD BE AN ISSUE WITH WEAPON COMPATIBILITY...
BUT YOUR GEAR SHOULD BE GOOD ENOUGH,
SO I DON'T THINK IT'S AS SIMPLE AS JUST NOT GETTING ENOUGH HITS IN.
IN THAT CASE, WHEN YOU'RE USING STRIKE ATTACKS,
FOCUS ON ATTACKING THE ENEMIES HEAD-ON—
YOU'LL HAVE A BETTER CHANCE OF CHIPPING AWAY AT THEIR LIFE, AND DEFEATING THEM.
[An analytical type]

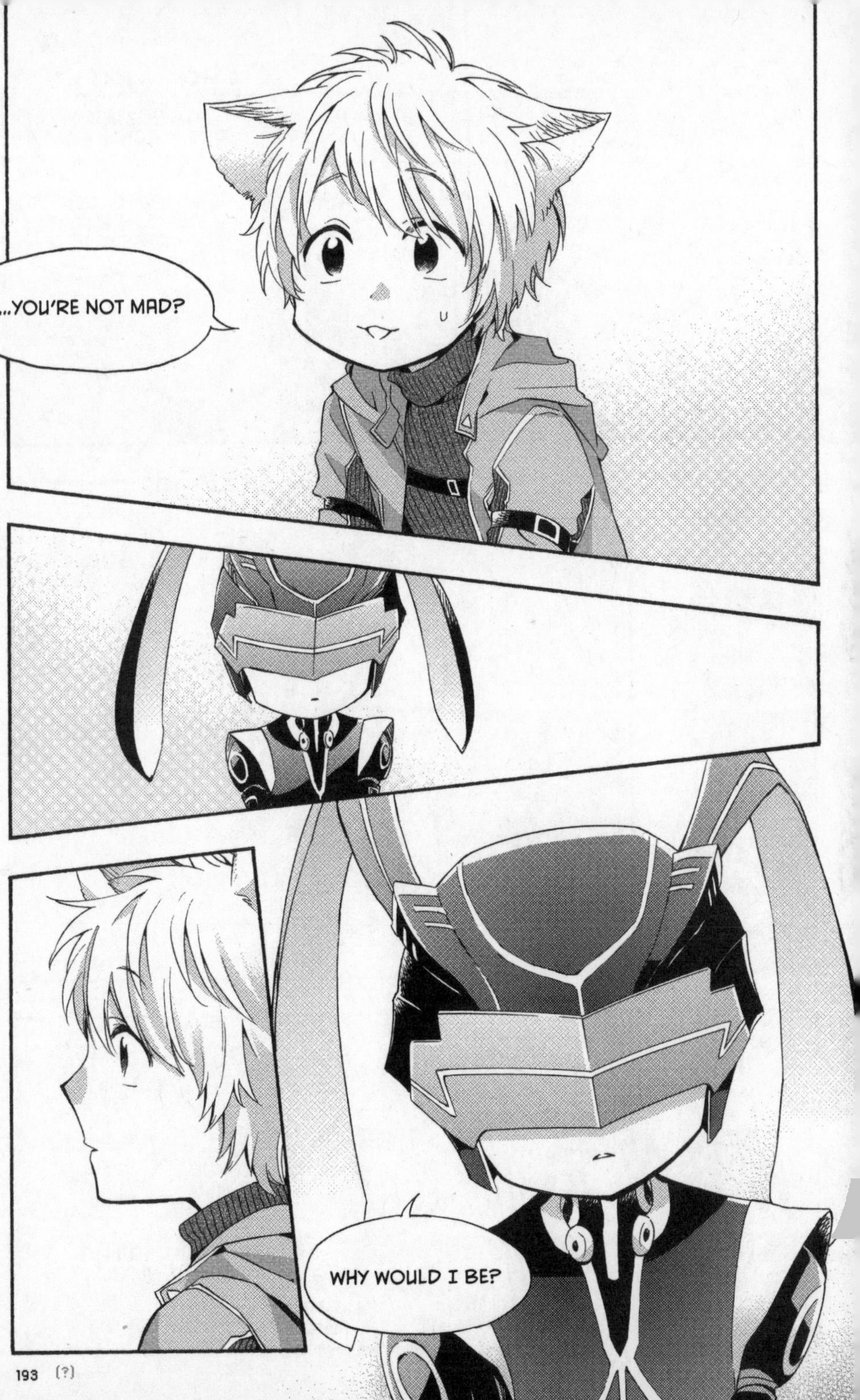
...YOU'RE NOT MAD?
WHY WOULD I BE?

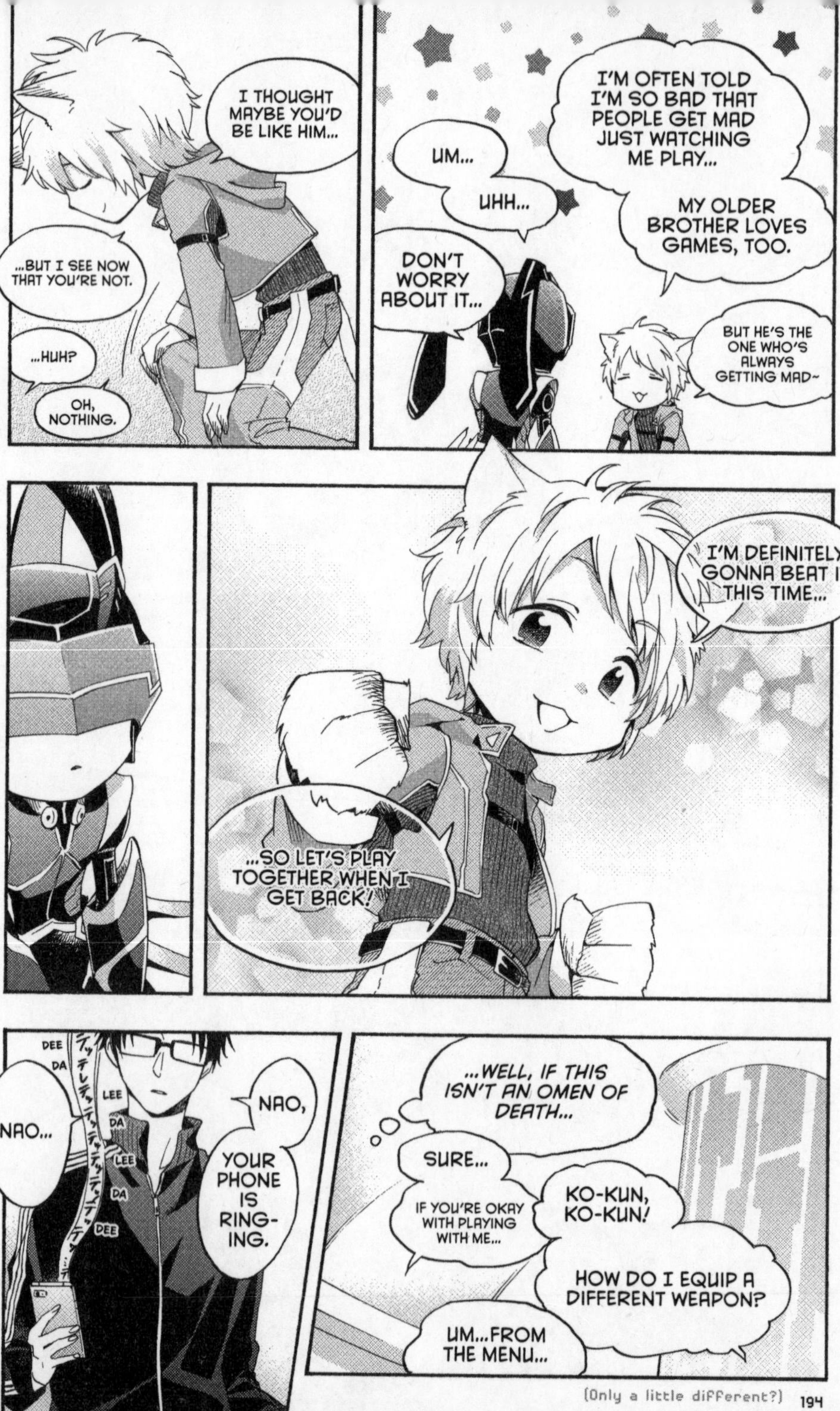
I'M OFTEN TOLD I'M SO BAD THAT PEOPLE GET MAD JUST WATCHING ME PLAY...
UM...
UHH...
MY OLDER BROTHER LOVES GAMES, TOO.
DON'T WORRY ABOUT IT...
BUT HE'S THE ONE WHO'S ALWAYS GETTING MAD~
I THOUGHT MAYBE YOU'D BE LIKE HIM...
...BUT I SEE NOW THAT YOU'RE NOT.
...HUH?
OH, NOTHING.
I'M DEFINITELY GONNA BEAT IT THIS TIME...
...SO LET'S PLAY TOGETHER WHEN I GET BACK!
...WELL, IF THIS ISN'T AN OMEN OF DEATH...
SURE...
IF YOU'RE OKAY WITH PLAYING WITH ME...
KO-KUN, KO-KUN!
HOW DO I EQUIP A DIFFERENT WEAPON?
UM...FROM THE MENU...
NAO,
YOUR PHONE IS RING-ING.
DEE DA LEE DA LEE DA DEE
NAO...

(Only a little different?)

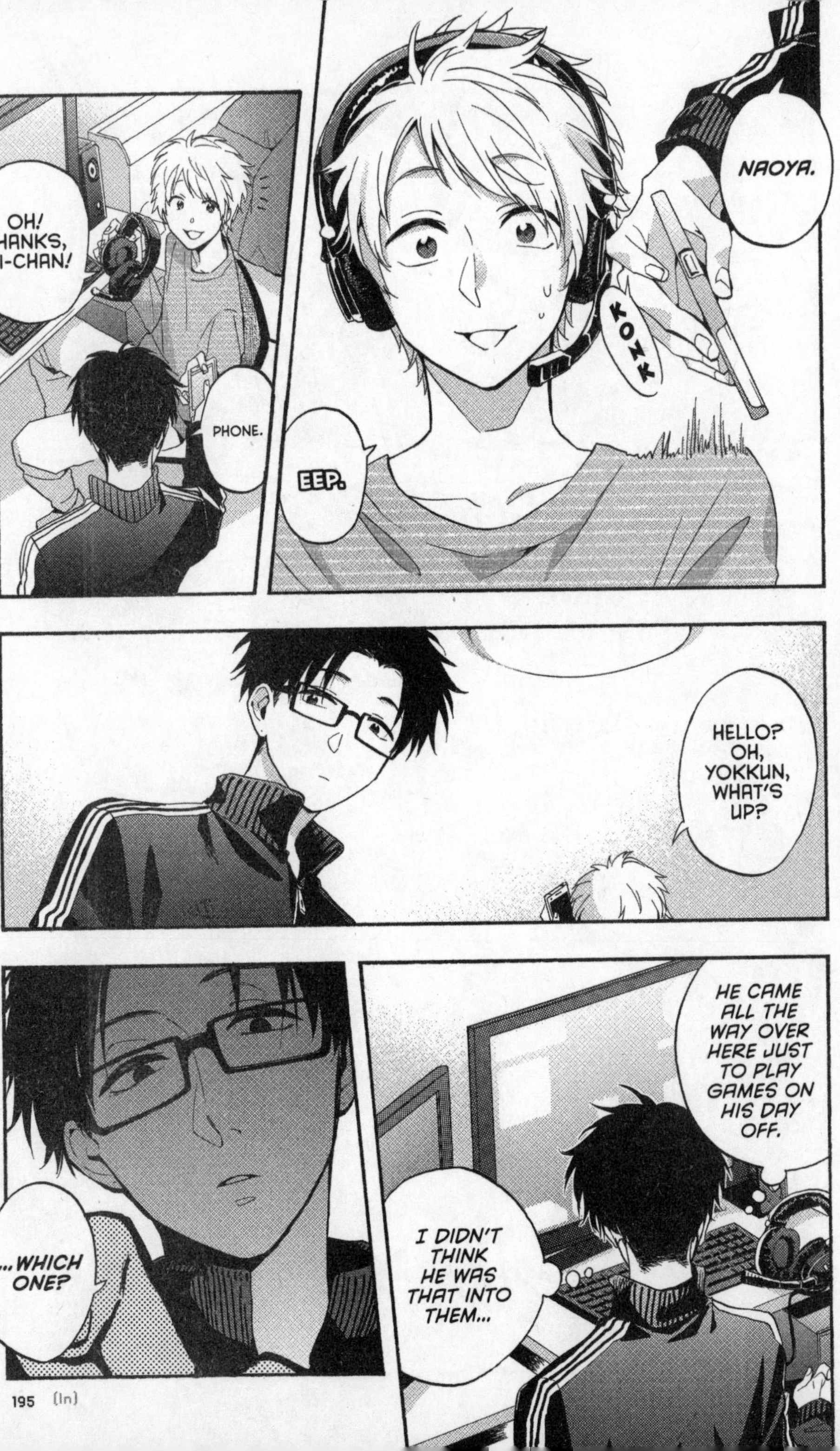
NAOYA.
KONK
EEP.
PHONE.
OH! THANKS, NII-CHAN!
HELLO? OH, YOKKUN, WHAT'S UP?
HE CAME ALL THE WAY OVER HERE JUST TO PLAY GAMES ON HIS DAY OFF.
I DIDN'T THINK HE WAS THAT INTO THEM...
...WHICH ONE?

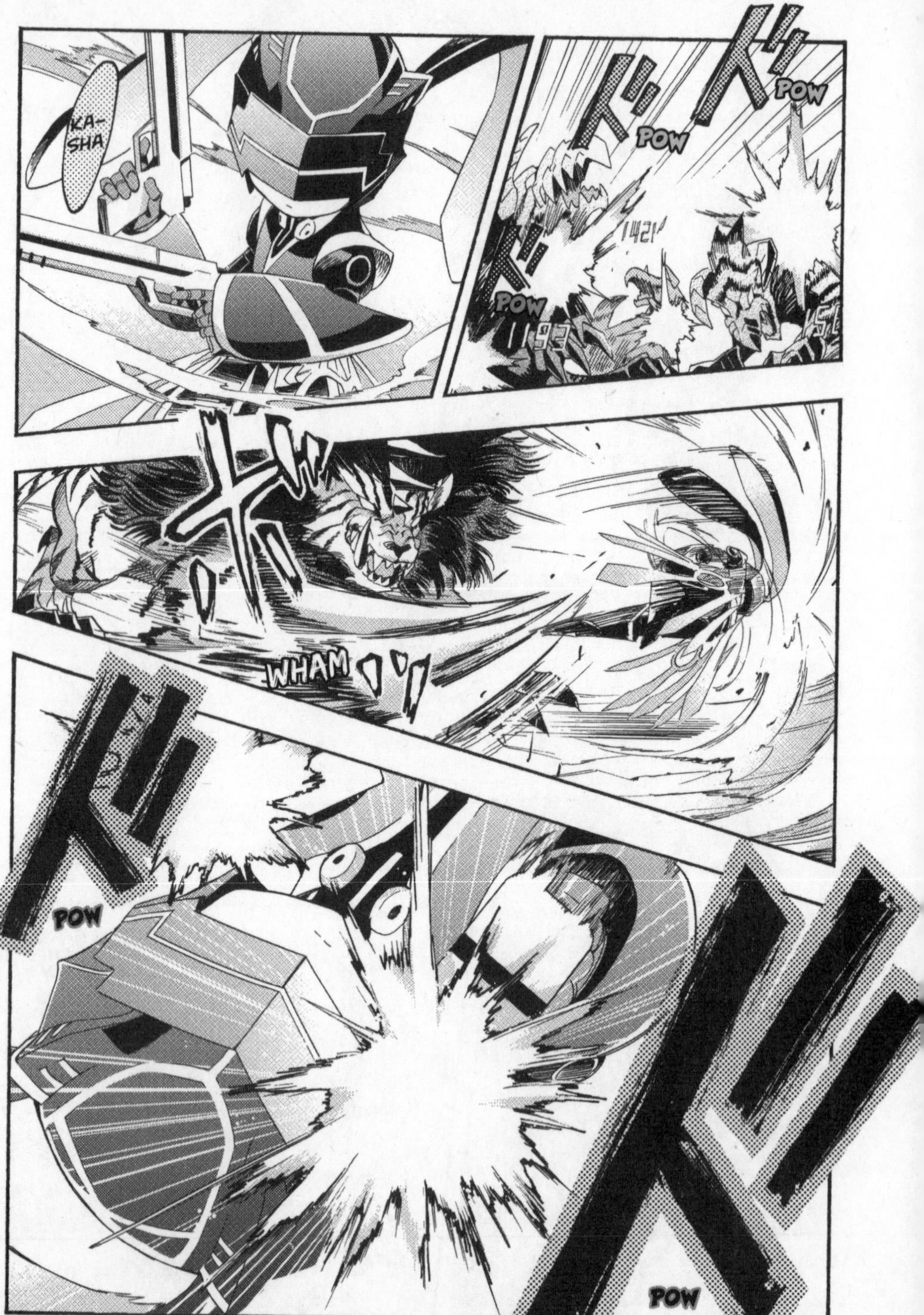
POW
POW
1421
POW
1193
KA-SHA
WHAM
POW
POW

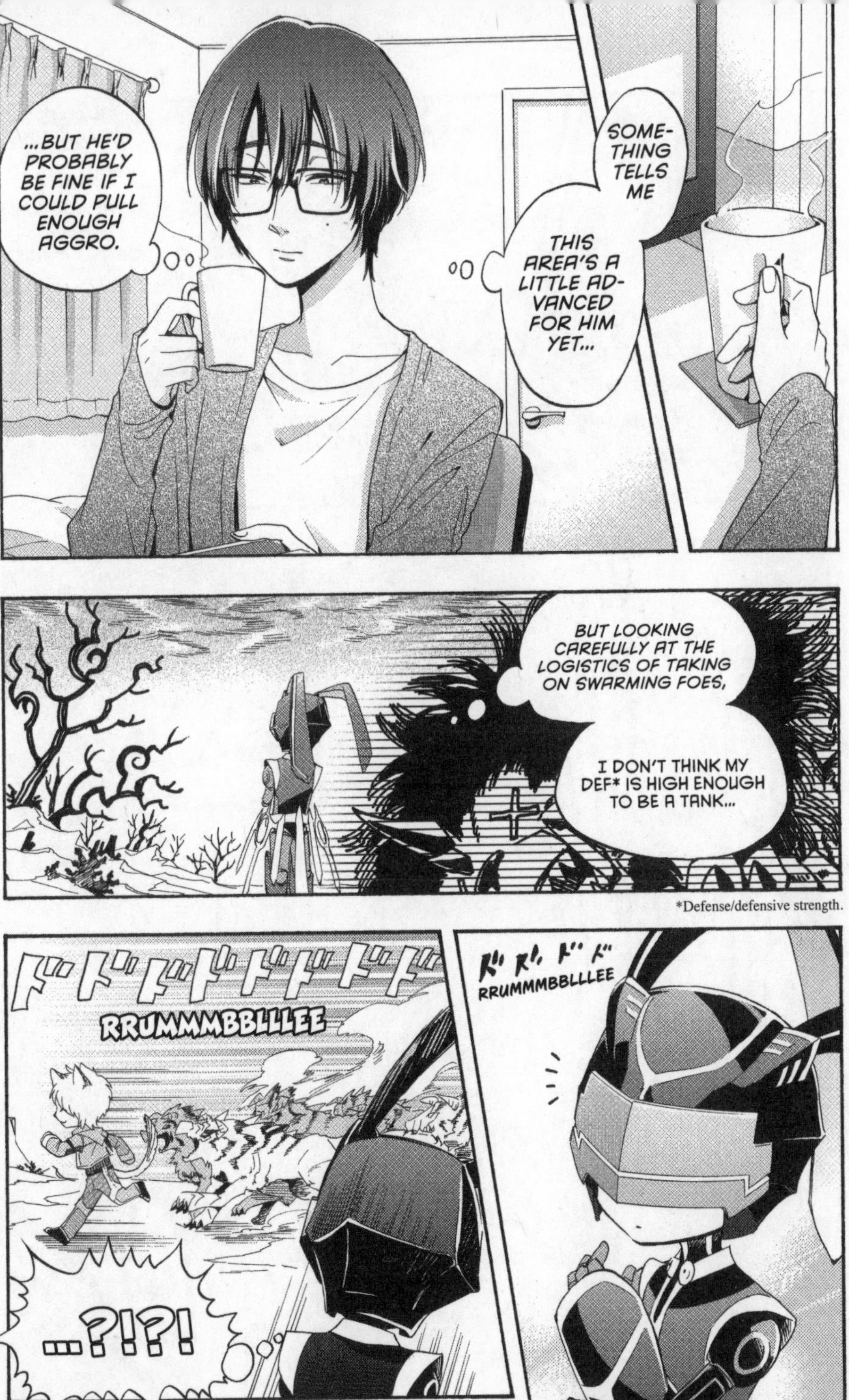
SOMETHING TELLS ME
THIS AREA'S A LITTLE ADVANCED FOR HIM YET...
...BUT HE'D PROBABLY BE FINE IF I COULD PULL ENOUGH AGGRO.
BUT LOOKING CAREFULLY AT THE LOGISTICS OF TAKING ON SWARMING FOES,
I DON'T THINK MY DEF* IS HIGH ENOUGH TO BE A TANK...
ドドドド
RRUMMMBBLLLEE
ドドドドドドドド
RRUMMMBBLLLEE
...?!?!

*Defense/defensive strength.

 (She still can't take swarms)

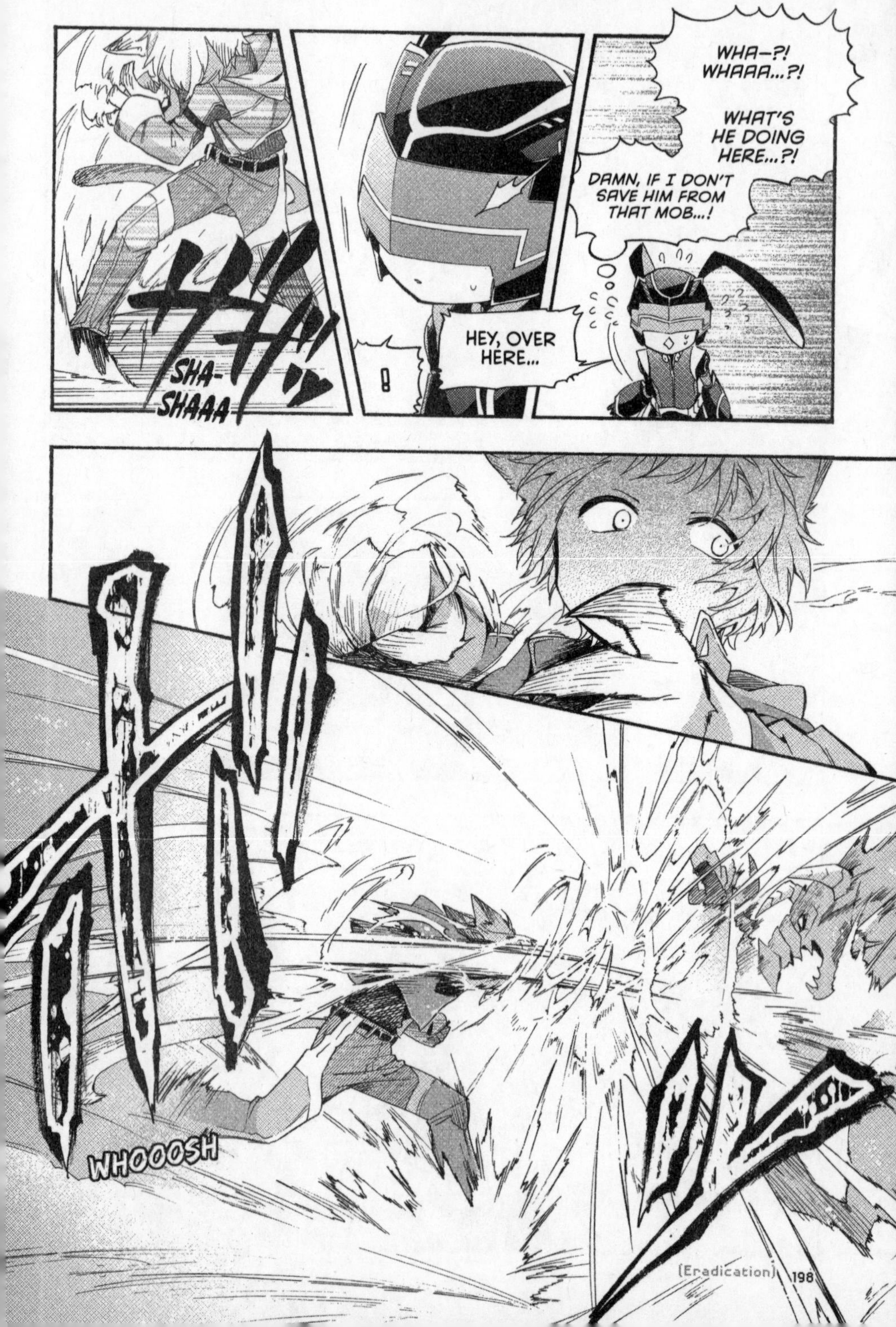
WHA-?! WHAAA...?!
WHAT'S HE DOING HERE...?!
DAMN, IF I DON'T SAVE HIM FROM THAT MOB...!
HEY, OVER HERE...
!
SHA-SHAAA
WHOOOSH

(Eradication)

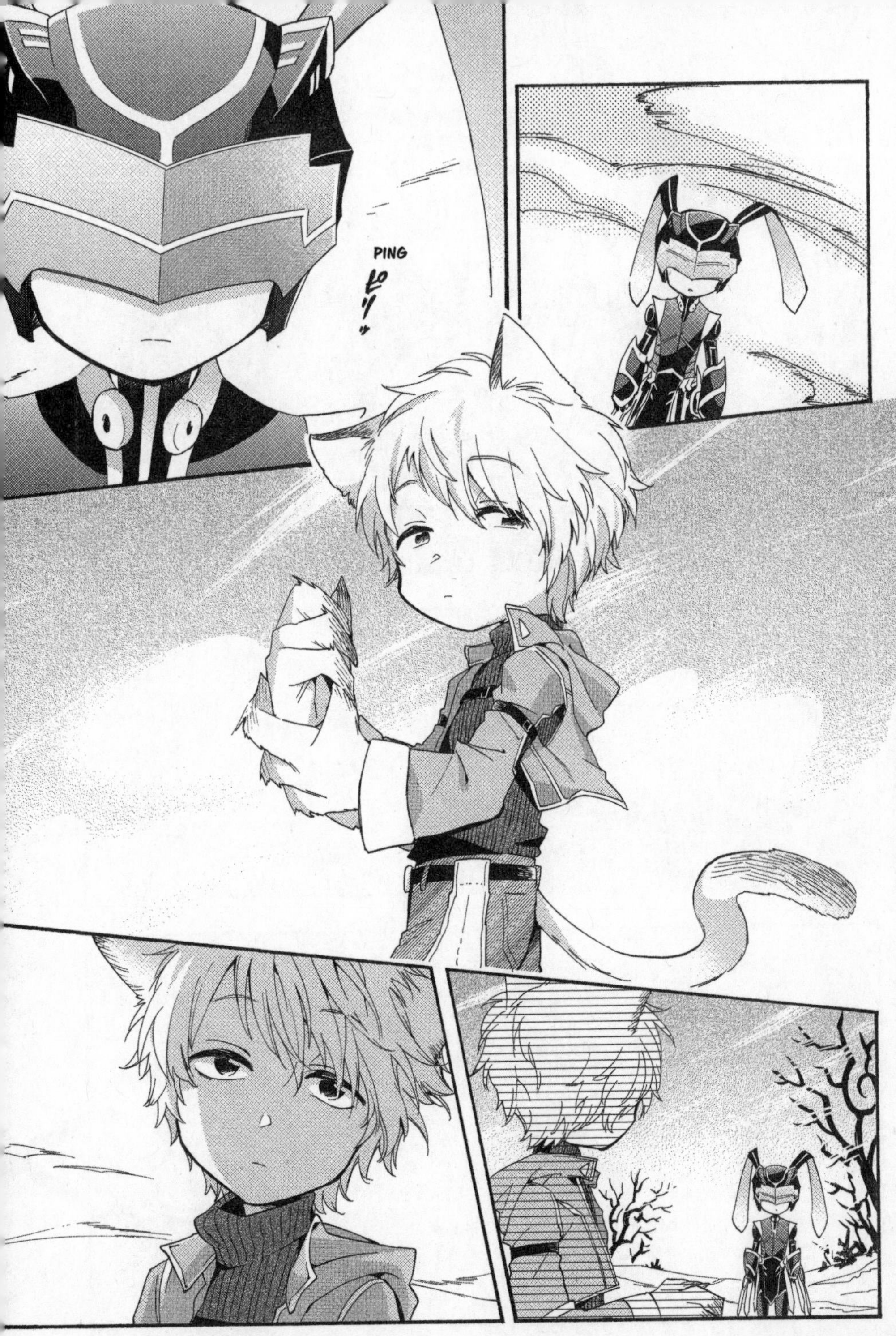
PING
ピリッ

 (Note the eyes)

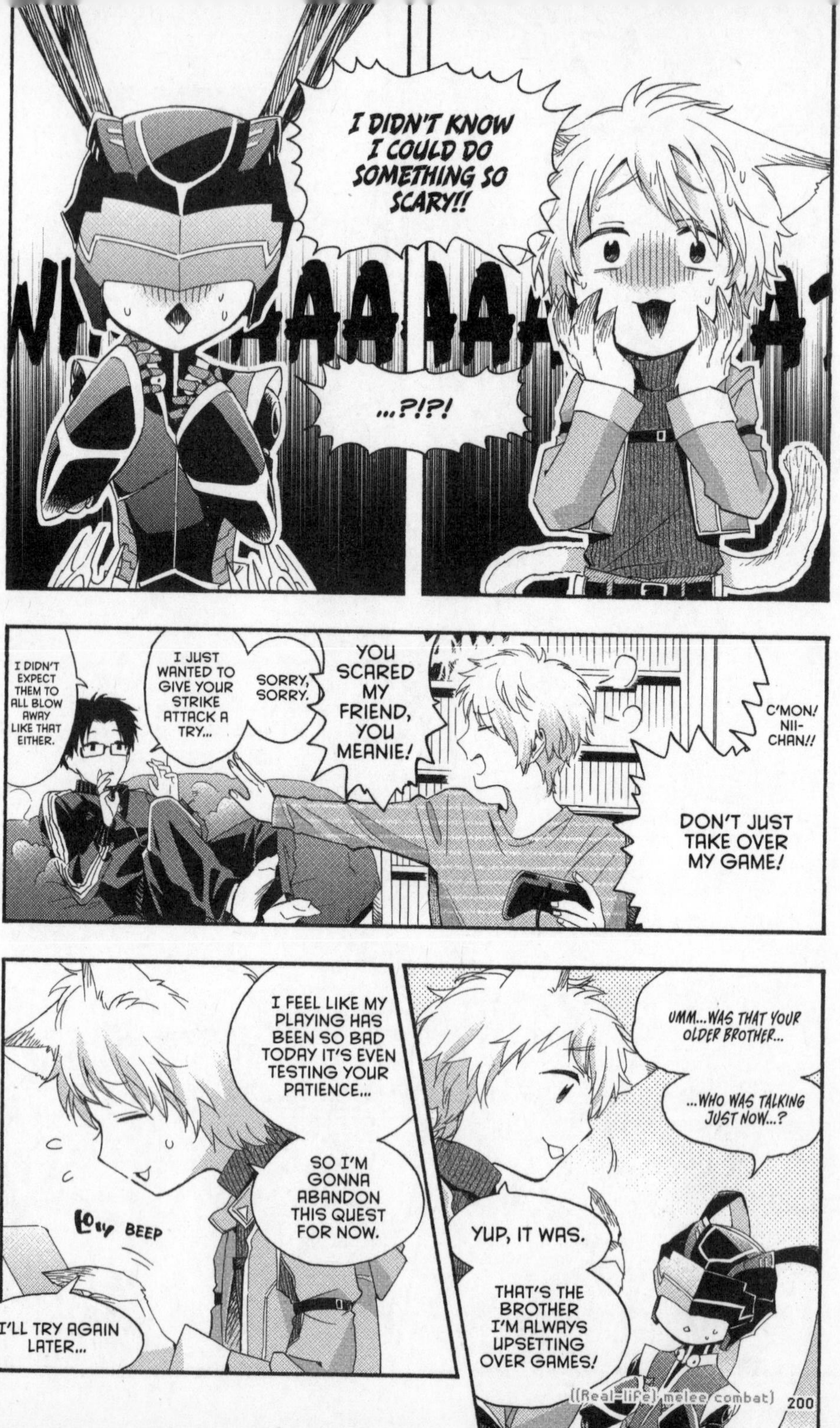
I DIDN'T KNOW I COULD DO SOMETHING SO SCARY!!
...?!?!
C'MON! NII-CHAN!!
DON'T JUST TAKE OVER MY GAME!
YOU SCARED MY FRIEND, YOU MEANIE!
SORRY, SORRY.
I JUST WANTED TO GIVE YOUR STRIKE ATTACK A TRY...
I DIDN'T EXPECT THEM TO ALL BLOW AWAY LIKE THAT EITHER.
UMM...WAS THAT YOUR OLDER BROTHER...
...WHO WAS TALKING JUST NOW...?
YUP, IT WAS.
THAT'S THE BROTHER I'M ALWAYS UPSETTING OVER GAMES!
I FEEL LIKE MY PLAYING HAS BEEN SO BAD TODAY IT'S EVEN TESTING YOUR PATIENCE...
SO I'M GONNA ABANDON THIS QUEST FOR NOW.
BEEP
I'LL TRY AGAIN LATER...

((Real-life) melee combat)

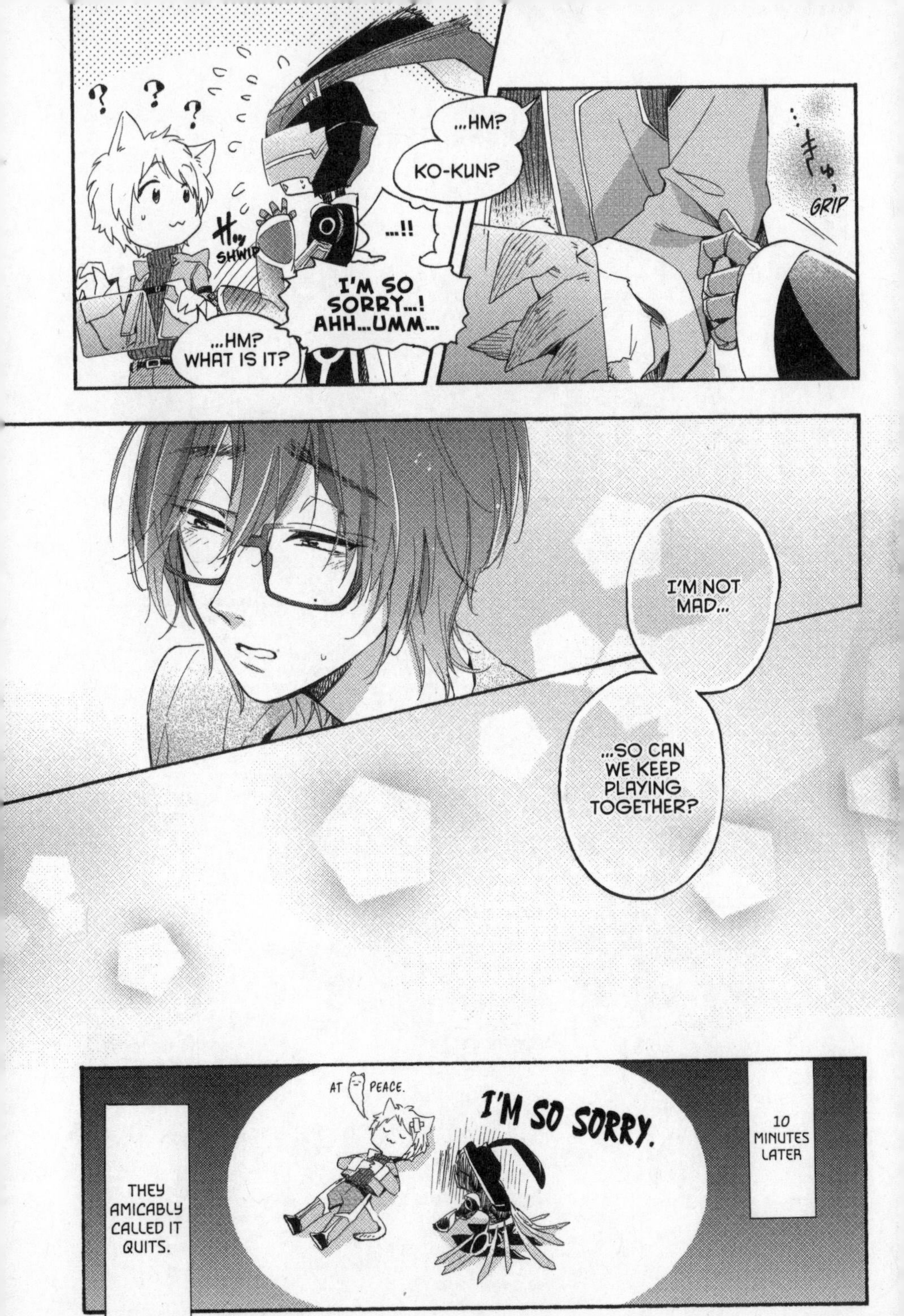
きゅ
GRIP
...HM?
KO-KUN?
...!!
I'M SO SORRY...! AHH...UMM...
SHWIP
...HM? WHAT IS IT?
I'M NOT MAD...
...SO CAN WE KEEP PLAYING TOGETHER?
10 MINUTES LATER
I'M SO SORRY.
AT PEACE.
THEY AMICABLY CALLED IT QUITS.

 (Yup, it's a little different)

CHARACTERS

二藤尚哉 / Naoya Nifuji

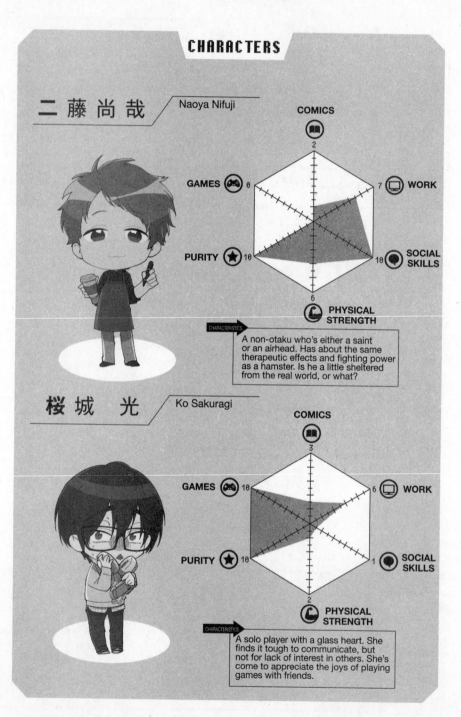

COMICS 2

GAMES 0

WORK 7

PURITY 10

SOCIAL SKILLS 10

PHYSICAL STRENGTH 6

CHARACTERISTICS
A non-otaku who's either a saint or an airhead. Has about the same therapeutic effects and fighting power as a hamster. Is he a little sheltered from the real world, or what?

桜城　光 / Ko Sakuragi

COMICS 3

GAMES 10

WORK 6

PURITY 10

SOCIAL SKILLS 1

PHYSICAL STRENGTH 2

CHARACTERISTICS
A solo player with a glass heart. She finds it tough to communicate, but not for lack of interest in others. She's come to appreciate the joys of playing games with friends.

Episode...28

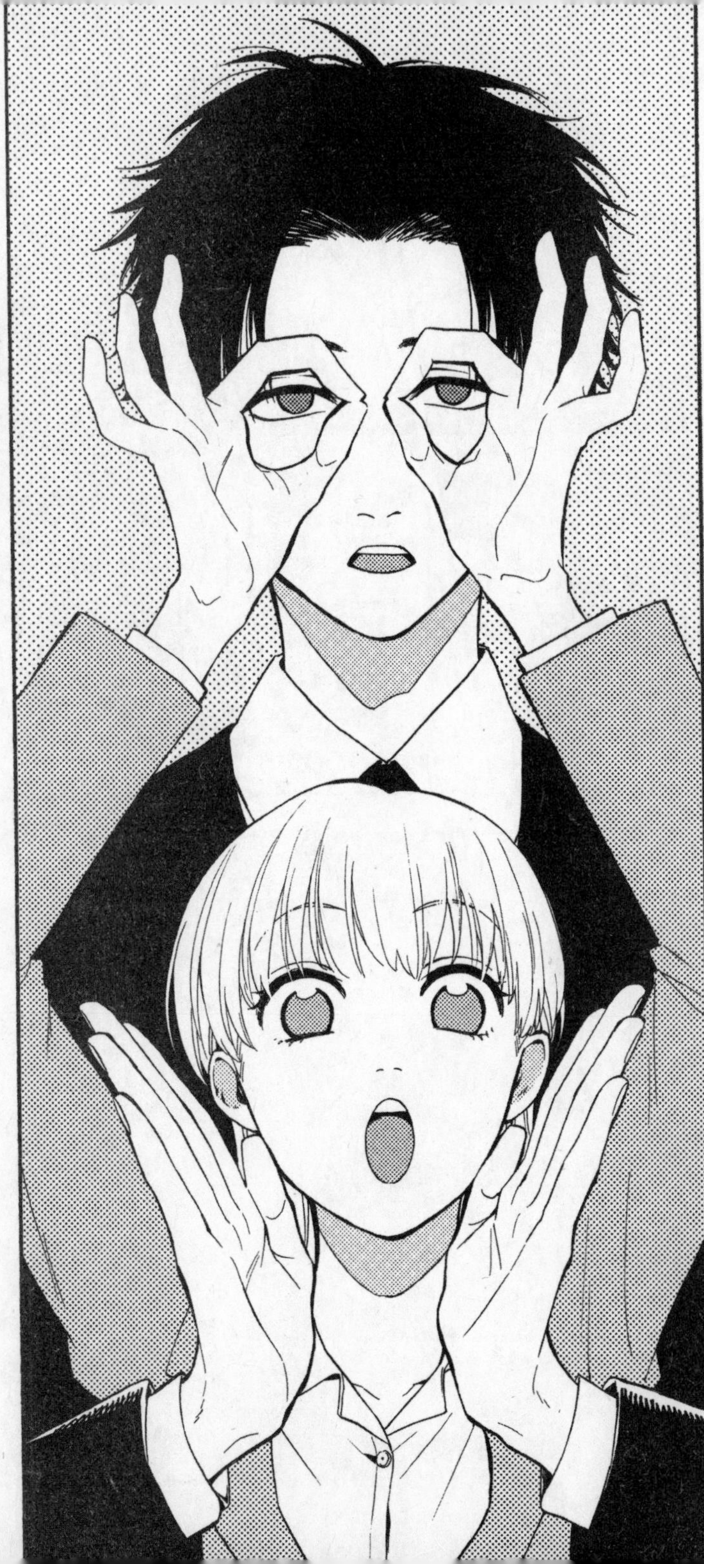

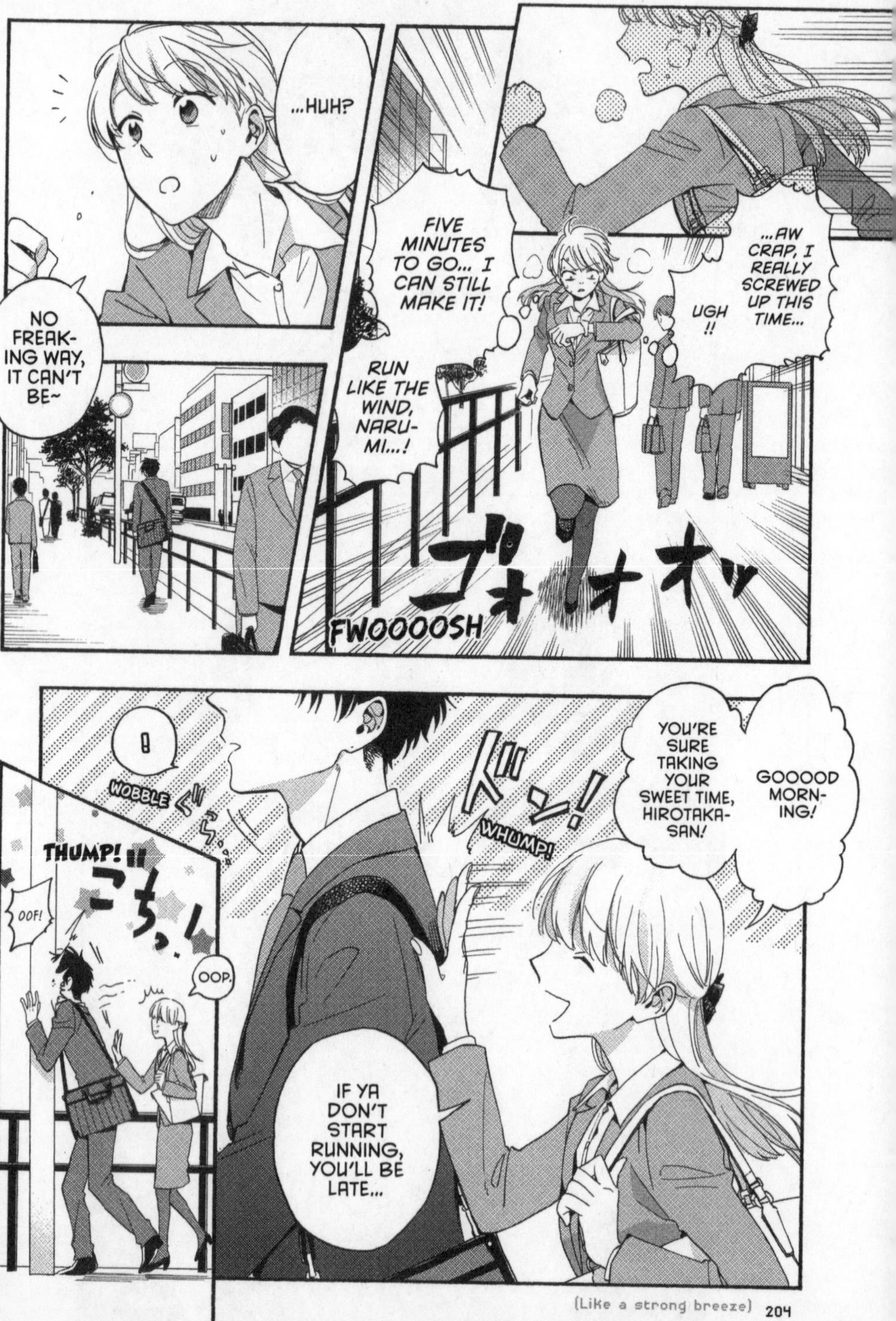
...AW CRAP, I REALLY SCREWED UP THIS TIME...
UGH !!
FIVE MINUTES TO GO... I CAN STILL MAKE IT!
RUN LIKE THE WIND, NARUMI...!
ゴォオオッ
FWOOOOSH
...HUH?
NO FREAKING WAY, IT CAN'T BE~
GOOOOD MORNING!
YOU'RE SURE TAKING YOUR SWEET TIME, HIROTAKA-SAN!
ドンッ!
WHUMP!
!
WOBBLE ぐらっ
IF YA DON'T START RUNNING, YOU'LL BE LATE...
THUMP! ごちっ!
OOF!
OOP.

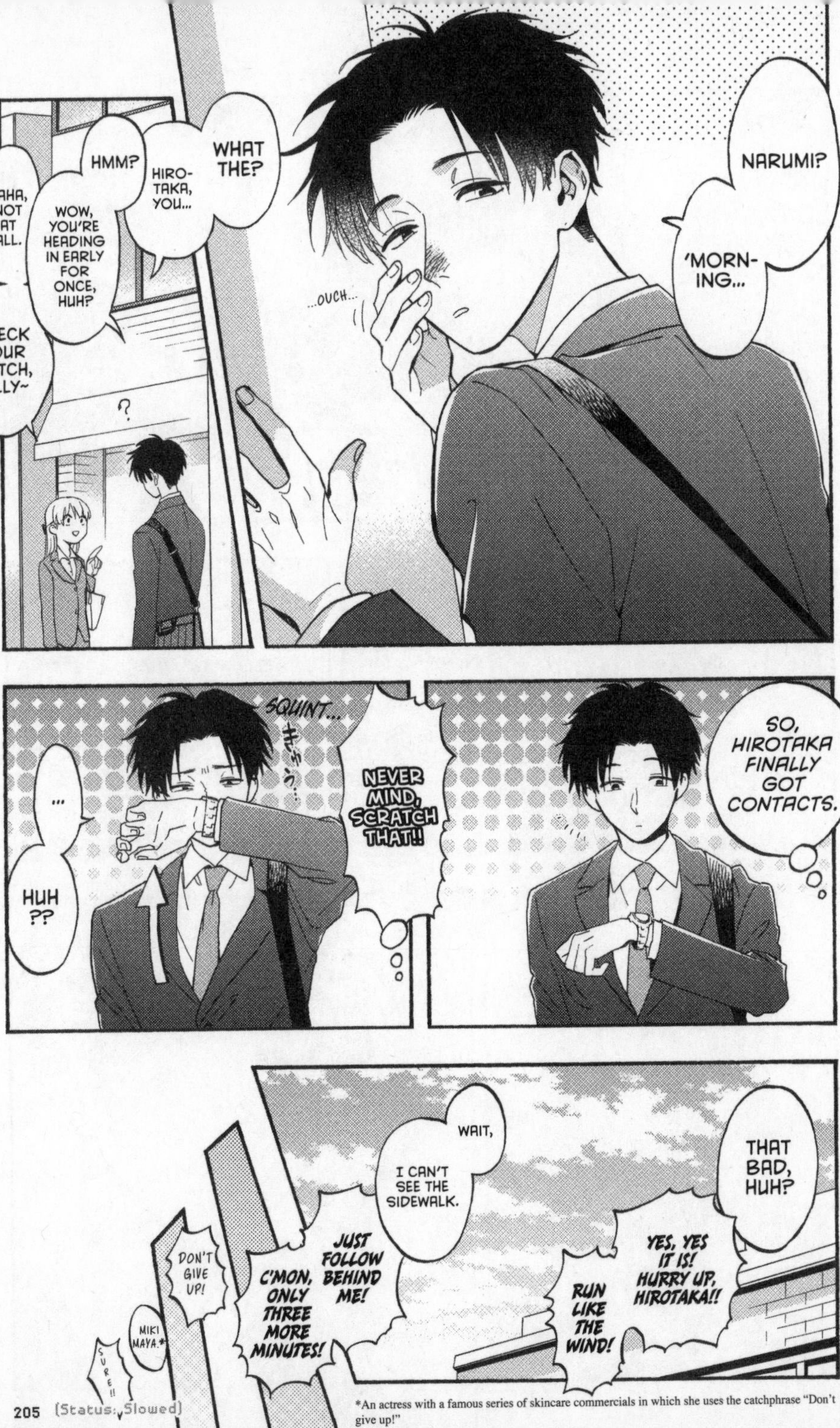
NARUMI?
'MORN-ING...
...OUCH...
WHAT THE?
HIRO-TAKA, YOU...
HMM?
WOW, YOU'RE HEADING IN EARLY FOR ONCE, HUH?
HAHA, NOT AT ALL.
CHECK YOUR WATCH, SILLY~
?
SO, HIROTAKA FINALLY GOT CONTACTS.
NEVER MIND, SCRATCH THAT!!
SQUINT...
...
HUH ??
THAT BAD, HUH?
YES, YES IT IS! HURRY UP, HIROTAKA!!
RUN LIKE THE WIND!
WAIT,
I CAN'T SEE THE SIDEWALK.
JUST FOLLOW BEHIND ME!
C'MON, ONLY THREE MORE MINUTES!
DON'T GIVE UP!
MIKI MAYA.*
SURE!!

*An actress with a famous series of skincare commercials in which she uses the catchphrase "Don't give up!"

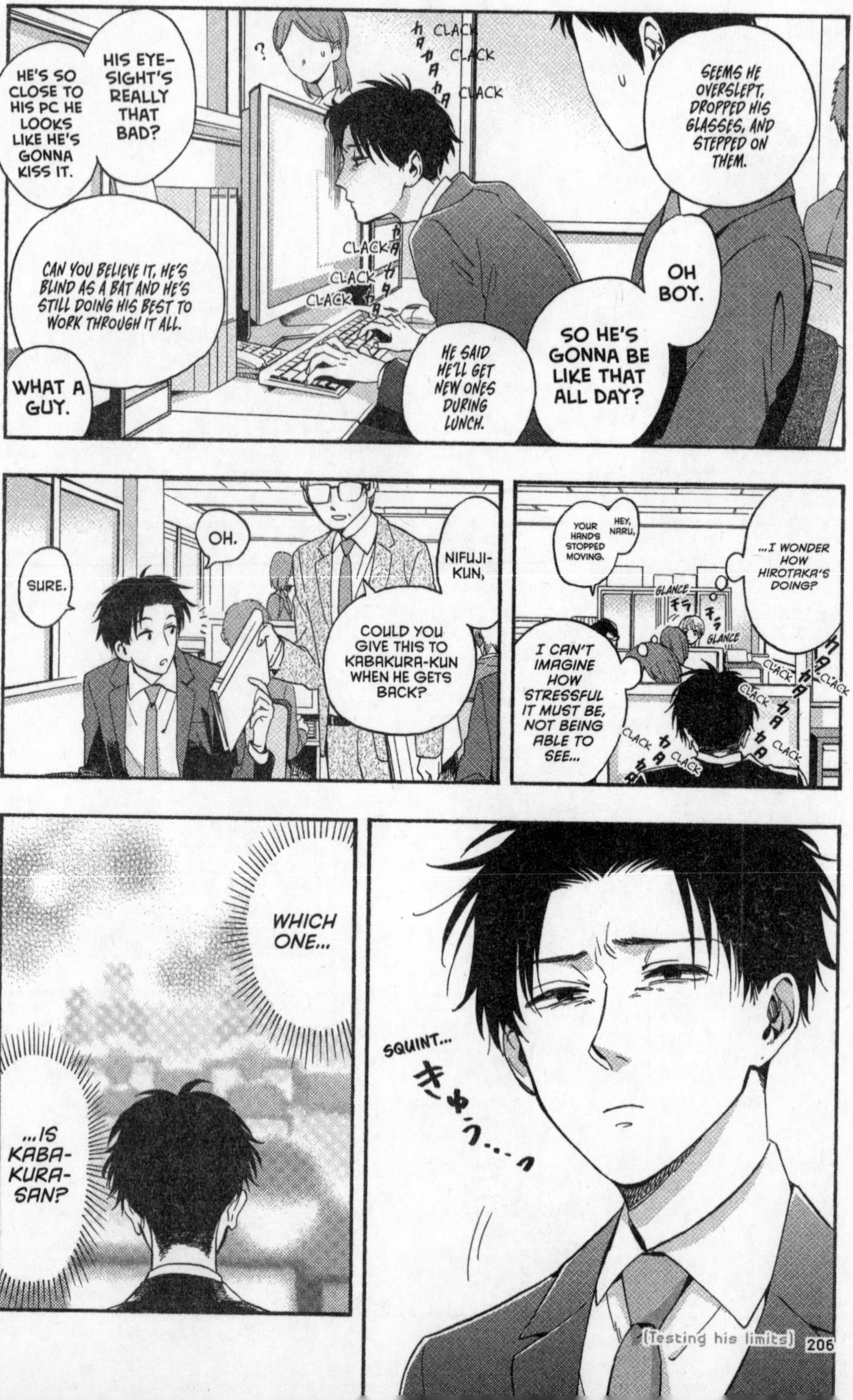

SEEMS HE OVERSLEPT, DROPPED HIS GLASSES, AND STEPPED ON THEM.
CLACK CLACK CLACK
OH BOY.
SO HE'S GONNA BE LIKE THAT ALL DAY?
HE SAID HE'LL GET NEW ONES DURING LUNCH.
CLACK CLACK CLACK
?
HIS EYE-SIGHT'S REALLY THAT BAD?
HE'S SO CLOSE TO HIS PC HE LOOKS LIKE HE'S GONNA KISS IT.
CAN YOU BELIEVE IT, HE'S BLIND AS A BAT AND HE'S STILL DOING HIS BEST TO WORK THROUGH IT ALL.
WHAT A GUY.
...I WONDER HOW HIROTAKA'S DOING?
HEY, NARU,
YOUR HAND'S STOPPED MOVING.
GLANCE GLANCE
I CAN'T IMAGINE HOW STRESSFUL IT MUST BE, NOT BEING ABLE TO SEE...
CLACK CLACK CLACK CLACK CLACK CLACK
NIFUJI-KUN,
COULD YOU GIVE THIS TO KABAKURA-KUN WHEN HE GETS BACK?
OH.
SURE.
SQUINT...
きゅう…っ
WHICH ONE...
...IS KABAKURA-SAN?

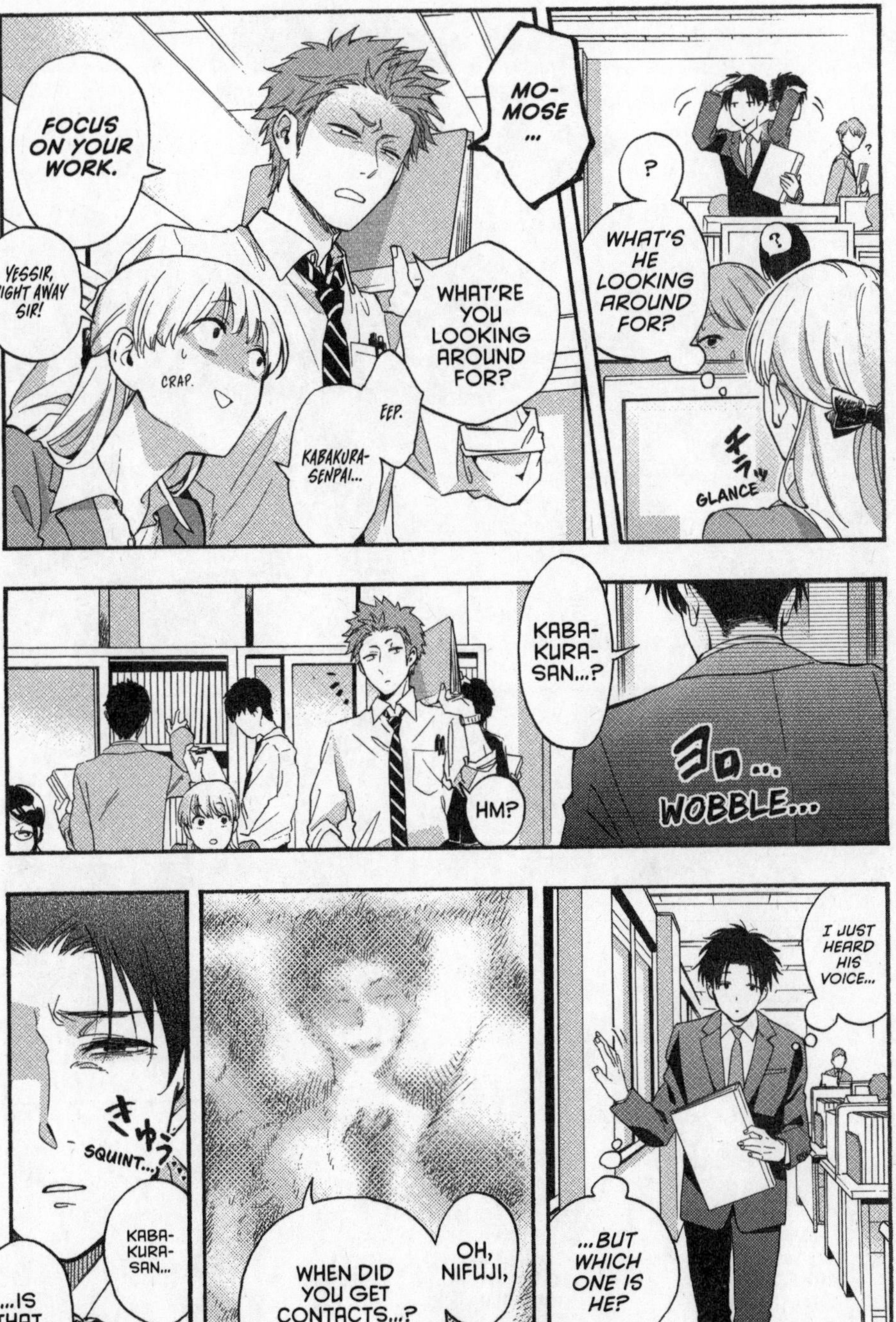
?
WHAT'S HE LOOKING AROUND FOR?
チラッ
GLANCE
MO-MOSE...
WHAT'RE YOU LOOKING AROUND FOR?
FOCUS ON YOUR WORK.
EEP.
KABAKURA-SENPAI...
YESSIR, RIGHT AWAY SIR!
CRAP.
KABA-KURA-SAN...?
ヨロ... WOBBLE...
HM?
I JUST HEARD HIS VOICE...
...BUT WHICH ONE IS HE?
OH, NIFUJI,
WHEN DID YOU GET CONTACTS...?
きゅう
SQUINT...
KABA-KURA-SAN...
...IS THAT YOU...?

 (Could that fuzzy outline be...)

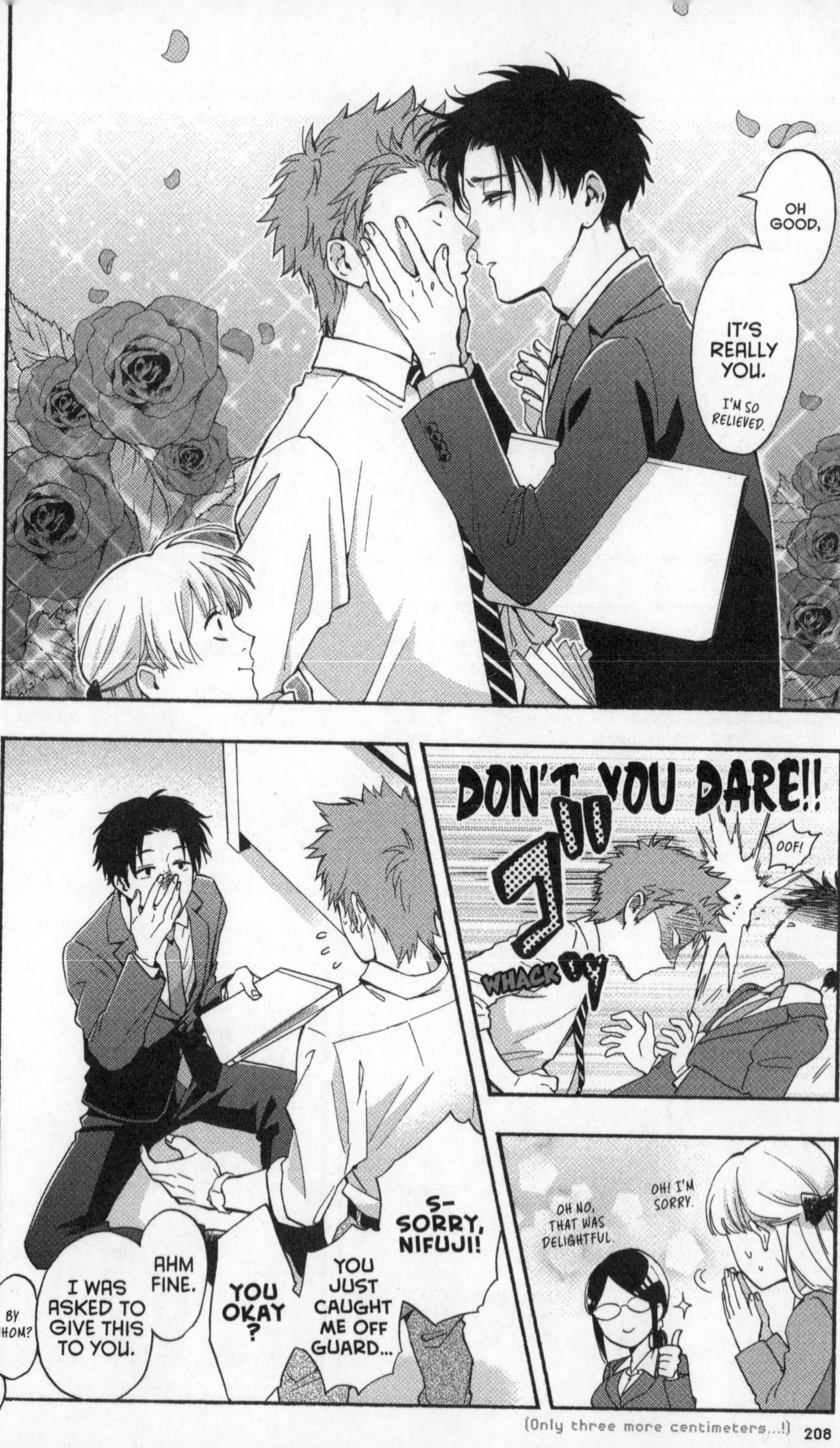
OH GOOD,
IT'S REALLY YOU.
I'M SO RELIEVED.
DON'T YOU DARE!!
OOF!
WHACK
OH! I'M SORRY.
OH NO, THAT WAS DELIGHTFUL.
S-SORRY, NIFUJI!
YOU JUST CAUGHT ME OFF GUARD...
YOU OKAY?
AHM FINE.
I WAS ASKED TO GIVE THIS TO YOU.
BY WHOM?
UHH.

(Only three more centimeters...!)

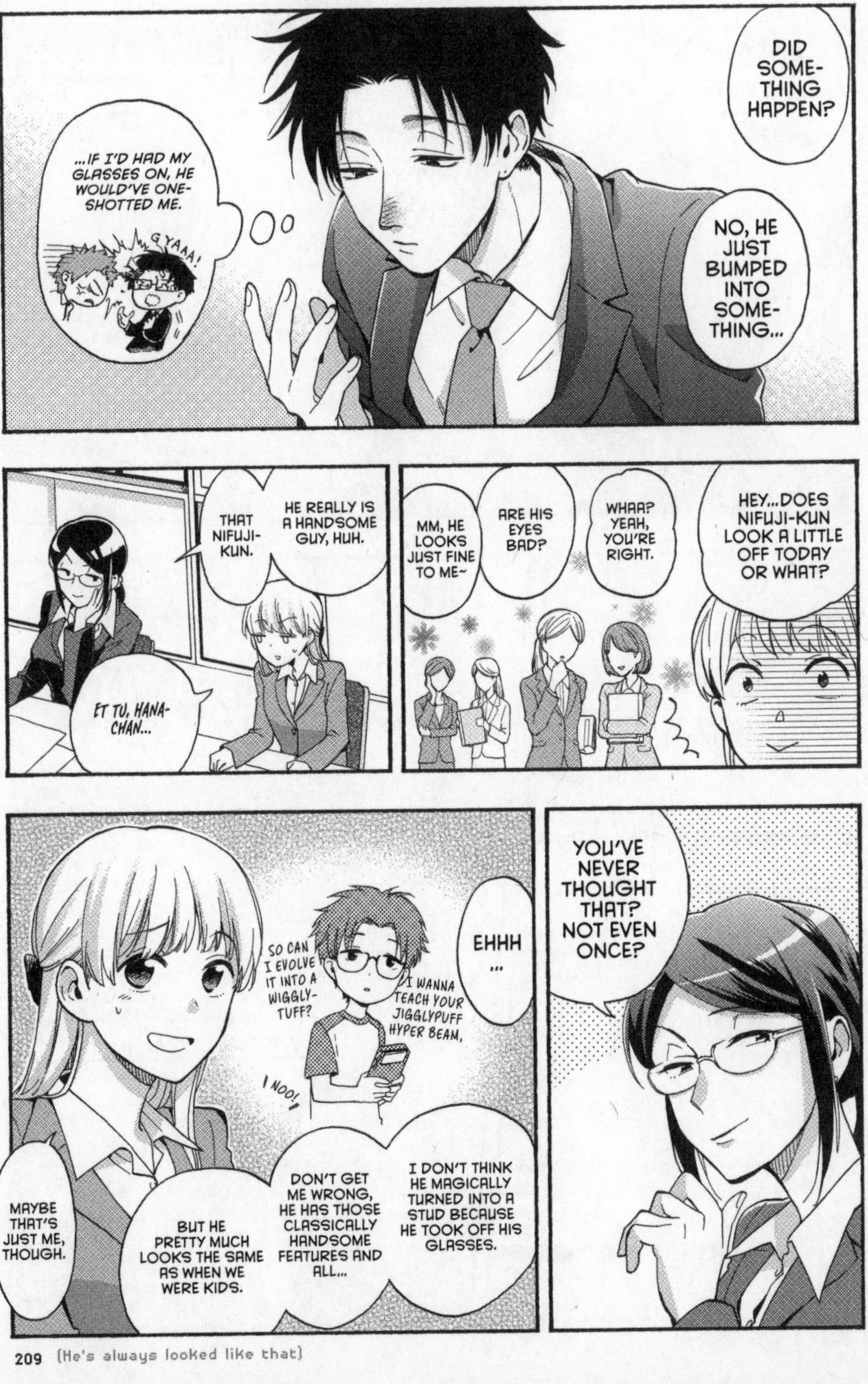
DID SOMETHING HAPPEN?
NO, HE JUST BUMPED INTO SOMETHING...
...IF I'D HAD MY GLASSES ON, HE WOULD'VE ONE-SHOTTED ME.
GYAAA!
HEY...DOES NIFUJI-KUN LOOK A LITTLE OFF TODAY OR WHAT?
WHAA? YEAH, YOU'RE RIGHT.
ARE HIS EYES BAD?
MM, HE LOOKS JUST FINE TO ME~
HE REALLY IS A HANDSOME GUY, HUH.
THAT NIFUJI-KUN.
ET TU, HANA-CHAN...
YOU'VE NEVER THOUGHT THAT? NOT EVEN ONCE?
EHHH...
I WANNA TEACH YOUR JIGGLYPUFF HYPER BEAM,
SO CAN I EVOLVE IT INTO A WIGGLYTUFF?
NOO!
I DON'T THINK HE MAGICALLY TURNED INTO A STUD BECAUSE HE TOOK OFF HIS GLASSES.
DON'T GET ME WRONG, HE HAS THOSE CLASSICALLY HANDSOME FEATURES AND ALL...
BUT HE PRETTY MUCH LOOKS THE SAME AS WHEN WE WERE KIDS.
MAYBE THAT'S JUST ME, THOUGH.

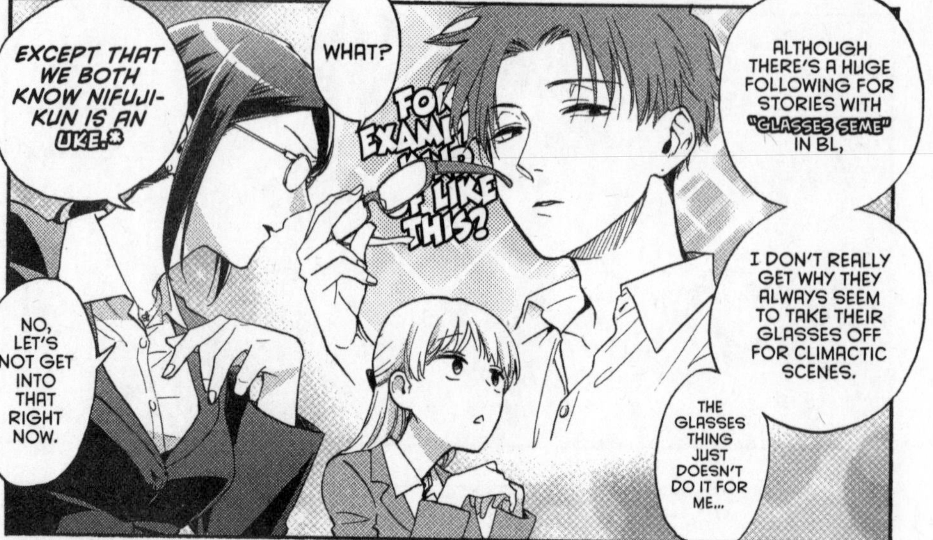
ALTHOUGH THERE'S A HUGE FOLLOWING FOR STORIES WITH "GLASSES SEME" IN BL,
I DON'T REALLY GET WHY THEY ALWAYS SEEM TO TAKE THEIR GLASSES OFF FOR CLIMACTIC SCENES.
THE GLASSES THING JUST DOESN'T DO IT FOR ME...
WHAT?
EXCEPT THAT WE BOTH KNOW NIFUJI-KUN IS AN UKE.*
NO, LET'S NOT GET INTO THAT RIGHT NOW.

*See page 35.

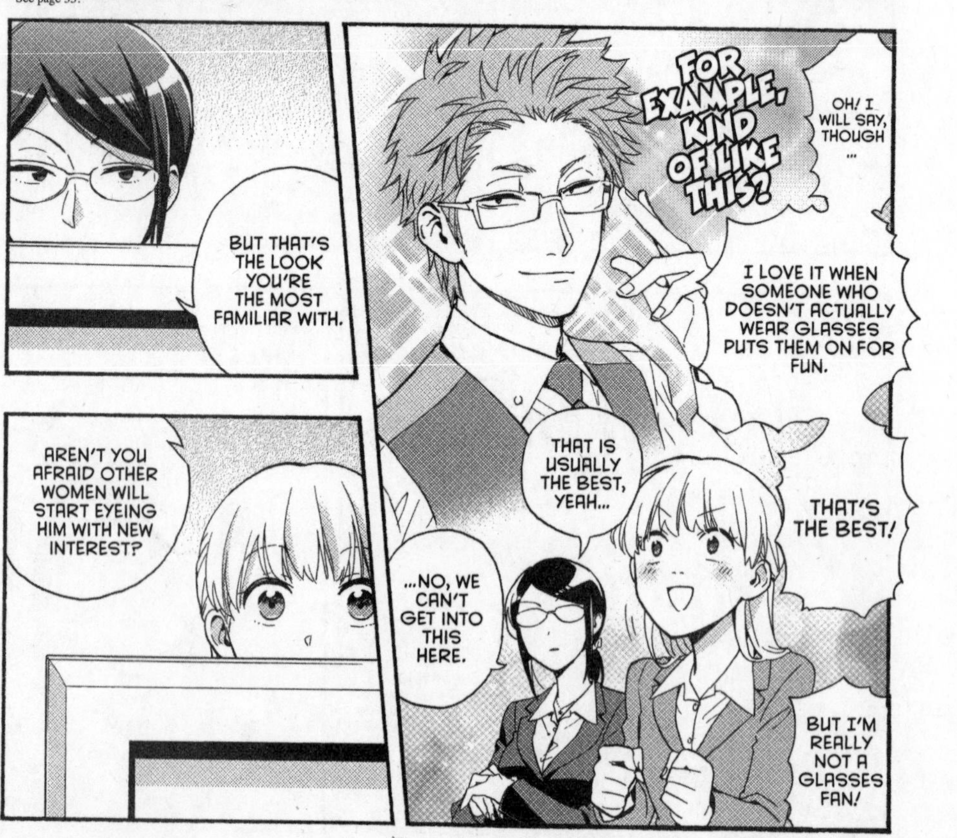
OH! I WILL SAY, THOUGH ...
FOR EXAMPLE, KIND OF LIKE THIS?
I LOVE IT WHEN SOMEONE WHO DOESN'T ACTUALLY WEAR GLASSES PUTS THEM ON FOR FUN.
THAT'S THE BEST!
THAT IS USUALLY THE BEST, YEAH...
BUT I'M REALLY NOT A GLASSES FAN!
...NO, WE CAN'T GET INTO THIS HERE.
BUT THAT'S THE LOOK YOU'RE THE MOST FAMILIAR WITH.
AREN'T YOU AFRAID OTHER WOMEN WILL START EYEING HIM WITH NEW INTEREST?

(The author isn't much of a glasses person either!)

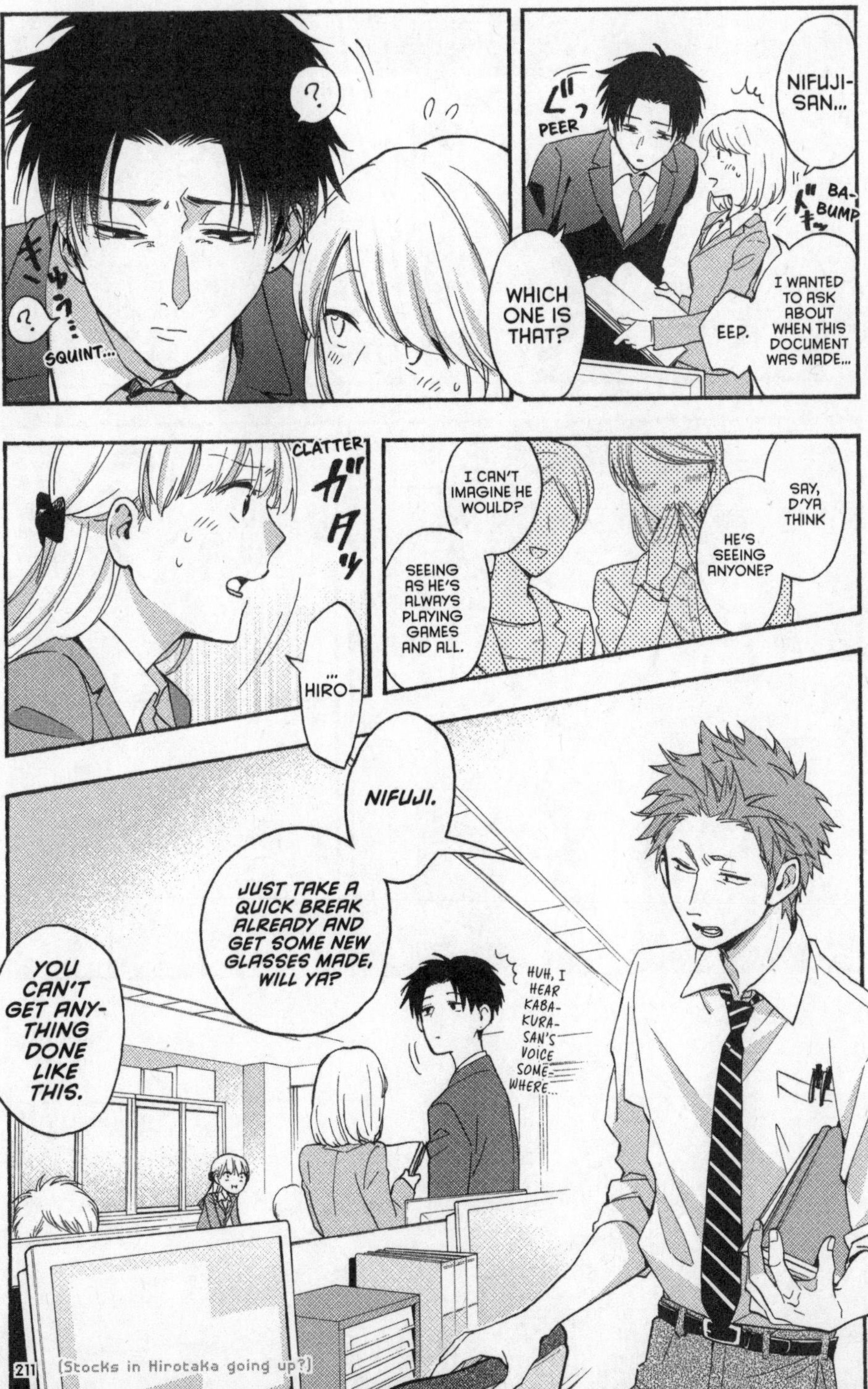
NIFUJI-SAN...
PEER
BA-BUMP
I WANTED TO ASK ABOUT WHEN THIS DOCUMENT WAS MADE...
EEP.
WHICH ONE IS THAT?
?
SQUINT...
?
SAY, D'YA THINK HE'S SEEING ANYONE?
I CAN'T IMAGINE HE WOULD?
SEEING AS HE'S ALWAYS PLAYING GAMES AND ALL.
CLATTER
...HIRO-
NIFUJI.
JUST TAKE A QUICK BREAK ALREADY AND GET SOME NEW GLASSES MADE, WILL YA?
YOU CAN'T GET ANYTHING DONE LIKE THIS.
HUH, I HEAR KABAKURA-SAN'S VOICE SOMEWHERE...

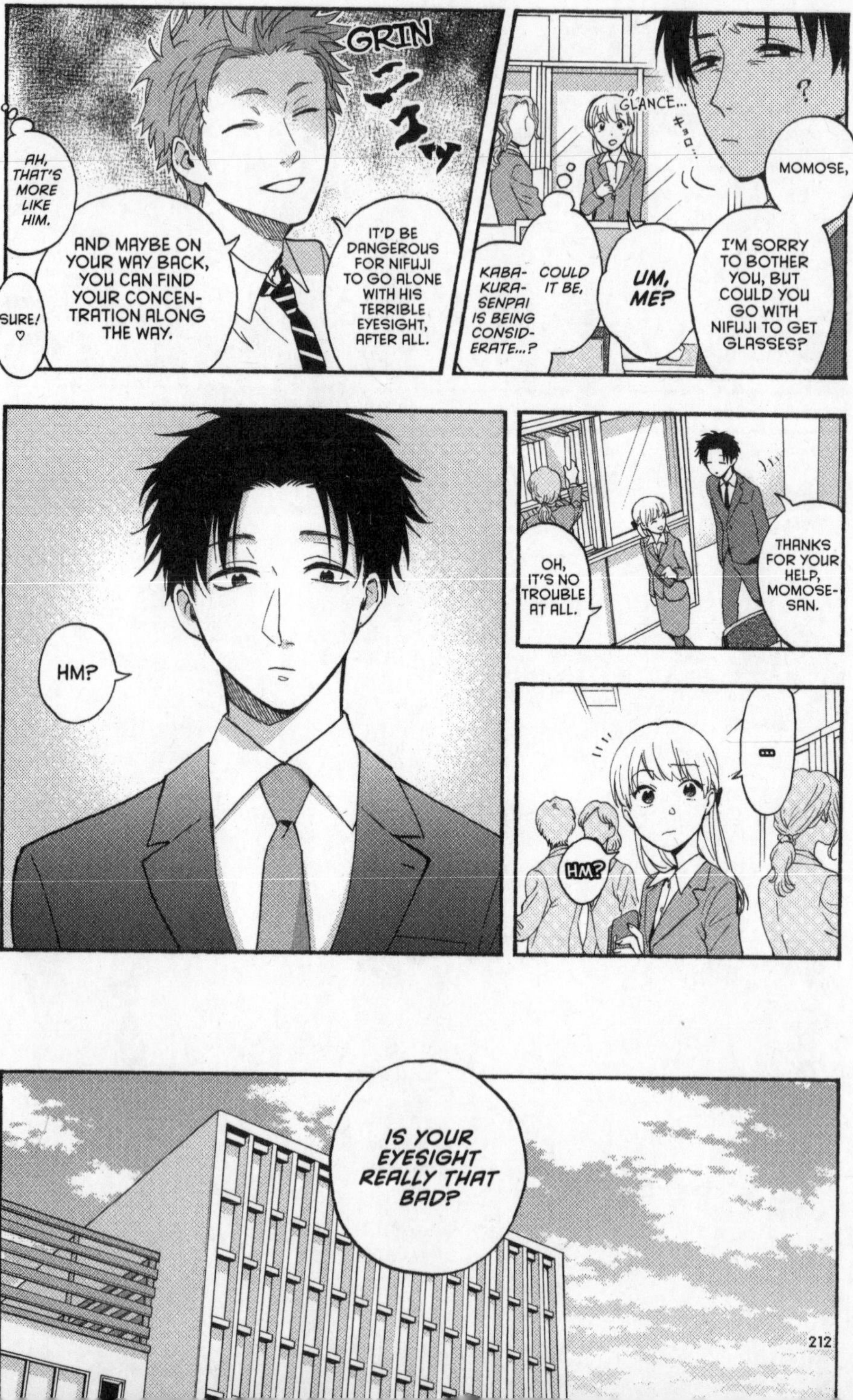
MOMOSE,
I'M SORRY TO BOTHER YOU, BUT COULD YOU GO WITH NIFUJI TO GET GLASSES?
UM, ME?
GLANCE... キョロ...
COULD IT BE, KABAKURA-SENPAI IS BEING CONSIDERATE...?
GRIN
ニコッ
IT'D BE DANGEROUS FOR NIFUJI TO GO ALONE WITH HIS TERRIBLE EYESIGHT, AFTER ALL.
AND MAYBE ON YOUR WAY BACK, YOU CAN FIND YOUR CONCENTRATION ALONG THE WAY.
AH, THAT'S MORE LIKE HIM.
SURE! ♡
THANKS FOR YOUR HELP, MOMOSE-SAN.
OH, IT'S NO TROUBLE AT ALL.
...
HM?
HM?
IS YOUR EYESIGHT REALLY THAT BAD?

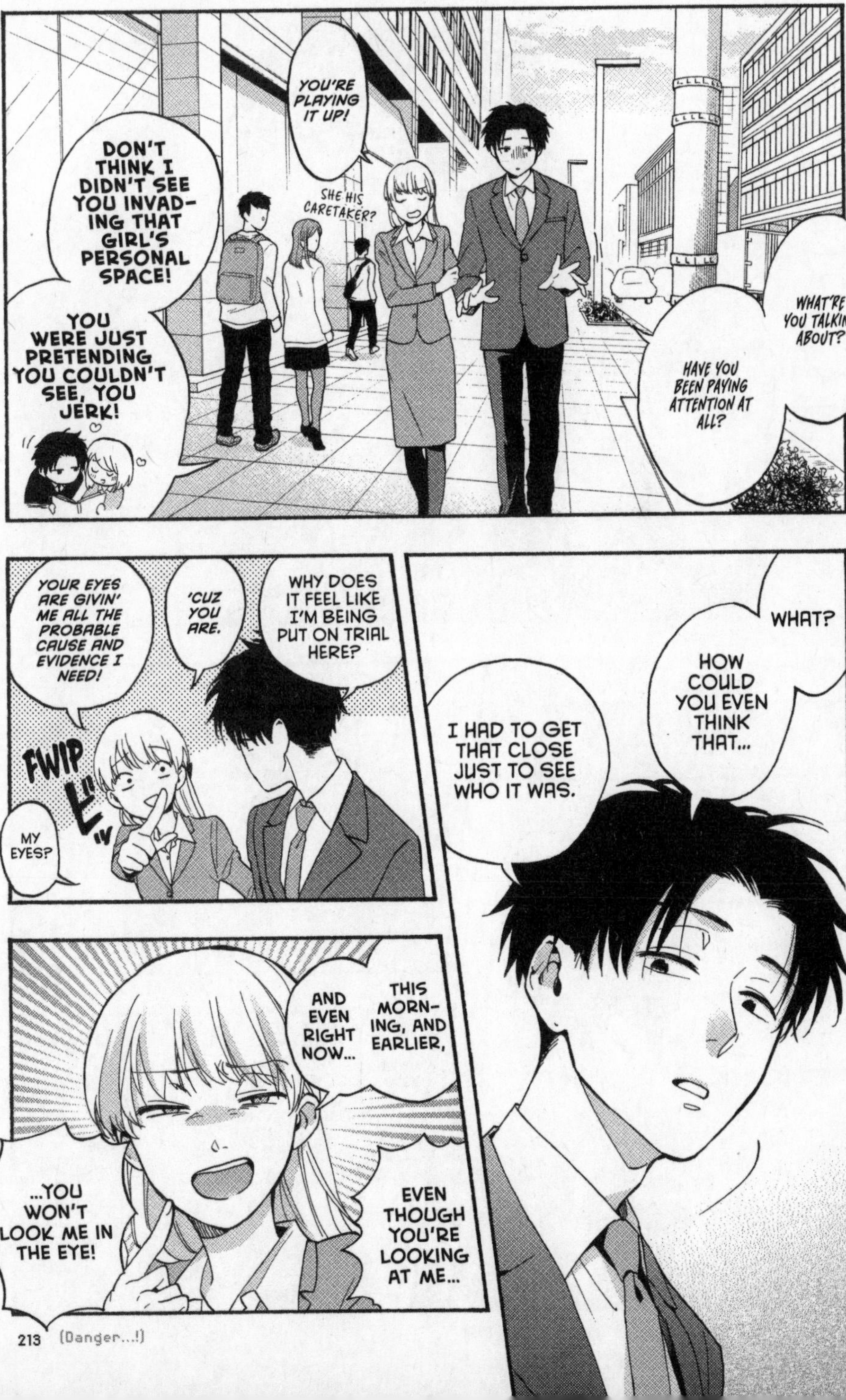
WHAT'RE YOU TALKING ABOUT?
HAVE YOU BEEN PAYING ATTENTION AT ALL?
YOU'RE PLAYING IT UP!
SHE HIS CARETAKER?
DON'T THINK I DIDN'T SEE YOU INVAD-ING THAT GIRL'S PERSONAL SPACE!
YOU WERE JUST PRETENDING YOU COULDN'T SEE, YOU JERK!
WHAT?
HOW COULD YOU EVEN THINK THAT...
I HAD TO GET THAT CLOSE JUST TO SEE WHO IT WAS.
WHY DOES IT FEEL LIKE I'M BEING PUT ON TRIAL HERE?
'CUZ YOU ARE.
YOUR EYES ARE GIVIN' ME ALL THE PROBABLE CAUSE AND EVIDENCE I NEED!
FWIP
MY EYES?
THIS MORN-ING, AND EARLIER,
AND EVEN RIGHT NOW...
EVEN THOUGH YOU'RE LOOKING AT ME...
...YOU WON'T LOOK ME IN THE EYE!

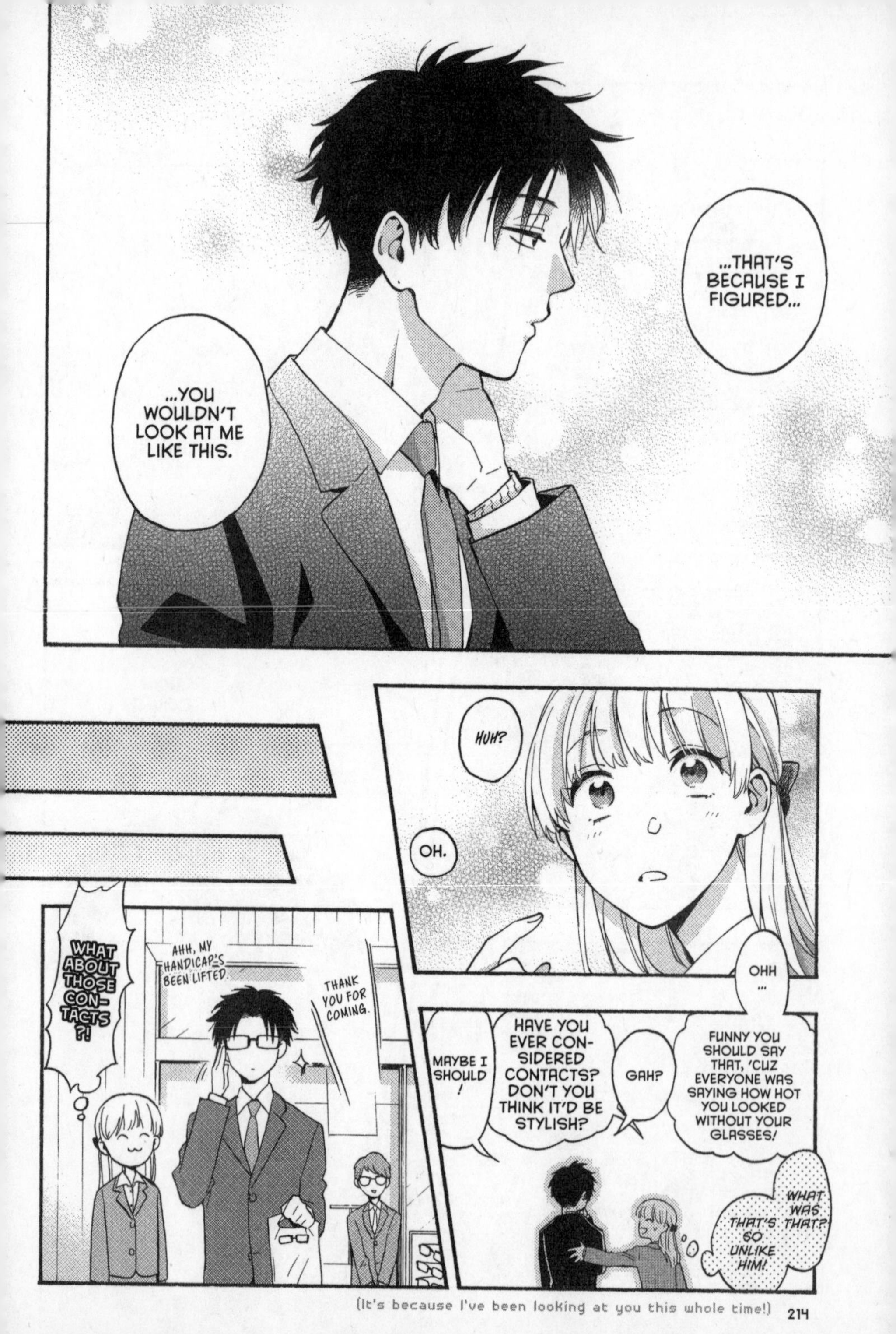
...THAT'S BECAUSE I FIGURED...
...YOU WOULDN'T LOOK AT ME LIKE THIS.
HUH?
OH.
OHH ...
FUNNY YOU SHOULD SAY THAT, 'CUZ EVERYONE WAS SAYING HOW HOT YOU LOOKED WITHOUT YOUR GLASSES!
GAH?
HAVE YOU EVER CONSIDERED CONTACTS? DON'T YOU THINK IT'D BE STYLISH?
MAYBE I SHOULD!
WHAT WAS THAT?
THAT'S SO UNLIKE HIM!
THANK YOU FOR COMING.
AHH, MY HANDICAP'S BEEN LIFTED.
WHAT ABOUT THOSE CONTACTS?!

(It's because I've been looking at you this whole time!)

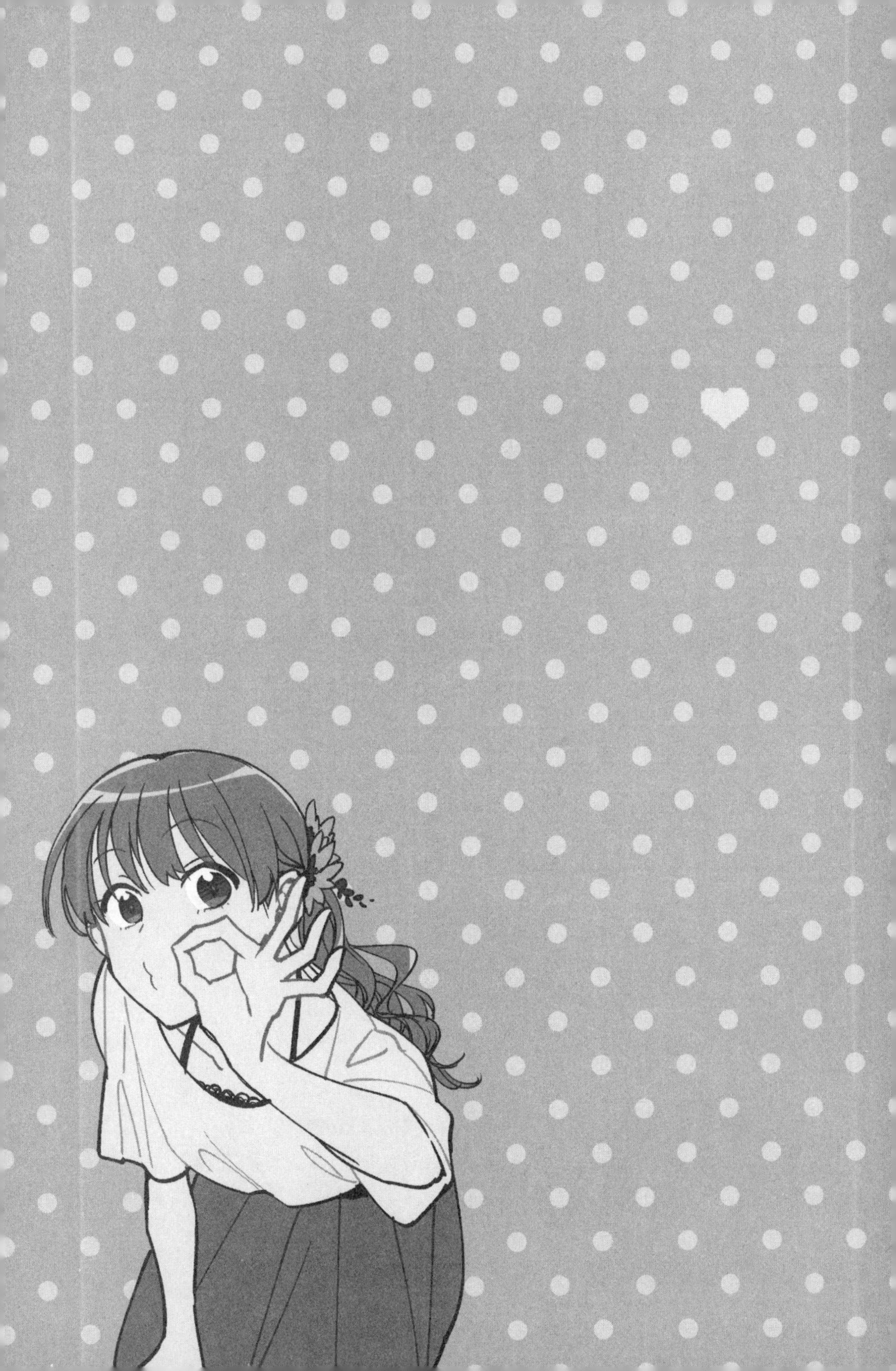

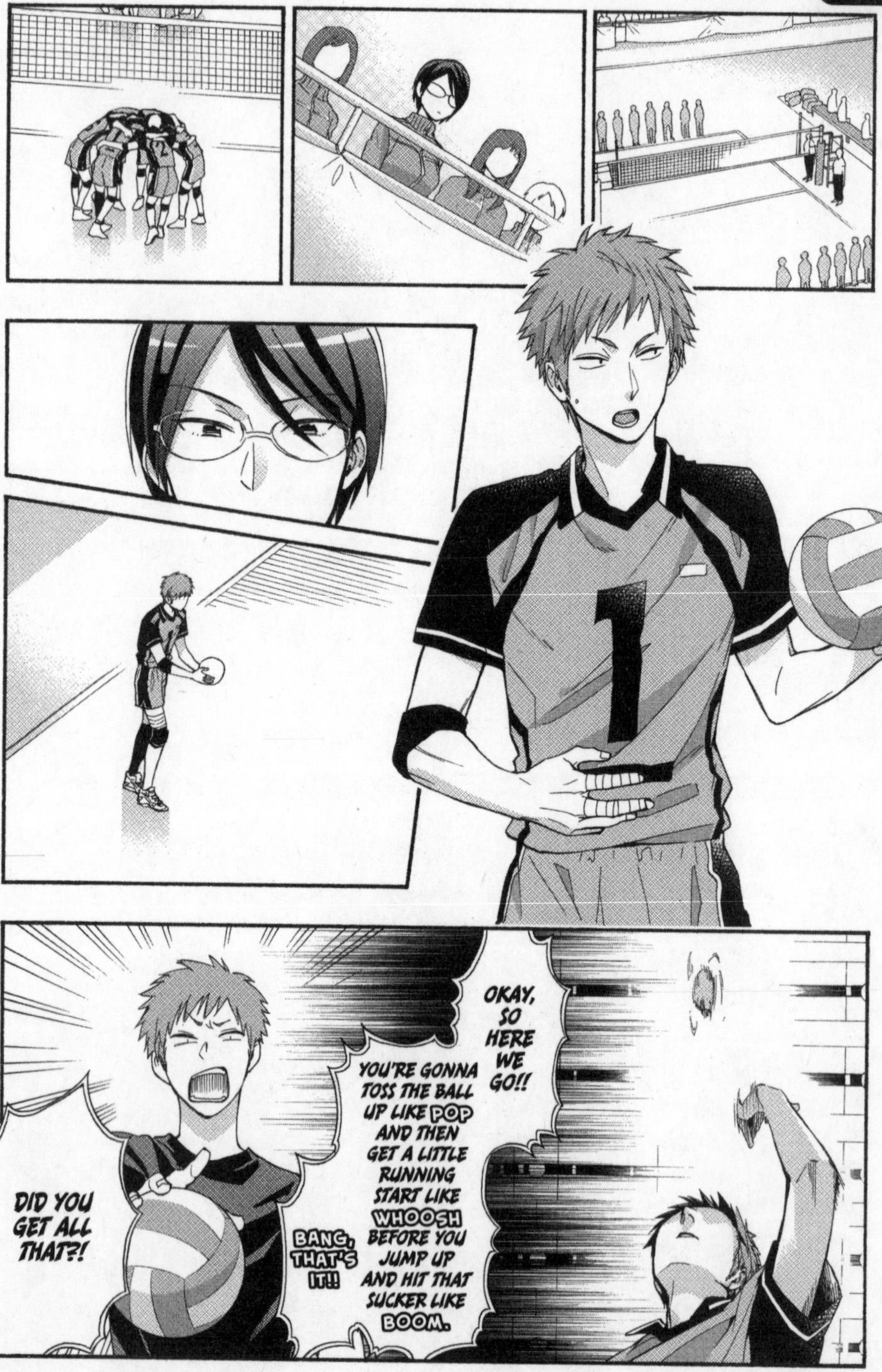
OKAY, SO HERE WE GO!!
YOU'RE GONNA TOSS THE BALL UP LIKE POP AND THEN GET A LITTLE RUNNING START LIKE WHOOSH BEFORE YOU JUMP UP AND HIT THAT SUCKER LIKE BOOM.
BANG, THAT'S IT!!
DID YOU GET ALL THAT?!

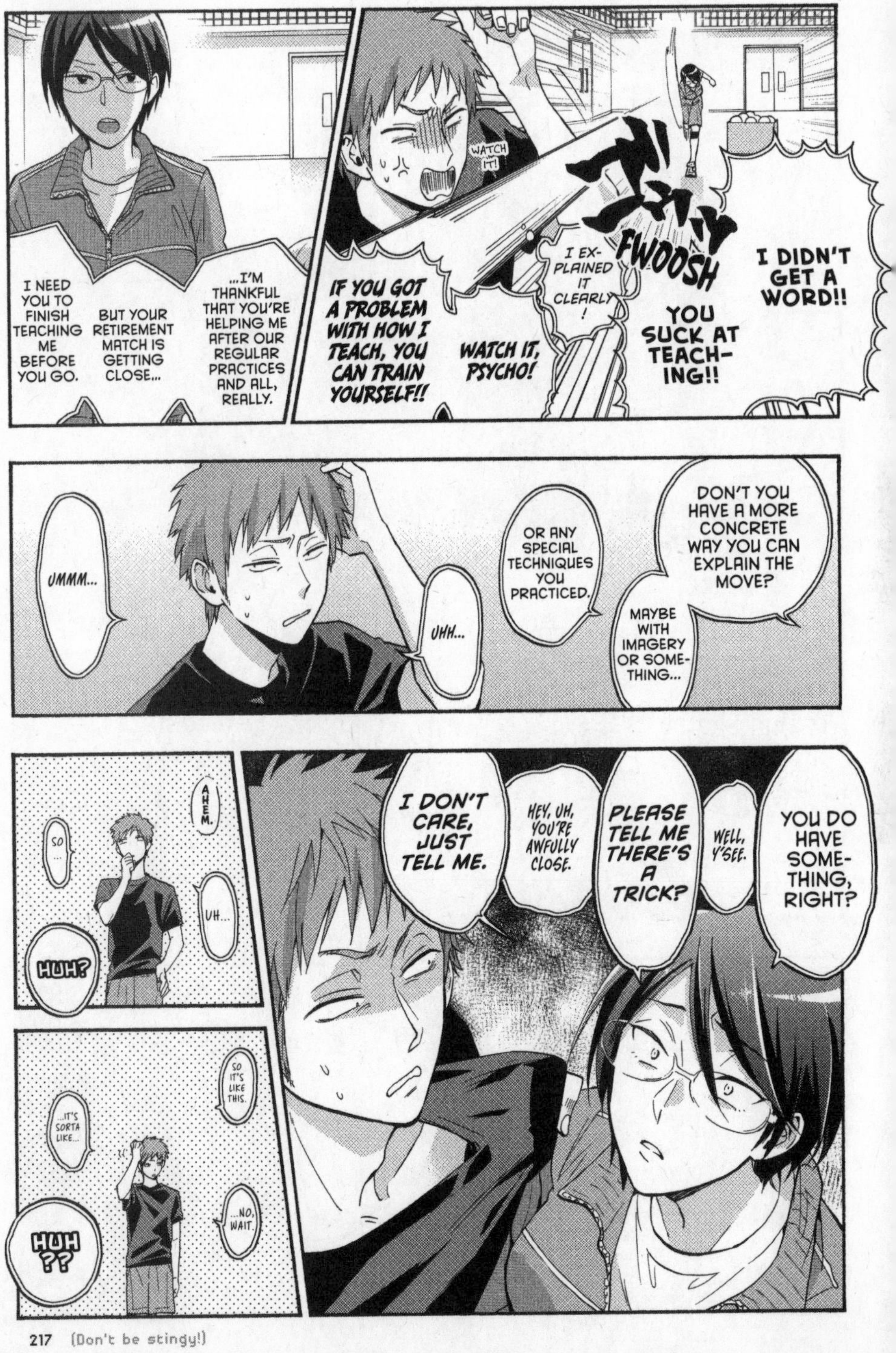
I DIDN'T GET A WORD!!
YOU SUCK AT TEACHING!!
FWOOSH
I EXPLAINED IT CLEARLY!
WATCH IT!
WATCH IT, PSYCHO!
IF YOU GOT A PROBLEM WITH HOW I TEACH, YOU CAN TRAIN YOURSELF!!
...I'M THANKFUL THAT YOU'RE HELPING ME AFTER OUR REGULAR PRACTICES AND ALL, REALLY.
BUT YOUR RETIREMENT MATCH IS GETTING CLOSE...
I NEED YOU TO FINISH TEACHING ME BEFORE YOU GO.
DON'T YOU HAVE A MORE CONCRETE WAY YOU CAN EXPLAIN THE MOVE?
MAYBE WITH IMAGERY OR SOMETHING...
OR ANY SPECIAL TECHNIQUES YOU PRACTICED.
UHH...
UMMM...
YOU DO HAVE SOMETHING, RIGHT?
WELL, Y'SEE.
PLEASE TELL ME THERE'S A TRICK?
HEY, UH, YOU'RE AWFULLY CLOSE.
I DON'T CARE, JUST TELL ME.
AHEM.
SO...
UH...
HUH?
SO IT'S LIKE THIS.
...IT'S SORTA LIKE...
...NO, WAIT.
HUH ??

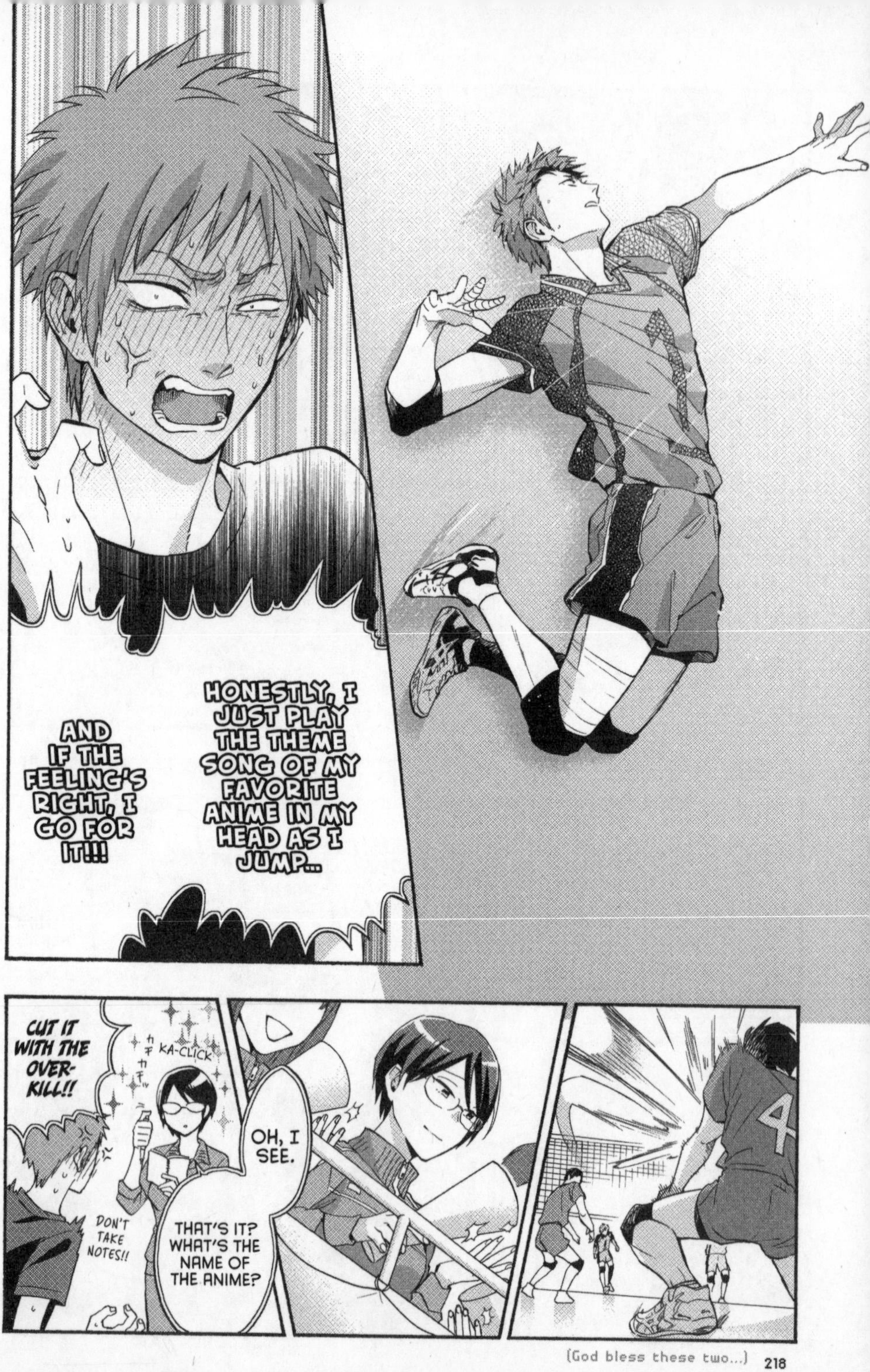
HONESTLY, I JUST PLAY THE THEME SONG OF MY FAVORITE ANIME IN MY HEAD AS I JUMP...
AND IF THE FEELING'S RIGHT, I GO FOR IT!!!
OH, I SEE.
THAT'S IT? WHAT'S THE NAME OF THE ANIME?
KA-CLICK
CUT IT WITH THE OVER-KILL!!
DON'T TAKE NOTES!!

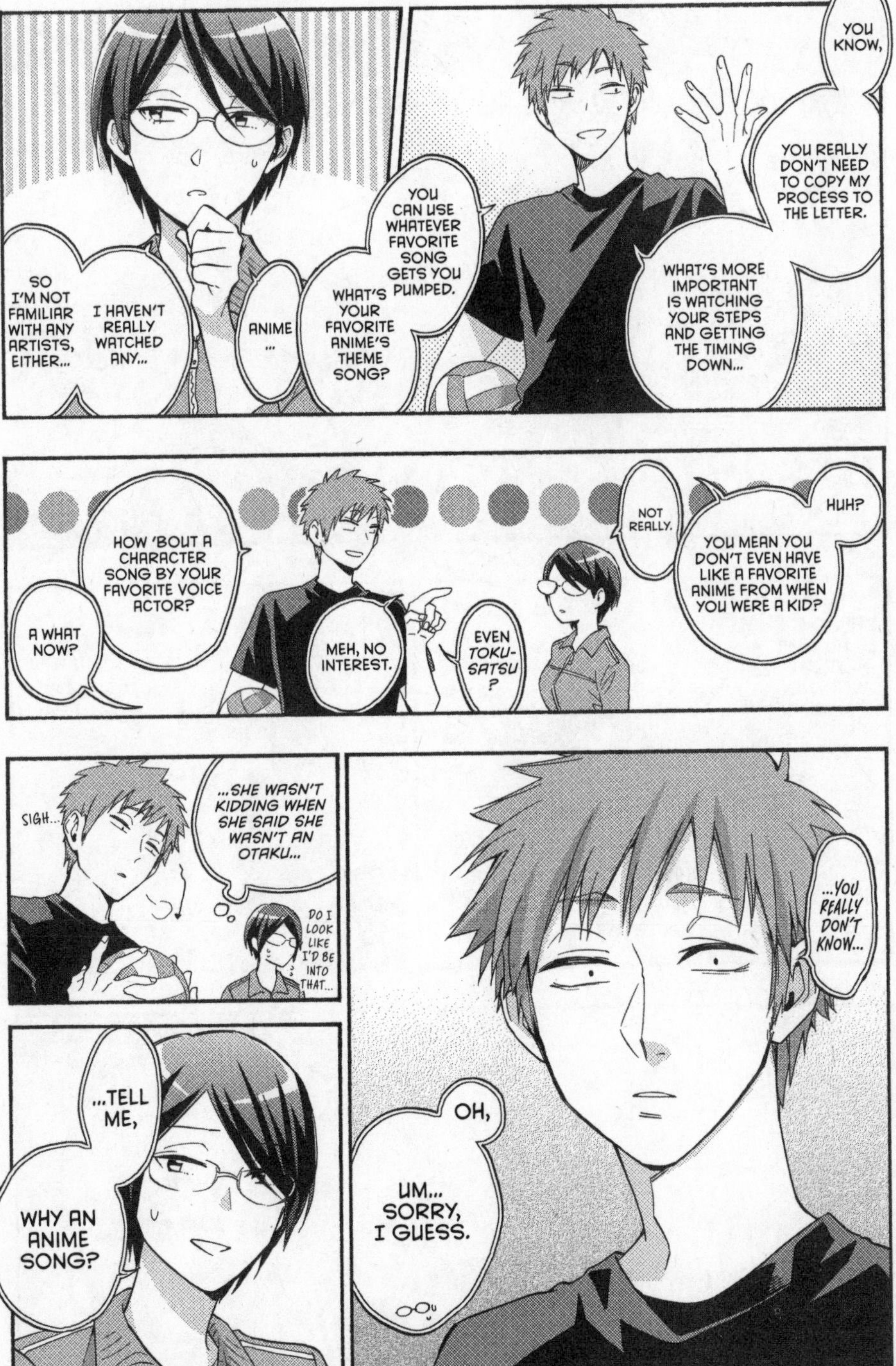
YOU KNOW,
YOU REALLY DON'T NEED TO COPY MY PROCESS TO THE LETTER.
WHAT'S MORE IMPORTANT IS WATCHING YOUR STEPS AND GETTING THE TIMING DOWN...
YOU CAN USE WHATEVER FAVORITE SONG GETS YOU PUMPED.
WHAT'S YOUR FAVORITE ANIME'S THEME SONG?
ANIME...
I HAVEN'T REALLY WATCHED ANY...
SO I'M NOT FAMILIAR WITH ANY ARTISTS, EITHER...
HUH?
YOU MEAN YOU DON'T EVEN HAVE LIKE A FAVORITE ANIME FROM WHEN YOU WERE A KID?
NOT REALLY.
EVEN TOKUSATSU?
MEH, NO INTEREST.
HOW 'BOUT A CHARACTER SONG BY YOUR FAVORITE VOICE ACTOR?
A WHAT NOW?
...YOU REALLY DON'T KNOW...
OH,
UM... SORRY, I GUESS.
...SHE WASN'T KIDDING WHEN SHE SAID SHE WASN'T AN OTAKU...
SIGH...
DO I LOOK LIKE I'D BE INTO THAT...
...TELL ME,
WHY AN ANIME SONG?

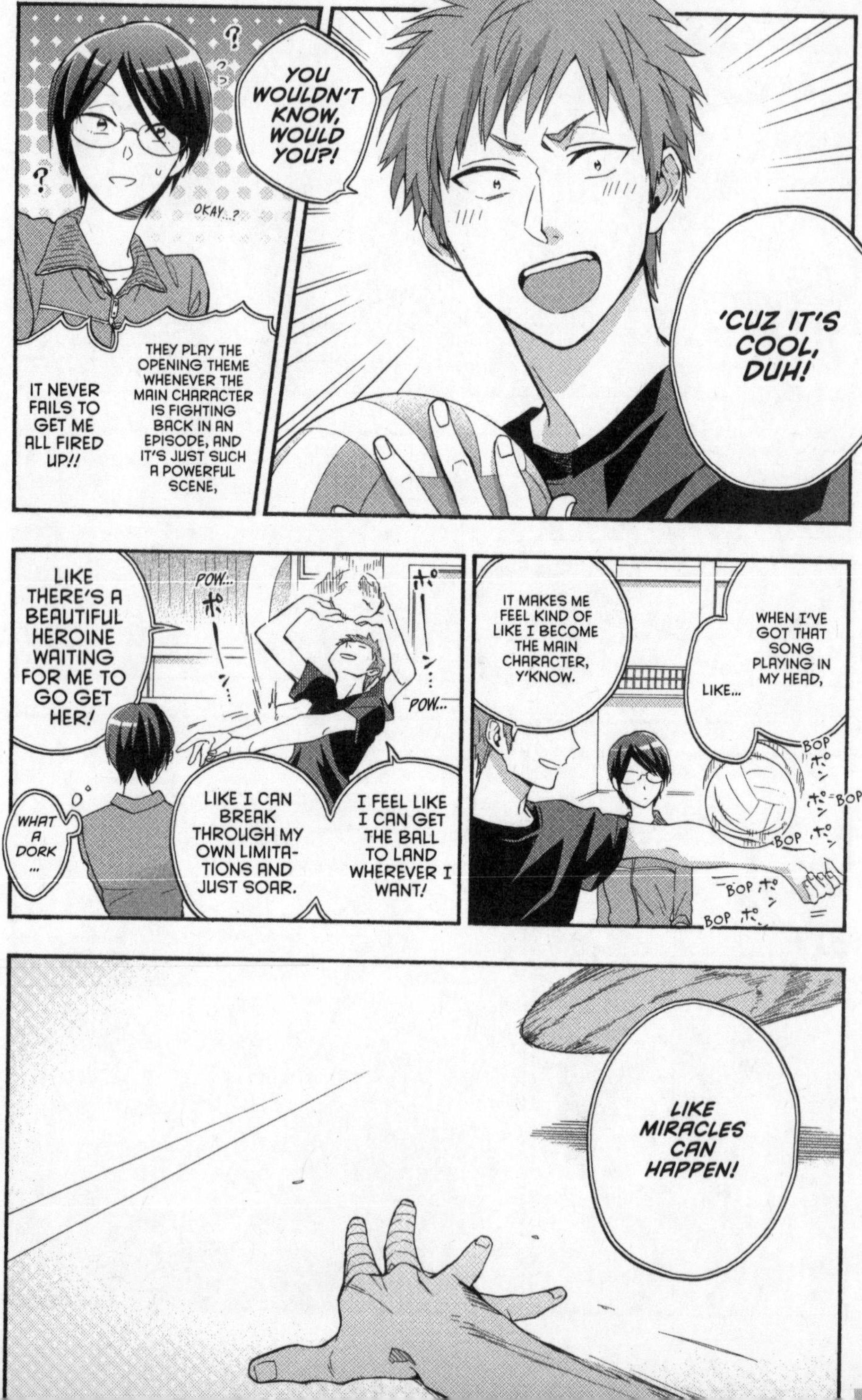
YOU WOULDN'T KNOW, WOULD YOU?!
'CUZ IT'S COOL, DUH!
OKAY...?
THEY PLAY THE OPENING THEME WHENEVER THE MAIN CHARACTER IS FIGHTING BACK IN AN EPISODE, AND IT'S JUST SUCH A POWERFUL SCENE,
IT NEVER FAILS TO GET ME ALL FIRED UP!!
WHEN I'VE GOT THAT SONG PLAYING IN MY HEAD,
LIKE...
IT MAKES ME FEEL KIND OF LIKE I BECOME THE MAIN CHARACTER, Y'KNOW.
BOP
BOP
BOP
BOP
BOP
POW...
POW...
I FEEL LIKE I CAN GET THE BALL TO LAND WHEREVER I WANT!
LIKE I CAN BREAK THROUGH MY OWN LIMITA- TIONS AND JUST SOAR.
LIKE THERE'S A BEAUTIFUL HEROINE WAITING FOR ME TO GO GET HER!
WHAT A DORK ...
LIKE MIRACLES CAN HAPPEN!

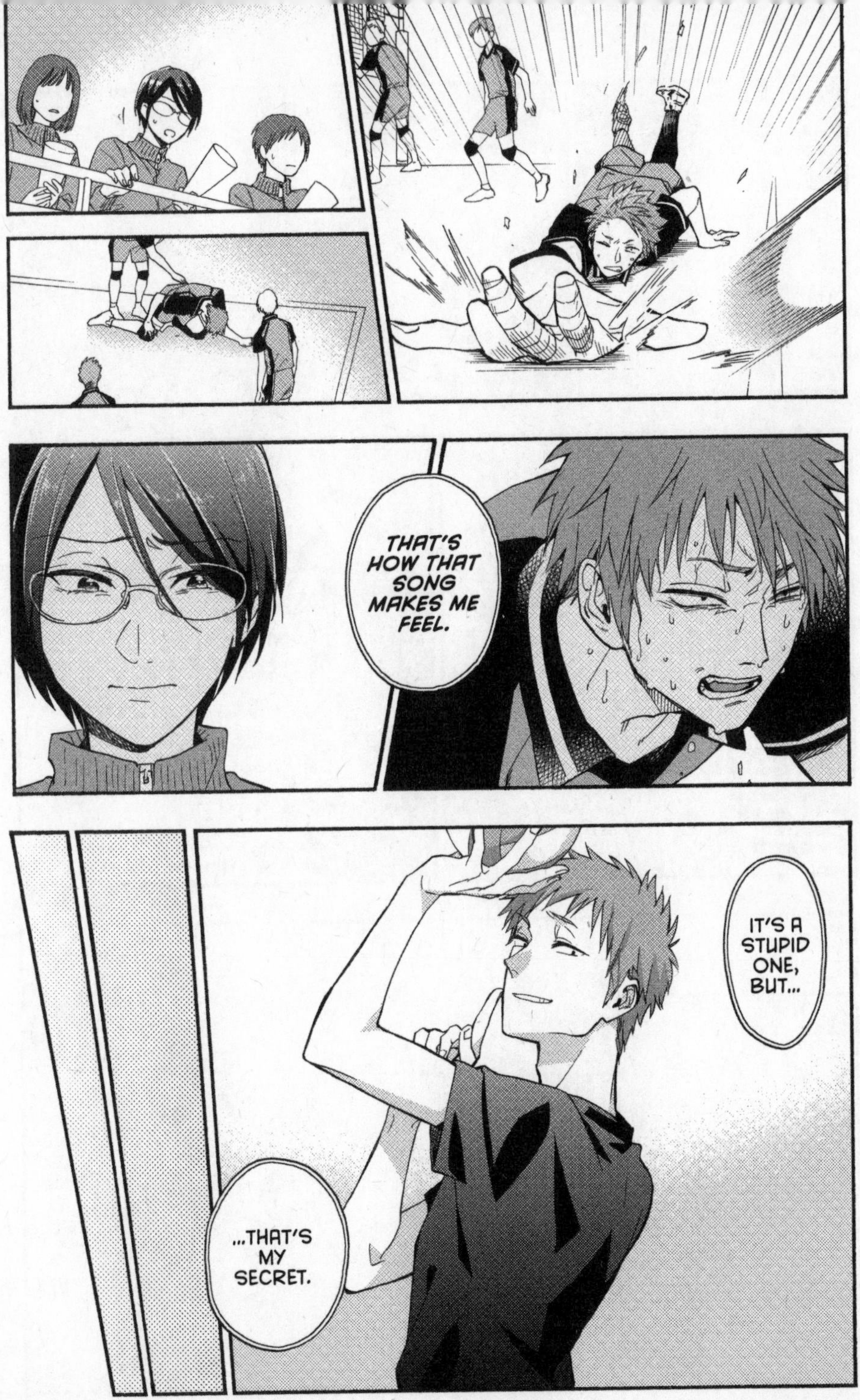
THAT'S HOW THAT SONG MAKES ME FEEL.
IT'S A STUPID ONE, BUT...
...THAT'S MY SECRET.

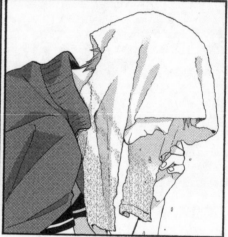

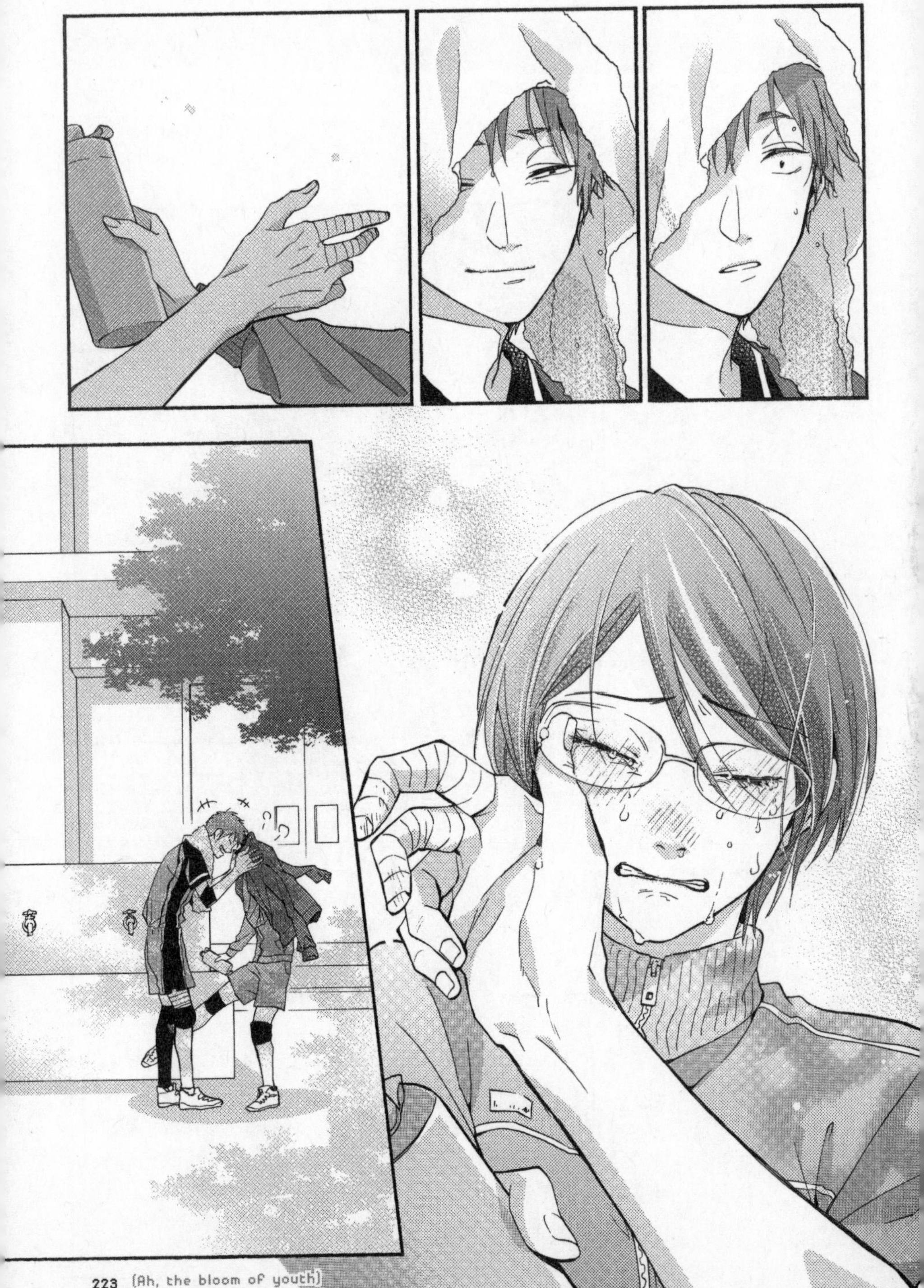

 (Ah, the bloom of youth)

← To be continued...

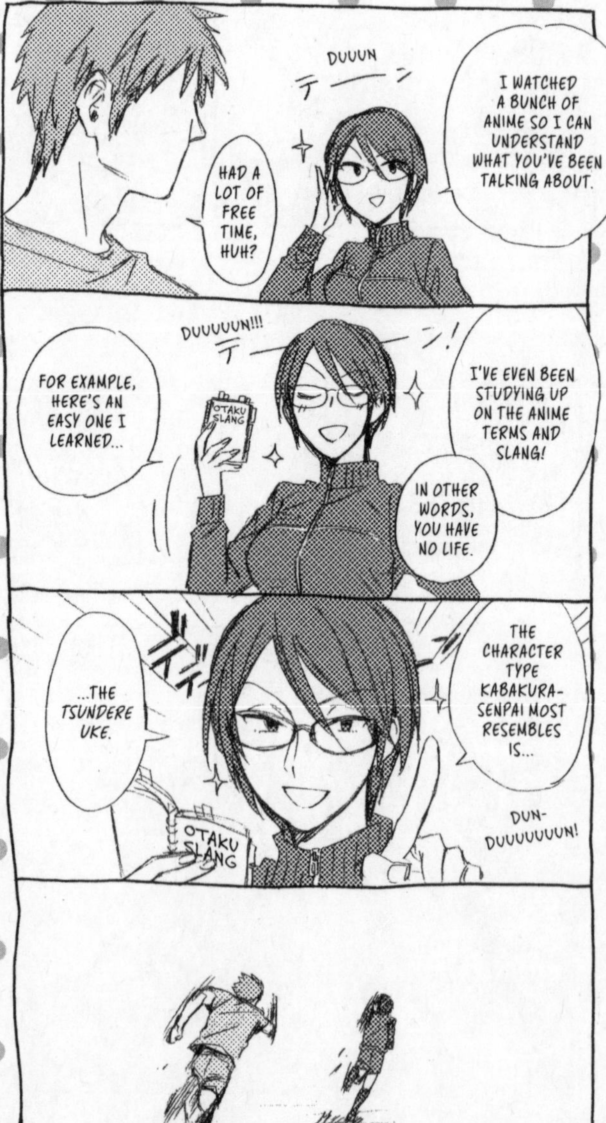
I WATCHED A BUNCH OF ANIME SO I CAN UNDERSTAND WHAT YOU'VE BEEN TALKING ABOUT.
DUUUN
HAD A LOT OF FREE TIME, HUH?
I'VE EVEN BEEN STUDYING UP ON THE ANIME TERMS AND SLANG!
DUUUUUN!!!
FOR EXAMPLE, HERE'S AN EASY ONE I LEARNED...
OTAKU SLANG
IN OTHER WORDS, YOU HAVE NO LIFE.
THE CHARACTER TYPE KABAKURA-SENPAI MOST RESEMBLES IS...
DUN-DUUUUUUUN!
...THE TSUNDERE UKE.
OTAKU SLANG

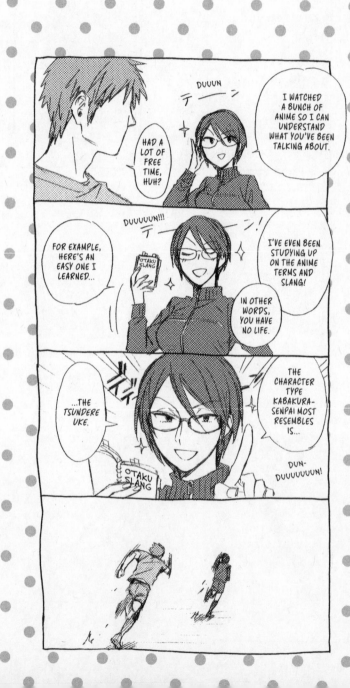

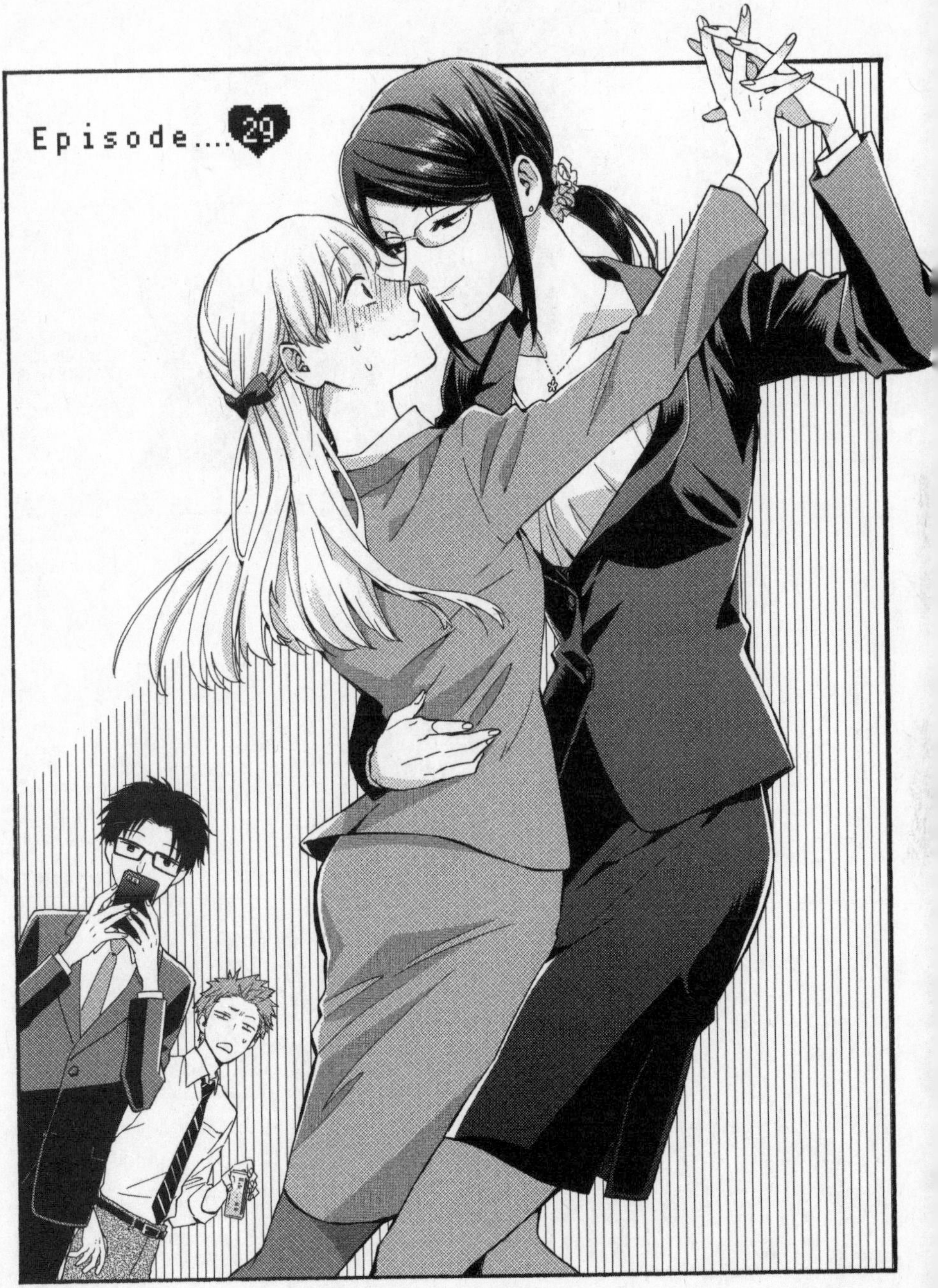
Episode.... 29

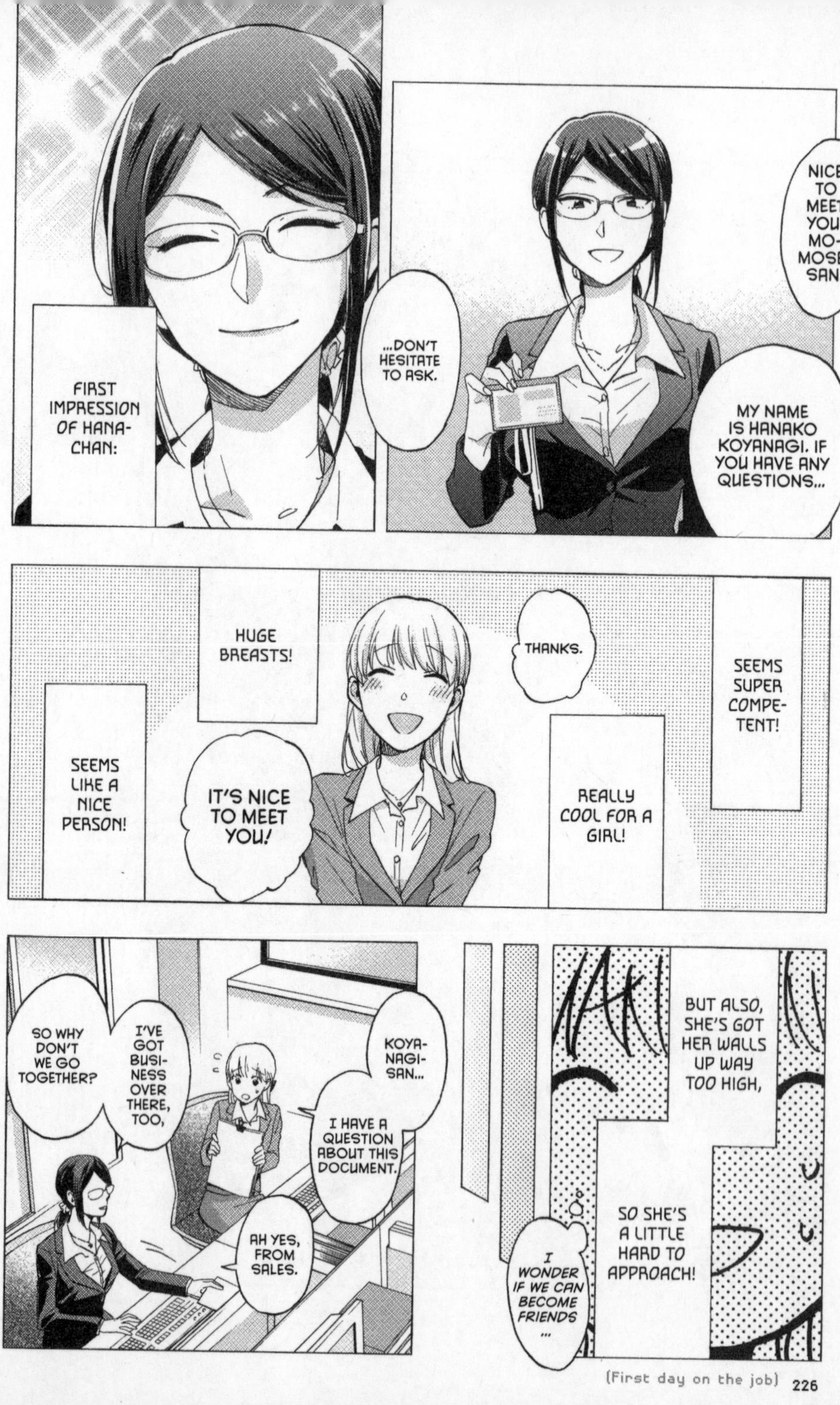
NICE TO MEET YOU, MOMOSE-SAN.
MY NAME IS HANAKO KOYANAGI. IF YOU HAVE ANY QUESTIONS...
...DON'T HESITATE TO ASK.
FIRST IMPRESSION OF HANA-CHAN:
SEEMS SUPER COMPETENT!
THANKS.
HUGE BREASTS!
REALLY COOL FOR A GIRL!
IT'S NICE TO MEET YOU!
SEEMS LIKE A NICE PERSON!
BUT ALSO, SHE'S GOT HER WALLS UP WAY TOO HIGH,
SO SHE'S A LITTLE HARD TO APPROACH!
I WONDER IF WE CAN BECOME FRIENDS...
KOYANAGI-SAN...
I HAVE A QUESTION ABOUT THIS DOCUMENT.
AH YES, FROM SALES.
I'VE GOT BUSINESS OVER THERE, TOO,
SO WHY DON'T WE GO TOGETHER?

(First day on the job)

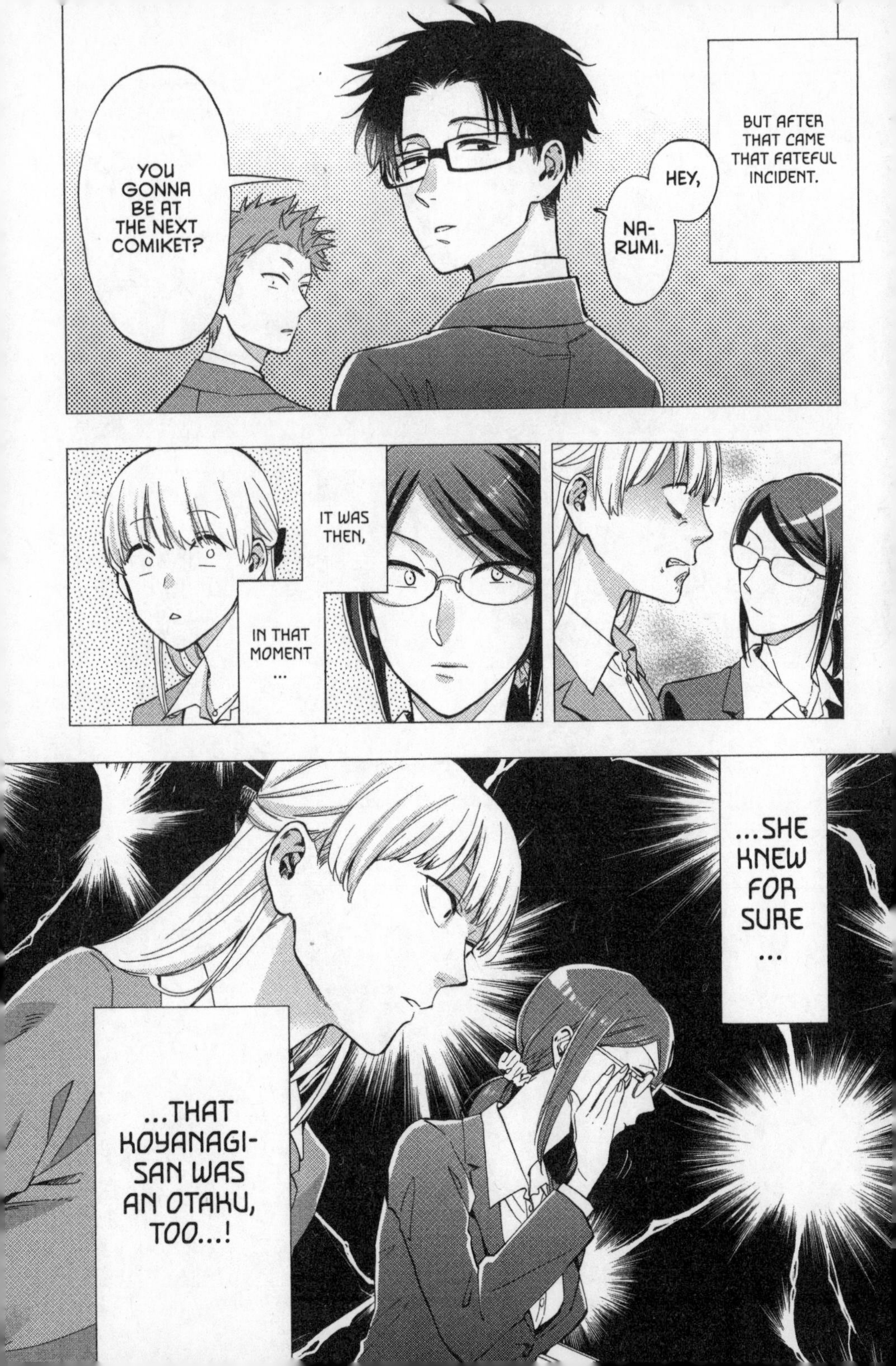
BUT AFTER THAT CAME THAT FATEFUL INCIDENT.
HEY, NA-RUMI.
YOU GONNA BE AT THE NEXT COMIKET?
IT WAS THEN,
IN THAT MOMENT ...
...SHE KNEW FOR SURE ...
...THAT KOYANAGI-SAN WAS AN OTAKU, TOO...!

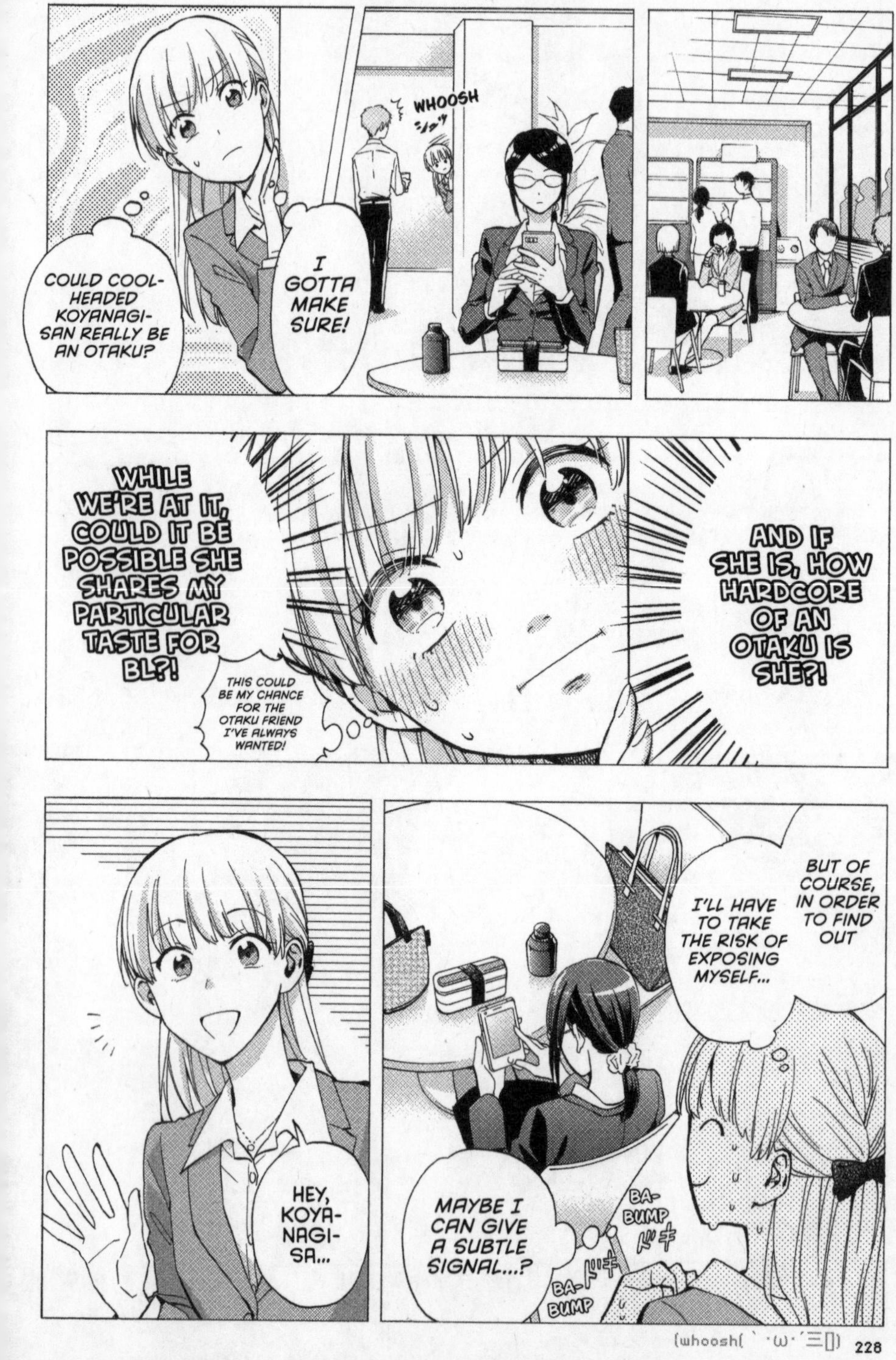
WHOOSH
シュッ
I GOTTA MAKE SURE!
COULD COOL-HEADED KOYANAGI-SAN REALLY BE AN OTAKU?
AND IF SHE IS, HOW HARDCORE OF AN OTAKU IS SHE?!
WHILE WE'RE AT IT, COULD IT BE POSSIBLE SHE SHARES MY PARTICULAR TASTE FOR BL?!
THIS COULD BE MY CHANCE FOR THE OTAKU FRIEND I'VE ALWAYS WANTED!
BUT OF COURSE, IN ORDER TO FIND OUT
I'LL HAVE TO TAKE THE RISK OF EXPOSING MYSELF...
BA-BUMP
ドキ
MAYBE I CAN GIVE A SUBTLE SIGNAL...?
BA-BUMP
ドキ
HEY, KOYANAGI-SA...

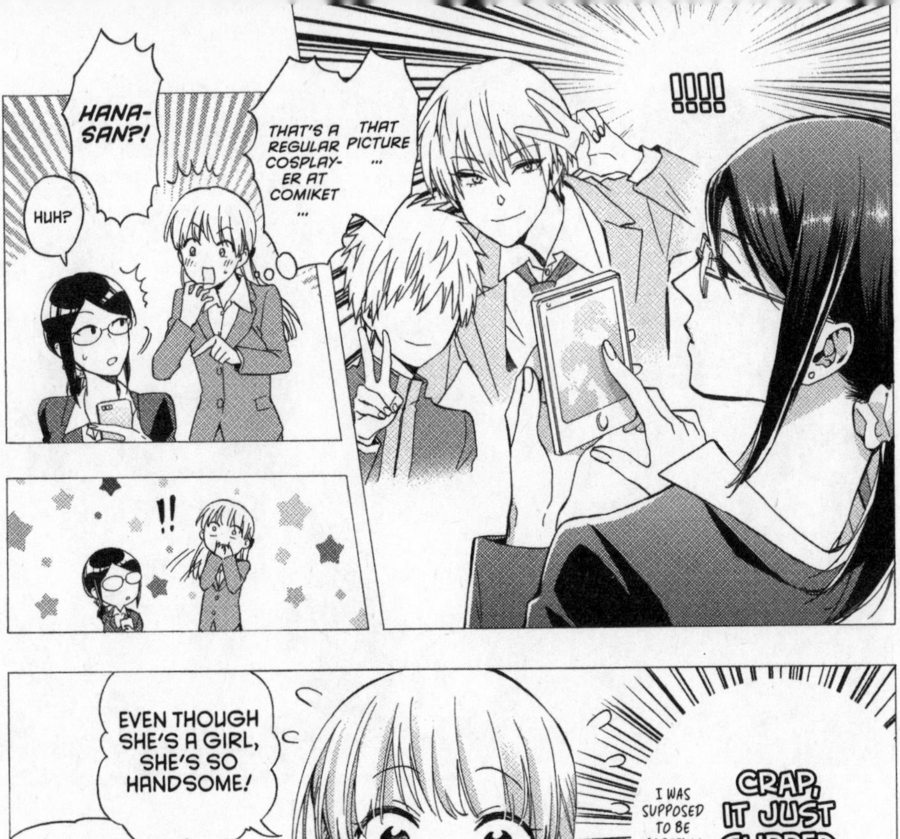
!!!!!
THAT PICTURE ...
THAT'S A REGULAR COSPLAYER AT COMIKET ...
HANA-SAN?!
HUH?
!!
CRAP, IT JUST SLIPPED OUT!
I WAS SUPPOSED TO BE CAREFUL!
OH, AH... SORRY TO SURPRISE YOU LIKE THAT!
I JUST SAW SOMEONE I RECOGNIZED IN YOUR PHOTO...
EVEN THOUGH SHE'S A GIRL, SHE'S SO HANDSOME!
I CAN'T TELL HER IT'S 'CUZ THAT COSPLAYER BOUGHT A BOOK FROM ME BACK WHEN I WAS INTO SOME OTHER STUFF...
I'M ALWAYS BROWSING YOUR SITE.
OH... WHOA... LIKE A GOD...

*An event for *dojinshi* artists to sell comics exclusively written about *Sengoku Basara*, a series of video games.

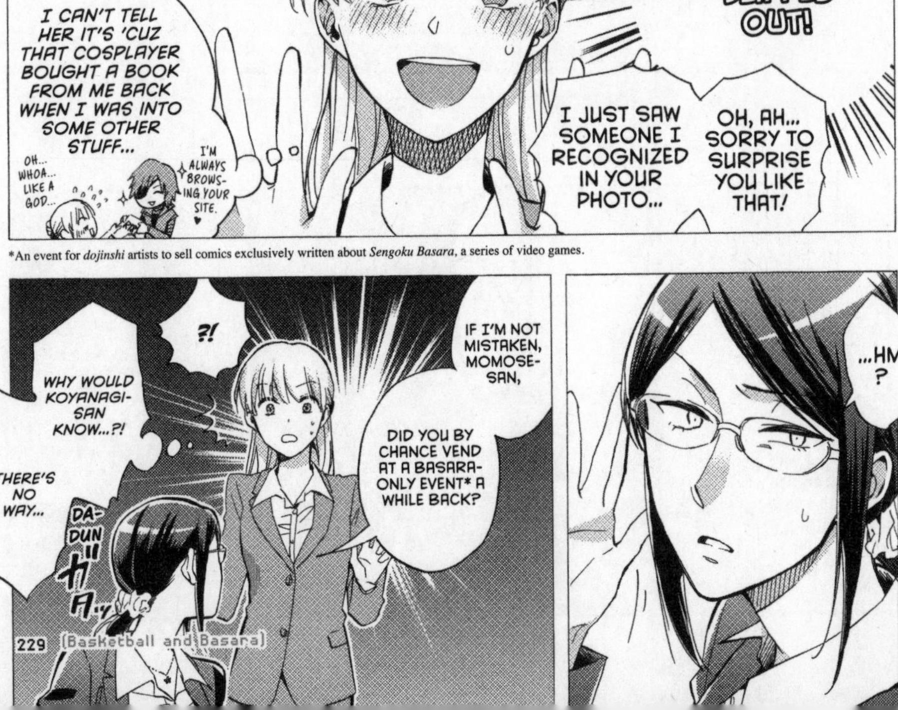
...HM?
IF I'M NOT MISTAKEN, MOMOSE-SAN,
DID YOU BY CHANCE VEND AT A BASARA-ONLY EVENT* A WHILE BACK?
?!
WHY WOULD KOYANAGI-SAN KNOW...?!
THERE'S NO WAY...
DA-DUN

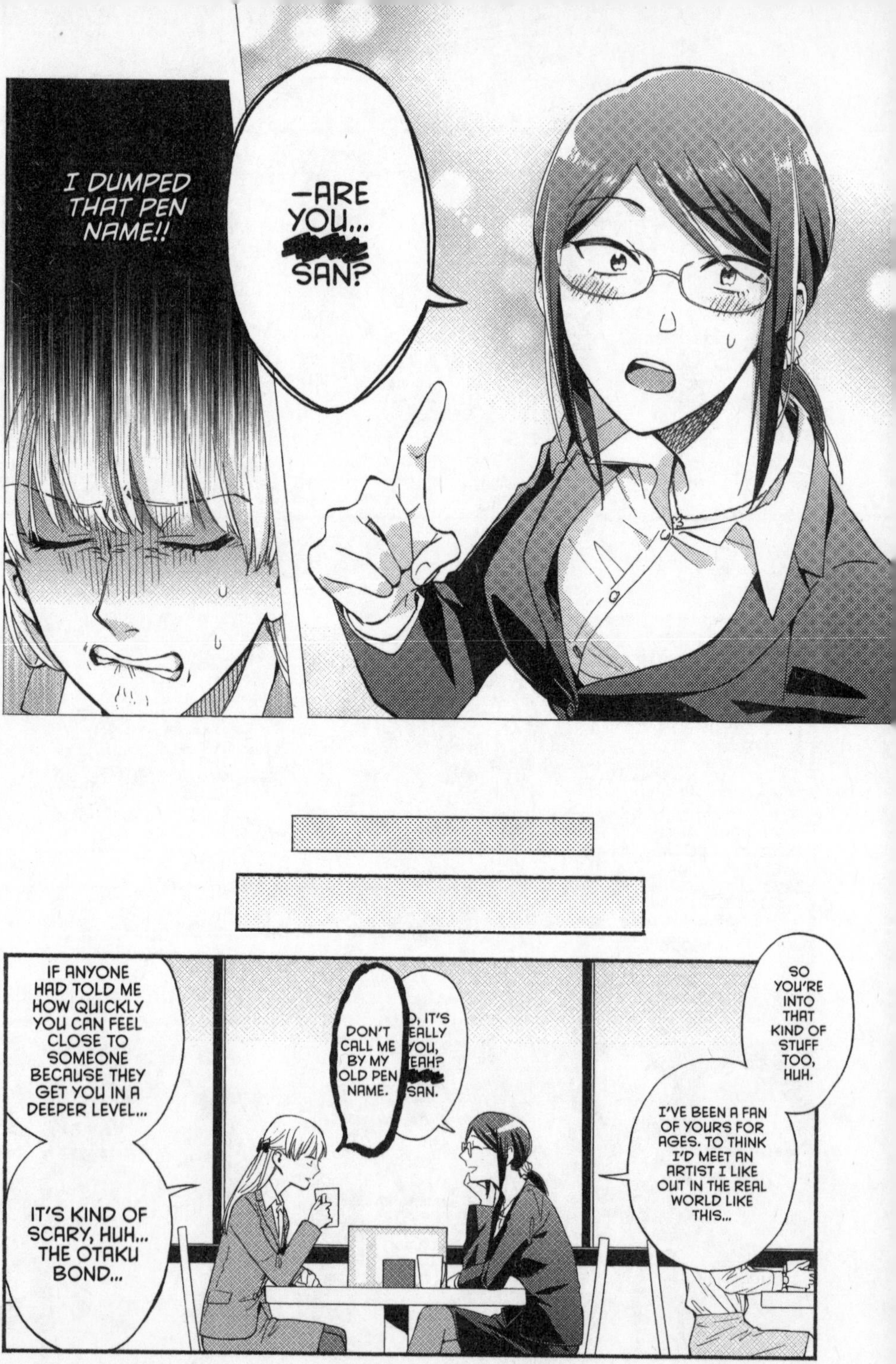
—ARE YOU... [redacted] SAN?
I DUMPED THAT PEN NAME!!
SO YOU'RE INTO THAT KIND OF STUFF TOO, HUH.
I'VE BEEN A FAN OF YOURS FOR AGES. TO THINK I'D MEET AN ARTIST I LIKE OUT IN THE REAL WORLD LIKE THIS...
O, IT'S EALLY YOU, EAH? [redacted] SAN.
DON'T CALL ME BY MY OLD PEN NAME.
IF ANYONE HAD TOLD ME HOW QUICKLY YOU CAN FEEL CLOSE TO SOMEONE BECAUSE THEY GET YOU IN A DEEPER LEVEL...
IT'S KIND OF SCARY, HUH... THE OTAKU BOND...

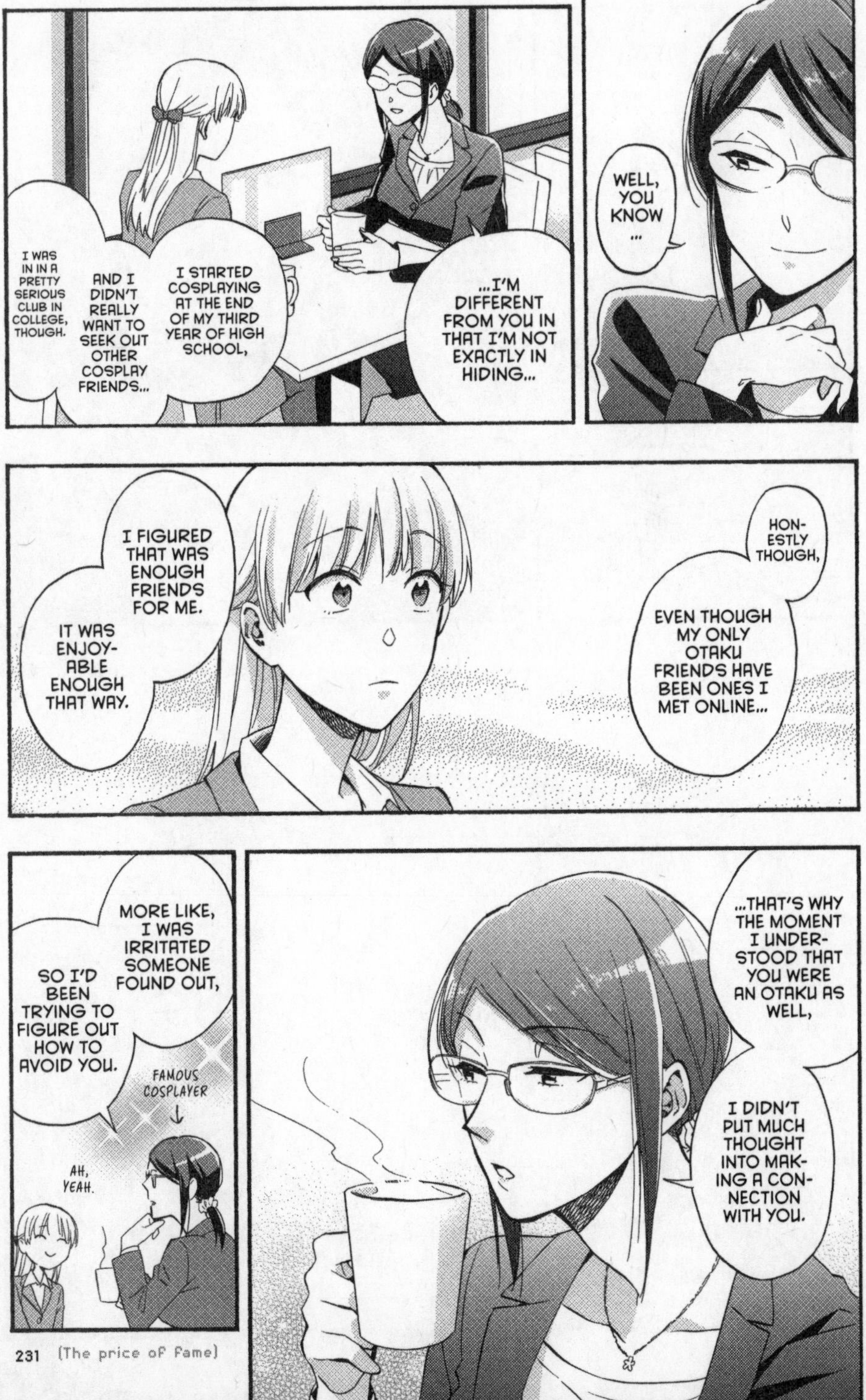
WELL, YOU KNOW ...
...I'M DIFFERENT FROM YOU IN THAT I'M NOT EXACTLY IN HIDING...
I STARTED COSPLAYING AT THE END OF MY THIRD YEAR OF HIGH SCHOOL,
AND I DIDN'T REALLY WANT TO SEEK OUT OTHER COSPLAY FRIENDS...
I WAS IN IN A PRETTY SERIOUS CLUB IN COLLEGE, THOUGH.
HON-ESTLY THOUGH,
EVEN THOUGH MY ONLY OTAKU FRIENDS HAVE BEEN ONES I MET ONLINE...
I FIGURED THAT WAS ENOUGH FRIENDS FOR ME.
IT WAS ENJOY-ABLE ENOUGH THAT WAY.
...THAT'S WHY THE MOMENT I UNDER-STOOD THAT YOU WERE AN OTAKU AS WELL,
I DIDN'T PUT MUCH THOUGHT INTO MAK-ING A CON-NECTION WITH YOU.
MORE LIKE, I WAS IRRITATED SOMEONE FOUND OUT,
SO I'D BEEN TRYING TO FIGURE OUT HOW TO AVOID YOU.
FAMOUS COSPLAYER ↓
AH, YEAH.

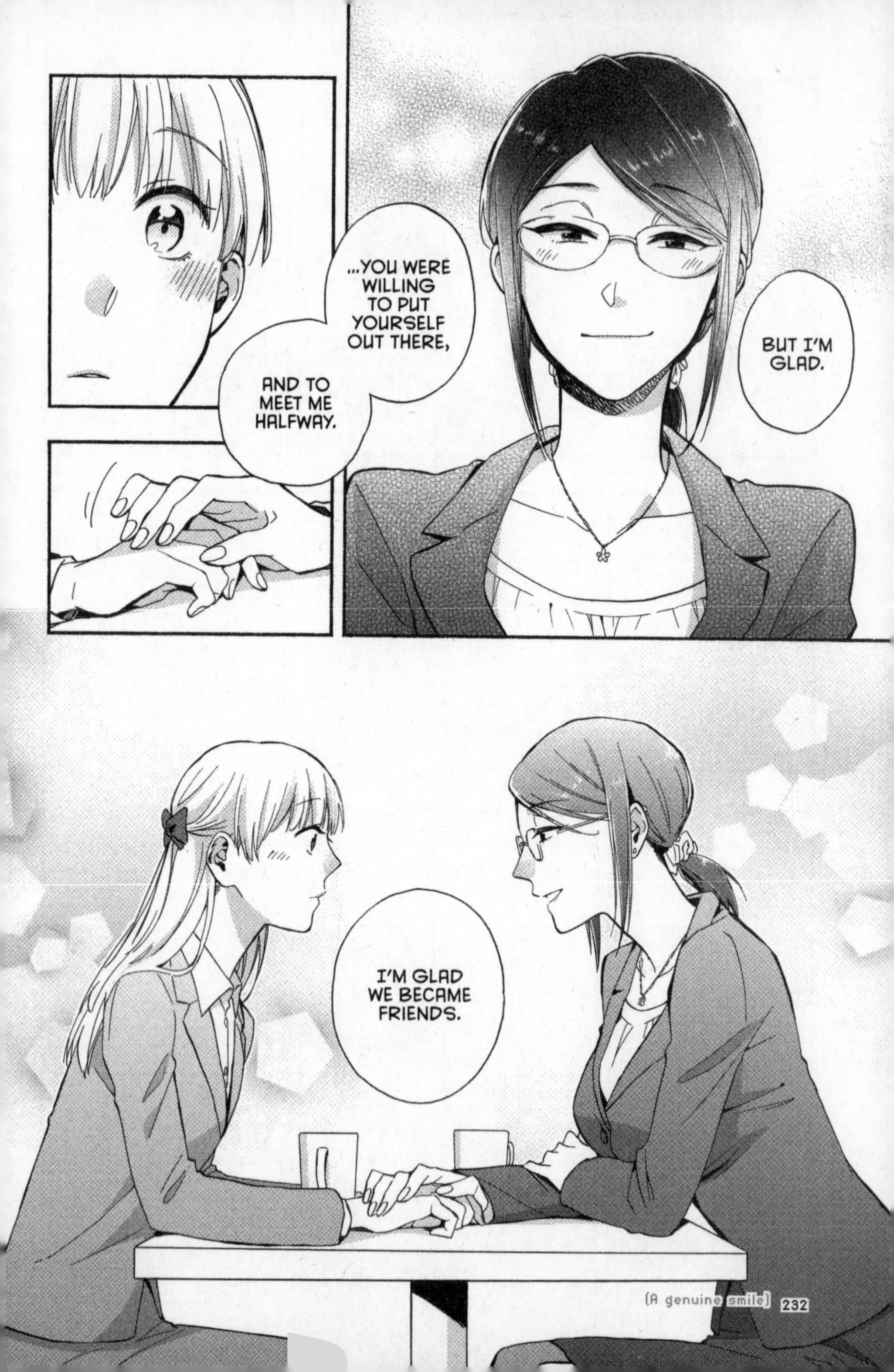
BUT I'M GLAD.
...YOU WERE WILLING TO PUT YOURSELF OUT THERE,
AND TO MEET ME HALFWAY.
I'M GLAD WE BECAME FRIENDS.
(A genuine smile)

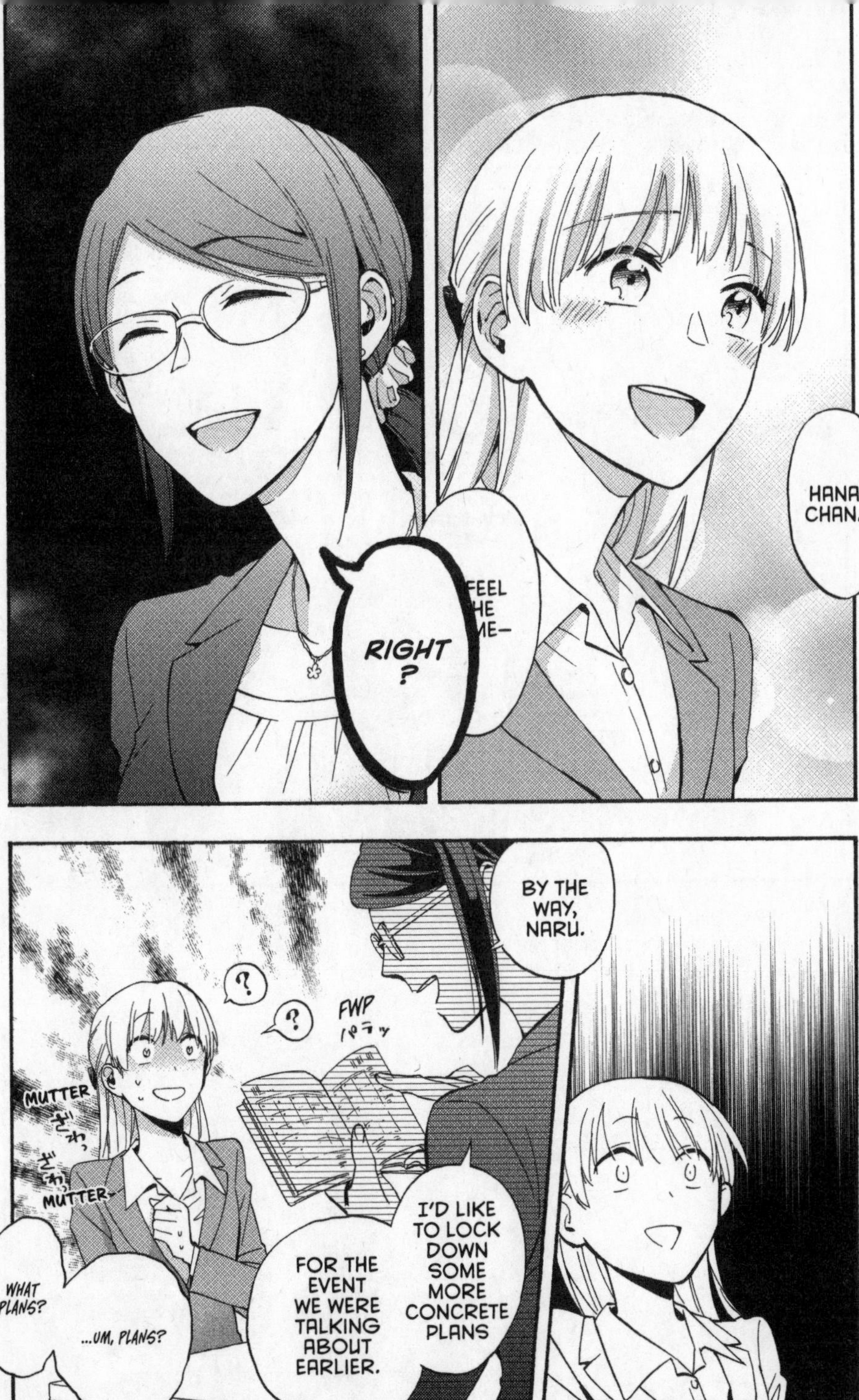
HANA-CHAN...
FEEL THE ME-
RIGHT?
BY THE WAY, NARU.
FWP
パラッ
?
?
I'D LIKE TO LOCK DOWN SOME MORE CONCRETE PLANS
FOR THE EVENT WE WERE TALKING ABOUT EARLIER.
MUTTER
MUTTER
...UM, PLANS?
WHAT PLANS?

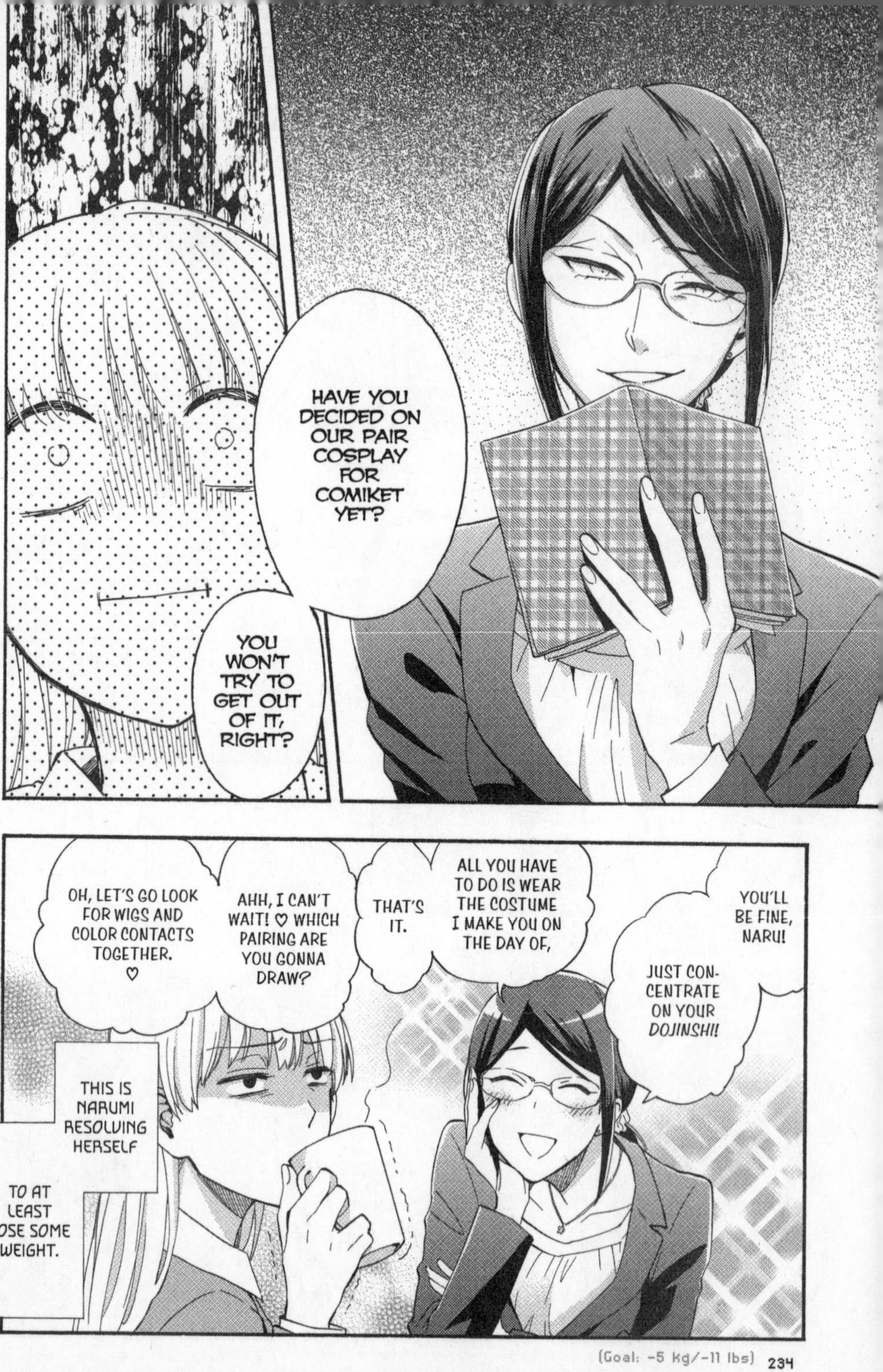
HAVE YOU DECIDED ON OUR PAIR COSPLAY FOR COMIKET YET?
YOU WON'T TRY TO GET OUT OF IT, RIGHT?
YOU'LL BE FINE, NARU!
JUST CONCENTRATE ON YOUR *DOJINSHI*!
ALL YOU HAVE TO DO IS WEAR THE COSTUME I MAKE YOU ON THE DAY OF,
THAT'S IT.
AHH, I CAN'T WAIT! ♡ WHICH PAIRING ARE YOU GONNA DRAW?
OH, LET'S GO LOOK FOR WIGS AND COLOR CONTACTS TOGETHER. ♡
THIS IS NARUMI RESOLVING HERSELF
TO AT LEAST LOSE SOME WEIGHT.

(Goal: -5 kg/-11 lbs)

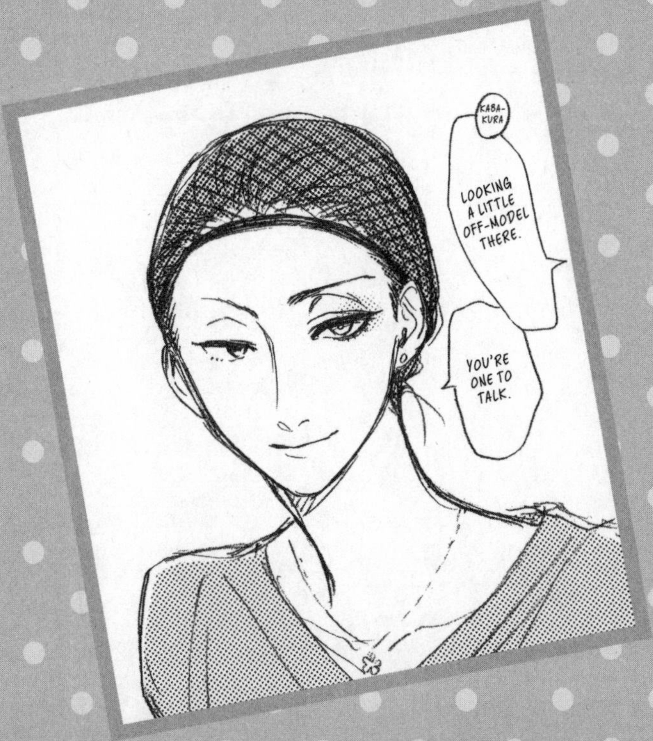
KABA-KURA
LOOKING A LITTLE OFF-MODEL THERE.
YOU'RE ONE TO TALK.

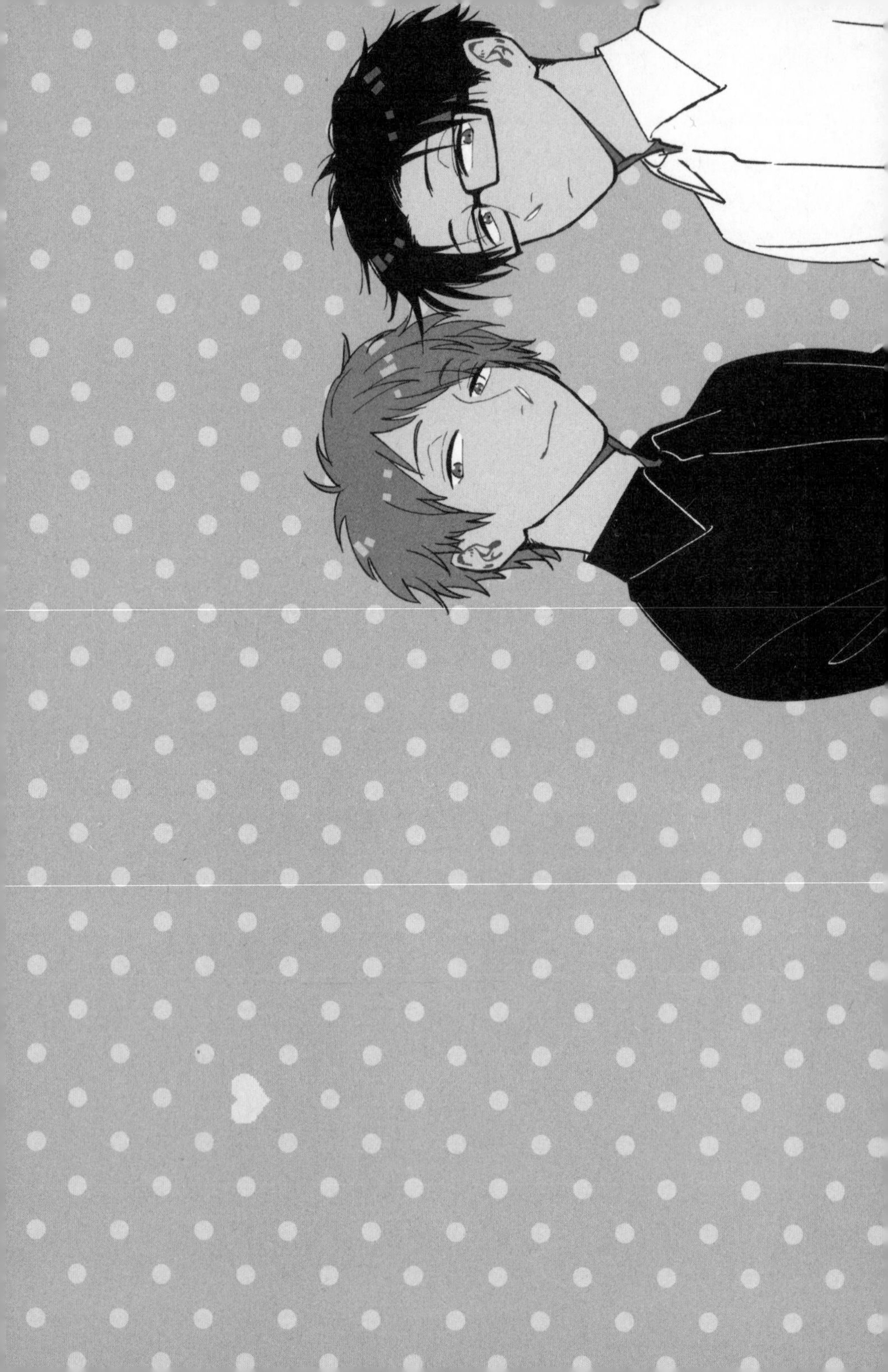

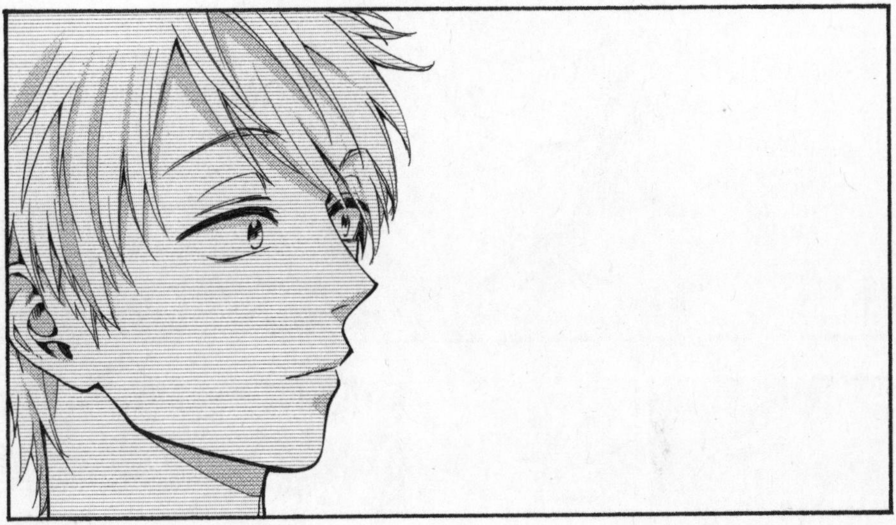

Episode.... 30

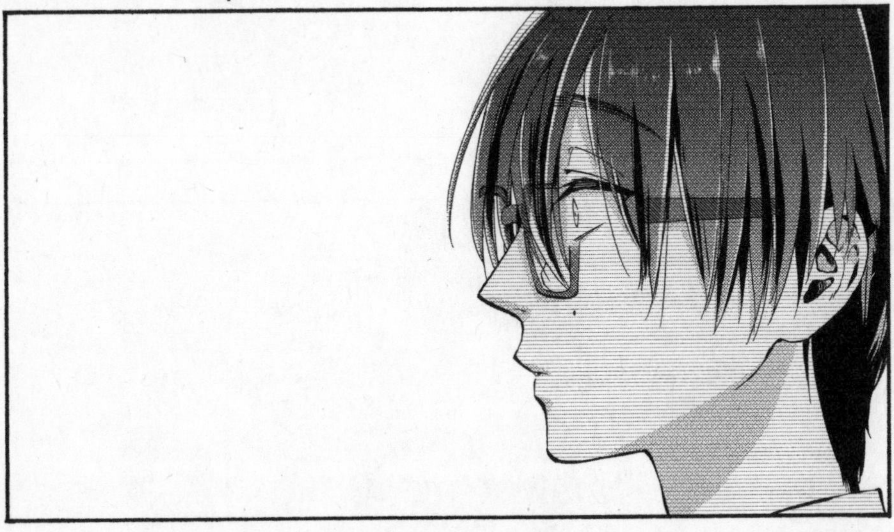

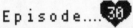

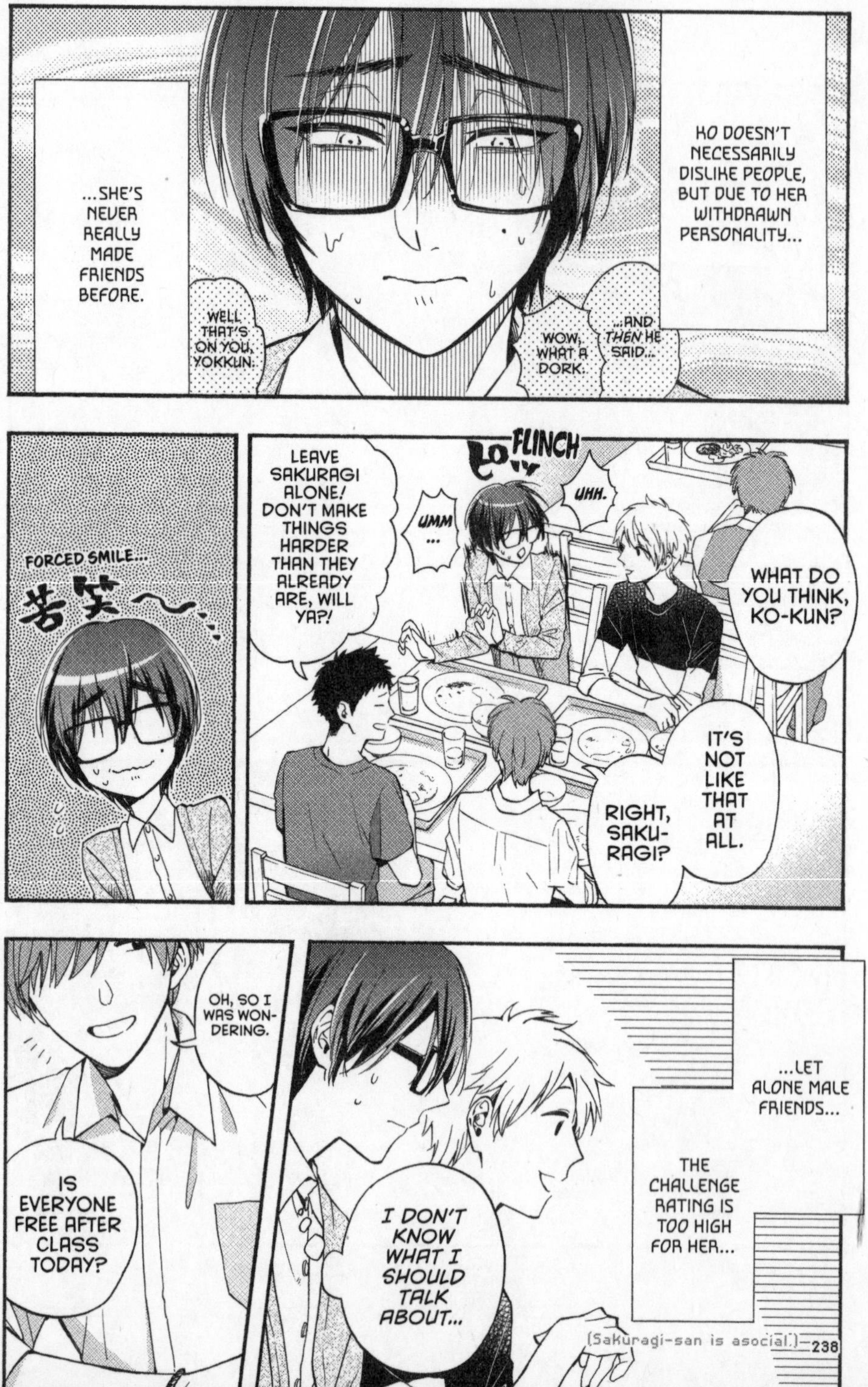
KO DOESN'T NECESSARILY DISLIKE PEOPLE, BUT DUE TO HER WITHDRAWN PERSONALITY...
...SHE'S NEVER REALLY MADE FRIENDS BEFORE.
...AND *THEN* HE SAID...
WOW, WHAT A DORK.
WELL THAT'S ON YOU, YOKKUN.
FLINCH
WHAT DO YOU THINK, KO-KUN?
IT'S NOT LIKE THAT AT ALL.
RIGHT, SAKURAGI?
UHH.
UMM...
LEAVE SAKURAGI ALONE! DON'T MAKE THINGS HARDER THAN THEY ALREADY ARE, WILL YA?!
FORCED SMILE...
苦笑〜
...LET ALONE MALE FRIENDS...
THE CHALLENGE RATING IS TOO HIGH FOR HER...
I DON'T KNOW WHAT I SHOULD TALK ABOUT...
OH, SO I WAS WONDERING.
IS EVERYONE FREE AFTER CLASS TODAY?

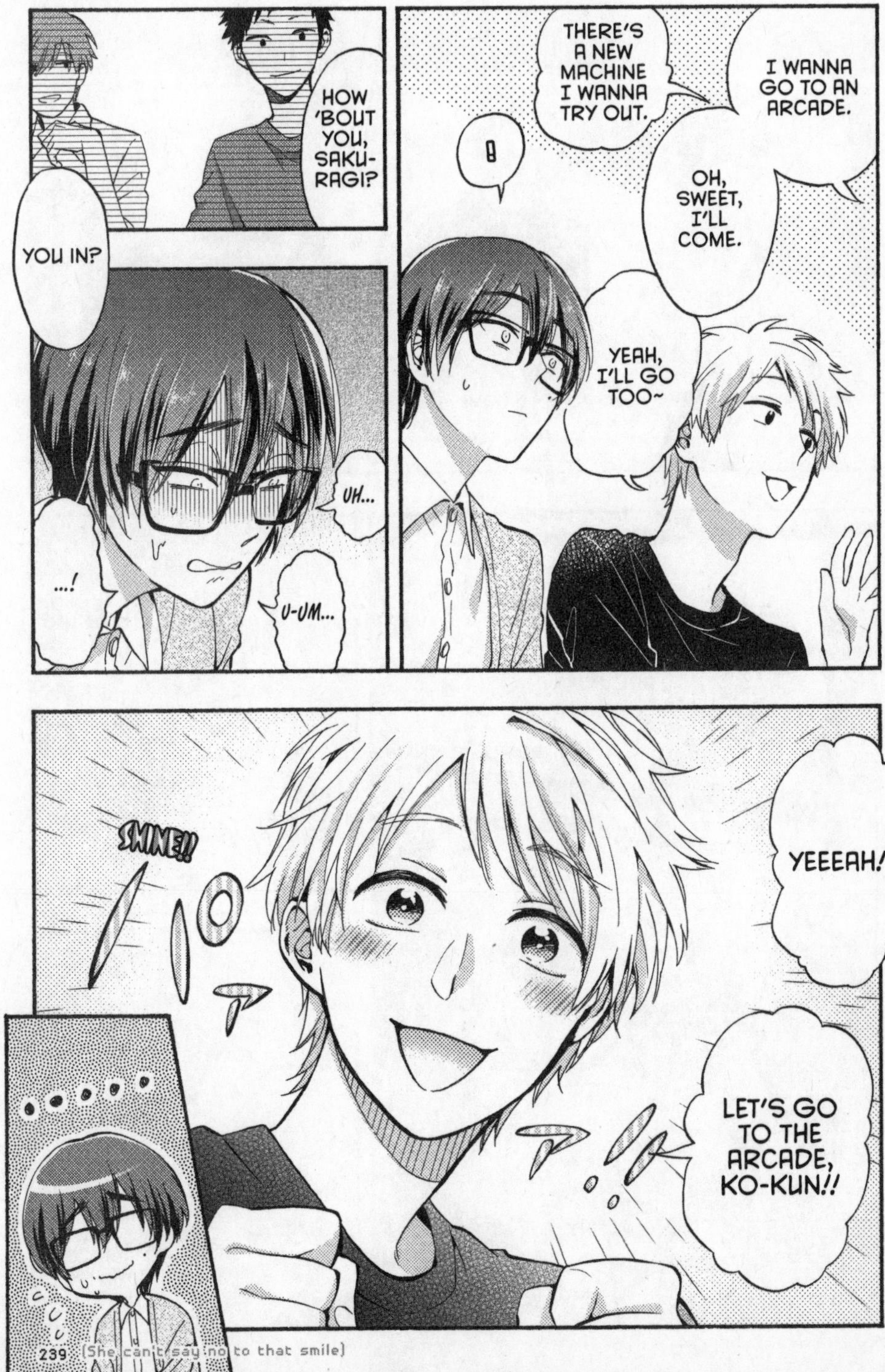
I WANNA GO TO AN ARCADE.
THERE'S A NEW MACHINE I WANNA TRY OUT.
!
OH, SWEET, I'LL COME.
YEAH, I'LL GO TOO~
HOW 'BOUT YOU, SAKURAGI?
YOU IN?
UH...
U-UM...
...!
YEEEAH!
LET'S GO TO THE ARCADE, KO-KUN!!
SHINE!!
.....

 [She can't say no to that smile]

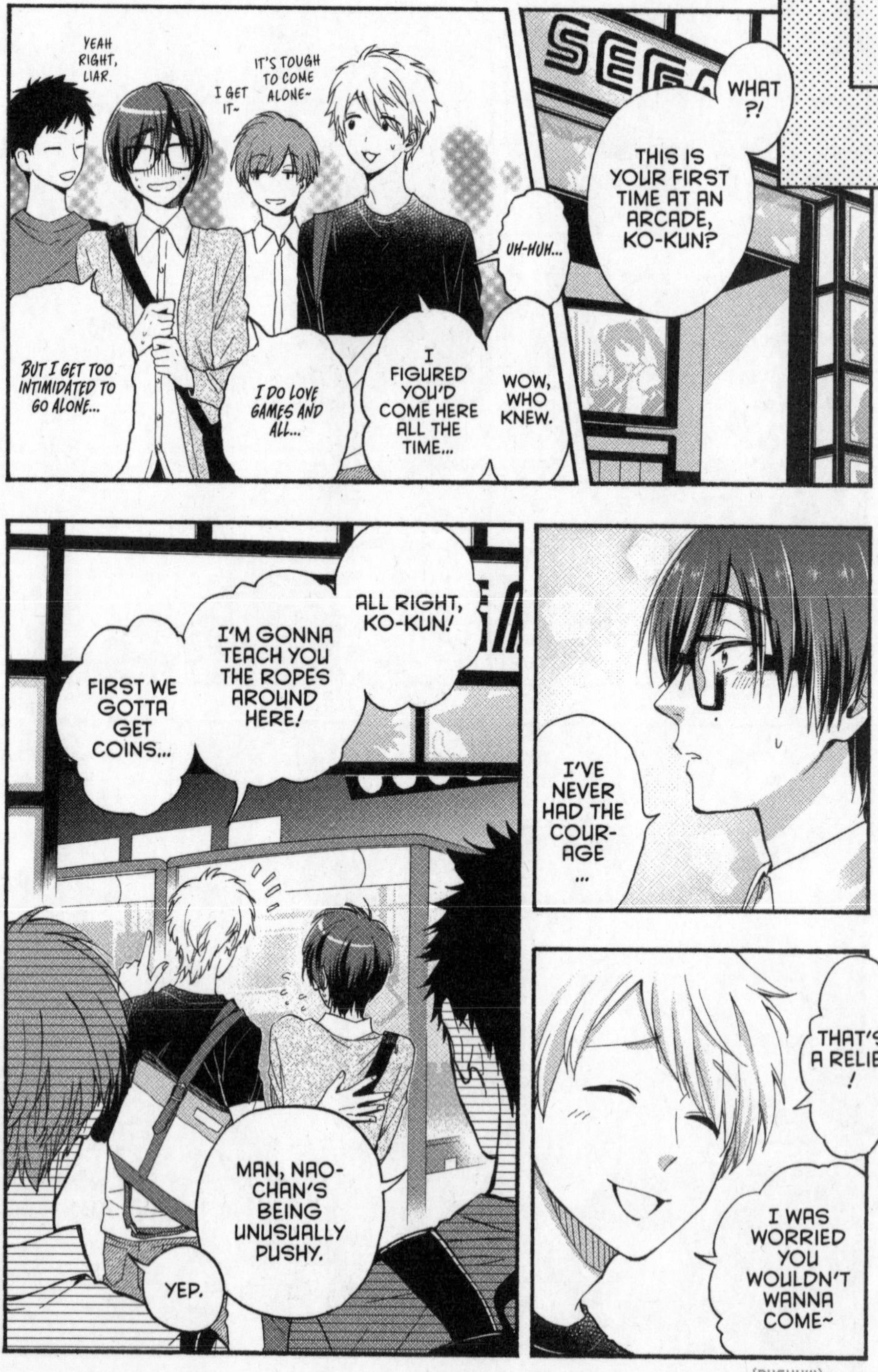
WHAT ?!
THIS IS YOUR FIRST TIME AT AN ARCADE, KO-KUN?
UH-HUH...
WOW, WHO KNEW.
I FIGURED YOU'D COME HERE ALL THE TIME...
I DO LOVE GAMES AND ALL...
BUT I GET TOO INTIMIDATED TO GO ALONE...
IT'S TOUGH TO COME ALONE~
I GET IT~
YEAH RIGHT, LIAR.
I'VE NEVER HAD THE COURAGE ...
THAT'S A RELIEF!
I WAS WORRIED YOU WOULDN'T WANNA COME~
ALL RIGHT, KO-KUN!
I'M GONNA TEACH YOU THE ROPES AROUND HERE!
FIRST WE GOTTA GET COINS...
MAN, NAO-CHAN'S BEING UNUSUALLY PUSHY.
YEP.

(PUSHY!!!)

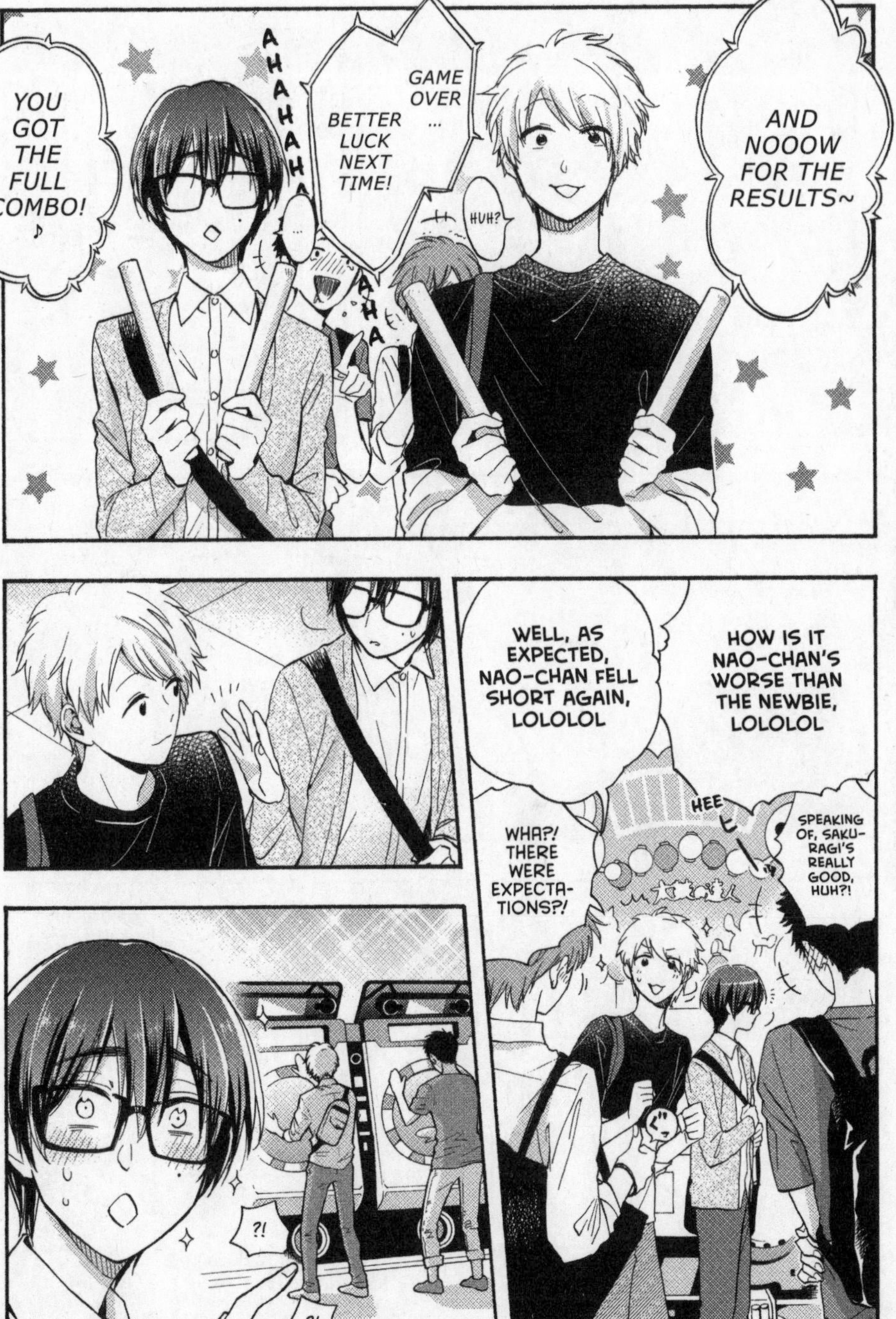

AND NOOOW FOR THE RESULTS~
HUH?
GAME OVER ...
BETTER LUCK NEXT TIME!
AHAHAHAHA
...
AHA
YOU GOT THE FULL COMBO! ♪
HOW IS IT NAO-CHAN'S WORSE THAN THE NEWBIE, LOLOLOL
WELL, AS EXPECTED, NAO-CHAN FELL SHORT AGAIN, LOLOLOL
SPEAKING OF, SAKU-RAGI'S REALLY GOOD, HUH?!
HEE
WHA?! THERE WERE EXPECTA-TIONS?!
?!
?!

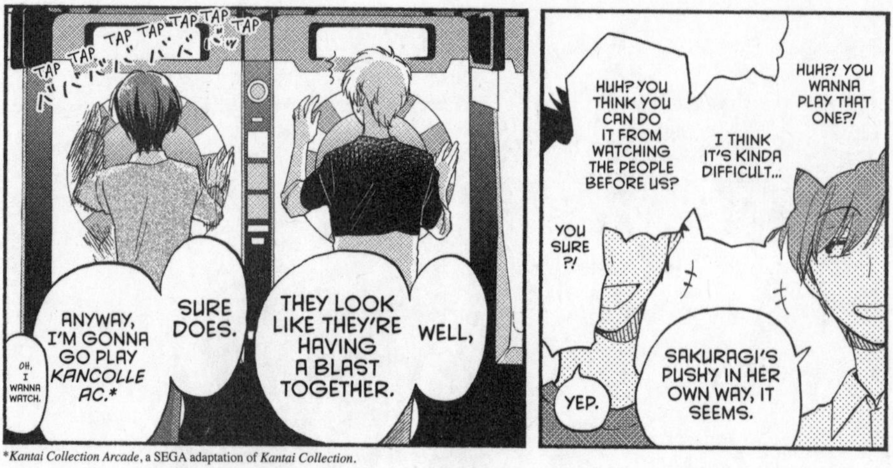
HUH?! YOU WANNA PLAY THAT ONE?!
I THINK IT'S KINDA DIFFICULT...
HUH? YOU THINK YOU CAN DO IT FROM WATCHING THE PEOPLE BEFORE US?
YOU SURE?!
SAKURAGI'S PUSHY IN HER OWN WAY, IT SEEMS.
YEP.
TAP TAP TAP TAP TAP TAP TAP TAP
WELL,
THEY LOOK LIKE THEY'RE HAVING A BLAST TOGETHER.
SURE DOES.
ANYWAY, I'M GONNA GO PLAY *KANCOLLE AC.**
OH, I WANNA WATCH.

**Kantai Collection Arcade*, a SEGA adaptation of *Kantai Collection*.

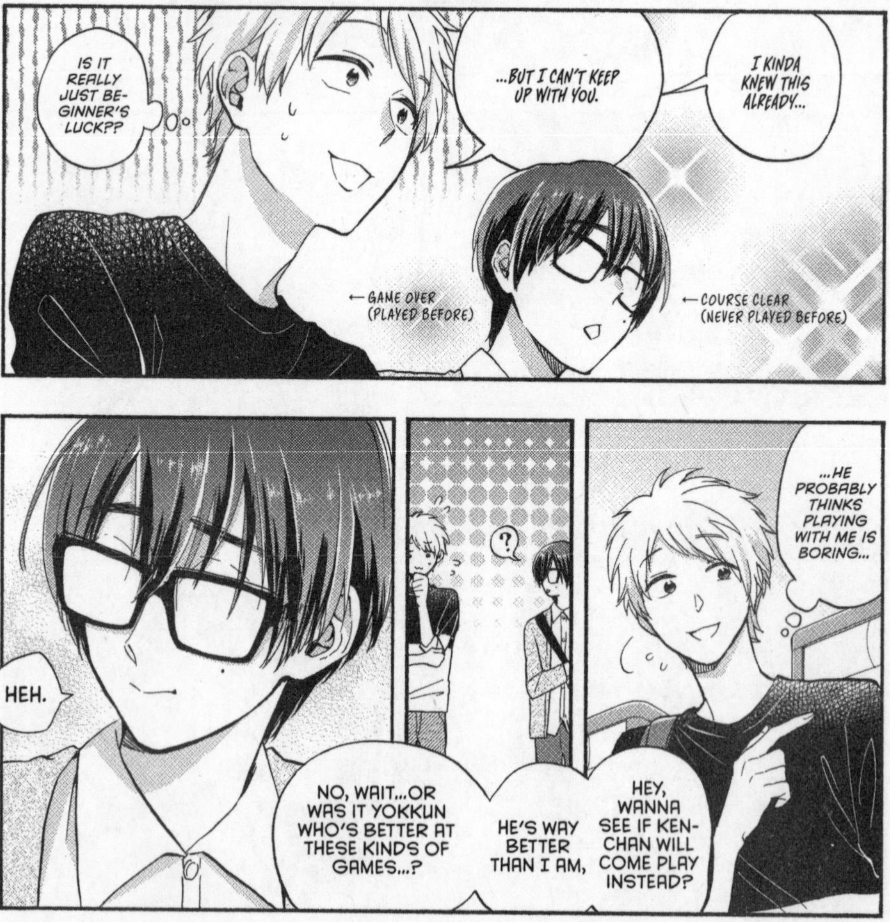
I KINDA KNEW THIS ALREADY...
...BUT I CAN'T KEEP UP WITH YOU.
IS IT REALLY JUST BEGINNER'S LUCK??
← COURSE CLEAR (NEVER PLAYED BEFORE)
← GAME OVER (PLAYED BEFORE)
...HE PROBABLY THINKS PLAYING WITH ME IS BORING...
HEY, WANNA SEE IF KEN-CHAN WILL COME PLAY INSTEAD?
HE'S WAY BETTER THAN I AM,
NO, WAIT...OR WAS IT YOKKUN WHO'S BETTER AT THESE KINDS OF GAMES...?
?
HEH.

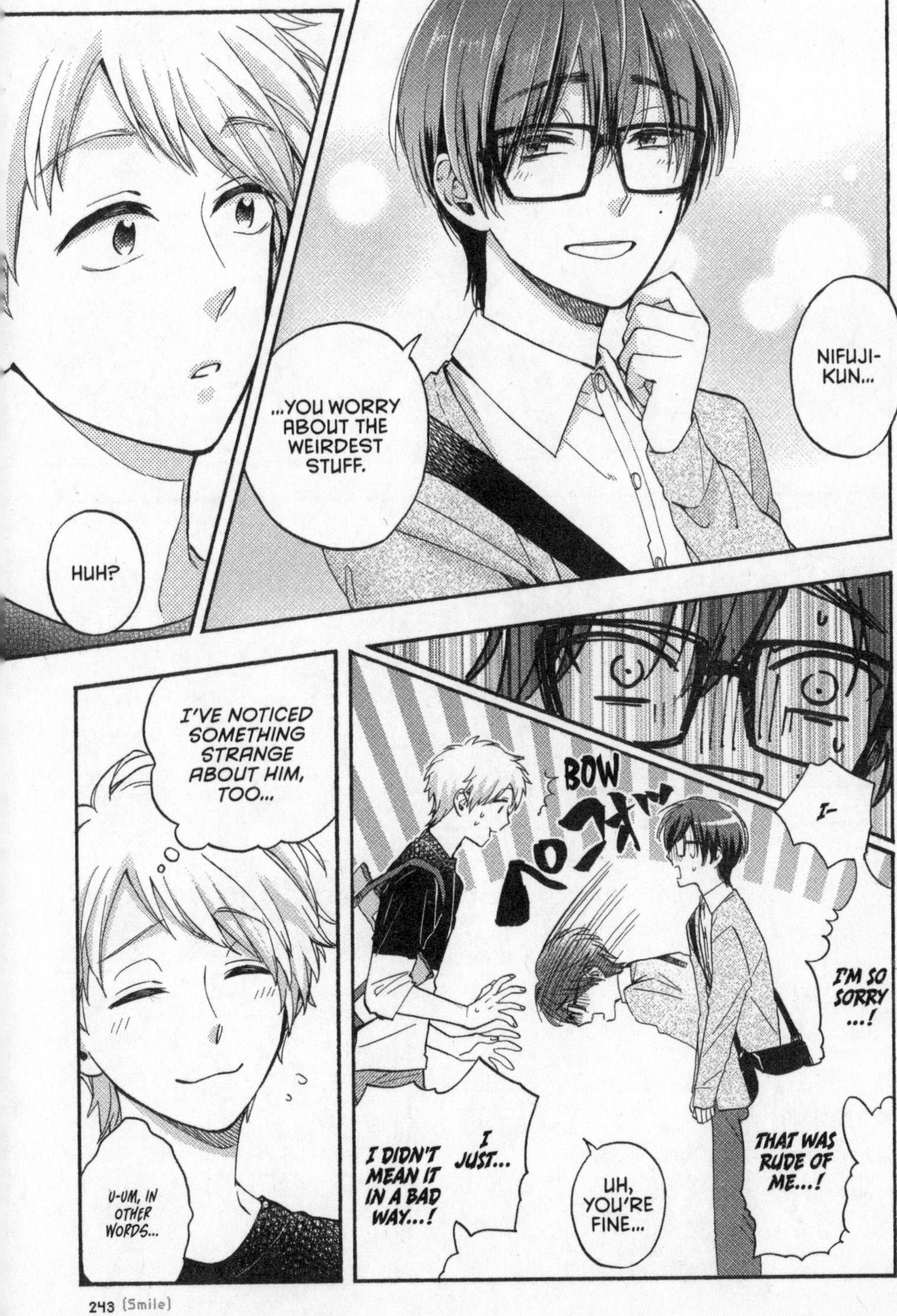
NIFUJI-KUN...
...YOU WORRY ABOUT THE WEIRDEST STUFF.
HUH?
I-
BOW
I'M SO SORRY...!
THAT WAS RUDE OF ME...!
UH, YOU'RE FINE...
I JUST...
I DIDN'T MEAN IT IN A BAD WAY...!
I'VE NOTICED SOMETHING STRANGE ABOUT HIM, TOO...
U-UM, IN OTHER WORDS...

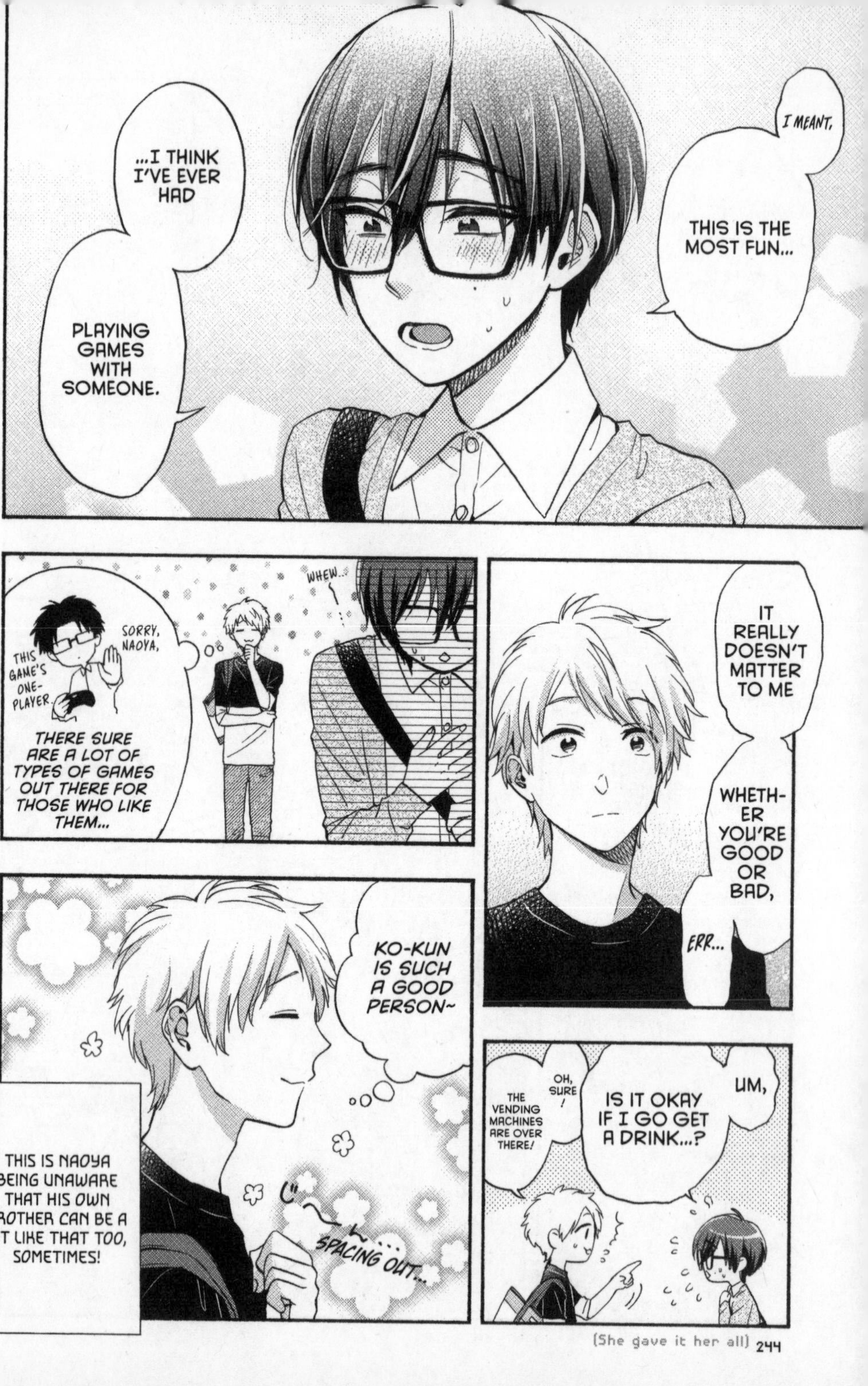
I MEANT,
THIS IS THE MOST FUN...
...I THINK I'VE EVER HAD
PLAYING GAMES WITH SOMEONE.
IT REALLY DOESN'T MATTER TO ME
WHETHER YOU'RE GOOD OR BAD,
ERR...
UM,
IS IT OKAY IF I GO GET A DRINK...?
OH, SURE!
THE VENDING MACHINES ARE OVER THERE!
WHEW..
SORRY, NAOYA,
THIS GAME'S ONE-PLAYER.
THERE SURE ARE A LOT OF TYPES OF GAMES OUT THERE FOR THOSE WHO LIKE THEM...
KO-KUN IS SUCH A GOOD PERSON~
SPACING OUT...
THIS IS NAOYA BEING UNAWARE THAT HIS OWN BROTHER CAN BE A BIT LIKE THAT TOO, SOMETIMES!

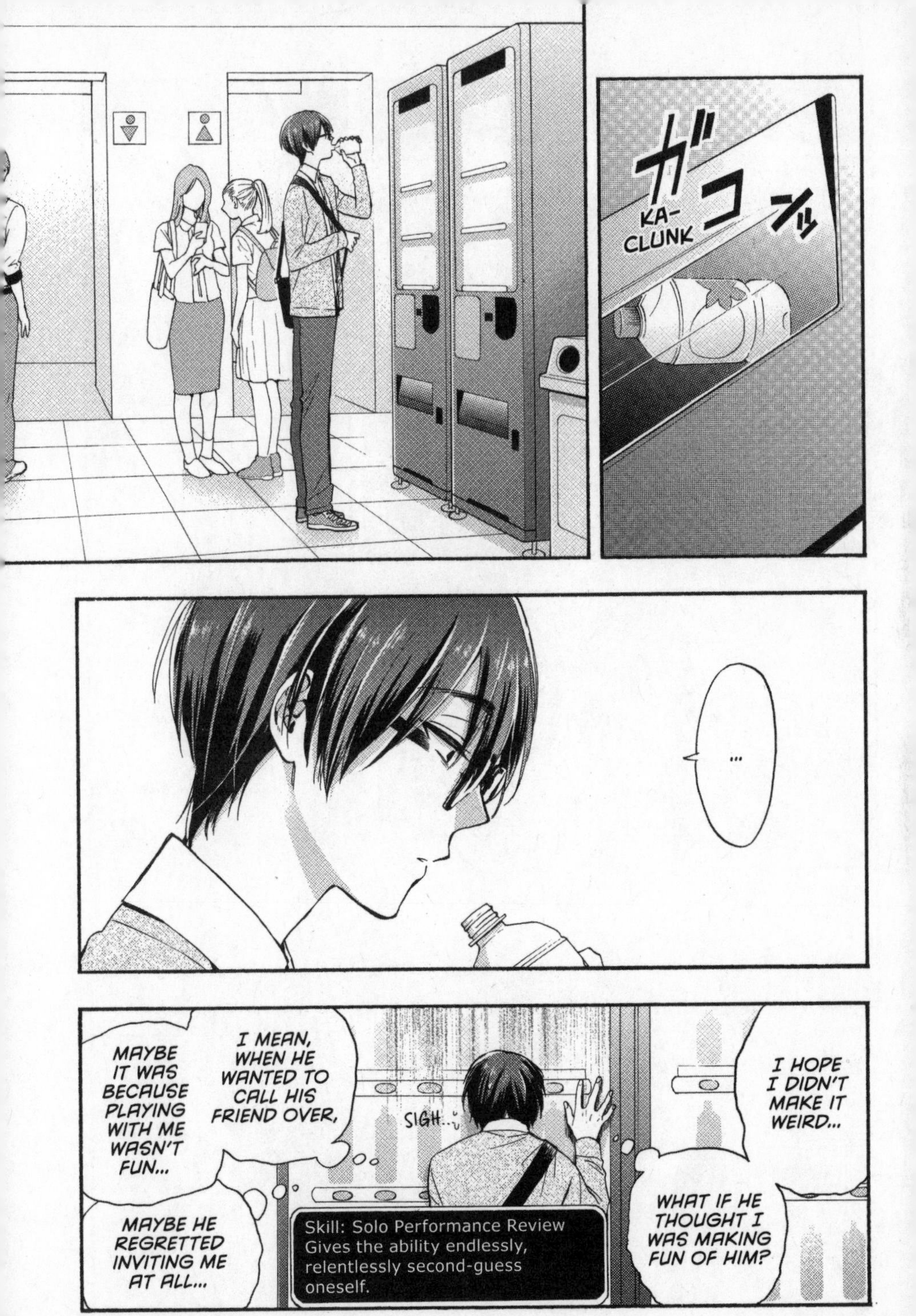
KA-CLUNK
...
I HOPE I DIDN'T MAKE IT WEIRD...
WHAT IF HE THOUGHT I WAS MAKING FUN OF HIM?
SIGH...
I MEAN, WHEN HE WANTED TO CALL HIS FRIEND OVER,
MAYBE IT WAS BECAUSE PLAYING WITH ME WASN'T FUN...
Skill: Solo Performance Review
Gives the ability endlessly, relentlessly second-guess oneself.
MAYBE HE REGRETTED INVITING ME AT ALL...

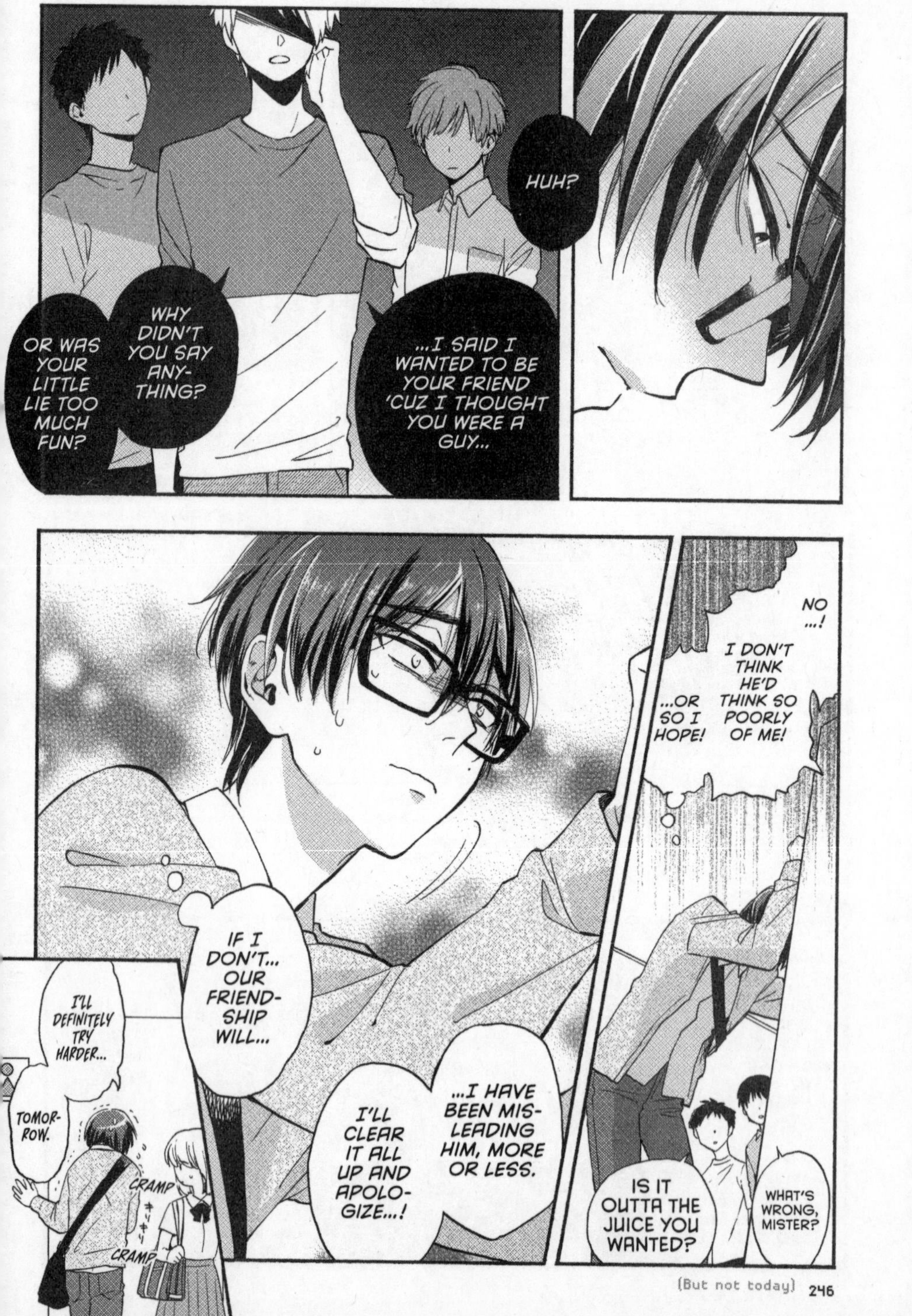
HUH?
...I SAID I WANTED TO BE YOUR FRIEND 'CUZ I THOUGHT YOU WERE A GUY...
WHY DIDN'T YOU SAY ANYTHING?
OR WAS YOUR LITTLE LIE TOO MUCH FUN?
NO ...!
I DON'T THINK HE'D THINK SO POORLY OF ME!
...OR SO I HOPE!
WHAT'S WRONG, MISTER?
IS IT OUTTA THE JUICE YOU WANTED?
IF I DON'T... OUR FRIENDSHIP WILL...
...I HAVE BEEN MISLEADING HIM, MORE OR LESS.
I'LL CLEAR IT ALL UP AND APOLOGIZE...!
I'LL DEFINITELY TRY HARDER...
TOMORROW.
CRAMP
キリキリ
CRAMP

(But not today)

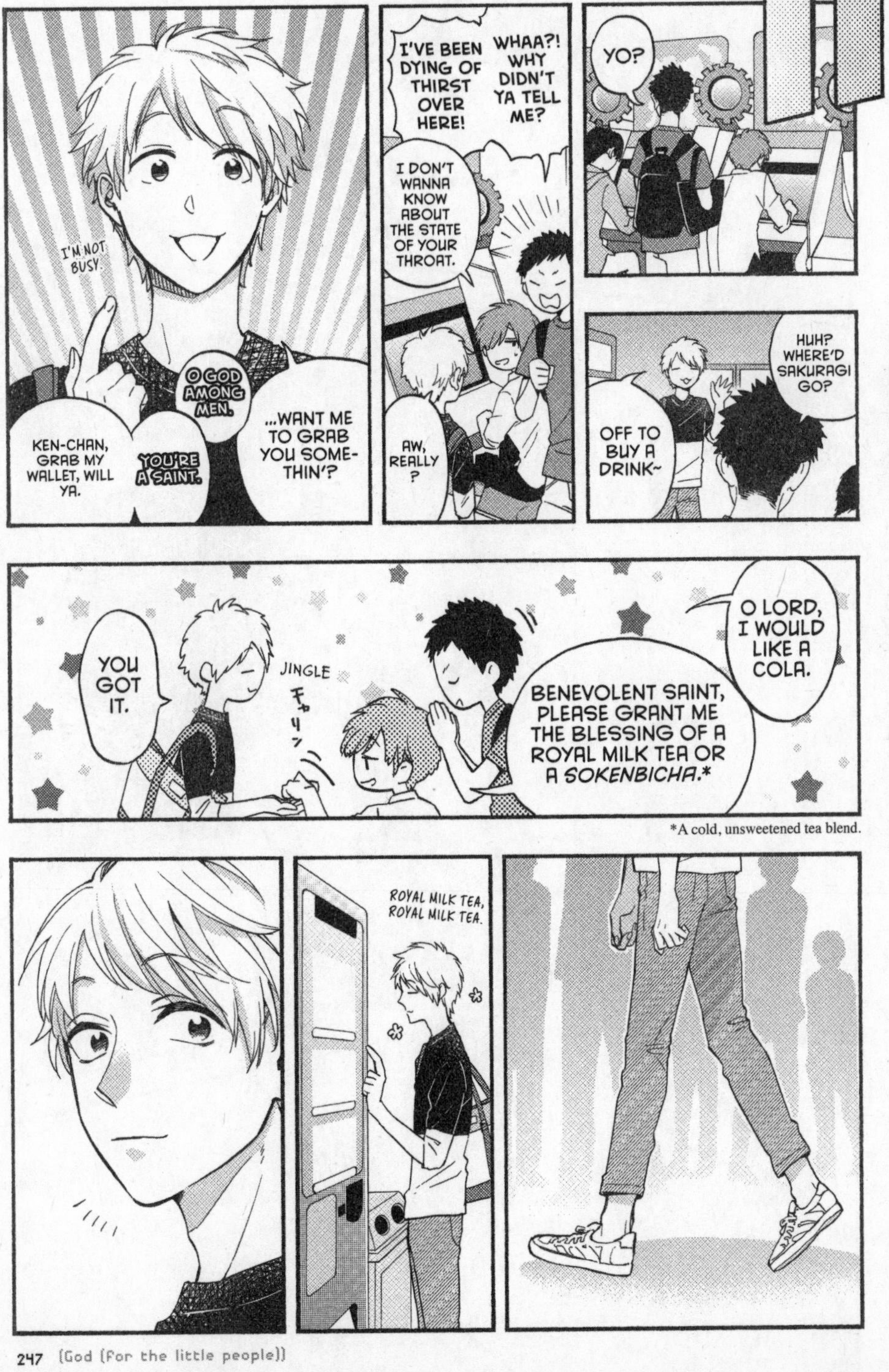
YO?
HUH? WHERE'D SAKURAGI GO?
OFF TO BUY A DRINK~
WHAA?! WHY DIDN'T YA TELL ME?
I'VE BEEN DYING OF THIRST OVER HERE!
I DON'T WANNA KNOW ABOUT THE STATE OF YOUR THROAT.
AW, REALLY?
I'M NOT BUSY.
...WANT ME TO GRAB YOU SOMETHIN'?
O GOD AMONG MEN.
YOU'RE A SAINT.
KEN-CHAN, GRAB MY WALLET, WILL YA.
O LORD, I WOULD LIKE A COLA.
BENEVOLENT SAINT, PLEASE GRANT ME THE BLESSING OF A ROYAL MILK TEA OR A *SOKENBICHA*.*
JINGLE
チャリン
YOU GOT IT.
ROYAL MILK TEA, ROYAL MILK TEA.

*A cold, unsweetened tea blend.

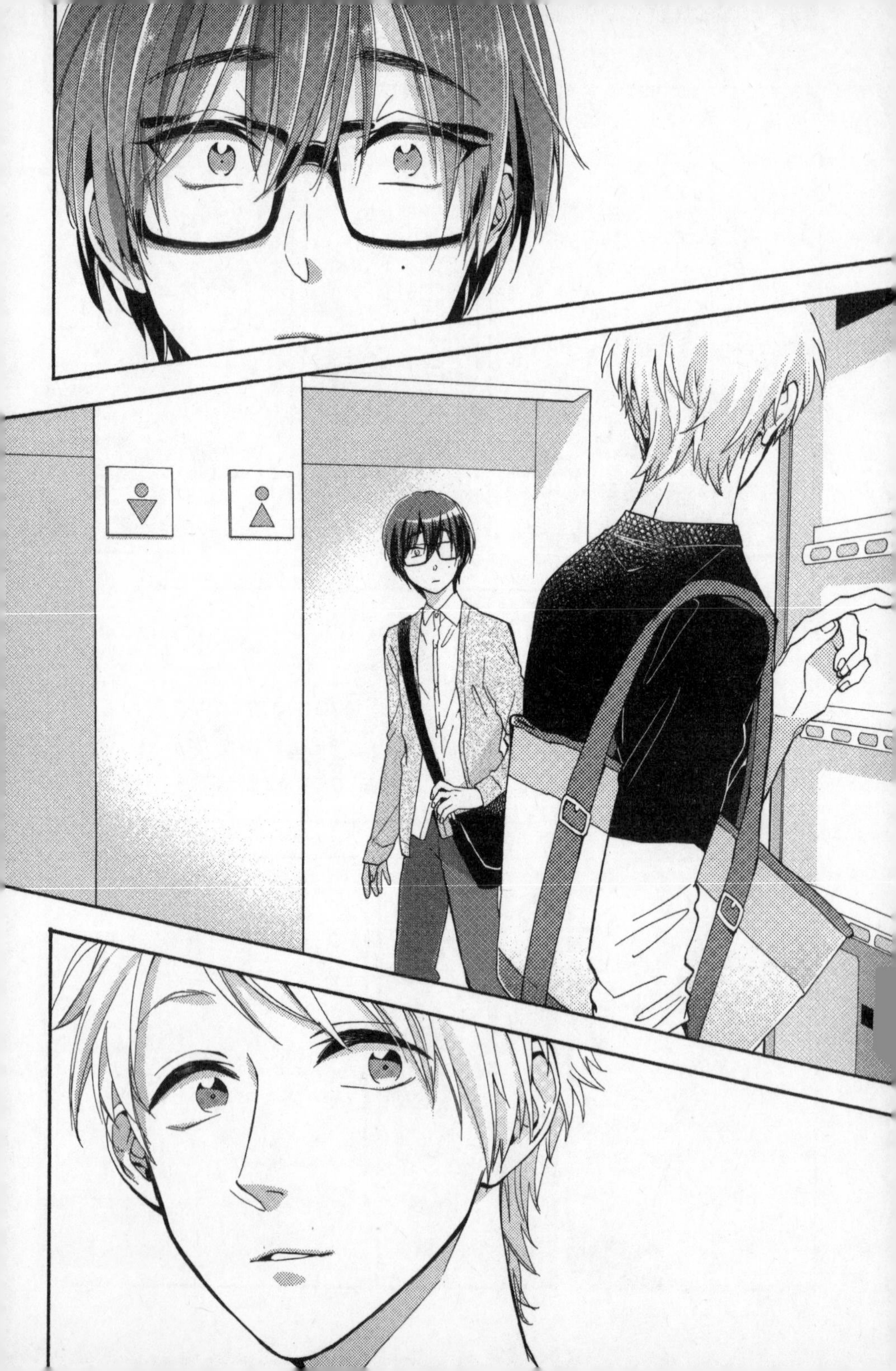

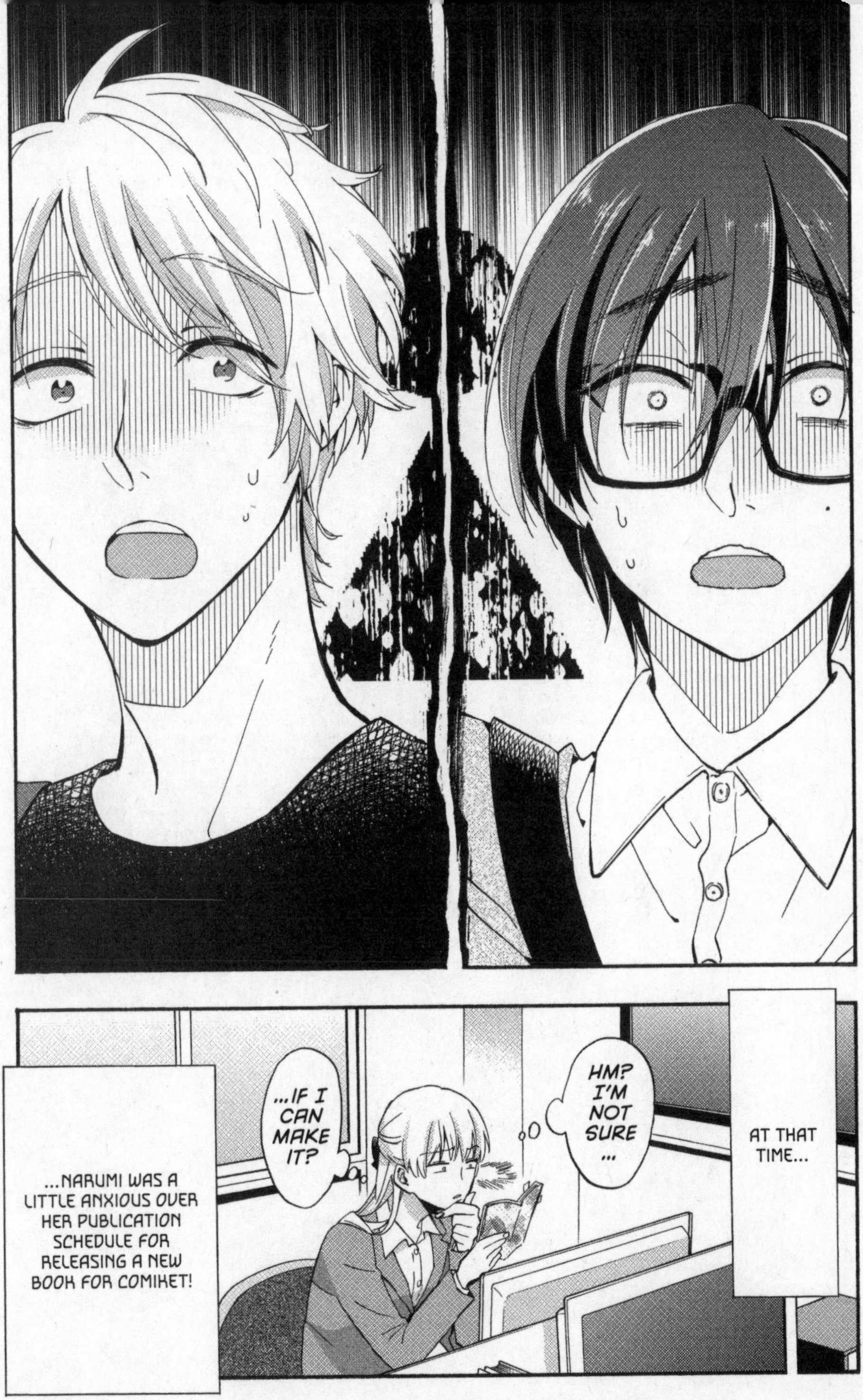
AT THAT TIME...
HM? I'M NOT SURE ...
...IF I CAN MAKE IT?
...NARUMI WAS A LITTLE ANXIOUS OVER HER PUBLICATION SCHEDULE FOR RELEASING A NEW BOOK FOR COMIKET!

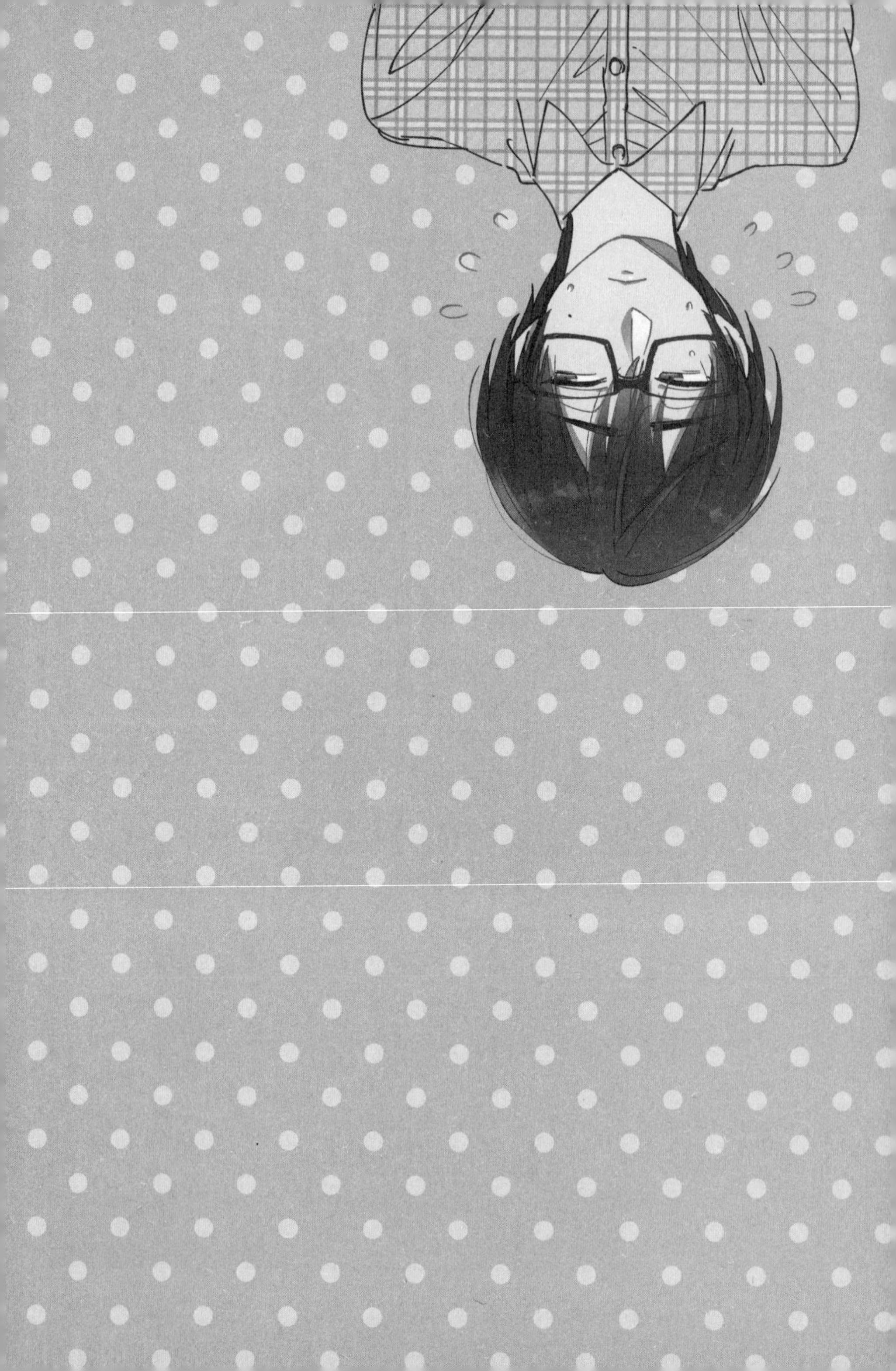

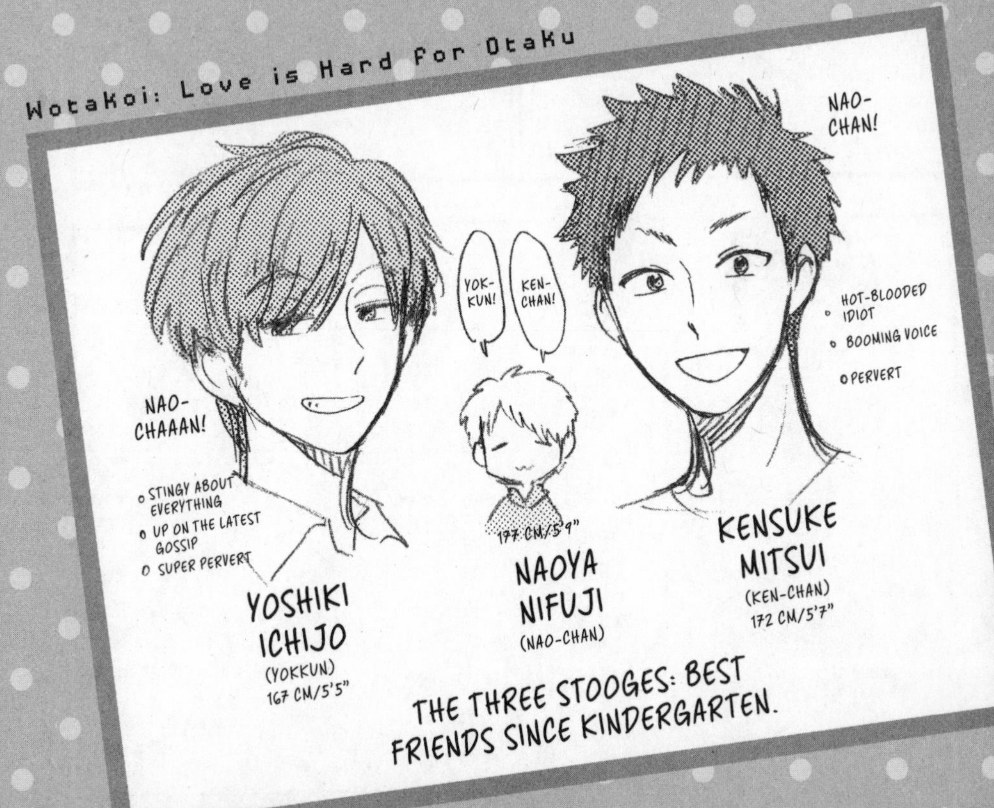
WotaKoi: Love is Hard for OtaKu
NAO-CHAN!
HOT-BLOODED IDIOT
BOOMING VOICE
PERVERT
KENSUKE MITSUI
(KEN-CHAN)
172 CM/5'7"
YOK-KUN!
KEN-CHAN!
177 CM/5'9"
NAOYA NIFUJI
(NAO-CHAN)
NAO-CHAAAN!
STINGY ABOUT EVERYTHING
UP ON THE LATEST GOSSIP
SUPER PERVERT
YOSHIKI ICHIJO
(YOKKUN)
167 CM/5'5"
THE THREE STOOGES: BEST FRIENDS SINCE KINDERGARTEN.

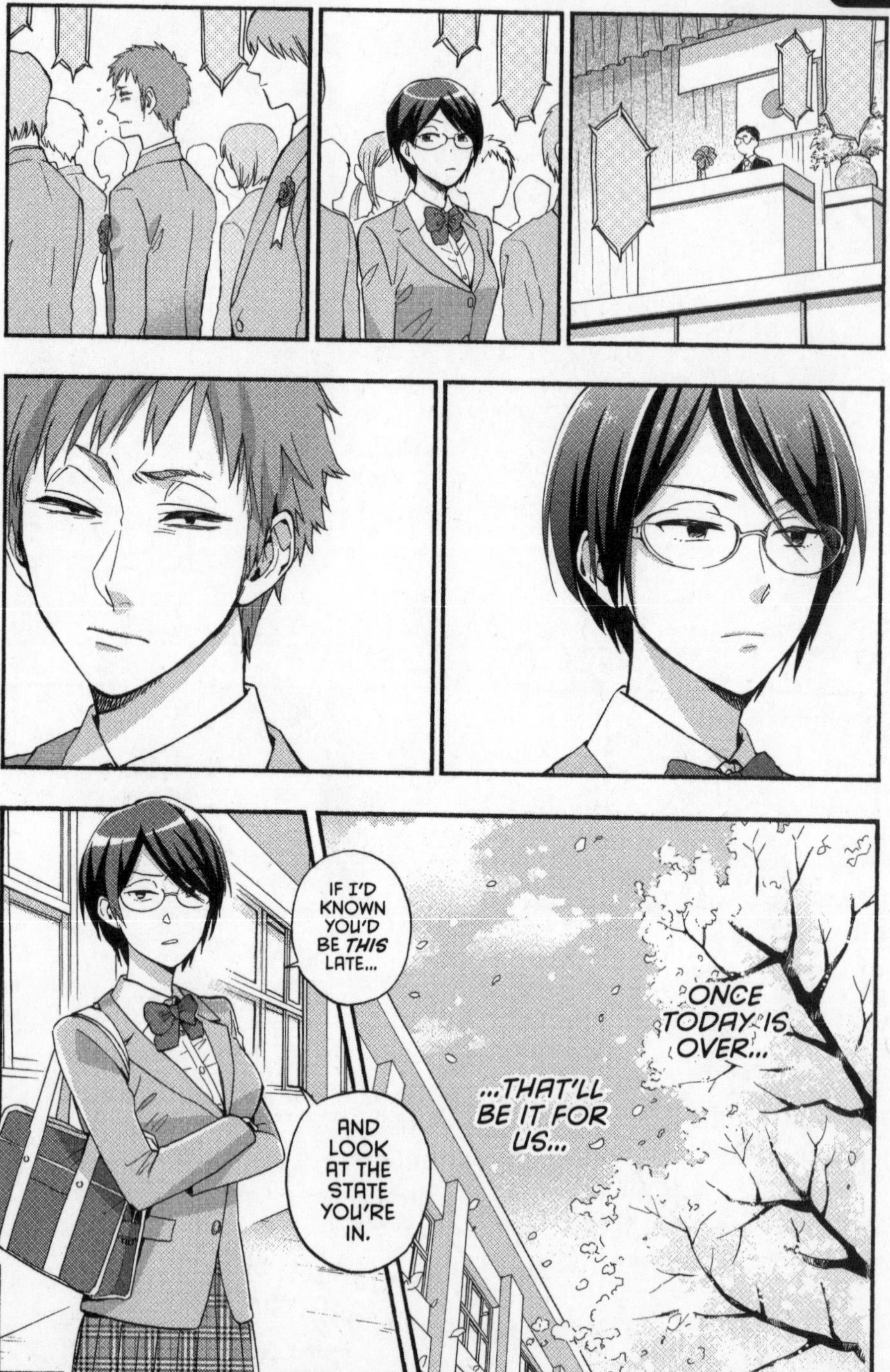
ONCE TODAY IS OVER...
...THAT'LL BE IT FOR US...
IF I'D KNOWN YOU'D BE *THIS* LATE...
AND LOOK AT THE STATE YOU'RE IN.

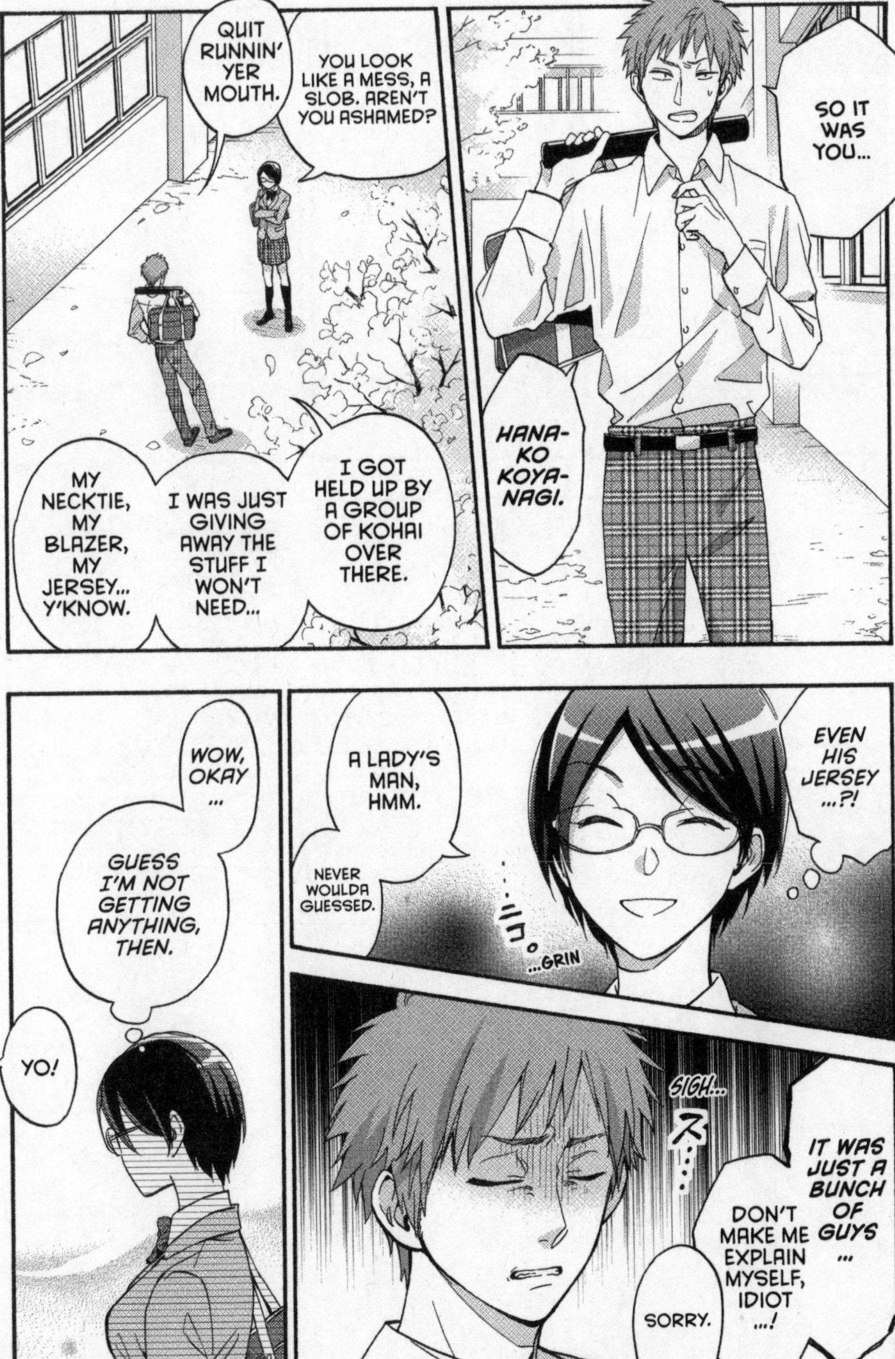
SO IT WAS YOU...
HANAKO KOYANAGI.
YOU LOOK LIKE A MESS, A SLOB. AREN'T YOU ASHAMED?
QUIT RUNNIN' YER MOUTH.
I GOT HELD UP BY A GROUP OF KOHAI OVER THERE.
I WAS JUST GIVING AWAY THE STUFF I WON'T NEED...
MY NECKTIE, MY BLAZER, MY JERSEY... Y'KNOW.
EVEN HIS JERSEY ...?!
...GRIN
A LADY'S MAN, HMM.
NEVER WOULDA GUESSED.
IT WAS JUST A BUNCH OF GUYS ...
SIGH...
DON'T MAKE ME EXPLAIN MYSELF, IDIOT ...!
SORRY.
WOW, OKAY ...
GUESS I'M NOT GETTING ANYTHING, THEN.
YO!

 (All the girls were afraid of him)

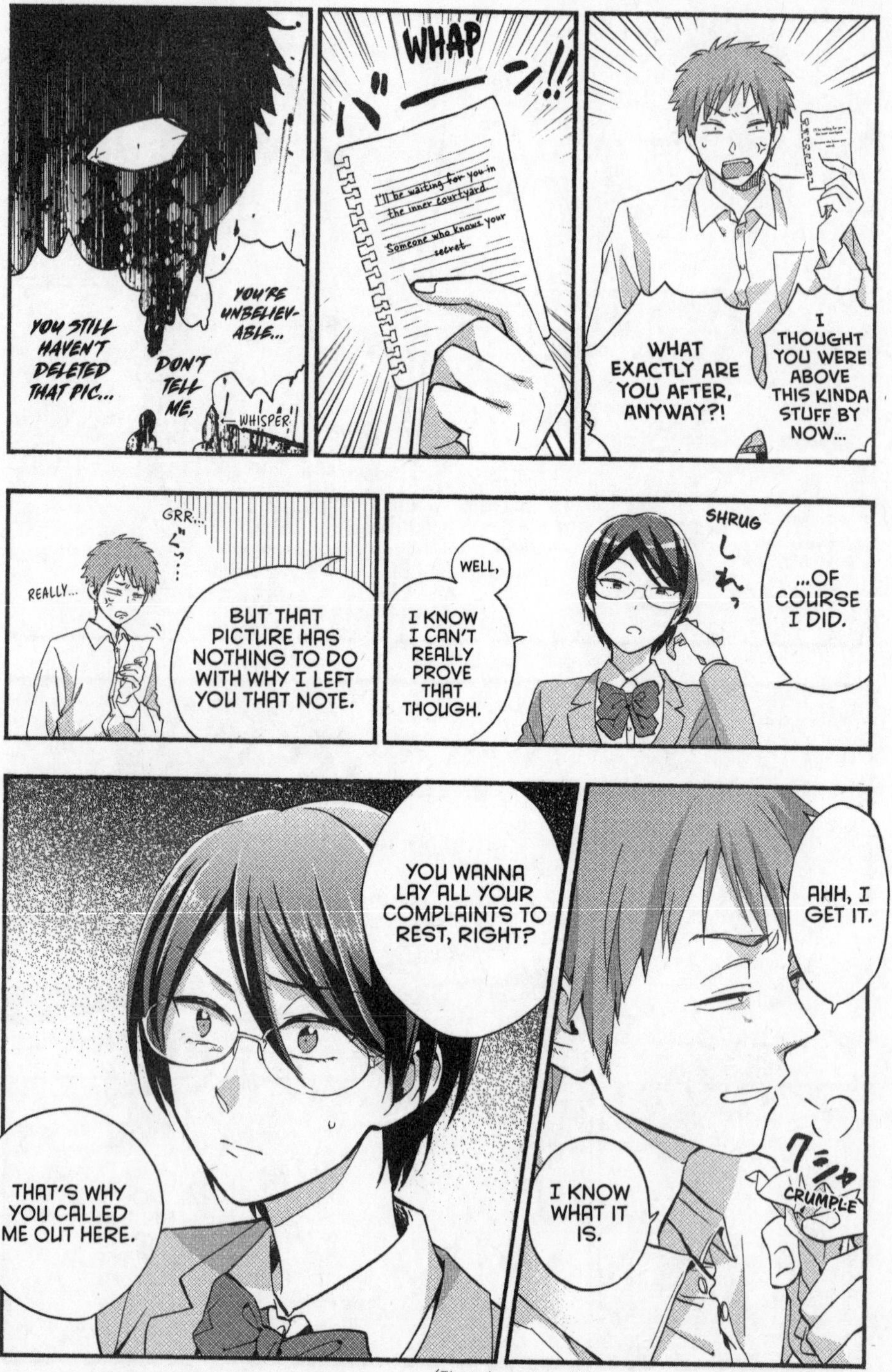
I THOUGHT YOU WERE ABOVE THIS KINDA STUFF BY NOW...
WHAT EXACTLY ARE YOU AFTER, ANYWAY?!
WHAP
I'll be waiting for you in the inner courtyard
Someone who knows your secret
YOU'RE UNBELIEVABLE...
DON'T TELL ME,
YOU STILL HAVEN'T DELETED THAT PIC...
WHISPER
SHRUG
...OF COURSE I DID.
WELL,
I KNOW I CAN'T REALLY PROVE THAT THOUGH.
BUT THAT PICTURE HAS NOTHING TO DO WITH WHY I LEFT YOU THAT NOTE.
GRR...
REALLY...
AHH, I GET IT.
I KNOW WHAT IT IS.
CRUMPLE
YOU WANNA LAY ALL YOUR COMPLAINTS TO REST, RIGHT?
THAT'S WHY YOU CALLED ME OUT HERE.

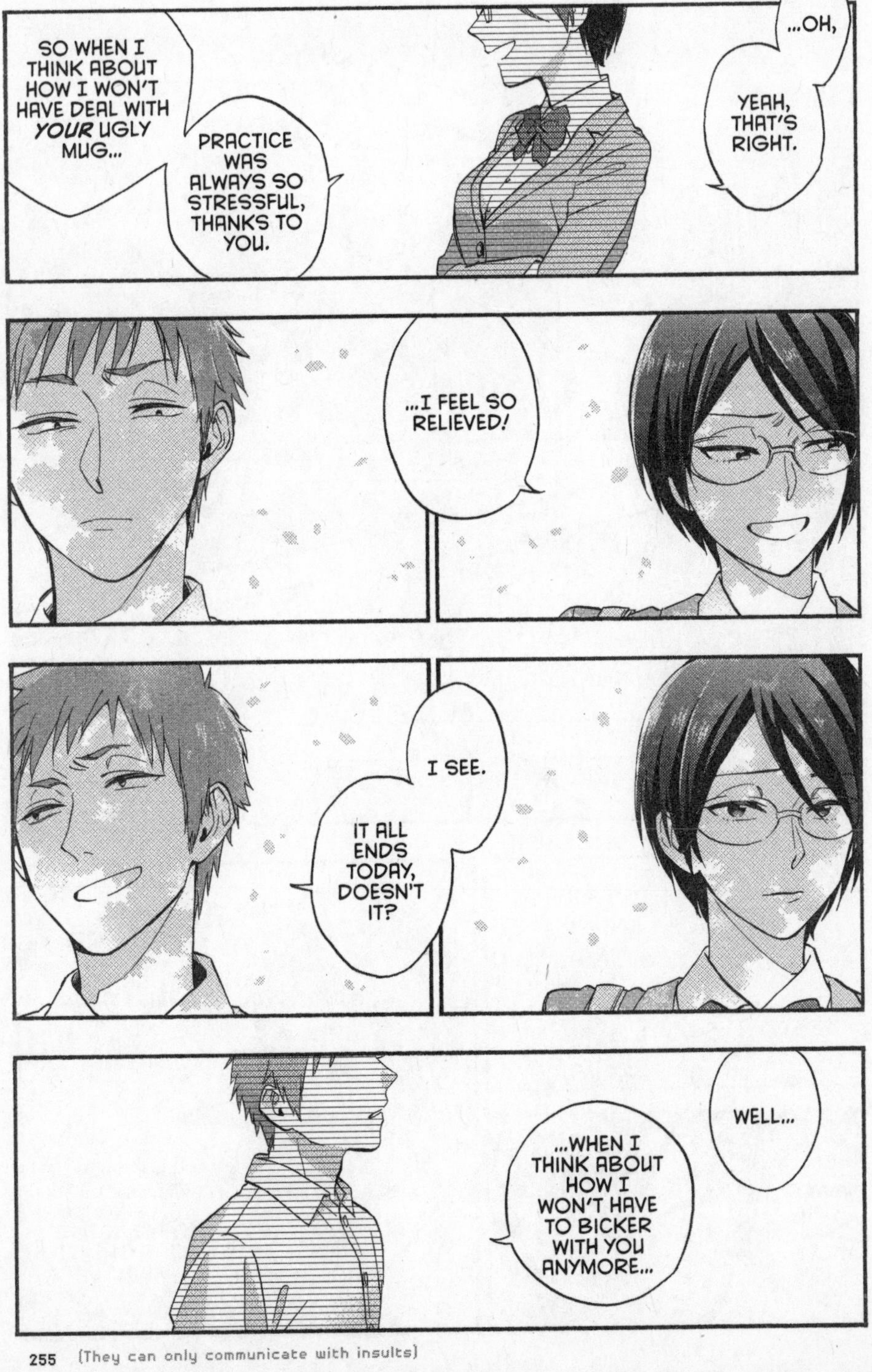
...OH,
YEAH, THAT'S RIGHT.
SO WHEN I THINK ABOUT HOW I WON'T HAVE DEAL WITH *YOUR* UGLY MUG...
PRACTICE WAS ALWAYS SO STRESSFUL, THANKS TO YOU.
...I FEEL SO RELIEVED!
I SEE.
IT ALL ENDS TODAY, DOESN'T IT?
WELL...
...WHEN I THINK ABOUT HOW I WON'T HAVE TO BICKER WITH YOU ANYMORE...

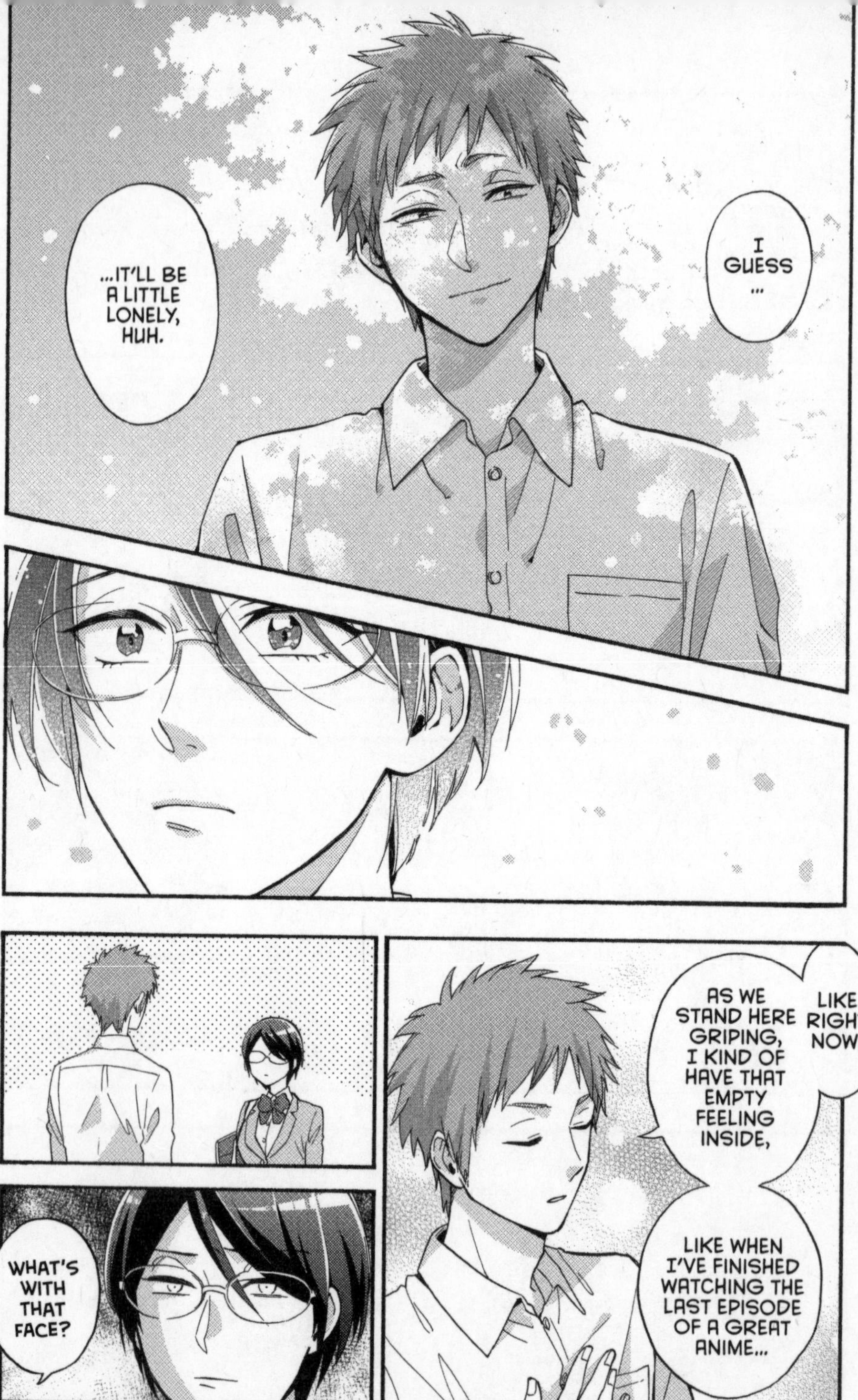
I GUESS ...
...IT'LL BE A LITTLE LONELY, HUH.
LIKE RIGHT NOW,
AS WE STAND HERE GRIPING, I KIND OF HAVE THAT EMPTY FEELING INSIDE,
LIKE WHEN I'VE FINISHED WATCHING THE LAST EPISODE OF A GREAT ANIME...
WHAT'S WITH THAT FACE?

(He said too much)

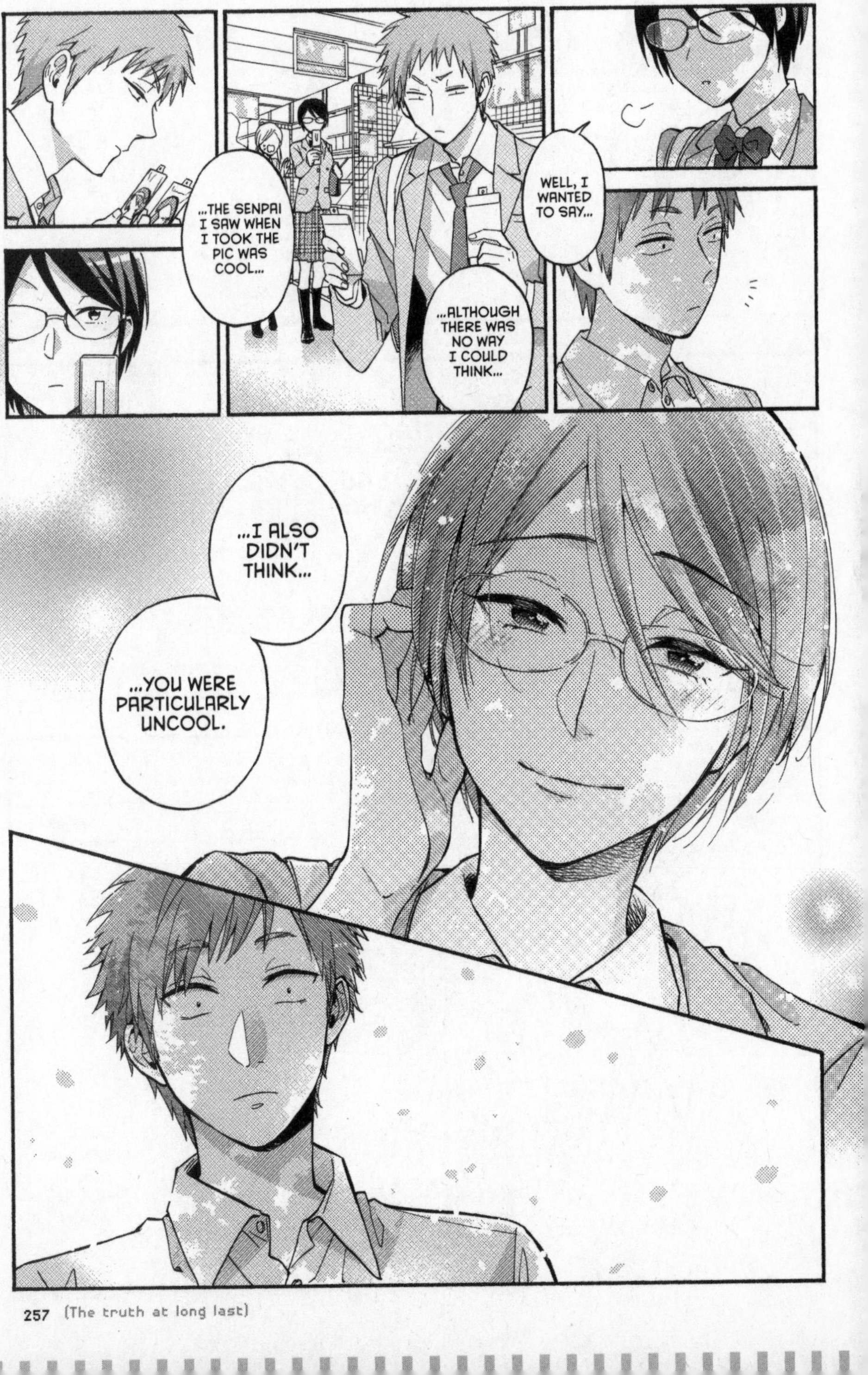
WELL, I WANTED TO SAY...
...ALTHOUGH THERE WAS NO WAY I COULD THINK...
...THE SENPAI I SAW WHEN I TOOK THE PIC WAS COOL...
...I ALSO DIDN'T THINK...
...YOU WERE PARTICULARLY UNCOOL.

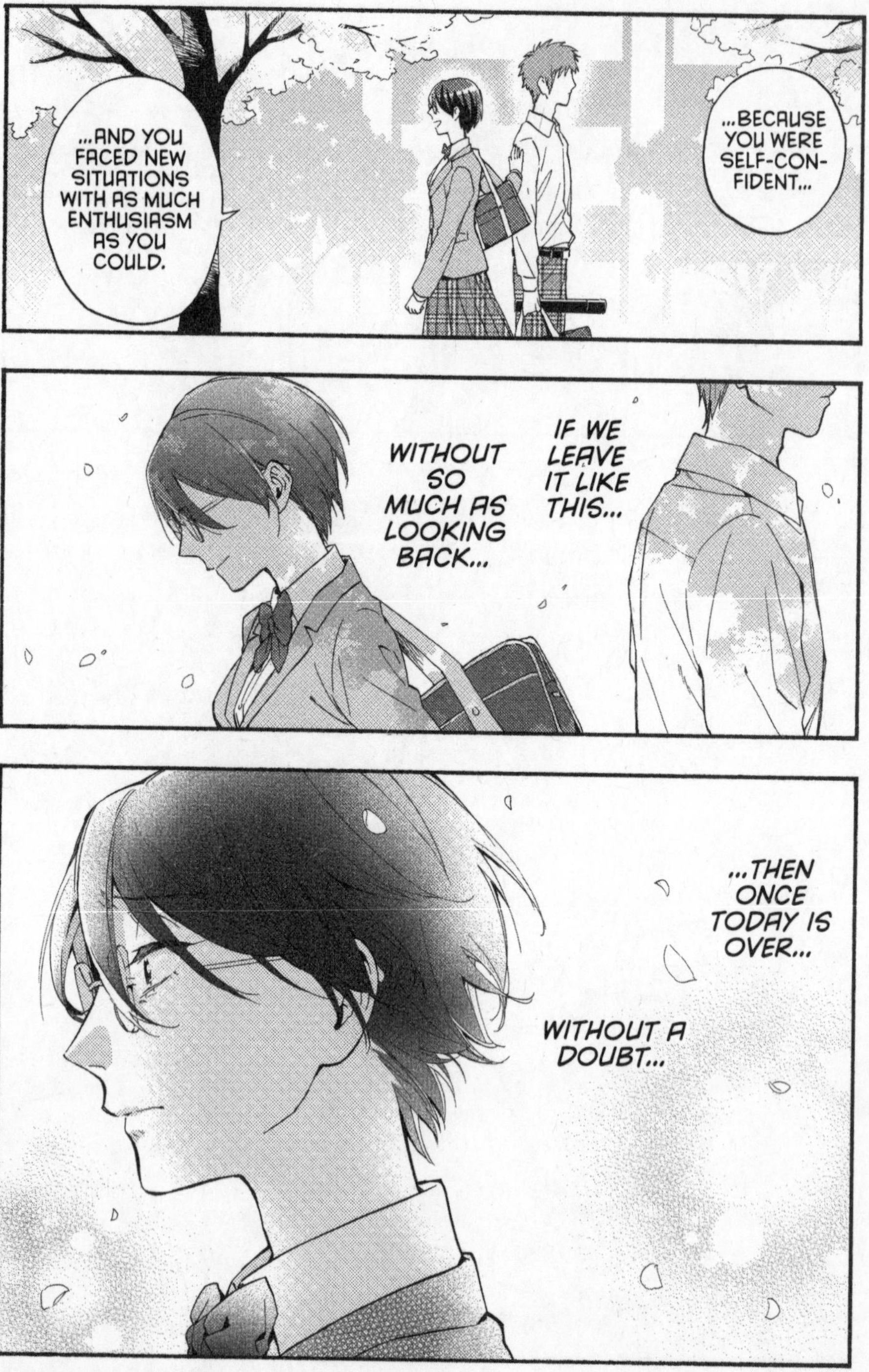
...BECAUSE YOU WERE SELF-CON-FIDENT...
...AND YOU FACED NEW SITUATIONS WITH AS MUCH ENTHUSIASM AS YOU COULD.
IF WE LEAVE IT LIKE THIS...
WITHOUT SO MUCH AS LOOKING BACK...
...THEN ONCE TODAY IS OVER...
WITHOUT A DOUBT...

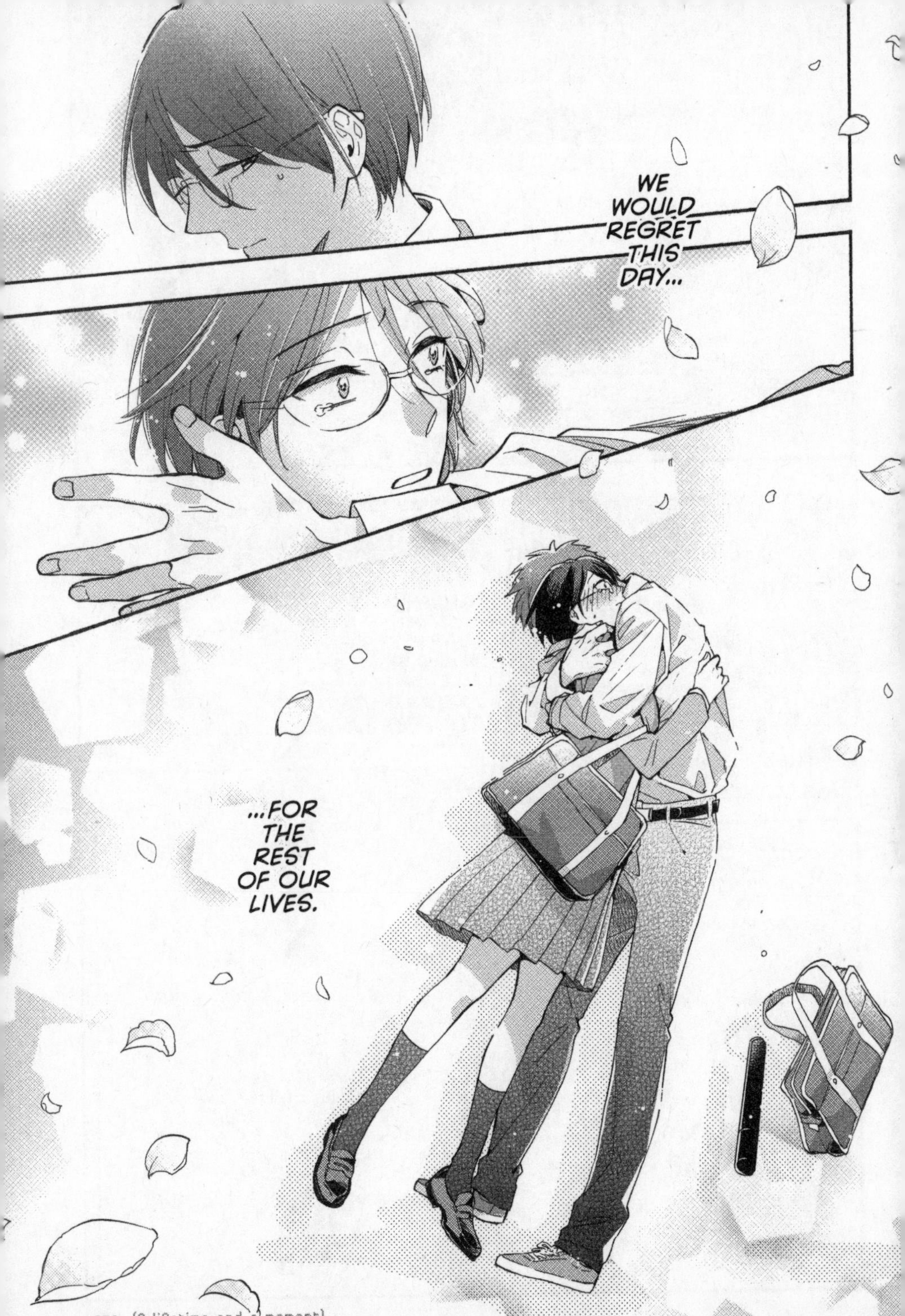
WE WOULD REGRET THIS DAY...
...FOR THE REST OF OUR LIVES.

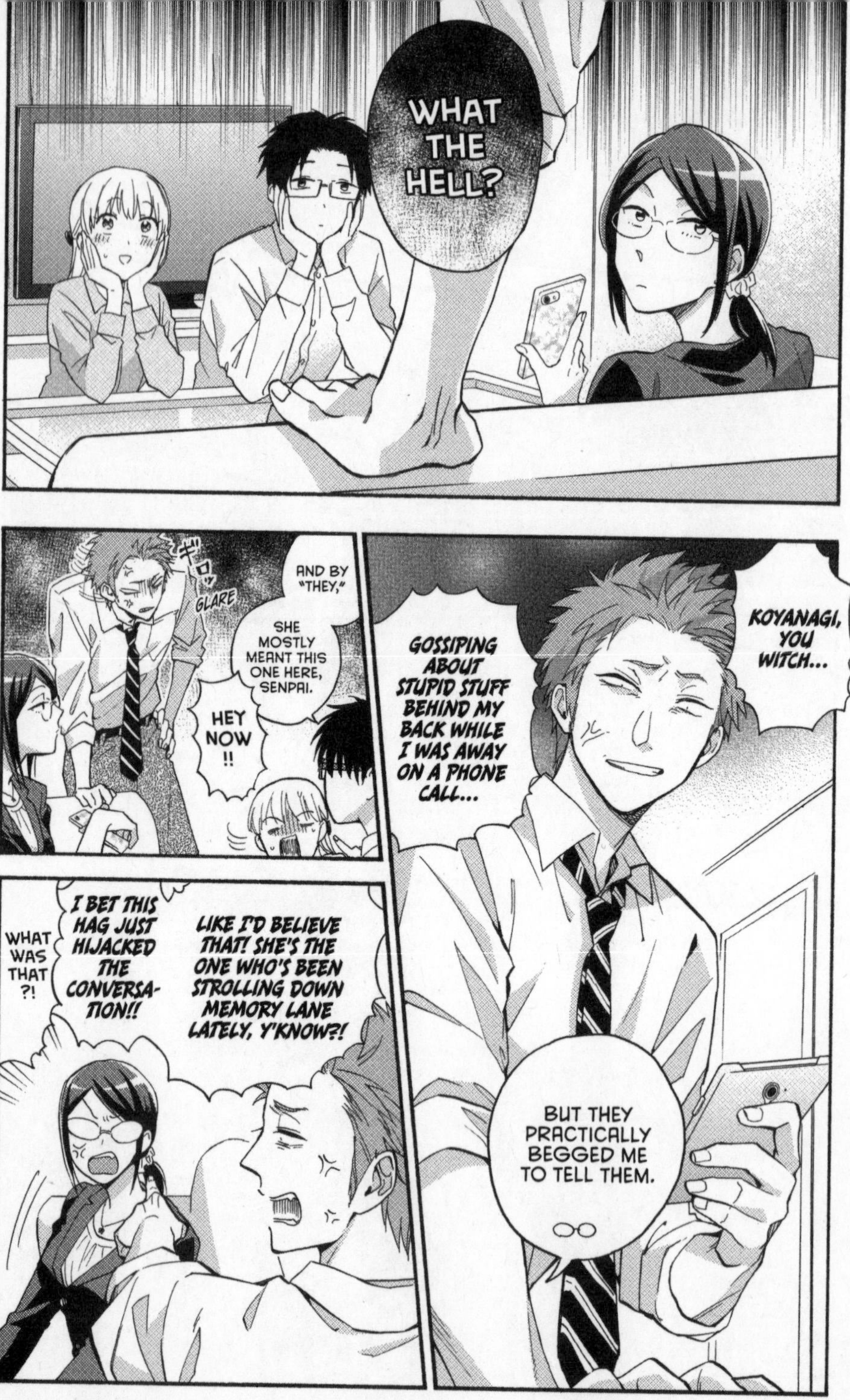
WHAT THE HELL?
KOYANAGI, YOU WITCH...
GOSSIPING ABOUT STUPID STUFF BEHIND MY BACK WHILE I WAS AWAY ON A PHONE CALL...
BUT THEY PRACTICALLY BEGGED ME TO TELL THEM.
AND BY "THEY,"
SHE MOSTLY MEANT THIS ONE HERE, SENPAI.
ギロッ
GLARE
HEY NOW!!
LIKE I'D BELIEVE THAT! SHE'S THE ONE WHO'S BEEN STROLLING DOWN MEMORY LANE LATELY, Y'KNOW?!
I BET THIS HAG JUST HIJACKED THE CONVERSATION!!
WHAT WAS THAT?!

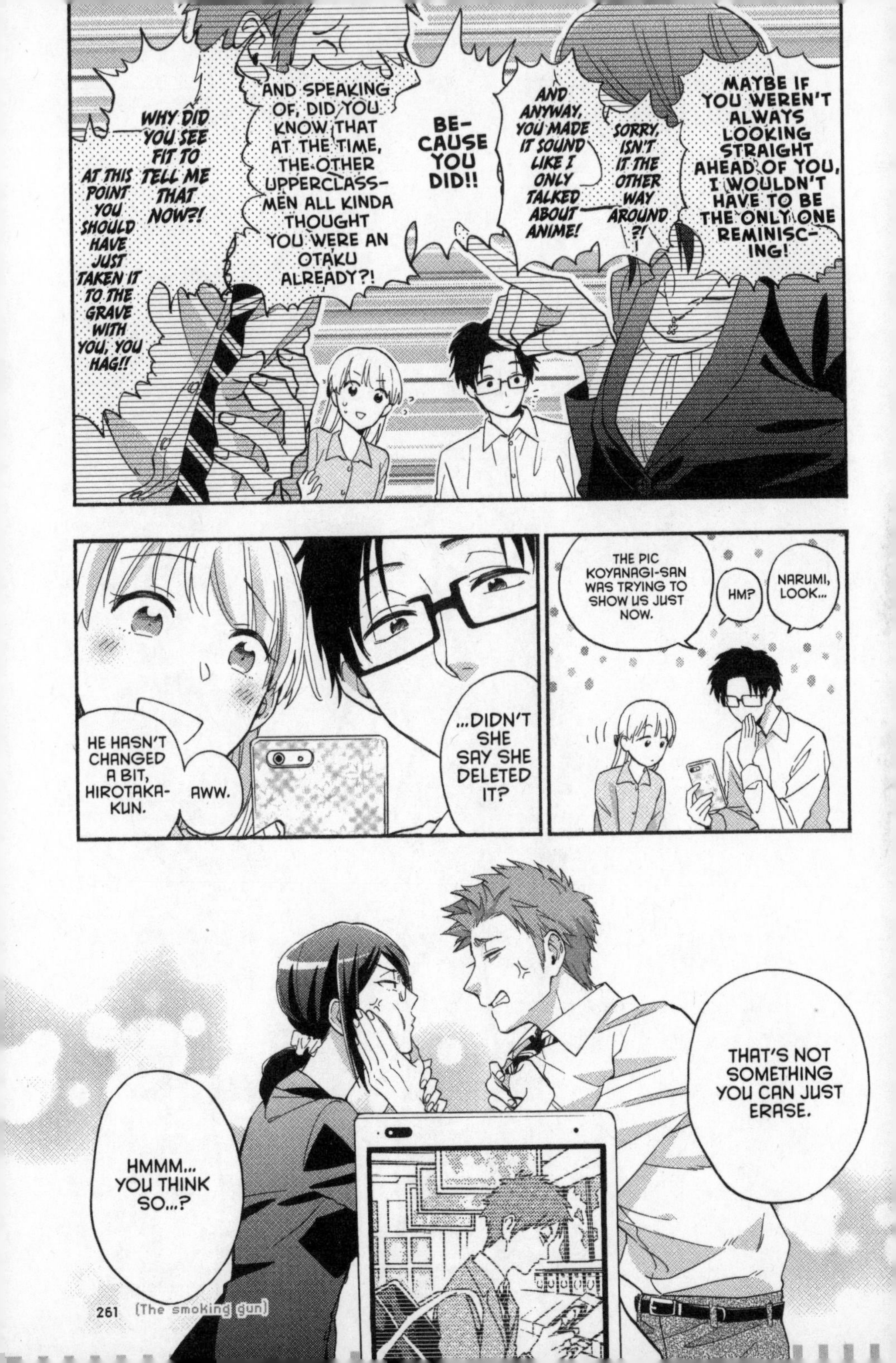
MAYBE IF YOU WEREN'T ALWAYS LOOKING STRAIGHT AHEAD OF YOU, I WOULDN'T HAVE TO BE THE ONLY ONE REMINISC-ING!
SORRY, ISN'T IT THE OTHER WAY AROUND?!
AND ANYWAY, YOU MADE IT SOUND LIKE I ONLY TALKED ABOUT ANIME!
BE-CAUSE YOU DID!!
AND SPEAKING OF, DID YOU KNOW THAT AT THE TIME, THE OTHER UPPERCLASS-MEN ALL KINDA THOUGHT YOU WERE AN OTAKU ALREADY?!
WHY DID YOU SEE FIT TO TELL ME THAT NOW?!
AT THIS POINT YOU SHOULD HAVE JUST TAKEN IT TO THE GRAVE WITH YOU, YOU HAG!!
NARUMI, LOOK...
HM?
THE PIC KOYANAGI-SAN WAS TRYING TO SHOW US JUST NOW.
...DIDN'T SHE SAY SHE DELETED IT?
AWW.
HE HASN'T CHANGED A BIT, HIROTAKA-KUN.
THAT'S NOT SOMETHING YOU CAN JUST ERASE.
HMMM... YOU THINK SO...?
[The smoking gun]

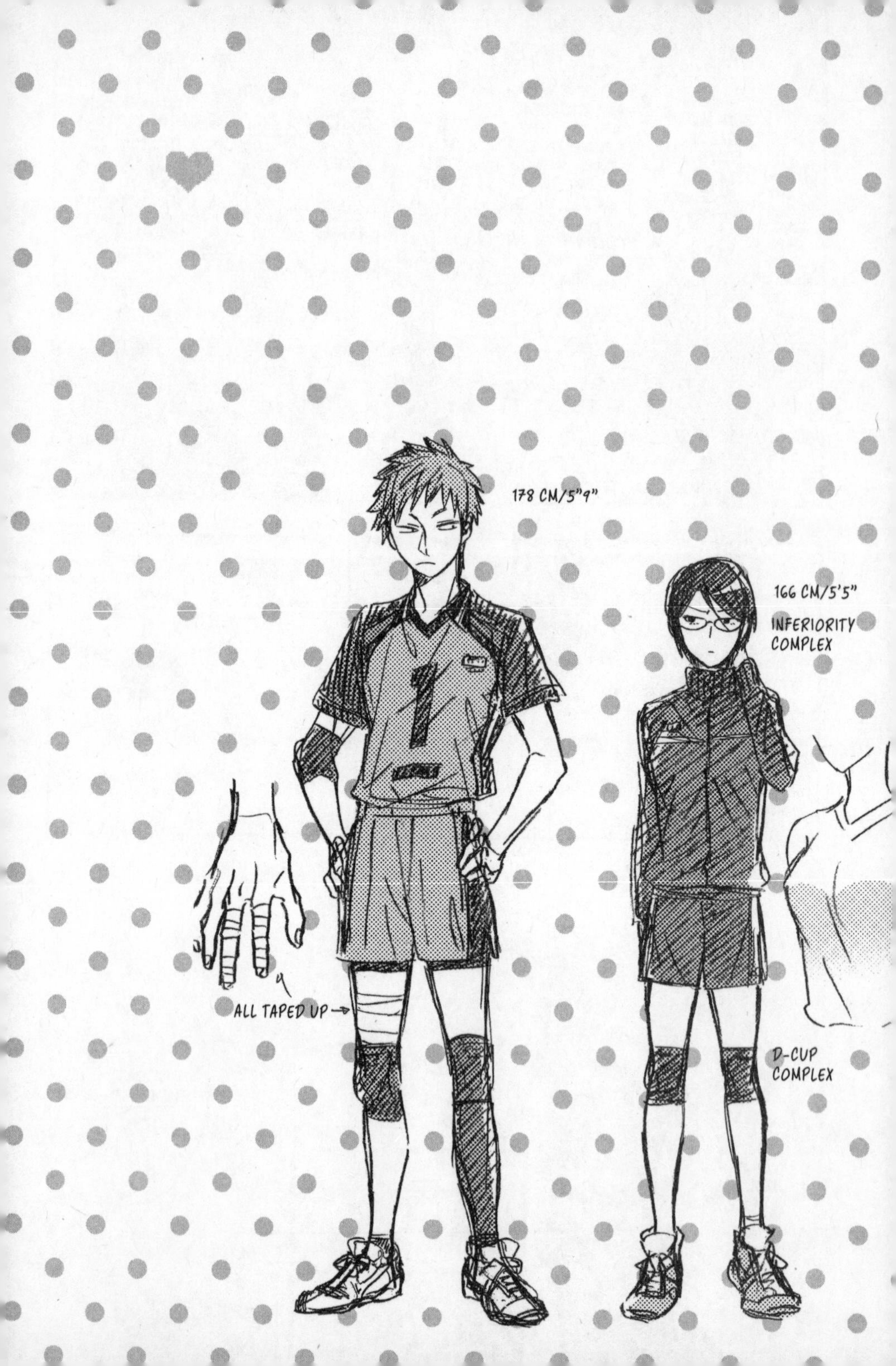
178 CM/5"9"
166 CM/5'5"
INFERIORITY COMPLEX
ALL TAPED UP
D-CUP COMPLEX

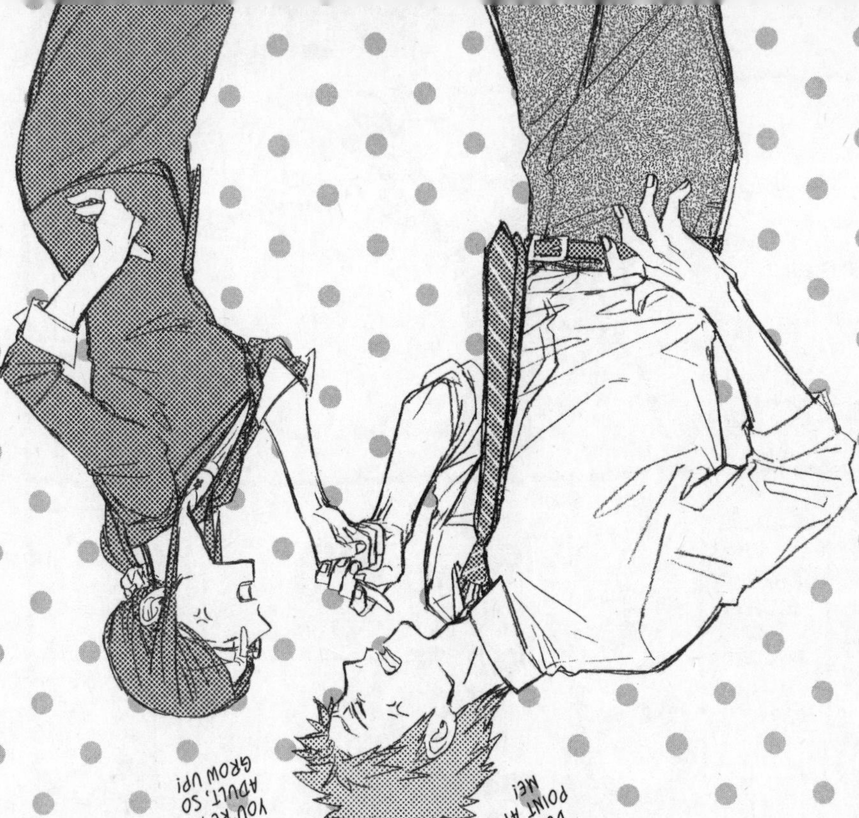
DON'T POINT AT ME!
YOU'RE AN ADULT, SO GROW UP!

Wotakoi: Love is Hard for Otaku

Afterword

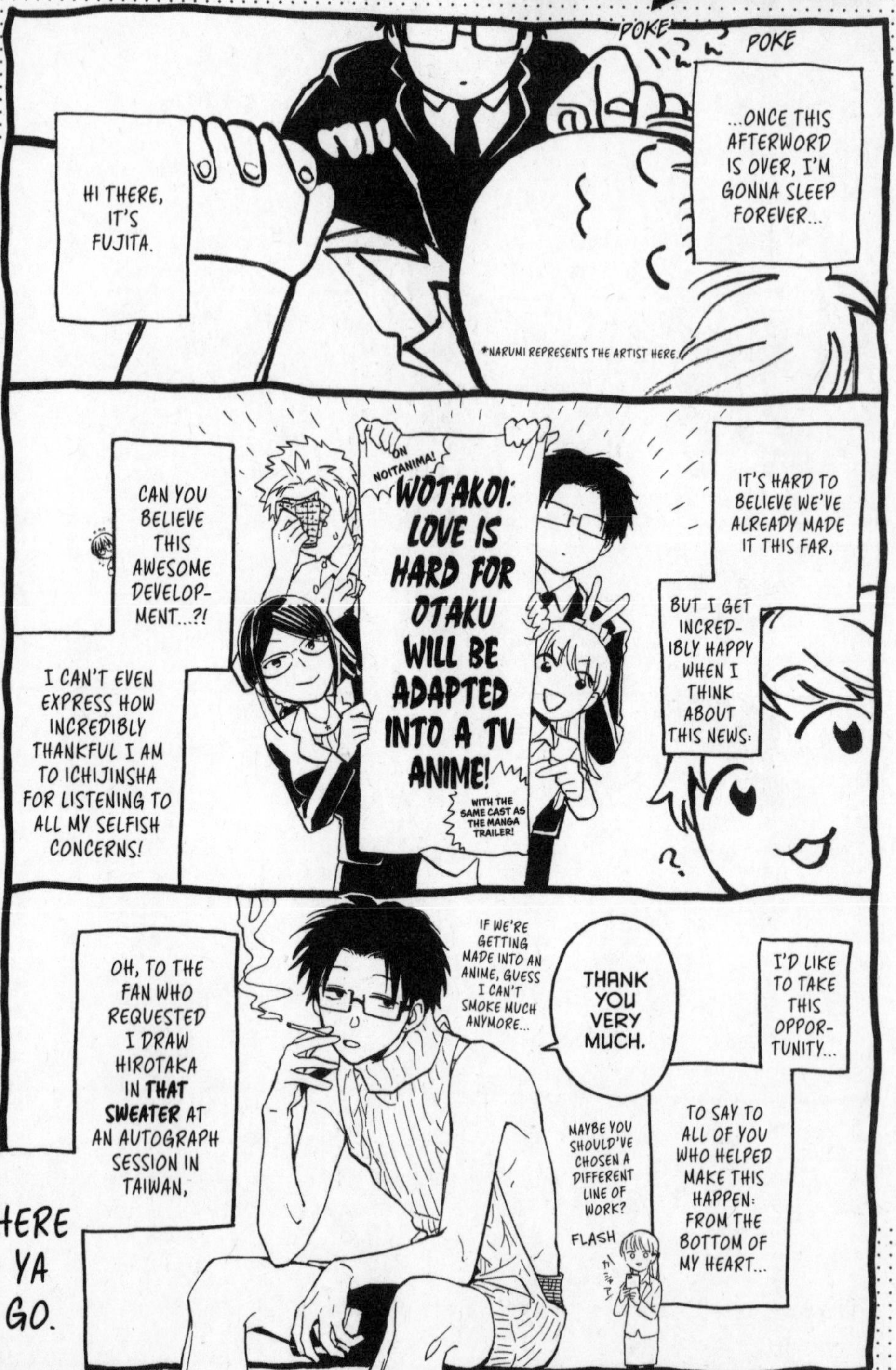
...ONCE THIS AFTERWORD IS OVER, I'M GONNA SLEEP FOREVER...
POKE
POKE
HI THERE, IT'S FUJITA.
*NARUMI REPRESENTS THE ARTIST HERE.
IT'S HARD TO BELIEVE WE'VE ALREADY MADE IT THIS FAR,
BUT I GET INCREDIBLY HAPPY WHEN I THINK ABOUT THIS NEWS:
?
ON NOITANIMA!
WOTAKOI: LOVE IS HARD FOR OTAKU WILL BE ADAPTED INTO A TV ANIME!
WITH THE SAME CAST AS THE MANGA TRAILER!
CAN YOU BELIEVE THIS AWESOME DEVELOPMENT...?!
I CAN'T EVEN EXPRESS HOW INCREDIBLY THANKFUL I AM TO ICHIJINSHA FOR LISTENING TO ALL MY SELFISH CONCERNS!
I'D LIKE TO TAKE THIS OPPORTUNITY...
TO SAY TO ALL OF YOU WHO HELPED MAKE THIS HAPPEN: FROM THE BOTTOM OF MY HEART...
THANK YOU VERY MUCH.
MAYBE YOU SHOULD'VE CHOSEN A DIFFERENT LINE OF WORK?
FLASH
IF WE'RE GETTING MADE INTO AN ANIME, GUESS I CAN'T SMOKE MUCH ANYMORE...
OH, TO THE FAN WHO REQUESTED I DRAW HIROTAKA IN THAT SWEATER AT AN AUTOGRAPH SESSION IN TAIWAN,
HERE YA GO.

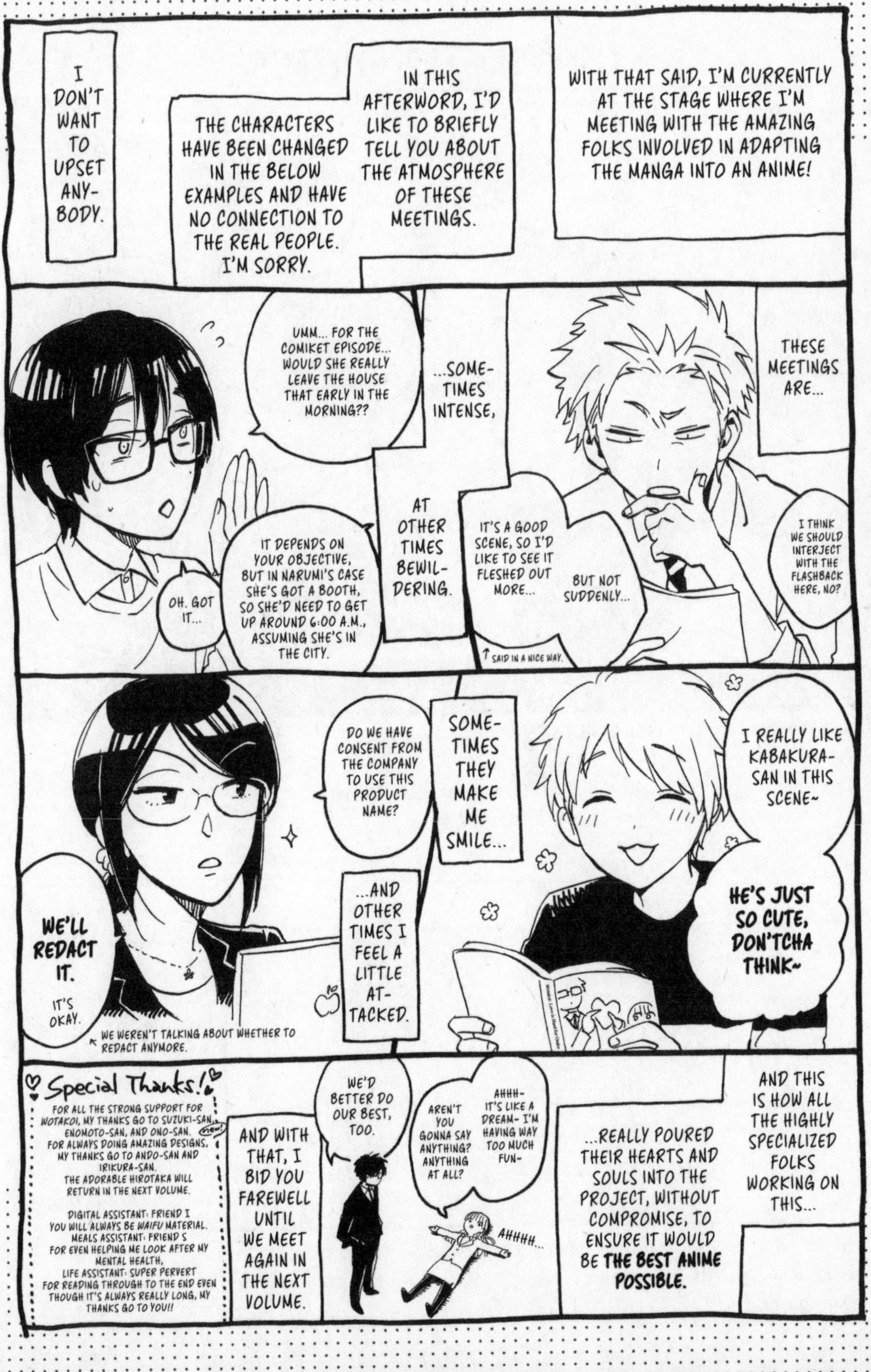
WITH THAT SAID, I'M CURRENTLY AT THE STAGE WHERE I'M MEETING WITH THE AMAZING FOLKS INVOLVED IN ADAPTING THE MANGA INTO AN ANIME!
IN THIS AFTERWORD, I'D LIKE TO BRIEFLY TELL YOU ABOUT THE ATMOSPHERE OF THESE MEETINGS.
THE CHARACTERS HAVE BEEN CHANGED IN THE BELOW EXAMPLES AND HAVE NO CONNECTION TO THE REAL PEOPLE. I'M SORRY.
I DON'T WANT TO UPSET ANYBODY.
THESE MEETINGS ARE...
I THINK WE SHOULD INTERJECT WITH THE FLASHBACK HERE, NO?
BUT NOT SUDDENLY...
IT'S A GOOD SCENE, SO I'D LIKE TO SEE IT FLESHED OUT MORE...
↑ SAID IN A NICE WAY.
...SOMETIMES INTENSE,
AT OTHER TIMES BEWILDERING.
UMM... FOR THE COMIKET EPISODE... WOULD SHE REALLY LEAVE THE HOUSE THAT EARLY IN THE MORNING??
IT DEPENDS ON YOUR OBJECTIVE, BUT IN NARUMI'S CASE SHE'S GOT A BOOTH, SO SHE'D NEED TO GET UP AROUND 6:00 A.M., ASSUMING SHE'S IN THE CITY.
OH. GOT IT...
I REALLY LIKE KABAKURA-SAN IN THIS SCENE~
HE'S JUST SO CUTE, DON'TCHA THINK~
SOMETIMES THEY MAKE ME SMILE...
...AND OTHER TIMES I FEEL A LITTLE ATTACKED.
DO WE HAVE CONSENT FROM THE COMPANY TO USE THIS PRODUCT NAME?
WE'LL REDACT IT.
IT'S OKAY.
↖ WE WEREN'T TALKING ABOUT WHETHER TO REDACT ANYMORE.
AND THIS IS HOW ALL THE HIGHLY SPECIALIZED FOLKS WORKING ON THIS...
...REALLY POURED THEIR HEARTS AND SOULS INTO THE PROJECT, WITHOUT COMPROMISE, TO ENSURE IT WOULD BE THE BEST ANIME POSSIBLE.
AHHH~ IT'S LIKE A DREAM~ I'M HAVING WAY TOO MUCH FUN~
AREN'T YOU GONNA SAY ANYTHING? ANYTHING AT ALL?
WE'D BETTER DO OUR BEST, TOO.
AHHHH...
AND WITH THAT, I BID YOU FAREWELL UNTIL WE MEET AGAIN IN THE NEXT VOLUME.
Special Thanks!
FOR ALL THE STRONG SUPPORT FOR WOTAKOI, MY THANKS GO TO SUZUKI-SAN, ENOMOTO-SAN, AND ONO-SAN. new!
FOR ALWAYS DOING AMAZING DESIGNS, MY THANKS GO TO ANDO-SAN AND IRIKURA-SAN.
THE ADORABLE HIROTAKA WILL RETURN IN THE NEXT VOLUME.
DIGITAL ASSISTANT: FRIEND I
YOU WILL ALWAYS BE WAIFU MATERIAL.
MEALS ASSISTANT: FRIEND S
FOR EVEN HELPING ME LOOK AFTER MY MENTAL HEALTH,
LIFE ASSISTANT: SUPER PERVERT
FOR READING THROUGH TO THE END EVEN THOUGH IT'S ALWAYS REALLY LONG, MY THANKS GO TO YOU!!

TRANSLATION NOTES

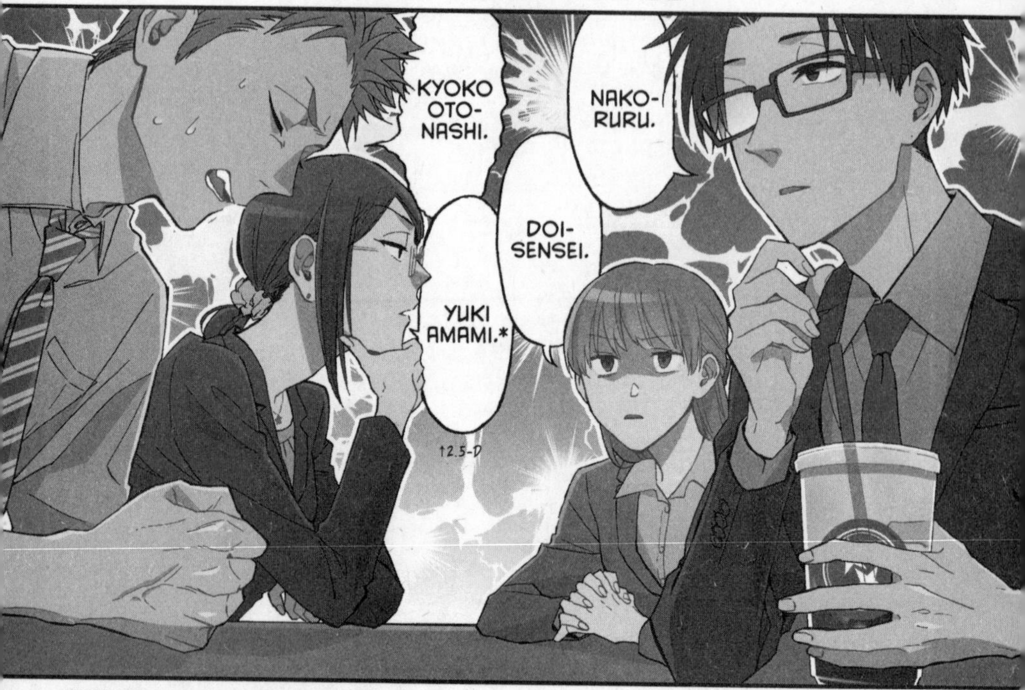

NAKO-RURU.
DOI-SENSEI.
KYOKO OTO-NASHI.
YUKI AMAMI.*
↑2.5-D

▲ TRY TO NAME THESE TITLES, PAGE 141

The characters the *Wotakoi* friends are referencing are:

- Nakoruru: *Samurai Shodown,* a video game
- Doi-sensei: *Nintama Rantaros,* an anime series
- Kyoko Otonashi: *Maison Ikkoku,* a manga series

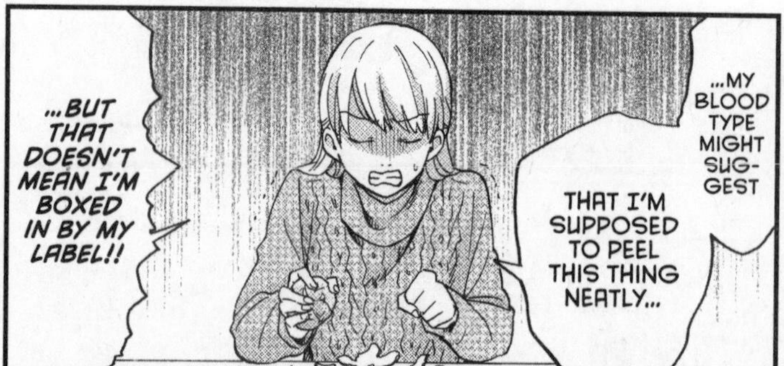

...MY BLOOD TYPE MIGHT SUG-GEST
THAT I'M SUPPOSED TO PEEL THIS THING NEATLY...
...BUT THAT DOESN'T MEAN I'M BOXED IN BY MY LABEL!!

◀ BLOOD TYPE, PAGE 162

Many Japanese believe that a person's blood type defines their personality. Nearly everyone in Japan knows their blood type, and it is common to ask friends and potential dates for theirs, as blood type is thought to determine compatibility. The common characteristics, both positive and negative, assigned to each blood type are:

• Type A: Organized, neat, and considerate, but high-strung and stubborn.
• Type B: Considered to be the least desirable blood type and sometimes subject to *buruhara* ("blood harassment"); creative and unconventional, but selfish and uncooperative.
• Type O: Easygoing, hardworking, and natural leaders, but insensitive and rude.
• Type AB: Calm and artistic, but eccentric and two-faced.

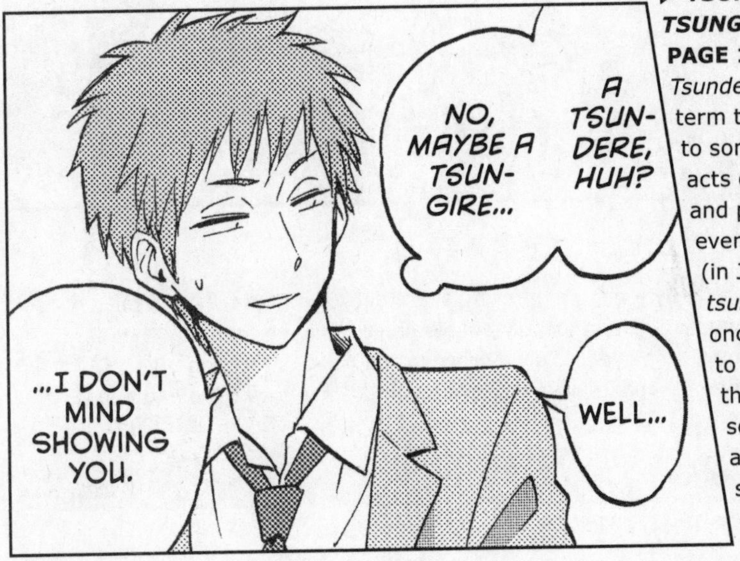
A TSUNDERE, HUH?
NO, MAYBE A TSUNGIRE...
WELL...
...I DON'T MIND SHOWING YOU.

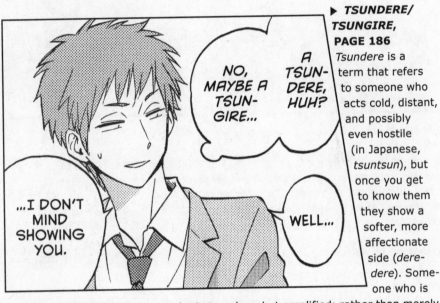

▶ *TSUNDERE/TSUNGIRE,* PAGE 186

Tsundere is a term that refers to someone who acts cold, distant, and possibly even hostile (in Japanese, *tsuntsun*), but once you get to know them they show a softer, more affectionate side (*deredere*). Someone who is *tsungire* is similar to someone who is *tsundere,* but amplified; rather than merely being cold or hostile, they may be emotionally abusive or violent, without a *dere* side at all.

▼ *TOKUSATSU,* PAGE 219

Literally "special effects," *tokusatsu* refers to a genre of TV shows and film that includes monster movies like *Godzilla,* mecha series like *Giant Robo,* and costumed superhero series like *Super Sentai* (the source material for the original *Power Rangers*). These shows are often the most popular with children.

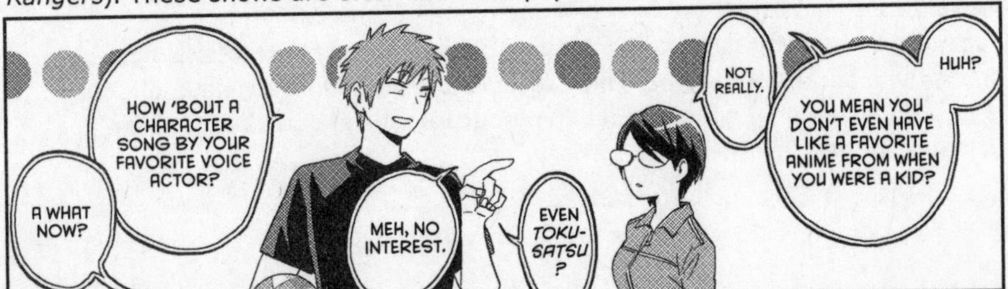
HUH?
YOU MEAN YOU DON'T EVEN HAVE LIKE A FAVORITE ANIME FROM WHEN YOU WERE A KID?
NOT REALLY.
EVEN TOKU-SATSU?
MEH, NO INTEREST.
HOW 'BOUT A CHARACTER SONG BY YOUR FAVORITE VOICE ACTOR?
A WHAT NOW?

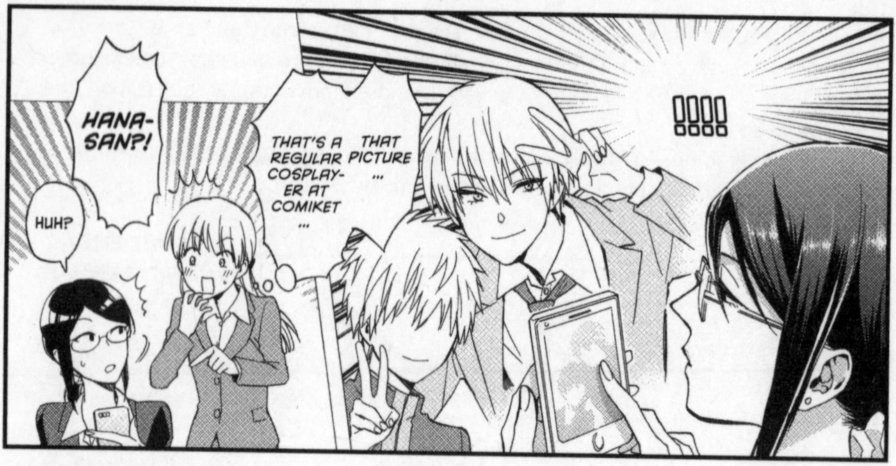
THAT PICTURE ...
THAT'S A REGULAR COSPLAY-ER AT COMIKET ...
HANA-SAN?!
HUH?

▲ HANA-SAN,
PAGE 229

Many cosplayers go by a handle different than their own name. This is to preserve anonymity, so their cosplay photos can't easily be found by friends, family, or potential employers. Narumi recognized Hanako through her cosplay, as it seems Hanako is a famous enough cosplayer to have name recognition.

BASKETBALL AND
BASARA,
PAGE 229

Basketball is a reference to the anime and manga *Kuroko's Basketball,* from which Hanako and her friend are cosplaying.

YOUR NAME,
PAGE 230

Your Name is a blockbuster anime movie by acclaimed director Makoto Shinkai, about two time-traveling, consciousness-swapping teens who are brought together by fate.

OFF-MODEL,
PAGE 235

Kabakura is referring to an animation mistake, where the character is not drawn quite according to spec. This usually happens when the animation team is on a tight deadline, and is something hardcore fans are quick to find and point out in their favorite shows.

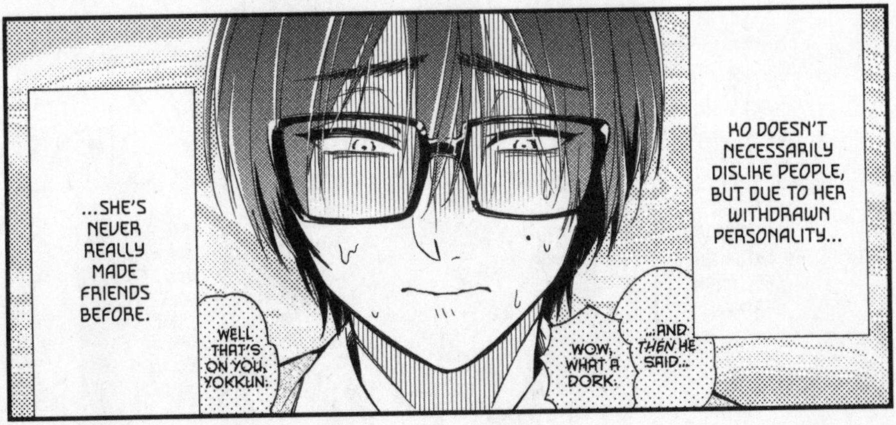
KO DOESN'T NECESSARILY DISLIKE PEOPLE, BUT DUE TO HER WITHDRAWN PERSONALITY...
...AND THEN HE SAID...
WOW, WHAT A DORK.
WELL THAT'S ON YOU, YOKKUN.
...SHE'S NEVER REALLY MADE FRIENDS BEFORE.

▲ ASOCIAL, PAGE 238

This is from *commubyo,* or literally "communication-illness" – slang for those who are a bit socially awkward or have trouble communicating.

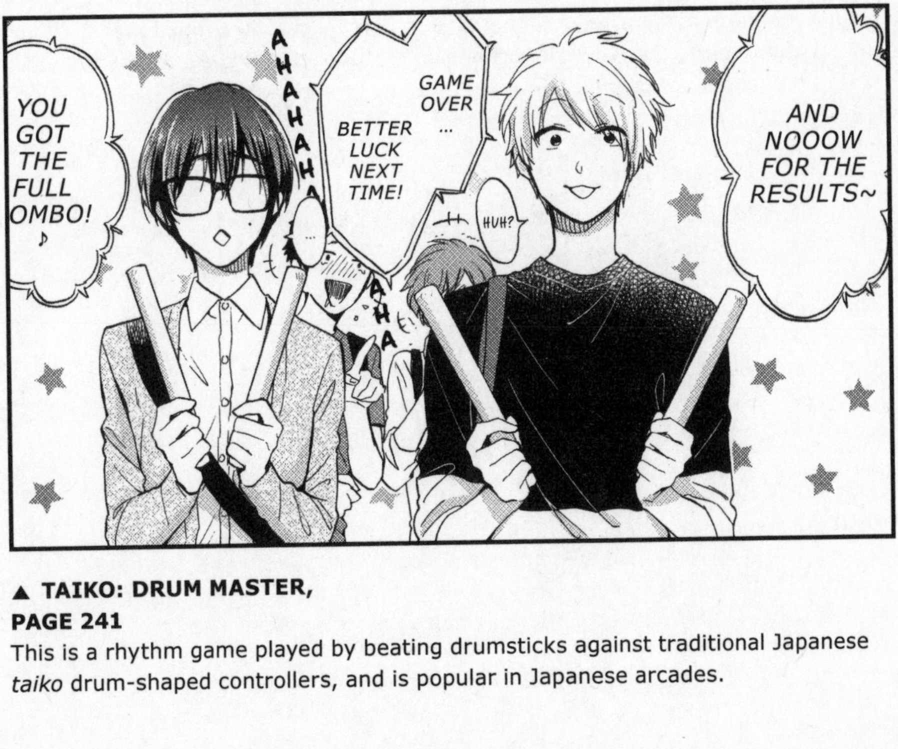
AND NOOOW FOR THE RESULTS~
HUH?
GAME OVER ...
BETTER LUCK NEXT TIME!
AHAHAHA
...
AHAHA
YOU GOT THE FULL OMBO! ♪

▲ TAIKO: DRUM MASTER, PAGE 241

This is a rhythm game played by beating drumsticks against traditional Japanese *taiko* drum-shaped controllers, and is popular in Japanese arcades.

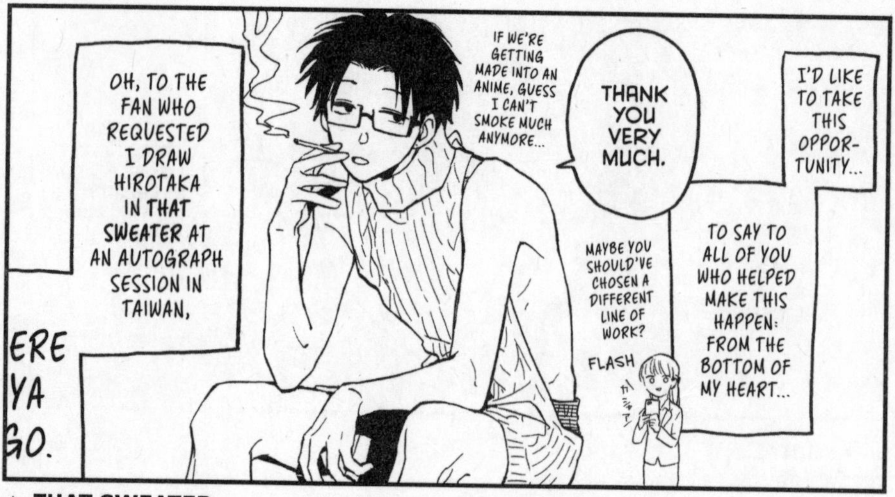
I'D LIKE TO TAKE THIS OPPOR-TUNITY...
TO SAY TO ALL OF YOU WHO HELPED MAKE THIS HAPPEN: FROM THE BOTTOM OF MY HEART...
THANK YOU VERY MUCH.
IF WE'RE GETTING MADE INTO AN ANIME, GUESS I CAN'T SMOKE MUCH ANYMORE...
MAYBE YOU SHOULD'VE CHOSEN A DIFFERENT LINE OF WORK?
FLASH
OH, TO THE FAN WHO REQUESTED I DRAW HIROTAKA IN THAT SWEATER AT AN AUTOGRAPH SESSION IN TAIWAN,
ERE YA GO.

▲ THAT SWEATER, PAGE 264

The unusual sweater Hirotaka is depicted in is referred to as "that sweater" or "the virgin-killing sweater," and is a well-known otaku meme. The sweater, based off a real-life garment, is featured prominently in fanart (especially erotic fanart), along with another meme, the "keyhole turtleneck" – modeled in *Wotakoi* by Narumi and Hanako on page 90 of Volume 1.

WOTAKOI:
LOVE IS HARD FOR OTAKU

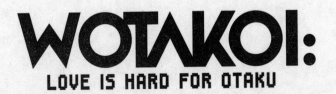

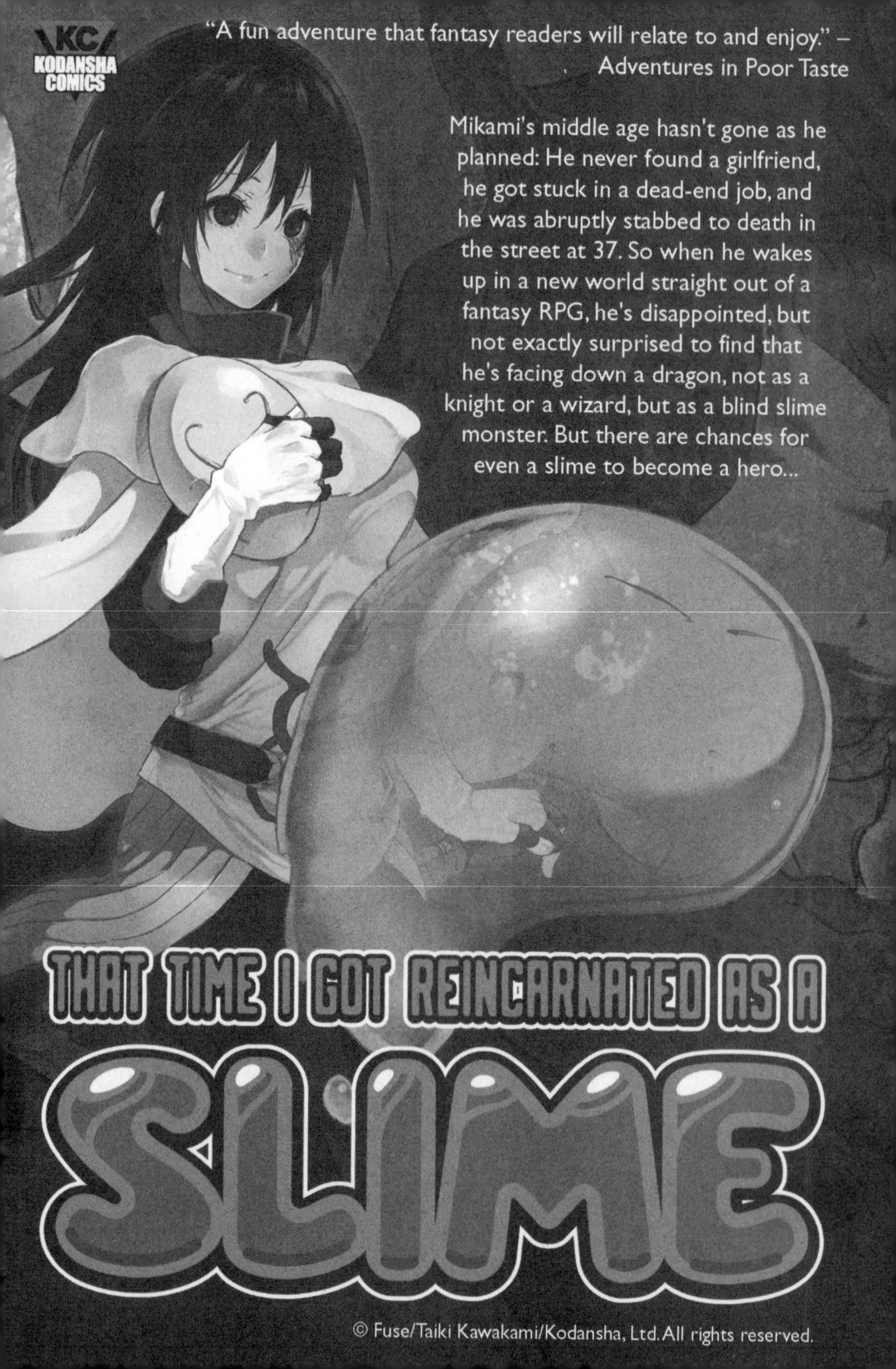
KC KODANSHA COMICS
"A fun adventure that fantasy readers will relate to and enjoy." – Adventures in Poor Taste
Mikami's middle age hasn't gone as he planned: He never found a girlfriend, he got stuck in a dead-end job, and he was abruptly stabbed to death in the street at 37. So when he wakes up in a new world straight out of a fantasy RPG, he's disappointed, but not exactly surprised to find that he's facing down a dragon, not as a knight or a wizard, but as a blind slime monster. But there are chances for even a slime to become a hero...
THAT TIME I GOT REINCARNATED AS A
SLIME
© Fuse/Taiki Kawakami/Kodansha, Ltd. All rights reserved.

Japan's most powerful spirit medium delves into the ghost world's greatest mysteries!

Story by Kyo Shirodaira, famed author of mystery fiction and creator of *Spiral*, *Blast of Tempest*, and *The Record of a Fallen Vampire*.

Both touched by spirits called yôkai, Kotoko and Kurô have gained unique superhuman powers. But to gain her powers Kotoko has given up an eye and a leg, and Kurô's personal life is in shambles. So when Kotoko suggests they team up to deal with renegades from the spirit world, Kurô doesn't have many other choices, but Kotoko might just have a few ulterior motives...

IN/SPECTRE

STORY BY KYO SHIRODAIRA
ART BY CHASHIBA KATASE

A Kodansha Comics Trade Paperback Original.

Published in the United States by Kodansha Comics, an imprint of Kodansha USA Publishing, LLC, New York.

Publication rights for this English edition arranged through Kodansha Ltd., Tokyo.

First published in Japan in 2017 by Ichijinsha Inc., Tokyo. as *Wotaku ni koi ha muzukashi* volumes 3 & 4

ISBN 978-1-63236-705-1

Printed in the United States of America.

www.kodansha.us

9 8

Translation: Jessica Sheaves
Lettering: AndWorld Design
Editing: Lauren Scanlan
Kodansha Comics edition cover design: Phil Balsman